P9-AZX-361

MICROECONOMICS

SECOND EDITION

WILLIAM BOYES

Arizona State University

MICHAEL MELVIN

Arizona State University

NEW HANOVER COUNTY
PUBLIC LIBRARY
201 CHESTNUT STREET
WILMINGTON, N C 28401

HOUGHTON MIFFLIN COMPANY   BOSTON   TORONTO
Geneva, Illinois   Palo Alto   Princeton, New Jersey

To our families

W.B.
M.M.

Sponsoring Editor: Denise Clinton
Development Editor: Julie Hogenboom
Project Editor: Susan Westendorf
Senior Production/Design Coordinator: Patricia Mahtani
Senior Manufacturing Coordinator: Marie Barnes
Marketing Manager: Michael Ginley

CREDITS

Cover design and illustration by Darci Mehall, Aureo Design, Boston, MA.

Chapter photos: p. 3 © Bob Daemmrich/The Image Works; p. 8 © R. Lord/The Image Works; p. 33 © Peter Freed/Sygma; p. 44 © Cameramann/The Image Works; p. 51 Cameramann International; p. 52 (left) © Ron McMillan/Gamma-Liaison; p. 52 (right) © David R. Frazier; p. 68 © Benelux/Photo Researchers; p. 83 © Haruyoshi Yamaguchi/Sygma; p. 101 (left) Andrew Popper/Picture Group; p. 101 (right) © Fujifotos/The Image Works; p. 111 © Bob Daemmrich; *(continued on p. C1)*

Copyright © 1994 by Houghton Mifflin Company. All rights reserved.

No part of this work may be reproduced or transmitted in any form or by any means, electronic or mechanical, including photocopying and recording, or by any information storage or retrieval system without the prior written permission of Houghton Mifflin Company unless such copying is expressly permitted by federal copyright law. Address inquiries to College Permissions, Houghton Mifflin Company, 222 Berkeley Street, Boston, MA 02116-3764.

Printed in the U.S.A.

Library of Congress Catalog Card Number: 93-78703

ISBN: 0-395-67543-X

EXAMINATION COPY ISBN: 0-395-69065-X

123456789-VH-97 96 95 94 93

Preface

We wrote the first edition of this book in response to a gap we saw between the real world and the world students were learning about in class. At that time no economics text fully incorporated the world economy into the principles course. We wrote a text with the idea in mind that instructors could not afford to leave "the rest of the world" out of discussion. *Economics* was dedicated to acknowledging this more complete picture, and bringing it to students and instructors in a friendly, accessible way.

The tremendous success of the first edition confirmed our belief that the principles market was ready for change. Hundreds of instructors adopted *Economics* for their courses. Three years later, as we near the end of the revision process, we have several reasons to believe that our second edition text is more appropriate for students than ever:

A call for the internationalization of the principles course at the American Economics Association meeting. A panel of economists at the AEA meeting in January, 1993, presented their ideas for internationalizing the principles course to a packed audience, illustrating the increased attention to the global economy by instructors, something we anticipated with the publication of *Economics* in 1990. (See *American Economic Review,* May, 1993.)

The increasing interrelatedness of world economies makes a closed economy course unrealistic today. We continue to see that the decisions made by a firm or a government in one part of the world will have far-reaching effects everywhere. The merging of East and West Germany, the successes and controversies within the European community, the freeing of restraints in Eastern Europe, Russia, and other parts of the communist world, the struggles in Latin America, the Middle East, and the Balkans, and the rapidly rising economic powers of Asia: all affect the U.S. economy, and the lives of U.S. citizens. Likewise, actions taken by the United States and by Americans individually alter economic patterns around the globe. Today's students come to class wanting to make sense of these global connections.

Student success with the first edition. Current users of *Economics* tell us that their students stumbled through other texts before settling comfortably into using Boyes/Melvin. They report that Boyes/Melvin *Economics* is the kind of book students can pick up and learn from independently, either to supplement lecture, or to replace it, when class time runs out and students are on their own to learn extra topics.

Recognizing that the world and the field of economics have changed over the past three years, we have updated this text to keep pace with those changes. At the same time, our goals in producing this edition remain essentially the same as when we began work on the first edition: to expand the traditional scope of the principles course and provide an arena in which economics educators could present and students could absorb the principles of the global economy.

We hope that this text well serves all the students who use it—those who major in business, psychology, education, engineering, English, and other fields, as well as those who choose to pursue economics. All of these readers will inevitably be faced with new issues and questions as the world's economic story continues to unfold.

Changes made for the second edition. Our conversations with instructors—both users and non-users—and an extensive reviewing program helped us isolate parts of the text where refinement was needed, as well as identify opportunities for the inclusion of modern, innovative topics. The revision has resulted in the most up-to-date treatment of topics possible while the carefully paced reading style and expansive art program, which proved to be such effective learning tools in the first edition, have been preserved.

■ *Improved organization of introductory chapters.* The first five introductory chapters have been revised to provide a more concise and meaningful welcome to the subject. Chapters 1 through 4 deal with the economic problem and private markets. Chapter 5 then introduces the public sector. This structure enables instructors to pursue as much of the role of government in the market economy as they like and from more than one perspective. Instructors may wish to minimize government at this stage, or they may decide to explore the role of government in either the public interest or as the result of rent seeking or special interests.

■ *Modern microeconomics.* More international applications and national comparisons appear in the second edition micro chapters. Topics in recent micro research have been included where possible, to show students the relevance of microeconomic theory and how it is used to explain human behavior. Strategic behavior is now treated as a separate section within the oligopoly chapter. The economics of personnel practices is a new topic covered in the labor market chapter. An entire new chapter has been added—Chapter 13, THE ECONOMICS OF INFORMATION—which addresses the role of information in the micro model. Key information topics such as moral hazard, asymmetric information, and adverse selection are presented, giving those students who are interested in continuing in economics a good introduction to material they will encounter at the intermediate level. On the other hand, reviewers told us less motivated students would also be comfortable with and interested in this material, even if there was no time to include the chapter in lecture.

The public choice chapter examines the process of collective decision making, and how this method of choosing government is used to explain government actions.

■ *Transitional Economies.* In recognition of the important and difficult transitions going on in the economies of Eastern Europe and the former Soviet Union, we have added a new chapter to the last section of the book, Chapter 26, THE TRANSITION FROM SOCIALISM TO CAPITALISM. The chapter addresses both the micro and macro issues involved in the momentous changes these economies are undergoing.

■ *Greatly Expanded Collection of End-of-Chapter Exercises.* The end-of-chapter exercises have been revised and greatly expanded to test student understanding. Students now have plenty of opportunity for the drill and practice they need to give them confidence in their understanding of chapter concepts. Each chapter has an average of 15 exercises.

■ *Revised and Up-to-Date Economically Speaking Pieces.* An end-of-chapter feature popular with our first edition users, ECONOMICALLY SPEAKING pairs a news article with some simple economic analysis—a *Commentary*—which serves to translate real events into economic terms for students. More than three-fourths of the Economically Speaking articles have been replaced with new articles, reporting on the kinds of current issues students will have heard much about in the media—NAFTA, the Oregon health care plan, and the U.S. trade deficit with Japan, among others.

■ *Art Program Fully Updated to Reflect Latest Data.* While the size, pedagogical color scheme, and careful art-table-caption correspondence that resulted in such a successful art program in the first edition have been maintained, charts and graphs were redrawn to incorporate the new data that's now available.

■ *New Photos Throughout the Second Edition.* With the first edition we were able to see the value photos can bring to learning about economics. Colorful photos featuring scenes and events students are familiar with provide another important layer of translation for students—of world events into economic terms, and the reverse.

CONTINUED SUCCESS FROM THE FIRST EDITION

In addition to the considerable updating and revising we did for the second edition, there are several unique features preserved from the first edition which instructors who are new to Boyes/Melvin will find interesting.

THOROUGHLY INTEGRATED INTERNATIONAL COVERAGE

Students understand that they live in a global economy—they can hardly shop, or watch the news, or read a major newspaper without understanding this basic fact. International examples are presented in almost every chapter. Because the international content is incorporated from the beginning, students will develop a far more realistic picture of the economy; they will not have to later alter their thinking to allow for international factors. Recognizing that some instructors may wish to reserve international concerns for the last section of their course, we provide international trade and finance chapters in the traditional place. These instructors can treat the international material in detail at the end of their course. In either case, the instructor is in no danger of omitting international coverage. This text offers the optimal opportunity for business programs to better answer the American Assembly of Collegiate Schools of Business (AACSB) call to prepare the student "for imaginative and responsible citizenship and leadership roles in business and society—domestic and worldwide."

Unique international elements of microeconomic coverage include

■ Introduction of exchange rates as a determinant of demand.

■ Extensive analyses of the effects of trade barriers, tariffs, and quotas.

■ Examination of strategic trade.

■ Examination of dumping as a special case of price discrimination.

■ Identification of problems faced by multinational firms.

■ Comparison of behavior, results, and institutions among nations with respect to consumption, production, firm size, government policies toward business, labor markets, health care, income distribution, environmental policy, and other issues.

MODERN MICROECONOMIC CONTENT AND ORGANIZATION

All too often microeconomics is presented as a succession of facts, graphs, and theories whose connections are not easily grasped or appreciated. Because students don't see the big picture, they find microeconomics difficult and unrelated to their lives. We give students a context for organizing and understanding the material covered and point out how it relates to their everyday experience. And we extend the application of economic principles to families, aging, health care, occupational choice, and discrimination.

Part II presents basic concepts such as supply, demand, and elasticity, that are needed for any study of markets and of an individual's economic choices. Parts III and IV both begin with overview chapters (Chapter 9 on product markets and Chapter 15 on

resource markets). These overviews give students a chance to look at the big picture before delving into details they often find confusing. Chapter 9, for instance, gives students an intuitive overview to the market structures before they explore each type of structure in more detail in succeeding chapters. These overview chapters can be omitted by instructors wishing to follow a more traditional sequence and to spend more time on the detailed chapters that follow.

Part V extends microeconomics to issues that are of high interest to students. Chapter 19 offers an analysis of the economics of aging and health care, two critical issues for the nineties. *Economics* continues to be the only text which treats the issues of aging and health care so fully. Chapter 20 lays out the tension between equity and efficiency as it examines the distribution of income and poverty, and Chapter 21 examines environmental issues. The last application chapter focuses on how decisions are made in the public sector.

AN EFFECTIVE AND PROVEN SYSTEM OF TEACHING AND LEARNING AIDS

This text is designed to make teaching easier by enhancing student learning. Tested pedagogy motivates students, emphasizes clarity, reinforces relationships, simplifies review, and fosters critical thinking.

In-text Referencing System

Sections are numbered for easy reference and to reinforce hierarchies of ideas. The numbering of sections serves as an outline of the chapter, allowing instructors flexibility in assigning reading, and making it easy for students to find topics to review. The key term list and summary at the end of the chapter refer students back to the appropriate *section*.

The section-numbering system appears throughout the Boyes/Melvin ancillary package. The Test Bank, Study Guide, and Instructor's Resource Manual are organized according to the same system.

In-text Study System

Pedagogical elements were designed to work together to enhance understanding and retention.

Fundamental Questions. These questions help to organize the chapter and highlight those issues that are critical to understanding. Students can preview chapters with these questions in mind, reading actively for understanding and retention. The Fundamental Questions reappear in the margin by the text discussion that helps students to answer the question. Fundamental Questions also serve to organize the chapter summaries. Brief paragraphs answering each of these questions are found in the *Study Guides* available as supplements to this text. They also serve as one of several criteria used to categorize questions in the *Test Bank*.

Preview. This motivating lead-in sets the stage for the chapter. Much more than a road map, it helps students identify real issues that relate to the concepts that will be presented.

Recaps. Briefly listing the main points covered, a recap appears at the end of each major section within a chapter. Students are reminded to quickly review what they have just read before going on to the next section.

Summary. The summary at the end of each chapter is organized along two dimensions. The primary organizational device is the list of Fundamental Questions. A brief synopsis of the discussion that helps students to answer those questions is arranged by section below each of the questions. Students are encouraged to create their own links between material as they keep in mind the connections between the "big picture" and the details that comprise it.

Reminders. Found in the text margin, these hints and comments highlight especially important concepts, point out common mistakes, and warn students of common pitfalls. They alert students to parts of the discussion that they should read with particular care.

Key Terms. Key terms appear in bold type in the text. They also appear with their definition in the margin and are listed at the end of the chapter for easy review. All key terms are included in the glossary at the end of the text.

Exercises

End-of-chapter exercises provide excellent self-checks for students and a homework assignment option for instructors. An average of 15 exercises appears at the end of every chapter.

The exercises ask students to work with the ideas presented in the chapter: Do they know how to apply the concepts? Can they perform necessary computations? Can they draw conclusions about the real world based on the theories presented?

FULL-COLOR ART PROGRAM

Over 300 figures rely on well-developed pedagogy and consistent use of color to reinforce understanding. Striking colors were chosen to enhance readability and provide visual interest. Experienced art editors developed a color palette that will help students recognize curves and grasp relationships. Specific curves were assigned specific colors. Each time a particular curve appears, it is shown in the same color.

Tables that provide data from which graphs are plotted are paired with their graphs. Where appropriate, color is used to show correlations between the art and the table, as can be seen in Figure 8 in Chapter 3. There the pale yellow screen in the area that shows a surplus echoes the screen over the top two rows of the table, which also show a surplus. The light blue screen designating the area of shortage in the graph echoes the screen over the bottom two rows of the table, which show shortage values.

Extensive captions clearly explain what is shown in the figures and draw explicit connections between the art and the text discussion. Because the critical information is contained in the caption, students can study the graph and caption independently from the text and get the whole picture.

Recognizing the importance of accuracy in a principles text with such an extensive art program, we incorporated a thorough accuracy review in the production process of the book. A team of reviewers was hired to verify the accuracy of curve shapes and their relationships, arithmetic accuracy in the art, and the correspondence between art, text, tables, and captions.

ENHANCED STUDENT RELEVANCE

With all the demands on today's students, it's no wonder that they resist spending time on a subject unless they see how the material relates to them and how they will benefit from mastering it. We worked hard to incorporate features throughout the text that would show economics as the relevant and necessary subject we know it to be.

Idea Maps

The Idea Map—"Making Sense of Microeconomics"—visually demonstrates the connections between the topics students are learning. The Idea Map helps students avoid feeling disjointed about the material as they move through the course. The map organizes what students have learned into a logical whole.

Real-world Examples

Students are rarely intrigued by a large manufacturer or a service company. Our text talks about people and firms that students recognize. We describe business decisions made by McDonald's and Pizza Hut, by General Motors and Shearson Lehman Hutton as well as the local hardware or grocery store. We discuss the policies of Bill Clinton, Boris Yeltsin, John Major, and other world leaders. These examples grab students' interest. Reviewers have repeatedly praised the use of novel examples to convey economic concepts.

Economic Insight

These short boxes bring in contemporary material from current periodicals and journals to illustrate or extend the discussion in the chapter. By reserving interesting but more technical sidelights for boxes, we lessen the likelihood that students will be confused or distracted by issues that are not critical to understanding the chapter. By including excerpts from articles we help students learn to move from theory to real-world example. And by including plenty of contemporary issues, we guarantee that students will see how economics relates to their own lives.

Economically Speaking

The objective of the principles course is to teach students how to translate the predictions that come out of economic models to the real world and to translate real-world events into an economic model in order to analyze and understand what lies behind the events. The Economically Speaking boxes present students with a model of this kind of analysis. First they read an article which appears on the left-hand page of a two-page spread at the end of each chapter. The commentary on the right-hand page shows how the facts and events in the article translate into a specific economic model or idea, thereby moving the student from reality back to theory.

Carefully Selected Photographs

Vibrant photos that tell a story and illustrate a concept appear throughout the text. Captions explain what is in the photo and draw connections between these images and the discussion in the text. Careful coordination between text, photograph, and caption help students make concepts concrete, enhancing retention of the material and increasing the relevance of the material.

A CLEARLY CODED LEARNING SYSTEM

In today's market no book is complete without a full complement of ancillaries. Our package provides the breadth and depth of support for both instructors and students that the market has a right to demand. The ancillary package for *Economics* is second to none. Throughout its development, we have kept today's economics instructor in mind. Those instructors who face huge classes find good transparencies (acetates) and transparency masters critical instructional tools. Others may find that computer simulations and tutorials are invaluable. *Economics* meets both challenges. And to foster the development of consistent teaching and study strategies, the ancillaries pick up pedagogical features of the text—like the fundamental questions—wherever appropriate.

Transparencies Available to adopters are 150 color acetates showing the most important figures in the text. Over 10 percent of these figures have one to three overlays, which in addition to adding clarity and flexibility to the discussion, allow instructors to visually demonstrate the dynamic nature of economics.

Instructor's Resource Manual Edward T. Merkel and Paul S. Estenson, two experienced and highly talented economists with a wealth of classroom experience, have collaborated to produce a manual that will streamline preparation for both new and experienced faculty. Preliminary sections cover class administration and alternative syllabi. Each chapter contains

■ Teaching Objectives. *What are the critical points to cover if your students are to succeed with later chapters?* You can ensure that the foundations are laid and that students see connections between topics.

What concepts are traditionally difficult for students to master? You can concentrate on these topics and develop classroom exercises to bring these topics into clearer focus.

What are the unique features of this chapter? You may wish to augment your lectures and treat these topics differently than you have in the past.

■ Fundamental Questions listed.

- Key Terms listed.

- Lecture Outline. The in-text reference system comes into play again in the lecture outline. The numbered heads are picked up from the main text. The authors have identified primary points to cover each section and have suggested examples and classroom activities that have worked well for them or that have been suggested by instructors who reviewed the text.

- Teaching Strategies. More general techniques and guidelines, essay topics, and other hints to enliven your classes are presented.

- Opportunities for Discussion. Thought provoking questions to assign students, or to use as a launch for in-class debate.

- Answers to End-of-Chapter Questions. Every exercise in this text is answered here.

- Transparency Masters. Significant figures that do not appear in the transparency package are included here.

Study Guides Janet L. Wolcutt and James E. Clark of the Center for Economic Education at Wichita State University have written study guides for *Macroeconomics* and *Microeconomics* that give students the practice they need to master this course. Written in a warm and lively style, the study guides should keep students on the right track. In each chapter:

- Fundamental Questions are answered in one or several paragraphs. For students who have trouble formulating their own answers to these questions after reading the text, the study guides provide an invaluable model.

- Key terms are listed.

- Quick Check Quiz is organized by section, so any wrong answers send the student directly to the relevant material in the text. These questions focus on vocabulary and basic concepts. They alert students to sections of the chapter that they forgot or didn't understand.

- Practice Questions and Problems, which is also organized by section, includes a variety of question formats—multiple choice, true/false, matching, and fill-in-the-blank. They test understanding of the concepts and ask students to construct graphs or perform computations.

- Thinking About and Applying . . . use newspaper headlines or some other real-life applications to test students' ability to reason in economic terms.

- Sample Tests. New to this edition, these tests appear at the end of each Study Guide part and consist of 25 to 50 questions similar to test bank questions. Taking the sample tests will help students determine whether or not they're really prepared for exams.

- Answers are provided to every question in the study guides. Students are referred back to relevant pages in the main text. Rejoinders are provided where appropriate to alert students to common mistakes or likely reasons for an incorrect answer.

Test Banks Test Banks for both *Macroeconomics* and *Microeconomics* are available. Over 7,000 test items in total provide a wealth of material for classroom testing. Features include

- True/false and essay questions, brand new to this edition, in every chapter to supplement multiple choice.

- 2,000 questions new to this edition, and marked for easy identification (multiple choice, true/false, and essay).

- An increased number of analytical, applied, and graphical questions appear in this edition.

- Identification of all test items according to topic, question type (factual, interpretive, or applied), level of difficulty, and applicable fundamental question.

- Identification of relevant page number in complete book, as well as in micro or macro splits, where the answer is found.

- Study Guide section of test which includes five test items taken directly from the Study Guide and five test items that parallel Study Guide questions, for the instructor who is interested in rewarding students for working through the Study Guide.

FOR THE COMPUTER

ESA TEST II for IBM Machines

New to this edition, this innovative test-assembly program renders precise, preprogrammed graphs on the computer quickly, easily, and accurately. You can select from among more than 7,000 questions, edit nongraphic items, peruse items in order, add your own questions to customize tests, and print out alternate versions using a number of variables. Individual items or tests in their entirety can be previewed before printing. The sophisticated data retrieval capabilities of the computerized test bank allow instructors to generate multiple versions of a test automatically and assure comparability of tests consisting of different test items. This program also allows importation of files from ASCII, WordStar, and WordPerfect. Available for IBM-PC®, PS/2, and compatible microcomputers.

LXR Test for Macintosh Machines

This state-of-the-art graphic test generator combines text-editing tools for creating or editing test questions with powerful layout features, graphic printing capabilities, and more. Multiple versions of a test can be generated quickly. Available for Macintosh® microcomputers.

Computerized Macroeconomics and Microeconomics Tutorial/Simulation Package

This software package has been updated to reflect the changes in the Second Edition. Each of the more than 35 modules reviews a major concept, then asks questions that require students to change variables and work with graphs. For questions answered incorrectly, page numbers refer students back to the appropriate text discussion. Scores are displayed at the end of each module. Available for IBM-PC®, PS/2, and compatible microcomputers.

Laserdisc: *Graphs!*

Our new laserdisc offers instructors the capability to show graphs and their movements in a dynamic way. Each set of graphs is introduced and motivated by interesting, brief video clips. Instructors can choose from a collection of key economic graphs. Each graph is easily accessed and controlled to provide optimal lecture support. Also available in VHS format for video projection.

ACKNOWLEDGMENTS

Writing a text of this scope is a challenge that requires the expertise and efforts of many. We are grateful to our friends and colleagues who have so generously given their time, creativity, and insight to help us create a text that best meets the needs of today's classroom.

Throughout the development of the text, there were many instructors who reviewed sections of the manuscript, sometimes more than once and often, many sections. We thank them for their candor and diligence in pointing out problems and offering solutions. Ted Scheinman of Mount Hood Community College, was particularly helpful by class-testing our revised macro manuscript with his principles students and sharing their opinions with us.

Participants in a focus group we held in Nashville gave us some good ideas for improving our manuscript. George Greenwade of Sam Houston State University, Yousef Mansur of Oklahoma City Community College, Bradley Braun of the University of Saint Cloud State University, all deserve our thanks for their time and energy.

We are very grateful for the work done by a group of adopters who compiled semester-long evaluations for us as they taught from the book. We would like to thank John Atkins of Pensacola Junior College, James T. Bennett of George Mason University, Cindy Cannon of North Harris College, John F. Ficks of the College of Dupage, John Kane of the State University of New York at Oswego, Thomas Maloy of Muskegon Community College, Nancy Roberts of Arizona State University, and Louise Wolitz of University of Texas at Austin, for their conscientious efforts.

The team of accuracy reviewers who reviewed art and page proof during the production process were also invaluable in their contributions to the Second Edition. We owe thanks to Kevin Baird of Montgomery County Community College, Duane Eberhardt of Missouri Southern State College, Martha Field of Greenfield Community College, Marcia Jones of Georgia Southern University, and Bettina Peiers of Arizona State University, for their keen eyes and intelligent comments.

Special thanks again go to Bettina Peiers and Karen Thomas-Brandt, both of Arizona State University, who were a tremendous help with the Test Bank. Their patience and skill contributed to an even more comprehensive testing tool for this edition. The important efforts made by Michael Couvillion of Plymouth State College in preparing the first edition Test Bank must also be acknowledged.

We also want to thank the many people at Houghton Mifflin Co. who devoted countless hours making this text the best it could be, including Denise Clinton, Mike Ginley, Julie Hogenboom, Susan Westendorf, Pat Mahtani, Nancy Murphy, and Ann Schroeder. From the beginning, we have been impressed with their expertise and energy. Through the mail, computer systems, phone, and sometimes by plane, we have managed to join forces continually for the last three years. We could not have completed this book without their enthusiasm and devotion.

Finally, we wish to thank our families and friends. The inspiration they provided through the conception and development of this book cannot be measured, but certainly was essential.

Our students at Arizona State University have helped us along the way: their many questions have given us invaluable insight into how best to present this intriguing subject. It is our hope that this textbook will bring a clear understanding of economic thought to many other students as well. We welcome any feedback for improvements.

W.B.
M.M.

REVIEWERS WHO HELPED SET THE STAGE FOR A SUCCESSFUL FIRST EDITION

Shahid Alam
Northeastern University

Lori Alden
California State University, Sacramento

Maurice Ballabon
City University of New York—Baruch College

Mark Berger
University of Kentucky

Donna Bialik
Indiana-Purdue University

Mary Bone
Pensacola Junior College

Bradley Braun
University of Central Florida

Jacqueline Brux
University of Wisconsin

Joan Buccino
Florida Southern College

Conrad Caligaris
Northeastern University

Michael Couvillion
Plymouth State College

Andy Dane
Angelo State University

Elynor Davis
Georgia Southern College

Gary Dymski
University of Southern California

Ana Eapen
William Paterson College

John Eckalbar
California State University, Chico

Paul Estenson
Gustavus Adolphus College

Paul Fahy
Eastern Illinois University

Joel Feiner
State University of New York at Old Westbury

Peter Garlick
State University of New York at New Paltz

John Gemello
San Francisco State University

Morton Hirsch
Kingsboro Community College

Beth Ingram
University of Iowa

David Jobson
Keystone Junior College

George Kelley
Worcester State College

Dick Kennedy
Odessa College

Barbara Killen
University of Minnesota

Michael Klein
Clark University

Keith Leeseberg
Manatee Community College

James Marchand
Radford University

James Mason
San Diego Mesa College

Edward Merkel
Troy State University

Irving Morrissett
University of Colorado

Denny Myers
Oklahoma City College

Joseph Nieb
Embry-Riddle Aeronautical University

Thomas Oberhofer
Eckerd College

Gerard O'Boyle
St. John's University

Erin O'Brien
San Diego Mesa College

Albert Okunade
Memphis State University

Paul Reali
Bryant & Stratton Business Institute

Robert Reinke
University of South Dakota

James Rigterink
Polk Community College

Randell Routt
Elizabethtown Community College

Gerald Sazama
University of Connecticut

Paul Schmitt
St. Clair County Community College

Carole Scott
West Georgia College

William Doyle Smith
University of Texas at El Paso

W.R. Smith
Georgia Southern College

Todd Steen
Hope College

Andrew Stern
California State University, Long Beach

Thomas Tacker
Embry-Riddle Aeronautical University

Eugenia Toma
University of Kentucky

William Trumbull
West Virginia University

Thomas Watkins
Eastern Kentucky University

Marc Zagara
Community College of the Finger Lakes

John Atkins
Pensacola Junior College

Kevin Baird
Montgomery County Community College

A. Paul Baroutsis
Slippery Rock University

Kari Battaglia
University of North Texas

James T. Bennett
George Mason University

Charles A. Bennett
Gannon University

Robert G. Bise
Orange Coast College

Bradley Braun
University of Central Florida

G.E. Breger
University of South Carolina

James A. Bryan
North Harris College

Evelyn Burkett
University of Arkansas at Pine Bluff

Judy Butler
Baylor University

Cindy Cannon
North Harris College

Shirley Cassing
University of Pittsburgh

Mitch Charklewicz
Central Connecticut State University

Barry Clark
University of Wisconsin, LaCrosse

Charles M. Clark
Saint John's University

Joseph Daboll-Lavoie
Nazareth College

Joseph Daniels
Marquette University

David Denslow
University of Florida

Mike Davoudi
North Harris College

Robert H. DeFina
Villanova University

John W. Dorsey
University of Maryland, College Park

Duane Eberhardt
Missouri Southern State College

James Eden
Portland Community College

Mary Edwards
Saint Cloud State University

Paul Estenson
Gustavus Adolphus College

Eleanor Fapohunda
State University of New York, Farmingdale

John F. Ficks
College of Dupage

Martha K. Field
Greenfield Community College

John Fizel
Pennsylvania State University at Erie, The Behrend College

Gregory Fleckenstein
Baker College of Muskegon

Jim Gerber
San Diego State University

James R. Gillette
Texas A&M University

Janet Griffin-Graves
Howard University

George Greenwade
Sam Houston State University

Robert G. Homa
Norwalk Community College

Calvin Hoy
County College of Morris

Marcia Jones
Georgia Southern University

B. Patrick Joyce
Michigan Technological University

Robert Kaestner
Rider College

John Kane
State University of New York, Oswego

Farida Khan
University of Wisconsin, Parkside

S.Y. Li
Virginia State University

Mark Maier
Glendale College

Thomas Maloy
Muskegon Community College

Yousef Mansur
Oklahoma City Community College

Donald Mar
San Francisco State University

Shannon Marting
Inver Hills Community College

Mark McNulty
San Diego State University

Edward T. Merkel
Troy State University

Timothy Nash
Northwood Institute

Gregory Ozimek
Eastern Illinois University

Lynn Pierson Doti
Chapman University

Nancy Roberts
Arizona State University

Jonathan Sandy
University of San Diego

Ted Scheinman
Mount Hood Community College

Richard Schiming
Mankato State University

Steven Shwiff
East Texas State University

Ajmer Singh
Western Oregon State College

Harlan Smith
Marshall University

Robert Sorenson
University of Missouri, Saint Louis

William Stine
Clarion University of Pennsylvania

Robert C. Stuart
Rutgers University

Timothy Sullivan
Towson State University

Jay Sultan
Bentley College

Anthony Viegbesie
Tallahassee Community College

Mark L. Wilson
University of Charleston

Mark Wohar
University of Nebraska

Louise Wolitz
University of Texas, Austin

Brief Contents

Contents

Contents

MICROECONOMICS

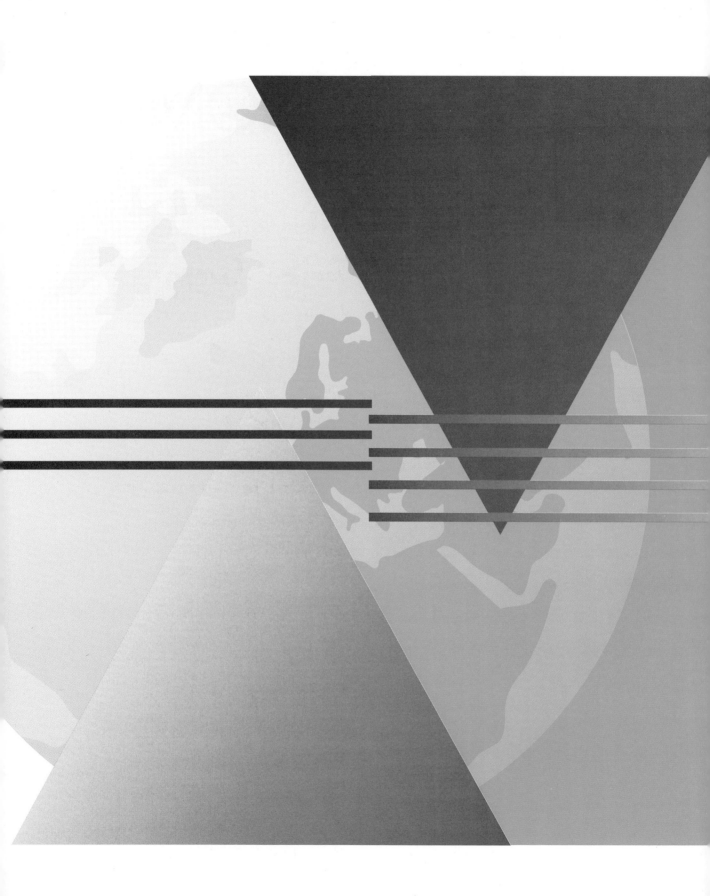

I

Introduction to the Price System

1

Economics: The World Around You

FUNDAMENTAL QUESTIONS

1. What is economics?
2. What are the principles of economics?
3. What is the economic approach?

PREVIEW

Y ou are a member of a very select group: you are attending college. Only about 25 percent of people in your age group in the United States are currently attending college. And, although this percentage is higher than it was back in the 1960s, it is actually lower than it was during the 1980s.

Why aren't more people attending college? Part of the reason may be the increased costs of college; during the 1980s, the direct expenses associated with college tripled. Yet, attending college and acquiring an education is more valuable today than it was during the 1970s and early 1980s. Technological change and increased international trade have placed a premium on a college education; more and more jobs require the skills acquired in college. As a result, the wage disparity between college-educated and non-college-educated workers is rising fairly rapidly. A college-educated person earns nearly twice as much as the person without a college degree.

Why are you attending college? Perhaps you've never really given it a great

deal of thought—your family always just assumed that college was a necessary step after high school; perhaps you analyzed the situation and decided that college was better than the alternatives. Whichever approach you took, you were practicing economics. You, or your family, were making choices and examining alternatives. This is what economics is about.

The objective of economics is to understand why the real world is what it is. This is not an easy proposition as the real world is very complex. After all, what happens in the real world is the result of human behavior, and humans are not simple creatures. Nonetheless, there are some fundamental regularities of human behavior that can help to explain the world we observe.

One such regularity is that people behave in ways that make themselves and those they care about better off and happier. Even without knowing that having a college education means your income will be higher than if you do not earn a college degree, you and your family knew or suspected that the college degree would mean a better lifestyle and a more secure or more prestigious job for you. However, what makes one person happy may not make others happy.

Knowing that it is the person without a college degree who is first laid off or unemployed during a recession, that the riskier jobs are held by those without a college degree, and that a person without a college degree is six times more likely to fall into poverty than a person with a college degree, we might be inclined to argue that the 75 percent of young people not attending college are making the wrong choice. But we can't say that. We don't know their circumstances; we don't know what makes them and their families happy. We only know that they do not believe the benefits of college outweigh the costs; otherwise they would be in college.

Knowing that most people behave in ways that make themselves better off and that most people compare costs and benefits in coming to a decision is powerful stuff. It allows us to explain much of the real world and to predict how that world might change if certain events occur.

This knowledge of human behavior is the subject matter of economics. To study economics is to seek answers not only for why people choose to go to college but also for why economies go through cycles, at times expanding and creating new jobs and at other times dipping into recessions; for why some people are thrown out of jobs to join the ranks of the unemployed while others are drawn out of the ranks of the unemployed into new jobs; for why some people live on welfare; for why some nations are richer than others; for why the illegal drug trade is so difficult to stop; for why health care is so expensive; or, in general, for why the world is what it is.

This chapter is the introduction to our study of economics. In it we present some of the terminology commonly used in economics and outline what the study of economics is.

What is economics?

I. THE DEFINITION OF ECONOMICS

What are the principles of economics?

People have unlimited wants—they always want more goods and services than they have or can purchase with their incomes. Whether they are wealthy or poor, what they have is never enough. Since people do not have everything they want, they must use their limited time and income to select those things they want most and forgo, or relinquish, the rest. The choices they make and the manner in which the choices are made explain much of why the real world is what it is. *Scarcity, choices, and how choices are made are the simple basics of human behavior called the principles of economics.*

I.a. Scarcity

scarcity:
the shortage that exists when less of something is available than is wanted at a zero price

economic good:
any item that is scarce

free good:
a good for which there is no scarcity

Neither the poor nor the wealthy have unlimited time, income, or wealth, and both must make choices to use these limited items in a way that best satisfies their wants. Because wants are unlimited and incomes, time, and other items are not, scarcity exists everywhere. **Scarcity** of something means that there is not enough of that item to satisfy everyone who wants it; it means that at a zero price the amount of an item that people want is greater than the amount that is available. Anything for which this condition holds is called an **economic good**. An economic good refers to *goods and services*—where goods are physical products, such as books or food, and services are nonphysical products, such as haircuts or golf lessons.

If there is enough of an item to satisfy wants, even at a zero price, the item is said to be a **free good**. It is difficult to think of examples of free goods. At one time people referred to air as free, but with air pollution control devices and other costly activities directed toward the maintenance of air quality

ECONOMIC INSIGHT

"Free" Air?

Although air might be what we describe as a free good, quality, breathable air is not free in many places in the world. One of the most successful new business ventures in Mexico City, in fact, is providing clean, breathable air. In this city of 19 million people and 3 million cars, dust, lead, and chemicals make the air unsafe to breathe more than 300 days a year. Private companies are now operating oxygen booths in local parks and malls. Breathable air, which costs more than $1.60 per minute, has become a popular product.

No city in the United States has resorted to oxygen boutiques, but there are large costs for air pollution abatement in many cities. It has been estimated that the cost of meeting federal air quality standards in Los Angeles will soon exceed $1,200 per year for every resident of the Los Angeles metropolitan area.

Sources: "Breathable Air for Swap or Sale," Peter Passell, *New York Times*, Jan. 30, 1992, p. D2; "Best Things in Life Aren't Always Free," Matt Moffett, *Wall Street Journal*, May 8, 1992, p. A1.

standards, "clean" air, at least, is not a free good, as noted in the Economic Insight "'Free' Air?"

If people would pay to have less of an item, that item is called an **economic bad**. It is not so hard to think of examples of bads: pollution, garbage, and disease fit the description.

Some goods are used to produce other goods. For instance, to make chocolate chip cookies we need flour, sugar, chocolate chips, butter, our own labor, and an oven. To distinguish between the ingredients of a good and the good itself, we call the ingredients **resources**. (Resources are also called **factors of production** and **inputs**; the terms are interchangeable.) The ingredients of the cookies are the resources, and the cookies are the goods.

As illustrated in Figure 1(a), economists have classified resources into four categories: land, labor, capital, and entrepreneurial ability.

1. **Land** includes all natural resources, such as minerals, timber, and water, as well as the land itself.

2. **Labor** refers to the physical and intellectual services of people and includes the training, education, and abilities of the individuals in a society.

3. **Capital** refers to products such as machinery and equipment that are used in production. Capital is a manufactured or created product used solely for the production of the goods and services that are consumed by individuals. You will often hear the term *capital* used to describe the financial backing for some project or the dollars used to finance some business. *Financial capital* refers to the money value of capital; *capital*, as the term is used in economics, is the physical entity—the machinery and equipment and the buildings, warehouses, and factories.

4. **Entrepreneurial ability** refers to the ability to recognize a profitable opportunity and the willingness and ability to organize the other resources and undertake the risk associated with the opportunity. It is

economic bad:
any item for which we would pay to have less

resources, factors of production, or inputs:
goods used to produce other goods, i.e., land, labor, capital, entrepreneurial ability

land:
all natural resources, such as minerals, timber, and water, as well as the land itself

labor:
the physical and intellectual services of people, including the training, education, and abilities of the individuals in a society

capital:
products such as machinery and equipment that are used in production

entrepreneurial ability:
the ability to recognize a profitable opportunity and the willingness and ability to organize land, labor, and capital and assume the risk associated with the opportunity

Figure 1
Flow of Resources and Income

Four types of resources are used to produce goods and services: land, labor, capital, and entrepreneurial ability. See 1(a). The owners of resources are provided income for selling their services. Land-owners are paid rent; laborers receive wages; capital receives interest; and entrepreneurs acquire profit. See 1(b). Figure 1(c) links Figures 1(a) and 1(b). People use their resources to acquire income with which they purchase the goods they want. Producers use the money received from selling the goods to pay for the use of the resources in making goods. Resources and income flow between certain firms and certain resource owners as people allocate their scarce resources to best satisfy their wants.

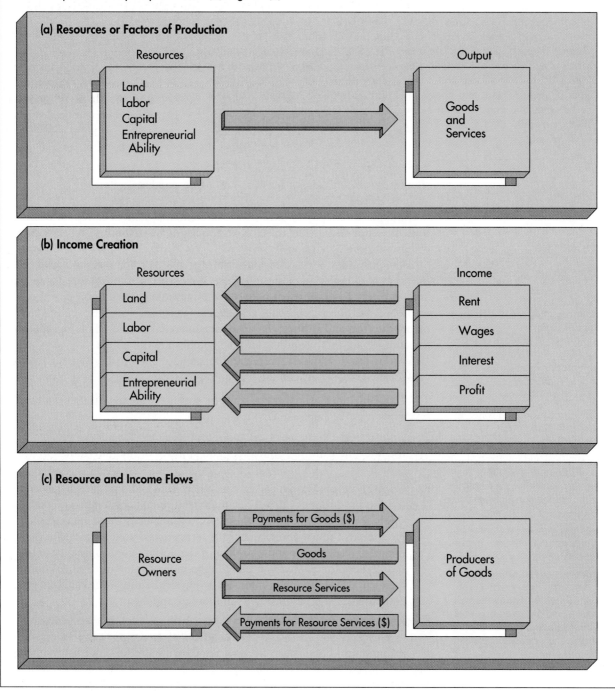

entrepreneur:
an individual with entre-
preneurial ability

a special talent few individuals have, and it plays such an important role in the economy that it is considered to be a resource on its own rather than just grouped together with labor. People who demonstrate entrepreneurial abilities are called **entrepreneurs**.

People obtain income by selling their resources or the use of their resources, as illustrated in Figure 1(b). Owners of land receive *rent*; when people provide labor services they are paid *wages*; owners of capital receive *interest*; and people with entrepreneurial ability receive the *profits* from starting, running, and operating businesses.

Figures 1(a) and 1(b) are linked because the income that resource owners acquire from selling the use of their resources provides them the ability to buy goods and services. And producers use the money received from selling their goods to pay for the resource services. In Figure 1(c), the flows of money are indicated along the outside arrows, and the flows of goods or resource services are indicated along the inside arrows. The resource services flow from resource owners to producers of goods in return for income; the flows of goods go from the producers of the goods to resource owners in return for the money payment for these goods.

1.b. Choices

Scarcity means that people have to make choices. People don't have everything they want; they do not have the time or the money to purchase everything they want. When people choose some things, they have to give up, or forgo, other things. *Economics is the study of how people choose to use their scarce resources to attempt to satisfy their unlimited wants.*

1.c. Rational Self-Interest

rational self-interest:
the term economists use to
describe how people make
choices

Rational self-interest is the term economists use to describe how people make choices. It means that people will make the choices that, at the time and with the information they have at their disposal, will give them the greatest amount of satisfaction.

You chose to attend college although 75 percent of those in your age group chose not to attend. All of you made rational choices based on what you perceived was in your best interest. How could it be in your best interest to do one thing and in another person's best interest to do exactly the opposite? Each person has unique goals and attitudes and faces different costs. Although your weighing of the alternatives came down on the side of attending college, another person weighed similar alternatives and came down on the side of not attending college. Both decisions were rational because in both cases the individual compared alternatives and selected the option that the *individual* thought was in his or her best interest.

It is important to note that rational self-interest depends on the information at hand and the individual's perception of what is in his or her best interest. People will make different choices even when facing the same information. Even though the probability of death in an accident is nearly 20 percent less if seat belts are worn, many people choose not to use them. Are these people rational? The answer is yes. Perhaps they do not want their clothes wrinkled or perhaps seat belts are just too inconvenient or perhaps they think the odds

When a college student volunteers to spend time with senior citizens in a local nursing home, she is giving up an afternoon that could be spent studying or forgoing the extra income she could earn at a part-time job. The opportunity costs of the time spent in volunteer activities are substantial. Yet, people who choose to do volunteer work find it more satisfying than the alternatives.

of getting in an accident are just too small to worry about. Whatever the reason, these people are choosing the option that at the time gives them the greatest satisfaction. *This is rational self-interest.*

If we told those people choosing not to wear seat belts that they definitely would have an accident and would suffer very serious injuries unless they wore the seat belts, their choice would probably be different. But because *we* think wearing seat belts is smart does not mean that others who choose not to wear seat belts are irrational or any less smart. Similarly, the expense of college and the commitment of four or more years of time might not make college seem like such a good choice to many people. Because some people choose not to attend college does not make them irrational. They are rational because they are comparing alternatives in order to select the option that *they* think will make them better off.

Economists think that most of the time most human beings are weighing alternatives, looking at costs and benefits, and making decisions in a way that they believe makes them better off. This is not to say that economists look upon human beings as androids lacking feelings and able only to carry out complex calculations like a computer. Rather, economists believe that the feelings and attitudes of human beings enter into people's comparisons of alternatives and help determine how people decide something is in their best interest.

Economists believe that human beings are self-interested, *not selfish.* People do contribute to charitable organizations and help others; people do make individual sacrifices because those sacrifices benefit their families or people they care about; soldiers do risk their lives to defend their country. All these acts are made in the name of rational self-interest.

Relying on the idea that most people, most of the time, are rationally self-interested allows economists to explain many real-world observations that otherwise might be inexplicable. Why, for instance, does the federal government spend $300 billion more each year than it takes in? Because, according to rational self-interest, the deficit is in the best interests of those receiving the benefits of the deficit. Why do people already living in apartments support limits on rents and rent increases, while landlords and those without apartments are opposed to such controls? Rational self-interest suggests that it is in the best interest of renters with apartments to have rent controls, while it is not in the best interest of landlords or potential renters without apartments to have rent controls. As we will see throughout the book, rational self-interest provides a valuable first step in analyzing issues and answering questions.

RECAP

1. Scarcity exists when people want more of an item than exists at a zero price.
2. Because people have unlimited wants, goods are scarce.
3. Goods are produced with resources (also called factors of production and inputs). Economists have classified resources into four categories: land, labor, capital, and entrepreneurial ability.
4. Choices have to be made because of scarcity. People cannot have or do everything they desire all the time. Economics is the study of how people choose to use their scarce resources in an attempt to satisfy their wants.
5. People make choices in a manner known as rational self-interest; people make the choices that at the time and with the information they have at their disposal will give them the greatest satisfaction.

2. THE ECONOMIC APPROACH

What is the economic approach?

Economists often refer to the "economic approach" or to "economic thinking." By this, they mean that the principles of scarcity, choice, and rational self-interest are used in a specific way to search out answers to questions about the real world. The specific way is to focus on positive analysis and apply the scientific method. In this section we will examine economic thinking.

2.a. Positive and Normative Analysis

In applying the principles of economics to questions about the real world, it is important to avoid imposing your opinions or value judgments on others. Analysis that does not impose the value judgments of one individual on the decisions of others is called **positive analysis**. If you demonstrate that unemployment in the automobile industry in the United States rises when people

positive analysis:
analysis of what is

normative analysis:
analysis of what ought to be

purchase cars produced in other countries instead of cars produced in the United States, you are undertaking positive analysis. However, if you claim that there ought to be a law to stop people from buying foreign-made cars, you are imposing your value judgments on the decisions and desires of others. That is not positive analysis. It is, instead, **normative analysis**. *Normative means "what ought to be"; positive means "what is."* If you demonstrate that the probability of death in an automobile accident is 20 percent higher if seat belts are not worn, you are using positive analysis. If you argue that there should be a law requiring seat belts to be worn, you are using normative analysis.

Conclusions based on opinion or value judgments do not advance one's understanding of events.

Economics involves mostly positive analysis because normative analysis does not explain the real world or lead to predictions about it. Normative analysis does, however, play a role in economic policy formation. Typically, policymakers discuss some aspects of human behavior and then make a proposal to change that behavior. For instance, many politicians believe that the United States consumes too much gasoline. They argue that a high tax should be placed on gasoline in order to change people's behavior. This is a normative approach; it is someone's opinion that too much gasoline is consumed.

The problem with normative analysis is that everything depends on the norm being used. For instance, suppose society decides to evaluate policies like the gas-tax proposal using the norm that if more people are helped than are hurt by a program then the program is beneficial. A program of taxing gas at the pump might meet this norm, but—and this is the key point—if the norm is changed, the result could change. Suppose the norm used to evaluate a program is that at least one person must be made better off by the program without harming anyone else. Then the gas-tax program would fail, since someone or some group—those who drive the most—would be made worse off by the tax scheme. The point here is that the outcome of normative analysis depends on the norms or value judgments being applied. Positive analysis is free of value judgments, so its outcome does not vary as norms change.

The outcome of normative analysis depends on the norm being applied; the outcome of positive analysis does not vary as norms change.

2.b. Scientific Method

scientific method:
a manner of analyzing issues that involves five steps: recognizing the problem, making assumptions, building a model, making predictions, and testing the model

As stated before, economists want to understand the real world and to be able to predict the results of certain events. These goals are hardly unique to economics—they are the same goals most scientists strive toward. A chemist may want to predict the results of combining certain chemicals, and an astronomer may want to predict the results of black holes on galaxy behavior. Similarly, an economist may want to predict the result of an increase in the tuition and fees of college or the result of an increase in taxes. The economist uses much the same methodology as the chemist and astronomer to examine the real world—the **scientific method**. There are five steps in the scientific method, as noted in Figure 2: (1) recognize the problem or issue, (2) cut away unnecessary detail by making assumptions, (3) develop a model or story of the problem or issue, (4) make predictions, and (5) test the model.

The first step in the scientific method, the recognition of the problem, means that an issue is identified—rise in unemployment, accelerated inflation, failure of a business, growth of social security taxes, increased cocaine addiction, the AIDS epidemic, the purchase of one cereal over another, the choice of one job over another, and on and on. Once the issue is identified,

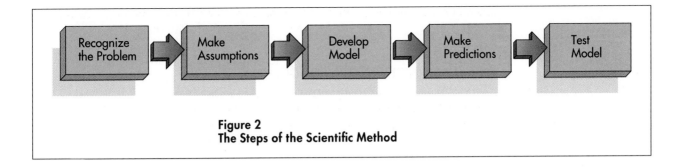

Figure 2
The Steps of the Scientific Method

the next step is to explain it. This step may seem simple enough, but often it is not. Each problem in economics is so complex that the task of explaining it seems impossible. Thousands, even hundreds of thousands, of details are involved in something as apparently straightforward as deciding why people choose one college over another. The location of the college relative to the home, the appearance of the college, the friendliness of the admissions officers, the reputation of the football team, the occupations of parents, whether friends are attending college, the weather during the day the college was visited, and whether the student was feeling well the day applications were submitted are all details involved in the decision. Economists, like biochemists, physicists, and paleontologists, can never take into account all the details surrounding an event they want to study. They have to reduce the complexity of the real world to manageable proportions using models and assumptions.

A **theory**, or **model**, is merely a simplification, or abstraction, of the real world that enables scientists to organize their thoughts. A paper airplane is a model of a real airplane; a computer simulation of space is a model of the galaxies. Each model can illustrate certain aspects of the real world but is not intended to capture every aspect of the real world. Good economic models are those that explain or predict well; poor models are those that do not explain or predict well.

An economic model uses assumptions. **Assumptions** are statements taken to be true without justification. One of the most commonly used assumptions is *everything else held constant*, referred to quite often in its Latin form, **ceteris paribus**. We might say that fewer people attend college as the tuition of college rises, ceteris paribus. This means that if only the tuition and number of people attending college are allowed to change, then a higher tuition means fewer people attend college. If we did not make the assumption of everything else held constant, then the statement could be grossly in error. If, for instance, incomes quadrupled while tuition rose a mere 5 percent, we could observe more people attending college even as the tuition rose. Similarly, if the income-earning potential of those with a college degree increased significantly, we might observe that more people attended college even as the tuition rose. Assumptions allow us to focus on the relationship between the variables in which we are interested, in this case tuition and the number of people attending college.

An economic model (or theory) is a tool used in the attempt to understand the real world. As with any theory, it must undergo a **test** to see whether it is

theory or model:
a simplification or abstraction of the real world that enables scientists to organize their thoughts

assumptions:
statements that are taken to be true without justification

ceteris paribus:
other things being equal, or everything else held constant

tests:
trials or measurements used to determine whether a theory is consistent with the facts

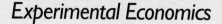
Experimental Economics

Experimentation in the scientific sense is described as "putting in action causes and agents over which we have control, and purposely varying their combinations and noticing what effects take place" (Herschel, *Study of Natural Philosophy*, p. 76). In sciences like physics and chemistry, this is the best form of discovery. Where easy manipulation is more difficult, the inquirer must rely on simple observation; instead of creating instances, the inquirer has to find them in nature or wait until they are presented to his or her view. This has been the predominant form of inquiry in economics.

About 1950, laboratory experimentation was introduced into economic methodology. Many of the initial experiments were run on students in economics classes. Since the early 1970s, hundreds of experiments have been run using both human and animal subjects; economic laboratories have been constructed and are used at institutions such as the University of Arizona, Indiana University, and Texas A & M University.

During the last fifteen years, experimental economics has become an important part of the field of economics. Experiments are being developed to study all topics in economics, from individual choice to how groups make decisions to the transition from Soviet-style economies to a U.S.-style economy.

consistent with the facts—whether it can be used to make accurate predictions. It is difficult to test economic models the way that chemists or physicists test their models, however. A chemist's model might predict that a certain combination of chemicals will cause an explosion. This model can be tested by combining the chemicals and observing the results. Economists, though, can seldom find naturally occurring conditions that provide a good test of a model, and it is difficult (although not always impossible, as noted in the Economic Insight "Experimental Economics") to conduct controlled laboratory experiments in economics. For instance, how would we test the economic model that predicts the number of people attending college will rise as the cost of college falls? A test of this model would be to reduce the cost of college while nothing else changes and see what happens to college enrollments. But things do change—changes occur in incomes, attitudes, international conditions, jobs, quality of cars, transportation systems, and millions of other items all the time. Testing theories is difficult; nevertheless, economists need to develop models in order to study human behavior, and they have to subject the models to whatever tests can be devised—they have to compare the predictions of the model to the real world.

Don't read this as an apology for the use of economic theory or models. Models are very powerful devices. They have allowed us to better understand the causes of unemployment and inflation, recessions and expansions, wage rates, income distributions, and the relative performances of different economies, among many other issues. Without models, scientists could not have sent a man to the moon or understood the impact of CFCs on the ozone; without models, economists could not have understood and predicted the collapse of the Soviet Union.

The Super Bowl Predictor

Football's Washington Redskins and the U.S. stock market had much in common in 1992: both looked as though they had long-lasting vigor last January; both had a brief down spell in the fall; and both had, overall, a good year.

This came as no surprise to fans of the Super Bowl Predictor, which has proven uncannily accurate in foretelling the stock market's direction for the year in which the game is played. Since Super Bowl I in 1967, whenever a team from the original National Football League (which includes old NFL teams now in the American Football Conference such as the Colts, Steelers, and Browns) wins the Super Bowl, the stock market usually has an up year. Conversely, the market tends to go down during years when an American Football Conference team is the winner. The Predictor missed in 1970, 1978, and 1988, but has been accurate in twenty-three out of the twenty-six Super Bowls played to date, when measured against the Dow Jones Average, for a performance percentage of 88 percent accuracy.

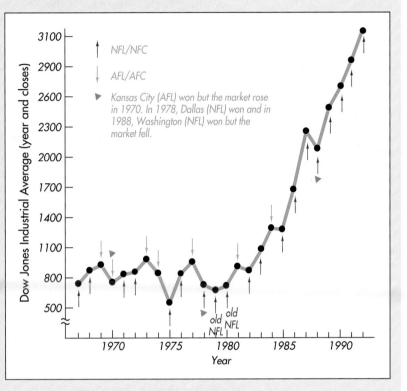

Source: Robert H. Stovall, "The Super Bowl Predictor," *Financial World*, Jan. 26, 1988, p. 72; data and story updated by authors. Reprinted by permission.

2.c. Common Mistakes

fallacy of composition:
the mistaken assumption that what applies in the case of one applies to the case of many

Many errors can be made in scientific analysis. Two common mistakes in economics are the fallacy of composition and interpreting association as causation. The **fallacy of composition** is the error of attributing what applies in the case of one to the case of many. If one person in a theater realizes a fire has begun and races to the exit, that one person is better off. If we assume that a thousand people in a crowded theater would be better off behaving exactly like the single individual, we would be committing the mistake known as the fallacy of composition.

association as causation:
the mistaken assumption that because two events seem to occur together, one causes the other

The mistaken interpretation of **association as causation** occurs when unrelated or coincidental events that occur at about the same time are believed to have a cause-and-effect relationship. For example, the result of the Super Bowl game is sometimes said to predict how the stock market will perform, as noted in the Economic Insight "The Super Bowl Predictor." According to this "theory," if the NFC team wins, the stock market will rise in the new year, but if the AFC team wins, the market will fall. This bit of folklore is a clear example of confusion between causation and association. Simply because two events seem to occur together does not mean that one causes the other. Clearly, a football game cannot cause the stock market to rise or fall.

2.d. Microeconomics and Macroeconomics

microeconomics:
the study of economics at the level of the individual

macroeconomics:
the study of the economy as a whole

Economics is the study of how people choose to allocate their scarce resources among their unlimited wants and involves the application of certain principles—scarcity, choice, rational self-interest—in a consistent manner using the scientific method. The study of economics is usually separated into two general areas, microeconomics and macroeconomics. **Micro-economics** is the study of economics at the level of the individual economic entity: the individual firm, the individual consumer, and the individual worker. In **macroeconomics**, rather than analyzing the behavior of an individual consumer, we look at the sum of the behaviors of all consumers, which is called the consumer sector, or household sector. Similarly, instead of examining the behavior of an individual firm, in macroeconomics we examine the sum of the behaviors of all firms, called the business sector.

RECAP

1. The objective of economics is to understand why the real world is what it is.

2. Positive analysis refers to what is, while normative economics refers to what ought to be.

3. The scientific method consists of five steps: recognition of the problem, assumptions, model, predictions, and tests of the model.

4. Assumptions are a means of simplifying the analysis; they are statements that are taken to be true without justification.

5. The fallacy of composition and interpreting association as causation are two commonly made errors in economic analysis.

6. The study of economics is typically divided into two parts, macroeconomics and microeconomics.

SUMMARY

▲▼ What is economics?

1. The objective of economics is to understand why the real world is what it is. §1.a

2. Economics is the study of how people choose to allocate scarce resources to satisfy their unlimited wants. §1.b

3. The resources that go into the production of goods are land, labor, capital, and entrepreneurial ability. §1.a

▲▼ **What are the principles of economics?**

4. Scarcity is universal; it applies to anything people would like more of than is available at a zero price. Because of scarcity, choices must be made, and choices are made in a way that is in the decision-maker's rational self-interest. §1.a, 1.b, 1.c

5. People make choices that, at the time and with the information at hand, will give them the greatest satisfaction. §1.c

▲▼ **What is the economic approach?**

6. Positive analysis is analysis of what is; normative analysis is analysis of what ought to be. §2.a

7. The scientific method consists of five steps: recognition of the problem, assumptions, model, predictions, and tests of the model. §2.b

8. Assumptions are a means of simplifying the analysis; they are statements that are taken to be true without justification. §2.b

9. The fallacy of composition and interpreting association as causation are two commonly made errors in economic analysis. §2.c

10. The study of economics is typically divided into two parts, macroeconomics and microeconomics. §2.d

KEY TERMS

scarcity §1.a
economic good §1.a
free good §1.a
economic bad §1.a
resources, factors of production, or inputs §1.a
land §1.a
labor §1.a
capital §1.a
entrepreneurial ability §1.a
entrepreneur §1.a
rational self-interest §1.c

positive analysis §2.a
normative analysis §2.a
scientific method §2.b
theory or model §2.b
assumptions §2.b
ceteris paribus §2.b
test §2.b
fallacy of composition §2.c
association as causation §2.c
microeconomics §2.d
macroeconomics §2.d

EXERCISES

1. Which of the following are economic goods? Explain why each is or is not an economic good.
   a. steaks
   b. houses
   c. cars
   d. garbage
   e. T-shirts

2. Many people go to a medical doctor every time they are ill; others never visit a doctor. Explain how a "model" of human behavior can include such opposite behaviors.

3. Erin has purchased a $35 ticket to a "Grateful Dead" concert. She is invited to a send-off party for a friend who is moving to another part of the country. The party is scheduled for

the same day as the concert. If she had known about the party before she bought the concert ticket, she would have chosen to attend the party. However, having purchased the ticket, Erin will choose to attend the concert. Evaluate this problem.

4. It is well documented in scientific research that smoking is harmful to our health. Smokers have higher incidences of coronary disease, cancer, and other catastrophic illnesses. Knowing this, about thirty percent of young people begin smoking and about twenty-five percent of the U.S. population smokes. Are the people who choose to smoke irrational? What do you think of the argument that we should ban smoking in order to protect these people from themselves?

5. Indicate which of the following statements is true or false. If the statement is false, change it to make it true.

a. Positive analysis imposes the value judgments of one individual on the decisions of others.

b. Ceteris paribus is Latin for "let the buyer beware."

c. Rational self-interest is the same thing as selfishness.

d. An economic good is scarce if it has a positive price.

e. An economic bad is an item that has a positive price.

f. A resource is the ingredient used to make factors of production.

6. Are the following statements normative or positive? If a statement is normative change it to a positive statement.

a. The government should provide free tuition to all college students.

b. An effective way to increase the skills of the work force is to provide free tuition to all college students.

c. The government must provide job training if we are to compete with other countries.

d. The North American Free Trade Act will increase the skill requirements of workers in the United States.

e. The North American Free Trade Act should not be supported because it will take jobs away from the United States.

7. In the *New York Times Magazine* in 1970, Milton Friedman, a Nobel Prize–winning economist, argued that "the social responsibility of business is to increase profits." How would Friedman's argument fit with the basic economic model that people behave in ways they believe are in their best self-interest?

8. Two economists crossed the street one day when one spied a twenty-dollar bill on the sidewalk. The first economist pointed out to the second economist that there was a twenty-dollar bill on the sidewalk. The second said, "No, there isn't a twenty-dollar bill there. If it were a twenty-dollar bill, somebody would have picked it up." In what sense does this joke describe the scientific methodology used by economists?

9. Use economics to explain why men's and women's restrooms tend to be located near each other in airports and other public buildings.

10. Use economics to explain why diamonds are more expensive than water, when water is necessary for survival and diamonds are not.

11. Use economics to explain why people leave tips in the following two cases: (a) at a restaurant they visit often; (b) at a restaurant they visit only once.

12. Use economics to explain why people contribute to charities.

13. Use economics to explain this statement: "Increasing the speed limit has, to some degree, compromised highway safety on interstate roads but enhanced safety on non-interstate roads."

More Cars, Going Faster, Closer Together

Remember the long and hot arguments over the national speed limits? It may be that we have not heard the last of the disputes over the "double nickel" (55 miles per hour) and its country cousin, the 65-mph limit, posted along rural sections of the nation's freeways five years ago.

As any traveler can testify, these limits are violated routinely. Yet speed violations evidently counted for little in the pleasant news of recent days that the death rate on the nation's highways has dropped yet again and now—at 2.1 fatalities per 100 million miles of travel recorded in 1990—is at a record low. . . .

Statistics do not diminish the personal tragedies that continue to occur on U.S. roadways. Far too many people are still dying on the highways and—because there are a lot more people on the road these days—total fatalities can (and do) grow even as the overall death rate declines.

Still, it was interesting that the announcements about the past year's highway-safety performance made no specific references to speed limits. Instead, officials in the federal Transportation Department and the National Highway Traffic Safety Administration (NHTSA) attributed the trend to other factors.

For example, Jerry Ralph Curry, head of the NHTSA, cited greater availability of automobile air bags and improved safety belts (plus increased use of seat belts of all kinds), along with more efficient emergency medical services and greater emphasis on motorcycle training and helmet use. Meantime, the campaign against the biggest highway menace of all, drinking drivers, goes on, too. . . .

Arguments across the nation over the 55-mph limit began soon after its enactment by Congress following the 1974 Arab oil embargo—not as a safety measure but as one way to conserve energy.

The promised energy savings were minimal—at best, about 1 percent of gasoline consumption, or roughly the same amount that could be saved by increasing radial-tire pressures from 24 to 26 pounds.

So, the "double nickel" was transformed into a safety symbol. "Stay alive at 55," the slogans read. And much publicity was given the striking decline in highway deaths —more than 15 percent—that had occurred in the first year of the lowered limit.

But skeptics said the lifesaving advantages were overstated. They said the especially dramatic drop in deaths during 1974 more likely was the result of high fuel prices and limited supplies that caused Americans to drive 25 to 30 percent fewer miles during the period.

Worse, millions of otherwise law-abiding citizens routinely began violating the 55-mph law, which was given very uneven enforcement. . . .

By the late 1980s, pressures on Congress from wide-open-spaces states produced the 65-mph law for sections of interstate freeways in lightly populated areas.

Safety proponents said the change would invite many more violations (many motorists around the country fudge on posted limits by about 10 mph no matter what the limit happens to be), and predicted a serious increase in fatal accidents. Fortunately, the forecasts were wrong.

Today, major freeways serving urban areas are experiencing a continuing rise in traffic volumes, the inevitable result of the population boom and—unless the Persian Gulf war proves otherwise—ample supplies of motor fuel. . . .

Highway experts say today's freeways were designed to handle a "maximum" of 2,000 vehicles per hour per lane at an average speed of 50 mph. But in several places around the state, the 2,000-car maximum has run up to more than 2,300 vehicles per lane with little reduction in speed.

In short, we have more cars traveling faster, and with less distance between them.

It's a dicey situation that could get worse. We need to slow things down a bit and—as a Washington State Patrol spokesman puts it—"to be more civil out there."

Source: Reprinted with permission of The Seattle Times Company.

Commentary

Why is there a speed limit on highways? This may strike you as a strange question, but in fact some highways, like the Autobahn in Germany, have no speed limit. Does this mean that people drive as fast as possible on the Autobahn? Alternatively, why don't people drive within the legal speed limit on interstate highways in the United States? Should the government try to influence the manner in which people drive by posting speed limits?

Economics is concerned with the manner in which people choose among different alternatives and with the implications of these choices. Economic analysis of an issue first considers how people select one option over another by focusing on the relative costs and benefits of different choices. The analysis may then look at the implications of these choices for the individual or for society as a whole. We can apply this type of analysis to the issue of speed limits.

What determines the speed at which you drive on an interstate highway? You weigh the benefits against the costs of driving within the speed limit. An obvious benefit of staying within the speed limit is that you avoid the risk of receiving a speeding ticket. Another benefit is that driving more slowly saves gas; in fact, one of the primary arguments for the initial imposition of the 55 mph limit in 1974, which came in the wake of increased oil prices, was that it would reduce the consumption of gasoline (and therefore imported oil) in the United States. As noted in the article, this argument was not supported by the facts; simply inflating tires would save more gas. Nevertheless, gas saving, no matter how little is saved, is one benefit of a lower speed limit. Other benefits are that driving more slowly reduces the wear and tear on your car. Also, driving slower, if everyone else is also driving slower, reduces your chances of having an accident. Nothing is free, however. The main cost to driving more slowly is time: the slower you travel, the longer your trip will take.

The actual speed that people travel on an interstate reflects their weighing of the benefits and costs of different speeds. As the costs or benefits of driving no faster than 55 mph change, we may expect to see a change in the average speed on the interstate. For example, if the fine for speeding increases, the cost of violating the speed limit rises and we would expect to see a decrease in the average speed on the interstate. If there is an increase in the number of police patrolling the highway, the likelihood of being caught speeding rises and this too would tend to decrease the average speed on the interstate. Policies that attempt to increase the costs of driving above the speed limit, such as by increasing fines, or that increase the likelihood of getting caught, for instance by outlawing radar detectors, would tend to make people drive more slowly on average. On the other hand, if fines are decreased or if radar detectors get more sophisticated or police are not allowed to use radar equipment, the costs of driving above the speed limit decline. Also, if the price of gas falls, the comparative cost of driving faster falls and the average speed on the interstate might very well increase.

Do increased speeds lead to increased highway deaths? To answer this question definitively, we would need to examine what happens on the highways when the speed limit is changed and everything else is held constant. The problem is that when the speed limit was changed, everything else was not held constant: Airbags, antilock brake systems, improved seat belts, and other safety features have been added to automobiles since the speed limit was lowered so that driving at any speed is safer than it used to be. Nevertheless, suppose that we could argue definitively that increased speed limits mean more highway deaths. Would we then argue that speed limits should be reduced to 25 or 15 mph? No one is in favor of more highway deaths, but there is a tradeoff. In this case, the tradeoff is between people's desire to drive at a certain speed and the reduction of highway deaths.

Speed limits, like other laws and public policies, carry costs and benefits to individuals and to society. Economic analysis helps us identify these costs and benefits and understand how people may react to them. Economic analysis serves as a useful tool in deciding among policies and courses of action.

1

Working with Graphs

According to the old saying, one picture is worth a thousand words. If that maxim is correct, and, in addition, if producing a thousand words takes more time and effort than producing one picture, it is no wonder that economists rely so extensively on pictures. The pictures that economists use to explain concepts are called *graphs*. The purpose of this appendix is to explain how graphs are constructed and how to interpret them.

1. READING GRAPHS

The three kinds of graphs used by economists are shown in Figures 1, 2, and 3. Figure 1 is a *line graph*. It is the most commonly used type of graph in eco-

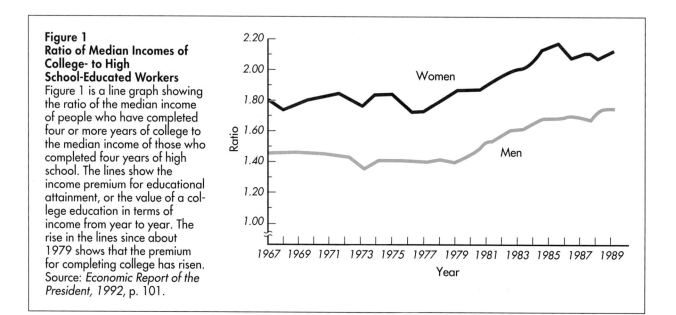

Figure 1
Ratio of Median Incomes of College- to High School-Educated Workers
Figure 1 is a line graph showing the ratio of the median income of people who have completed four or more years of college to the median income of those who completed four years of high school. The lines show the income premium for educational attainment, or the value of a college education in terms of income from year to year. The rise in the lines since about 1979 shows that the premium for completing college has risen. Source: *Economic Report of the President, 1992*, p. 101.

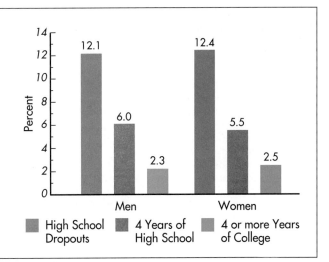

Figure 2
Unemployment and Education
Figure 2 is a bar graph indicating the unemployment rate by educational attainment. The blue refers to high school dropouts, the red refers to those with four years of high school, and the green refers to those with four or more years of college. One set of bars is presented for males and one set for females. The bars are arranged in order, with the highest incidence of unemployment shown first, the next highest second, and the lowest located third. This arrangement is made only for ease in reading and interpretation. The bars could be arranged in any order. Sources: *Economic Report of the President, 1992. Statistical Abstract of the United States, 1991* (Washington, D.C.: Government Printing Office).

nomics. Figure 2 is a *bar graph*. It is probably used more often in popular magazines than any other kind of graph. Figure 3 is a *pie graph*, or *pie chart*. Although it is less popular than the bar and line graphs, it appears often enough that you need to be familiar with it.

1.a. Relationships Between Variables

Figure 1 is a line graph showing the ratio of the median income of people who have completed four or more years of college to the median income of those who have completed just four years of high school. The lines show the value of a college education in terms of the additional income earned relative to the income earned without a college degree on a year-to-year basis. You can see that the premium for completing college has risen in recent years and that it is higher for women than men.

Figure 2 is a bar graph indicating the unemployment rate by educational attainment. The blue refers to high school dropouts, the red refers to those with four years of high school, and the green refers to those with four or more years of college. One set of bars is presented for males and one set for females. The bars are arranged in order, with the highest incidence of unemployment depicted first, the next highest second, and the lowest located third. This arrangement is made only for ease in reading and interpretation. The bars could be arranged in any order. The graph illustrates that unemployment strikes those with less education more than it does those with more education.

Figure 3 is a pie chart showing the percentage of the U.S. population completing various years of schooling. Unlike line and bar graphs, a pie chart is not actually a picture of a relationship between two variables. Instead, the pie represents the whole, 100 percent of the U.S. population, and the pieces of the pie represent parts of the whole—the percentage of the population completing one to four years of elementary school only, five to seven years of elementary school, and so on up to four or more years of college.

Because a pie chart does not show the relationship between variables, it is

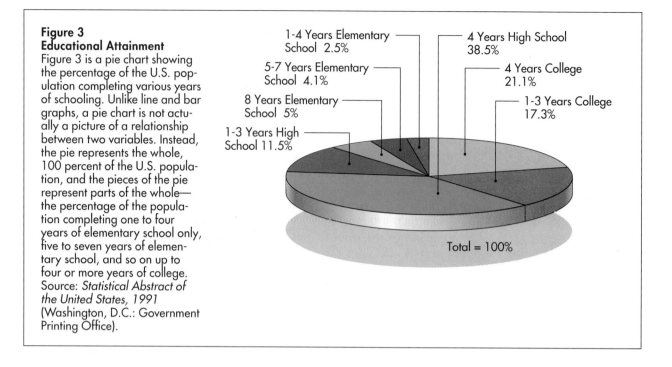

Figure 3
Educational Attainment
Figure 3 is a pie chart showing the percentage of the U.S. population completing various years of schooling. Unlike line and bar graphs, a pie chart is not actually a picture of a relationship between two variables. Instead, the pie represents the whole, 100 percent of the U.S. population, and the pieces of the pie represent parts of the whole—the percentage of the population completing one to four years of elementary school only, five to seven years of elementary school, and so on up to four or more years of college. Source: *Statistical Abstract of the United States, 1991* (Washington, D.C.: Government Printing Office).

1-4 Years Elementary School 2.5%
5-7 Years Elementary School 4.1%
8 Years Elementary School 5%
1-3 Years High School 11.5%
4 Years High School 38.5%
4 Years College 21.1%
1-3 Years College 17.3%
Total = 100%

not as useful for explaining economic concepts as line and bar graphs. Line graphs are used more often than bar graphs to explain economic concepts.

1.b. Independent and Dependent Variables

independent variable:
the variable whose value does not depend on the value of other variables

dependent variable:
the variable whose value depends on the value of the independent variable

Most line and bar graphs involve just two variables, an **independent variable** and a **dependent variable**. An independent variable is one whose value does not depend on the values of other variables; a dependent variable, on the other hand, is one whose value does depend on the values of other variables. The value of the dependent variable is determined after the value of the independent variable is determined.

In Figure 2, the *independent* variable is the educational status of the man or woman, and the *dependent* variable is the incidence of unemployment (percentage of group that is unemployed). The incidence of unemployment depends on the educational attainment of the man or woman.

1.c. Direct and Inverse Relationships

direct or positive relationship:
the relationship that exists when the values of related variables move in the same direction

inverse or negative relationship:
the relationship that exists when the values of related variables move in opposite directions

If the value of the dependent variable increases as the value of the independent variable increases, the relationship between the two types of variables is called a **direct**, or **positive**, **relationship**. If the value of the dependent variable decreases as the value of the independent variable increases, the relationship between the two types of variables is called an **inverse**, or **negative**, **relationship**.

In Figure 2, unemployment and educational attainment are inversely, or negatively, related: as people acquire more education, they are less likely to be unemployed.

2. CONSTRUCTING A GRAPH

Let's now construct a graph. We will begin with a consideration of the horizontal and vertical axes, or lines, and then we will put the axes together. We are going to construct a *straight-line curve*. This sounds contradictory, but it is common terminology. Economists often refer to the demand or supply *curve*, and that curve may be a straight line.

2.a. The Axes

It is important to understand how the *axes* (the horizontal and vertical lines) are used and what they measure. Let's begin with the horizontal axis, the line running across the page in a horizontal direction. Notice in Figure 4(a) that the line is divided into equal segments. Each point on the line represents a quantity, or the value of the variables being measured. For example, each segment could represent one year or 10,000 pounds of diamonds or some other value. Whatever is measured, the value increases from left to right, beginning with negative values, going on to zero, which is called the *origin*, and then moving on to positive numbers.

Figure 4
The Axes, the Coordinate System, and the Positive Quadrant
Figure 4(a) shows the vertical and horizontal axes. The horizontal axis has an origin, measured as zero, in the middle. Negative numbers are to the left of zero, positive numbers to the right. The vertical axis also has an origin in the middle. Positive numbers are above the origin, negative numbers below. The horizontal and verti- cal axes together show the entire coordinate system. Positive numbers are in quadrant I, negative numbers in quadrant III, and combinations of negative and positive numbers in quadrants II and IV.

Figure 4(b) shows only the positive quadrant. Because most economic data are positive, often only the upper right quadrant, the positive quadrant, of the coordinate system is used.

(a) The Coordinate System

(b) The Positive Quadrant

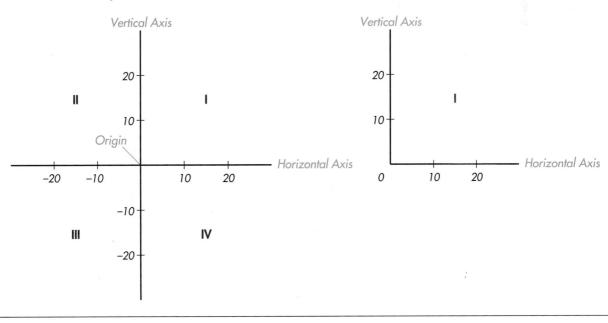

A number line in the vertical direction can be constructed as well, also shown in Figure 4(a). Zero is the origin, and the numbers increase from bottom to top. Like the horizontal axis, the vertical axis is divided into equal segments; the distance between 0 and 10 is the same as the distance between 0 and –10, between 10 and 20, and so on.

In most cases, the variable measured along the horizontal axis is the independent variable. This isn't always true in economics, however. Economists often measure the independent variable on the vertical axis. Do not assume that the variable on the horizontal axis is independent and the variable on the vertical axis is dependent.

Putting the horizontal and vertical lines together lets us express relationships between two variables graphically. The axes cross, or intersect, at their origins, as shown in Figure 4(a). From the common origin, movements to the right and up, in the area—called a quadrant—marked I, are combinations of positive numbers; movements to the left and down, in quadrant III, are combinations of negative numbers; movements to the right and down, in quadrant IV, are negative values on the vertical axis and positive values on the horizontal axis; and movements to the left and up, in quadrant II, are positive values on the vertical axis and negative values on the horizontal axis.

Economic data are typically positive numbers: the unemployment rate, the inflation rate, the price of something, the quantity of something produced or sold, and so on. Because economic data are usually positive numbers, the only part of the coordinate system that usually comes into play in economics is the upper right portion, quadrant I. That is why economists may simply sketch a vertical line down to the origin and then extend a horizontal line out to the right, as shown in Figure 4(b). Once in a while, economic data are negative—for instance, profit is negative when costs exceed revenues. When data are negative, quadrants II, III, and IV of the coordinate system could be used.

2.b. Constructing a Graph from a Table

Now that you are familiar with the axes, that is, the coordinate system, you are ready to construct a graph using the data in the table in Figure 5. The table lists a series of possible tuition levels per semester at a given college and the corresponding number of students who would choose to attend that college and pay that tuition. The data are only hypothetical; they are not drawn from actual cases. In column 2 of the table is the list of possible tuitions. In column 3 is the number of students who are willing and able to pay the tuition and attend the college at each tuition level.

The information given in the table is graphed in Figure 5. We begin by marking off and labeling the axes. The vertical axis is the list of possible tuition levels. We begin at zero and move up the axis at equal increments of $1,000. The horizontal axis is the number of students. We begin at zero and move out the axis at equal increments of 1,000 students. According to the information presented in the table, if the tuition is $10,000 per year, no one attends college. The combination of $10,000 and 0 people is point A on the graph. To plot this point, find the quantity zero on the horizontal axis (it is at the origin), and then move up the vertical axis from zero to a tuition level of $10,000. (Note that we have measured the units in the table and on the graph

Figure 5
Tuition and College Attendance
The information given in the table is graphed in Figure 5. We begin by marking off and labeling the axes. The vertical axis is the list of possible tuition levels. The horizontal axis is the number of students. Beginning at zero, the axes are marked at equal increments of 1,000. According to the information presented in the table, if the tuition is $10,000 per year, no one attends college. The combination of $10,000 and 0 people is point A on the graph. At a tuition of $9,000, there are 1,000 students choosing to attend college. This is point B. The final step in constructing a line graph is to connect the points that are plotted. When the points are connected, the straight line slanting downward showing the relationship between the tuition of college and the number of students attending college is obtained.

Point	Tuition per Semester (thousands)	Number of Students Attending the College (thousands)
A	$10	0
B	9	1
C	8	2
D	7	3
E	6	4
F	5	5
G	4	6
H	3	7
I	2	8
J	1	9

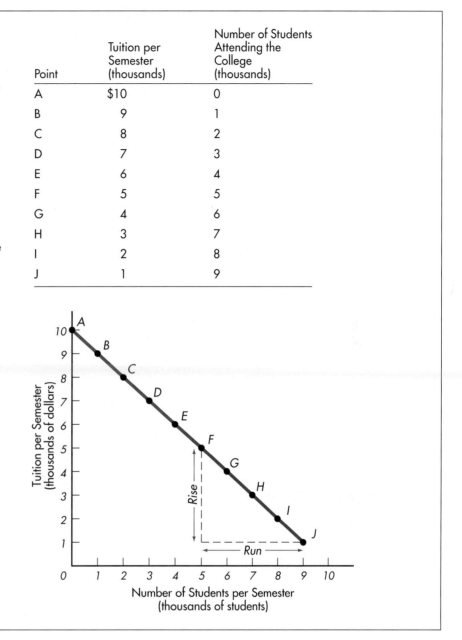

in thousands.) At a tuition of $9,000, there are 1,000 students choosing to attend college. To plot the combination of $9,000 tuition and 1,000 students, find 1,000 units on the horizontal axis and then measure up from ere to a tuition of $9,000. This is point B. Point C represents a tuition of $8,000 and 2,000 students attending college. Point D represents a tuition of $7,000 and 3,000 students attending college. Each combination of tuition and students attending college listed in the table is plotted in Figure 5.

The final step in constructing a line graph is to connect the points that are plotted. When the points are connected, the straight line slanting downward from left to right in Figure 5 is obtained. It shows the relationship between the tuition of college and the number of students attending college.

2.c. Interpreting Points on a Graph

Let's use Figure 5 to demonstrate how points on a graph may be interpreted. Suppose the current tuition is $6,000 per year. Are you able to tell how many students are attending college at this tuition level? By tracing that tuition level from the vertical axis over to the curve and then down to the horizontal axis, you find that 4,000 students choose to pay the $6,000 tuition and attend the college. You can also find what happens to the attendance if the tuition falls from $6,000 to $5,000. By tracing the price from $5,000 to the curve and then down to the horizontal axis, you discover that 5,000 students attend college. Thus, according to the graph, a decrease in the tuition from $6,000 to $5,000 results in an increase in the number of people attending college.

3. SLOPES

A curve may represent an inverse, or negative, relationship or a direct, or positive, relationship. The slope of the curve reveals the kind of relationship that exists between two variables.

3.a. Positive and Negative Slopes

slope:
the steepness of a curve, measured as the ratio of the rise to the run

The **slope** of a curve is its steepness, the rate at which the value of a variable measured on the vertical axis changes with respect to a given change in the value of the variable measured on the horizontal axis. If the value of a variable measured on one axis goes up when the value of the variable measured on the other axis goes down, the variables have an inverse (or negative) relationship. If the values of the variables rise or fall together, the variables have a direct (or positive) relationship. Inverse relationships are represented by curves that run downward from left to right; direct relationships by curves that run upward from left to right.

Slope is calculated by measuring the amount by which the variable on the vertical axis changes and dividing that figure by the amount by which the variable on the horizontal axis changes. The vertical change is called the *rise*, and the horizontal change is called the *run*. Slope is referred to as the *rise over the run*:

$$\text{Slope} = \frac{\text{rise}}{\text{run}}$$

The slope of any inverse relationship is negative. The slope of any direct relationship is positive.

Let's calculate the slope of the curve in Figure 5. Tuition (P) is measured on the vertical axis, and quantity of students attending college (Q) is measured on the horizontal axis. The rise is the change in tuition (ΔP), the change in the value of the variable measured on the vertical axis. The run is the change in quantity of students attending college (ΔQ), the change in the value of the variable measured on the horizontal axis. The symbol Δ means "change in"; it is the Greek letter delta, so ΔP means "change in P" and ΔQ means "change in Q." Remember that slope equals the rise over the run. Thus the equation for the slope of the straight-line curve running downward from left to right in Figure 5 is

$$\text{Slope} = \frac{\Delta P}{\Delta Q}$$

As the tuition (P) declines, the number of students attending college (Q) increases. The rise is negative, and the run is positive. Thus, the slope is a negative value.

The slope is the same anywhere along a straight line. Thus, it does not matter where we calculate the changes along the vertical and horizontal axes. For instance, from 0 to 9,000 on the horizontal axis—a change of 9,000—the vertical change is a negative $9,000 (from $10,000 down to $1,000). Thus, the rise over the run is –9,000/9,000, or –1. Similarly, from 5,000 to 9,000 in the horizontal direction, the corresponding rise is $5,000 to $1,000, or –$4,000, so that the rise over the run is –4,000/4,000, or –1.

Remember that direct, or positive, relationships between variables are represented by lines that run upward from left to right. These lines have positive slopes. Figure 6 is a graph showing the number of spaces the college makes available for students at various tuition levels. The curve represents the relationship between the two variables, number of spaces and tuition. It shows that as tuition rises, so does the number of spaces. The slope of the curve is positive. The change in the rise (the vertical direction) that comes with an increase in the run (the horizontal direction) is positive. Because the graph is a straight line, you can measure the rise and run using any two points along the curve and the slope will be the same. We find the slope by calculating the

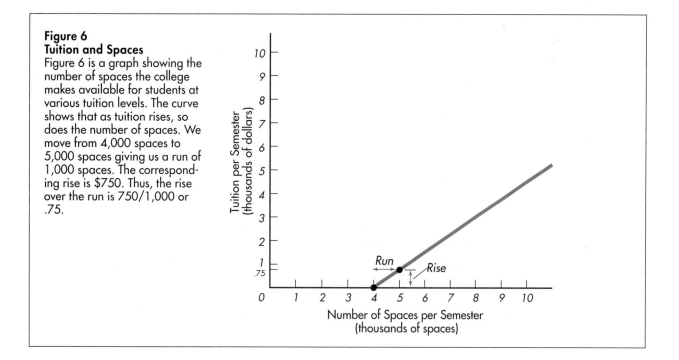

Figure 6
Tuition and Spaces
Figure 6 is a graph showing the number of spaces the college makes available for students at various tuition levels. The curve shows that as tuition rises, so does the number of spaces. We move from 4,000 spaces to 5,000 spaces giving us a run of 1,000 spaces. The corresponding rise is $750. Thus, the rise over the run is 750/1,000 or .75.

rise that accompanies the run. Moving from 4,000 to 5,000 spaces gives us a run of 1,000. Looking at the curve, we see that the corresponding rise is 750. Thus, the rise over the run is 750/1,000, or .75.

3.b. Equations

Graphs and equations can be used to illustrate the same topics. Some people prefer to use equations rather than graphs, or both equations and graphs, to explain a concept. Since a few equations are used in this book, we need to briefly discuss how they demonstrate the same things as a graph.

The general equation of a straight line has the form: $Y = a + bX$, where Y is the dependent variable, X is the independent variable, a defines the intercept (the value of Y when $X = 0$), and b is the slope. If b is negative, the line slopes downward. If b is positive, the line slopes upward. In the case of Figure 5, the tuition, P, is the independent variable, and the number of people attending the college, Q, is the dependent variable. The number of people attending the college depends on the tuition. In equation form, substituting Q for Y and P for X, the relationship between tuition and college attendance is $Q = a + bP$. We already know that the slope, b, is negative. For each $1,000 decline in semester tuition, 1,000 more people choose to attend the college. The slope, b, is -1. The value of a represents the value of Q when P is zero. When the tuition is zero, 10,000 people would choose to attend the college each semester. Thus, $a = 10,000$. The equation of Figure 5 is $Q = 10,000 + -1P$.

The equation can be used to tell us how many students will attend the college at any given tuition. Suppose the tuition is $P = \$4,000$. Substituting $4,000 for P in the equation yields:

$$Q = 10,000 - 1(4,000)$$
$$= 6,000$$

The equation for the curve in Figure 6 is:

$$Q = 4,000 + .75P$$

To demonstrate that this equation is the algebraic representation of Figure 6, you can substitute various tuition levels for P and solve for Q. The combinations of P and Q will lie along the curve in Figure 6.

4. MAXIMUM AND MINIMUM POINTS

The slope of a straight line is the same at all points on the line. The slope of a curve that is not a straight line changes at every point on the curve. Because the slope changes, it can be used to discover the maximum or minimum points. Figure 7(a) shows the total profit a store selling videocassette recorders (VCRs) earns depending on the number of VCRs sold. Total dollars of profit is measured on the vertical axis, and quantity of VCRs sold is measured on the horizontal axis. From 0 to 7 VCRs, the slope is positive; from 7 to 8, the slope is zero (the rise is zero because profit does not change); and from 8 on, the slope is negative. Total profit is at a *maximum* at 7 and 8 VCRs. When the slope is initially positive, then becomes zero, and

Figure 7
Maximum and Minimum Points
In Figure 7(a), a curve showing the total profit for a VCR producer is drawn. The curve has a positive slope until 7 units are produced. From 7 to 8 units, the curve has a zero slope; and from 8 units on, the curve has a negative slope. The maximum occurs at the point where the slope is zero.

In Figure 7(b), a curve showing the costs of producing VCRs is drawn. It has a negative slope followed by a zero slope and then a positive slope. The minimum point occurs at the zero slope.

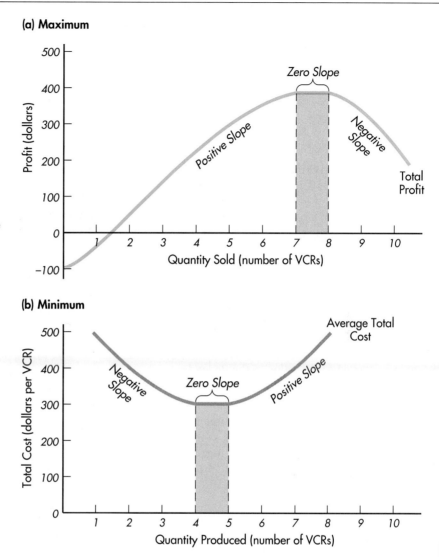

(a) Maximum

(b) Minimum

finally becomes negative when going from smaller to larger numbers along the horizontal axis, we know that the variable measured along the vertical axis has reached a maximum and that the maximum occurs at the point of the zero slope.

Figure 7(b) shows a curve that measures the cost of producing each VCR. Cost in dollars is measured on the vertical axis, and quantity of VCRs produced is measured on the horizontal axis. From 0 to 4 VCRs, the curve has a negative slope. The slope is zero from 4 to 5 VCRs, and beyond 5 it is positive. The *minimum* average total cost occurs at 4 and 5 VCRs. When a curve has a negative slope followed by a zero slope and then a positive slope, the minimum point of the variable measured along the vertical axis occurs at the point where the slope is zero.

Finding the places where the slope is zero identifies possible maximum or minimum points. To know whether the point is really a maximum or minimum, you must calculate the slope before the point and following the point. Then, whether the slope changes from positive to negative or from negative to positive will determine whether the point is a maximum or minimum.

SUMMARY

1. There are three commonly used types of graphs: the line graph, the bar graph, and the pie chart. §1

2. An independent variable is a variable whose value does not depend on the values of other variables. The values of a dependent variable do depend on the values of other variables. §1.b

3. A direct, or positive, relationship occurs when the value of the dependent variable increases as the value of the independent variable increases. An indirect, or negative, relationship occurs when the value of the dependent variable decreases as the value of the independent variable increases. §1.c

4. Most economic data are positive numbers, so often only the upper right quadrant of the coordinate system is used in economics. §2.a

5. The slope of a curve is the rise over the run: the change in the variable measured on the vertical axis that corresponds to a change in the variable measured on the horizontal axis. §3.a

6. The slope of a straight-line curve is the same at all points along the curve. §3.a

7. The equation of a straight line has the general form: $Y = a + bX$, where Y is the dependent variable, X the independent variable, a the value of Y when X equals zero, and b the slope. §3.b

8. A maximum or minimum occurs when the slope is zero. If the slope goes from positive to zero to negative along the curve, a maximum occurs. If the slope goes from negative to zero to positive along the curve, a minimum occurs. §4

KEY TERMS

independent variable §1.b

dependent variable §1.b

direct or positive relationship §1.c

inverse or negative relationship §1.c

slope §3.a

EXERCISES

1. Listed below are two sets of figures: the total quantity of Mexican pesos in circulation (the total amount of Mexican money available) and the peso price of a dollar (how many pesos are needed to purchase one dollar). Values are given for the years 1980 through 1986 for each variable.

   a. Plot each variable by measuring time (years) on the horizontal axis and, in the first graph, pesos in circulation on the vertical axis and, in the second graph, peso price of a dollar on the vertical axis.

b. Plot the combinations of variables by measuring pesos in circulation on the horizontal axis and peso prices of a dollar on the vertical axis.

c. In each of the graphs in parts a and b, what are the dependent and independent variables?

d. In each of the graphs in parts a and b, indicate whether the relationship between the dependent and independent variables is direct or inverse.

e. Calculate the slope of each graph in part a between 1980 and 1981, between 1984 and 1985, and between 1985 and 1986.

f. Using your answers in part e, indicate what the slope would have to have done for the year 1985 to have been a maximum.

Year	Pesos in Circulation (billions)	Peso Price of a Dollar
1980	477	23.26
1981	635	26.23
1982	1,031	96.48
1983	1,447	143.93
1984	2,315	192.56
1985	3,462	371.70
1986	5,790	923.50

2

Choice, Opportunity Costs, and Specialization

FUNDAMENTAL
QUESTIONS

1.   What are opportunity costs?
2.   What is a production possibilities curve?
3.   How are specialization and opportunity costs related?
4.   Why does specialization occur?
5.   What are the benefits of trade?

n the previous chapter you learned that the existence of scarcity forces people to make choices. This occurs whether we are speaking of individuals or of societies. Individuals must allocate their scarce resources to attempt to satisfy their unlimited wants, and societies must allocate their scarce resources to satisfy the unlimited wants of their citizens.

To many people the end of the Cold War seemed to offer one such choice: a costless opportunity to focus more on social and domestic issues than on war-related activities—the "peace dividend," as many called it. Instead of making rockets and bombs, nations could choose to improve the environment, provide better health care and education, and build highways and bridges.

PREVIEW

In the United States, the rate of growth of defense spending declined dramatically in the late 1980s and early 1990s, and spending on health care and other nonmilitary areas rose. This choice was not costless, however. Regions of the United States, such as southern California, experienced serious economic downturns as many workers in defense-related industries lost their jobs.

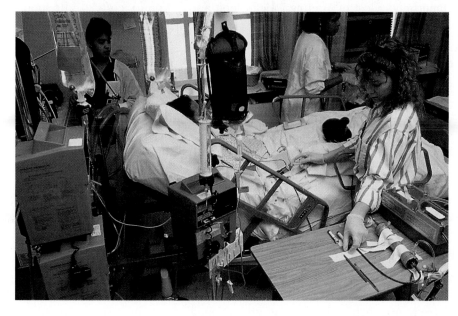

There are costs involved in any choice. As the old saying goes, "There is no free lunch." In every choice, alternatives are forgone, or sacrificed. Having nearly 4 million people in the armed forces, as the United States did in 1969, meant that these 4 million people were not employed in producing automobiles, health care, or other nondefense-related items. The nondefense goods and services not produced—forgone—during that period are part of the costs of choosing to focus on military activities. However, reducing the numbers employed in the military and in military-related activities, as occurred in the early 1990s, is not free either, as the term "peace dividend" might imply. The equipment and the skills people had acquired that were useful only in the production of military goods became worthless.

All choices, then, have both costs and benefits. This chapter explains how to calculate these costs and benefits from the perspective of both the individual and society as a whole.

I. OPPORTUNITY COSTS

What are opportunity costs?

A choice is simply a comparison of alternatives: to attend college or not to attend college, to change jobs or not to change jobs, to purchase a new car or to keep the old one. An individual compares the benefits that one option is expected to yield to the benefits that another option would be expected to bring and selects the one with the greatest *anticipated* benefits. Of course, when one option is chosen, the benefits of the alternatives are forgone. You choose not to attend college and you forgo the benefits of attending college; you buy a new car and forgo the benefits of having the money to use in other ways. *Economists refer to the forgone opportunities or forgone benefits of the next best alternative as* **opportunity costs**—the highest-valued alternative that must be forgone when a choice is made.

opportunity costs:
the highest-valued alternative that must be forgone when a choice is made

The cost of any item or activity includes the opportunity cost involved in its purchase.

Opportunity costs are part of every decision and activity. Your opportunity costs of reading this book are whatever else you could be doing—perhaps watching TV, talking with friends, working, or listening to music. Your opportunity costs of attending college are whatever else you could be doing—perhaps working full time or traveling around the world. Each choice means giving up something else. Even waiting in line to see a performer or to visit a doctor involves opportunity costs, as described in the Economic Insight "The Opportunity Cost of Waiting." Let's look at opportunity costs a little more closely.

1.a. The Opportunity Cost of Going to College

Suppose you decided to attend a college where the tuition and other expenses add up to $4,290 per year. Are these your total costs of attending college? If you answer yes, you are ignoring opportunity costs. Remember that you must account for forgone opportunities. If instead of going to college you could have worked full time, then the benefits of full-time employment are your opportunity costs. If you could have obtained a position paying $10 per hour and worked 52 weeks a year for 40 hours per week, your annual income would have been $20,800. The actual cost of college is the $4,290 of direct expenses plus the $20,800 of forgone salary, or $25,090.

1.b. Trade-Offs and Decisions at the Margin

trade-off:
the giving up of one good or activity in order to obtain some other good or activity

Life is a continuous sequence of decisions, and every single decision involves choosing one thing over another or trading off something for something else. A **trade-off**, then, means giving up one good or activity in order to obtain some other good or activity. Each term you must decide whether to register for college or not. You could work full time and not attend college, attend college and not work, or work part time and attend college. The time you devote to college will decrease as you devote more time to work. You trade off hours spent at work for hours spent in college; in other words, you compare the additional benefits you think you will get from going to college this term with the additional costs of college this term. Once you decide to go to college, you must constantly decide how much to study. Once you sit down and begin studying, you are constantly deciding whether to continue studying or to do something else. You compare the benefit of devoting *additional* time to studying to the cost of not devoting that time to another activity. As long as the *additional* benefit is greater than the *additional* cost, you devote the time to studying. **Marginal** and *additional* mean the same thing, but economists use the term *marginal* more often than they use *additional*. Thus, economists say that making choices involves comparing the **marginal costs** (additional costs) and the **marginal benefits** (additional benefits).

marginal:
additional

marginal cost:
additional cost

marginal benefit:
additional benefit

The Opportunity Cost of Waiting

Standing in line has never been a popular activity, but today it seems that Americans are even more impatient about waiting in line. According to a recent Louis Harris survey, Americans' leisure time has shrunk by 37 percent in the last two decades. With leisure time more valuable, the opportunity cost of waiting in lines is much higher.

Businesses recognize that people choose their products on the basis of the full opportunity cost, not just the price of the good or service. By keeping people waiting, businesses may be losing customers. They are finding that people will choose one establishment over another because of shorter lines. As a result, businesses are focusing their marketing efforts on what marketers call time utility—providing products and services in ways that do not consume valuable time or providing values to offset the time losses. When the multiple-line approach—customers line up behind the teller or clerk of their choice—is used in banks and stores, people get frustrated because they often find themselves in the slowest line. Single lines, where customers wait in one line that allows the first person in line to go to the next available server, do not move any quicker, but they reduce the variance of the wait and thus reduce frustration. As a result, most types of businesses in which several service people handle customers have switched to the single-server line.

Firms have tried several other approaches to dealing with lines. Chemical Bank began a program where any customer who had to wait in a teller line for more than seven minutes was given $5. Hospital emergency rooms in Los Gatos, California, now offer a "no waiting" guarantee: if you wait longer than five minutes for emergency-room care, the billing department knocks 25 percent off your bill. The Manhattan Savings Bank offers live entertainment during noontime banking hours. Some hotels and office buildings have mirrors on their elevator doors in an attempt to distract people while waiting.

Sometimes just telling people how long they have to wait cheers them up. Disneyland has had to learn to comfort those in line, since a popular attraction like Star Tours can attract as many as 1,800 people in a line. Like many amusement parks, Disneyland provides entertainment for those standing in line, but it also gives people updates, in the form of signs noting "From this point on the wait is 30 minutes." Distractions such as these help people forget how they could be spending their time if they weren't waiting in line.

Sources: N. R. Kleinfield, "Companies Try a Trick or Two to Conquer Those Killer Queues," *New York Times,* Sept. 25, 1988, p. F-11. "It'll Only Hurt for a Very Little While," *Business Week,* Feb. 8, 1988, p. 34; Danny N. Bellenger and Pradeep K. Korganokar, "Profiling the Recreational Shopper," *Journal of Retailing,* Vol. 56 (Fall 1980), pp. 77–92.

1.c. The Production Possibilities Curve

What is a production possibilities curve?

production possibilities curve (PPC):
a graphical representation showing the maximum quantity of goods and services that can be produced using limited resources to the fullest extent possible

Societies, like individuals, face scarcities and must make choices. And societies, like individuals, forgo opportunities each time they make a particular choice and must compare the marginal costs and marginal benefits of each alternative.

The trade-offs facing a society can be illustrated in a graph known as the **production possibilities curve (PPC)**. The production possibilities curve shows the maximum quantity of goods and services that can be produced using limited resources to the fullest extent possible. Figure 1 shows a production possibilities curve based on the information (see table) about the production of defense goods and services and nondefense goods and services by a nation such as the United States. Defense goods and services include guns, ships, bombs, personnel, and so forth, that are used for national defense. Nondefense goods and services include education, housing, and food that are

Combination	Defense Goods and Services (millions of units)	Nondefense Goods and Services (millions of units)
A_1	200	0
B_1	175	75
C_1	130	125
D_1	70	150
E_1	0	160
F_1	130	25
G_1	200	75

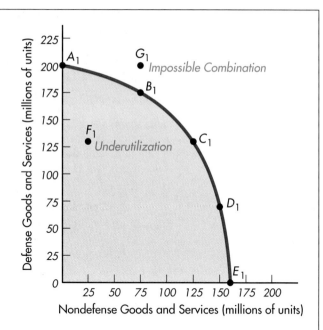

Figure 1
The Production Possibilities Curve
With a limited amount of resources, only certain combinations of defense and nondefense goods and services can be produced. The maximum amounts that can be produced, given various trade-offs, are represented by points A_1 through E_1. Point F_1 lies inside the curve and represents the underutilization of resources. More of one type of goods and less of another could be produced, or more of both types could be produced. Point G_1 represents an impossible combination. There are insufficient resources to produce quantities lying beyond the curve.

not used for national defense. All societies allocate their scarce resources in order to produce some combination of defense and nondefense goods and services. Because resources are scarce, a nation cannot produce as much of everything as it wants. When it produces more health care, it must forgo the production of education or automobiles; when it devotes more of its resources to the military area, fewer are available to devote to health care.

If we could draw or even visualize many dimensions, we could draw a PPC that has a specific good measured along the axis in each dimension. Since we can't, we typically just draw a two-dimensional graph and thus can have just two classes of goods. In Figure 1 the two classes are defense-type goods and nondefense-type goods. But we could just as easily draw a PPC for health care and all other goods or for education and all other goods. These PPCs would look like Figure 1 except that the axes would measure units of health care and other goods or units of education and other goods.

A production possibilities curve shows that more of one type of good can be produced only by reducing the quantity of other types of goods that are produced; it shows that a society has scarce resources; and it shows what the marginal costs and marginal benefits of alternative decisions are. In what way does the PPC show these things? We can answer that question by looking more carefully at Figure 1. In this figure, units of defense goods and services are measured on the vertical axis; units of nondefense goods and

Part I / Introduction to the Price System

services on the horizontal axis. If all resources are allocated to producing defense goods and services, then 200 million units can be produced, but the production of nondefense goods and services will cease. The combination of 200 million units of defense goods and services and 0 units of nondefense goods and services is point A_1, a point on the vertical axis. At 175 million units of defense goods and services, 75 million units of nondefense goods and services can be produced (point B_1). Point C_1 represents 125 million units of nondefense goods and services and 130 million units of defense goods. Point D_1 represents 150 million units of nondefense goods and services and 70 million units of defense goods and services. Point E_1, a point on the horizontal axis, shows the combination of no production of defense goods and services and total production of nondefense goods and services.

The production possibilities curve represents the maximum, or the outer limit, of what can be produced.

The production possibilities curve shows the *maximum* output that can be produced with a limited quantity and quality of resources. The PPC is a picture of the trade-offs facing society. Only one combination of goods and services can be produced at any one time. All other combinations are forgone.

1.c.1. Points Inside the Production Possibilities Curve   Suppose a nation produces 130 million units of defense goods and services and 25 million units of nondefense goods and services. That combination, Point F_1 in Figure 1, lies inside the production possibilities curve. A point lying inside the production possibilities curve indicates that resources are not being fully or efficiently used. If the existing work force is employed only 20 hours per week, it is not being fully used. If two workers are used when one would be sufficient—say, two people in each Domino's Pizza delivery car—then resources are not being used efficiently. If there are resources available for use, society can move from point F_1 to a point on the PPC, such as point C_1. The move would gain 100 million units of nondefense goods and services with no loss of defense goods and services.

1.c.2. Points Outside the Production Possibilities Curve   Point G_1 in Figure 1 represents the production of 200 million units of defense goods and services and 75 units of nondefense goods and services. Point G_1, however, represents the use of more resources than are available—it lies outside the production possibilities curve. Unless more resources can be obtained and/or the quality of resources improved so that the nation can produce more with the same quantity of resources, there is no way the society can currently produce 200 million units of defense goods and 75 million units of nondefense goods.

1.c.3. Shifts of the Production Possibilities Curve   If a nation obtains more resources, points outside its current production possibilities curve become attainable. Suppose a country discovers new sources of oil within its borders and is able to greatly increase its production of oil. Greater oil supplies would enable the country to increase production of all types of goods and services.

Figure 2 shows the production possibilities curve before (PPC_1) and after (PPC_2) the discovery of oil. PPC_1 is based on the data given in Figure 1. PPC_2 is based on the data given in Figure 2 (see table), which shows the increase in production of goods and services that results from the increase in oil supplies. The first combination of goods and services on PPC_2, point A_2, is 220 million units of defense goods and 0 units of nondefense goods. The second point, B_2, is a combination of 200 million units of defense goods and 75 million units of nondefense goods. C_2 through F_2 are the combinations shown in the table of Figure 2. Connecting these points yields the bowed-out curve, PPC_2. Because of the availability of new supplies of oil, the nation is

Combination	Defense Goods and Services (millions of units)	Nondefense Goods and Services (millions of units)
A_2	220	0
B_2	200	75
C_2	175	125
D_2	130	150
E_2	70	160
F_2	0	165

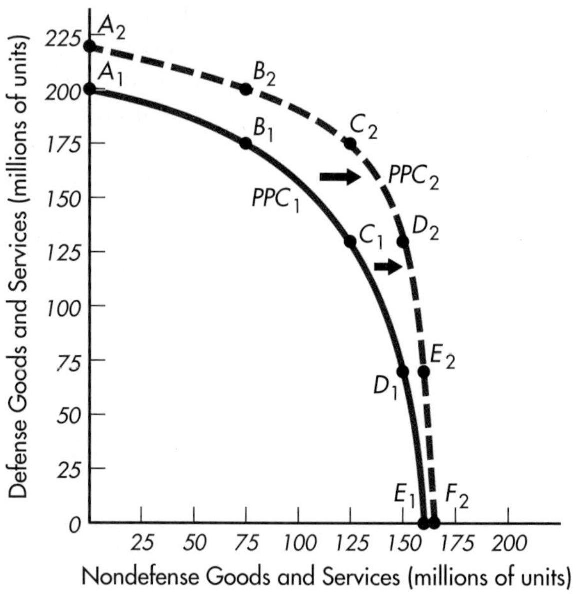

Figure 2
A Shift of the Production Possibilities Curve
Whenever the ceteris paribus conditions change, the curve shifts. In this case, an increase in the quantity of a resource enables the society to produce more of both types of goods. The curve shifts out, away from the origin.

able to increase production of all goods, as shown by the *shift* from PPC_1 to PPC_2. A comparison of the two curves shows that more goods and services for both defense and nondefense are possible along PPC_2 than along PPC_1.

The outward shift of the PPC can be the result of an increase in the quantity of resources, but it also can occur because the quality of resources improves. For instance, a technological breakthrough could conceivably improve the way that communication occurs, thereby requiring fewer people and machines and less time to produce the same quantity and quality of goods. The work force could become more literate, thereby requiring less time to produce the same quantity and quality of goods. Each of these quality improvements in resources could lead to an outward shift of the PPC.

The outward shift of the PPC illustrates that the capacity, or potential, of the economy has grown. However, being able to produce more of all goods doesn't mean that a society will do that. A society might produce at a point on the PPC, inside the PPC, or even attempt to produce at a point outside the PPC. In the early 1990s, for example, the United States was producing at a point inside its PPC. Resources were not being used fully and efficiently. Resources became more fully and efficiently utilized in 1992, and the United States moved out toward its PPC. Conversely, there are times when a society tries to produce a combination of goods and services that are beyond its capacity—a point outside its current PPC. The result can be similar to that when individuals attempt to carry out physical exertion that is beyond their capabilities. They become overheated and can damage internal organs. Such was the case for the United States in the late 1960s when it attempted to pay for the Vietnam War and to increase expenditures on social programs.

Knowing that the opportunity costs include the entire PPC plus the forgone production of those resources not fully or efficiently used, why would a society produce at a point inside the PPC? Almost as puzzling is why a society might try to produce beyond its capacity, something it cannot sustain, when the opportunity costs include not only the entire PPC but the possible damage to the society's "internal organs." The answers to these questions are far from straightforward; in fact, a significant part of macroeconomics is devoted to answering them.

RECAP

1. Opportunity costs are the benefits that are forgone due to a choice. When you choose one thing you must give up—forgo—others.

2. Opportunity cost is an individual concept but can be used to demonstrate scarcity and choice for a society as a whole.

3. The production possibilities curve represents all combinations of goods and services that can be produced using limited resources efficiently to their full capabilities.

4. Points inside the production possibilities curve represent the underutilization or inefficient use of resources—more goods and services could be produced by using the limited resources more fully or efficiently.

5. Points outside the production possibilities curve represent combinations of goods and services that are unattainable given the limitation of resources. More resources would have to be obtained, or a more efficient means of production through the development of technology or innovative management techniques would have to be discovered, to produce quantities of goods and services outside the current production possibilities curve.

2. SPECIALIZATION AND TRADE

No matter which combination of goods and services a society chooses to produce, other combinations of goods are forgone. The PPC illustrates what these forgone combinations are. The PPC also illustrates how easily a society can transfer resources from one activity to another. As the Preview indicated, it is neither easy nor costless to switch from the production of defense-related products to the production of nondefense goods and services. If someone is equally productive making either rocket launchers or medical equipment, total output will not change as that person moves from producing one type of product to producing the other type. However, a specialist in the design of rocket launchers might not be very good at designing medical equipment. By taking that specialist from the production of defense goods and placing her into the health-care industry, many rocket launchers may have to be forgone with little additional production in the health-care industry. We describe how specialization affects the shape of the PPC curve in the following section.

2.a. Marginal Opportunity Cost

marginal opportunity cost:
the amount of one good or service that must be given up to obtain one additional unit of another good or service, no matter how many units are being produced

The shape of the PPC illustrates the ease with which resources can be transferred from one activity to another. If it becomes increasingly more difficult or costly to move resources from one activity to another, the PPC will have the bowed-out shape of Figure 1. With each successive increase in the production of nondefense goods, we see that some amount of defense goods has to be given up. The incremental amounts of defense production given up with each increase in the production of nondefense goods are known as marginal opportunity costs. **Marginal opportunity cost** is the amount of one good or service that must be given up to obtain one additional unit of another good or service, no matter how many units are being produced.

The bowed-out shape shows that for each additional nondefense good, more and more defense goods have to be forgone. According to the table and graph in Figure 3, we see that moving from point A to point B on the PPC means increasing nondefense production from 0 to 25 million units and decreasing defense production from 200 million to 195 million units, resulting in a marginal opportunity cost of 5 million units of defense goods and services for each 25 million units of nondefense goods and services. Moving from point B to point C means increasing nondefense production from 25 to 50 million units, decreasing defense production from 195 to 188 million units and creating a marginal opportunity cost of 7 million units. Moving from point C to point D causes nondefense production to increase from 50 to 75 million units, a decrease in defense production from 188 million to 175 million units and a marginal opportunity cost of 11 million units. As you can see from the table for Figure 3, marginal opportunity costs increase with each successive increase of nondefense production. In other words, it gets more and more costly to produce nondefense goods. The increased marginal opportunity costs occur as a result of specialization. The first resources switched from defense to nondefense production are those who are least specialized in the production of defense goods. Switching these resources is less costly (less has to be given up) than switching the specialists. An accountant can do accounting in either defense- or nondefense-related industries equally well; an expert rocket physicist cannot work as efficiently in health care as in the defense area. But as more and more nondefense goods are produced, the more specialized resources have to be switched as well. This means higher opportunity costs, and increasing amounts of nondefense goods have to be forgone.

2.b. Specialize Where Opportunity Costs Are Lowest

How are specialization and opportunity costs related?

Why does specialization occur?

Why does specialization occur? Every coach, every band director, and every manager of a firm knows the answer to this question. Each has a limited number of talented people and must decide where to position each person in order to create the best team, band, or firm. A band director doesn't expect one person to play the clarinet, trumpet, and drums, even if that person has the ability to play all three instruments, because that would not result in the best band. A coach doesn't expect one person to play every position, and a manager doesn't expect one worker to do every task. Each of these leaders must allocate the scarce resources to best perform the job.

We also have to decide how to use our own scarce resources. We must choose where to devote our energies. Few of us are jacks-of-all-trades.

Figure 3
The Production Possibilities Curve and Marginal Opportunity Costs

With a limited amount of resources, only certain combinations of defense and nondefense goods and services can be produced. The maximum amounts that can be produced are represented by points A through H. With each increase of nondefense production, marginal opportunity costs increase. This occurs as a result of specialization. The first resources switched from defense to nondefense production are those who are least specialized in the production of defense goods. But as more and more nondefense goods are produced, the more specialized resources have to be switched as well. This means higher opportunity costs; increasing amounts of nondefense goods have to be forgone.

Combination	Defense Goods and Services (millions of units)	Marginal Opportunity Costs (defense units forgone per 25 units of nondefense units gained)	Nondefense Goods and Services (millions of units)
A	200		0
		5	
B	195		25
		7	
C	188		50
		11	
D	175		75
		20	
E	155		100
		30	
F	125		125
		50	
G	75		150
		75	
H	0		160

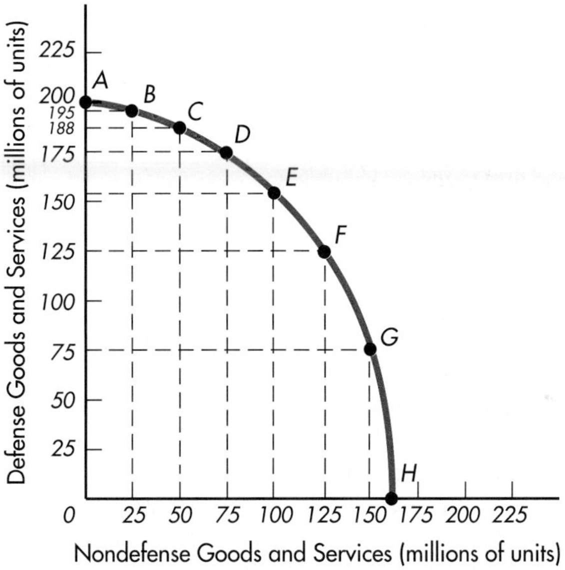

Individuals, firms, and nations select the option with the lowest opportunity cost.

Nations, similarly, have limited amounts of resources and must choose where to devote those resources.

How do we decide where to devote our energies? The answer for nations, and for us as individuals, is to *specialize in activities in which opportunity costs are lowest*. A plumber does plumbing and leaves teaching to the teachers. The teacher teaches and leaves electrical work to the electrician. A country such as Grenada, which has abundant rich land suitable for the cultivation and production of nutmeg and other spices, will specialize in spice production. Mexico, which has an abundant supply of low-skilled labor, will specialize in the production of goods that use low-skilled labor. If we, as individuals or as a society, specialize, however, how do we get the other things we want? The answer is that we trade, or exchange goods and services.

2.b.1. Trade By specializing in activities in which opportunity costs are lowest and then trading, each country or individual will end up with more than if each tried to produce everything. Consider a simple example, as given in Figure 4, which concerns two countries, Haiti and the Dominican Republic, that share an island. Assume Haiti and the Dominican Republic must decide how to allocate their resources between food production and health care. Haiti's daily production possibilities curve is plotted using the data in columns 2 and 3 of the table. If Haiti devotes all of its resources to health care, then it would be able to provide 1,000 people adequate care each day but would have no resources with which to produce food. If it devotes half of its available resources to each activity, then it would provide 500 people adequate health care and produce 7 tons of food. Devoting all of its resources to food production would mean that Haiti could produce 10 tons of food but would have no health care. The Dominican Republic's production possibilities curve is plotted using the data in columns 4 and 5 of the table. If the Dominican Republic devotes all of its resources to health care, it could provide adequate care to 500 people daily but would be unable to produce any food. If it devotes

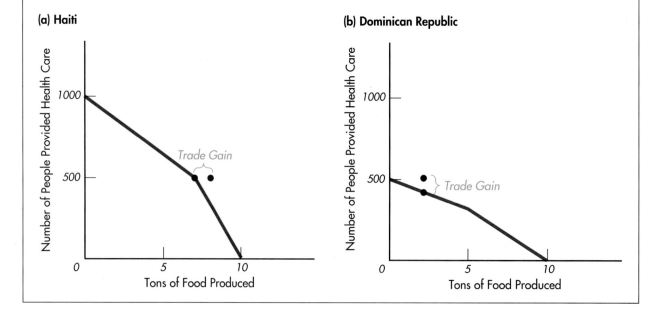

Figure 4
The Benefits of Trade
The trade point of providing health care to 500 people and 2 tons of food is beyond the Dominican Republic's PPC; similarly, the trade point of providing health care to 500 people and 8 tons of food is beyond Haiti's PPC. However, through specialization and trade, these points are achieved by the two nations.

Allocation of Resources to Health Care	Haiti		Dominican Republic	
	Health Care (no. of people provided care)	Food (tons)	Health Care (no. of people provided care)	Food (tons)
100%	1,000	0	500	0
50	500	7	300	5
0	0	10	0	10

(a) Haiti

(b) Dominican Republic

half of its resources to each activity then it could provide 300 people health care and produce 5 tons of food; and if it devotes all of its resources to food production, it could produce 10 tons of food but no health care.

Suppose that Haiti and the Dominican Republic each want 500 people per day provided adequate health care. By itself, the Dominican Republic would be unable to grow any food if it devoted resources to health care for 500 people. However, if the Dominican Republic and Haiti could agree to some type of exchange, perhaps the Dominican Republic could get some food and give the 500 people the health care. But who produces what? The answer depends on opportunity costs. If the Dominican Republic decides to provide health care to 500 people, it must forgo 10 tons of food; Haiti, on the other hand, must forgo only 3 tons of food if it decides to provide health care to 500 people. Haiti's opportunity cost for devoting its resources to providing 500 people health care, 3 tons of food, is lower than the Dominican Republic's, 10 tons. Conversely, if the Dominican Republic produces 10 tons of food, it forgoes providing health care for only 500 people while Haiti forgoes health care for 1,000 people. Clearly, the Dominican Republic's opportunity costs of producing food are lower than Haiti's.

Given the differences in opportunity costs, it would make sense for Haiti to devote its resources to health care and for the Dominican Republic to devote its resources to food production. In this case, Haiti would provide 1,000 people health care and produce no food and the Dominican Republic would produce 10 tons of food but no health care. The two nations would then trade. The Dominican Republic might give 8 tons of food to Haiti in exchange for health care for 500 people. Under this scheme, where each country gets health care for 500 people, the Dominican Republic would be better off by the 2 tons of food it would also get, while Haiti would be better off by the 8 rather than 7 tons of food it would get if it provided the 500 people health care using its own resources. Each is made better off by specialization and trade.

Specialization and trade enable individuals, firms, or nations to acquire combinations of goods that lie beyond their own resource capabilities. This is shown in Figure 4: the trade point of 500 people being provided health care and 2 tons of food is beyond the Dominican Republic's PPC. Similarly, the trade point of 500 people being provided health care and 8 tons of food is beyond Haiti's PPC. Even though one person or one nation is limited to the combinations of goods it can produce using its own resources along or inside its own PPC, through specialization and trade more goods can be acquired. This is why people, firms, and nations trade; this is why there are buyers and sellers.

2.c. Comparative Advantage

comparative advantage:
the ability to produce a good or service at a lower opportunity cost than someone else

We have seen that the choice of which area or activity to specialize in is made on the basis of opportunity costs. Economists refer to the ability of one person or nation to do something with a lower opportunity cost than another as **comparative advantage**. In the example shown in Figure 4, the Dominican Republic had a comparative advantage in food production and Haiti had a comparative advantage in health-care provision. You may be better at both computer programming and literature than your roommate, but you may be much better at computer programming and only slightly better at literature. You, then, have a comparative advantage in computers. Your room-

The fruit of the prickly pear cactus is popular in salads and drinks. Recently, the extract from the cactus leaves has been found to relieve some of the symptoms of diabetes. Physicians in Mexico and Japan prescribe the extract as a substitute for insulin in some cases and as an enhancement to insulin in others. Though the prickly pear cactus grows in southwestern United States as well, the harvesting of the cacti occurs mainly in Mexico because most of the prickly pear cactus forests are in Mexico, and the labor-intensive harvesting process is less costly in Mexico than it would be in the United States. Mexico has a comparative advantage in the harvesting of the cacti.

mate has a comparative advantage as well, in literature. Remember, comparative advantage depends on opportunity costs. Just because you are better than your roommate at both activities, you do not have the same opportunity costs in both. Like Haiti and the Dominican Republic, you and your roommate are better off specializing and then trading (helping each other) than if each of you do all the studying all by yourselves. You both get better grades and have more time to devote to other activities.

2.d. Specialization and Trade Occur Everywhere

What are the benefits of trade?

Individuals specialize in the activity in which their opportunity costs are lowest.

Each of us will specialize in some activity, earn an income, and then trade our output (or income) for other goods and services we want. Specialization and trade ensure that we are better off than doing everything ourselves. A firm, a team, or a band can be thought of as an organization in which people specialize according to their comparative advantage and then trade or exchange their output. This ensures that the organization gets the greatest output at the lowest cost. Nations also are better off if they devote resources to the production of goods and services in which they have a comparative advantage and then exchange those goods and services. *Specialization according to comparative advantage followed by trade, that is, the exchange of goods produced, allows everyone to acquire more of the goods they want.*

We have now explored the basics of economics. We know that scarcity means that choices must be made. We have learned that choices are made according to rational self-interest. And we just discovered that specialization according to comparative advantage followed by trade ensures that people are as well off as they can possibly be. Trade usually refers to the exchange of goods and services by nations, but trade is also what you do when you purchase goods and services. You trade money for the goods and services. You acquired the money as a payment for the resource services you provided—

working, owning land, providing funds for capital, or being an entrepreneur. Thus, you are in essence trading your resource services for the goods and services others provide.

RECAP

1. Marginal opportunity cost is the amount of one good or service that must be given up to obtain one additional unit of another good or service.

2. The rule of specialization is: the individual (firm, region, or nation) will specialize in the production of the good or service that has the lowest opportunity cost.

3. Comparative advantage exists whenever one person (firm, country) can do something with fewer opportunity costs than some other individual (firm, nation) can.

4. Specialization and trade enable individuals, firms, and nations to get more than they could without specialization and trade.

SUMMARY

▲▼ *What are opportunity costs?*

1. Opportunity costs are the forgone opportunities of the next best alternative. Choice means both gaining something and giving up something. When you choose one option you forgo all others. The benefits of the next best alternative are the opportunity costs of your choice. §1

▲▼ *What is a production possibilities curve?*

2. A production possibilities curve represents the trade-offs involved in the allocation of scarce resources. It shows the maximum quantity of goods and services that can be produced using limited resources to the fullest extent possible. §1.c

3. The bowed-out shape of the PPC occurs because of specialization and increasing marginal opportunity costs. §2.a

▲▼ *How are specialization and opportunity costs related?*

4. Comparative advantage is when one person (one firm, one nation) can perform an activity or produce a good with fewer opportunity costs than someone else. §2.c

▲▼ *Why does specialization occur?*

5. Comparative advantage accounts for specialization. We specialize in the activities in which we have the lowest opportunity costs, that is, in which we have a comparative advantage. §2.c

▲▼ *What are the benefits of trade?*

6. Specialization and trade enable those involved to acquire more than they could by not specializing and engaging in trade. §2.d

KEY TERMS

opportunity costs §1

trade-offs §1.b

marginal §1.b

marginal cost §1.b

marginal benefit §1.b

production possibilities curve (PPC) §1.c

marginal opportunity cost §2.a

comparative advantage §2.c

EXERCISES

1. In the 1992 presidential campaign, critics of the Bill Clinton/Al Gore team argued that it is impossible for them to fulfill their promises. Clinton and Gore promised more and better health care, a better environment, only minor reductions in defense, better education, and a better and improved system of roads, bridges, sewer systems, water systems, and so on. Accepting the promises as facts, what economic concept are the critics claiming that Clinton and Gore ignored?

2. Janine is an accountant who makes $30,000 a year. Robert is a college student who makes $8,000 a year. All other things being equal, who is more likely to stand in a long line to get a concert ticket?

3. Back in the 1960s, President Lyndon Johnson passed legislation that increased expenditures both for the Vietnam War and for social problems in the United States. Since the U.S. economy was operating at its full employment level when President Johnson did this, he appeared to be ignoring what economic concept?

4. The following numbers measure the trade-off between grades and income.

Total Hours	Hours Studying	GPA	Hours Working	Income
60	60	4.0	0	$ 0
60	40	3.0	20	100
60	30	2.0	30	150
60	10	1.0	50	250
60	0	0.0	60	300

a. Calculate the marginal opportunity cost of an increase in the number of hours spent studying in order to earn a 3.0 grade point average (GPA) rather than a 2.0 GPA.

b. Is the opportunity cost the same for a move from a 0.0 GPA to a 1.0 GPA as it is for a move from a 1.0 GPA to a 2.0 GPA?

c. What is the opportunity cost of an increase in salary from $100 to $150?

5. Suppose a second individual has the following trade-offs between income and grades:

Total Hours	Hours Studying	GPA	Hours Working	Income
60	50	4.0	10	$ 60
60	40	3.0	20	120
60	20	2.0	40	240
60	10	1.0	50	300
60	0	0.0	60	360

a. Define comparative advantage.

b. Does either individual (the one in question 4 or the one in question 5) have a comparative advantage in both activities?

c. Who should specialize in studying and who should specialize in working?

6. A doctor earns $250,000 per year while a professor earns $40,000. They play tennis against each other each Saturday morning, each giving up a morning of relaxing, reading the paper, and playing with their children. They could each decide to work a few extra hours on Saturday and earn more income. But they choose to play tennis or to relax around the house. Are their opportunity costs of playing tennis different?

7. Plot the PPC given by the following data.

Combination	Health Care	All Other Goods
A	0	100
B	25	90
C	50	70
D	75	40
E	100	0

a. Calculate the marginal opportunity cost of each combination.

b. What is the opportunity cost of combination C?

c. Suppose a second nation has the following PPC. Plot the PPC and then determine which nation has the comparative advantage in which activity. Show whether the two nations can gain from specialization and trade.

Combination	Health Care	All Other Goods
A	0	50
B	20	40
C	40	25
D	60	5
E	65	0

8. A doctor earns $200 per hour, a plumber $40 per hour, and a professor $20 per hour. Everything else the same, which one will devote more hours to negotiating the price of a new car?

9. Perhaps you've heard of the old saying "There is no such thing as a free lunch." What does it mean? If someone invites you to a lunch and offers to pay for it, is it free to you?

10. You have waited 30 minutes in a line for the Star Tours ride at Disneyland. You see a sign that says, "From this point on your wait is 45 minutes." You must decide whether to continue in line or to move elsewhere. On what basis do you make the decision? Do the 30 minutes you've already stood in line come into play?

11. The university is deciding between two meal plans. One plan charges a fixed fee of $600 per semester and allows students to eat as much as they want. The other plan charges a fee based on the quantity of food consumed. Under which plan will students eat the most?

12. Evaluate this statement: "You are a natural athlete, an attractive person who learns easily and communicates well. Clearly, you can do every-thing better than your friends and acquaintances. As a result, the term specialization has no meaning for you. Specialization would cost you rather than benefit you."

13. During China's Cultural Revolution in the late 1960s and early 1970s, many people with a high school or college education were forced to move to farms and work in the fields. Some were common laborers for eight or more years. What does this policy say about specialization and the PPC? Would you predict that the policy would lead to an increase in output?

14. In elementary schools and through middle schools most students have the same teacher throughout the day and for the entire school year. Then, beginning in high school different subjects are taught by different teachers. In college, the same subject is often taught at different levels, freshman, sophomore, junior-senior, or graduate, by different faculty. Is education taking advantage of specialization only from high school on? Comment on the differences between elementary school and college and the use of specialization.

15. The top officials in federal government and high-ranking officers of large corporations often have chauffeurs to drive them around the city or from meeting to meeting. Is this simply part of the largesse of their positions or is the use of chauffeurs something justifiable on the basis of comparative advantage?

Low Prices Reflect High Sales Goals

The most popular value-marketing strategy these days is purely bottom line: price cutting.

Lower prices are the bluntest way to reach penny-pinching consumers, marketing consultants say:

Procter & Gamble launched its "Cleans clothes clean for less" campaign for Dash detergent, priced 30% to 40% below premium brands. P&G is slicing prices 7% on Pampers and Luvs disposable diapers.

Honda plans to launch a less expensive, "value-priced" Accord to help the model remain No. 1 among U.S. cars.

P.F. Flyers cut sneakers prices to $20 a pair and reintroduced them through mass merchandisers such as WalMart. A year ago, Flyers cost $45 at Nordstrom and other department stores. Marketing manager Teresa Giacalone hopes the move will triple '92 sales to 10 million pairs.

Gap ignited a denim war by cutting the price of its basic jeans $10 last month. Last week, Gap announced more cuts on a broader array of apparel in an attempt to boost revenue.

Price cutting may work for firms able to absorb lower profit margins by boosting volume. But for others, it could be shortsighted.

"The danger is that consumers get used to a certain price so it's almost impossible to raise prices or become a premium-priced brand again," says brand and packaging consultant John Lister.

Moreover, widespread price cutting could prompt shakeouts in some industries.

"Being the low-price guy and hanging in there and not letting market share go down is idiotic," says David Aaker, author of *Managing Brand Equity*. "In the long run, it's a bankrupt strategy."

Source: Gary Strauss, "Low Prices Reflect High Sales Goals," *USA Today*, Sept. 29, 1992, p. 2B. Copyright 1992, USA TODAY. Reprinted with permission.

USA Today/September 29, 1992

Commentary

As you learned in this chapter, opportunity costs represent the benefits forgone by choosing one option rather than another. This article illustrates a particular application of the concept of opportunity costs: the opportunity cost to a firm of lowering the price of the products the firm sells. You might be thinking: "How can there be an opportunity cost to a lower price? Everyone likes lower prices. Customers pay less; firms sell more." However, there are opportunity costs to every decision and every action.

One part of the opportunity cost of the lower price decision could be lower profits. Suppose that although the lower price does cause sales to rise, costs rise as well. Then, like the old joke that "while the firm is losing money on each item, it is making it up in volume," the firms would be losing money. The article points this out by quoting author David Aaker: "Being the low-price guy and hanging in there and not letting market share go down is idiotic. In the long run, it's a bankrupt strategy."

Another opportunity cost of the lower price strategy might be the loss of reputation. Perhaps a firm has built up a reputation as a quality firm. The lower prices might make people think that the firm's quality has decreased as well. As the article says, it may be impossible to correct this impression if it is created: "The danger is that consumers get used to a certain price so it's almost impossible to raise prices or become a premium-priced brand again."

Still another possibility is that the lower price could alienate former customers who purchased a particular product for the status of its brand name. A consumer may have purchased clothing from the Gap, for instance, because it was expensive. Simply wearing Gap products sends a signal that the consumer has money. With a lower price, this attitude does not arise, and perhaps some customers are lost.

It is likely that these firms have studied what their prices mean to customers. It is likely that the firms know how consumers will react to the lower prices. In other words, it is likely that the firms know what the opportunity costs of the decision to lower prices are.

Opportunity cost is of central importance in a decision whether to raise or lower the price of a product a company sells, or for that matter in any economic decision. The proper application of the principle of opportunity cost considers *all* opportunities forgone by a certain course of action, even though putting an actual dollar value on these opportunities may sometimes pose a challenge.

3

Markets, Demand and Supply, and the Price System

FUNDAMENTAL
QUESTIONS

1. What is a market?
2. What is demand?
3. What is supply?
4. How is price determined by demand and supply?
5. What causes price to change?

f you decided to vacation in Phoenix, Arizona, from January 10 through March 15, you could spend $319 per person per night for a first-class resort. If your vacation to Phoenix occurred in August, the same luxurious treatment could be yours for less than half the price. During the winter in Vail, Colorado, you could have accommodations for $280 per person; in the summer that price would be $150 per person. For $400 per night per person you could have an ocean view at the Ritz-Carlton in Laguna Niguel, California, any time of the year—but sorry, it is booked up for more than the next full year.

If you wanted to see *The Phantom of the Opera* on Broadway or in Los Angeles in 1992, you couldn't purchase tickets from the usual places. The show was sold out for more than a year. You could, however, get tickets if you were willing to pay more than ten times the face value and search out those people, called scalpers, who had tickets for sale.

Many restaurants don't take reservations. You simply arrive and take your

turn. If you arrive at 7:30 in the evening, you have at least an hour wait. Notwithstanding that fact, a few people arrive, speak quietly with the maitre d', hand him some money, and are promptly seated. At some restaurants that do take reservations, there is a month wait for a Saturday evening, three weeks for a Friday evening, two weeks for Tuesday through Thursday, and virtually no wait for a Sunday or Monday evening.

In the Soviet Union before its collapse, long lines at all stores were a common sight. After the collapse, the lines were not as evident, but prices were many times higher than their precollapse levels.

Do you see any similarities among these examples? Each deals with the allocation of goods and services, with price, and with demand and supply. However, in some of the examples, price changes seem to allocate scarce goods to buyers, while in others, price doesn't seem to function as an allocating device. Phoenix is a great place in the winter—75 degrees and sunny. Phoenix in August can be an oppressive 108 degrees with humidity of 50 percent. It makes sense that resort prices would be higher in winter than in summer in Phoenix. Why doesn't the same logic apply to rooms at the Ritz-Carlton, or tables at a restaurant, or tickets to shows? Does it apply to the Russian situation?

In the previous chapters you learned that as a result of scarcity, choices have to be made. Individuals, organizations, and nations must select certain uses for their scarce resources and forgo others. On what basis do we make choices? In market-based economies, prices play a key role in defining opportunity costs and determining choices. But, as in the examples just described, prices do not always serve this role. In this chapter we discuss the role that prices play in allocating goods and services, what economists mean by price, what a market is, and how demand and supply in a market work to determine price.

1. MARKETS

What is a market?

The supermarket, the stock market, the market for foreign exchange, and all other markets are similar in that well-defined goods and services are exchanged. A market may be a specific location, such as the supermarket or the stock market, or it may be the exchange of particular goods or services at many different locations, such as the foreign exchange market. The stock and foreign exchange markets are discussed in the Economic Insight "The Stock Market."

1.a. Market Definition

market:
a place or service that enables buyers and sellers to exchange goods and services

A **market** makes possible the exchange of goods and services between buyers and sellers. Buyers and sellers communicate with each other about the quantity and quality of a product, what the buyers are willing and able to pay, and what the sellers must receive. Food, shares of stock, and various national monies are bought and sold in, respectively, the supermarket, the stock market, and the foreign exchange market.

Markets may be general or specialized, large or small, localized or global; they may consist of one or many buyers and sellers, but a well-defined commodity is always traded. A market may be a formally organized exchange, such as the New York Stock Exchange, or it may be loosely organized like the market for used bicycles or automobiles. A market may be confined to one location, as in the case of a supermarket or the stock market, or it may encompass a city, a state, a country, or the entire world. The market for agricultural products, for instance, is international, but the market for labor services is mostly local or national.

A market arises when buyers and sellers exchange a well-defined good or service. In stock markets, buyers and sellers exchange their "goods," or stocks, solely through electronic connections. Shoppers at a fish market can examine the day's catch and make their choices.

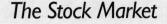
The Stock Market

Stock markets are specific places where people buy and sell shares of stock, or shares of ownership in corporations. A share of stock represents a piece of the firm. For instance, if you buy Ford Motor Company stock, you are one of the owners of Ford. The price of stock is determined by the expectations of buyers and sellers, whose exchange of shares reflects their beliefs about whether the firm will be more or less profitable in the future and whether the firm will perform better or worse than other firms.

There are several stock exchanges in the United States. The largest and best known is the New York Stock Exchange, located on Wall Street in lower Manhattan. In addition to the New York Stock Exchange, there are the American Stock Exchange, also located in New York, and regional exchanges such as the Philadelphia Exchange and the Pacific Exchange, located in San Francisco. Stock exchanges in other nations include the London Exchange and the Tokyo Exchange.

The stock of only a small proportion of the total number of firms is listed on the exchanges, but the firms that are listed are the largest ones and those whose shares are most commonly traded. The markets for stocks offered by other firms are not as formally structured as the stock exchanges. Such stocks are bought and sold through dealers and brokers or through word of mouth in what is called the *over-the-counter market*.

1.b. Barter and Money Exchanges

barter:
the direct exchange of goods and services without the use of money

The purpose of markets is to facilitate the exchange of goods and services between buyers and sellers. In some cases money changes hands; in others only goods and services are exchanged. The exchange of goods and services directly, without money, is called **barter**. Barter occurs when a plumber fixes a leaky pipe for a lawyer in exchange for the lawyer's work on a will, and when a Chinese citizen provides fresh vegetables to an American visitor in exchange for a pack of American cigarettes. See the Economic Insight "Barter is Big Business" for a description of bartering on a large-scale basis.

double coincidence of wants:
the situation that exists when A has what B wants and B has what A wants

transaction costs:
the cost involved in making an exchange

Most markets involve money because goods and services can be exchanged more easily with money than without it. When IBM purchases microchips from Yakamoto of Japan, IBM and Yakamoto don't exchange goods directly. Neither firm may have what the other wants. Barter requires a **double coincidence of wants**: IBM must have what Yakamoto wants, and Yakamoto must have what IBM wants. The **transaction costs** (the costs associated with making an exchange) of finding a double coincidence of wants for barter transactions are typically very high. Money reduces these transaction costs. To obtain the microchips, all IBM has to do is provide dollars to Yakamoto. Yakamoto is willing to accept the money since it can spend it to obtain the goods that it wants.

1.c. Relative Price

relative price:
the price of one good expressed in terms of the price of another good

When people agree to trade or exchange, they must agree on the rate of exchange, or the price. The price of an exchange is a **relative price**—the price of one good expressed in terms of the price of another good. In a barter exchange a relative price is established between the goods traded. When the

Barter is Big Business

In Southern California, barter is big business. An estimated 15,000 to 20,000 businesses from San Diego to Bakersfield, including law firms, hotels, contractors, and doctors, are involved in barter worth approximately $20 million a month.

Carl Farless, a North Hollywood dentist, claims, "With barter, you don't feel the searing bite you would feel if you spent cash." He has bartered $20,000 a year for the past seven years, obtaining, among other things, an $18,000 set of Erté limited edition prints and a holiday office party for his staff at Ocean Seafood in Chinatown.

Barter exchange firms keep track of who's swapping what for a 10 to 15 percent commission on each trade. People offer goods and services for "credits" that can be exchanged for other goods and services. Some exchanges use barter scrip; others use "credit cards." And when tax time rolls around, barter is considered "wages, tips and other compensation"; the exchanges report all transactions to the IRS. According to the president of BX International, a Burbank-based barter company with 52 branches nationwide, one individual recently made a $150,000 down payment on an office building in San Francisco entirely with barter.

Barter does not involve just small sole practitioners either. The television syndication market is about 25 percent barter. A network will purchase the rights to, say, "Cheers" in exchange for advertising time.

Source: David Drum, *Los Angeles Times Magazine*, March 29, 1992, p. 10; Elizabeth Jensen, "Networks Gain in Syndication Dispute, But Many Fear Rerun of Battle Ahead," *Wall Street Journal*, Nov. 9, 1992, p. B1.

---

lawyer exchanges 2 hours of work for 1 hour of the plumber's work, the relative price established is 2/1. In a money exchange the relative price is more implicit. You pay a money price of $1 for a carton of milk. But, with that purchase you are forgoing everything else you could get for that dollar. Thus, the carton of milk is worth 1/3 of a $3 box of Quaker Oats 100% Natural cereal, 1/200 of a $200 used Diamond Back mountain bike, 20 sticks of $.05/stick Trident gum, and so on. These are the relative prices of the milk. Relative prices are a measure of what you must give up to get 1 unit of a good or service and are, therefore, a measure of opportunity costs. Since opportunity costs are what decisions are based on, when economists refer to the price of something, it is the relative price they have in mind.

The relative price is the price that affects economic decision making.

RECAP

1. A market is not necessarily a specific location or store. Instead, the term *market* refers to buyers and sellers communicating with each other regarding the quality and quantity of a well-defined product, what buyers are willing and able to pay for a product, and what sellers must receive in order to produce and sell a product.

2. Barter refers to exchanges made without the use of money.

3. Money makes it easier and less expensive to exchange goods and services.

4. The price of a good or service is a measure of what you must give up to get one unit of that good or service.

2. DEMAND

What is demand?

demand:
the amount of a product that people are willing and able to purchase at every possible price

quantity demanded:
the amount of a product that people are willing and able to purchase at a specific price

Demand and supply determine the price of any good or service. To understand how a price level is determined and why a price rises or falls, it is necessary to know how demand and supply function. We begin by considering demand alone, then supply, and then we put the two together. Before we begin, we discuss some economic terminology that is often confusing.

Economists distinguish between the terms **demand** and **quantity demanded**. When they refer to the *quantity demanded* they are talking about the amount of a product that people are willing and able to purchase at a *specific* price. When they refer to *demand* they are talking about the amount that people would be willing and able to purchase at *every possible* price. Demand is the quantities demanded at every price. Thus, the statement that "the demand for U.S. white wine rose after a 300 percent tariff was applied to French white wine" means that at each price for U.S. white wine, more people were willing and able to purchase U.S. white wine. And the statement that "the quantity demanded of white wine fell as the price of white wine rose in 1992" means that people were willing and able to purchase less white wine because the price of the wine rose.

2.a. The Law of Demand

law of demand:
as the price of a good or service rises (falls), the quantity of that good or service that people are willing and able to purchase during a particular period of time falls (rises), everything else held constant

Consumers and merchants know that if you lower the price of a good or service without altering its quality or quantity, people will beat a path to your doorway. This simple truth is referred to as the **law of demand**.

According to the law of demand, people purchase more of something when the price of that item falls. More formally, the law of demand states that the quantity of some item that people are willing and able to purchase, during a particular period of time, decreases as the price rises, and vice versa.

The more formal definition of the law of demand can be broken down into five phrases:

1. the quantity of a well-defined good or service that
2. people are willing and able to purchase
3. during a particular period of time
4. decreases as the price of that good or service rises and increases as the price falls
5. everything else held constant

The first phrase ensures that we are referring to the same item, that we are not mixing different goods. A watch is a commodity defined and distinguished from other goods by several characteristics: quality, color, and design of the watch face, to name a few. The law of demand applies to the well-defined good, in this case, a watch. If one of the characteristics should change, the good would no longer be well-defined—in fact, it would be a different good. A Rolex watch is different from a Timex watch; Polo brand golf shirts are different goods than generic brand golf shirts; Mercedes-Benz automobiles are different goods than Yugo automobiles.

The second phrase indicates that people must not only *want* to purchase some good, they must be *able* to purchase that good in order for their wants to be counted as part of demand. For example, Sue would love to buy a membership to the Paradise Valley Country Club, but because the membership costs $35,000, she is not able to purchase the membership. Though willing, she is not able. At a price of $5,000, however, she is willing and able to purchase the membership.

The third phrase points out that the demand for any good is defined for a specific period of time. Without reference to a time period, a demand relationship would not make any sense. For instance, the statement that "at a price of $3 per Happy Meal, 13 million Happy Meals are demanded" provides no useful information. Are the 13 million meals sold in one week or one year? Think of demand as a rate of purchase at each possible price over a period of time—2 per month, 1 per day, and so on.

The fourth phrase points out that price and quantity demanded move in opposite directions; that is, as the price rises, the quantity demanded falls, and as the price falls, the quantity demanded rises.

determinants of demand:
factors other than the price of the good that influence demand—income, tastes, prices of related goods and services, expectations, and number of buyers

Demand is a measure of the relationship between the price and quantity demanded of a particular good or service, when the determinants of demand do not change. The **determinants of demand** are income, tastes, prices of related goods and services, expectations, and the number of buyers. If any one of these items changes, demand changes. The final phrase, everything else held constant, ensures that the determinants of demand do not change.

2.b. The Demand Schedule

demand schedule:
a table or list of the prices and the corresponding quantities demanded of a particular good or service

A **demand schedule** is a table or list of the prices and the corresponding quantities demanded of a particular good or service. The table in Figure 1 is a demand schedule for video rentals (movies). It shows the number of videos that a consumer named Bob would be willing and able to rent at each price during the year, everything else held constant. As the rental price of the videos gets higher relative to the prices of other goods, Bob would be willing and able to rent fewer videos.

At the high price of $5 per video, Bob indicates that he will rent only 10 videos during the year. At a price of $4 per video, Bob tells us that he will rent 20 videos during the year. As the price drops from $5 to $4 to $3 to $2 and to $1, Bob is willing and able to rent more videos. At a price of $1, Bob would rent 50 videos during the year, nearly 1 per week.

2.c. The Demand Curve

demand curve:
a graph of a demand schedule that measures price on the vertical axis and quantity demanded on the horizontal axis

A **demand curve** is a graph of the demand schedule. The demand curve shown in Figure 1 is plotted from the information given in the demand schedule. Price is measured on the vertical axis, quantity per unit of time on the horizontal axis. The demand curve slopes downward because of the inverse relationship between the rental price of the videos and the quantity an individual is willing and able to purchase (rent). Point A in Figure 1 corresponds to combination A in the table: a price of $5 and 10 videos demanded. Similarly, points B, C, D, and E in Figure 1 represent the corresponding combinations in the table. The line connecting these points is Bob's demand curve for videos.

All demand curves slope down because of the law of demand: as price falls, quantity demanded increases. The demand curves for bread, electricity, automobiles, colleges, labor services, and any other good or service you can think of slope down. You might be saying to yourself, "That's not true. What

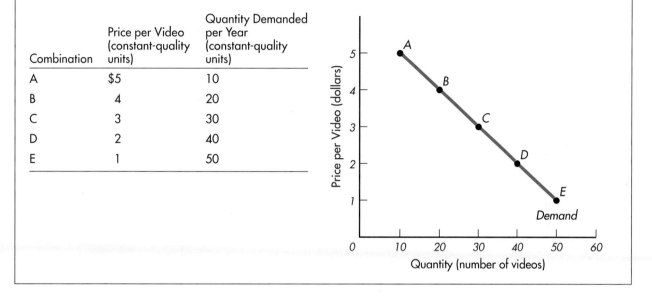

Figure 1
Bob's Demand Schedule and Demand Curve for Videos
The number of videos that Bob is willing and able to rent at each price during the year is listed in the table, or demand schedule. The demand curve is derived from the combinations given in the demand schedule. The price-quantity combination of $5 per video and 10 videos is point A. The combination of $4 per video and 20 videos is point B. Each combination is plotted, and the points are connected to form the demand curve.

Combination	Price per Video (constant-quality units)	Quantity Demanded per Year (constant-quality units)
A	$5	10
B	4	20
C	3	30
D	2	40
E	1	50

When speaking of the demand curve or demand schedule, we are using constant-quality units. The quality of a good does not change as the price changes along a demand curve.

about the demand for Mercedes-Benz cars or Gucci bags? As their price goes up, they become more prestigious and the quantity demanded actually rises." To avoid confusion in such circumstances, we say "everything else held constant." With this statement we are assuming that tastes don't change and that, therefore, the goods *cannot* become more prestigious as the price changes. Similarly, we do not allow the quality or the brand name of a product to change as we define the demand schedule or demand curve. We concentrate on the one quality or the one brand; so when we say that the price of a good has risen, we are talking about a good that is identical at all prices.

2.d. From Individual Demand Curves to a Market Curve

Bob's demand curve for video rentals is plotted in Figure 1. Unless Bob is the only renter of the videos, his demand curve is not the total, or market demand, curve. Market demand is the sum of all individual demands. To derive the market demand curve, then, the individual demand curves of all consumers in the market must be added together. The table in Figure 2 lists the demand schedules of three individuals, Bob, Helen, and Art. Because in this example the market consists only of Bob, Helen, and Art, their individual demands are added together to derive the market demand. The market demand is the last column of the table.

Bob's, Helen's, and Art's demand schedules are plotted as individual demand curves in Figure 2(a). In Figure 2(b) their individual demand curves have been added together to obtain the market demand curve. (Notice that we add in a horizontal direction—that is, we add quantities at each price, not the prices at each quantity.) At a price of $5, we add the quantity Bob would buy,

Figure 2
The Market Demand Schedule and Curve for Videos
The market is defined to consist of three individuals:
Bob, Helen, and Art. Their demand schedules are listed
in the table and plotted as the individual demand
curves shown in Figure 2(a). By adding the quantities
that each demands at every price, we obtain the market
demand curve shown in Figure 2(b). At a price of $1 we
add Bob's quantity demanded of 50 to Helen's quantity
demanded of 25 to Art's quantity demanded of 27 to
obtain the market quantity demanded of 102. At a
price of $2 we add Bob's 40 to Helen's 20 to Art's 24
to obtain the market quantity demanded of 84. To obtain the market demand curve, for every price we sum
the quantities demanded by each market participant.

Price per Video	Quantities Demanded per Year by						Market Demand
	Bob		Helen		Art		
$5	10	+	5	+	15	=	30
4	20		10		18		48
3	30		15		21		66
2	40		20		24		84
1	50		25		27		102

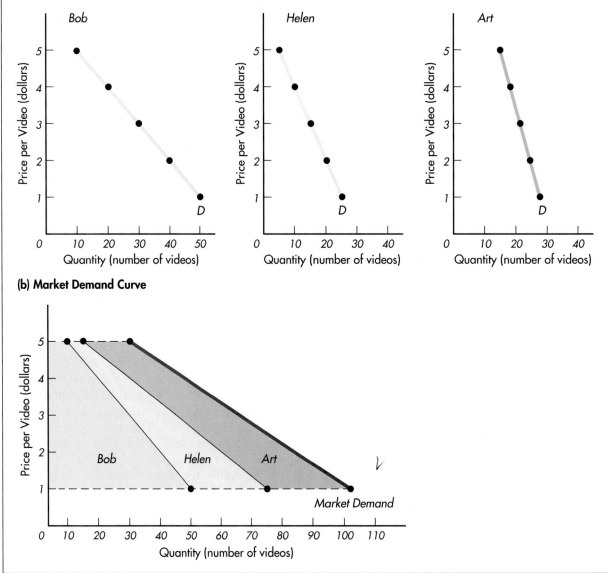

(a) Individual Demand Curves

(b) Market Demand Curve

10, to the quantity Helen would buy, 5, to the quantity Art would buy, 15, to get the market demand of 30. At a price of $4, we add the quantities each of the consumers is willing and able to buy to get the total quantity demanded of 48. At all prices, then, we add the quantities demanded by each individual consumer to get the total, or market quantity, demanded.

2.e. Changes in Demand and Changes in Quantity Demanded

When one of the determinants of demand—income, tastes, prices of related goods, expectations, or number of buyers—is allowed to change, the demand for a good or service changes as well. What does it mean to say that demand changes? Demand is the entire demand schedule, or demand curve. When we say that demand changes, we are referring to a change in the quantities demanded at each and every price.

A change in the quantity demanded is a movement along the demand curve. A change in demand is a shift of the demand curve.

For example, if Bob's income rises, then his demand for video rentals rises. At each and every price, the number of videos Bob is willing and able to rent each year rises. This increase is shown in the last column of the table in Figure 3. A change in demand is represented by a shift of the demand curve, as shown in Figure 3(a). The shift to the right, from D_1 to D_2, indicates that Bob is willing and able to rent more videos at every price.

Figure 3
A Change in Demand and a Change in the Quantity Demanded
According to the table, Bob's demand for videos has increased by 5 videos at each price level. In Figure 3(a), this change is shown as a shift of the demand curve from D_1 to D_2. Figure 3(b) shows a change in the quantity demanded. The change is an increase in the quantity that consumers are willing and able to purchase at a lower price. It is shown as a movement along the demand curve from point A to point B.

Price per Video	Quantity Demanded per Year	
	Before	After
$5	10	15
4	20	25
3	30	35
2	40	45
1	50	55

(a) Change in Demand

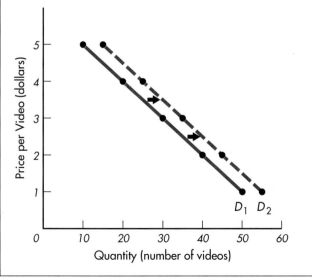

(b) Change in Quantity Demanded

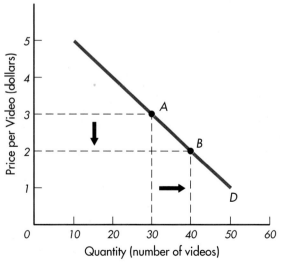

When the price of a good or service is the only factor that changes, the quantity demanded changes but the demand curve does not shift. Instead, as the price of the rentals is decreased (increased), everything else held constant, the quantity that people are willing and able to purchase increases (decreases). This change is merely a movement from one point on the demand curve to another point on the same demand curve, not a shift of the demand curve. *Change in the quantity demanded* is the phrase economists use to describe the change in the quantities of a particular good or service that people are willing and able to purchase as the price of that good or service changes. A change in the quantity demanded, from point *A* to point *B* on the demand curve, is shown in Figure 3(b).

The demand curve shifts when income, tastes, prices of related goods, expectations, or the number of buyers changes. Let's consider how each of these determinants of demand affects the demand curve.

Income   The demand for any good or service depends on income. The higher someone's income is, the more goods and services that person can purchase at any given price. The increase in Bob's income causes his demand to increase. This change is shown in Figure 3(a) by the shift to the right from the curve labeled D_1 to the curve labeled D_2. Increased income means a greater ability to purchase goods and services. At every price, more videos are demanded along curve D_2 than along curve D_1.

Tastes   The demand for any good or service depends on individuals' tastes and preferences. For decades, the destination of choice for college students in the East and Midwest during spring break was Fort Lauderdale, Florida. In the early 1990s, many students decided that Mexico offered a more exciting destination than Fort Lauderdale. Regardless of the prices of the Fort Lauderdale and Mexican vacations, tastes changed so that more students went to Mexico. The demand curve for the Mexican vacation shifted to the right while that for the Fort Lauderdale vacation shifted to the left.

Prices of Related Goods and Services   Goods and services may be related in two ways. **Substitute goods** can be used for each other, so that as the price of one rises, the demand for the other rises. Bread and crackers, BMWs and Acuras, video rentals and theater movies, universities and community colleges, electricity and natural gas are, more or less, pairs of substitutes. As the price of cassette tapes rises, everything else held constant, the demand for CDs will rise and the demand curve for CDs will shift to the right. As the price of theater movies increases, the demand for video rentals will rise and the demand curve for the videos will shift to the right.

Complementary goods are used together, and as the price of one rises, the demand for the other falls. Bread and margarine, beer and peanuts, cameras and film, shoes and socks, CDs and CD players, video rentals and VCRs are examples of pairs of complementary goods. As the price of cameras rises, people tend to purchase fewer cameras, but they also tend to purchase less film. As the price of VCRs rises, people tend to purchase fewer VCRs, but they also demand fewer video rentals. The demand curve for a complementary good shifts to the left when the price of the related good increases.

Expectations   Expectations about future events can have an effect on demand today. People make purchases today because they expect their

substitute goods:
goods that can be used in place of each other; as the price of one rises, the demand for the other rises

complementary goods:
goods that are used together; as the price of one rises, the demand for the other falls

A change in demand is represented by a shift of the demand curve.

income level to be a certain amount in the future, or they expect the price of certain items to be higher in the future. A change in expected income or expected prices can have an effect on today's expenditures. For instance, you might be planning to purchase a car, some furniture, or a house today thinking that your income will be a certain amount next year. If for some reason you change your expectation of next year's income, you may also change your current expenditures. In November 1992, the United States threatened to impose a 300 percent tariff on French white wine beginning in December 1992. The tariff would have increased white wine prices in the United States from about $8 a bottle to $24. Expecting the higher prices in December, U.S. consumers immediately went out and stockpiled French white wine. The effect of changed expectations on demand is represented by a shift of the demand curve. The demand for a good or service may rise (fall) and the demand curve may shift to the right (left) because of a change in expectations.

Number of Buyers   Market demand consists of the sum of the demands of all individuals. The more individuals there are with income to spend, the greater the market demand is likely to be. For example, the populations of Florida and Arizona are much larger during the winter than they are during the summer. The demand for any particular good or service in Arizona and Florida rises (the demand curve shifts to the right) during the winter and falls (the demand curve shifts to the left) during the summer.

2.f. International Effects

exchange rate:
the rate at which monies of different countries are exchanged

The law of demand says the amount of a good or service that people are willing and able to purchase during a particular period of time falls as the price rises and rises as the price falls. It does not indicate whether those people are residents of the United States or some other country. The demand for a product that is available to residents of other countries as well as to residents of the United States will consist of the sum of the demands by U.S. and foreign residents. However, because nations use different monies or currencies, the demand will be affected by the rate at which the different currencies are exchanged. As pointed out in the Economic Insight "The Foreign Exchange Market," an **exchange rate** is the rate at which monies of different countries are exchanged. If the exchange rate changes, then the foreign price of a good produced in the United States will change. To illustrate this, let's consider an example using Levi's blue jeans sold to both U.S. and Japanese customers. The Japanese currency is the yen (¥). In November 1992, it took 124 yen to purchase one dollar. Suppose that a pair of Levi's blue jeans is priced at $20 in the United States. That dollar price in terms of yen is ¥2,480. The exchange rate between the yen and the dollar means that ¥2,480 converts to $20; ¥2,480 = $20 × 124¥/$. Suppose the exchange rate changes to ¥110 per dollar and nothing else changes. The U.S. price of the blue jeans remains at $20. In Japan, the yen value of the blue jeans falls to $20 × 110¥/$ = ¥2,200. Since the blue jeans are now less expensive in Japan because of the exchange rate change, even though the U.S. price of blue jeans did not change, the demand for U.S. blue jeans rises. Thus, changes in exchange rates can affect the demand for goods. At constant U.S. prices, demand curves for U.S. goods will shift around as exchange rates change and foreign purchases fluctuate.

The Foreign Exchange Market

Most countries have their own national currency. Germany has the deutsche mark, France the franc, England the pound sterling, Japan the yen, the United States the dollar, and so on. The citizens of each country use their national currency to carry out transactions. For transactions among nations to occur, however, some exchange of foreign currencies is necessary.

Americans buy Toyotas and Nissans from Japan, while American computer companies sell pocket calculators to businesses in Mexico. Some Americans open bank accounts in Switzerland, while American real estate companies sell property to citizens in England. These transactions require the acquisition of a foreign currency. An English businessman who wants to buy property in the United States will have to exchange his money, pounds sterling, for dollars. An American car distributor who imports Toyotas will have to exchange dollars for yen in order to pay the Toyota manufacturer.

The exchange of currency and the determination of the value of national currencies occur in the foreign exchange market. This is not a tightly organized market operating in a building in New York. Usually, the term *foreign exchange market* refers to the trading that occurs among large international banks. Such trading is global and is done largely through telephone and computer communication systems. If, for example, a foreign exchange trader at First Chicago Bank calls a trader at Bank of Tokyo to buy $1 million worth of Japanese yen, that is a foreign exchange market transaction. Banks buy and sell currencies according to the needs and demands of their customers. Business firms and individuals rely largely on banks to buy and sell foreign exchange for them.

The price of one currency expressed in terms of another currency is called a *foreign exchange rate*, or just *exchange rate*. You can think of an exchange rate as the number of dollars it costs to purchase one unit of another country's currency. For instance, how many dollars does it take to purchase one unit of Japan's currency, the yen? One yen (¥) costs about $.008, or eight-tenths of a cent. The list that follows shows the number of U.S. dollars it took to purchase one unit of several different nations' currencies in November 1992.

Number of U.S. Dollars Needed to Purchase One

Australian dollar	.6947
Belgian franc	.03042
Canadian dollar	.7954
French franc	.18153
Deutsche mark	.6254
Italian lira	.000731
Japanese yen	.00806
Dutch guilder	.5559
Spanish peseta	.008737
Swedish krona	.1665
Swiss franc	.6978

RECAP

1. According to the law of demand, as the price of any good or service rises (falls), the quantity demanded of that good or service falls (rises), during a specific period of time, everything else held constant.

2. A demand schedule is a listing of the quantity demanded at each price.

3. The demand curve is a downward-sloping line plotted using the values of the demand schedule.

4. Market demand is the sum of all individual demands.

5. Demand changes when one of the determinants of demand changes. A demand change is a shift of the demand curve.

6. The quantity demanded changes when the price of the good or service changes. This is a change from one point on the demand curve to another point on the same demand curve.

7. The determinants of demand are income, tastes, prices of related goods and services, expectations, and number of buyers.

8. The exchange rate also is a determinant of demand when a good is sold in both the United States and other countries.

3. SUPPLY

Why is the price of hotel accommodations higher in Phoenix in the winter than in the summer? Demand AND supply. Why is the price of beef higher in Japan than in the United States? Demand AND supply. Why did the price of the dollar in terms of other countries' currencies rise during 1989? Demand AND supply. Both demand and supply determine price, neither demand nor supply alone. We now discuss supply.

3.a. The Law of Supply

What is supply?

supply:
the amount of a good or service that producers are willing and able to offer for sale at each possible price during a period of time, everything else held constant

quantity supplied:
the amount sellers are willing to offer at a given price, during a particular period of time, everything else held constant

law of supply:
as the price of a good or service that producers are willing and able to offer for sale at each possible price during a particular period of time rises (falls), the quantity of that good or service rises (falls), everything else held constant

Just as demand is the relation between the price and the quantity demanded of a good or service, supply is the relation between price and quantity supplied. **Supply** is the amount of the good or service producers are willing and able to offer for sale at each possible price during a period of time, everything else held constant. **Quantity supplied** is the amount of the good or service producers are willing and able to offer for sale at a *specific* price, during a period of time, everything else held constant. According to the **law of supply**, as the price of a good or service rises, the quantity supplied rises, and vice versa.

The formal statement of the law of supply consists of five phrases:

1. the quantity of a well-defined good or service that
2. producers are willing and able to offer for sale
3. during a particular period of time
4. increases as the price of the good or service increases and decreases as the price decreases
5. everything else held constant

The first phrase is the same as the first phrase in the law of demand. The second phrase indicates that producers must not only *want* to offer the product for sale but must be *able* to offer the product. The third phrase points out that the quantities producers will offer for sale depend on the period of time being considered. For instance, the prices at which producers of personal computers would sell their products in January 1992 were significantly different than in January 1993. The fourth phrase points out that more will be supplied at higher than at lower prices. The final phrase ensures that the **determinants of supply** do not change. The determinants of supply are those factors that influence the willingness and ability of producers to offer their goods and services for sale other than the price of the good or service— the prices of resources used to produce the product, technology and productivity, expectations of producers, the number of producers in the market, and the prices of related goods and services. If any one of these should change, supply changes.

determinants of supply:
factors other than the price of the good that influence supply—prices of resources, technology and productivity, expectations of producers, number of producers, and the prices of related good and services

3.b. The Supply Schedule and Supply Curve

supply schedule:
a table or list of prices and corresponding quantities supplied of a particular good or service

supply curve:
a graph of a supply schedule that measures price on the vertical axis and quantity supplied on the horizontal axis

A **supply schedule** is a table or list of the prices and the corresponding quantities supplied of a good or service. The table in Figure 4 presents MGA's supply schedule of videos. The schedule lists the quantities that MGA is willing and able to supply at each price, everything else held constant. As the price increases, MGA is willing and able to offer more videos for rent.

A **supply curve** is a graph of the supply schedule. Figure 4 shows MGA's supply curve of videos. The price and quantity combinations given in the supply schedule correspond to the points on the curve. For instance, combination A in the table corresponds to point *A* on the curve; combination B in the table corresponds to point *B* on the curve, and so on for each price-quantity combination.

MGA's supply curve slopes upward. This means that MGA is willing and able to supply more at higher prices than it is at lower prices. Recall from Chapter 2 that as society puts more and more resources into the production of any specific item, the opportunity cost of each additional unit of production rises because more specialized resources are transferred to activities in which they are relatively less productive. MGA, too, finds that as it increases production, the opportunity costs of additional production rise. Hence, the only way that MGA, or any producer, is willing and able to produce more is if the price rises sufficiently to cover these increasing opportunity costs.

Figure 4
MGA's Supply Schedule and Supply Curve for Videos
The quantity that MGA is willing and able to offer for sale at each price is listed in the supply schedule and shown on the supply curve. At point *A*, the price is $5 per video and the quantity supplied is 60 videos. The combination of $4 per video and 50 videos is point *B*. Each price-quantity combination is plotted, and the points are connected to form the supply curve.

Combination	Price per Video (constant-quality units)	Quantity Supplied per Year (constant-quality units)
A	$5	60
B	4	50
C	3	40
D	2	30
E	1	20

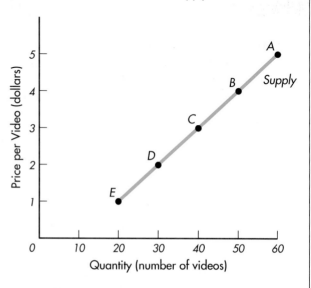

3.c. From Individual Supply Curves to the Market Supply

To derive market supply, the quantities that each producer supplies at each price are added together, just as the quantities demanded by each consumer are added together to get market demand. The table in Figure 5 lists the supply schedules of three video rental stores: MGA, Motown, and Blockmaster. For our example, we assume that these three are the only video rental stores. (We are also assuming that the brand names are not associated with quality or any other differences.)

The supply schedule of each producer is plotted in Figure 5(a). Then in Figure 5(b) the individual supply curves have been added together to obtain the market supply curve. At a price of $5, the quantity supplied by MGA is 60, the quantity supplied by Motown is 30, and the quantity supplied by Blockmaster is 12. This means a total quantity supplied in the market of 102. At a price of $4, the quantities supplied are 50 by MGA, 25 by Motown, and 9 by Blockmaster for a total market quantity supplied of 84. The market supply schedule is the last column in the table. The plot of the price and quantity combinations listed in this column is the market supply curve. The market supply curve slopes up because each of the individual supply curves has a positive slope. The market supply curve tells us that the quantity supplied in the market increases as the price rises.

3.d. Changes in Supply and Changes in Quantity Supplied

A change in the quantity supplied is a movement along the supply curve. A change in the supply is a shift of the supply curve.

When we draw the supply curve, we allow only the price and quantity supplied of the good or service we are discussing to change. Everything else that might affect supply is assumed not to change. If any of the determinants of supply—the prices of resources used to produce the product, technology and productivity, expectations of producers, the number of producers in the market, and the prices of related goods and services—changes, the supply schedule changes and the supply curve shifts.

Prices of Resources If labor costs—one of the resources used to produce video rentals—rise, higher rental prices will be necessary to induce each store to offer as many videos as it did before the cost of the resource rose. The higher cost of resources causes a decrease in supply, meaning a leftward shift of the supply curve, from S_1 to S_2 in Figure 6(a).

Two interpretations of a leftward shift of the supply curve are possible. One comes from comparing the old and new curves in a horizontal direction; the other comes from comparing the curves in a vertical direction. In the vertical direction, the decrease in supply informs us that sellers want a higher price to produce any given quantity. Compare, for example, point A on curve S_1 with C on curve S_2. A and C represent the same quantity but different prices. Sellers will offer 66 videos at a price of $3 per video according to supply curve S_1. But if the supply curve shifts to the left, then the sellers want more ($3.50) for 66 units.

In the horizontal direction, the decrease in supply means that sellers will offer less for sale at any given price. This can be seen by comparing point B on curve S_2 with A on curve S_1. Both points correspond to a price of $3, but along curve S_1, sellers are willing to offer 66 units for sale, while curve S_2 indicates that sellers will offer only 57 videos for rent.

Figure 5
The Market Supply Schedule and Curve for Videos

The market supply is derived by summing the quantities that each producer is willing and able to offer for sale at each price. In this example, there are three producers: MGA, Motown, and Blockmaster. The supply schedules of each are listed in the table and plotted as the individual supply curves shown in Figure 5(a). By adding the quantities supplied at each price, we obtain the market supply curve shown in Figure 5(b). For instance, at a price of $5, MGA offers 60 units, Motown 30 units, and Blockmaster 12 units, for a market supply quantity of 102. The market supply curve reflects the quantities that each producer is able and willing to supply at each price.

Price per Video	Quantities Supplied per Year by							Market Supply
	MGA		Motown		Blockmaster			
$5	60	+	30	+	12	=		102
4	50		25		9			84
3	40		20		6			66
2	30		15		3			48
1	20		10		0			30

(a) Individual Supply Curves

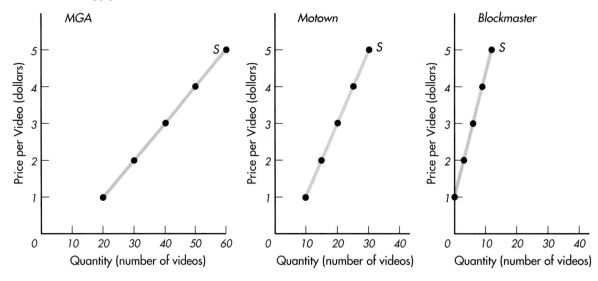

(b) Market Supply Curve

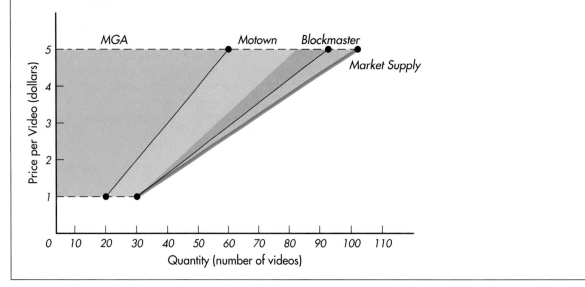

Figure 6
A Shift of the Supply Curve
Figure 6(a) shows a decrease in supply and the shift of the supply curve to the left, from S_1 to S_2. The decrease is caused by a change in one of the determinants of video supply—an increase in the price of labor. Because of the increased price of labor, producers are willing and able to offer fewer videos for rent at each price than they were before the price of labor rose. Supply curve S_2 shows that at a price of $3 per video, suppliers will offer 57 videos. That is 9 units less than the 66 videos at $3 per video indicated by supply curve S_1. Conversely, to offer a given quantity, producers must receive a higher price per video than they previously were getting: $3.50 per video for 66 videos (on supply curve S_2) instead of $3 per video (on supply curve S_1).

Figure 6(b) shows an increase in supply. A technological improvement or an increase in productivity causes the supply curve to shift to the right, from S_1 to S_2. At each price, a higher quantity is offered for sale. At a price of $3, 66 units were offered, but with the shift of the supply curve, the quantity of units for sale at $3 apiece increases to 84. Conversely, producers can reduce prices for a given quantity—for example, charging $2 per video for 66 units.

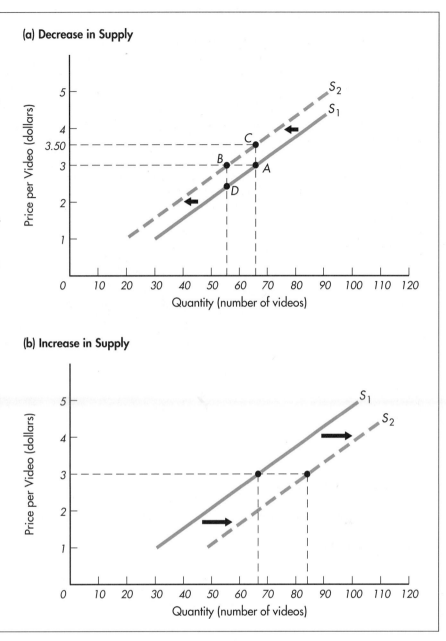

(a) Decrease in Supply

(b) Increase in Supply

If resource prices declined, then supply would increase. That combination would be illustrated by a rightward shift of the supply curve.

Technology and Productivity   If resources are used more efficiently in the production of a good or service, more of that good or service can be produced for the same cost, or the original quantity can be produced for a lower cost. As a result, the supply curve shifts to the right, as in Figure 6(b).

The move from horse-drawn plows to tractors or from mainframe computers to personal computers meant that each worker was able to produce more. The increase in output produced by each unit of a resource is called a *productivity increase*. **Productivity** is defined as the quantity of output produced

productivity:
the quantity of output produced per unit of resource

Before computers, businesses had to manually count their inventories, keeping track of those items that needed to be reordered and those that were not selling. Today, businesses can monitor their inventories with bar codes and scanners. Bar codes allow warehouse stock pickers to locate parts quickly and accurately. This and similar inventory control processes have automated businesses and made them able to produce and offer a larger quantity for sale at the same or lower prices. The supply curve has shifted out as technology has improved.

per unit of resource. Improvements in technology cause productivity increases, which lead to an increase in supply.

Expectations of Producers Sellers may choose to alter the quantity offered for sale today because of a change in expectations regarding future prices or the determinants of supply. If producers change their expectations of the future level of consumer income, they may change the quantities supplied of goods and services they produce today. If producers become pessimistic about future income levels, they might expect to sell less in the future and will decrease production today. This would be shown as a leftward shift of the supply curve.

A change in expectations about the price of a product can also affect a producer's current willingness to supply. For example, during the 1980s, some owners of oil wells in Texas may have kept their wells capped (not pumping) because they expected the price of oil to rise and they wanted to wait to sell at the higher price. If these owners had been more pessimistic about oil prices they might have decided to increase the number of wells in operation, causing the supply curve to shift to the right.

Number of Producers When more people decide to produce a good or service, the market supply increases. More is offered for sale at each and every price, causing a rightward shift of the supply curve.

Prices of Related Goods or Services The opportunity cost of producing and selling any good or service is the forgone opportunity to produce any other good or service. If the price of an alternative good changes, then the opportunity cost of producing a particular good changes. This could cause

Figure 7
A Change in Supply and a Change in the Quantity Supplied
In Figure 7(a), the quantities that producers are willing and able to offer for sale at every price decrease, caus-

ing a leftward shift of the supply curve from S_1 to S_2. In Figure 7(b), the quantities that producers are willing and able to offer for sale increase, due to an increase in the price of the good, causing a movement along the supply curve from point A to point B.

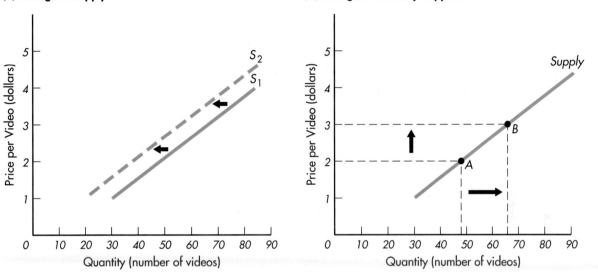

(a) Change in Supply

(b) Change in Quantity Supplied

the supply curve to change. For instance, if the video store can offer videos or arcade games with equal ease, an increase in the price of the arcade games could induce the store owner to offer more arcade games and fewer videos. The supply curve of videos would then shift to the left.

A *change in supply* occurs when the quantity supplied at each and every price changes or there is a shift in the supply curve—like the shift from S_1 to S_2 in Figure 7(a). A change in one of the determinants of supply brings about a change in supply.

When only the price changes, a greater or smaller quantity is supplied. This is shown as a movement along the supply curve, not as a shift of the curve. A change in price is said to cause a *change in the quantity supplied*. An increase in quantity supplied is shown in the move from point A to point B on the supply curve of Figure 7(b).

RECAP

1. According to the law of supply, the quantity supplied of any good or service is directly related to the price of the good or service, during a specific period of time, everything else held constant.

2. Market supply is found by adding together the quantities supplied at each price by every producer in the market.

3. Supply changes if the prices of relevant resources change, if technology or productivity changes, if producers' expectations change, if the number of producers changes, or if the prices of related goods and services change.

4. Changes in supply are reflected in shifts of the supply curve. Changes in the quantity supplied are reflected in movements along the supply curve.

4. EQUILIBRIUM: PUTTING DEMAND AND SUPPLY TOGETHER

equilibrium:
the point at which quantity demanded and quantity supplied are equal at a particular price

The demand curve shows the quantity of a good or service that buyers are willing and able to purchase at each price. The supply curve shows the quantity that producers are willing and able to offer for sale at each price. Only where the two curves intersect is the quantity supplied equal to the quantity demanded. This intersection is the point of **equilibrium**.

4.a. Determination of Equilibrium

How is price determined by demand and supply?

Figure 8 brings together the market demand and market supply curves for video rentals. The supply and demand schedules are listed in the table and the curves are plotted in the graph in Figure 8. Notice that the curves intersect at only one point, labeled *e*, a price of $3 and a quantity of 66. The intersection point is the equilibrium price, the only price at which the quantity demanded and quantity supplied are the same. You can see that at any other price the quantity demanded and quantity supplied are not the same. These are called **disequilibrium** points.

disequilibrium:
a point at which quantity demanded and quantity supplied are not equal at a particular price

surplus:
a quantity supplied that is larger than the quantity demanded at a given price; it occurs whenever the price is greater than the equilibrium price

shortage:
a quantity supplied that is smaller than the quantity demanded at a given price; it occurs whenever the price is less than the equilibrium price

Whenever the price is greater than the equilibrium price, a **surplus** arises. For example, at $4, the quantity of videos demanded is 48 and the quantity supplied is 84. Thus, at $4 per video there is a surplus of 36 videos—that is, 36 videos are not rented. Conversely, whenever the price is below the equilibrium price, the quantity demanded is greater than the quantity supplied and there is a **shortage**. For instance, if the price is $2 per video, consumers will want and be able to pay for more videos than are available. As shown in the table in Figure 8, the quantity demanded at a price of $2 is 84 but the quantity supplied is only 48. There is a shortage of 36 videos at the price of $2.

Neither a surplus nor a shortage exists for long if the price of the product is free to change. Producers who are stuck with videos sitting on the shelves getting brittle and out of style will lower the price and reduce the quantities they are offering for rent in order to eliminate a surplus. Conversely, producers whose shelves are empty even as consumers demand videos will acquire more videos and raise the rental price to eliminate a shortage. Surpluses lead to decreases in the price and the quantity supplied and increases in the quantity demanded. Shortages lead to increases in the price and the quantity supplied and decreases in the quantity demanded.

Note that a shortage is not the same thing as scarcity. A shortage exists only when the quantity that people are willing and able to purchase at a particular price is more than the quantity supplied at that price. Scarcity applies to everything at every price. The only goods that are not scarce are free goods—a greater quantity exists than people are willing and able to purchase even when the price is zero.

Figure 8
Equilibrium
Equilibrium is established at the point where the quantity that suppliers are willing and able to offer for sale is the same as the quantity that buyers are willing and able to purchase. Here, equilibrium occurs at the price of $3 per video and the quantity of 66 videos. It is shown as point *e* at the intersection of the demand and supply curves. At prices above $3, the quantity supplied is greater than the quantity demanded, and the result is a surplus. At prices below $3, the quantity supplied is less than the quantity demanded, and the result is a shortage.

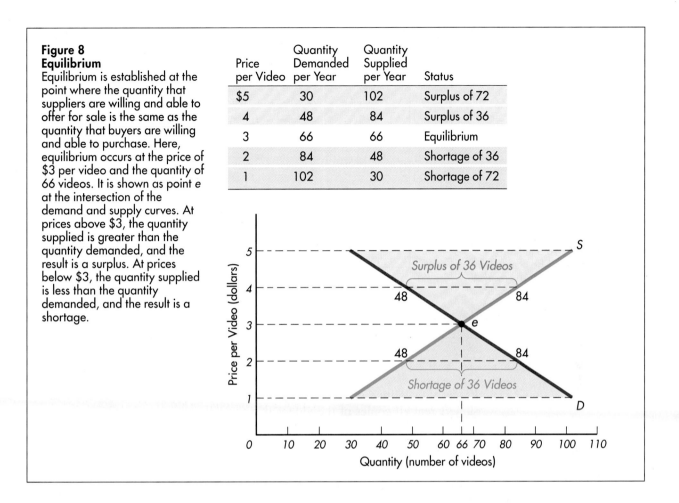

Price per Video	Quantity Demanded per Year	Quantity Supplied per Year	Status
$5	30	102	Surplus of 72
4	48	84	Surplus of 36
3	66	66	Equilibrium
2	84	48	Shortage of 36
1	102	30	Shortage of 72

4.b. Changes in the Equilibrium Price: Demand Shifts

What causes price to change?

Equilibrium is the combination of price and quantity at which the quantities demanded and supplied are the same. Once an equilibrium is achieved, there is no incentive for producers or consumers to move away from it. An equilibrium price changes only when demand and/or supply changes—that is, when the determinants of demand or determinants of supply change.

Let's consider a change in demand and what it means for the equilibrium price. Suppose that experiments on rats show that watching videos causes brain damage. As a result, a large segment of the human population decides not to rent videos. Stores find that the demand for videos has decreased, as shown in Figure 9 by a leftward shift of the demand curve, from curve D_1 to curve D_2.

Once the demand curve has shifted, the original equilibrium price of $3 per video at point e_1 is no longer equilibrium. At a price of $3, the quantity supplied is still 66, but the quantity demanded has declined to 48 (look at the demand curve D_2 at a price of $3). There is, therefore, a surplus of 18 videos at the price of $3.

With a surplus comes downward pressure on the price. This downward pressure occurs because producers acquire fewer videos to offer for rent and reduce the rental price in an attempt to rent the videos sitting on the shelves.

Figure 9
The Effects of a Shift of the Demand Curve
The initial equilibrium price ($3 per video) and quantity (66 videos) are established at point e_1, where the initial demand and supply curves intersect. A change in the tastes for videos causes demand to decrease, and the demand curve shifts to the left. At $3 per video, the initial quantity supplied, 66 videos, is now greater than the quantity demanded, 48 videos. The surplus of 18 units causes producers to reduce production and lower the price. The market reaches a new equilibrium, at point e_2, $2.50 per video and 57 videos.

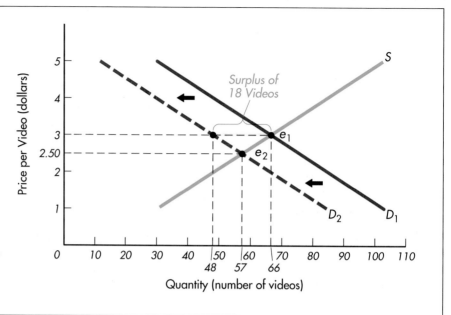

Producers continue reducing the price and the quantity available until consumers rent all copies of the videos that the sellers have available, or until a new equilibrium is established. That new equilibrium occurs at point e_2 with a price of $2.50 and a quantity of 57.

The decrease in demand is represented by the leftward shift of the demand curve. A decrease in demand results in a lower equilibrium price and a lower equilibrium quantity as long as there is no change in supply. Conversely, an increase in demand would be represented as a rightward shift of the demand curve and would result in a higher equilibrium price and a higher equilibrium quantity as long as there is no change in supply.

4.c. Changes in Equilibrium Price: Supply Shifts

The equilibrium price and quantity may be altered by a change in supply as well. If the price of relevant resources, technology and productivity, expectations of producers, the number of producers, or the price of related products change, supply changes.

Let's consider an example. Petroleum is a key ingredient in videotapes. Suppose the quantity of oil available is reduced by 40 percent, causing the price of oil to rise. Every video manufacturer has to pay more for oil, which means that the rental stores must pay more for each videotape. To purchase the videos and offer them for rent, the rental stores must receive a higher rental price in order to cover their higher costs. This is represented by a leftward shift of the supply curve in Figure 10.

The leftward shift of the supply curve, from curve S_1 to curve S_2, leads to a new equilibrium price and quantity. At the original equilibrium price of $3 at point e_1, 66 videos are supplied. After the shift in the supply curve, 48 videos are offered for rent at a price of $3 apiece, and there is a shortage of 18

Figure 10
The Effects of a Shift of the Supply Curve
The initial equilibrium price and quantity are $3 and 66 units, at point e_1. When the price of labor increases, suppliers are willing and able to offer fewer videos for rent at each price. The result is a leftward (upward) shift of the supply curve, from S_1 to S_2. At the old price of $3, the quantity demanded is still 66, but the quantity supplied falls to 48. The shortage is 18 videos. The shortage causes suppliers to acquire more videos to offer for rent and to raise the rental price. The new equilibrium, e_2, the intersection between curves S_2 and D, is $3.50 per video and 57 videos.

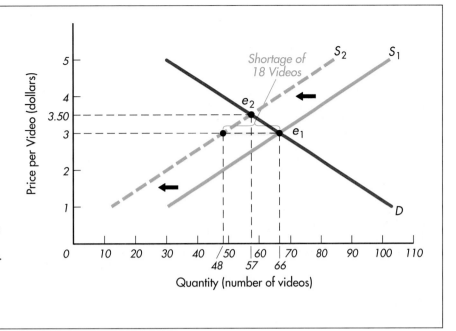

videos. The shortage puts upward pressure on price. As the price rises, consumers decrease the quantities that they are willing and able to rent, and sellers increase the quantities that they are willing and able to supply. Eventually, a new equilibrium price and quantity is established at $3.50 and 57 videos at point e_2.

The decrease in supply is represented by the leftward shift of the supply curve. A decrease in supply with no change in demand results in a higher price and a lower quantity. Conversely, an increase in supply would be represented as a rightward shift of the supply curve. An increase in supply with no change in demand would result in a lower price and a higher quantity.

4.d. Equilibrium in Reality

We have examined a hypothetical (imaginary) market for video rentals in order to represent what goes on in real markets. We have established that the price of a good or service is defined by equilibrium between demand and supply. We noted that an equilibrium could be disturbed by a change in demand or a change in supply and the equilibrium could also be disturbed by simultaneous changes in demand and supply. The important point of this discussion is to demonstrate that when not in equilibrium, the price and the quantities demanded and/or supplied change until equilibrium is established. The market is always attempting to reach equilibrium.

Looking at last year's sweaters piled up on the sale racks, waiting over an hour for a table at a restaurant, or finding that the VCR rental store never has a copy of the movie you want to rent in stock may make you wonder whether equilibrium is ever established. In fact, it is not uncommon to observe situations where quantities demanded and supplied are not equal. But this observation does not cast doubt on the usefulness of the equilibrium concept. Even if all markets do not clear, or reach equilibrium, all the time, we can be assured that market forces are operating so that the market is moving toward an equilibrium. The market forces exist even when the price is not allowed to change, as illustrated in the following section.

price floor:
a situation where the price is not allowed to decrease below a certain level

4.d.1. Price Ceilings and Price Floors

A **price floor** is the situation where the price is not allowed to decrease below a certain level. Consider Figure 11 representing the market for sugar. The equilibrium price of sugar is $.10 a pound, but because the government has set a price floor of $.20 a pound, as shown by the solid yellow line, the price is not allowed to move to its equilibrium level. A surplus of 250,000 pounds of sugar results from the price floor. Sugar growers produce 1 million pounds of sugar and consumers purchase 750,000 pounds of sugar.

We saw previously that whenever the price is above the equilibrium price, market forces work to decrease the price. The price floor interferes with the functioning of the market; a surplus exists because the government will not allow the price to drop. How does the government ensure that the price floor remains in force? It has to purchase the excess sugar. The government must purchase the surplus so that its price floor of $.20 per pound remains in force.

What would occur if the government had set the price floor at $.09 a pound? Since at $.09 a pound a shortage of sugar would result, the price would rise. A price floor only keeps the price from falling, not rising. So the price rises to its equilibrium level of $.10. Only if the price floor is set above the equilibrium price is it an effective price floor.

price ceiling:
a situation where the price is not allowed to rise above a certain level

A **price ceiling** is the situation where a price is not allowed to rise to its equilibrium level. L.A., San Francisco, Boston, and New York are among over 125 U.S. cities that have *rent controls*. A rent control law places a ceiling on the rents that landlords can charge for apartments. Figure 12 is a demand

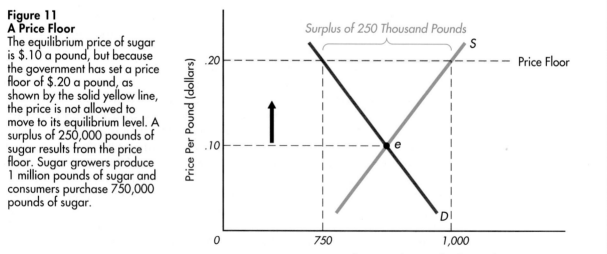

Figure 11
A Price Floor
The equilibrium price of sugar is $.10 a pound, but because the government has set a price floor of $.20 a pound, as shown by the solid yellow line, the price is not allowed to move to its equilibrium level. A surplus of 250,000 pounds of sugar results from the price floor. Sugar growers produce 1 million pounds of sugar and consumers purchase 750,000 pounds of sugar.

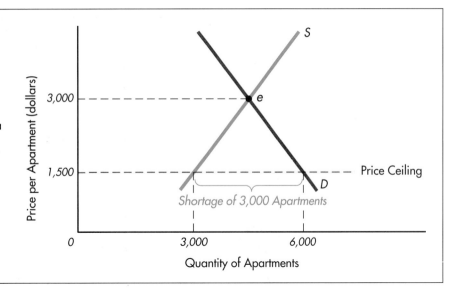

Figure 12
Rent Controls
A demand and supply graph representing the market for apartments in New York City is shown. The equilibrium price is $3,000 a month. The government has set a price of $1,500 a month. The government's price ceiling is shown by the solid yellow line. At the government's price, 3,000 apartments are available but consumers want 6,000. There is a shortage of 3,000 apartments.

and supply graph representing the market for apartments in New York. The equilibrium price is $3,000 a month. The government has set a price of $1,500 a month as the maximum that can be charged. The price ceiling is shown by the solid yellow line. At the rent control price of $1,500 per month, 3,000 apartments are available but consumers want 6,000 apartments. There is a shortage of 3,000 apartments.

The shortage means that not everyone willing and able to purchase the apartment will be allowed to. Since the price is not allowed to ration the apartments, something else will have to. It may be that those willing and able to stand in line the longest get the apartments. Perhaps bribing an important official might be the way to get an apartment. Perhaps relatives of officials or important citizens will get the apartments. Whenever a price ceiling exists, a shortage results and some rationing device other than price will arise.

Had the government set the rent control price at $4,000 per month, the price ceiling would not have had an effect. Since the equilibrium is $3,000 a month, the price would not have risen to $4,000. Only if the price ceiling is below the equilibrium price will it be an effective price ceiling.

Price ceilings are not uncommon features in the U.S. or in other economies. China had a severe housing shortage for thirty years because the price of housing was kept below equilibrium. Faced with unhappy citizens and realizing the cause of the shortage, officials began to lift the restrictions on housing prices in 1985. The shortage has diminished. In the former Soviet Union prices on all goods and services were defined by the government. For most consumer items, the price was set below equilibrium; shortages existed. The long lines of people waiting to purchase food or clothing were the result of the price ceilings on all goods and services. In the United States, price ceilings on all goods and services have been imposed at times. During the first and second world wars and during the Nixon Administration of the early 1970s, wage and price controls were imposed. These were price ceilings on all goods and services. As a result of the ceilings, people were unable to purchase many of the products they desired. The Organization of Petroleum Exporting Countries (OPEC) restricted the quantity of oil in the early 1970s and drove its price up considerably. The United States government responded by placing a price ceiling on gasoline. The result was long lines at gas stations—shortages of gasoline.

Price floors are quite common features in economies as well. The agricultural policies of most of the developed nations are founded on price floors—the government guarantees that the price of an agricultural product will not fall below some level. Price floors result in surpluses and this has been the case with agricultural products as well. The surpluses in agricultural products in the United States have resulted in cases where dairy farmers dumped milk in the river, where grain was given to other nations at taxpayer expense, and where citrus ranchers picked and then discarded thousands of tons of citrus, all to reduce huge surpluses.

There are many reasons other than price ceilings and price floors why we observe excess supplies or demands in the real world. In most cases, the excess demands or supplies are due to the difficulty of changing prices rapidly or to the desires of either the demanders or suppliers not to have prices change rapidly. We shall consider many such cases in the text. The important part of the discussion in this chapter is to keep in mind that unless the price is not allowed to change, surpluses and shortages will put pressure on the price to move to its equilibrium level.

RECAP

1. Equilibrium occurs when quantity demanded and quantity supplied are equal: it is the price-quantity combination where the demand and supply curves intersect.

2. A price that is above the equilibrium price creates a surplus. Producers are willing and able to offer more for sale than buyers are willing and able to purchase.

3. A price that is below the equilibrium price leads to a shortage, because buyers are willing and able to purchase more than producers are willing and able to offer for sale.

4. When demand changes, price and quantity change in the same direction—both rise as demand increases and both fall as demand decreases.

5. When supply changes, price and quantity change but not in the same direction. When supply increases, price falls and quantity rises. When supply decreases, price rises and quantity falls.

6. When both demand and supply change, the direction of the change in price and quantity depends on the relative sizes of the changes of demand and supply.

7. A price floor is a situation where a price is set above the equilibrium price. This creates a surplus.

8. A price ceiling is a case where a price is set below the equilibrium price. This creates a shortage.

SUMMARY

▲▼ *What is a market?*

1. A market is where buyers and sellers trade a well-defined commodity. §1

▲▼ *What is demand?*

2. Demand is the quantities that buyers are willing and able to buy at alternative prices. §2

3. The quantity demanded is a specific amount at one price. §2

4. The law of demand states that as the price of a well-defined commodity rises (falls) the quantity demanded during a given period of time will fall (rise), everything else held constant. §2.a

5. Demand will change when one of the determinants of demand changes, that is, when income, tastes, prices of related goods, expectations, or number of buyers change. In addition, the demand may change when exchange rates change. A demand change is illustrated as a shift of the demand curve. §2.e and f

▲▼ *What is supply?*

6. Supply is the quantities that sellers will offer for sale at alternative prices. §3.a

7. The quantity supplied is the amount sellers offer for sale at one price. §3.a

8. The law of supply states that as the price of a well-defined commodity rises (falls) the quantity supplied during a given period of time will rise (fall), everything else held constant. §3.a

9. Supply changes when one of the determinants of supply changes, that is, when prices of resources, technology and productivity, expectations of producers, the number of producers, or the prices of related goods or services change. A supply change is illustrated as a shift of the supply curve. §3.a and b

▲▼ *How is price determined by demand and supply?*

10. Together, demand and supply determine the equilibrium price and quantity. §4

▲▼ *What causes price to change?*

11. A price that is above equilibrium creates a surplus, which leads to a lower price. A price that is below equilibrium creates a shortage, which leads to a higher price. §4.a

12. A change in demand or a change in supply (a shift of either curve) will cause the equilibrium price and quantity to change. §4.b and c

13. Markets are not always in equilibrium, but forces work to move them toward equilibrium. §4.d

14. A price floor is a situation where a price is not allowed to decrease below a certain level—it is set above the equilibrium price. This creates a surplus. A price ceiling is a case where a price is not allowed to rise—it is set below the equilibrium price. This creates a shortage. §4.d

KEY TERMS

market §1.a

barter §1.b

double coincidence of wants §1.b

transaction costs §1.b

relative price §1.c

demand §2

quantity demanded §2

law of demand §2.a

determinants of demand §2.a

demand schedule §2.b

demand curve §2.c

substitute goods §2.e

complementary goods §2.e

exchange rate §2.f

supply §3.a

quantity supplied §3.a

law of supply §3.a

determinants of supply §3.a

supply schedule §3.b

supply curve §3.b

productivity §3.d

equilibrium §4

disequilibrium, §4.a

surplus §4.a

shortage §4.a

price floor §4.d

price ceiling §4.d

EXERCISES

1. Illustrate each of the following events using a demand and supply diagram for bananas.

   a. Reports surface that imported bananas are infected with a deadly virus.

   b. Consumers' incomes drop.

   c. The price of bananas rises.

   d. The price of oranges falls.

   e. Consumers expect the price of bananas to decrease in the future.

2. Answer true or false and if the statement is false change it to make it true. Illustrate your answers on a demand and supply graph.

   a. An increase in demand is represented by a movement up the demand curve.

   b. An increase in supply is represented by a movement up the supply curve.

   c. An increase in demand without any changes in supply will cause the price to rise.

   d. An increase in supply without any changes in demand will cause the price to rise.

3. Using the following schedules, define the equilibrium price and quantity. Describe the situation at a price of $10. What will occur? Describe the situation at a price of $2. What will occur?

Price	Quantity Demanded	Quantity Supplied
$ 1	500	100
2	400	120
3	350	150
4	320	200
5	300	300
6	275	410
7	260	500
8	230	650
9	200	800
10	150	975

4. Suppose the government imposed a minimum price of $7 in the schedules of question 3. What would occur? Illustrate.

5. In question 3, indicate what the price would have to be to represent an effective price ceiling. Point out the surplus or shortage that results. Illustrate a price floor and provide an example of a price floor.

6. A common feature of skiing is waiting in lift lines. Does the existence of lift lines mean that the price is not working to allocate the scarce resource? If so, what should be done about it?

7. Why don't we observe barter systems as often as we observe the use of currency?

8. A severe drought in California has resulted in nearly a 30 percent reduction in the quantity of citrus grown and produced in California. Explain what effect this event might have on the Florida citrus market.

9. According to a 1992 law, freon for air conditioning will not be produced after 1995. All 1995 automobiles will have non-freon-based air conditioning systems. Explain what the 1992 law will mean for freon in 1995. Explain what the 1995 result might mean for freon in 1992.

10. The prices of the Ralph Lauren "Polo" line of clothing is considerably higher than comparable quality lines. Yet, it sells more than a JC Penney brand line of clothing. Does this violate the law of demand?

11. In December, the price of Christmas trees rises and the quantity of trees sold rises. Is this a violation of the law of demand?

12. In recent years, the price of artificial Christmas trees has fallen while the quality has risen. What impact has this event had on the price of cut Christmas trees?

13. Many restaurants don't take reservations. You simply arrive and wait your turn. If you arrive at 7:30 in the evening, you have at least an hour wait. Notwithstanding that fact, a few people arrive, speak quietly with the maitre d', hand him some money, and are promptly seated. At some restaurants that do take reservations, there is a month wait for a Saturday evening, three weeks for a Friday evening, two weeks for Tuesday through Thursday, and virtually no wait for Sunday or Monday evening. How do you explain these events using demand and supply?

14. Evaluate the following statement: "The demand for U.S. oranges has increased because the quantity of U.S. oranges demanded in Japan has risen."

15. In December 1992, the federal government began requiring that all foods display information about fat content and other ingredients on food packages. The displays had to be verified by independent laboratories. The price of an evaluation of a food product could run as much as $20,000. What impact will this law have on the market for meat?

Panel Denies Rent Hike Request Because of Complaints on Upkeep

CANYON COUNTRY—Managers of a mobile-home park were denied the rent increase they requested because residents complained about the park's upkeep.

The Manufactured Home Rent Stabilization Panel, the city commission that oversees rent at mobile home parks, approved a 4 percent rent increase at the Soledad Trailer Lodge, rather than the 13.7 percent hike the manager proposed.

The higher increase was rejected because the management had failed to take good care of the park, panel member Leslee Bowman said.

"It's a slum," she said. "The roads are cracking, the septic tanks are leaking. The wiring appears to be inadequate." . . .

The park deserved the bigger hike because management had not raised rents since 1989, and maintenance costs have increased, park manager William Reed said.

Over the past couple of years, many improvements have been made to the 30-home park, including repainting the laundry room and upgrading the sewage system, he said.

"I don't think management has been unresponsive," Reed said. "When we have a problem, we try to fix it."

But several park residents said the park has deteriorated.

Parts of the roof on the newly painted laundry room, for example, have dry-rotted, said Don Johnson, president of the Soledad Trailer Lodge Mobile Home Owners Association.

Also, the park has had two large sewage spills in the past two years, he said.

"There's been a lack of it [maintenance] throughout many years," said Johnson, standing astride cracks in the park's driveway. . . .

The city sent an inspector to the park in late September after receiving a complaint from a resident, said code enforcement officer Kyle Lancaster. Inspectors found the property littered with debris and broken cars, according to a letter sent to the state dated Oct. 1. Park management later addressed many of the concerns, Lancaster said.

The state regulates mobile-home parks and is responsible for code enforcement, Lancaster added.

City code permits annual rate hikes up to 6 percent or the consumer price index increase, whichever is lower. Bigger raises are permitted in "extraordinary circumstances," said Kevin Michel, city senior planner.

Park residents pay an average of $250 a month. The Canyon Country park has operated for more than 30 years.

Source: Marc Ballon, "Panel Denies Rent Hike Request Because of Complaints on Upkeep," *Daily News*, Dec. 17, 1992, p. SC1. Reprinted with permission of the Los Angeles Daily News.

Commentary

Rent control—the attempt to make housing available to more people by controlling its cost—is among the most hotly contested local political issues in America. Since 1960, the number of jurisdictions with rent-control ordinances has swelled to more than 125, and the decision to adopt such laws is being debated in still more communities.

Rent controls, at their simplest, can be represented as a price ceiling (see figure, left). A rent control could be represented as a maximum, or ceiling price, of P_m, which is less than the equilibrium price P_1. This price ceiling creates a shortage: At the rent-control price P_m, the quantity of housing units demanded is Q_d while the quantity of housing units supplied is only Q_s. The difference, $Q_d - Q_s$, is the number of families willing and able to rent a house at price P_m but for whom there are no homes available.

How is this excess demand resolved? Two things occur. One is that something other than price serves as the allocater. Common replacements for price are: first come, first served; preferences of the landlord; or black market or under-the-table payoffs. The second is that the landlord decreases the maintenance on the existing rentals, and new rental units are not brought to the market. As the landlord expe-

riences a lower return on the rental housing, he or she has a lower incentive to devote resources to the upkeep of the unit. As a result, the quality of the housing deteriorates.

This is what occurred at the Soledad Trailer Lodge. Unable to secure what it considered a fair return, the management of the park let it deteriorate. When the landlord asked for a 13.7 percent rent hike in order to increase the quality of the park, the city commission said no because the park had deteriorated. The landlord will not receive increased compensation until the maintenance and upkeep are improved, but the landlord has no incentive to make improvements at the low, rent-controlled price.

Not only does rent control lead to deterioration but the lower return on the rental housing means that some landlords may convert their units to condominiums or to commercial properties and sell them. Over time, the supply of rental housing declines. The supply curve shifts in, to S_2 in Figure, right, creating an even greater excess demand.

If rent control provides the same return as the free market would, there is no rent control. If the law provides a lower return, then the benefits to tenants rise, but the incentives for deterioration of the housing market also rise.

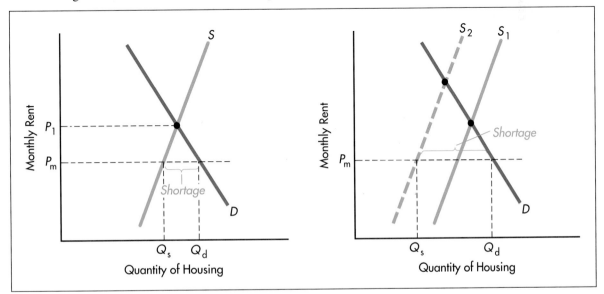

4

The Market System and the Private Sector

FUNDAMENTAL QUESTIONS

1. In a market system, who decides what goods and services are produced and how they are produced, and who obtains the goods and services that are produced?

2. What is a household, and what is household income and spending?

3. What is a business firm, and what is business spending?

4. How does the international sector affect the economy?

5. How do the three private sectors—households, businesses, and the international sector—interact in the economy?

You ou decide to buy a new Toyota, so you go to a Toyota dealer and exchange money for the car. The Toyota dealer has rented land and buildings and hired workers in order to make cars available to you and other members of the public. The employees earn incomes paid by the Toyota dealer and then use their incomes to buy food from the grocery store. This transaction generates revenue for the grocery store, which hires workers and pays them incomes that they then use to buy groceries and Toyotas. Your expenditure for the Toyota is part of a circular flow. Revenue is received by the Toyota dealer, who pays employees, who, in turn, buy goods and services.

Of course, the story is complicated by the fact that the Toyota is originally manufactured and purchased in Japan and then shipped to the United States before it can be sold by the local Toyota dealer. Your purchase of the Toyota creates revenue for the local dealer as well as for the manufacturer in Japan, who pays Japanese autoworkers to produce Toyotas. Furthermore, when you buy your Toyota, you must pay a tax to the government, which uses tax revenues to pay for police protection, national defense, the legal system, and other services. Many people in different areas of the economy are involved.

An economy is made up of individual buyers and sellers. Economists could discuss the neighborhood economy that surrounds your university, the economy of the city of Chicago, or the economy of the state of Massachusetts. But typically it is the national economy, the economy of the United States, that is the center of their attention. To clarify the operation of the national economy, economists usually group individual buyers and sellers into three sectors: households, businesses, and government. Omitted from this grouping, however, is an important source of activity, the international sector. Since the U.S. economy affects, and is affected by, the rest of the world, to understand how the economy functions we must include the international sector.

In a market system, who decides what goods and services are produced and how they are produced, and who obtains the goods and services that are produced?

We begin this chapter by examining the way that buyers and sellers interact in a market system. The impersonal forces of supply and demand operate to answer the following questions: Who determines what is produced? How things are produced? Who gets the output that is produced? The answers are given by the market system and involve the private-sector participants: households, business firms, and the international sector. Government also plays a major role in answering these questions, but we leave government and its role for the next chapter.

Following the discussion of the market system, we examine basic data and information on each individual sector with the objective of answering some general questions: What is a household, and how do households spend their incomes? What is a business firm, and how does a corporation differ from a partnership? What does it mean if the United States has a trade deficit?

After describing the three sectors that make up the private sector of the national economy, we present a simple economic model to illustrate the interrelationships linking all the individual sectors into the national economy.

1. THE MARKET SYSTEM

As you learned in Chapter 2, the production possibilities curve represents all possible combinations of goods and services that a society can produce if its resources are used fully and efficiently. Which combination, that is, which point on the PPC, will society choose? The answer is given by demand and supply.

1.a. Consumer Sovereignty

After World War II, incomes rose and people began to enjoy more leisure time. Instead of eating three square meals a day at home, families began to go to restaurants once in a while. In the 1950s and 1960s, consumers wanted more and more restaurants and fast-food outlets. As a result, McDonald's, Wendy's, Big Boy, White Castle, Pizza Hut, Godfather's Pizza, and other fast-food outlets flourished. The trend toward eating away from home reached fever pitch in the late 1970s, when the average number of meals per person eaten out (excluding brown-bag lunches and other meals prepared at home but eaten elsewhere) exceeded one per day. In the 1980s, people chose to spend more time at home with their families; the demand for restaurants decreased and was replaced by a demand for food delivered to the home.

By emphasizing delivery, Domino's Pizza and a few other fast-food outlets became very successful. However, the star of this story is not Domino's, Pizza Hut, or Wendy's. It is the consumer. In a market system, if consumers are willing and able to pay for more restaurant meals, more restaurants appear. If consumers are willing and able to pay for food delivered to their homes, food is delivered to their homes.

Why does the consumer wield such power? The name of the game for business is profit, and the only way business can make a profit is by satisfying consumer wants. The consumer, not the politician or the business firm, ultimately determines what is to be produced. A firm that produces something that no consumers want will not remain in business very long. **Consumer sovereignty**—the authority of consumers to determine what is produced through their purchases of goods and services—dictates what goods and services will be produced.

consumer sovereignty:
the authority of consumers to determine what is produced through their purchases of goods and services

1.b. Profit and the Allocation of Resources

Competitive firms produce in the manner that minimizes costs and maximizes profits.

When a good or service seems to have the potential to generate a profit, someone with entrepreneurial ability will be eager to put together the resources needed to produce that good or service. Recall from Chapter 1 that economists classify the resources used to produce goods and services into four general groups: land, labor, capital, and entrepreneurial ability. The returns to the owners of these resources are *rent* for the use of land, *wages* and *salaries* for the use of labor, *interest* for the use of capital, and *profits* for the use of entrepreneurial ability. An individual with entrepreneurial ability aims to earn a profit by renting land, hiring labor, and using capital to produce a good or service that can be sold for more than the sum of rent, wages, and interest. If the potential profit turns into a loss, the entrepreneur stops buying resources and turns to some other occupation or project. The resources used in the losing operation are then available for use in an activity where they are more highly valued.

Ownership of resources determines who gets what goods and services in a market system.

To illustrate how resources get allocated in the market system, let's look at the market for fast foods. Figure 1 shows a change in demand for meals eaten in restaurants. The initial demand curve, D_1, and supply curve, S, are shown in Figure 1(a). With these demand and supply curves, the equilibrium price (P_1) is $8, and the equilibrium quantity (Q_1) is 100 units (meals). At this price-quantity combination, the number of meals demanded equals the number of meals sold; equilibrium is reached, so we say the market clears (there is no shortage or surplus).

As already noted, consumer tastes changed during the late 1980s and early 1990s. Consumers preferred to have more food delivered to their homes instead of eating out. This change in tastes caused the demand for fast-food restaurants to decline and is represented by a leftward shift of the demand curve, from D_1 to D_2, in Figure 1(b). The demand curve shifted to the left because fewer in-restaurant meals were demanded at each price. Consumer tastes, not the price of in-restaurant meals, changed first. (A price change would have led to a change in the quantity demanded and would be represented by a move *along* demand curve D_1.) The change in tastes caused a

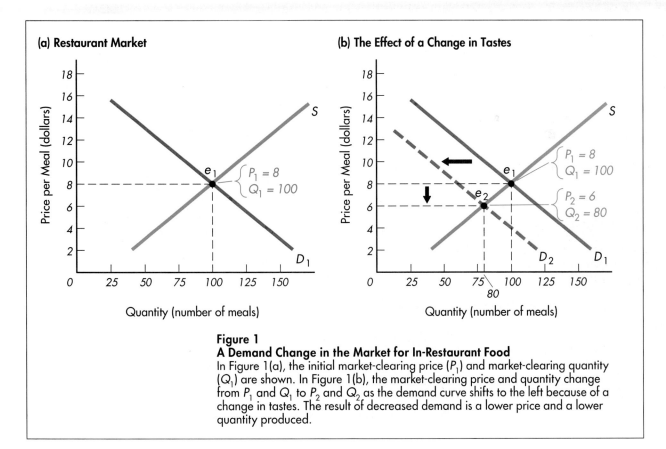

Figure 1
A Demand Change in the Market for In-Restaurant Food
In Figure 1(a), the initial market-clearing price (P_1) and market-clearing quantity (Q_1) are shown. In Figure 1(b), the market-clearing price and quantity change from P_1 and Q_1 to P_2 and Q_2 as the demand curve shifts to the left because of a change in tastes. The result of decreased demand is a lower price and a lower quantity produced.

change in demand and a leftward shift of the demand curve. The shift from D_1 to D_2 created a new equilibrium point. The equilibrium price (P_2) decreased to $6, and the equilibrium quantity (Q_2) decreased to 80 units (meals).

While the market for in-restaurant food was changing, so was the market for delivered food. People substituted meals delivered to their homes for meals eaten in restaurants. Figure 2(a) shows the original demand for food delivered to the home. Figure 2(b) shows a rightward shift of the demand curve, from D_1 to D_2, representing increased demand for home delivery. This demand change resulted in a higher market-clearing price for food delivered to the home, from $10 to $12.

The changing profit potential of the two markets induced existing firms to switch from in-restaurant service to home delivery and for new firms to offer delivery from the start. Domino's Pizza, which is a delivery-only firm, grew from a one-store operation to become the second largest pizza chain in the United States, with sales exceeding $2 billion per year. Little Caesar's, another take-out chain, grew from $63.6 million in sales in 1980 to nearly $1 billion in 1987. Pizza Hut, which at first did not offer home delivery, had to play catch-up; and by 1992, about two-thirds of Pizza Hut's more than 5,000 restaurants were delivering pizza.

As the market-clearing price of in-restaurant fast food fell (from $8 to $6 in Figure 1), the quantity of in-restaurant meals sold also declined (from 100 to 80) because the decreased demand, lower price, and resulting lower profit induced some firms to decrease production. In the delivery business, the

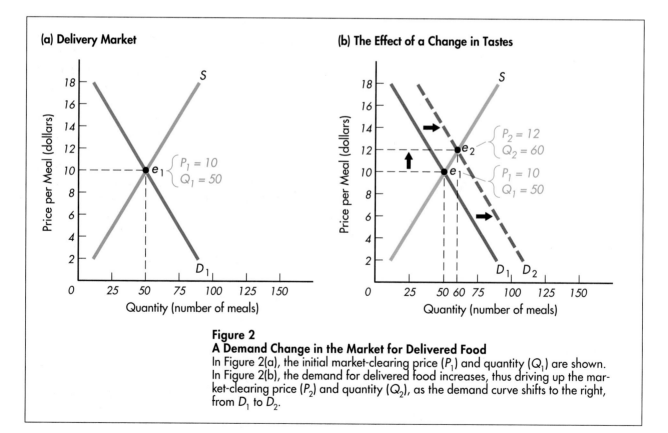

Figure 2
A Demand Change in the Market for Delivered Food
In Figure 2(a), the initial market-clearing price (P_1) and quantity (Q_1) are shown. In Figure 2(b), the demand for delivered food increases, thus driving up the market-clearing price (P_2) and quantity (Q_2), as the demand curve shifts to the right, from D_1 to D_2.

Part I/Introduction to the Price System

opposite occurred. As the market-clearing price rose (from $10 to $12 in Figure 2[b]), the number of meals delivered also rose (from 50 to 60). The increased demand, higher price, and resulting higher profit induced firms to increase production.

Why did the production of delivered foods increase while the production of meals at restaurants decrease? Not because of government decree. Not because of the desires of the business sector, especially the owners of restaurants. The consumer—consumer sovereignty—made all this happen. Businesses that failed to respond to consumer desires and failed to provide the desired good at the lowest price failed to survive.

I.c. The Flow of Resources

After demand shifted to home-delivered food, the resources that had been used to produce pizzas consumed in the restaurants were available for use elsewhere. A few former waiters, waitresses, and cooks were able to get jobs in the delivery firms. Some of the equipment used in eat-in restaurants—ovens, pots, and pans—was purchased by the delivery firms; and some of the ingredients that previously would have gone to the eat-in restaurants were bought by the delivery firms. A few former employees of the eat-in restaurants became employed at department stores, at local pubs, and at hotels. Some of the equipment was sold as scrap; other equipment was sold to other restaurants. In other words, the resources moved from one activity where their value was relatively low to another activity where they were more highly valued. No one commanded the resources to move. They moved because they could earn more in some other activity.

Adam Smith described this phenomenon in his 1776 treatise *The Wealth of Nations*, saying it was as if an invisible hand reached out and guided the resources to their most-valued use. That invisible hand is the self-interest that drives firms to provide what consumers want to buy, leads consumers to use their limited incomes to buy the goods and services that bring them the greatest satisfaction, and induces resource owners to supply resource services where they are most highly valued. (See the Economic Insight "Adam Smith.")

Firms produce the goods and services and use the resources that enable them to generate the highest profits. If one firm does this better than others, then that firm earns a greater profit than others. Seeing that success, other firms copy or mimic the first firm. If a firm cannot be as profitable as the others, it will eventually go out of business or move to another line of business where it can be successful. In the process of firms always seeking to lower costs and make higher profits, society finds that the goods and services buyers want are produced in the least costly manner. Consumers not only get the goods and services they want and will pay for, but they get these products at the lowest possible price.

I.d. The Determination of Income

Consumer demands dictate *what* is produced, and the search for profit defines *how* goods and services are produced. *For whom* are the goods and services produced, that is, who gets the goods and services? Those who have the ability to pay for the products. Your income determines your ability to

Adam Smith

Adam Smith was born in 1723 and reared in Kirkcaldy, Scotland, near Edinburgh. He went to the University of Glasgow when he was fourteen, and three years later began studies at Oxford, where he stayed for six years. In 1751, Smith became professor of logic and then moral philosophy at Glasgow. From 1764 to 1766, he tutored the future duke of Buccleuch in France, and then he was given a pension for the remainder of his life. Between 1766 and 1776, Smith completed *The Wealth of Nations*. He became commissioner of customs for Scotland and spent his remaining years in Edinburgh. He died in 1790.

Economists date the beginning of their discipline from the publication of *The Wealth of Nations* in 1776. In this major treatise, Smith emphasizes the role of self-interest in the functioning of markets, specialization, and division of labor.

According to Smith, the funda-mental explanation of human behavior is found in the rational pursuit of self-interest. Smith uses it to explain how men choose occupations, how farmers till their lands, and how leaders of the American Revolution were led by it to rebellion. Smith did not equate self-interest with selfishness but broadened the definition of self-interest, believing that a person is interested "in the fortune of others and renders their happiness neces-sary to him, though he derives nothing from it, except the plea-sure of seeing it." On the basis of self-interest, Smith constructed a theory of how markets work: how goods, once produced, are sold to the highest bidders, and how the quantities of the goods that are produced are governed by their costs and selling prices. But Smith's insight showed that this self-inter-est resulted in the best situation for society as a whole. In a cele-brated and often-quoted passage

from the treatise Smith says:

> But man has almost constant occasion for the help of his brethren, and it is in vain for him to expect it from their benevolence only. He will be more likely to prevail if he can interest their self-love in his favour, and show them that it is for their own advantage to do for him what he requires of them. . . . It is not from the benevolence of the butcher, the brewer, or the baker, that we can expect our dinner, but from their regard to their own inter-est.

Source: *An Inquiry into the Nature and Causes of the Wealth of Nations,* edited and with an introduction, notes, mar-ginal summary, and index by Edwin Cannan, with a preface by George J. Stigler (Chicago: University of Chicago Press, 1976). Reprinted by permission of the publisher.

pay, but where does income come from? Income is obtained by selling the services of resources. When you sell your labor services, your money income reflects your wage rate or salary level. When you sell the services of the capi-tal you own, you receive interest; and when you sell the services of the land you own, you receive rent. A person with entrepreneurial ability earns profit as a payment for services. Thus, we see that buyers and sellers of goods and services and resource owners are linked together in an economy: the more one buys, the more income or revenue the other receives. In the remainder of this chapter, we learn more about the linkages among the sectors of the econ-omy. We classify the buyers and the resource owners into the household sec-tor; the sellers or business firms are the business sector; households and firms in other countries, who may also be buyers and sellers of this country's goods and services, are the international sector. These three sectors—house-holds, business firms, and the international sector—constitute the private sector of the economy. In this chapter we focus on the interaction among the components of the private sector. In the next chapter we focus on the public sector, government, and examine its role in the economy.

RECAP

1. In a market system, consumers are sovereign and decide by means of their purchases what goods and services will be produced.

2. In a market system, firms decide how to produce the goods and services that consumers want. In order to earn maximum profits, firms use the least-cost combinations of resources.

3. Income and prices determine who gets what in a market system. Income is determined by the ownership of resources.

2. HOUSEHOLDS

What is a household, and what is household income and spending?

household:
one or more persons who occupy a unit of housing

A **household** consists of one or more persons who occupy a unit of housing. The unit of housing may be a house, an apartment, or even a single room, as long as it constitutes separate living quarters. A household may consist of related family members, like a father, mother, and children, or it may comprise unrelated individuals, like three college students sharing an apartment. The person in whose name the house or apartment is owned or rented is called the *householder*.

2.a. Number of Households and Household Income

In 1990, there were more than 93 million households in the United States. The breakdown of households by age of householder is shown in Figure 3. Householders between 35 and 44 years old make up the largest number of households. Householders between 45 and 54 years old have the largest median income. The *median* is the middle value—half of the households in an age group have an income higher than the median and half have an income lower than the median. Figure 3 shows that households in which the householder is between 45 and 54 years old have a median income of

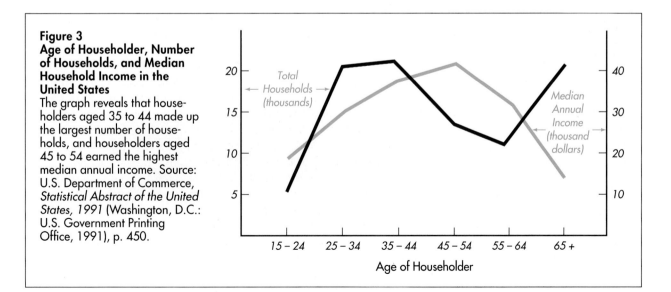

Figure 3
Age of Householder, Number of Households, and Median Household Income in the United States
The graph reveals that householders aged 35 to 44 made up the largest number of households, and householders aged 45 to 54 earned the highest median annual income. Source: U.S. Department of Commerce, *Statistical Abstract of the United States, 1991* (Washington, D.C.: U.S. Government Printing Office, 1991), p. 450.

$41,523, substantially higher than the median incomes of other age groups. Typically, workers in this age group are at the peak of their earning power. Younger households are gaining experience and training; older households include retired workers.

The size distribution of households in the United States is shown in Figure 4. Thirty-two percent of all households, or 30,114,000, are two-person households. The stereotypical household of husband, wife, and two children accounts for only 16 percent of all households. There are relatively few large households in the United States. Of the more than 93 million households in the country, only 1,295,000 (1 percent) have seven or more persons.

2.b. Household Spending

consumption:
household spending

Household spending is called **consumption**. Householders consume housing, transportation, food, entertainment, and other goods and services. The pattern of household spending (also called *consumer spending*) in the United States between 1959 and 1991 is shown in Figure 5. The pattern is one of steady increase. This spending by the household sector is the largest component of total spending in the economy—rising to almost $4 trillion in 1991.

RECAP

1. A household consists of one or more persons who occupy a unit of housing.
2. An apartment or house is rented or owned by a householder.
3. As a group, householders between the ages of 45 and 54 have the highest median incomes.
4. Household spending is called *consumption*.

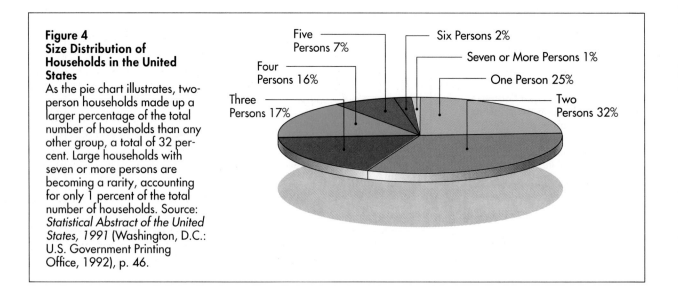

Figure 4
Size Distribution of Households in the United States
As the pie chart illustrates, two-person households made up a larger percentage of the total number of households than any other group, a total of 32 percent. Large households with seven or more persons are becoming a rarity, accounting for only 1 percent of the total number of households. Source: *Statistical Abstract of the United States, 1991* (Washington, D.C.: U.S. Government Printing Office, 1992), p. 46.

Five Persons 7%
Six Persons 2%
Four Persons 16%
Seven or More Persons 1%
Three Persons 17%
One Person 25%
Two Persons 32%

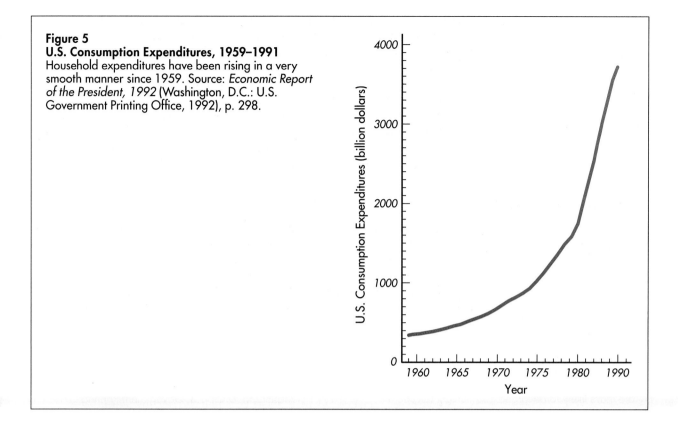

Figure 5
U.S. Consumption Expenditures, 1959–1991
Household expenditures have been rising in a very
smooth manner since 1959. Source: *Economic Report
of the President, 1992* (Washington, D.C.: U.S.
Government Printing Office, 1992), p. 298.

3. BUSINESS FIRMS

What is a business firm, and
what is business spending?

A **business firm** is a business organization controlled by a single management. The firm's business may be conducted at more than one location. The
terms *company*, *enterprise*, and *business* are used interchangeably with *firm*.

3.a. Forms of Business Organizations

business firm:
a business organization controlled by a single management

sole proprietorship:
a business owned by one person
who receives all the profits and
is responsible for all the debts
incurred by the business

partnership:
a business with two or more
owners who share the firm's
profits and losses

corporation:
a legal entity owned by shareholders whose liability for the
firm's losses is limited to the
value of the stock they own

Firms are organized as sole proprietorships, partnerships, or corporations. A
sole proprietorship is a business owned by one person. This type of firm
may be a one-person operation or a large enterprise with many employees. In
either case, the owner receives all the profits and is responsible for all the
debts incurred by the business.

A **partnership** is a business owned by two or more partners who share
both the profits of the business and responsibility for the firm's losses. The
partners could be individuals, estates, or other businesses.

A **corporation** is a business whose identity in the eyes of the law is distinct from the identity of its owners. State law allows the formation of corporations. A corporation is an economic entity that, like a person, can own
property and borrow money in its own name. The owners of a corporation
are shareholders. If a corporation cannot pay its debts, creditors cannot seek
payment from the shareholders' personal wealth. The corporation itself is
responsible for all its actions. The shareholders' liability is limited to the
value of the stock they own.

Many firms are global in their operations even though they may have been founded and may be owned by residents of a single country. Firms typically first enter the international market by selling products to foreign countries. As revenues from these sales increase, the firms realize advantages by locating subsidiaries in foreign countries. A **multinational business** is a firm that owns and operates producing units in foreign countries. The best-known U.S. corporations are multinational firms. Ford, IBM, PepsiCo, and McDonald's all own operating units in many different countries. Ford Motor Company, for instance, is the parent firm of sales organizations and assembly plants located around the world. As transportation and communication technology progress, multinational business activity will grow.

multinational business:
a firm that owns and operates producing units in foreign countries

3.b. Business Statistics

Figure 6(a) shows that in the United States there are far more sole proprietorships than partnerships or corporations. Figure 6(a) also compares the

---

Figure 6
Number and Revenue of Business Firms
As the first graph illustrates, most sole proprietorships and partnerships are small firms, with nearly 70 percent of all proprietorships falling into the less-than-$25,000 category, and over 60 percent of all partnerships falling into the same lowest revenue category. Corporations are more likely to be larger—33 percent fall into the $100,000 to $499,000 category. The second graph shows that most sole proprietorship revenues are earned by the larger proprietorships, those in the $100,000 to $499,000 category. By contrast, the small number of partnerships in the top revenue category is enough to account for 79 percent of all partnership revenues. The same is true of corporations, to a greater degree. Source: *Statistical Abstract of the United States, 1991* (Washington, D.C.: U.S. Government Printing Office, 1991), p. 525.

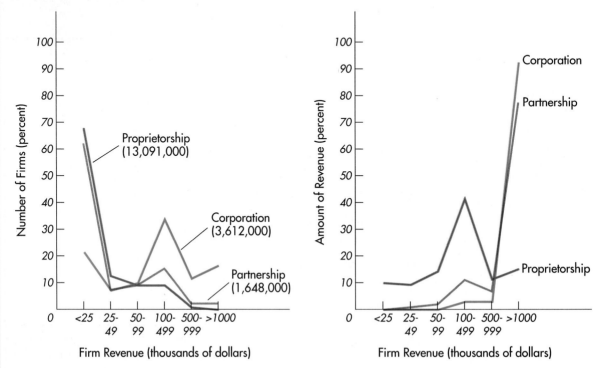

(a) Number of Business Firms

(b) Revenue of Business Firms

revenues earned by each type of business. The great majority of sole proprietorships are small businesses, with revenues under $25,000 a year. Similarly, over half of all partnerships also have revenues under $25,000 a year, but only 22 percent of the corporations are in this category.

Figure 6(b) shows that the 69 percent of sole proprietorships that earn less than $25,000 a year account for only 10 percent of the revenue earned by proprietorships. The 0.3 percent of proprietorships with revenue of $1 million or more account for 15 percent. Even more striking are the figures for partnerships and corporations. The 64 percent of partnerships with the smallest revenue account for only 0.5 percent of the total revenue earned by partnerships. At the other extreme, the 3.3 percent of partnerships with the largest revenue account for 79 percent of total partnership revenue. The 22 percent of corporations in the smallest range account for only 0.1 percent of total corporate revenue, while the 17 percent of corporations in the largest range account for 93 percent of corporate revenue.

The message of Figure 6 is that big business is important in the United States. There are many small firms, but large firms and corporations account for the greatest share of business revenue. Although there are only about one-third as many corporations as sole proprietorships, corporations have more than fifteen times the revenue of sole proprietorships.

3.c. Firms Around the World

Big business is a dominant force in the United States. Many people believe that because the United States is the world's largest economy, U.S. firms are the largest in the world. Figure 7 shows that this is not true. Of the ten largest corporations in the world, five are Japanese and one is European. Big business is not just an American phenomenon.

Figure 7
The World's Ten Largest Public Companies
As shown in the chart, nine out of ten of the world's largest companies are located in either the United States or Japan.
Source: "The World's 100 Largest Public Companies," *Wall Street Journal*, Sept. 20, 1991, p. R8.

Rank	Firm (country)	Market Value (millions)
1	NTT (Japan)	$96,749
2	Exxon (U.S.)	72,656
3	Royal Dutch/Shell (Netherlands, U.K.)	69,296
4	General Electric (U.S.)	64,611
5	Industrial Bank of Japan (Japan)	60,110
6	Philip Morris (U.S.)	58,815
7	IBM (U.S.)	55,614
8	Fuji Bank (Japan)	53,822
9	Mitsubishi Bank (Japan)	53,039
10	Dai-Ichi Kangyo Bank (Japan)	51,890

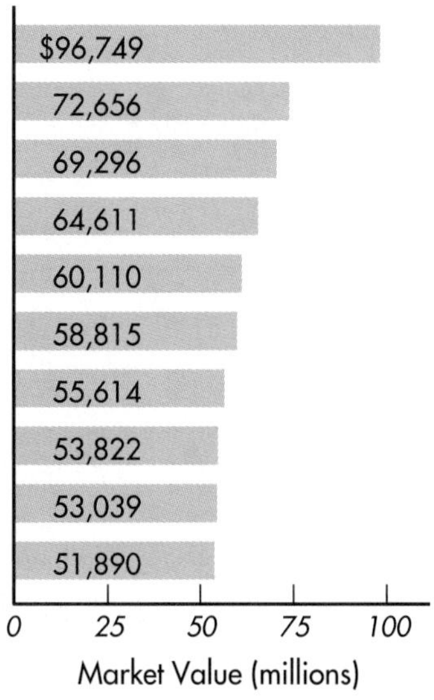

3.d. Entrepreneurial Ability

The emphasis on bigness should not hide the fact that many new firms are started each year. Businesses are typically begun as small sole proprietorships. The people who begin new firms are called *entrepreneurs*. Recall from Chapter 1 that an entrepreneur is an individual with the ability to organize resources in order to produce a product and the willingness to take the risk to pursue a profitable opportunity. Entrepreneurs are responsible for many advances in technology and services. Yet many of them are forced to go out of business within a year or two. Businesses survive in the long run only if they provide a good or service that people want enough to yield a profit for the entrepreneur. Although there are fabulous success stories, the failure rate among new firms is high. (See the Economic Insight "The Successful Entrepreneur.")

Regardless of the business they choose, entrepreneurs tend to agree about the incentives and problems associated with starting a business. The results of a survey of entrepreneurs after their first year of business are summarized in Table 1. Several of the responses suggest the small size of the typical new business. That 47 percent of entrepreneurs surveyed could hire employees by "word of mouth" while 15.5 percent used relatives for employees indicates that the firms generally required a small number of employees. It is clear that the entrepreneurs undertook personal risks to begin their businesses: 81 percent used personal assets to finance the business. Relatively few, 6 percent, received **venture capital**—a loan provided by an individual or firm that specializes in lending to new, unproven businesses. (Venture capitalists speculate on the success of the new business.) Only 3 percent received loans from the Small Business Administration (SBA), a government agency that assists small firms.

venture capital:
funds provided by a firm or individual that specializes in lending to new, unproven firms

That many new businesses fail is a fact of economic life. In the U.S. economy, anyone with an idea and sufficient resources has the freedom to open a business. However, if buyers do not respond to the new offering, the business fails. Only firms that satisfy this "market test" survive. Entrepreneurs thus try to ensure that as wants change, goods and services are produced to satisfy those wants.

3.e. Business Spending

investment:
spending on capital goods to be used in producing goods and services

Investment is the expenditure by business firms for capital goods—machines, tools, and buildings—that will be used to produce goods and services. The economic meaning of *investment* is different from the everyday meaning, "a financial transaction such as buying bonds or stocks." In economics, the term *investment* refers to business spending for capital goods.

Investment spending in 1991 was $725.3 billion, an amount equal to roughly one-fifth of consumption, or household spending. Investment spending between 1959 and 1991 is shown in Figure 8. Compare Figures 5 and 8 and notice the different patterns of spending. Investment increases unevenly, actually falling at times and then rising very rapidly. Even though investment spending is much smaller than consumption, the wide swings in investment spending mean that business expenditures are an important factor in determining the economic health of the nation.

TABLE I

Results of a Survey of Entrepreneurs

How Entrepreneurs Choose New Business Sites

Factor	Percentage of entrepreneurs
Near customers	53.9
Reasonable rent	52.6
Near freeway or major street	40.5
Near home	34.5
Near suppliers	9.9
Near similar businesses	8.2

How Entrepreneurs Find Employees

Method	Percentage of entrepreneurs
Word of mouth	47.0
Newspaper ad	21.1
Other	20.3
Relatives	15.5
Employment agency	4.3
Management consultants	1.3

How Entrepreneurs Financed New Firms

Method	Percentage of entrepreneurs
Personal assets	81.0
Bank loans	38.4
Relatives	17.7
Forgone wages	15.5
Venture capital	6.0
Friends	3.9
SBA loans	3.0

Most Difficult Problems Facing Entrepreneurs

Problem	Percentage of entrepreneurs
Financing and cash flow	29.7
Becoming known	19.8
Keeping good employees	14.2
Government (permits, taxes, etc.)	9.5

Source: *Arizona Business*, October 1987, p. 6. From *ARIZONA BUSINESS*, a monthly publication of the Center for Business Research, College of Business, Arizona State University, Tempe, AZ 85287. Reprinted by permission of *Arizona Business*.

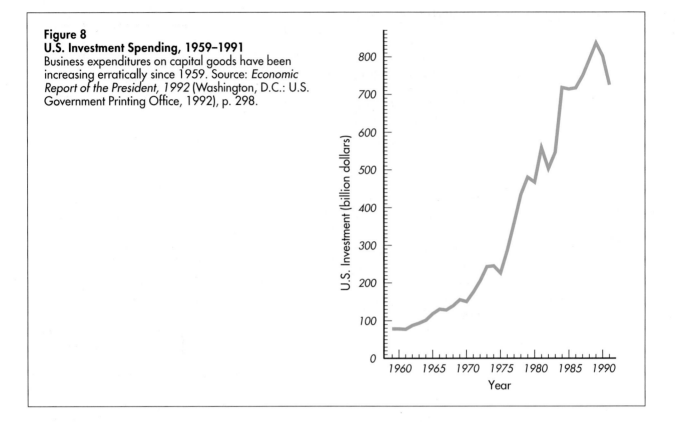

Figure 8
U.S. Investment Spending, 1959–1991
Business expenditures on capital goods have been increasing erratically since 1959. Source: *Economic Report of the President, 1992* (Washington, D.C.: U.S. Government Printing Office, 1992), p. 298.

RECAP

1. Business firms may be organized as sole proprietorships, partnerships, or corporations.

2. Large corporations account for the largest fraction of total business revenue.

3. Entrepreneurs are business organizers and risk-takers.

4. Business investment spending fluctuates widely over time.

THE INTERNATIONAL SECTOR

How does the international sector affect the economy?

Years ago, only U.S. households and businesses were included in discussions of the private-sector participants in the economy because the international aspects of the U.S. economy were so small. Today, however, foreign buyers and sellers have a significant effect on economic conditions in the United States, and developments in the rest of the world often influence U.S. buyers and sellers. We saw in Chapter 3, for instance, how exchange rate changes can affect the demand for U.S. goods and services.

4.a. Types of Countries

The nations of the world may be divided into two categories: industrial countries and developing countries. Developing countries greatly outnumber

The Successful Entrepreneur (Sometimes It's Better to Be Lucky Than Good)

Entrepreneurs do not always develop an abstract idea into reality when starting a new firm. Sometimes people stumble onto a good thing by accident and then are clever enough and willing to take the necessary risk to turn their lucky find into a commercial success.

In 1875, a Philadelphia pharmacist on his honeymoon tasted tea made from an innkeeper's old family recipe. The tea, made from sixteen wild roots and berries, was so delicious that the pharmacist asked the innkeeper's wife for the recipe. When he returned to his pharmacy, he created a solid concentrate of the drink that could be sold for home consumption.

The pharmacist was Charles Hires, a devout Quaker, who intended to sell "Hires Herb Tea" to hard-drinking Pennsylvania coal miners as a nonalcoholic alternative to beer and whiskey. A friend of Hires suggested that miners would not drink anything called "tea" and recommended that he call his drink "root beer."

The initial response to Hires Root Beer was so enthusiastic that Hires soon began nationwide distribution. The yellow box of root beer extract was a familiar sight in homes and drugstore fountains across America. By 1895, Hires, who started with a $3,000 loan, was operating a business valued at half a million dollars (a lot of money in 1895) and bottling ready-to-drink root beer across the country.

Hires, of course, is not the only entrepreneur clever enough to turn a lucky discovery into a business success. In 1894, in Battle Creek, Michigan, a sanitarium handyman named Will Kellogg was helping his older brother prepare wheat meal to serve to patients in the sanitarium's dining room. The two men would boil wheat dough and then run it through rollers to produce thin sheets of meal. One day they left a batch of the dough out overnight. The next day, when the dough was run through the rollers, it broke up into flakes instead of forming a sheet.

By letting the dough stand overnight, the Kelloggs had allowed moisture to be distributed evenly to each individual wheat berry. When the dough went through the rollers, the berries formed separate flakes instead of binding together. The Kelloggs toasted the wheat flakes and served them to the patients. They were an immediate success. In fact, the brothers had to start a mail-order flaked-cereal business because patients wanted flaked cereal for their households.

Kellogg saw the market potential for the discovery and started his own cereal company (his brother refused to join him in the business). He was a great promoter who used innovations like four-color magazine ads and free-sample promotions. In New York City, he offered a free box of corn flakes to every woman who winked at her grocer on a specified day. The promotion was considered risqué, but Kellogg's sales in New York increased from two railroad cars of cereal a month to one car a day.

Will Kellogg, a poorly paid sanitarium worker in his mid-forties, became a daring entrepreneur after his mistake with wheat flour led to the discovery of a way to produce flaked cereal. He became one of the richest men in America because of his entrepreneurial ability.

Source: Based on Joseph J. Fucini and Suzy Fucini, *Entrepreneurs* (Boston: Hall and Co., 1985).

industrial countries (see Figure 9). The World Bank (an international organization that makes loans to developing countries) groups countries according to per capita income (income per person). Low-income economies are those with per capita incomes of $610 or less. Middle-income economies have per capita incomes of $611–$7,619. High-income economies—oil exporters and industrial market economies—are distinguished from the middle-income economies and have per capita incomes of greater than $7,620. Some countries are not members of the World Bank and so are not categorized, and information about a few small countries is so limited that the World Bank is unable to classify them.

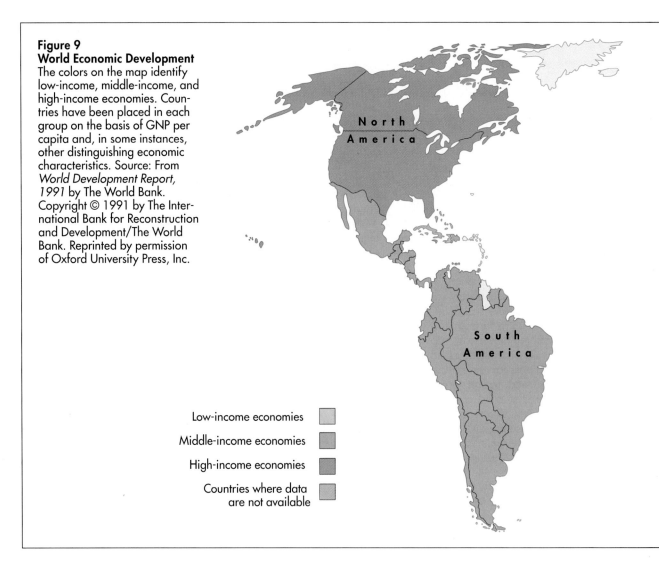

Figure 9
World Economic Development
The colors on the map identify low-income, middle-income, and high-income economies. Countries have been placed in each group on the basis of GNP per capita and, in some instances, other distinguishing economic characteristics. Source: From *World Development Report, 1991* by The World Bank. Copyright © 1991 by The International Bank for Reconstruction and Development/The World Bank. Reprinted by permission of Oxford University Press, Inc.

North America

South America

Low-income economies
Middle-income economies
High-income economies
Countries where data are not available

It is readily apparent from Figure 9 that low-income economies are heavily concentrated in Africa and Asia. Countries in these regions have a low profile in U.S. trade, although they may receive aid from the United States. U.S. trade is concentrated with its neighbors Canada and Mexico, along with the major industrial powers. Nations in each group present different economic challenges to the United States.

4.a.1. The Industrial Countries The World Bank uses per capita income to classify nineteen countries as "industrial market economies." They are listed in the bar chart in Figure 10. The nineteen countries listed in Figure 10 are among the wealthiest countries in the world. Not appearing on the list are the high-income oil-exporting nations like Libya, Saudi Arabia, Kuwait, and the United Arab Emirates. The World Bank considers those countries to be "still developing."

The economies of the industrial nations are highly interdependent. As conditions change in one nation, business firms and individuals looking for the best return or interest rate on their funds may shift large sums of money

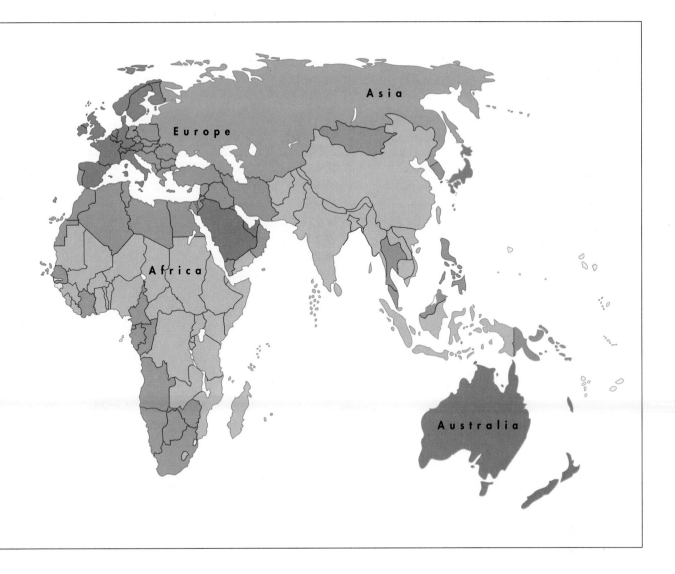

between countries. As the funds flow from one country to another, economic conditions in one country spread to other countries. As a result, the industrial countries, particularly the major economic powers like the United States, Germany, and Japan, are forced to pay close attention to each other's economic policies.

4.a.2. The Developing Countries The developing countries (sometimes referred to as *less developed countries*, or *LDCs*) provide a different set of problems for the United States than do the industrial countries. In the 1980s, the debts of the developing countries to the developed nations reached tremendous heights. For instance, at the end of 1989, Brazil owed foreign creditors $111.3 billion, Mexico owed $95.6 billion, and Argentina owed $64.7 billion. In each case, the amounts owed were more than several times the annual sales of goods and services by those countries to the rest of the world. The United States had to arrange loans at special terms and establish special trade arrangements in order for those countries to be able to buy U.S. goods.

The United States tends to buy, or *import*, primary products such as agri-

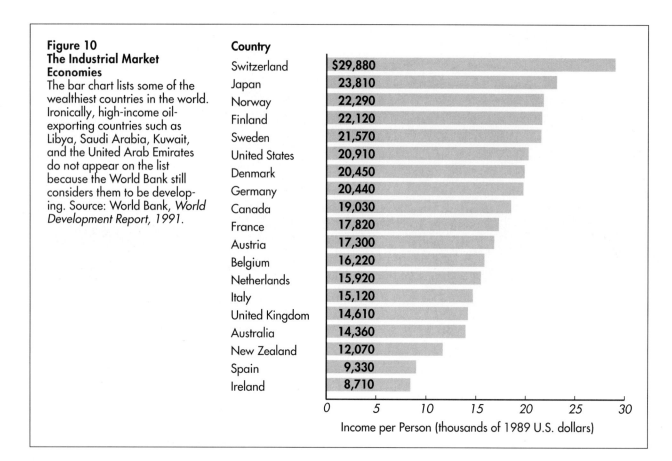

**Figure 10
The Industrial Market Economies**
The bar chart lists some of the wealthiest countries in the world. Ironically, high-income oil-exporting countries such as Libya, Saudi Arabia, Kuwait, and the United Arab Emirates do not appear on the list because the World Bank still considers them to be developing. Source: World Bank, *World Development Report, 1991.*

Country

Country	Income
Switzerland	$29,880
Japan	23,810
Norway	22,290
Finland	22,120
Sweden	21,570
United States	20,910
Denmark	20,450
Germany	20,440
Canada	19,030
France	17,820
Austria	17,300
Belgium	16,220
Netherlands	15,920
Italy	15,120
United Kingdom	14,610
Australia	14,360
New Zealand	12,070
Spain	9,330
Ireland	8,710

Income per Person (thousands of 1989 U.S. dollars)

cultural produce and minerals from the developing countries. Products that a country buys from another country are called **imports**. The United States tends to sell, or *export*, manufactured goods to developing countries. Products that a country sells to another country are called **exports**. The United States is the largest producer and exporter of grains and other agricultural output in the world. The efficiency of U.S. farming relative to farming in much of the rest of the world gives the United States a comparative advantage in many agricultural products.

4.b. International Sector Spending

U.S. economic activity with the rest of the world includes U.S. spending on foreign goods and foreign spending on U.S. goods. Figure 11 shows how U.S. exports and imports are spread over different countries. Notice that two countries, Canada and Japan, account for roughly one-third of U.S. exports and more than one-third of U.S. imports. Trade with the industrial countries is approximately twice as large as trade with the developing countries, and U.S. trade with Eastern Europe is trivial.

When exports exceed imports, a **trade surplus** exists. When imports exceed exports, a **trade deficit** exists. Figure 11 shows that the United States is importing much more than it exports.

The term **net exports** refers to the difference between the value of exports and the value of imports: net exports equals exports minus imports. Figure

imports:
products that a country buys from other countries

exports:
products that a country sells to other countries

trade surplus:
the situation that exists when imports are less than exports

trade deficit:
the situation that exists when imports exceed exports

net exports:
the difference between the value of exports and the value of imports

The trade partnership between the United States and Japan is important to both countries economically and politically. The United States is the most important export market for Japan. Even subway cars used in the New York subway system are made by Kawasaki of Japan. When Toys "R" Us first tried to establish stores in Japan, local Japanese toy stores blocked their entry claiming their business would be hurt by the new competition. This policy received much attention in the United States. The resulting outcry over the Japanese unwillingness to allow U.S. competition resulted in a change in Japanese policy. Toys "R" Us opened their first store in Japan in 1992.

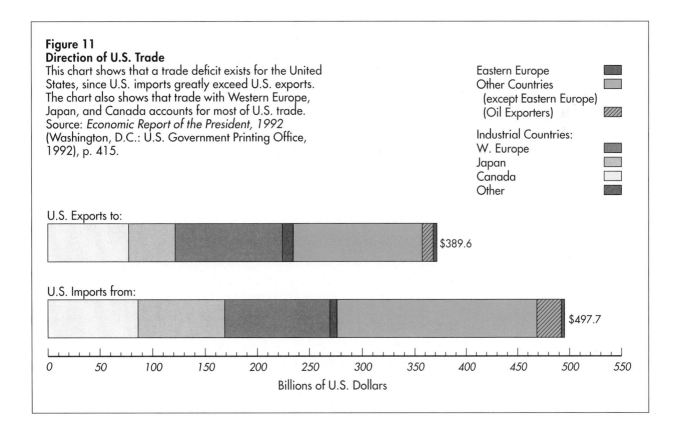

Figure 11
Direction of U.S. Trade
This chart shows that a trade deficit exists for the United States, since U.S. imports greatly exceed U.S. exports. The chart also shows that trade with Western Europe, Japan, and Canada accounts for most of U.S. trade.
Source: *Economic Report of the President, 1992* (Washington, D.C.: U.S. Government Printing Office, 1992), p. 415.

Eastern Europe
Other Countries
(except Eastern Europe)
(Oil Exporters)

Industrial Countries:
W. Europe
Japan
Canada
Other

U.S. Exports to: $389.6

U.S. Imports from: $497.7

0   50   100   150   200   250   300   350   400   450   500   550
Billions of U.S. Dollars

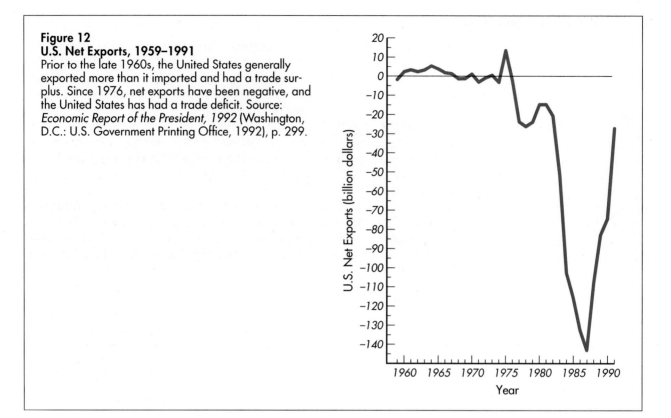

Figure 12
U.S. Net Exports, 1959–1991
Prior to the late 1960s, the United States generally exported more than it imported and had a trade surplus. Since 1976, net exports have been negative, and the United States has had a trade deficit. Source: *Economic Report of the President, 1992* (Washington, D.C.: U.S. Government Printing Office, 1992), p. 299.

12 traces U.S. net exports for the period 1959 to 1991. Positive net exports represent trade surpluses; negative net exports represent trade deficits. The trade deficits (indicated by negative net exports) of the 1980s were unprecedented. Reasons for this pattern of international trade are discussed in later chapters.

RECAP

1. The majority of U.S. trade is with the industrial market economies.
2. Exports are products sold to foreign countries; imports are products bought from foreign countries.
3. Exports minus imports equals net exports.
4. Positive net exports signal a trade surplus; negative net exports signal a trade deficit.

5. LINKING THE SECTORS

How do the three private sectors—households, businesses, international—interact in the economy?

How are the major players in the private sector of the economy—households, businesses, and the international sector—linked together? We first examine the simplest possible economy, one with only households and firms; then we add the international sector. In the next chapter, we will add government so that we end up with an economic model that brings together all four sectors.

5.a. Households and Firms

Households own all the basic resources, or factors of production, in the economy. The resources are the land, labor, capital, and entrepreneurial ability that are combined to produce other goods and services. Household members own land and provide labor, and they are the entrepreneurs, stockholders, proprietors, and partners who own business firms.

Households and businesses interact with each other by means of buying and selling. Businesses, hoping to earn profits, employ the services of resources in order to produce goods and services. Business firms pay for the use of resources, and because it is the households who own the resources, firms pay households.

Households sell the resource services to businesses in exchange for money payments. The flow of resource services from households to businesses is shown by the blue-green line at the bottom of Figure 13. The flow of money payments from firms to households is shown by the gold line at the bottom of Figure 13. Households use the money payments to buy goods and services from firms. These money payments are the firms' revenues. The flow of

Figure 13
The Circular Flow: Households and Firms
The diagram indicates that income is equal to the value of output. Firms hire resources from households. The payments for these resources represent household income. Households spend their income for goods and services produced by the firms. Household spending represents revenue for firms. Households save some of their income. This income reenters the circular flow as investment spending. Financial intermediaries like banks take in the saving of households and then lend this money to business firms for investment spending.

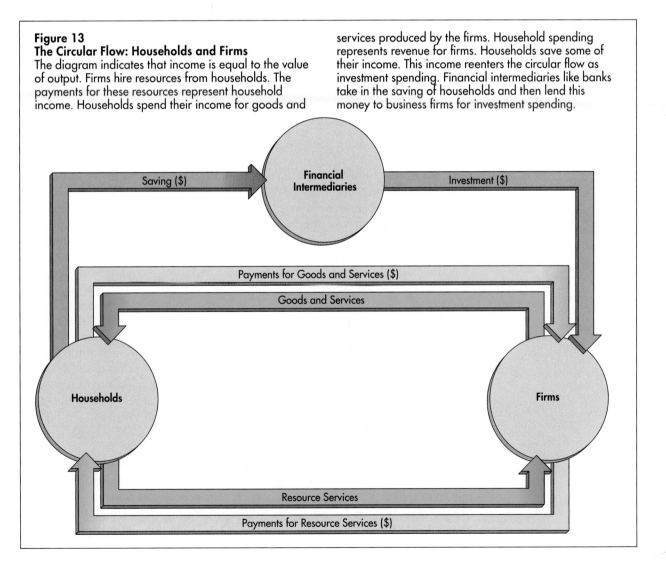

money payments from households to firms is shown by the gold line at the top of the diagram. The flow of goods and services from firms to households is shown by the blue-green line at the top of Figure 13. There is, therefore, a flow of money and goods and services from one sector to the other. The payments made by one sector are the receipts taken in by the other sector. Money, goods, and services flow from households to firms and back to households in a circular flow.

Households do not spend all of the money they receive. They save some fraction of their income. In Figure 13, we see that household saving is deposited in **financial intermediaries** like banks, credit unions, and saving and loan firms. A financial intermediary accepts deposits from savers and makes loans to borrowers. The money that is saved by the households reenters the economy in the form of investment spending as business firms borrow for expansion of their productive capacity.

The **circular flow diagram** represented in Figure 13 indicates that income is equal to the value of output. Money flows to the household sector are the sum of the payments to the resource owners, including the payments to entrepreneurs. Money flows to firms are the revenue that firms receive when they sell the goods and services they produce. Revenue minus the costs of land, labor, and capital is profit. Profit represents the payment to entrepreneurs and other owners of corporations, partnerships, and sole proprietorships. Thus, household income is equal to business revenue—the value of goods and services produced.

financial intermediaries:
institutions that accept deposits from savers and make loans to borrowers

circular flow diagram:
a model showing the flow of output and income from one sector of the economy to another

5.b. Households, Firms, and the International Sector

The international sector must be included in order to properly describe the economy. Figure 14 includes foreign countries in the circular flow. To simplify the circular flow diagram, let's assume that households are not directly engaged in international trade and that only business firms are buying and selling goods and services across international borders. This assumption is not far from the truth for the industrial countries and for many developing countries. We typically buy a foreign-made product from a local business firm rather than directly from the foreign producer.

A line labeled "net exports" connects firms and foreign countries in Figure 14, as well as a line labeled "payments for net exports." Notice that neither line has an arrow indicating the direction of flow as do the other lines in the diagram. The reason is that net exports of the home country may be either positive (a trade surplus) or negative (a trade deficit). When net exports are positive, there is a net flow of goods from the firms of the home country to foreign countries and a net flow of money from foreign countries to the firms of the home country. When net exports are negative, the opposite occurs. A trade deficit involves net flows of goods from foreign countries to the firms of the home country and net money flows from the domestic firms to the foreign countries. If exports and imports are equal, net exports are zero because the value of exports is offset by the value of imports.

Figure 14 shows the circular flow linking the major private sectors of the economy. This model is a simplified view of the world, but it highlights the important interrelationships. The value of output equals income, as always; but spending may be for foreign as well as domestic goods. Domestic firms may produce for foreign as well as domestic consumption. In the next chapter, the government sector is added to complete the analysis.

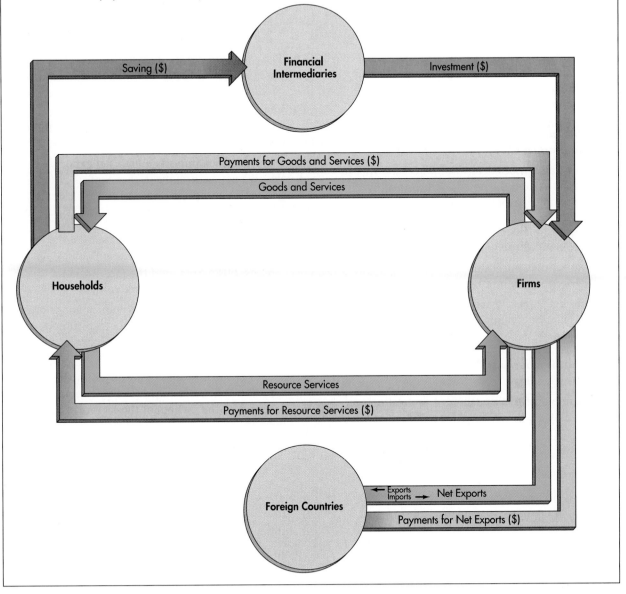

Figure 14
The Circular Flow: Households, Firms, and Foreign Countries
The diagram assumes that households are not directly engaged in international trade. The flow of goods and services between countries is represented by the line labeled "net exports." Neither the net-exports line nor the line labeled "payments for net exports" has an arrow indicating the direction of the flow because the flow can go from the home country to foreign countries or vice versa. When the domestic economy has positive net exports (a trade surplus), goods and services flow out of the domestic firms toward foreign countries and money payments flow from the foreign countries to the domestic firms. With negative net exports (a trade deficit), the reverse is true.

RECAP

1. The circular flow diagram illustrates how the main sectors of the economy fit together.
2. The circular flow diagram shows that the value of output is equal to income.

SUMMARY

KEY TERMS

EXERCISES

1. What is consumer sovereignty? What does it have to do with determining what goods and services are produced? Who determines how goods and services are produced? Who receives the goods and services in a market system?

2. Is a family a household? Is a household a family?

3. What is the median value of the following series?
   4, 6, 8, 3, 9, 10, 10, 1, 5, 7, 12

4. Which sector (households, business, or international) spends the most? Which sector spends the least? Which sector, because of volatility, has importance greater than is warranted by its size?

5. What does it mean if net exports are negative?

6. Why does the value of output always equal the income received by the resources that produced the output?

7. Total spending in the economy is equal to consumption plus investment plus government spending plus net exports. If households want to save and thus do not use all of their income for consumption, what will happen to total spending? Because total spending in the economy is equal to total income and output, what will happen to the output of goods and services if households want to save more?

8. People sometimes argue that imports should be limited by government policy. Suppose a government quota on the quantity of imports causes net exports to rise. Using the circular flow diagram as a guide, explain why total expenditures and national output may rise after the quota is imposed. Who is likely to benefit from the quota? Who will be hurt?

9. Draw the circular flow diagram linking households, business firms, and the international sector. Use the diagram to explain the effects of a decision by the household sector to increase saving.

10. Suppose there are three countries in the world. Country A exports $11 million worth of goods to country B and $5 million worth of goods to country C; country B exported $3 million worth of goods to country A and $6 million worth of goods to country C; and country C exported $4 million worth of goods to country A and $1 million worth of goods to country B.

    a. What are the net exports of countries A, B, and C?

    b. Which country is running a trade deficit? A trade surplus?

11. Over time, there has been a shift away from outdoor drive-in movie theaters to indoor movie theaters. Use supply and demand curves to illustrate and explain how consumers can bring about such change when tastes change.

12. Figure 3 indicates that the youngest and the oldest households have the lowest household incomes. Why should middle-aged households have higher incomes than the youngest and oldest?

13. The chapter provides data indicating that there are many more sole proprietorships than corporations or partnerships. Why are there so many sole proprietorships? Why is the revenue of the average sole proprietorship less than that of the typical corporation?

14. List the four sectors of the economy along with the type of spending associated with each sector. Order the types of spending in terms of magnitude and give an example of each kind of spending.

15. The circular flow diagram of Figure 14 excludes the government sector. Draw a new version of the figure that includes this sector with government spending and taxes added to the diagram. Label your new figure and be sure to include arrows to illustrate the direction of flows.

Movie Theaters Take Commercial Break

You're in a darkened movie theater, gazing at the screen. The glamorous and brave heroine is running across the top of a moving train, struggling to return to the arms of the hand-some hero. It's an ad for Diet Sprite. You throw popcorn at the screen.

Advertising in the movie theater enrages some and entertains others.

"As long as a campaign is enter-taining and kicks off or precedes a television campaign, it does well in the theater," says Alex Szabo of Screenvision Cinema Network, which sells ads on 6,500 screens nationally (at a cost of $800,000 for a 28-day run).

The 1,587-screen AMC Theater chain doesn't run ads. "Customers don't like it," says Marc Mery, cor-porate marketing director for the chain. "Once the house lights go down, that's when the customers' perception is that the entertainment they paid for should start."

Booing at ads in New York City theaters is so loud and persistent that Screenvision has dropped some movie houses from its network. "Manhattan is a tough crowd," Szabo says.

Among those booing is Ron Collins, co-founder of the Center for the Study of Commercialism. "There are fewer and fewer places in our society where you can go that are commercial-free."

Source: Martha T. Moore, "Movie Theaters Take Commercial Break," *USA Today*, Oct. 5, 1992, p. 2B. Copyright 1993, USA TODAY. Reprinted with permission.

USA Today/October 5, 1992

Commentary

What lies behind the move toward advertising in movie theaters? Does it correspond to consumer sovereignty, with firms providing what the moviegoer "desires"? Or is it more a case of sovereign businesses foisting extra costs on an unwilling public?

In a competitive market, additional services are provided if they result in greater profit. This means the customer must be willing and able to pay for them. It also means that customers must be willing and able to pay for not having some services, those the customers find distasteful. If customers want commercial-free movies, they must be willing and able to pay for those movies; conversely, if the customers do not care whether the movies have commercials or even find the commercials entertaining, then they would not be willing to pay extra to do without the commercials.

In the following diagram, S_1 represents the supply of movies with ads and S_2 represents the supply of movies without ads. The ads enable the firm to offer the movies at a lower cost, and thus the supply curve S_1 lies below the curve S_2. D_1 represents the demand for movies with commercials and D_2 represents the demand for movies without commercials. According to the demand curves, people are strongly opposed to the commercials; perhaps this market represents the Manhattan crowds mentioned in the article. The equilibrium price and quantity of movies with commercials is given by the intersection between S_1 and D_1, point e_1, while the price and quantity of movies without commercials is given by the intersection between S_2 and D_2, point e_2. If the price and quantity of movies without commercials is greater than the price and quantity of movies with commercials, the theaters have an incentive not to provide commercials. As stated in the article, the commercials are not shown in many New York theaters.

If customers realized that the commercials might result in lower costs for the movie theaters and that some of these lower costs would result in lower ticket prices, then the distaste toward the commercials might change. Or, in some cases, moviegoers actually find the commercials entertaining. In this case, the demand curve for movies without commercials might be no different from the demand curve for movies with commercials, D_1. Then, the intersection of the supply curves with D_1 would tell us that customers would be able to purchase ticket prices at P_1 and watch more movies because of the commercials than if there were no commercials.

Customers do reign supreme. No profit-maximizing firm will ignore customer desires. The firms will try new cost-reducing gimmicks or revenue-enhancing techniques, but if these reduce demand sufficiently, they will be discarded. Perhaps commercials will enter the movie theaters through displays in the lobby or on the popcorn containers even if customers do not want to see them on the screen. It all depends on what the customer wants.

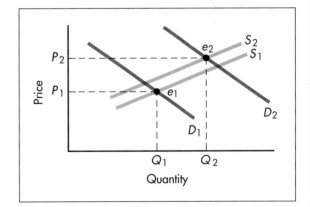

5

The Public Sector

FUNDAMENTAL
         QUESTIONS

1. How does the government interact with the other sectors of the economy?
2. What is the economic role of government?
3. Why is the public sector such a large part of a market economy?
4. What does the government do?
5. How do the sizes of public sectors in various countries compare?

From conception to death, we are affected by the activities of the government. Many mothers receive prenatal care through government programs. We are born in hospitals that are subsidized or run by the government. We are delivered by doctors who received training in subsidized colleges. Our births are recorded on certificates filed with the government. Ninety percent of us attend public schools. Many of us live in housing that is directly subsidized by the government or whose mortgages are insured by the government. Most of us at one time or another put savings into accounts that are insured by the government. Virtually all of us, at some time in our lives, receive money from the government—from student loan programs, unemployment compensation, disability insurance, Social Security, or Medicare. Twenty percent of the work force is employed by the government. The prices of wheat, corn, sugar, and dairy products are controlled or strongly influenced by the government. The prices we pay for cigarettes, alcohol, automobiles, utilities, water, gas, and a multitude of other goods are directly or indirectly influenced by the government. We travel on public roads and publicly subsidized or controlled airlines, airports, trains, and ships. Our legal structure provides a framework in which we all live and act; the national defense ensures our rights of citizenship and protects our private property.

According to virtually any measure, government in the United States has been a growth industry since 1930. The number of people employed by the local, state, and federal governments combined grew from 3 million in 1930 to 17 million in 1992; there are now more people employed in government than there are in manufacturing. Annual expenditures by the federal government rose from $3 billion in 1930 to over $1.3 trillion in 1992, and total government (federal, state, and local) expenditures now equal about $2 trillion annually. In 1929, government spending constituted less than 2.5 percent of total spending in the economy. By 1992, it had increased to nearly 25 percent. The number of rules and regulations created by the government is so large that it is measured by the number of telephone-book-sized pages needed just to list them, and that number is more than 67,000. The cost of all federal rules and regulations is estimated to be somewhere between $4,000 and $17,000 per U.S. household each year, and the number of federal employees required to police these rules is about 125,000.

There is no doubt that the government (often referred to as the *public sector*) is a major player in the United States economy. But in the last few chapters we have been learning about the market system and how well it works. If the market system works so well, why is the public sector such a large part of the economy? In this chapter we discuss the public sector and the role government plays in a market economy.

1. THE CIRCULAR FLOW

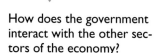

How does the government interact with the other sectors of the economy?

Government in the United States exists at the federal, state, and local levels. Local government includes county, regional, and municipal units. Economic discussions tend to focus on the federal government because national economic policy is set at that level. Nevertheless, each level affects us through its taxing and spending decisions, and laws regulating behavior.

To illustrate how the government sector affects the economy, let's add government to the circular flow model presented in the previous chapter. Government at the federal, state, and local levels interacts with both households and firms. Because the government employs factors of production to produce government services, households receive payments from the government in exchange for the services of the factors of production. The flow of resource services from households to government is illustrated by the blue-green line flowing from the households to government in Figure 1. The flow of money from government to households is shown by the gold line flowing from government to households. We assume that government, like a household, does not trade directly with foreign countries but obtains foreign goods from domestic firms who do trade with the rest of the world.

Households pay taxes to support the provision of government services, such as national defense, education, and police and fire protection. In a sense, then, the household sector is purchasing goods and services from the government as well as from private businesses. The flow of tax payments from households and businesses to government is illustrated by the gold lines flowing from households and businesses to government, and the flow of government services to households and businesses is illustrated by the purple lines flowing from government.

The addition of government brings significant changes to the model. Households have an additional place to sell their resources for income, and businesses have an additional market for goods and services. The value of *private* production no longer equals the value of household income. Households receive income from government in exchange for providing resource services to government. The total value of output in the economy is equal to the total income received, but government is included as a source of income and a producer of services.

RECAP

1. The circular flow diagram illustrates how the main sectors of the economy fit together.
2. Government interacts with both households and firms. Households get government services and pay taxes; they provide resource services and receive income. Firms sell goods and services to government and receive income.

Figure 1
The Circular Flow: Households, Firms, Government, and Foreign Countries
The diagram assumes that households and government are not directly engaged in international trade. Domestic firms trade with firms in foreign countries. The government sector buys resource services from house-holds and goods and services from firms. This government spending represents income for the households and revenue for the firms. The government uses the resource services and goods and services to provide government services for households and firms. Households and firms pay taxes to the government to finance government expenditures.

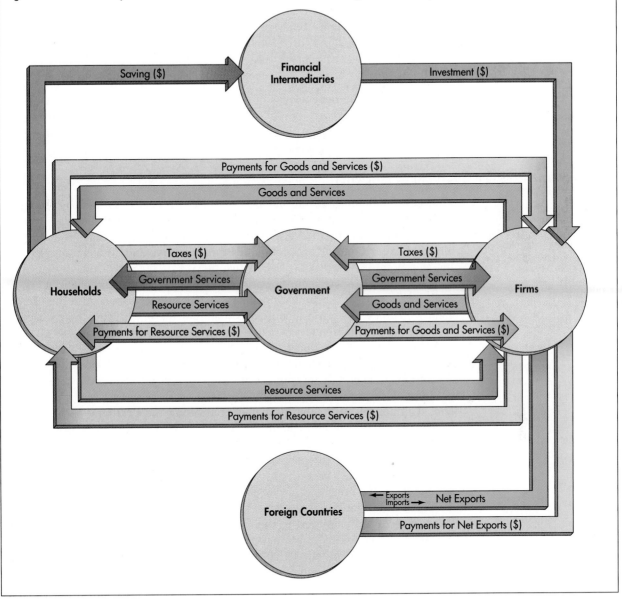

2. THE ROLE OF GOVERNMENT IN THE MARKET SYSTEM

What is the economic role of government?

We have learned that consumers use their limited incomes to buy the goods and services that give them the greatest satisfaction; that resource owners offer the services of their resources to the highest bidder; and that firms produce the goods and services and use the resources that enable them to generate the highest profits. In other words, everyone—consumers, firms, resource suppliers—attempts to get the most benefits for the least cost.

This apparently narrow, self-interested behavior is converted by the market into a social outcome in which no one can be made better off without making someone else worse off. Any resource allocation that could make someone better off and no one any worse off would increase efficiency. When all such allocations have been realized, so that the *only* way to make one person better off would harm someone else, then we have realized the best allocation society can achieve. Wholly unaware of the effects of their actions, self-interested individuals act as if driven by an *invisible hand* to produce the greatest social good. In what might be the most widely quoted passage from Adam Smith's *Wealth of Nations*, Smith captured this aspect of the market system:

> It is not from the benevolence of the butcher, the brewer, or the baker that we expect our dinner, but from their regard to their own interest. We address ourselves not to their humanity, but to their self-love, and never talk to them of our necessities, but of their advantage.

2.a. Government as the Guardian of Efficiency

economic efficiency:
a situation where no one in society can be made better off without making someone else worse off

technical efficiency:
producing at a point on the PPC

Economic efficiency is the name given to the events described by Adam Smith. Efficiency can mean many things to many different people. Even within economics there are different definitions of efficiency. We have already talked about the production possibilities curve and efficiency; operating at a point on the PPC is called **productive** or **technical efficiency**. A firm is said to be operating efficiently when it produces a given quantity and quality of goods at the lowest possible cost. Consumers are said to be efficient when they are getting the greatest bang for the buck, using their scarce resources to get the greatest benefits. *Economic efficiency* encompasses all of these definitions of efficiency. When *one person cannot be made better off without harming someone else*, then we say economic efficiency prevails.

Somewhat amazingly, economic efficiency occurs in a market system simply through the self-interested individual actions of participants in that system. It is not because some despot is controlling the economy and telling people what they can and cannot do, but because of individual actions that the market system results in efficiency. The higher profits go, the more income is earned by people with entrepreneurial ability. In order to earn profits, entrepreneurs have to provide, at the lowest possible cost, the goods and services that consumers want and are able to buy. This means that the least-cost combination of resources is used by each firm, but it also means that resources are employed in their most highly valued uses. Any reallocation of resources results in a situation that is worse—some resources will not be used where they are most highly valued, and some consumers will be less satisfied with the goods and services they can purchase.

As we saw in the Preview, the government plays a significant role in the U.S. economy; governmental influence is even larger in other market economies, and is especially large in the socialist economies of Cuba, China, Vietnam, and the former Soviet Union. Why, if the actions of individuals in the market system results in the best social outcome, does the government play such a large role?

Why is the public sector such a large part of a market economy?

There are two justifications given for the government's role in a market economy. One is based on cases where the market may not always result in economic efficiency. The second is based on the idea that people who do not

Part I/Introduction to the Price System

like the market outcome use the government to change the outcome. Sections 2.b through 2.f are brief discussions of some cases where the market system may fail to achieve economic efficiency. Section 2.g is a brief discussion of cases where people manipulate the market outcome.

2.b. Information and the Price System

As you learned in Chapters 3 and 4, a market is a place or service that allows buyers and sellers to exchange information on what they know about a product, what buyers are willing and able to pay for a product, and what sellers want to receive in order to produce and sell a product. A market price is a signal indicating when more or less of a good is desired. When the market price rises, buyers know that the quantity demanded at the prior equilibrium price exceeded the quantity supplied.

A market price is only as good an indicator as the information that exists in the market. It takes time for people to gather information about a product. It takes time to go to a market and purchase an item. It takes time for producers to learn what people want and bring together the resources necessary to produce that product. Thus, people are not likely to be perfectly informed, nor will everyone have the same information. This means that not all markets will adjust instantaneously or even at the same speed to a change in demand or supply. It also means that some people may pay higher prices for a product than others pay. Some people may be swindled by a sharp operator, and some firms may fail to collect debts owed them.

market imperfection:
a lack of efficiency that results from imperfect information in the marketplace

When information is not perfect, **market imperfections** may result. As a result of market imperfections, least-cost combinations of resources may not be used, or resources may not be used where they have the highest value. Often in such cases, people have argued for the government to step in with rules and regulations concerning the amount of information that must be provided. The government requires, for example, that specific information be provided on the labels of food products, that warning labels be placed on cigarettes and alcohol products, and that statements about the condition of a used car be made available to buyers. The government also declares certain actions by firms or consumers to be fraudulent or illegal. It also tests and licenses pharmaceuticals and members of many professions—medical doctors, lawyers, beauticians, barbers, nurses, and others.

2.c. Externalities

The market system works efficiently only if the market price reflects the full costs and benefits of producing and consuming a particular good or service. Recall that people make decisions on the basis of their opportunity costs and the market price is a measure of what must be forgone to acquire some good or service. If the market price does not reflect the full costs, then decisions cannot reflect opportunity costs. For instance, when you use air conditioners, you contaminate the ozone layer with Freon but you don't pay the costs of that contamination. When you drive, you don't pay for all of the pollution created by your car. When you have a loud, late-night party, you don't pay for the distractions you impose on your neighbors. When firms dump wastes or create radioactive by-products, they don't pay the costs. When homeowners allow their properties to become rundown, they reduce the value of neighboring properties but they don't pay for the loss of value. When society is educated, it costs less to produce signs, ballots, tax forms, and other information tools. Literacy enables a democracy to function effectively, and higher education may stimulate scientific discoveries that improve the welfare of society. When you acquire an education, however, you do not get a check in the amount of savings your education will create for society. All these side effects—some negative and some positive—which are not covered by the market price, are called **externalities**.

externalities:
costs or benefits of a transaction that are borne by someone not directly involved in the transaction

Externalities are the costs or benefits of a market activity borne by someone who is not a direct party to the market transaction. When you drive, you pay only for gasoline and car maintenance. You don't pay for the noise and pollutants that your car emits. You also don't pay for the added congestion and delays that you impose on other drivers. Thus, the *market* price of driving understates the *full* cost of driving to society; as a result, people drive more frequently than they would if they had to pay the full cost. (See the Economic Insight "Gridlock on the Highways.")

The government is often called upon to intervene in the market to resolve externality problems. Government agencies, such as the Environmental Protection Agency, are established to set and enforce air quality standards, and taxes are imposed to obtain funds to pay for external costs or subsidize external benefits. Thus, the government provides education to society at below-market prices because the positive externality of education benefits everyone.

2.d. Public Goods

The market system works efficiently only if the benefits derived from consuming a particular good or service are available only to the consumer who buys the good or service. You buy a pizza, and only you receive the benefits of eating that pizza. What would happen if you weren't allowed to enjoy that pizza all by yourself? Suppose your neighbors have the right to come to your home when you have a pizza delivered and share your pizza. How often would you buy a pizza? There is no way to exclude others from enjoying the benefits of some of the goods you purchase. These types of goods are called **public goods**, and they create a problem for the market system.

public goods:
goods whose consumption cannot be limited only to the person who purchased the good

Radio broadcasts are public goods. Everyone who tunes in a station enjoys the benefits. National defense is also a public good. You could buy a missile to protect your house, but your neighbors, as well as you, would benefit from the protection it provided. A pizza, however, is not a public good. If you pay for it, only you get to enjoy the benefits. Thus, you have an incentive to purchase pizza. You don't have that incentive to purchase public goods. If you and I both benefit from the public good, who will buy it? I'd prefer that you buy it so that I receive its benefits at no cost. Conversely, you'd prefer that I buy it. The result may be that no one will buy it.

Fire protection provides a good example of the problem that occurs with public goods. Suppose that as a homeowner you have the choice of subscribing to fire protection services from a private firm or having no fire protection. If you subscribe and your house catches fire, the fire engines will arrive as soon as possible and your house may be saved. If you do not subscribe, your house will burn. Do you choose to subscribe? You might say to yourself that as long as your neighbors subscribe, you need not do so. The fact that your neighbors subscribe means that fires in their houses won't cause a fire in

Gridlock on the Highways

The health of an economy depends on the quality of its transportation systems. Concern is growing that the transportation system of the United States is failing because of congestion and age. In just ten years, congestion on urban highways nationwide has increased by over 50 percent. The labor loss attributable to congestion delays equals 17 percent of the average workday.

The solution does not seem to be increases in highway capacity. Indeed, highway congestion grew just as rapidly in the United States between 1960 and 1970 as it did between 1970 and 1980, even though spending on highways in the earlier decade was almost double the spending that occurred in the later decade. Moreover, highway construction is very expensive; one new lane-mile for the morning rush-hour commute can cost $40,000 per commuter in an urban area.

Most consumers accept the principle that the prices they pay for goods and services should reflect the full cost of providing those goods and services. If they buy goods in a shop, for example, they understand that the price includes compensation for the salesperson's time and the cost of the premises, in addition to the cost of the goods purchased. Consumers also accept the principle that the price of goods and services varies with the strength of demand relative to the available supply. Virtually everywhere in the economy, prices are highest during periods of peak demand. Neither of these principles, however, has been adopted by transportation policymakers. Indeed, highways usually are not priced directly at all and are financed instead with gasoline or other taxes. The exceptions are toll bridges and toll highways.

Transportation facilities are beleaguered by an externalities problem. The use of a highway by one additional vehicle adversely affects the amount of time that other users must spend to make their trips. Because no driver has to compensate other travelers for their lost time, each trip-making decision ignores the externalities imposed on others. During rush hours, the externalities can be extremely large.

Congestion delays are a cost imposed on others and should be reflected in the price of the facility. Only a few states in the United States have begun to implement this full-cost pricing idea with the use of toll roads that will be built and operated by private investors, but several other countries have had such a pricing scheme in practice for some time. The United Kingdom, Singapore, and Hong Kong have implemented full-cost pricing of some roads by setting tolls at appropriate levels or by issuing license tags that indicate when a car is allowed on the road.

Sources: "Unlocking Gridlock," Federal Reserve Bank of San Francisco, Weekly Letter, Dec. 9, 1988; "Be Prepared to Pay," *The Economist,* May 20, 1989, p. 63; Wendy White, "States Give Private Toll Roads Green Light," *Investor's Daily,* Jan. 17, 1990, pp. 1, 32.

---

yours, and you do not expect a fire to begin in your house. If many people made decisions in this way, fire protection services would not be available because not enough people would subscribe to make the services profitable.

The problem with a public good is the communal nature of the good. No one has a **private property right** to a public good. If you buy a car, you must pay the seller an acceptable price. Once this price is paid, the car is all yours and no one else can use it without your permission. The car is your private property, and you make the decisions about its use. In other words, you have the private property right to the car. Public goods are available to all because no one individual owns them or has property rights to them.

When goods are public, people have an incentive to try to obtain a **free ride**—the enjoyment of the benefits of a good without paying for the good. Your neighbors would free-ride on your purchases of pizza if you didn't have the private property rights to the pizza. People who enjoy public radio and

private property right:
the limitation of ownership to an individual

free ride:
the enjoyment of the benefits of a good by a producer or consumer without having to pay for it

public television stations without donating money to them are getting free rides from those people who do donate to them. People who benefit from the provision of a good whether they pay for it or not have an incentive not to pay for it.

Typically, in the absence of private property rights to a good, people call on the government to claim ownership and provide the good. For instance, governments act as owners of police departments and specify how police services are used.

2.e. Monopoly

monopoly:
a situation where there is only one producer of a good

If only one firm produces a good that is desired by consumers, then that firm might produce a smaller amount of the good in order to charge a higher price. In this case, resources might not be used in their most highly valued manner and consumers might not be able to purchase the goods they desire. A situation where there is only one producer of a good is called a **monopoly**. The existence of a monopoly can imply the lack of economic efficiency. The government is often called on to regulate the behavior of firms that are monopolies or even to run the monopolies as government enterprises.

2.f. Business Cycles

business cycles:
fluctuations in the economy between growth and stagnation

People are made better off by economic growth. Economic growth increases the number of jobs and draws people out of poverty and into the mainstream of economic progress. Economic stagnation and ill health, on the other hand, throw the relatively poor out of their jobs and into poverty. These fluctuations in the economy are called **business cycles**. People call on the government to protect them against the periods of economic ill health and to minimize the damaging effects of business cycles. Government agencies are established to control the money supply and other important parts of the economy, and government-financed programs are implemented to offset some of the losses that result during bad economic times.

2.g. The Public Choice Theory of Government

The efficiency basis for government intervention in the economy discussed in sections 2.b through 2.f implies that the government is a monolithic unit functioning in much the same way that a benevolent dictator would. This monolith intervenes in the market system only to correct the ills created by the market. Not all economists agree with this view of government. Many claim that the government is not a benevolent dictator looking out for the best interests of society, but is instead merely a collection of individuals who respond to the same economic impulses we all do—that is, the desire to satisfy our own interests.

Economic efficiency does not mean that everyone is as well off as they desire. Economic efficiency merely means that someone or some group cannot be made better off without harming some other person or group of people. People always have an incentive to attempt to make themselves better off. If their attempts result in the transfer of benefits to themselves and away from others, however, economic efficiency has not increased. Moreover, the resources devoted to enacting the transfer of benefits are not productive; they

rent seeking:
the use of resources to transfer income from one sector to another

public choice:
the study of how government actions result from the self-interested behaviors of voters and politicians

do not create new income and benefits but merely transfer income and benefits. Such activity is called **rent seeking**. Rent seeking refers to cases where people devote resources to attempting to create income transfers to themselves. Rent seeking includes the expenditures on lobbyists in Congress, the time and expenses that health-care professionals devote to fighting nationalized health care, the time and expenses farmers devote to improving their subsidies, and millions of other examples.

A group of economists, referred to as **public choice** economists, argue that government is more the result of rent seeking than it is market failure. The study of public choice focuses on how government actions result from the self-interested behaviors of voters and politicians. Whereas the efficiency justification of government argues that it is only in cases where the market does not work that the government steps in, the public choice theory says that the government may be brought into the market system whenever someone or some group can benefit, even if efficiency is not served.

According to the public choice economists, price ceilings or price floors may be enacted for political gain rather than market failure; government spending or taxing policies may be enacted not to resolve a market failure but instead to implement an income redistribution from one group to another; government agencies such as the Food and Drug Administration may exist not to improve the functioning of the market but to enact a wealth transfer from one group to another. Each such instance of manipulation leads to a larger role for government in a market economy. Moreover, government employees have the incentive to increase their role and importance in the economy and therefore transfer income or other benefits to themselves.

The government sector is far from a trivial part of the market system. Whether the government's role is one of improving economic efficiency or the result of rent seeking is a topic for debate, and in later chapters we discuss this debate in more detail. For now, it is satisfactory just to recognize how important the public sector is in the market system and what the possible reasons for its prevalence are.

RECAP

1. The government's role in the economy may stem from the inefficiencies that exist in a market system.

2. The market system does not result in economic efficiency when there are market imperfections such as imperfect information or when the costs or benefits of the transaction are borne by parties not directly involved in the transaction. Such cases are called externalities. Also, the market system may not be efficient when private ownership rights are not well defined. The government is called upon to resolve these inefficiencies that exist in the market system.

3. The government is asked to minimize the problems that result from business cycles.

4. The public choice school of economics maintains that the government's role in the market system is more the result of rent seeking than of reducing market inefficiencies.

3. OVERVIEW OF THE UNITED STATES GOVERNMENT

What does the government do?

When Americans think of government policies, rules, and regulations, they typically think of Washington, D.C., because their economic lives are regulated and shaped more by policies made there than by policies made at the local and state levels. Who actually is involved in economic policymaking? Important government institutions that shape U.S. economic policy are listed in Table 1. This list is far from inclusive, but it includes the agencies with the broadest powers and greatest influence.

Economic policy involves macroeconomic issues like government spending and control of the money supply and microeconomic issues aimed at providing public goods like police and military protection, correcting externalities like pollution, and maintaining a competitive economy.

3.a. Microeconomic Policy

Government provides public goods to avoid the free-rider problem that would occur if private firms provided the goods.

One reason for government's microeconomic role is the free-rider problem associated with the provision of public goods. If an army makes all citizens safer, then all citizens should pay for it. But even if one person does not pay taxes, the army still protects this citizen from foreign attack. To minimize free riding, the government collects mandatory taxes to finance public goods. Congress and the president determine the level of public goods needed and how to finance them.

Government taxes or subsidizes some activities that create externalities.

Microeconomic policy also deals with externalities. Activities that cause air or water pollution impose costs on everyone. For instance, a steel mill may generate air pollutants that have a negative effect on the surrounding population. A microeconomic function of government is to internalize the externality—that is, to force the steelmaker to bear the full cost to society of producing steel. In addition to assuming the costs of hiring land, labor, and capital, the mill should bear the costs associated with polluting the air.

"It's the economy, stupid!" was the rallying cry of the Clinton campaign. As President of the United States, Bill Clinton has focused on the economy and health care, proposing an increased public sector role in the economy in general and health care in particular. The President, with Treasury Secretary Bentsen on his right and Labor Secretary Reich on his left, discusses the lack of job growth and what the government should do about it with Commerce Secretary Brown and other cabinet members.

TABLE 1
U.S. Government Economic Policymakers and Related Agencies

Institution	Role
Fiscal policymakers	
President	Provides leadership in formulating fiscal policy
Congress	Sets government spending and taxes and passes laws related to economic conduct
Monetary policymaker	
Federal Reserve	Controls money supply and credit conditions
Related agencies	
Council of Economic Advisors	Monitors the economy and advises the president
Office of Management and Budget	Prepares and analyzes the federal budget
Treasury Department	Administers the financial affairs of the federal government
Commerce Department	Administers federal policy regulating industry
Justice Department	Enforces legal setting of business
Comptroller of the Currency	Oversees national banks
International Trade Commission	Investigates unfair international trade practices
Federal Trade Commission	Administers laws related to fair business practices and competition

Congress and the president determine which externalities to address and the best way of taxing or subsidizing each activity in order to ensure that the amount of the good produced and its price reflect the true value to society.

Government regulates industries where free market competition may not exist and polices other industries to promote competition.

Another of government's microeconomic roles is to promote competition. Laws to restrict the ability of business firms to engage in practices that limit competition exist and are monitored by the Justice Department and the Federal Trade Commission. Some firms, such as public utilities, are monopolies and face no competition. The government defines the output, prices, and profits of many monopolies. In some cases, the monopolies are government-run enterprises.

3.b. Macroeconomic Policy

monetary policy:
policy directed toward control of money and credit

The focus of the government's macroeconomic policy is monetary and fiscal policy. **Monetary policy** is policy directed toward control of money and credit. The major player in this policy arena is the Federal Reserve, com-

Federal Reserve:
the central bank of the United States

monly called "the Fed." The **Federal Reserve** is the central bank of the United States. It serves as a banker for the U.S. government and regulates the U.S. money supply.

The Federal Reserve System is run by a seven-member Board of Governors. The most important member of the Board is the chairman, who is appointed by the president for a term of four years. The Board meets regularly (from ten to twelve times a year) with a group of high-level officials to review the current economic situation and set policy for the growth of U.S. money and credit. The Federal Reserve exercises a great deal of influence on U.S. economic policy.

fiscal policy:
policy directed toward government spending and taxation

Government has the responsibility of minimizing the damage from business cycles.

Fiscal policy, the other area of macroeconomic policy, is policy directed toward government spending and taxation. In the United States, fiscal policy is determined by laws that are passed by Congress and signed by the president. The relative roles of the legislative and executive branches in shaping fiscal policy vary with the political climate, but usually it is the president who initiates major policy changes. Presidents rely on key advisers for fiscal policy information. These advisers include Cabinet officers such as the secretary of the treasury and the secretary of state as well as the director of the Office of Management and Budget. In addition, the president has a Council of Economic Advisers made up of three economists—usually a chairman, a macroeconomist, and a microeconomist—who, together with their staff, monitor and interpret economic developments for the president. The degree of influence wielded by these advisers depends on their personal relationship with the president.

Figure 2
Federal, State, and Local Government Expenditures for Goods and Services, 1959–1992
In the 1950s and early 1960s, federal government spending was above state and local government spending. In 1969, state and local expenditures rose above federal spending and have remained higher ever since. Source: data are from the *Economic Report of the President, 1992* (Washington, D.C.: U.S. Government Printing Office, 1992), p. 299.

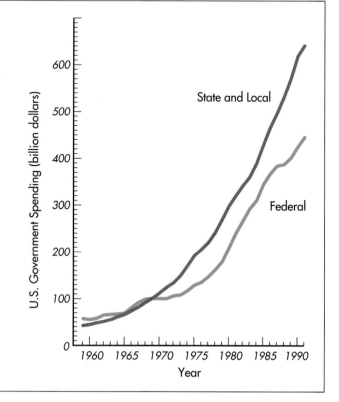

3.c. Government Spending

Federal, state, and local government spending for goods and services between 1959 and 1992 is shown in Figure 2. Except during times of war in the 1940s and 1950s, federal expenditures were roughly similar in size to state and local expenditures until 1969. Since 1969, state and local spending has been growing more rapidly than federal spending.

Combined government spending on goods and services is larger than investment spending but much smaller than consumption. In 1991, combined government spending was $1,086.9 billion, investment spending was $725.3 billion, and consumption was $3,886.8 billion.

transfer payments:
the transfer of money by the government from taxpayers with higher incomes to those with lower incomes

Besides government expenditures on goods and services, government also serves as an intermediary, taking money from taxpayers with higher incomes and transferring this income to those with lower incomes. Such **transfer payments** are a part of total government expenditures, so that the total government budget is much larger than the expenditures on goods and services reported in Figure 2. In 1991, total expenditures of federal, state, and local government for goods and services was $1,086.9 billion. In this same year, transfer payments paid by all levels of government were $699 billion.

The magnitude of federal government spending relative to federal government revenue from taxes has become an important issue in recent years. Figure 3 shows that the federal budget was roughly balanced until the early 1970s. The budget is a measure of spending and revenue. A balanced budget occurs when federal spending is approximately equal to federal revenue. This

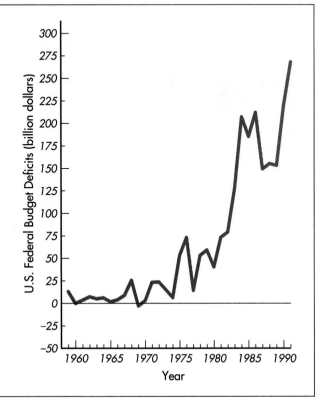

Figure 3
U.S. Federal Budget Deficits, 1959–1992
The budget deficit is equal to the excess of government spending over tax revenue. If taxes are greater than government spending, a budget surplus (shown as a negative deficit) exists. The United States has run a budget deficit for all but two years in the period 1959–1991. Source: data are from the *Economic Report of the President, 1992* (Washington, D.C.: U.S. Government Printing Office, 1992), p. 385.

budget surplus:
the excess that results when government spending is less than revenue

budget deficit:
the shortage that results when government spending is greater than revenue

was the case through the 1950s and 1960s. If federal government spending is less than tax revenue, a **budget surplus** exists. The U.S. government last had a budget surplus in 1969. By the early 1980s, federal government spending was much larger than revenue, so a large **budget deficit** existed. The federal budget deficit grew very rapidly to around $200 billion by the mid-1980s. When spending is greater than revenue, the excess spending must be covered by borrowing, and this borrowing can have effects on investment and consumption as well as on economic relationships with other countries.

RECAP

1. The microeconomic functions of government include correcting externalities, redistributing income from high-income groups to lower-income groups, enforcing a competitive economy, and providing public goods.

2. Macroeconomic policy attempts to control the economy through monetary and fiscal policy.

3. The Federal Reserve conducts monetary policy. Congress and the president formulate fiscal policy.

4. Government spending is larger than investment spending but much smaller than consumption spending.

5. When government spending exceeds tax revenue, a budget deficit exists. When government spending is less than tax revenue, a budget surplus exists.

4. GOVERNMENT IN OTHER ECONOMIES

How do the sizes of public sectors in various countries compare?

centrally planned economy:
an economic system in which the government determines what goods and services are produced and the prices at which they are sold

The government plays a role in every economy, and in most the public sector is a much larger part of the economy than it is in the United States. In some economies, referred to as **centrally planned**, or nonmarket, economies, the public sector is the principal component of the economy. There are significant differences between the market system and the centrally planned systems. In market economies, people can own businesses, be private owners of land, start new businesses, and purchase what they want as long as they can pay the price. They may see their jobs disappear as business conditions worsen, but they are free to take business risks and to reap the rewards if taking these risks pays off. Under centrally planned systems, people are not free to own property other than a house, a car, and personal belongings. They are not free to start a business. They work as employees of the state. Their jobs are guaranteed regardless of whether their employer is making the right or wrong decisions and regardless of how much effort they expend on the job. Even though they might have money in their pockets, they may not be able to buy many of the things they want. Money prices are often not used to ration goods and services, so people may spend much of their time standing in lines to buy the products available on the shelves of government stores. Waiting in line is a result of charging a money price lower than equilibrium and imposing a quantity limit on how much a person can buy. The time costs, along with the money price required to buy goods, will ration the limited supply.

The Soviet Union implemented a centrally planned economy in the 1920s, following its October 1917 revolution. During, and especially following, World War II, the Soviet system expanded into Eastern Europe, China, North Korea, and Vietnam. At the peak of Soviet influence, about one-third of the world's population lived in countries generally described as having centrally planned economic systems. The 1980s and 1990s ushered in a new world order, however. The Soviet Union's economy failed and ultimately led to the fall of the communist governments in Eastern Europe, the disintegration of the Soviet Union, the end of the Cold War, and the reunification of West and East Germany.

4.a. Overview of Major Market Economies

Figure 4 shows the size of government and the type of economy for several countries. The United States and Canada are representative of nations that are market economies with relatively small public sectors. Cuba and Vietnam are representative of nations that are primarily centrally planned. Although China has some pockets of a market economy, it is more like the centrally planned economy. Germany, Japan, and the United Kingdom are market economies but the public sector plays a larger role than it does in the United States. The nations of the former Soviet Union and those of Eastern Europe are not shown because they currently are in transition from centrally planned to market-oriented systems.

4.a.1. France The public sector in France is much larger than it is in the United States. France is a market economy in which a national economic plan has been used to influence resource allocation. The French plan, however, unlike the Soviet counterpart, does not order firms to do things. The plan is indicative; it offers suggested targets. The state uses its budget and its ownership of firms to attempt to further the implementation of the plan. Government ownership is concentrated in banking, coal, gas and electricity, transportation, and auto and aircraft production. The government-sector share of the economy is quite large; total government expenditures were nearly 50 percent of total output in 1990.

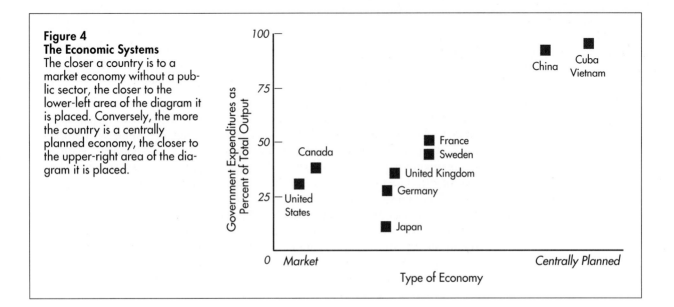

Figure 4
The Economic Systems
The closer a country is to a market economy without a public sector, the closer to the lower-left area of the diagram it is placed. Conversely, the more the country is a centrally planned economy, the closer to the upper-right area of the diagram it is placed.

The extent of government involvement in the economy varies from country to country. The government's role in the European economies is larger than it is in the United States. For instance, the French government owns Aerospatiale Usine Airbus, the Toulouse, France firm that produces the airbus. The airbus is a direct competitor to private firms in the United States, Boeing and McDonnell-Douglas. As a result, many U.S. politicians and others associated with the aerospace industry have called on the U.S. government to provide some protection to the private firms in the U.S. that compete with the government enterprises or government-subsidized firms of other nations.

4.a.2. United Kingdom   The role of the public sector in the United Kingdom is significant but not exceptional by European standards. Great Britain is an island economy with a land area slightly greater than that of the state of Minnesota and a population of just over 57 million persons. The resource base of the economy is quite limited, and the British economy is tied very closely to other economies. The British concept of an appropriate role for the public sector in economic affairs is more limited than that prevailing in France. Government spending in 1990 was about 37 percent of total output in the United Kingdom, not much larger than in the United States.

4.a.3. Germany   There is no significant planning apparatus in Germany, and the public sector owns few businesses, but the public sector intervenes a great deal to foster social programs. For instance, the government regulates business hours, supports minimum prices for brand-name articles, imposes rent controls, regulates the hiring and firing of employees, regulates vacations, and has a series of other laws protecting workers and renters. State expenditures were about 30 percent of total output in 1990. The unification of the East and West German economies and the merging of two different types of systems has led to additional government intervention.

4.a.4. Japan   Japan is a capitalist economy whose postwar rate of economic growth is the highest among the major industrialized countries. Japan is a small country with adequate labor but generally limited supplies of natural resources and land. Like Great Britain, Japan is an island economy. With a population of approximately 123 million and a land area slightly smaller than that of the state of California, Japan is densely populated. The public sector appears on the surface to have a relatively small role in the Japanese economy: government spending as a percent of total output was only about 17 percent in 1990. But this statistic understates the reality. The public sector plays a very important role through the Japanese industrial families known as *keiretsu*. The government wields its influence on the keiretsu through various ministries. For example, the Ministry of International Trade and Industry (MITI) is responsible for international trade, domestic production, and domestic industrial structure. MITI guides and influences economic decisions by promoting key sectors of the economy and carefully phasing out other, low-productivity sectors. MITI uses government funds for research and development and to provide assistance for organizational change, such as mergers. Economic planning has not been an important element in the Japanese economy. Japan has had a planning agency since the late 1940s and has assembled numerous plans, but the plans are neither binding nor involuntarily implemented.

4.a.5. Sweden   The Swedish economic system and its performance are of interest because Sweden is viewed as a system that has been able, over an extended period of time, to sustain economic progress through the efficiency of the market while at the same time ensuring that incomes are equally distributed. Sweden is a relatively small but highly industrialized country. It has a total area of roughly 450,000 square kilometers (somewhat larger than the state of California) and a population of just over 8.5 million. Foreign trade is of vital importance to Sweden, accounting for more than 70 percent of its total output. The Swedish economy looks like a market economy in the production of goods and services, but the government accounts for nearly 50 percent of total purchases in Sweden. To support such expenditures, taxes in Sweden are very high—about 43 percent of Sweden's total output. The comparable figure for the United States is about 20 percent.

RECAP

1. No economy is purely private. The public sector plays a role in every economy.
2. A market economy relies on prices and individual actions to solve economic problems. In centrally planned economies, the government decides what is produced, how it is produced, and who gets what.

SUMMARY

▲▼ *How does the government interact with the other sectors of the economy?*

1. The circular flow diagram illustrates the interaction among all sectors of the economy—households, businesses, the international sector, and the public sector. §1

▲▼ *What is the economic role of government?*

2. The market system results in economic efficiency. Economic efficiency means that in an economy one person cannot be made better off without harming someone else. §2.a

3. The market system does not result in economic efficiency when there are market imperfections, externalities, or public goods. Market imperfections occur when information is imperfect. §§2.b–2.g

▲▼ *Why is the public sector such a large part of a market economy?*

4. Two general reasons are given for the government's participation in the economy: the government may resolve the inefficiencies that occur in a market system, or the government may be the result of rent seeking. §2.b–2.g

5. Economic efficiency means that some people cannot be made better off without others being made worse off. Some people do not like the result of the market outcome and want to alter it. In such cases, resources are devoted to creating a transfer of income. This is called rent seeking. §2.g

6. The government carries out microeconomic and macroeconomic activities. The microeconomic activities include resolving market imperfections, externalities, and public goods problems. The macroeconomic activities are directed toward monetary and fiscal policy and minimizing disruptions due to business cycles. §3

7. Governments often provide public goods and services such as fire protection, police protection, and national defense. Governments place limits on what firms and consumers can do in certain types of situations. Governments tax externalities or otherwise attempt to make price reflect the full cost of production and consumption. §3.a

8. Governments carry out monetary and fiscal policy to attempt to control business cycles. In the United States, monetary policy is the province of the Federal Reserve, and fiscal policy is up to the Congress and the president. §3.b

▲▼ **How do the sizes of public sectors in various countries compare?**

9. Market systems rely on the decisions of individuals. Centrally planned systems rely on the government to answer economic questions for all individuals. §4

10. The size and influence of the public sector ranges from the market economies of the United States and Canada to the centrally planned economies of Cuba, Vietnam, and China. §4.a

KEY TERMS

economic efficiency §2.a
technical efficiency §2.a
market imperfection §2.b
externalities §2.c
public goods §2.d
private property right §2.d
free ride §2.d
monopoly §2.e
business cycles §2.f

rent seeking §2.g
public choice §2.g
monetary policy §3.b
Federal Reserve §3.b
fiscal policy §3.b
transfer payments §3.c
budget surplus §3.c
budget deficit §3.c
centrally planned economies §4

EXERCISES

1. Illustrate productive or technical efficiency using a production possibilities curve. Can you illustrate economic efficiency? Are you able to show the exact point where economic efficiency would occur?

2. Why would an externality be referred to as a market failure? Explain how your driving on a highway imposes costs on other drivers. Why is this an externality? How might the externality be resolved or internalized?

3. What is the difference between a compact disc recording of a rock concert and a radio broad

cast of that rock concert? Why would you spend $12 on the CD but refuse to provide any support to the radio station?

4. "The American buffalo disappeared because they were not privately owned." Evaluate this statement.

5. Which of the following economic policies are the responsibility of the Federal Reserve? Congress and the president?

   a. An increase in the rate of growth of the money supply

   b. A decrease in the rate of interest

c. An increase in taxes on the richest two percent of Americans

d. A reduction in taxes on the middle class

e. An increase in the rate of growth of spending on health care

6. "The Department of Justice plans to file a lawsuit against major airlines, claiming they violated price-fixing laws by sharing plans for fare changes through a computer system, officials said Friday." This statement was reported in newspapers December 12, 1992. Is this a microeconomic or macroeconomic policy?

7. People sometimes argue that imports should be limited by government policy. Suppose a government quota on the quantity of imports causes net exports to rise. Using the circular flow diagram as a guide, explain why total expenditures and national output may rise after the quota is imposed. Who is likely to benefit from the quota? Who will be hurt? Explain why the government would become involved in the economy through its imposition of quotas.

8. Most highways are "free" ways: there is no toll charge for using them. What problem does free access create? How would you solve this?

9. Explain why the suggested government action may or may not make sense in each of the following scenarios.

a. People purchase a VCR with a guarantee provided by its maker, only to find that within a year the company has gone out of business. Consumers demand that the government provide the guarantee.

b. Korean microchip producers are selling the microchips at a price that is below the cost of making the microchips in the United States. The government must impose quotas on the Korean producers.

c. The economy has slowed down, unemployment has risen, and interest rates are high. The government should provide jobs and force interest rates down.

d. Fully 15 percent of all United States citizens are without health insurance. The government must provide health care for all Americans.

e. The falling value of the dollar is making it nearly impossible for U.S. manufacturers to sell their products to other nations. The government must increase the value of the dollar.

f. The rich got richer at a faster rate than the poor got richer during the 1980s. The government must increase the tax rate on the rich to equalize the income distribution.

g. The AIDS epidemic has placed such a state of emergency on health care that the only solution is to provide some pharmaceutical firm with a monopoly on any drugs or solutions discovered to HIV or AIDS.

10. Many nations of Eastern Europe are undergoing a transition from a centrally planned to a market economic system. An important step in the process is to define private property rights in countries where they did not exist before. What does this mean? Why is it necessary to have private property rights?

11. Using the circular flow diagram, illustrate the effects of an increase in taxes imposed on the household sector.

12. Using the circular flow diagram, explain how the government can continually run budget deficits, that is, spend more than it receives in revenue from taxes.

13. Suppose you believe that government is the problem, not the solution. How would you explain the rapid growth of government during the past few decades?

14. The government intervenes in the private sector by imposing laws that ban smoking in all publicly used buildings. As a result, smoking is illegal in bars, restaurants, hotels, dance clubs, and other establishments. Is such a ban justified by economics?

15. Relying on question 14, we could say that before a ban is imposed the owners of businesses owned the private property right to the air in their establishments. As owners of this valuable asset they would ensure it is used to earn them the greatest return. Thus, if their customers desired nonsmoking, then they would provide nonsmoking environments. How then does the ban on smoking improve things? Doesn't it merely transfer ownership of the air from the business owners to the nonsmokers?

Economically Speaking

Wisconsin Private-School Program Learns Lesson in Supply and Demand

MILWAUKEE—The nation's first private school choice program, designed to shake up public education by subjecting it to the bracing effects of marketplace competition, has itself been shaken by unexpected shortages of both supply and demand.

"The whole thing hasn't amounted to a good-sized flea on the tail of a dog," said Steven Dold, assistant state superintendent of public instruction. The pilot program allows inner-city students here to attend non-sectarian private schools with taxpayer-financed vouchers of $2,500. . . .

When the Wisconsin legislature created a private school choice program here last year, it capped participation at 1,000 Milwaukee students, fearing that without such a ceiling, there might be an exodus from the troubled public school system. It turns out lawmakers needn't have worried.

Even though nearly 60,000 of Milwaukee's 98,000 public school students meet the program's income eligibility requirements (they qualify for federally subsidized free lunches), a mere 600 applied for the vouchers.

At the same time, only seven of the 21 non-sectarian private schools in the city chose to accept voucher students from the public schools, meaning that the light demand was still too great for the small supply. A lottery had to be held to apportion the 400 available voucher slots. . . .

Voucher advocates attribute the wobbly start to the opposition of public school teachers and administrators and civil rights groups, who are parties to a lawsuit—pending before the state Supreme Court—that seeks to have the program declared illegal for failing to meet the "public purpose" standard of the state constitution.

"The foxes guarding the henhouse have had ulterior motives," said Clint Bolick, director of Landmark Legal Foundation's Center for Civil Rights, a Washington, D.C.-based conservative group that is defending the program against the suit. "You wish they would have applied the energy they've spent fighting this program into fixing the schools."

But others, including an independent evaluator selected by the state, say the voucher program here has been undersubscribed for a more complex mix of reasons—including consumer allegiance to neighborhood public schools—that raise doubt whether private school vouchers can ever be the educational panacea some of its champions envision.

"The idea of bringing marketplace competition into education may sound like a wonderful theory, especially for a nation that has its ears tuned to the bottom line, but I think we're in the process of discovering that it doesn't have much to do with the reality of urban education," said Diane Neicheril, principal of Clarke Street School, an inner-city public elementary school.

It's not difficult to understand why educators such as Neicheril feel threatened by vouchers: For every $2,500 voucher that follows a Milwaukee public school student into a private school, the city public school system loses that much in state aid.

Public school educators say this will produce a "creaming" effect—the most motivated students will take the money and run, leaving behind a "dumping ground for the poorest and neediest students, all concentrated in one place," said Neicheril. "And meantime, we also lose financial resources and political support."

Voucher advocates say that it's precisely this dire prospect they're after—because only then, they argue, will a top-heavy, calcified public education bureaucracy be forced to improve its product. "The goal of this program isn't just to give vouchers to a few students—it's to be a tail that wags the dog, the whole Milwaukee public school system," said Larry Harwell, chief aide to state Rep. Annette "Polly" Williams, a Milwaukee Democrat who is the political godmother of the voucher program.

Paul Taylor, "Wisconsin Private-School Program Learns Lesson in Supply and Demand," *St. Paul Pioneer Press Dispatch*, May 26, 1991, p. 1B. © 1991, The Washington Post. Reprinted with permission.

Commentary

Studies that compare private and public education conclude that private school students generally outperform public school students on standardized math and language tests. Many people ask why the public sector finances and controls education when the private sector seems better able to do the job.

The argument in favor of public education is based on externalities. The demand for education is represented by the downward-sloping curve labeled D in the figure on the left. The higher the cost of education, that is, the higher P is, the lower the quantity demanded. The supply of education is represented by the upward-sloping curve labeled S. The quantity of education purchased and the price of that education should be where the demand and supply curves intersect, point e.

However, if education provides benefits to society in addition to the benefits it provides to the individual, then the private-market solution is biased toward too little education. The supply curve, S_s, reflects not only the private benefits of education, such as better jobs and higher standards of living, but also the social benefits of a better-run and more efficient country. If all of the benefits of education are taken into account, the quantity of education purchased would be Q_s instead of Q_e. However, Q_e won't occur at price P_e because the suppliers of

education are not paid enough. The only way that the "right" quantity of education, Q_s, is provided is if the public sector provides a subsidy equal to the distance $A - B$. You can see that the difference between S and S_s calls for a *subsidy*, not the complete takeover of education by the public sector.

If the positive externalities argument does not justify publicly provided education, then why does it exist? Perhaps the public provision of education is the result of rent seeking on the part of those employed in public education. The figure on the right illustrates the market for teachers, where the demand and supply curves intersect at point e. Suppose that the teachers are able to get a law implemented that reduces the supply of teachers relative to the demand for teachers, as illustrated by an inward shift of the supply curve, from S to S_1. The result of the rent seeking would be higher wages for the teachers, W_1 compared to W_e.

Thus, the positive externalities of education could be handled through subsidies to parents; and the rent seeking by educators, administrators, and others in the public education system could result in restrictions to entry and higher wages. Neither necessity means publically provided education. Do you think that allowing market forces to work in education might solve some of the problems of public education?

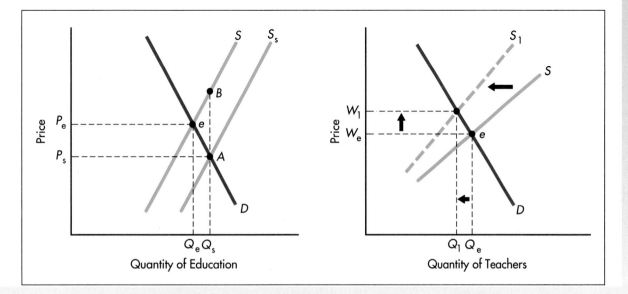

Quantity of Education

Quantity of Teachers

MAKING SENSE OF MICROECONOMICS

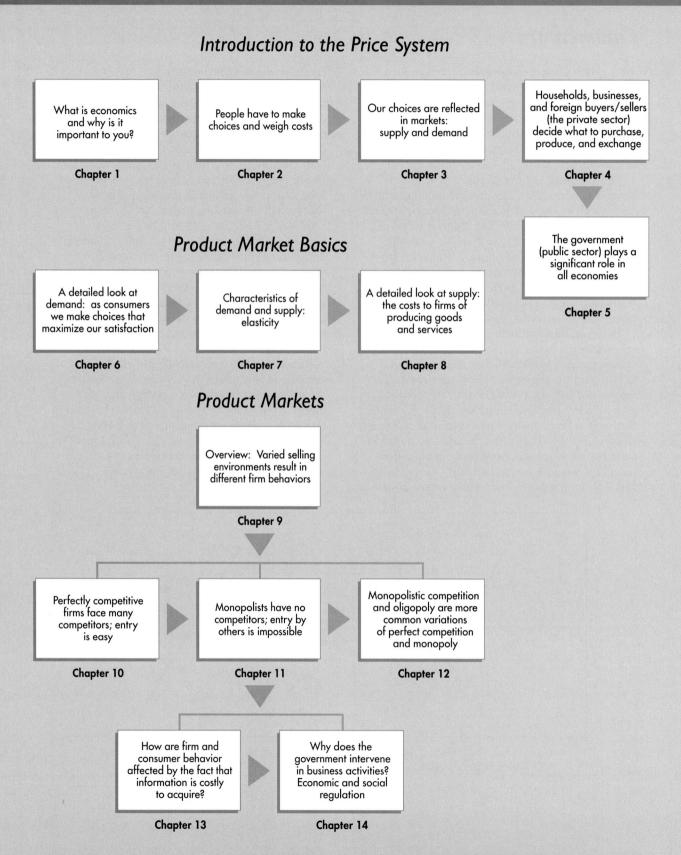

Introduction to the Price System

What is economics and why is it important to you?

Chapter 1

People have to make choices and weigh costs

Chapter 2

Our choices are reflected in markets: supply and demand

Chapter 3

Households, businesses, and foreign buyers/sellers (the private sector) decide what to purchase, produce, and exchange

Chapter 4

The government (public sector) plays a significant role in all economies

Chapter 5

Product Market Basics

A detailed look at demand: as consumers we make choices that maximize our satisfaction

Chapter 6

Characteristics of demand and supply: elasticity

Chapter 7

A detailed look at supply: the costs to firms of producing goods and services

Chapter 8

Product Markets

Overview: Varied selling environments result in different firm behaviors

Chapter 9

Perfectly competitive firms face many competitors; entry is easy

Chapter 10

Monopolists have no competitors; entry by others is impossible

Chapter 11

Monopolistic competition and oligopoly are more common variations of perfect competition and monopoly

Chapter 12

How are firm and consumer behavior affected by the fact that information is costly to acquire?

Chapter 13

Why does the government intervene in business activities? Economic and social regulation

Chapter 14

Resource Markets

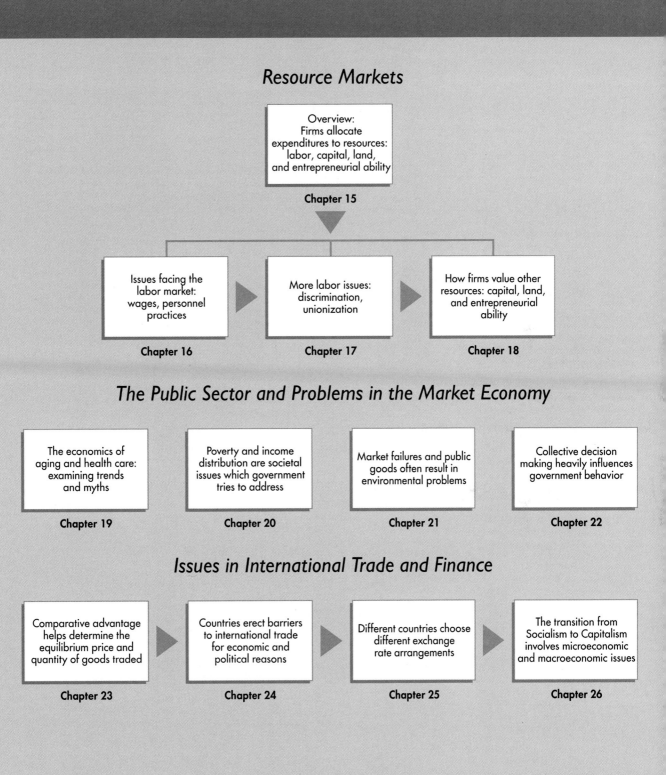

Overview:
Firms allocate expenditures to resources: labor, capital, land, and entrepreneurial ability

Chapter 15

Issues facing the labor market: wages, personnel practices

Chapter 16

More labor issues: discrimination, unionization

Chapter 17

How firms value other resources: capital, land, and entrepreneurial ability

Chapter 18

The Public Sector and Problems in the Market Economy

The economics of aging and health care: examining trends and myths

Chapter 19

Poverty and income distribution are societal issues which government tries to address

Chapter 20

Market failures and public goods often result in environmental problems

Chapter 21

Collective decision making heavily influences government behavior

Chapter 22

Issues in International Trade and Finance

Comparative advantage helps determine the equilibrium price and quantity of goods traded

Chapter 23

Countries erect barriers to international trade for economic and political reasons

Chapter 24

Different countries choose different exchange rate arrangements

Chapter 25

The transition from Socialism to Capitalism involves microeconomic and macroeconomic issues

Chapter 26

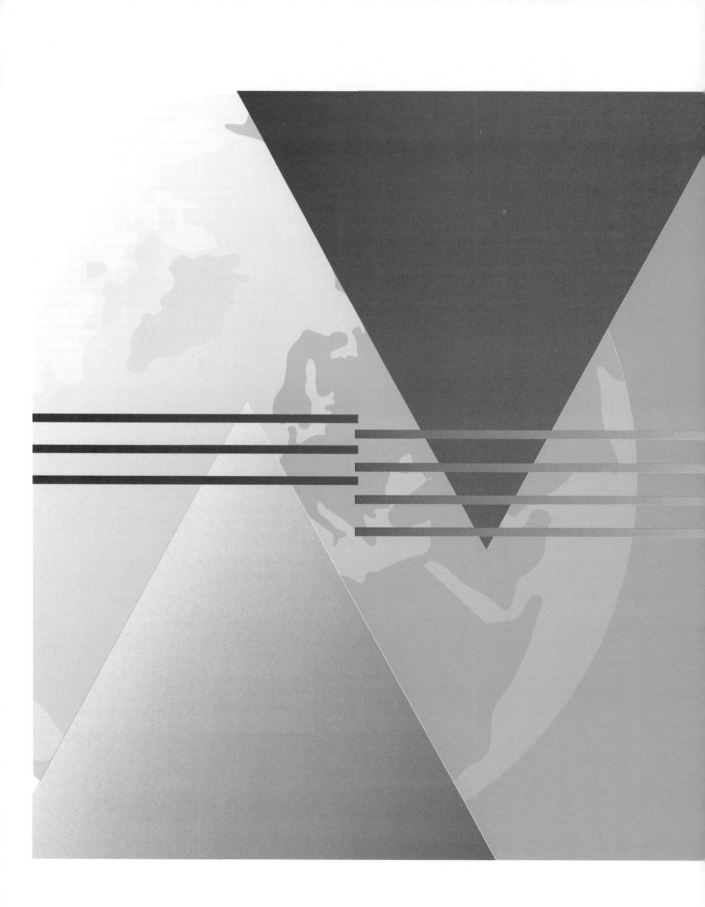

II

Product Market Basics

6

Consumer Choice

1. Does one more dollar mean less to a millionaire than to a pauper?
2. What does "all you can eat" really mean?
3. How do consumers allocate their limited incomes among the billions of goods and services that exist?
4. Why do Disneyland, Sea World, and other businesses charge an admission fee and then provide the use of the facilities for no extra charge?

everal students who had just completed their final exam in economics were joking that any lab animal could be trained to get an A in economics. It would only have to answer "demand and supply" to every question. The students' sarcasm demonstrated both their grasp and lack of understanding of economics. There is no doubt that demand and supply are at the heart of economics, but unless you know *why* demand and supply behave as they do, can you be confident about what they imply? Can firms be sure they will sell more if they lower the price of their product? Should producers confidently assume that when income grows, demand will increase? Can managers rely on a direct relation between price and quantity supplied? To grasp how the economy functions, it is necessary to understand what lies behind demand and supply.

In this and the next chapter we take a close look at demand. Here we examine how and why consumers make choices and what factors influence their choices. In the chapter "Elasticity: Demand and Supply," we examine the magnitude of consumer response to changes in those factors. Then in the chapter "Supply: The Costs of Doing Business," we turn to the supply side and discuss what decisions and factors lie behind the relation between quantities supplied and price.

I. DECISIONS

Do we go to college or get a job? Do we get married or remain single? Do we live in the dorm, a house, or an apartment? "Decisions, decisions, decisions! Don't we ever get a break from the pressure of making choices?" Not unless scarcity disappears will we be freed of having to make choices. Although scarcity and choice are pervasive, how people make decisions is a question that has eluded scientific explanation. Some decisions seem to be based on feelings, or come from the heart, while others seem more calculated. Some are quick and impulsive, while others take months or years of research. Is it the appeal of the book cover that makes you decide to buy one book over another? Does a television commercial affect your decision? Are you more influenced by your spouse, your family, your friends, or your coworkers?

The answers to these questions depend on your values, on your personality, on where you were raised, on how others might react to your decision, and on many other factors. Although the important factors of a decision may vary from person to person, everyone makes decisions in much the same way. People tend to compare perceived costs and benefits of alternatives and select those that they believe give them the greatest relative benefits. This is not to say everyone walks around with a computer into which they continually feed data and out of which comes the answer: "Buy this," or "Do that." Instead, whether the decision is made on the basis of emotion or on the basis of an accountant's balance sheet, people are comparing what they perceive to be the costs and benefits. To explain how these comparisons are made, philosophers and economists of the nineteenth century developed a concept called *utility*. That concept can help us understand consumer decision-making today.

I.a. Utility

utility:
a measure of the satisfaction received from possessing or consuming goods and services

Individuals behave so as to maximize their utility.

Utility describes the degree to which goods and services satisfy wants. You are nourished by a good meal, entertained by a concert, proud of a fine car, and comforted by a nice home and warm clothing. Whatever feelings are described by *nourishment, entertainment, pride*, and *comfort* are captured in the term *utility*. Utility is another term for *satisfaction*.

Consumers make choices that give them the greatest satisfaction; they maximize their utility. Whether one item is preferable to another depends on how much utility each provides. If you enjoy a hot fudge sundae more than a piece of angel food cake, you choose the sundae. You select it because it gives you more utility than the angel food cake.

The utility you derive from experiencing some activity or consuming some good depends on your tastes and preferences. You may love opera and intensely dislike country music. You may have difficulty understanding how anyone can eat tripe, but you love hot chilies. We shall have little to say about why some people prefer country music and others classical music; we simply *assume* that tastes and preferences are given and use those given tastes and preferences to describe the process of decision-making.

I.b. Diminishing Marginal Utility

To illustrate how utility maximization can be useful, we must create a hypothetical world where we can measure the satisfaction that people receive from consuming goods and services. Suppose that a chocolate cake is cut into 20 equal pieces and that a consumer named Stephanie can eat as much of the cake as she wishes during the course of the day. Assume that Stephanie is hooked up to a computer that measures satisfaction in units called *utils*. The utils that Stephanie associates with each piece of cake and the total utility she receives from the total amount of cake eaten in a day are presented in Table 1.

Several important concepts associated with consumer choice can be observed in Table 1. First, each *additional* piece of cake yields Stephanie less satisfaction (fewer utils) than the previous piece. According to Table 1, the first piece of cake yields 200 utils, the second 98, the third 50, the fourth 10, and the fifth none. Each additional piece of cake, until the fifth piece, adds to total utility; but Stephanie enjoys each additional piece just a little bit less than she enjoyed the prior piece. This relationship is called **diminishing marginal utility**.

diminishing marginal utility:
the principle that the more of a good that one obtains in a specific period of time, the less is the additional utility yielded by an additional unit of that good

marginal utility:
the extra utility derived from consuming one more unit of a good or service

Marginal utility is the change in total utility that occurs because one more unit of the good is consumed or acquired;

$$\text{Marginal utility} = \frac{\text{change in total utility}}{\text{change in quantity}}$$

According to the principle of diminishing marginal utility, the more of a good or service that someone consumes during a particular period of time,

TABLE 1
The Utility of Chocolate Cake

Pieces of Cake per Day	Util of Each Piece (marginal utility)	Total Utility
1	200	200
2	98	298
3	50	348
4	10	358
5	0	358
6	−70	288
7	−200	88

disutility:
dissatisfaction

total utility:
a measure of the total satisfaction derived from consuming a quantity of some good or service

the less satisfaction another unit of that good or service provides that individual. Imagine yourself sitting down to a plate piled high with cake. The first piece is delicious, and the second tastes good but not as good as the first. The fourth piece doesn't taste very good at all, and the sixth piece nearly makes you sick. Instead of satisfaction, the sixth piece of cake yields dissatisfaction, or **disutility**.

Notice that we are speaking of diminishing *marginal* utility, not diminishing *total* utility. **Total utility**, the measure of the total satisfaction derived from consuming a quantity of some good or service, climbs until dissatisfaction sets in. For Stephanie, total utility rises from 200 to 298 to 348 and reaches 358 with the fourth piece of cake. From the fifth piece on, total utility declines. Marginal utility, however, is the additional utility gained from consuming an additional piece of cake, and it declines from the first piece on.

To illustrate the relation between marginal and total utility, we have plotted the data from Table 1 in Figure 1(a). The total utility curve rises as quantity rises until the fifth piece of cake. After 5 pieces of cake, the total utility curve declines. The reason total utility rises at first is that each additional piece of cake provides a little more utility. The marginal utility of the first piece of cake is 200; the marginal utility of the second piece is 98; of the third, 50; of the fourth, 10; and of the fifth, zero. By the fifth piece, total utility is 200 + 98 + 50 + 10 + 0 = 358.

We have plotted marginal utility in Figure 1(b), directly below the total utility curve of Figure 1(a). Marginal utility declines with each successive unit, reaches zero, and then turns negative. As long as marginal utility is positive, total utility rises. When marginal utility becomes negative, total utility declines. Marginal utility is zero at the point where total utility is at its maximum (unit 5 in this case).

1.c. Diminishing Marginal Utility and Time

The concept of diminishing marginal utility makes sense only if we define the *period of time* during which consumption is occurring. If Stephanie ate the cake over a period of several days, we would not observe diminishing marginal utility until she had eaten more than 5 pieces. Usually, the shorter the time period, the more quickly marginal utility diminishes. Once the time

Figure 1
Total and Marginal Utility

Figure 1(a) shows the total utility obtained from consuming pieces of cake. Total utility reaches a maximum and then declines as additional consumption becomes distasteful. For the first piece of cake the marginal and total utilities are the same. For the second piece of cake, the marginal utility is the additional utility provided by the second unit. The total utility is the sum of the marginal utilities of the first and second units. The second unit provides less utility than the first unit, the third less than the second, and so on, in accordance with the law of diminishing marginal utility. But total utility, the sum of marginal utilities, rises as long as marginal utility is positive. Figure 1(b) shows marginal utility. Notice that when marginal utility is zero, total utility is at its maximum. When marginal utility is negative, total utility declines.

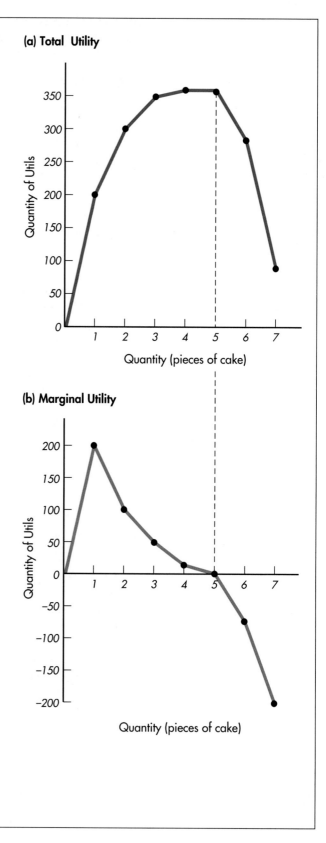

(a) Total Utility

(b) Marginal Utility

period has been defined, diminishing marginal utility will apply; it applies to everyone and to every good and service, except perhaps to income itself, as discussed in the Economic Insight "Does Money Buy Happiness?"

I.d. Consumers Are Not Identical

Does one more dollar mean less to a millionaire than to a pauper?

All consumers experience diminishing marginal utility, but the rate at which marginal utility declines is not identical for all consumers. This is where tastes and preferences enter the discussion. The rate at which marginal utility diminishes depends on an individual's tastes and preferences. Stephanie clearly enjoys chocolate cake. For a person who dislikes the calories associated with the cake, the first piece might yield 200 utils and the second might yield none.

I.e. An Illustration: "All You Can Eat"

What does "all you can eat" really mean?

The principle of diminishing marginal utility says something about "all you can eat" specials. It says that you will stop eating when marginal utility is zero. At some restaurants consumers who pay a fixed charge may eat as much as they desire. The only restriction is that the restaurant does not allow "doggy bags." Because diminishing marginal utility eventually sets in, all consumers eventually stop eating when their marginal utility is zero. This is the point at which their total utility is at a maximum: one more bite would be distasteful and would decrease utility. The restaurant must determine what fixed price to charge. Knowing that no consumer will eat forever—that each will stop when his or her marginal utility is zero—the restaurant must set a price that yields a profit from the average consumer.

RECAP

1. Utility is a concept used to represent the degree to which goods and services satisfy wants.
2. Total utility is the total satisfaction that a consumer obtains from consuming a particular good or service.
3. Marginal utility is the utility that an additional unit of a good or service yields.
4. Total utility increases until dissatisfaction sets in. When another unit of a good would yield disutility, the consumer has been filled up with the good—more will not bring greater satisfaction.
5. According to the principle of diminishing marginal utility, marginal utility declines with each additional unit of a good or service that the consumer obtains. When marginal utility is zero, total utility is at its maximum.

How do consumers allocate their limited incomes among the billions of goods and services that exist?

2. UTILITY AND CHOICE

Can we simply conclude that people will consume goods until the marginal utility of each good is zero? No, we cannot, for we would be ignoring opportunity costs. No one has enough income to purchase everything until the

Does Money Buy Happiness?

Diminishing marginal utility affects consumer purchases of every good. Does diminishing marginal utility affect income as well? This question has been a topic of economic debate for years. The case for progressive taxation—the more income you have, the greater the percentage of each additional dollar that you pay in taxes—is based on the idea that the marginal utility of income diminishes. In theory, if each additional dollar brings less utility to a person, the pain associated with giving up a portion of each additional dollar will decline. And as a result of taxing the rich at a higher rate than the poor, the total pain imposed on society from a tax will be less than it would be if the same tax rate were applied to every dollar.

Economists have attempted to confirm or disprove the idea of the diminishing marginal utility of income, but doing so has proved difficult. Experiments have even been carried out on the topic. In one experiment, laboratory rats were trained to work for pay. They had to hit a bar several times to get a piece of food or a drink of water. After a while, after obtaining a certain amount of food and water, the rats reduced their work efforts, choosing leisure instead of more food and water. Thus, the rats did react as if their "income"—food and water—had a diminishing marginal utility.

Economists have also turned to the literature of psychology. Psychologists have carried out many surveys to measure whether people are more or less happy under various circumstances. One survey back in the 1960s asked

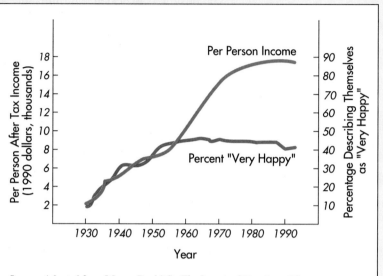

Source: Adapted from Myers, David G., *The Pursuit of Happiness* (New York: William Morrow and Company, Inc., 1992).

people in different income brackets whether they were unhappy, pretty happy, or very happy. The results indicated that the higher income is, the happier people are. A more recent study by David Myers in 1992, however, examined why people are happy and found some results that contradicted the earlier study. Although citizens of the more wealthy nations tend to be happier than citizens of the less wealthy nations, this relationship is not very strong. More important than wealth is the history of democracy; the longer a nation has been democratic, the happier are its citizens. Within any one country, there is only a modest link between well-being and being well-off. "Once we're comfortable, more money therefore provides diminishing returns. The second

helping never tastes as good as the first," says Myers. "The second fifty thousand dollars of income means much less than the first." Myers uses a figure something like the accompanying one to illustrate his findings. Notice how income and percentage who are happy both rise until a 1990 income level of about $7,000 per person after tax is reached. After that income level, as income rises, the percentage who are happy does not change much.

Sources: David G. Myers, *The Pursuit of Happiness* (New York: William Morrow and Company, Inc., 1992); and N. M. Bradburn and D. Caplovitz, *Reports on Happiness* (Chicago: Aldine, 1965), p. 9.

marginal utility of each item is zero. Because incomes are limited, purchasing one thing means not purchasing other things. Stephanie, our cake fancier, might be able to get more utility by purchasing some other good than by buying additional pieces of cake.

To illustrate the effect of opportunity costs on consumption, let's turn again to Stephanie and ask her to allocate a limited income—$10—among three goods: cake, coffee, and mineral water.

2.a. Consumer Choice

Stephanie has a budget of $10 to spend on cake, coffee, and mineral water. How many units of each will she purchase? The answer is in Table 2.

The price (P) of each piece of cake is $2; the price of each cup of coffee is $1; the price of each bottle (6-ounce bottles) of mineral water is $3. The marginal utility (MU) provided by each unit and the ratio of the marginal utility to the price (MU/P) are presented at the top of the table. In the lower part of the table are the steps involved in allocating income among the three goods.

The first purchase involves a choice among the first unit of each of the three goods. The first piece of cake yields a marginal utility (MU) of 200 and costs $2; thus, per dollar of expenditure, the first piece of cake yields 100 utils (MU/P = 100). The first cup of coffee yields a marginal utility per dollar of expenditure of 200. The coffee yields 200 utils and costs $1. The first bottle of water yields a marginal utility per dollar of expenditure of 50; it yields 150 utils and costs $3. Which does Stephanie choose?

To find the answer, compare the ratios of the marginal utility per dollar of expenditure (MU/P), *not* the marginal utility of each good (MU). The ratio of marginal utility to price puts the goods on the same basis (utility per dollar) and allows us to make sense of Stephanie's decisions. Looking only at marginal utilities would not do this. For instance, another diamond might yield 10,000 utils and another apple might yield only 100 utils; but if the diamond costs $100,000 and the apple costs $1, the marginal utility per dollar of expenditure on the apple is greater than the marginal utility per dollar of expenditure on the diamond, and thus a consumer is better off purchasing the apple.

As indicated in Table 2, Stephanie's first purchase is the cup of coffee. It yields the greatest marginal utility per dollar of expenditure; and because it costs $1, Stephanie has $9 left to spend.

The second purchase involves a choice among the first unit of cake, the second unit of coffee, and the first unit of water. The ratios of marginal utility per dollar of expenditure are 100 for cake, 150 for coffee, and 50 for water. Thus, Stephanie purchases the second cup of coffee and has $8 left.

For the third purchase Stephanie must decide between the first unit of cake, the first unit of water, and the third cup of coffee. Because cake yields a ratio of 100 and both the coffee and the water yield ratios of 50, she purchases the cake. The cake costs $2, so she has $6 left to spend.

A utility-maximizing consumer like Stephanie always chooses the purchase that yields the greatest marginal utility per dollar of expenditure. If two goods offer the same marginal utility per dollar of expenditure, the consumer will be indifferent between the two—that is, the consumer won't care

TABLE 2
The Logic of Consumer Choice

Cake (P = $2)			Coffee (P = $1)			Water (P = $3)		
Units	MU	MU/P	Units	MU	MU/P	Units	MU	MU/P
1	200	100	1	200	200	1	150	50
2	98	49	2	150	150	2	90	30
3	50	25	3	50	50	3	60	20
4	10	5	4	30	30	4	30	10
5	0	0	5	0	0	5	9	3
6	−70	−35	6	−300	−300	6	0	0
7	−200	−100	7	−700	−700	7	−6	−2

Steps	Choices		Decision	Remaining Budget
1st purchase	1st cake:	$MU/P = 100$	Coffee	$10 − $1 = $9
	1st coffee:	$MU/P = 200$		
	1st water:	$MU/P = 50$		
2nd purchase	1st cake:	$MU/P = 100$	Coffee	$9 − $1 = $8
	2nd coffee:	$MU/P = 150$		
	1st water:	$MU/P = 50$		
3rd purchase	1st cake:	$MU/P = 100$	Cake	$8 − $2 = $6
	3rd coffee:	$MU/P = 50$		
	1st water:	$MU/P = 50$		
4th purchase	2nd cake:	$MU/P = 49$	Coffee	$6 − $1 = $5
	3rd coffee:	$MU/P = 50$		
	1st water:	$MU/P = 50$		
5th purchase	2nd cake:	$MU/P = 49$	Water	$5 − $3 = $2
	4th coffee:	$MU/P = 30$		
	1st water:	$MU/P = 50$		
6th purchase	2nd cake:	$MU/P = 49$	Cake	$2 − $2 = 0
	4th coffee:	$MU/P = 30$		
	2nd water:	$MU/P = 30$		

Note: Purchases made with $10: 2 pieces of cake, 3 cups of coffee, and 1 bottle of mineral water.

which is chosen. For example, Table 2 indicates that for the fourth purchase another unit of either coffee or water would yield 50 utils per dollar. The consumer is completely indifferent between the two and so arbitrarily selects coffee. Water is chosen for the fifth purchase. With the sixth purchase, the total budget is spent. For $10, Stephanie ends up with 2 pieces of cake, 3 cups of coffee, and 1 bottle of mineral water.

In this example, Stephanie is portrayed as a methodical, robot-like consumer who calculates how to allocate her scarce income among goods and services in a way that ensures that each additional dollar of expenditure yields the greatest marginal utility. This picture is more than a little far-fetched, but it does describe the result if not the process of consumer choice.

ECONOMIC INSIGHT

Rats and Demand

Economists have been troubled by the apparent limitation that economics is a nonexperimental science. Unlike chemists or physicists, economists cannot, it is argued, carry out controlled experiments in which one element is changed while all others remain constant. Several economists have recently challenged that assumption by carrying out experiments with laboratory animals.

In one experiment, rats isolated in cages were given water, root beer, and Collins Mix as consumption alternatives. The water was free, but the rats had to pay for the other drinks. Payment was in the form of pushes on a lever—so many pushes to get a squirt of beverage. Each rat was given a "budget"—a given number of pushes per day—and was then allowed to allocate its income between root beer and Collins Mix. The rats settled into their own consumption patterns. The researchers then experimented with price changes—altering the number of pushes per drink—and income changes—changing the total number of pushes allowed each day. The rats responded to the changes in a manner that would have been predicted by utility maximization and consumer choice. The higher the price, or the more pushes required, the smaller the quantity purchased. The higher the income, the more of both kinds of drinks purchased.

Source: J. H. Kagel, H. Rachlin, L. Green, R. C. Bartalio, R. L. Bassman, and W. R. Klemm, "Experimental Studies of Consumer Demand Behavior Using Laboratory Animals," *Economic Inquiry*, vol. 13, March 1975. Reprinted by permission.

People do have to decide which goods and services to purchase with their limited incomes, and people do select the options that give them the greatest utility. (Lab animals do, too—see the Economic Insight "Rats and Demand.")

2.b. Consumer Equilibrium

equimarginal principle (consumer equilibrium): to maximize utility, consumers must allocate their scarce incomes among goods so as to equate the marginal utilities per dollar of expenditure on the last unit of each good purchased

With $10, Stephanie purchases 2 pieces of cake, 3 cups of coffee, and 1 bottle of water. For the second piece of cake, the marginal utility per dollar of expenditure is 49; for the third cup of coffee, it is 50; and for the first bottle of mineral water, it is 50. Is it merely a fluke that the marginal utility per dollar of expenditure ratios are nearly equal? No. *In order to maximize utility, consumers must allocate their limited incomes among goods and services in such a way that the marginal utilities per dollar of expenditure on the last unit of each good purchased will be as nearly equal as possible.* This is called the **equimarginal principle** and also represents **consumer equilibrium**. It is consumer equilibrium because the consumer will not change from this point unless something changes income, marginal utility, or price.

In our example, the ratios are not equal at consumer equilibrium—49, 50, 50—but they are as close to equal as possible because Stephanie (like all consumers) had to purchase whole portions of food and beverage. Consumers cannot spend a dollar on any good or service and always get the fractional amount a dollar buys—one-tenth of a tennis lesson, or one-third of a bottle of water. Instead, consumers have to purchase goods and services in whole units—1 piece or 1 ounce or 1 package—and pay the per unit price.

The equimarginal principle is simply common sense. Consumers spend an additional dollar on the good that gives the greatest satisfaction. At the prices given in Table 2, with an income of $10, and with the marginal utilities given, Stephanie maximizes her utility by purchasing 2 pieces of cake, 3 cups of coffee, and 1 bottle of mineral water. Everything else held constant, no other allocation of the $10 would yield Stephanie more utility.

Consumers are in equilibrium when they have no incentive to reallocate their limited budget or income. With MU standing for marginal utility and P for price, the general rule for consumer equilibrium is

$$\frac{MU_{cake}}{P_{cake}} = \frac{MU_{water}}{P_{water}} = \frac{MU_{coffee}}{P_{coffee}} = \cdots = \frac{MU_x}{P_x}$$

MU_x/P_x is the marginal utility per dollar of expenditure on any good other than cake, water, or coffee. It represents the opportunity cost of spending $1 on cake, mineral water, or coffee.

RECAP

1. To maximize utility, consumers must allocate their limited incomes in such a way that the marginal utilities per dollar obtained from the last unit consumed are equal among all goods and services; this is the equimarginal principle.

2. As long as the marginal utilities per dollar obtained from the last unit of all products consumed are the same, the consumer is in equilibrium and will not reallocate income.

3. Consumer equilibrium, or utility maximization, is summarized by a formula that equates the marginal utilities per dollar of expenditure on the last item purchased of all goods:

$$MU_a/P_a = MU_b/P_b = MU_c/P_c = MU_x/P_x$$

3. THE DEMAND CURVE AGAIN

We have shown how consumers make choices—by allocating their scarce incomes among goods in order to maximize their utility. The next step is to relate consumer choices to the demand curve.

3.a. The Downward Slope of the Demand Curve

The demand curve or schedule can be derived from consumer equilibrium by altering the price of one good or service.

Recall from Chapter 3 that as the price of a good falls, the quantity demanded of that good rises. This inverse relation between price and quantity demanded arises from diminishing marginal utility and consumer equilibrium.

Consumers allocate their income among goods and services in order to maximize their utility. A consumer is in equilibrium when the total budget is expended and the marginal utilities per dollar of expenditure on the last unit of each good are the same. A change in the price of one good will disturb the consumer's equilibrium; the ratios of marginal utility per dollar of expenditure on the last unit of each good will no longer be equal. The consumer will then reallocate her income among the goods in order to increase total utility.

In the example presented in Table 2, the price of cake is $2 per piece, the price of coffee is $1 per cup, and the price of mineral water is $3 per bottle. With $10, Stephanie purchases 2 pieces of cake, 3 cups of coffee, and 1 bottle of water. The marginal utility per dollar of expenditure on each of the goods is approximately 50. Now suppose the price of cake falls to $1 while the prices of coffee and water and Stephanie's budget of $10 remain the same. Common sense tells us that Stephanie will probably alter the quantities purchased by buying more cake. To find out if she does—and whether the equimarginal principle holds—let's trace her purchases step by step.

The units of each good, their marginal utilities, and the ratios of the marginal utility to price are listed at the top of Table 3. Only the *MU/P* ratio for cake is different from the corresponding figure at the top of Table 2. According to Table 3, at the old consumer equilibrium of 2 pieces of cake, 3 cups of coffee, and 1 bottle of mineral water, the marginal utility per dollar of expenditure (*MU/P*) on each good is:

$$\text{Cake: } 98/\$1 = 98/\$1 \quad \text{Coffee: } 50/\$1 = 50/\$1 \quad \text{Water: } 150/\$3 = 50/\$1$$

Clearly, the ratios are no longer equal. In order to maximize utility, Stephanie must reallocate her budget among the goods. Her choices are shown in the lower portion of Table 3.

Stephanie's first choice now involves the first piece of cake, which yields 200 utils per dollar; the first cup of coffee, which also yields 200 utils per dollar; and the first bottle of water, which yields 50 utils per dollar. She is indifferent between the first piece of cake and the first cup of coffee; we will assume that she chooses cake. Her remaining budget is $9. For her second purchase, she chooses the coffee, and her remaining budget is then $8. When all $10 is spent, Stephanie finds that she has purchased 3 pieces of cake, 4 cups of coffee, and 1 bottle of mineral water. The lower price of cake has induced her to purchase an additional piece of cake. Stephanie's behavior illustrates what you already know: the quantity demanded of cake increases as the price of cake decreases.

If the price of cake were increased to $3 per piece and we traced Stephanie's purchases again, we would find that Stephanie demands only 1 piece of cake. The three prices ($1, $2, $3) and the corresponding quantities of cake purchased give us Stephanie's demand for cake, which is shown in Figure 2. At $3 she is willing and able to buy 1 piece; at $2 she is willing and able to buy 2 pieces; and at $1 she is willing and able to buy 3 pieces.

Stephanie's demand curve is the line connecting points *A*, *B*, and C in Figure 2. This demand curve shows that at a price of $3, Stephanie would purchase 1 piece of cake; at a price of $2, Stephanie would purchase 2 pieces of cake; and at a price of $1, 3 pieces of cake are bought. The demand curve was derived by changing the price of cake *while income, tastes and preferences, prices of related goods, the time period over which consumption occurred, and expectations were held constant.*

3.b. Income and Substitution Effects of a Price Change

When the price of one good falls while everything else is held constant, two things occur: (1) other goods become relatively *more* expensive so consumers buy more of the less expensive good and less of the more expensive goods; and (2) the good purchased prior to the price change now costs less so the consumer can buy more of all goods.

TABLE 3
A Price Change

Cake (P = $1)			Coffee (P = $1)			Water (P = $3)		
Units	MU	MU/P	Units	MU	MU/P	Units	MU	MU/P
1	200	200	1	200	200	1	150	50
2	98	98	2	150	150	2	90	30
3	50	50	3	50	50	3	60	20
4	10	10	4	30	30	4	30	10
5	0	0	5	0	0	5	9	3
6	−70	−70	6	−300	−300	6	0	0
7	−200	−200	7	−700	−700	7	−6	−2

Steps	Choices		Decision	Remaining Budget
1st purchase	1st cake:	$MU/P = 200$	Cake	$10 − $1 = $9
	1st coffee:	$MU/P = 200$		
	1st water:	$MU/P = \ 50$		
2nd purchase	2nd cake:	$MU/P = \ 98$	Coffee	$9 − $1 = $8
	1st coffee:	$MU/P = 200$		
	1st water:	$MU/P = \ 50$		
3rd purchase	2nd cake:	$MU/P = \ 98$	Coffee	$8 − $1 = $7
	2nd coffee:	$MU/P = 150$		
	1st water:	$MU/P = \ 50$		
4th purchase	2nd cake:	$MU/P = \ 98$	Cake	$7 − $1 = $6
	3rd coffee:	$MU/P = \ 50$		
	1st water:	$MU/P = \ 50$		
5th purchase	3rd cake:	$MU/P = \ 50$	Water	$6 − $3 = $3
	3rd coffee:	$MU/P = \ 50$		
	1st water:	$MU/P = \ 50$		
6th purchase	3rd cake:	$MU/P = \ 50$	Cake	$3 − $1 = $2
	3rd coffee:	$MU/P = \ 50$		
	2nd water:	$MU/P = \ 30$		
7th purchase	4th cake:	$MU/P = \ 10$	Coffee	$2 − $1 = $1
	3rd coffee:	$MU/P = \ 50$		
	2nd water:	$MU/P = \ 30$		
8th purchase	4th cake:	$MU/P = \ 10$	Coffee	$1 − $1 = \ 0
	4th coffee:	$MU/P = \ 30$		
	2nd water:	$MU/P = \ 30$		

Note: Purchases made with $10: 3 pieces of cake, 4 cups of coffee, and 1 bottle of mineral water.

The substitution effect indicates that following a decrease in the price of a good or service, an individual will purchase more of the now less-expensive good and less of other goods.

When a good becomes relatively less expensive, it yields more satisfaction per dollar than before, so consumers buy more of it than before as they decrease their expenditures on other goods. This is the *substitution effect* of a price change.

Figure 2 shows that at the price of $2 per piece of cake, Stephanie spends $4 on cake. When the price falls to $1, she spends only $2 for those two

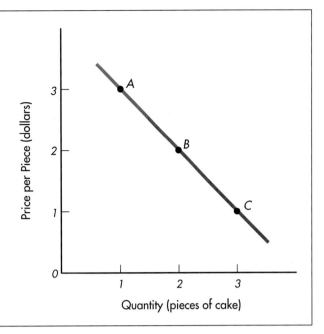

Figure 2
Stephanie's Demand Curve for Cake
The demand curve shows that Stephanie purchases 1 piece of cake at a price of $3, 2 pieces at a price of $2, and 3 pieces at a price of $1.

The income effect of a price change indicates that an individual's income can buy more of all goods when the price of one good declines, everything else held constant.

pieces of cake. As a result, Stephanie can purchase more of all goods, including the good whose price has fallen. This is the *income effect* of a price change.

The income and substitution effects of a price change usually refer to one specific good, but as discussed in the Economic Insight "Exchange Rates, Foreign Goods, and Income and Substitution Effects," they can apply to all the goods produced in one country.

3.c. Consumer Surplus

An individual's demand curve measures the value that the individual consumer places on each unit of the good being considered. For example, the value that Stephanie places on the first piece of cake is the price she would be willing and able to pay for it. The price Stephanie would be willing to pay for one piece of cake is $3, as shown in Figure 3. Interestingly, Stephanie does not have to pay as much for the cake as she is willing to pay. She only has to pay $2 for the piece of cake. At a price of $2, Stephanie purchases two pieces of cake. She is willing to pay $3 for the first piece and $2 for the second piece, but she gets both pieces for $2 each. She gets a bonus because the value she places on the cake is higher than the price she has to pay for it. This bonus is called *consumer surplus*.

consumer surplus:
the difference between what the consumer is willing to pay for a unit of a good and the price that the consumer actually has to pay

Consumer surplus is a measure of the difference between what a consumer is willing and able to pay and the market price of a good. At a market price of $2, Stephanie's consumer surplus is equal to ($3 − $2) + ($2 − $2) = $1, shown as the blue area in Figure 3. At a price of $1, Stephanie is willing and able to purchase 3 pieces of cake, but only the third piece is worth only $1 to her. The first two pieces are worth more than the $1 she has to pay for them. When she purchases the cake, she gets a bonus of ($3 − $1) + ($2 − $1) + ($1 − $1) = $3, shown as the sum of the yellow and blue areas.

Figure 3
Consumer Surplus and the Demand for Cake
The demand curve shown in Figure 2 is reproduced
here. Stephanie is willing and able to pay $3 for the
first piece of cake. She is willing to pay $2 for the sec-
ond piece of cake. If the market price of cake is $2, she
can buy both the first and the second pieces for $2
each; and she receives a bonus on the first piece, paying less for it than she is willing and able to pay. This
bonus, the consumer surplus, is indicated by the blue
area. At a price of $1, the consumer surplus is both the
blue and yellow areas.

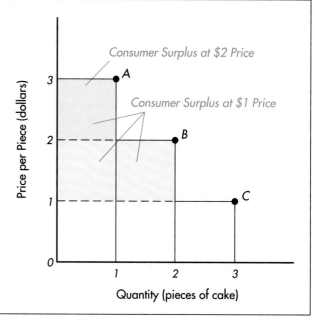

3.d. Disneyland and Consumer Surplus

Why do Disneyland, Sea
World, and other businesses
charge an admission fee and
then provide the use of the
facilities for no extra charge?

Consumer surplus provides a basis for explaining aspects of consumer, producer, and government behavior. Let's consider how consumer surplus can
play a part in determining a firm's pricing strategy.

Disneyland has experimented with several different pricing schemes since
opening its gates 40 years ago. At one stage patrons paid a small admission
fee and could purchase ride or exhibit tickets one by one. Now Disneyland,
Disney World, and the Disney Worlds in France and Japan have forgone the
pricing of individual rides and exhibits for a larger admission fee. Consumers
pay an admission fee that enables them to go on any ride or in any exhibit as
many times as desired.

Suppose consumers enjoy the rides at Disneyland according to the utility
schedule shown in Table 4. If Disneyland does not charge for rides, consumers who enter the park will want to take in no more than 7 rides, since
the seventh ride provides them zero marginal utility. At a price above zero,
consumers will participate in rides until the marginal utility of a ride is equal
to the marginal utility of anything else that money could be used for, presum-
ably a number of rides less than 7.

The consumers' demand schedule and demand curve for rides at
Disneyland are shown in Figure 4. At $7 per ride, no one wants to ride. At $6
per ride, each consumer purchases 1 ride and Disneyland obtains the total
revenue that results when the price listed is multiplied by the quantity. That
amount is the area bounded by A, B, J, L in the graph in Figure 4. At a price
of $5 per ride, each consumer buys 2 rides and Disneyland earns the total
revenue in area A, C, I, M. At a price of $2 per ride, each consumer buys 5
rides and Disneyland earns the revenue in area A, D, F, N. What should
Disneyland charge? If Disneyland wants to maximize its total revenue, it must
get the consumer to pay an amount equal to the value the consumer places on
the rides—that is, Disneyland must collect the entire consumer surplus.

TABLE 4
The Utility of Rides at Disneyland

Number of Rides	Marginal Utility	Total Utility
1	100	100
2	90	190
3	70	260
4	50	310
5	25	335
6	10	345
7	0	345
8	−10	335
9	−20	315

Consumer surplus varies from individual to individual, but let's assume that Figure 4 represents the average individual's demand curve for rides. The consumer surplus is the area that lies below the demand curve and above the per ride price. Figure 4 shows that at $5 per ride, 2 rides are purchased and consumer surplus is the area bounded by *M, I, K*. At $2 per ride, 5 rides are purchased and consumer surplus is the area bounded by *N, F, K*.

Figure 4
Consumer Surplus and the Demand for Rides at Disneyland
The demand schedule and demand curve for rides at Disneyland are shown. Disneyland wants to set a price that extracts as much of the consumer surplus as possible. The consumer surplus at a zero price per ride is shown as the area bounded by *A, E, K*. By setting an admission price equal to the consumer surplus and a zero price per ride, Disneyland can extract the full consumer surplus, the area below the demand curve and above the price.

Price per Ride	Quantity Demanded
$7	0
6	1
5	2
4	3
3	4
2	5
1	6
0	7

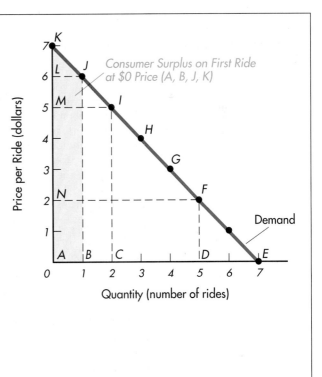

Exchange Rates, Foreign Goods, and Income and Substitution Effects

Typically when the price of a good or service falls, people purchase more of that good because of the income and substitution effects of the price change. For instance, when the price of hardcover books falls, consumers will purchase more hardcover books. The lower price of the hardcover books means that more consumers will give up purchases of softcover books to purchase the hardcover books. In addition, because the price of the hardcover books has fallen, consumers who would have paid the higher price now have more income available to spend on all goods. But the income and substitution effects refer to consumer responses to the change in a price of one specific good or service. What occurs when the prices of *all* of a nation's goods rise?

The value of the dollar refers to the number of units of foreign currency it takes to buy one dollar, that is, the exchange rate. During the early 1980s, the dollar was rising in value relative to the Japanese yen and the German mark, and U.S. manufacturers were complaining about the negative impacts of the rising dollar on their sales. Why? Suppose one dollar costs 150 yen and then the dollar rises in value so that one dollar costs 160 yen. A shirt priced at $20 in the United States would be priced at ¥3,000 in Japan before the exchange rate change and ¥3,200 after. Japanese households, facing higher prices for goods made in the United States, would purchase Japanese-made goods instead—the substitution effect. Japanese households also would have had less dis-

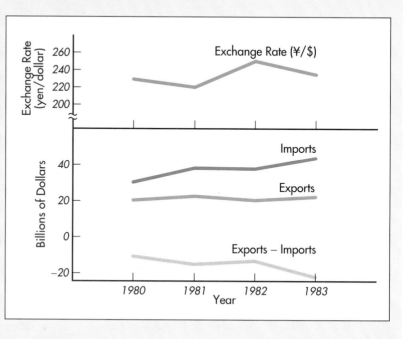

cretionary income had they purchased the same amount of U.S.-made goods. So they would purchase fewer U.S.-made goods— the income effect of the exchange rate change. At the same time, U.S. households would face lower prices for Japanese-made goods. When the dollar rises in value relative to foreign currencies, foreign currencies cost fewer dollars. A Japanese car priced at $15,000 in the United States before the exchange rate change would be $14,063 after the change. Thus, U.S. households would substitute Japanese-made products for U.S.-made products—the substitution effect. And, because they now had more discretionary income, U.S. households would purchase more of all goods, including perhaps some U.S. goods, but also Japanese

goods—the income effect of the exchange rate change. The two effects together would mean fewer total sales of U.S.-made products. It would seem understandable that the U.S. manufacturers were upset by the rising value of the dollar.

The exchange rate between the dollar and the yen, the sales of U.S. goods to Japan (exports), the purchases of Japanese goods by the United States (imports), and the difference between exports and imports are shown in the figure for the years 1980–1983. Notice that as the dollar rose in the early 1980s and then remained high, increasingly more was purchased from Japan than was sold to Japan, as suggested by our discussion of income and substitution effects of the exchange rate change.

TABLE 5
Consumer Surplus and the Demand
for Rides at Disneyland

Ride	Consumer Surplus
1	$6 − $0 = $ 6
2	5 − 0 = 5
3	4 − 0 = 4
4	3 − 0 = 3
5	2 − 0 = 2
6	1 − 0 = 1
7	0 − 0 = 0
Total	$21

If Disneyland charges nothing per ride, total demand is satisfied but Disneyland's revenue is zero. However, by placing an admission charge equal to total consumer surplus, Disneyland is able to collect the entire consumer surplus. At a per ride price of zero, the consumer surplus is about $21. The consumer surplus is calculated in Table 5 by subtracting a zero price from the price the consumer is willing and able to pay for each unit. For instance, the consumer is willing and able to pay $6 for the first ride. Consumer surplus for the first ride, if the price of that ride equals zero, is $6 − $0 = $6. The consumer is willing and able to pay $5 for the second ride; thus, the consumer surplus of that second ride, at a zero price, is $5. Calculating the total consumer surplus at a zero price tells Disneyland that the admission charge has to be about $21 to pick up the entire consumer surplus.

The admission policy is compared to a policy of charging per ride in Table 6. The greatest revenue is obtained when a price of either $3 or $4 is set. There, total revenue is $12. You can see in this example how the per-ride pricing policy generates significantly less revenue than the admission-only pricing policy.

TABLE 6
Pricing Policies

Price per Ride	Rides Taken	Revenue
$7	0	$ 0
6	1	6
5	2	10
4	3	12
3	4	12
2	5	10
1	6	6

RECAP

1. The principle of diminishing marginal utility and the equimarginal principle account for the inverse relation between the price of a product and the quantity demanded.

2. A price change triggers the substitution effect and the income effect.

3. The substitution effect occurs because once a good becomes less expensive, it yields more satisfaction per dollar than before and consumers buy more of it than before. They do this by decreasing their purchases of other goods. The income effect of the price change occurs because a lower price raises real income (total utility) and the consumer purchases more of all goods.

4. Consumer surplus is the excess of the amount consumers are willing and able to pay for an item over the price they actually pay.

4. MARKET DEMAND

By assuming that everyone wants to maximize his or her utility, we are able to examine the quantities of a good that an individual consumer is willing and able to buy at various prices. We know that consumers will reach the consumer equilibrium point, a point where they have expended their budget and where one dollar of additional expenditure on any good or service will yield the same marginal utility. Using this consumer equilibrium point, we are able to see what occurs to the quantity demanded of a good or service as the price of that good or service changes. A change in the price of one good or service changes the ratio of MU/P for that good or service, thereby throwing the consumer out of equilibrium. The consumer will reallocate her budget until she again reaches a consumer equilibrium point.

The process of changing the price of a good and allowing the consumer to reallocate her income among all goods and services until a new equilibrium point is reached allows us to derive the individual's demand curve. This process identifies the determinants of demand, those factors that cause the demand curve to shift. For instance, to derive the demand curve for a good, the only thing that we allowed to change was the price of that good. Tastes and preferences, represented as MU, did not change; income did not change. Thus, anything that changes tastes and preferences or income causes the demand curve to shift.

A different consumer equilibrium point is likely to occur for each individual. We do not have the same tastes and preferences, nor do we have the same incomes. Yet, for all consumers, the process of allocating their limited income among all the goods and services they would like to have in order to maximize their utility is the same.

4.a. From Individual Demands to Market Demand

The market demand curve is the sum of all the individual demand curves. If there are only two consumers, Stephanie and Roger, the demand for cake by Stephanie plus the demand by Roger is the market demand for cake. Figure 5 shows Stephanie's and Roger's individual demand schedules and curves, and

Figure 5
Market Demand
Market demand is the summation of the individual consumer demands. In this example, the market consists of two consumers, Stephanie and Roger, and the market demand is merely the sum of their individual demands. At $2, Stephanie purchases 2 units, Roger 3, so the market quantity demanded is 5. Similarly, the individual consumer surpluses may be added together to obtain the market consumer surplus. Stephanie's consumer surplus at a price of $2 is the area under her demand curve and above $2; Roger's consumer surplus is the area under his demand curve and above $2. The total consumer surplus is the area under the market demand curve and above the $2 price line in Figure 5(c).

| | Quantities Demanded by | | |
Price	Stephanie	Roger	Market Demand
$4	0	1	1
3	1	2	3
2	2	3	5
1	3	5	8
0.5	4	7	11

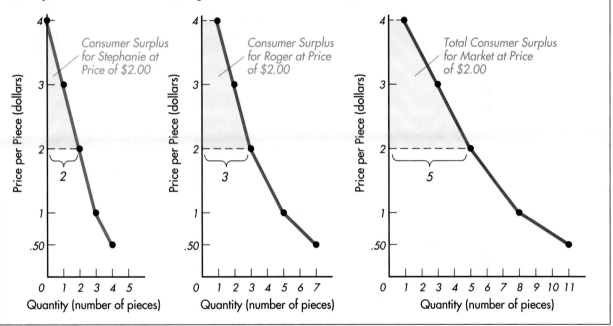

(a) Stephanie's Demand   **(b) Roger's Demand**   **(c) Market Demand**

the market demand schedule and curve. As the price of cake gets higher and higher, the quantity demanded in the market declines because fewer consumers purchase the good and because the consumers who do purchase it purchase fewer units. The market demand schedule shows that at $4, Stephanie buys no cake and Roger buys just 1 piece. At $3, Stephanie demands 1 piece, Roger 2 pieces, so the market quantity demanded at $3 is 3.

The market demand is the sum of individual demands. The total consumer surplus is the sum of individual consumer surpluses. The consumer surplus for Stephanie is the area under her demand curve and above the price line, and the consumer surplus for Roger is the area under his demand curve and above the price line. Thus, for the entire market, the consumer surplus is the area under the market demand curve and above the price line. In Figure 5(a), Stephanie's consumer surplus at a price of $2 is the area under her demand

Consumers have many choices. They can purchase the lowest-priced items, the highest-quality items, items with different colors or shapes, items that cause pollution when they are produced, or items that are biodegradeable. Believing that the environment is important to the consumers of the industrial nations, The Body Shop sells only green products. Green refers to environmentally safe products. The British company has branched to several nations with its bodycare products that are environmentally safe and are not animal tested. Although the products are more expensive than many substitute products, enough consumers prefer the green products that The Body Shop has been very successful.

curve and above $2; in Figure 5(b), Roger's consumer surplus is the area under his demand curve and above $2. The total consumer surplus is the sum of the consumer surplus for both Stephanie and Roger. It is the area under the market demand curve and above the $2 price line in Figure 5(c).

4.b. Review of the Determination of Market Demand

Individual demand comes from utility maximization. Individuals allocate their scarce incomes among goods in order to get the greatest utility; this occurs when consumer equilibrium is reached, represented in symbols as $MU_a/P_a = MU_b/P_b = \ldots = MU_x/P_x$. As the price of a good or service is changed, consumer equilibrium is disturbed. In response to the price change, individuals alter their purchases so as to achieve maximum utility. The process of changing the price of one good or service while income, tastes and preferences, and the prices of related goods are held constant, defines the individual's demand for that good or service.

Should income, tastes and preferences, or prices of related goods and services change, then the individual's demand will change. More or less income means more or less goods and services can be purchased. But buying more of everything does not mean you are in equilibrium because the rates of diminishing marginal utility vary from good to good. Thus, a change in income affects the ratios of MU/P and thus disturbs consumer equilibrium. When the price of a related good changes, the ratio of marginal utility to price for that good changes, thus disturbing consumer equilibrium. And changes in tastes and preferences, represented as changes in the MUs, also alter consumer equilibrium. In each case a new consumer equilibrium point will be reached. Then, based on the new consumer equilibrium, a new demand curve for a good or service can be derived. The new demand curve will lie inside or outside the former demand curve; thus, the demand curve will have shifted.

Consumer equilibrium shows that the nonprice determinants of demand have their effects through the MUs or the prices of other goods and services.

The market demand curve is the sum of all the individual demand curves. This means that anything that affects the individual curves also affects the market curve. In addition, when we combine the individual demand curves into a market demand curve, the number of individuals to be combined determines the position of the market demand curve. Changes in the number of consumers alters the market demand curve. We thus say that the determinants of demand are tastes and preferences, income, prices of related goods, and number of consumers. Also, recall that diminishing marginal utility is defined for consumption during a specific period of time. Since consumer equilibrium and thus the demand curve depend on diminishing marginal utility, the demand curve is also defined for consumption over a specific period of time. Changes in the time period or changes in expectations will therefore also alter demand.

RECAP

1. The market demand curve is the summation of all individual demand curves.

2. Economists derive the market demand curve for a good by assuming that individual incomes are fixed, that the prices of all goods except the one in question are constant, that each individual's tastes remain fixed, that expectations do not change, that the number of consumers is constant, and that the time period under consideration remains unchanged. A change in any one of these determinants causes the demand curve to shift.

SUMMARY

▲▼ Does one more dollar mean less to a millionaire than to a pauper?

1. Utility is a measure of the satisfaction received from possessing or consuming a good. §1.a

2. *Diminishing marginal utility* refers to the decline in utility received from each additional unit of a good that is consumed during a particular period of time. The more of some good a consumer has, the less desirable is another unit of that good. §1.b

▲▼ What does "all you can eat" really mean?

3. Even if a good is free a consumer will eventually reach a point where one more unit of the good would be undesirable or distasteful, and he or she will not consume that additional unit. §1.e

▲▼ How do consumers allocate their limited incomes among the billions of goods and services that exist?

4. *Consumer equilibrium* refers to the utility-maximizing situation in which the consumer has allocated his or her budget among goods and services in such a way that the marginal utilities per dollar of expenditure on the last unit of any good are the same for all goods. It is represented in symbols as: $MU_a/P_a = MU_b/P_b = MU_c/P_c = \ldots = MU_x/P_x$. §2.b

5. The demand curve slopes down because of diminishing marginal utility and consumer equilibrium. §3.a

6. The income and substitution effects of a price change occur because of diminishing marginal utility and the equimarginal principle. When the price of one good falls while all other

prices remain the same, it yields more satisfaction per dollar than before, so consumers buy more of it than before. §3.b

▲▼ **Why do Disneyland, Sea World, and other businesses charge an admission fee and then provide the use of the facilities for no extra charge?**

7. Consumer surplus is the difference between what a consumer is willing and able to pay for a good and what the consumer must pay for the good. §3.c

8. Consumer surplus is the area under the market demand curve and above the price line. The pricing strategy of an admission fee and no charge per ride is an attempt to extract as much of the consumer surplus as possible. §§3.d, 4.a

9. Market demand is the summation of individual demands. §4.a

KEY TERMS

utility §1.a

diminishing marginal utility §1.b

marginal utility §1.b

disutility §1.b

total utility §1.b

equimarginal principle §2.b

consumer equilibrium §2.b

consumer surplus §3.c

EXERCISES

1. Using the following information, calculate total utility and marginal utility.

   a. Plot the total utility curve.

   b. Plot marginal utility directly below total utility.

   c. At what marginal utility value does total utility reach a maximum?

Number of utils for the 1st unit	300
Number of utils for the 2nd unit	250
Number of utils for the 3rd unit	220
Number of utils for the 4th unit	160
Number of utils for the 5th unit	100
Number of utils for the 6th unit	50
Number of utils for the 7th unit	20
Number of utils for the 8th unit	0
Number of utils for the 9th unit	−50

2. Is it possible for marginal utility to be negative and total utility positive? Explain.

3. Suppose Mary is in consumer equilibrium. The marginal utility of good A is 30 and the price of good A is $2.

   a. If the price of good B is $4, the price of good C is $3, the price of good D is $1, and the price of all other goods and services is $5,

   what is the marginal utility of each of the goods Mary is purchasing?

   b. If Mary has chosen to keep $10 in savings, what is the ratio of MU to P for savings?

4. Using the following utility schedule, derive a demand curve for pizza.

   a. Assume income is $10, the price of each slice of pizza is $1, and the price of each glass of beer is $2. Then change the price of pizza to $2 per slice.

   b. Now change income to $12 and derive a demand curve for pizza.

Slices of Pizza	Total Utility	Glasses of Beer	Total Utility
1	200	1	500
2	380	2	800
3	540	3	900
4	600	4	920
5	630	5	930

5. Using utility explain the following commonly made statements:

   a. I couldn't eat another bite.

b. I'll never get tired of your cooking.

c. The last drop tastes as good as the first.

d. I wouldn't eat broccoli if you paid me.

e. My kid would eat nothing but junk food if I allowed her.

f. Any job worth doing is worth doing well.

6. How would guests' behavior likely differ at a BYOB (bring your own bottle) party and one at which the host provides the drinks? Explain your answer.

7. Consider the Disneyland example discussed in section 3.d.

a. With an admission charge and no charge per ride, we would expect each consumer who enters the park to take more rides than he or she would take if there were a charge per ride. Why?

b. At Disneyland the typical wintertime wait for a ride on the Star Tours or Matterhorn exhibit is 45 minutes, and that wait can triple during the summer. If the park charged for each ride, would you expect shorter or longer waits?

8. A round of golf on a municipal golf course usually takes about 5 hours. At a private country club golf course a round takes less than 4 hours. What accounts for the difference? Would the time spent playing golf be different if golfers paid only an admission fee (membership fee) and no monthly dues or if they paid only a charge per round and no monthly dues?

9. To increase marginal utility, you must decrease consumption (everything else held constant). This statement is correct even though it sounds strange. Explain why.

10. Suppose that the marginal utility of good A is 4 times the marginal utility of good B, but the price of good A is only 2 times larger than the price of good B. Is this point consumer equilibrium? If not, what will occur?

11. Last Saturday you went to a movie and ate a large box of popcorn and two candy bars and drank a medium soda. This Saturday you went to a movie and ate a medium box of popcorn and one candy bar and drank a large soda. Your tastes and preferences did not change. What could explain the different combinations of goods you purchased?

12. Peer pressure is an important influence on the behavior of youngsters. For instance, many preteens begin smoking because their friends pressure them into being "cool" by smoking. Using utility theory, how would you explain peer pressure?

13. Many people who earn incomes below some level receive food stamps from the government. Economists argue that these people would be better off if the government gave them the cash equivalent of the food stamps rather than the food stamps. What is the basis of the economists' argument?

14. Suppose you are in consumer equilibrium and have chosen to work 10 hours a day, leaving the other 14 hours each day for leisure activities (leisure includes sleeping and anything other than working on the job).

a. How might you change your behavior if your wage rate per hour rises?

b. What are the income and substitution effects of the price change?

c. What would occur if the income effect is larger than the substitution effect?

15. What is the impact on charitable giving of a reduction in the tax rate on income? Will the lower tax rate lead to more or to less charitable giving?

"'Made in America' Becomes Hard to Label"

The recent buy-America binge has raised the question of just which common products are, in fact, made by American companies. Here's a quiz:

1. The parent company of Braun household appliances is:
   a. Swiss
   b. German
   c. American
   d. Japanese

2. Bic pens are:
   a. Japanese
   b. Czech
   c. American
   d. French

3. The maker of Haagen-Dazs ice cream is based in:
   a. France
   b. Sweden
   c. Britain
   d. America

4. RCA televisions are made by a company based in:
   a. Japan
   b. America
   c. France
   d. Korea

5. The parent of Green Giant vegetables is:
   a. German
   b. Italian
   c. American
   d. British

6. Godiva chocolate is:
   a. French
   b. Belgian
   c. Swiss
   d. American

7. Vaseline's owner is:
   a. American
   b. French
   c. Anglo-Dutch
   d. German

8. Wrangler jeans are:
   a. American
   b. French
   c. Korean
   d. Canadian

9. Holiday Inns are owned by a company based in:
   a. France
   b. America
   c. Britain
   d. Saudi Arabia

10. Tropicana orange juice is owned by a company based in:
    a. Brazil
    b. Canada
    c. Mexico
    d. America

Answers. 1. c (Gillette Co.), 2. d (Bic SA), 3. c (Grand Metropolitan PLC), 4. c (Thomson SA), 5. d (Grand Metropolitan), 6. d (Campbell Soup Co.), 7. c (Unilever PLC), 8. a (VF Corp.), 9. c (Bass PLC), 10. b (Seagram Co. Ltd)

NEW YORK—What's an American product? Is it a TV made by U.S. based Zenith at a Mexican plant? A General Motors car assembled at a California factory half owned by Toyota? A Gap polo shirt sewn in Honduras from cloth cut in the United States?

To truly be American, you can't drive a Chevrolet Lumina sedan (assembled in Canada), eat at Burger King (owned by a British company) or buy groceries at the A&P (German-controlled). And don't think of munching a Nestle's Crunch bar (Swiss) while watching a Columbia Pictures movie (Japanese) at a Cineplex Odeon theater (Canadian).

Identical products on a store shelf may be imported or domestic depending on when they were ordered. Seemingly American brands often are foreign owned. And foreign brands can be made in the United States.

"Almost any one product weighing more than 10 pounds and costing more than $10 these days is a global composite, combining parts or services from many different nations," says Robert B. Reich, a Harvard political economist [currently President Clinton's Labor Secretary]. . . .

Members of Congress have backed legislation to protect the U.S. auto industry. Business groups have aired "pro-American" ads. . . . Cities and towns have canceled orders to Japan.

"We're losing our shirts in this country. We're losing our dresses too," begins a television ad by the Crafted With Pride in the U.S.A. Council, a textile industry marketing group.

"The worst part is we're doing this to ourselves because we're buying so many imports," the voice-over says. "The time to look out for ourselves is now. Buy American, and we won't have to throw in the towel."

"'Made in America' Becomes Hard to Label," Stefan Fatsis and Bart Ziegler, *San Francisco Examiner*, Feb. 2, 1992, pp. E–1, E–4. 1992 © Fatsis and Ziegler

San Francisco Examiner/February 2, 1992

Commentary

The logic of consumer choice indicates that consumers will allocate their limited budgets among the goods and services they desire until the marginal utility from spending an additional dollar on any good or service is the same. This point is known as consumer equilibrium:

$$MU_a/P_a = MU_b/P_b = MU_c/P_c = \ldots MU_x/P_x$$

All factors that affect the ratios of marginal utility to price affect consumer choice. For instance, if good a represents American goods and goods b, c, etc., are foreign goods, and if American consumers develop a preference for goods made in America, then the ratio of MU_a/P_a rises relative to the ratios MU_b/P_b, etc. Specifically, MU_a rises and MU_b, MU_c and others decline. Consumer equilibrium is disturbed and changes in consumer purchases will result.

Since the consumer can gain more utility by spending a dollar on American goods than can be gained spending a dollar on foreign goods, the consumer purchases more American goods. The demand curve for American goods shifts out while the demand curve for foreign goods shifts in. These shifts mean that more American goods are sold, more resources are necessary to produce more American goods (more jobs are created), and more income is generated by those involved in producing and selling the American goods. Conversely, with fewer foreign goods sold, fewer resources are required by the producers of the foreign goods and less income is generated by those involved in producing and selling the foreign goods.

While the frenzy over "buy American" has induced many American consumers to buy what they thought were American products, this fervor has not been well placed. Although consumer tastes and preferences were altered, the reality is that purchasing decisions have not been fully informed. It is difficult in this global economy to know just what *is* American. Switching purchases from a good that seems to be foreign to a good that seems to be American may benefit some Americans and harm others. A switch from Hondas to Geos would benefit those affiliated with Geo and harm those affiliated with Honda, but there may be as many Americans affiliated with Honda as there are with Geo.

Another result of the "buy American" campaign was that Congress restricted the flow of foreign goods into the United States. This import limitation affects consumer equilibrium. In one sense, it says that fewer goods will be available to American consumers than the consumers desire; with smaller quantities of good b, the ratio of MU_b/P_b will be higher than it would be in equilibrium. As consumers attempt to purchase good b, the price of the good will rise. P_b will continue to rise until consumer equilibrium is re-established. The price rise means that consumer equilibrium is re-established but possibly at a level that includes less of all goods, including the American good, a. The restriction on consumer choice by Congress ends up harming consumers and American producers as well.

6

Indifference Analysis

Indifference analysis is an alternative approach to utility theory for explaining consumer choice but does not require us to rely on the concept of utility. Some economists prefer to use indifference analysis instead of utility theory to explain consumer choice, and some prefer to present both approaches. Since both approaches yield the same results, we just briefly discuss indifference analysis.

1. INDIFFERENCE CURVES

In Figure 1, the four combinations of cake and coffee listed in the table are plotted in Figure 1(a). Rationally preferring more to less, the consumer will clearly prefer *C* to the other combinations. Combination *C* is preferred to *B* because *C* offers one more cup of coffee and the same amount of cake as *B*. Combination *C* is preferred to *A* because *C* offers 1 more piece of cake and 1 more cup of coffee than *A*. And combination *C* is preferred to *D* because one more piece of cake is obtained with no loss of coffee. Combinations *B* and *D* are preferred to *A*; however, it is not obvious whether *B* is preferred to *D* or *D* is preferred to *B*.

indifferent:
lacking any preference

indifference curve:
a curve showing all combinations of two goods that the consumer is indifferent among

Let's assume that the consumer has no preference between *B* and *D*. We thus say that the consumer is **indifferent** between combination *B* (2 pieces of cake and 1 cup of coffee) and combination *D* (1 piece of cake and 2 cups of coffee). Connecting points *B* and *D*, as in Figure 1(b), produces an indifference curve. An **indifference curve** shows all the combinations of two goods that the consumer is indifferent among, or, in other words, an indifference curve shows all the combinations of goods that will give the consumer the same level of total utility.

The quantity of goods increases as the distance from the origin increases. Thus, any combination lying on the indifference curve (like *B* or *D*) is preferred to any combination falling below the curve, or closer to the origin (like *A*). Any combination appearing above the curve, or farther from the origin (like *C*), is preferred to any combination lying on the curve.

1.a. The Shape of Indifference Curves

The most reasonable shape for an indifference curve is a downward slope from left to right, indicating that as less of one good is consumed, more of

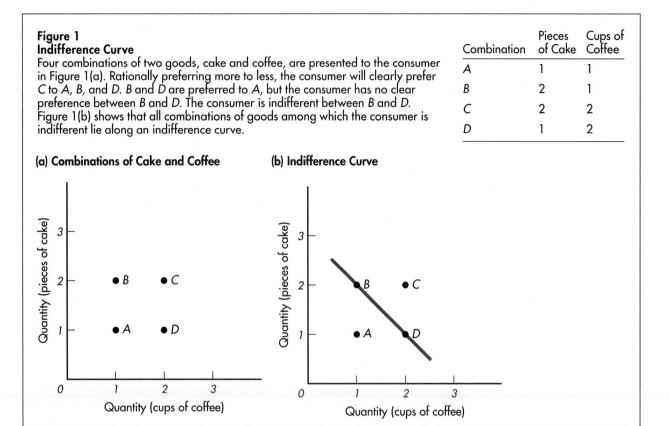

Figure 1
Indifference Curve
Four combinations of two goods, cake and coffee, are presented to the consumer in Figure 1(a). Rationally preferring more to less, the consumer will clearly prefer C to A, B, and D. B and D are preferred to A, but the consumer has no clear preference between B and D. The consumer is indifferent between B and D. Figure 1(b) shows that all combinations of goods among which the consumer is indifferent lie along an indifference curve.

Combination	Pieces of Cake	Cups of Coffee
A	1	1
B	2	1
C	2	2
D	1	2

(a) Combinations of Cake and Coffee

(b) Indifference Curve

another good is consumed. Indifference curves are not likely to be vertical, horizontal, or upward sloping. They do not touch the axes, and they do not touch each other.

An indifference curve that is a vertical line, like the one labeled I_v in Figure 2(a), would mean that the consumer is indifferent to combinations B and A. For most goods this will not be the case because combination B provides more of one good with no less of the other good.

Similarly, horizontal indifference curves, such as line I_h in Figure 2(b), are ruled out for most goods. People are not likely to be indifferent between combinations A and B along the horizontal curve since B provides more of one good with no less of the other good than A.

An upward-sloping curve, such as I_u in Figure 2(c), would mean that the consumer is indifferent between a combination of goods that provides less of everything and a combination that provides more of everything (compare points A and B). Rational consumers tend to prefer more to less.

1.b. The Slope of Indifference Curves

The slope, or steepness, of indifference curves is determined by consumer preferences. The amount of one good that a consumer must give up to get an additional unit of the other good and remain equally satisfied changes as the consumer trades off one good for the other. The less a consumer has of a good, the more the consumer values an additional unit of that good. This preference is shown by an indifference curve that bows in toward the origin,

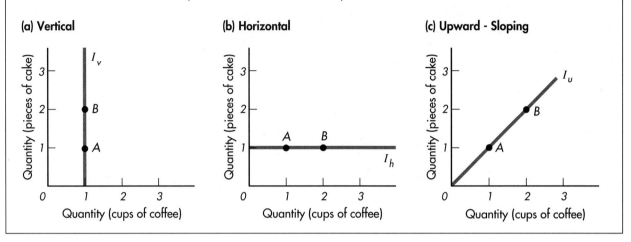

Figure 2
Unlikely Shapes of Indifference Curves
A vertical indifference curve, as in Figure 2(a), would violate the condition that more is preferred to less, as would a horizontal indifference curve, as in Figure 2(b), or an upward-sloping curve, as in Figure 2(c). Thus, indifference curves are not likely to have any of these shapes.

(a) Vertical

(b) Horizontal

(c) Upward - Sloping

like the curve shown in Figure 3. A consumer who has 4 pieces of cake and 1 cup of coffee (point *D*) may be willing to give up 2 pieces of cake for 1 more cup of coffee, moving from *D* to *E*. But a consumer who has only 2 pieces of cake may be willing to give up only 1 piece to get that additional cup of coffee. This preference is shown as the move from *E* to *F*.

1.c. Indifference Curves Cannot Cross

Indifference curves do not intersect. If the curves crossed, two combinations of goods that are clearly not equally preferred by the consumer would seem to be equally preferred. According to Figure 4, the consumer is indifferent

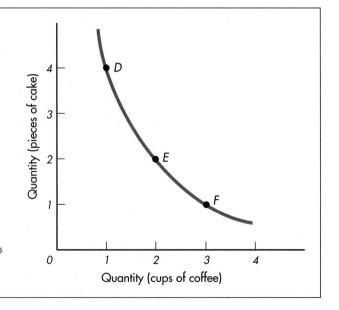

Figure 3
Bowed-in Indifference Curve
Indifference curves slope down from left to right and bow in toward the origin. They bow in because consumers value a good relatively more if they have less of it, ceteris paribus. At the top of the curve, where a little coffee and a lot of cake are represented by point *D*, the consumer is willing to give up 2 pieces of cake to get 1 cup of coffee. But lower down on the curve, such as at point *E*, the consumer has more coffee and less cake than at point *D* and thus is willing to give up less cake to get 1 more cup of coffee.

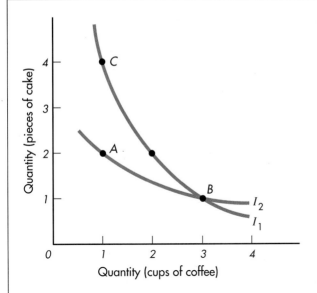

Figure 4
Indifference Curves Do Not Cross
If two indifference curves intersected, such as at point B, then the consumer would be indifferent to all points on each curve. But point C clearly provides more cake than point A and no less coffee, so the consumer will prefer C to A. If the consumer prefers more to less, the indifference curves will not cross.

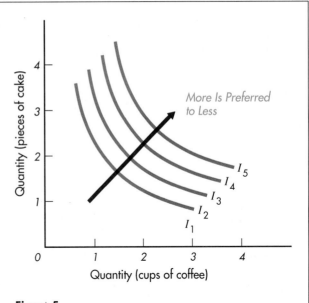

Figure 5
Indifference Map
Indifference curves cover the entire positive quadrant. As we move away from the origin, more is preferred to less: I_5 is preferred to I_4; I_4 is preferred to I_3; and so on.

between A and B along indifference curve I_2 and indifferent between B and C along indifference curve I_1. Thus, the consumer appears to be indifferent among A, B, and C. Combination C, however, offers more cake and no less coffee than combination A. Clearly, the consumer, preferring more to less, will prefer C to A. Thus, indifference curves are not allowed to cross.

I.d. An Indifference Map

indifference map:
a complete set of indifference curves

An **indifference map**, located in the positive quadrant of a graph, indicates the consumer's preferences among all combinations of goods and services. The farther from the origin an indifference curve is, the more the combinations of goods along that curve are preferred. The arrow in Figure 5 indicates the ordering of preferences: I_2 is preferred to I_1; I_3 is preferred to I_2 and I_1; I_4 is preferred to I_3, I_2, and I_1; and so on.

2. BUDGET CONSTRAINT

budget line:
a line showing all the combinations of goods that can be purchased with a given level of income

The indifference map reveals only the combinations of goods and services that a consumer prefers or is indifferent among—what the consumer is *willing* to buy. It does not tell us what the consumer is *able* to buy. Consumers' income levels or budgets limit the amount that they can purchase. Let's suppose a consumer has allocated $6 to spend on coffee and cake. Figure 6 shows the **budget line**, a line giving all the combinations of goods that a budget can buy at given prices.

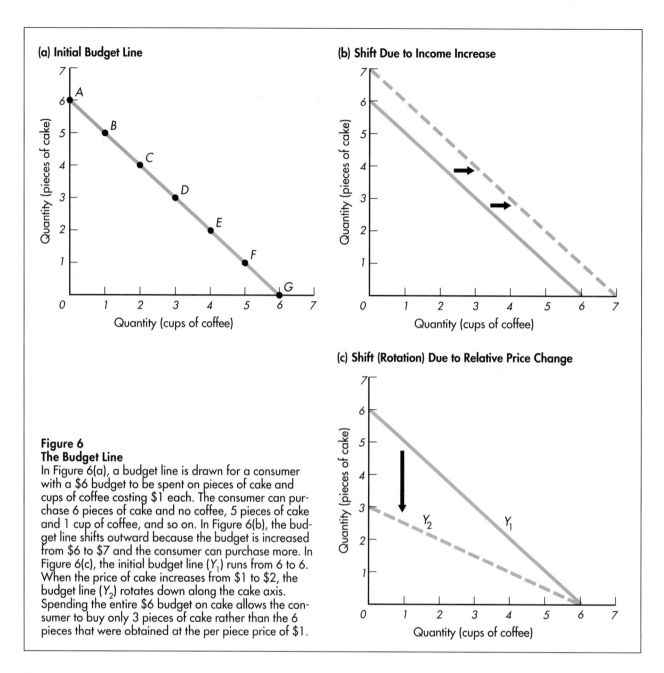

Figure 6
The Budget Line
In Figure 6(a), a budget line is drawn for a consumer with a $6 budget to be spent on pieces of cake and cups of coffee costing $1 each. The consumer can purchase 6 pieces of cake and no coffee, 5 pieces of cake and 1 cup of coffee, and so on. In Figure 6(b), the budget line shifts outward because the budget is increased from $6 to $7 and the consumer can purchase more. In Figure 6(c), the initial budget line (Y_1) runs from 6 to 6. When the price of cake increases from $1 to $2, the budget line ($Y_2$) rotates down along the cake axis. Spending the entire $6 budget on cake allows the consumer to buy only 3 pieces of cake rather than the 6 pieces that were obtained at the per piece price of $1.

Anywhere along the budget line in Figure 6(a), the consumer is spending $6. When the price of cake is $1 per piece and the price of coffee is $1 per cup, the consumer can choose among several different combinations of cake and coffee that add up to $6. If only cake is purchased, 6 pieces of cake can be purchased (point A). If only coffee is purchased, 6 cups of coffee can be purchased (point G). At point B, 5 pieces of cake and 1 cup of coffee can be purchased. At point C, 4 pieces of cake and 2 cups of coffee can be purchased. At point F, 1 piece of cake and 5 cups of coffee can be purchased.

An increase in the consumer's income or budget is shown as an outward shift of the budget line. Figure 6(b) shows an increase in income from $6 to

$7. The budget line shifts out to the line running from 7 to 7. A change in income or in the consumer's budget causes a parallel shift of the budget line.

A change in the price of one of the goods causes the budget line to rotate. For example, with a budget of $6 and the prices of both cake and coffee at $1, we have the budget line Y_1 of Figure 6(c). If the price of cake rises to $2, only 3 pieces of cake can be purchased if the entire budget is spent on cake. As a result, the budget line (Y_2) is flatter, running from 3 on the vertical axis to 6 on the horizontal axis. Conversely, a rise in the price of coffee would cause the budget line to become steeper.

3. CONSUMER EQUILIBRIUM

Putting the budget line on the indifference map allows us to determine the one combination of goods and services that the consumer is both *willing* and *able* to purchase. Any combination of goods that lies on or below the budget line is within the consumer's budget. Which combination will the consumer choose in order to yield the greatest satisfaction (utility)?

The budget line in Figure 7 indicates that most of the combinations along indifference curve I_1 and point C on indifference curve I_2 are attainable. Combinations along indifference curve I_3 are preferred to combinations along I_2, but the consumer is *not able* to buy combinations along I_3 because they cost more than the consumer's budget. Therefore, point C represents the maximum level of satisfaction, or utility, available to the consumer. Point C is the point where the budget line is tangent to (just touches) the indifference curve.

The demand curve for a good can be derived from indifference curves and budget lines by changing the price of one of the goods, leaving everything else the same, and finding the consumer equilibrium points. Budget line Y_1, running from 6 on the vertical axis to 6 on the horizontal axis in Figure 8(a), is the initial budget, in which the price of each piece of cake is $1 and the price of each cup of coffee is $1. We then increase the price of each cup of

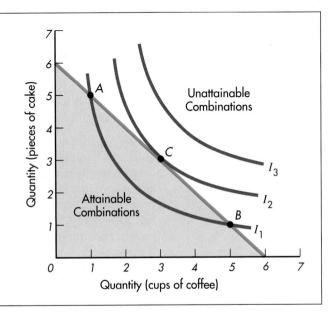

Figure 7
Consumer Equilibrium
The consumer maximizes satisfaction by purchasing the combination of goods that is on the indifference curve farthest from the origin but attainable given the consumer's budget. The combinations along I_1 are attainable, but so are the combinations that lie above I_1. Combinations beyond the budget line, such as those along I_3, cost more than the consumer's budget. Point C, where the indifference curve I_2 just touches, or is tangent to, the budget line, is the chosen combination and the point of consumer equilibrium.

Figure 8
The Demand Curve
By changing the price of one of the goods and leaving everything else the same, we can derive the demand curve. Figure 8(a) shows that as the price of a cup of coffee increases from $1 to $2, the budget line rotates in toward the cake axis. Consumer equilibrium occurs at point E instead of at point C. The consumer is purchasing only 2 cups of coffee at the $2 per cup price, whereas the consumer purchased 3 cups of coffee at the $1 per cup price. Plotting the price of coffee and the number of cups of coffee directly below, in Figure 8(b), yields the demand curve for coffee.

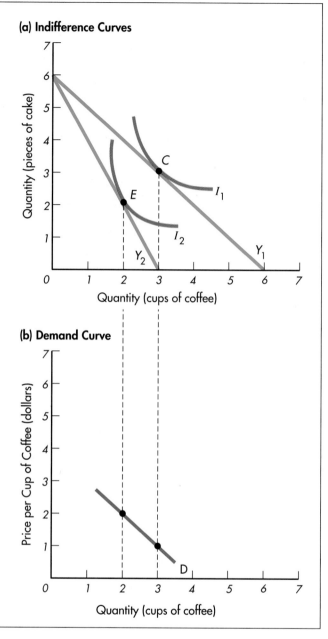

(a) Indifference Curves

(b) Demand Curve

coffee to $2 and draw the second budget line, Y_2, running from 6 units of cake to 3 units of coffee. For each budget (income) line, we draw the indifference curve that is tangent. For Y_1 it is curve I_1; for Y_2 it is curve I_2. The original consumer equilibrium is point C, the tangency between the initial budget line and curve I_1. The point at which the new budget line is just tangent to an indifference curve is the new consumer equilibrium point. This is point E.

At point C, 3 cups of coffee are purchased; at point E, 2 cups of coffee are purchased. By plotting the combinations of price and quantity demanded below the indifference curves, as in Figure 8(b), we trace out the demand curve for coffee.

SUMMARY

1. Indifference curves show all combinations of two goods that give the consumer the same level of total utility. §1

2. An indifference map is a complete set of indifference curves filling up the positive quadrant of a graph. §1.d

3. The indifference curve indicates what the consumer is willing to buy. The budget line indicates what the consumer is able to buy. Together they determine the combination of goods the consumer is willing and able to buy. §§1, 2

4. Consumer equilibrium occurs at the point where the budget line just touches, or is tangent to, an indifference curve. §3

5. The demand curve can be derived from the indifference curves and budget lines. A change in the relative price causes the budget line to rotate and become tangent to an indifference curve at a different quantity of goods. As the price of one good rises relative to the price of another, the quantity demanded of the higher-priced good falls. §3

KEY TERMS

indifferent §1
indifference curve §1

indifference map §1.d
budget line §2

EXERCISES

1. Use these combinations to answer a and b questions:

Combination	Clothes	Food
A	1 basket	1 pound
B	1 basket	2 pounds
C	1 basket	3 pounds
D	2 baskets	1 pound
E	2 baskets	2 pounds
F	2 baskets	3 pounds
G	3 baskets	1 pound
H	3 baskets	2 pounds
I	3 baskets	3 pounds

a. If more is preferred to less, which combinations are clearly preferred to other combinations? Rank the combinations in the order of preference.

b. Some clothes-food combinations cannot be clearly ranked. Why not?

2. Explain why two indifference curves cannot cross.

3. Using the data that follow, plot two demand curves for cake. Then explain what could have led to the shift of the demand curve.

I. Price of Cake	Quantity of Cake Demanded	II. Price of Cake	Quantity of Cake Demanded
$1	10	$1	14
$2	8	$2	10
$3	4	$3	8
$4	3	$4	6
$5	1	$5	5

7

Elasticity: Demand and Supply

FUNDAMENTAL QUESTIONS

1. How do we measure whether and how much consumers alter their purchases in response to a price change?

2. How does a business determine whether to increase or decrease the price of the product it sells in order to increase revenues?

3. Why might senior citizens or children receive price discounts relative to the rest of the population?

4. What determines whether consumers alter their purchases a little or a lot in response to a price change?

5. How do we measure whether and how much income changes or changes in the prices of related goods affect consumer purchases?

6. How do we measure whether and how much producers respond to a price change?

The cleanup of Boston Harbor has been enormously expensive. To help pay for it, the city of Boston imposed huge increases in water rates. The city soon learned, however, that the fee increase did not generate the amount of revenue it had anticipated. The soaring water rates induced firms like Legal Sea Foods and even some households to drill their own wells to avoid paying the high fees. Should Boston city officials fear that their fee increases will actually result in *lower* revenues?

In 1992, the Gap, Ford Motor Company, Procter & Gamble, and Compaq Computers implemented a strategy of reducing prices on all their products in order to increase sales. Was this a good strategy? Did sales rise for these companies?

Few doubt that consumers *do* respond to price changes. The question is, how large is their response? The answer to this question is vitally important to businesses and government agencies trying to determine whether and by how much to raise prices. The law of demand tells us that consumers will

buy less of a product if the price of that product rises, but the law of demand does not indicate *how much* sales will decline. Economists have devised measures of how much consumers alter their purchases in response to price changes. These measures are called *elasticities*.

Elasticity is a measure of responsiveness. It is used most often to measure the magnitude of consumer responses to price changes, but it can also be used to measure consumer responses to changes in the determinants of demand or to measure seller responses to price changes. You will see that elasticity is important not only to firms in setting and changing price but to the government in setting certain policies.

I. THE PRICE ELASTICITY OF DEMAND

How do we measure whether and how much consumers alter their purchases in response to a price change?

The price elasticity of demand is a measure of the magnitude by which consumers alter the quantity of some product they purchase in response to a change in the price of that product. The more price-elastic demand is, the more responsive consumers are to a price change—that is, the more they will adjust their purchases of a product when the price of that product changes. Conversely, the less price-elastic demand is, the less responsive consumers are to a price change.

Grocery shopping in many nations does not resemble the once-a-week trip to the super-market most households in the United States make. This Indian woman and her child make a daily trip to the stores and shops looking for the best produce and the best bargains. Having more time available to devote to grocery shopping means that the price elasticity of demand for the grocery items is higher. A small price change may induce the woman to make a trip to another store; a small price change for someone without the time to make additional trips to the store will not affect purchases.

1.a. The Definition of Price Elasticity

price elasticity of demand: the percentage change in the quantity demanded of a product divided by the percentage change in the price of that product

The **price elasticity of demand** is the percentage change in the quantity demanded of a product divided by the percentage change in the price of that product. For instance, if the quantity of videotapes that are rented falls by 3 percent whenever the price of a videotape rental rises by 1 percent, the price elasticity of demand is 3.

According to the law of demand, whenever the price of a good rises, the quantity demanded of that good falls. Thus, the price elasticity of demand is always negative, which can be confusing when referring to a "very high elasticity"—actually, a large negative number—or to a "low elasticity"—a small negative number. To avoid this confusion, economists use the absolute value of the price elasticity of demand and thus ignore the negative sign. Absolute value, denoted as | |, turns the negative number into a positive one. Thus, denoting the price elasticity of demand as e_d, we have:

$$e_d = |-3\%/1\%| = |-3| = 3$$

Demand can be elastic, unit-elastic, or inelastic. When the price elasticity of demand is greater than 1, demand is said to be *elastic*. For instance, the demand for videotape rentals, according to the example of $e_d = 3$, is elastic. When the price elasticity of demand is 1, demand is said to be *unit-elastic*. For example, if the price of private education rises by 1 percent and the quantity of private education purchased falls by about 1 percent, the price elasticity of demand is

$$e_d = |-1\%/1\%| = 1$$

When the price elasticity of demand is less than 1, demand is said to be *inelastic*. In this case, a 1 percent rise in price brings forth a smaller than 1 percent decline in quantity demanded. For example, if the price of gasoline rises by 1 percent and the quantity of gasoline purchased falls by 0.2 percent, the price elasticity of demand is

$$e_d = |-0.2\%/1\%| = 0.2$$

1.b. Demand Curve Shapes and Elasticity

perfectly elastic demand curve:
a horizontal demand curve indicating that consumers can and will purchase all they want at one price

A **perfectly elastic demand curve** is a horizontal line that shows that consumers can purchase any quantity they want at the single prevailing price. In Figure 1(a), a perfectly elastic demand curve represents the demand for the wheat harvested by a single farmer in Canada. The Canadian farmer is only one small producer of wheat who, because he is just one among many, is unable to charge a price that differs from the price of wheat in the rest of the world. If this farmer's wheat is even slightly more expensive than wheat elsewhere, consumers will shift their purchases away from this farmer and buy the wheat produced by other farmers in Canada and the rest of the world. A perfectly elastic demand means that even the smallest price change will cause consumers to change their consumption by a huge amount, in fact, totally switching purchases to the producer with the lowest prices.

perfectly inelastic demand curve:
a vertical demand curve indicating that there is no change in the quantity demanded as the price changes

A **perfectly inelastic demand curve** is a vertical line illustrating the idea that consumers cannot or will not change the quantity of a good they purchase when the price of the product is changed. Perhaps heroin to an addict is a reasonably vivid example of a good whose demand is perfectly inelastic. The addict will pay almost any price to get the quantity that satisfies the

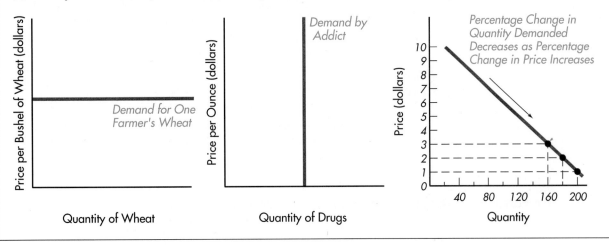

Figure 1
The Price Elasticity of Demand
Figure 1(a), a perfectly elastic demand curve, represents the demand for one farmer's wheat. Because there are so many other suppliers, buyers purchase wheat from the least expensive source. If this farmer's wheat is priced ever so slightly above other farmers' wheat, buyers will switch to another source. Also, because this farmer is just one small producer in a huge market, he can sell everything he wants at the market price. Figure 1(b), a perfectly inelastic demand curve, represents the demand for heroin by a drug addict. A certain quantity is necessary to satisfy the addiction regardless of the price. Figure 1(c) shows that the price elasticity of demand varies along a straight-line demand curve. As we move down the demand curve, the price elasticity varies from elastic to unit-elastic to inelastic.

(a) Perfectly Elastic Demand Curve

(b) Perfectly Inelastic Demand Curve

(c) Straight-Line Demand Curve

addiction. Of course, this behavior holds only over a certain price range. Eventually, the price rises enough that even the addict will have to decrease the quantity demanded. Figure 1(b) shows a perfectly inelastic demand curve.

In between the two extreme shapes of demand curves are the demand curves for most products. Figure 1(c) shows a downward-sloping straight-line demand curve. This type of demand curve is used to illustrate the demand for most goods and services. It is neither perfectly elastic nor perfectly inelastic, but instead, the price elasticity of demand varies from point to point along the downward-sloping straight-line demand curve.

1.b.1. Price Elasticity Along a Straight-Line Demand Curve

The price elasticity of demand declines as we move down a straight-line demand curve.

The price elasticity of demand varies along a straight-line downward-sloping demand curve, declining as we move down the curve. The reason that elasticity changes along the straight-line demand curve is due to the way that elasticity is calculated, not to some intuitive economic explanation.

Along a straight-line demand curve, equal changes in price mean equal changes in quantity. For instance, if price changes by $1 in Figure 1(c), quantity demanded changes by 20 units: as price changes from $1 to $2, quantity demanded falls from 200 to 180; as price changes from $2 to $3, quantity demanded falls from 180 to 160; and so on. Each $1 change in price means a 20-unit change in quantity demanded. But those same amounts (constant amounts of $1 and 20 units) do not translate into constant percentage changes.

A $1 change at the top of the demand curve is a significantly different percentage change from a $1 change at the bottom of the demand curve. A $1 change from $10 is a 10 percent change, but a $1 change from $2 is a 50 percent change. Thus, as we move down the demand curve from higher to lower prices, a given dollar change becomes a larger and larger percentage change in price. The opposite is true of quantity changes. As we move downward along the demand curve, the same change in quantity becomes a smaller and smaller percentage change. A 10-unit change from 20 is a 50 percent change, while a 10-unit change from 200 is a 5 percent change. As we move down the straight-line demand curve, the percentage change in quantity demanded declines while the percentage change in price increases. Because the price elasticity of demand is the ratio of the percentage change in quantity demanded to the percentage change in price, the price elasticity of demand moves close to zero as we move down the straight-line demand curve.

The terms elastic and inelastic refer to a price range, not to the entire demand curve.

The downward-sloping straight-line demand curve is divided into three parts by the price elasticity of demand: the *elastic region*, the *unit-elastic point*, and the *inelastic region*. The demand is elastic from the top of the curve to the unit-elastic point. At all prices below the unit-elastic point, the price elasticity of demand lies between 1 and 0. This is the inelastic portion of the curve.

elastic	$e_d > 1$
unit-elastic	$e_d = 1$
inelastic	$0 < e_d < 1$

1.c. The Price Elasticity of Demand Is Defined in Percentage Terms

By measuring the price elasticity of demand in terms of percentage changes, economists are able to compare how consumers respond to changes in the prices of different products. For instance, the impact of a 1 percent increase in the price of gasoline (measured in gallons) can be compared to the impact of a 1 percent change in the price of videotape rentals (measured in number of rentals). Or the impact of a 1 percent increase in the price of college tuition can be compared to the impact of a 1 percent rise in the price of a Big Mac.

Percentage changes ensure that we are comparing apples to apples, not apples to oranges. What sense could be made of a comparison between the effects on quantity demanded of a $1 rise in the price of college tuition, from $5,000 to $5,001, and a $1 rise in the price of Big Macs, from $2 to $3? The dollar change would mean that tuition increases by .02 percent, and the hamburger price increases by 50 percent.

1.d. Average or Arc Elasticity

One of the problems of measuring elasticity is that the value depends on the base, or the starting point. An increase from $5 to $6 is a 20 percent change [($6 − $5)/$5 = 1/5], but a decrease from $6 to $5 is a 16.67 percent change [($5 − $6)/$6 = 1/6]. The result differs according to whether we start from $5 or $6—that is, according to whether the base is $5 or $6. Because the value of the price elasticity of demand varies depending on the base, economists use the average price and average quantity demanded to calculate elasticity. The elasticity obtained when the midpoint, or average, price and quantity are used is often called the **arc elasticity**. The formula used to calculate arc elasticity is

arc elasticity:
the price elasticity of demand measured over a price range using the midpoint, or average, as the base

$$e_d = \frac{|(Q_2 - Q_1)/[(Q_1 + Q_2)/2]|}{|(P_2 - P_1)/[(P_1 + P_2)/2]|}$$

Let's use this formula to calculate an elasticity. At a price of $6 per ticket, the average moviegoer demands 2 tickets per month. At a price of $4 per ticket, the average moviegoer purchases 6 tickets per month. Thus,

$$P_1 = \$6 \qquad Q_1 = 2$$
$$P_2 = \$4 \qquad Q_2 = 6$$

The *change* in quantity demanded is $Q_2 - Q_1 = 6 - 2 = 4$. The *percentage change* is the change divided by the base. The base is the average, or midpoint between the two quantities, the sum of the two quantities divided by 2: $(Q_1 + Q_2)/2 = (6 + 2)/2 = 4$. With 4 as the base, the percentage change in quantity is 4/4, or 100 percent. We can say that the quantity of movie tickets sold rose by an average of 100 percent as the price of a ticket declined from $6 to $4.

The change in price is −$2, from $6 to $4, and the average price is $(P_1 + P_2)/2 = (\$6 + \$4)/2 = \$5$. The percentage change in price is −$2/$5 = −40 percent.

Because the numerator of the price elasticity of demand is 100 percent and the denominator is −40 percent, the price elasticity is

$$e_d = |100/-40| = 2.5$$

According to these calculations, the price elasticity of demand for movie tickets, over the price range from $6 to $4, is 2.5. We can say that demand is elastic over this price range.

RECAP

1. The price elasticity of demand is a measure of the degree to which consumers will alter the quantities of a product they purchase in response to changes in the price of that product.

2. Because the quantity demanded always declines as price rises, the price elasticity of demand is always a negative number. To avoid confusion when discussing price elasticity of demand, we use the absolute value—that is, the negative sign is ignored.

3. The price elasticity of demand is a ratio of the percentage change in the quantity demanded to the corresponding percentage change in the price.

4. When the price elasticity of demand is greater than 1, demand is said to be *elastic*. When the price elasticity of demand is equal to 1, demand is said to be *unit-elastic*. When the price elasticity of demand is less than 1, demand is said to be *inelastic*.

5. The elasticity obtained by using average price and average quantity demanded is called the *arc elasticity*.

2. THE USE OF PRICE ELASTICITY OF DEMAND

The price elasticity of demand for a product plays an important role in determining whether, and by how much, suppliers raise or lower the prices of their products. Let's consider a few examples.

2.a. Total Expenditures, Total Revenue, and Price Elasticity

How does a business determine whether to increase or decrease the price of the product it sells in order to increase revenues?

total revenue (TR):
$TR = P \times Q$

"Ford Motor Ventures into Value Pricing," "Gap Cuts Again in Price War," "Low Prices Reflect High Sales Goals," read the headlines recently.[1] All three headlines indicate that firms are reducing price to increase revenues. But does a reduction in price guarantee an increase in revenues? The answer is no. Whether a reduction in price leads to increased revenues depends on the price elasticity of demand.

The amount by which the total expenditures on a product change when the price of the product changes depends on the price elasticity of demand. Total expenditures on a product and the total revenue obtained from selling a product are the same thing. **Total revenue (TR)** equals the price of a product multiplied by the quantity sold: $TR = P \times Q$. If P rises by 10 percent and Q falls by more than 10 percent, then total revenue declines as a result of the price rise. If P rises by 10 percent and Q falls by less than 10 percent, then total revenue rises as a result of the price rise. And if P increases by 10 percent and Q falls by 10 percent, total revenue does not change as the price changes. Thus, total revenue increases as price is increased if demand is inelastic, decreases as price is increased if demand is elastic, and does not change as price is increased if demand is unit-elastic.

Whenever the price elasticity of demand for a product is in the elastic region, the product supplier must decrease price in order to increase revenue.

---

[1]*Wall Street Journal*, Sept. 18, 1991, p. B1; *USA Today*, Sept. 29, 1992, p. 2B; and *USA Today*, Sept. 25, 1992, p. B1.

TABLE 1
Some Products and Their Estimated Price Elasticities of Demand

Product	Estimated Price Elasticity of Demand
Inelastic	
Salt	0.1
Matches	0.1
Toothpicks	0.1
Electricity	0.1
Gasoline	0.2
Coffee	0.25
Telephone	0.25
Cigarettes	0.35
Taxi service	0.4
Residential natural gas	0.5
Legal services	0.5
Physicians' services	0.6
Tires	0.6
Approximate Unitary Elasticity	
Housing	0.9
Private education	1.1
China and tableware	1.1
Beer	1.13
Elastic	
Automobiles	1.2
Marijuana	1.51
Airline travel	2.4
Motion pictures	2.5
Fresh green peas	2.8
Chevrolet cars	4.0
Foreign travel	4.0
Fresh tomatoes	5.0

Sources: Hendrik S. Houthakker and Lester D. Taylor, *Consumer Demand in the United States, 1929–1970* (Cambridge, Mass.: Harvard University Press, 1970), pp. 166–167; Douglas R. Bohi, *Analyzing Demand Behavior* (Baltimore: Johns Hopkins University Press, 1981); T. C. Misket and F. Vakil, "Some Estimates of Price and Expenditure Elasticities Among UCLA Students," *The Review of Economics and Statistics* (Nov. 1972), pp. 473–474; T. F. Hogart and K. G. Elzinga, "The Demand for Beer," *The Review of Economics and Statistics* (May 1972), pp. 195–198; Paul J. Feldstein, *Health Care Economics* (New York: John Wiley & Sons, Inc.), 1983, pp. 96–97.

Table 1 lists estimated price elasticities of demand for several products. The table shows that the price elasticity of demand for airline travel is 2.4. This means that, over some price range, for each 1 percent increase in the price of an airline ticket, the quantity of tickets demanded will decline by 2.4 percent.

In the fall of 1992, a trip could be made from New York to Los Angeles for $250 each way, if you included a Saturday night stay. If the airlines had increased the fare by 10 percent, to $275 each way, they would have sold 24 percent (2.4 × .10) fewer tickets. As a result, their total revenue would have fallen. The revenue from selling 3,000 tickets per day for the trip between New York and Los Angeles at a fare of $250 was $750,000 per day. At a fare of $275, the quantity of tickets demanded would have declined by 720 to 2,280 per day (3,000 × .24 = 720), and revenue would have fallen to $627,000 per day. As long as the price elasticity of demand exceeds 1, total revenue is decreased if the price is increased.

As long as the price elasticity of demand exceeds 1, total revenue is decreased if the price is increased.

As long as demand is elastic, price must be decreased to increase total revenue. But by how much should the price be lowered? Since the price elasticity of demand declines as the price falls along a straight-line demand curve, eventually price reaches a point where demand becomes unit-elastic. Further price decreases at this stage would cause total revenue to fall. Thus, total revenue can be maximized by setting the price where the demand is unit-elastic.

The table in Figure 2 is a demand schedule for airline tickets listing the price and quantity of tickets sold and the total revenue ($P \times Q$). Figure 2(a) shows a straight-line demand curve representing the demand for air travel. Total revenue is plotted in Figure 2(b), directly below the demand curve. You can see that total revenue rises as price falls in the elastic range of the demand curve, while in the inelastic range of the demand curve, total revenue declines as price falls. *The unit-elastic point is the price at which revenue is at a maximum.* Remember that this is revenue, not profit, we are discussing. A firm may or may not want to maximize revenue, as noted in the Economic Insight "Price, Revenue, and Profit."

2.b. Price Discrimination

Why might senior citizens or children receive price discounts relative to the rest of the population?

price discrimination: charging different customers different prices for the same product

Ads and marquees proudly proclaim that "kids stay free" or that "senior discounts apply," and it is well known that airlines sell vacation travelers tickets for significantly less than the business traveler pays. The price elasticity of demand might explain why firms will not always increase revenue if they lower their prices, but what explains why firms charge different customers different prices for the same product? It is exactly the same principle. When demand is elastic, a price decrease causes total revenue to increase; and when demand is inelastic, a price increase causes total revenue to rise. If different groups of customers have different price elasticities of demand for the same product, and if the groups are easily identifiable and can be kept from trading with each other, then the seller of the product can increase total revenue by charging each group a different price. Charging different prices to different customers for the same product is called **price discrimination**. Price discrimination occurs when senior citizens purchase movie tickets at a lower price than younger citizens or when business travelers pay more for airline tickets than vacation travelers.

Senior citizens are frequently offered movie tickets at lower prices than younger people. The reason for the discount is that, on average, older people are more inclined than younger people to respond to a change in the price of admission to a movie.

Suppose everyone pays the same ticket price of $5 and the price elasticity of demand by senior citizens is 2.0, while that by nonsenior citizens is 0.5. Lowering the price of a movie ticket by 10 percent would cause senior citizens to increase their purchases of movie tickets by 20 percent, but nonsenior citizens would increase their purchases by only 5 percent. Total revenue from senior citizens would rise, but that from nonsenior citizens would fall. It

Figure 2
Total Revenue and Price Elasticity
The demand schedule provides data for plotting the straight-line demand curve, Figure 2(a), and the total revenue curve, Figure 2(b). In the elastic region of the demand curve, a price decrease will increase total revenue. At the unit-elastic point, a price decrease will not change total revenue. In the inelastic region of the demand curve, a price decrease will decrease total revenue.

Price per Ticket	Quantity of Tickets Sold per Day	Total Revenue
$1,000	200	$200,000
900	400	360,000
800	600	480,000
700	800	560,000
600	1,000	600,000
500	1,200	600,000
400	1,400	560,000
300	1,600	480,000
200	1,800	360,000
100	2,000	200,000

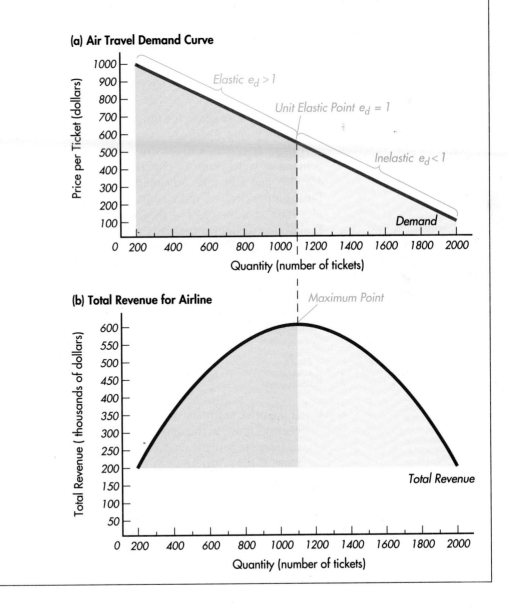

(a) Air Travel Demand Curve

(b) Total Revenue for Airline

ECONOMIC INSIGHT

Price, Revenue, and Profit

Profit is defined as revenue minus costs. If revenue rises but costs rise more, then profit declines. Whether a price reduction leads to more profits or not depends on how revenue and costs respond to the price change. With the price elasticity of demand we are looking *only* at the response of revenue to price changes. We do not know what costs are doing. (We will examine costs in the next chapter.)

Many people confuse revenue and profit; and sometimes even businesspeople embark on a strategy of increasing market share but lose sight of the "bottom line," that is, profit. Consider Stan Shih, who has had a strategy of making his Taiwan-based computer firm, founded in 1983, one of the top five companies by 1995. Shih's firm, known as Acer, entered the United States by purchasing companies in the Silicon Valley. It began producing a low-cost line of PCs known as Acros in 1992. Sales were expected to reach $100 million in the first year. However, those sales mean little if the firm is not making a profit. The sales goal was reached, but the company was not particularly pleased. It seemed the company lost sight of profits. According to Peter A. Janssen, Acer America's marketing vice president, "The revenues are huge. The problem is profitability."*

*Statement by Janssen reported in *Business Week*, May 18, 1992, p. 129.

would make more sense for the theater to lower the price for senior citizens but not for younger people.

Airline discounts are constructed on the basis of the price elasticity of demand as well. Families planning a vacation know their schedules well in advance and can take advantage of the least expensive means of travel. Business travelers are more constrained. They often do not know their schedules days in advance, and they usually want to travel on Monday through Friday. The airlines recognize that the demand for air travel by vacationers is much more elastic than the demand by business travelers. As a result, airlines offer discounts to travelers who purchase tickets well in advance and stay over a *Saturday night*. For instance, in the fall of 1992, a cross-country round-trip fare was $840 unless the trip included an overnight stay on Saturday. Then the fare dropped to $360. If tickets were purchased two weeks in advance, the fare dropped to $240.

RECAP

1. If the price elasticity of demand is greater than 1, revenue and price changes move in the opposite direction. An increase in price causes a decrease in revenue, and a decrease in price causes an increase in revenue. If the price elasticity of demand is less than 1, revenue and price move in the same direction. If the price elasticity of demand is 1, revenue does not change as price changes.

2. When the price elasticity of demand for one product differs among different groups of easily identified customers, firms can increase revenues by charging each group a different price. The groups with elastic demands will receive lower prices than those with inelastic demands.

3. DETERMINANTS OF THE PRICE ELASTICITY OF DEMAND

What determines whether consumers alter their purchases a little or a lot in response to a price change?

Different groups of consumers—such as senior and nonsenior citizens and business and vacation travelers—may have different price elasticities of demand for the same product. The demand for a product may be elastic or inelastic over a relevant price range, and not all products have the same price elasticity of demand. The degree to which the price elasticity of demand is inelastic or elastic depends on the following factors, which differ among products and among consumers:

■ The existence of substitutes

■ The importance of the product in the consumer's total budget

■ The time period under consideration

3.a. The Existence of Substitutes

Consumers who can switch from one product to another without losing quality or some other attribute associated with the original product will be very sensitive to a price change. Their demand will be elastic. Such consumers will purchase a substitute rather than the original product whenever the relative price of the original product rises.

A senior citizen discount is offered at movie theaters because of the different price elasticities of demand by senior citizens and nonsenior citizens. Why are their elasticities different? More substitutes may be available to senior citizens than to younger folks. Retirees have more time to seek out alternative entertainment activities than do people who are working full time. Retirees can go to movies during the early part of the day or on weekdays when the theater runs a special.

The more substitutes there are for a product, the greater the price elasticity of demand.

In contrast, drug addicts have few substitutes that satisfy the addiction, and business travelers have few substitutes for the airlines. As a result, their demands are relatively inelastic. The more substitutes there are for a product, the greater the price elasticity of demand.

3.b. The Importance of the Product in the Consumer's Total Budget

Because a new car and a European vacation are quite expensive, even a small percentage change in their prices can take a significant portion of a household's income. As a result, a 1 percent increase in price may cause many households to delay the purchase of a car or vacation. Coffee, on the other hand, accounts for such a small portion of a household's total weekly expenditures that a large percentage increase in the price of coffee will probably have little effect on the quantity of coffee purchased. The demand for vacations is most likely quite a bit more elastic than the demand for coffee. The greater the portion of the consumer's budget a good constitutes, the more elastic is the demand for the good.

The greater the portion of the consumer's budget a good constitutes, the more elastic the demand for the good.

3.c. The Time Period Under Consideration

If we are speaking about a day or an hour, then the demand for most goods and services will have a low price elasticity. If we are referring to a year or to several years, then the demand for most products will be more price-elastic than in a shorter period. For instance, the demand for gasoline is very nearly perfectly inelastic over a period of a month. No good substitutes are available in so brief a period. Over a ten-year period, however, the demand for gasoline is much more elastic, as discussed in the Economic Insight "What Goes Up Must Come Down?" The additional time allows consumers to alter their behavior to make better use of gasoline and to find substitutes for gasoline. The longer the period under consideration, the more elastic is the demand for any product. Another illustration of the time dimension in elasticity is given in the Economic Insight "Exchange Rate Changes and the Price Elasticities of Demand."

The longer the period under consideration, the more elastic the demand for the good.

RECAP

1. The price elasticity of demand depends on how readily and easily consumers can switch their purchases from one product to another.

2. Everything else held constant, the greater the number of close substitutes, the greater is the price elasticity of demand.

3. Everything else held constant, the greater the proportion of a householder's budget a good constitutes, the greater is the householder's elasticity of demand for that good.

4. Everything else held constant, the longer the time period under consideration, the greater is the elasticity of demand.

4. OTHER DEMAND ELASTICITIES: CROSS-PRICE AND INCOME

How do we measure whether and how much income changes or changes in the prices of related goods affect consumer purchases?

The price elasticity of demand is a measure of how consumers adjust their purchases of a commodity when the price of that commodity changes. Two other elasticities are used to describe demand curves. The *cross-price elasticity of demand* is a measure of how consumers adjust their purchases of a commodity when the price of some other commodity changes. The *income elasticity of demand* is a measure of how consumers adjust their purchases of a commodity when their incomes change.

4.a. The Cross-Price Elasticity of Demand

cross-price elasticity of demand:
the percentage change in the quantity demanded for one good divided by the percentage change in the price of a related good, everything else held constant

The **cross-price elasticity of demand** measures the degree to which goods are substitutes or complements (for a discussion of substitutes and complements, see Chapter 3). The cross-price elasticity of demand is defined as the percentage change in the quantity demanded of one good divided by the percentage change in the price of a related good, everything else held constant:[2]

$$\text{Cross-price elasticity of demand} = \frac{\text{percentage change in quantity demanded of good } j}{\text{percentage change in the price of good } k}$$

---

[2]Remember that a change in any of the determinants of demand (other than price of the good being considered) causes the entire demand curve to shift—a change in demand, not a change in quantity demanded. However, to calculate elasticity, particular prices and quantities must be selected; the entire demand curve cannot be used to calculate an elasticity. Thus, the definition of cross-price and income elasticities of demand refer to changes in quantity demanded rather than changes in demand.

What Goes Up Must Come Down?

The time element in the price elasticity of demand for gasoline is often misunderstood by politicians and the public, who claim that the large oil companies are gouging the public by raising prices at the pump whenever crude oil prices rise but not lowering the pump price when the crude oil price declines. This perception of price gouging is only partly correct, however. In fact, the lag in price changes results from a relatively inelastic demand for gasoline in the short run. Gasoline operators and wholesalers know that gasoline sales will not vary much as the price increases or decreases in the short run. Hence, to increase their revenues, they tend to raise prices. Yet, in the longer run, when the price elasticity is higher, an increase in the pump price will induce people to consume less gasoline. As a result, pump prices do tend to rise and fall as the crude oil price rises and falls.

In 1973, the Organization of Petroleum Exporting Countries (OPEC) successfully held enough oil off the market to drive the price per barrel of oil up from about $2 to $10 and then to more than $30 in the next few years, as shown in the figure. Expenditures on oil increased substantially because of the inelastic demand, and consumers were forced to decrease their expenditures on other goods and services. Over time, however, the price elasticity of demand increased as consumers began to use alternatives for petroleum and gasoline, producers began seeking other sources of oil, and manufacturers began producing more efficient cars and power generators that depended on alternative sources of fuel.

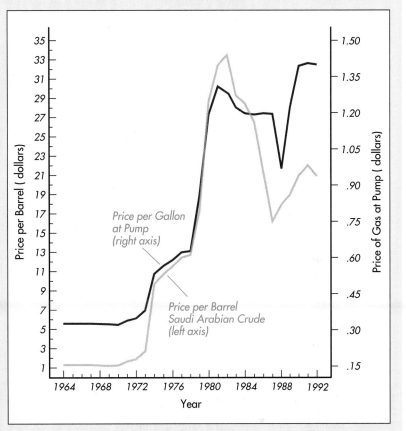

Producers also responded to the price increase. Major oil discoveries occurred in Prudhoe Bay, Alaska, and in the North Sea near Great Britain. In addition, oil wells drilled throughout the United States and in parts of Latin America increased the quantity of available oil. Nuclear power plants were constructed as alternatives to plants using oil to generate electricity. The result was an increased number of substitutes for oil and an increase in the price elasticity of demand. Consequently, the high price eventually resulted in a decreased quantity demanded and falling total revenues for the oil-producing countries. The result was a decline in the price of oil. The price of petroleum stabilized in 1981 and began falling again in 1984. By 1989 the price had dropped more than 40 percent from its 1981 high and it has remained relatively low since, although it did rise during the invasion of Kuwait by Iraq.

Source: Data provided by International Monetary Fund, *International Financial Statistics, Yearbook,* 1987.

When the cross-price elasticity of demand is positive, the goods are substitutes; and when the cross-price elasticity of demand is negative, the goods are complements. If a 1 percent *increase* in the price of a movie ticket leads to a 5 percent *increase* in the quantity of videotapes that are rented, movies and videotapes are substitutes. If a 1 percent *rise* in the price of a movie ticket leads to a 5 percent *drop* in the quantity of popcorn consumed, movies and popcorn are complements.

The cross-price elasticities of demand for food, clothing, and shelter are shown in Table 2. The cross-price elasticities are negative, indicating that an increase in the price of one good leads to a decrease in the quantity demanded of the other good. Thus, the goods are complements. For instance, when the price of clothing increases by 1 percent, the quantity demanded of food decreases by .03 percent.

Knowledge of how changes in economic events outside a firm's control affect sales is crucial in order for the firm to respond most effectively to competitors' policies and plan its own best growth strategy. For example, if a firm estimates that the cross-price elasticity of demand for its product with respect to the price of a competitor's product is very high, it will be quick to respond to a competitor's price reduction. If it were not quick, it would lose a great deal of its sales. However, the firm would think twice before being the first to lower its price, for fear of starting a price war. It knows that competitors will respond quickly to a price decrease and offset any advantage that a lower price might yield. If the cross-price elasticity is low, a firm would not care much about whether the other product's price is raised or lowered.

4.b. The Income Elasticity of Demand

income elasticity of demand: the percentage change in the demand for a good divided by the percentage change in income, everything else held constant

The income elasticity of demand measures the magnitude of consumer responsiveness to income changes. The **income elasticity of demand** is defined as the percentage change in demand for a product divided by the percentage change in income, everything else held constant:

$$\text{Income elasticity of demand} = \frac{\text{percentage change in quantity demanded for good } j}{\text{percentage change in income}}$$

TABLE 2
Cross-Price Elasticities of Demand

Elasticity of Demand of the Good on the Left with Respect to the Price of Each Good Listed Along the Top:			
	Clothing	**Transportation**	**Shelter**
Food	−.03	−.01	−.09
Clothing		−.01	−.09
Transportation			−.12

Source: E. Lazear and R. Michael, "Family Size and the Distribution of Real per Capita Income," *American Economic Review* (March 1980), pp. 91–108.

Exchange Rate Changes and the Price Elasticities of Demand

In the previous chapter we discussed the income and substitution effects of an exchange rate change. We saw that in the early 1980s, the rising value of the dollar meant higher prices of U.S. goods and lower prices of Japanese goods. As a result, the sales of Japanese goods rose while sales of U.S. goods fell, resulting in what is called a *balance-of-trade deficit*.

The *balance of trade* between Japan and the United States measures the difference between the sales of U.S. goods and services to Japan and the sales of Japanese goods and services to the United States. Whether the United States sells more to Japan than it buys from Japan (a trade surplus) or buys more from Japan than it sells to Japan (a trade deficit) is of great importance to U.S. politicians. Additionally, U.S. politicians are concerned about the jobs of U.S. workers that would be lost if sales of U.S. goods decline.

How a change in exchange rate affects the balance of trade depends on the price elasticities of demand. If the price elasticity of demand for Japanese goods in the United States is low, then an exchange rate change that raises the price of Japanese goods (a lower value of the dollar) will actually increase the total value of sales of Japanese goods (increase Japan's revenue). Similarly, if the price elasticity of demand for U.S. goods in Japan is low, then a lower value of the dollar will lower the total value of sales of U.S. goods (lower U.S. revenue).

In the early 1980s, the value of the dollar rose and the trade deficit grew as U.S. consumers bought more Japanese goods. In 1987, though, the value of the dollar declined by more than 33 percent, which made Japanese goods quite a bit more expensive to U.S. consumers. However, because the price elasticity of demand for Japanese goods by U.S. consumers was low, sales of Japanese goods did not decline, and the trade deficit worsened. But, because the price elasticity of demand in the longer period is higher than it is in the shorter period, after a period of time consumers switched to other goods and suppliers began to offer competing products. The trade deficit did begin to decline in 1988 and continued to decline throughout the rest of the 1980s. Although, to the dismay of many politicians, the trade balance for the U.S. remained in deficit even as the value of the dollar declined by nearly 50 percent from its peak value. Even the long-run U.S. price elasticity of demand for Japanese goods was not sufficiently large to have the trade deficit with Japan disappear.

normal goods:
goods for which the income elasticity of demand is positive

Several products and their estimated income elasticities are presented in Table 3. These goods are called **normal goods**. Any good whose income elasticity of demand is greater than zero is a normal good. Notice in Table 3 that products often called necessities have lower income elasticities than products known as luxuries. Food, gas, electricity, health-oriented drugs, and physicians' services might be considered necessities. On the other hand, people tend to view dental services, automobiles, and private education as luxury goods.

inferior goods:
goods for which the income elasticity of demand is negative

Consumers could have a negative income elasticity of demand for some goods: less of those goods would be consumed as income rose. Such goods are called **inferior goods**. It is difficult to think of examples of inferior goods. Some people claim that potatoes, rice, and hamburger are inferior goods because people who have very low levels of income eat large quantities of these goods but give up those items and begin eating fruit, fish, and higher-quality meats as their incomes rise. The problem with calling these

TABLE 3
Estimates of the Income Elasticity of Demand for Several Products

Product	Estimated Income Elasticity of Demand
Fuel	.38
Electricity, gas	.50
Food	.51
Drugs (health)	.61
Tobacco	.63
Charitable donations	.70
Physicians' services	.75
Beer	.93
Clothing	1.02
Housing	1.04
Dentists' services	1.41
Books	1.44
Furniture	1.48
Alcoholic beverages	1.54
New cars	2.45
Private education	2.46

Sources: Hendrik S. Houthakker and Lester D. Taylor, *Consumer Demand in the United States, 1929–1970* (Cambridge, Mass.: Harvard University Press, 1970), pp. 260–263; M. Feldstein and A. Taylor, "The Income Tax and Charitable Contributions," *Econometrica*, vol. 44, no. 6 (Nov. 1976), pp. 1201–1221.

products inferior is that many higher-income households consume large quantities of potatoes, rice, and hamburger.

The income elasticity of demand provides useful information to a firm. If management knows that the income elasticity of the firm's product is very low, it may want to upgrade the quality of its product or move into new product lines for which the income elasticity of demand is higher. The reason is that as incomes rise over time, a firm whose products have a low income elasticity of demand will not experience the sales growth of a firm whose products have a higher income elasticity of demand.

Japan's Ministry of International Trade and Industry (MITI) directed much of Japan's economic growth during the past 30 years, selecting specific industries that the government subsidized or protected from competition until they were strong and growing. MITI failed to rely on the income elasticity of demand for products to make its selections. For example, it forecast that incomes in the developed nations would continue to grow at substantial rates in the 1960s, 1970s, and 1980s, but failed to support industries whose products had high income elasticities of demand. MITI did not focus on consumer electronics, goods that had high income elasticities of demand. As a result, MITI's performance was dismal. The consumer electronics industry became one of the largest in the world, and it is now dominated by Japanese firms because industry executives did not follow MITI directives.

What used to fill an entire room now can be held on a lap. The laptop, or notebook, computer is capable of carrying out calculations that only twenty years ago required a computer of 10 feet by 12 feet. And, the notebook of today is being superceded by a machine capable of 100 times the power; the work of twenty 486 laptop computers today will not match one laptop machine in five years. When initially introduced, the personal computer and the laptop version appealed primarily to high income earners—the income elasticity of demand was high. The machine was looked on as an expensive toy. Today, with computers a necessity in nearly every business, the income elasticity of demand is lower than it used to be.

RECAP

1. The cross-price elasticity of demand is the percentage change in the quantity demanded of one product divided by the percentage change in the price of a related product, everything else held constant. If the cross-price elasticity of demand is positive, the goods are substitutes. If the cross-price elasticity of demand is negative, the goods are complements.

2. The income elasticity of demand is the percentage change in the quantity demanded of one product divided by the percentage change in income, everything else held constant. If the income elasticity of a good is greater than zero, the good is called a *normal good*. If the income elasticity of a good is negative, the good is called an *inferior good*.

5. SUPPLY ELASTICITIES

How do we measure whether and how much producers respond to a price change?

Although this chapter is largely about demand, it is convenient in the context of the discussion of elasticity to spend a little time on the price elasticity of supply. We will discuss the price elasticity of supply in more detail in our discussion of supply in the following chapters.

5.a. The Price Elasticity of Supply

Elasticity is a measure of responsiveness. The response of buyers to price changes is measured by the price elasticity of demand. The response of sellers to price changes can also be measured by elasticity. The *price elasticity of supply* is a measure of how sellers adjust the quantity of a good they offer for sale when the price of that good changes.

price elasticity of supply:
the percentage change in the quantity supplied divided by the percentage change in price, everything else held constant

The **price elasticity of supply** is the percentage change in the quantity supplied of a good divided by the percentage change in the price of that good, everything else held constant. The price elasticity of supply is usually a positive number because the quantity supplied typically rises when the price rises. Supply is said to be elastic over a price range if the price elasticity of supply is greater than 1 over that price range. It is said to be inelastic over a price range if the price elasticity of supply is less than 1 over that price range.

$$\text{Price elasticity of supply} = \frac{\text{percentage change in the quantity supplied}}{\text{percentage change in the price}}$$

The price elasticity of supply depends on the length of time producers have to vary their output in response to price changes. Usually, the greater the time period, the more elastic is supply. There are some special types of goods for which supply cannot change no matter the length of time allowed for change—land surface, ocean surface, Monet paintings, Beethoven symphonies. For such goods, supply is perfectly inelastic. For most other goods, supply becomes more elastic the longer the period of time being considered.

The price elasticity of supply depends on the ability of firms to change their production techniques or switch from the production of one good to another. A bakery that can switch from producing cupcakes to muffins within a day has a large price elasticity of supply for cupcakes or muffins; a small increase in the price of muffins relative to cupcakes will cause the bakery to switch from cupcakes to muffins. An automobile manufacturing plant that requires several months or years to switch from one type of car to another will have a relatively inelastic supply. A large increase in the price of large to small cars may have no effect on the firm's production of large and small cars for several months or years.

5.b. The Long and Short Runs

short run:
a period of time short enough that the quantities of all resources cannot be varied

Economists view time in terms of two distinct periods: the short run and the long run. The **short run** is a period of time long enough for existing firms to change the quantity of output they produce by changing the quantities of *some* of the resources they use to produce the output, but not long enough for the firms to change the quantities of *all* of the resources. In particular, firms cannot change their capital resources (such as by constructing new buildings or purchasing new offices) in the short run. In addition, in the short run, new firms do not have the time to build factories or rent buildings and begin producing the product.

long run:
a period of time just long enough that the quantities of all resources can be varied

The **long run** is a period of time long enough for existing firms to change the quantities of all resources they use and for new firms to begin producing a product. The durations of the short and long runs vary from industry to industry. The long run for oil refining is seven to eight years; for personal computers, perhaps a year; for basket making, probably no longer than one day.

Three supply curves are shown in Figure 3. The perfectly inelastic supply curve in Figure 3(a) indicates that no matter the price, the quantity supplied

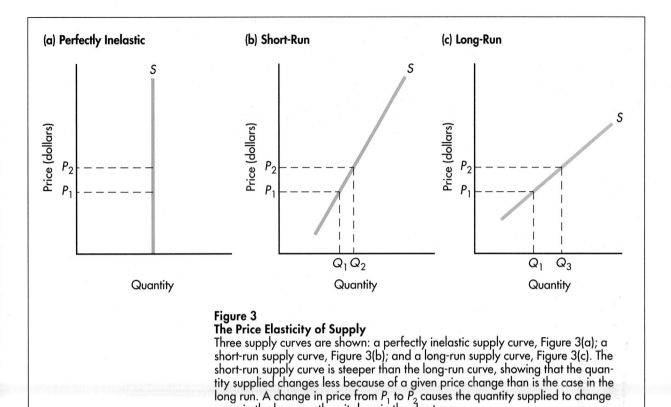

(a) Perfectly Inelastic

(b) Short-Run

(c) Long-Run

Figure 3
The Price Elasticity of Supply
Three supply curves are shown: a perfectly inelastic supply curve, Figure 3(a); a short-run supply curve, Figure 3(b); and a long-run supply curve, Figure 3(c). The short-run supply curve is steeper than the long-run curve, showing that the quantity supplied changes less because of a given price change than is the case in the long run. A change in price from P_1 to P_2 causes the quantity supplied to change more in the long run than it does in the short run.

cannot change. The short-run supply curve is illustrated in Figure 3(b), and the long-run supply curve is shown in Figure 3(c). In the short run, the quantity supplied increases as the price rises, but not as much as it does in the long run. Compare the effect on quantity supplied due to a change from P_1 to P_2 in the three curves. With the perfectly inelastic curve, the quantity supplied does not change as the price changes. In the short run, the quantity supplied increases from Q_1 to Q_2, and in the long run, the quantity supplied rises from Q_1 to Q_3.

5.c. Price Elasticities of Demand and Supply: Who Pays the Tax?

In the early 1990s, the state of California was reeling from its most serious recession in decades. Instead of providing an increasing array of services, state and local governments could not fund existing services. All levels of government were looking for new sources of revenue. Calls for taxes on business, on gasoline, on liquor and cigarettes, and on other items were commonplace. Perhaps the most controversial of California's new taxes was the so-called "snack" tax, a levy of about 8 percent on the sales price of food items classified as snacks. Snacks included potato chips, crackers, nuts, popcorn, Twinkies, cupcakes, and other items. Some consumer groups were upset about the tax, claiming that the snack tax was a tax on the poor. Others supported the tax as a tax on nonessential businesses.

Who actually pays a tax levied on some item or some business? Is it the business, or does the consumer ultimately pay? The answer seems straightforward enough: "Clearly, the consumer pays the tax since the consumer takes the item to the checkout counter and forks out the money." The answer is not that straightforward, however. Who pays the tax depends on the price elasticities of demand and supply.

Suppose that the price elasticity of supply for the item being taxed is large and the demand for that item is price-inelastic. In this case, the firm can raise the price without losing sales, or the government can impose a tax that raises the price and the firm will not lose sales. Moreover, the firm can switch from producing the taxed good to producing a nontaxed good relatively easily. Since the firm will not lose sales as a result of the tax, the firm does not need to worry about lowering the price and thus paying a portion of the tax. Regardless of whether the tax is imposed on the firm or on the consumer, it is the consumer who actually pays the tax. We say that the **tax incidence** falls on the consumer. Cigarettes are an example. If smokers will buy the same quantity of cigarettes even if the price rises by 20 percent, then an 8 percent tax levied on cigarettes will not affect sales. Firms would not need to reduce price to keep sales the same.

If, on the other hand, supply is price-inelastic and demand price-elastic, then a price increase means a revenue decrease for the firm. Since the firm cannot raise price without losing sales and cannot readily switch to producing another good, the firm must incorporate the tax in the original price and offer the same total cost to consumers after the tax is levied as before the tax. Hence, the firm will lower the price of the product enough that the price plus the new tax will just about equal the original (before tax) price. In this case, it is the business who pays the tax; the tax incidence falls on the business. If the price elasticity of demand for potato chips was high and the price elasticity of supply low, then an 8 percent tax on potato chips would reduce sales unless the business reduced the price of the chips. Because the business has to lower the price to maintain its sales, it actually pays the tax.

In general, the more elastic the demand and the less elastic the supply, everything else held constant, the more the incidence falls on businesses and the less on consumers.

tax incidence:
a measure of who pays a tax

RECAP

1. The price elasticity of supply is the percentage change in the quantity supplied of one product divided by the percentage change in the price of that product, everything else held constant. The price elasticity of supply increases as the time period under consideration increases.

2. The long run is a period of time just long enough that the quantities of all resources can be varied. The short run is a period of time just short enough that the quantity of at least one of the resources cannot be varied.

3. The interaction of demand and supply determines the price and quantity produced and sold; the relative size of demand and supply price elasticities determines how the market reacts to changes. For instance, the size of supply relative to demand price elasticities determines the incidence of a tax.

SUMMARY

▲▼ **How do we measure whether and how much consumers alter their purchases in response to a price change?**

1. The price elasticity of demand is a measure of the responsiveness of consumers to changes in price. It is defined as the percentage change in the quantity demanded of a good divided by the percentage change in the price of the good. §1.a

2. The price elasticity of demand is always a negative number because price and quantity demanded are inversely related. To avoid confusion about what large or small elasticity means, the price elasticity of demand is calculated as the absolute value of the percentage change in the quantity demanded of a good divided by the percentage change in the price of the good. §1.a

3. As the price is lowered along a straight-line demand curve, the price elasticity of demand declines. §1.b.1

4. The straight-line demand curve consists of three segments: the top part, which is elastic; the unit-elastic region; and the bottom part, which is inelastic. §1.b.1

5. The price elasticity of demand is calculated as the arc, or average, elasticity to avoid the problems created in choosing a starting point, or base. §1.d

▲▼ **How does a business determine whether to increase or decrease the price of the product it sells in order to increase revenues?**

6. If the price elasticity of demand is greater than 1, total revenue and price changes move in opposite directions. An increase in price causes a decrease in total revenue, and a decrease in price causes an increase in total revenue. If demand is inelastic, total revenue and price move in the same direction. §2.a

▲▼ **Why might senior citizens or children receive price discounts relative to the rest of the population?**

7. When the price elasticity of demand for one product differs among different groups of easily identifiable customers, firms can increase total revenue by resorting to price discrimination. The customers with the more elastic demands will receive lower prices than the customers with less elastic demands. §2.b

▲▼ **What determines whether consumers alter their purchases a little or a lot in response to a price change?**

8. Everything else held constant, the greater the number of close substitutes, the greater the price elasticity of demand. §3.a

9. Everything else held constant, the greater the proportion of a household's budget a good constitutes, the greater the household's elasticity of demand for that good. §3.b

10. Everything else held constant, the longer the time period under consideration, the greater the price elasticity of demand. §3.c

▲▼ **How do we measure whether and how much income changes, or changes in the prices of related goods affect consumer purchases?**

11. The cross-price elasticity of demand is defined as the percentage change in the quantity demanded of one good divided by the percentage change in the price of a related good, everything else held constant. §4.a

12. The income elasticity of demand is defined as the percentage change in the quantity demanded of a good divided by the percentage change in income, everything else held constant. §4.b

▲▼ **How do we measure whether and how much producers respond to a price change?**

13. The price elasticity of supply is defined as the percentage change in the quantity supplied of a good divided by the percentage change in the price of that good, everything else held constant. §5.a

14. The incidence of a tax depends on the price elasticities of demand and supply. In general, the more elastic the demand and the less elastic the supply, everything else held constant, the more the incidence falls on businesses and the less on consumers. §5.c

KEY TERMS

price elasticity of demand §1.a

perfectly elastic demand curve §1.b

perfectly inelastic demand curve §1.b

arc elasticity §1.d

total revenue (TR) §2.a

price discrimination §2.b

cross-price elasticity of demand §4.a

income elasticity of demand §4.b

normal goods §4.b

inferior goods §4.b

price elasticity of supply §5.a

short run §5.b

long run §5.b

tax incidence §5.c

EXERCISES

Use the following hypothetical demand schedule for movies to do exercises 1–4.

Quantity Demanded	Price	Elasticity
100	$ 5	
80	10	
60	15	
40	20	
20	25	
10	30	

1. a. Determine the price elasticity of demand at each quantity demanded using the starting price and quantity as the bases. Next, do the same using the ending price and quantity as the bases; then, use the average price and quantity.

   b. Redo problem 1.a using price changes of $10 rather than $5.

   c. Plot the price and quantity data given in the demand schedule. Indicate the price elasticity value at each quantity demanded using the average price and quantity demanded as the bases. Explain why the elasticity value gets smaller as you move down the demand curve.

2. Below the demand curve plotted in exercise 1, plot the total revenue curve, measuring total revenue on the vertical axis and quantity on the horizontal axis.

3. What would a 10 percent increase in the price of movie tickets mean for the revenue of a movie theater if the price elasticity of demand was 0.1, 0.5, 1.0, and 5.0?

4. Using the demand curve plotted in exercise 1, illustrate what would occur if the income elasticity of demand was .05 and income rose by 10 percent. If the income elasticity of demand was 3.0 and income rose by 10 percent, what would occur?

5. Which is easier: to list five substitutes for each of the products listed under the elastic portion of Table 1 or five substitutes for the goods listed under the inelastic portion? Explain.

6. Are the following pairs of goods substitutes or complements? Indicate whether their cross-price elasticities are negative or positive.

   a. Bread and butter

   b. Bread and potatoes

   c. Socks and shoes

   d. Tennis racket and golf clubs

   e. Bicycles and automobiles

   f. Foreign investments and domestic investments

   g. Cars made in Japan and cars made in the United States

7. Suppose the price elasticity of demand for movies by teenagers is 0.2 and that by adults is 2.0. What policy would the movie theater implement to increase total revenue? Use hypothetical data to demonstrate your answer.

8. Using Table 3, explain how consumers will react to a job loss. What will be the first goods they will do without?

9. Explain why senior citizens can obtain special discounts at movie theaters, drugstores, and other businesses.

10. Calculate the income elasticity of demand from the following data (use the midpoint or average):

Income	Quantity Demanded
$15,000	20,000
20,000	30,000

a. Explain why the value is a positive number.

b. Explain what would happen to a demand curve as income changes if the income elasticity were 2.0. Compare that outcome to the situation that would occur if the income elasticity of demand were 0.2.

11. The poor tend to have a price elasticity of demand for movie tickets that lies above 1. Why don't you see signs offering "poor people discounts" similar to the signs offering "senior citizen discounts"?

12. Suppose a tax is imposed on a product that has a completely inelastic supply curve. Who pays the tax?

13. During the budget crisis in California, many households called for increasing taxes on businesses. Explain why a 40 percent across-the-board tax on businesses might not benefit the households of California.

14. Explain what must occur for the strategies suggested by the following headlines to be successful.

a. "Ford to go nationwide with plan for one-price selling of Escorts."

b. "P.F. Flyers cut sneaker prices to $20 a pair in a move to triple 1992 sales to 10 million pairs."

c. "Honda plans to launch a less expensive 'value-priced' Accord."

d. "Procter & Gamble cut prices of Dash detergent 30 to 40 percent."

15. Suppose the demand for cocaine consists of two types of consumers, the addicts and the first-time users. Suppose the price elasticity of demand for the addicts is .01 and that for the first-time users is 4.0. Explain how the government might design an antidrug campaign to reduce cocaine consumption and demand.

Tobacco tax a bad source of revenue, experts say

It seems to make perfect sense: If cigarettes rob Americans of their health, why not tax smokers more to help pay for health insurance?

Because revenues from tobacco taxes are crumbling along with the percentage of Americans who smoke. They're butting out for health reasons or because tax increases make smoking too expensive. Either way, the public treasury is taking a hit.

A 50-state survey by Associated Press bureaus found 20 states reporting tobacco-product tax revenues in decline, and 11 others in which revenues were declining until the excise tax was raised. Revenues in the rest generally were static.

The same goes for federal tobacco revenues, which fell until the excise tax rose to 20 cents from 16 cents a pack in 1991. It went up to 24 cents this year.

Although tobacco taxes yield lots of ready money at first, they're unlikely to provide long-term funding for as something large and growing as universal health care.

In 1965, the year after the first U.S. surgeon general's report to link smoking to cancer, 42.4 percent of Americans age 19 and older smoked. By 1990, that figure had dropped to 25.5 percent.

Government treasuries have since reduced their dependence on tobacco. Among the states, tobacco taxes peaked in 1968, providing 5.2 percent of state revenues. That share has fallen to 1.9 percent. Smokers' current $5.8 billion contribution to the federal pot is 0.4 percent of all revenues, down from 1.39 percent in 1968.

This pattern of sliding revenues has two chief causes, economists say.

Tobacco taxes don't grow with the economy, necessitating regular increases. Also, when tobacco taxes get high enough, some smokers quit and would-be smokers don't start.

The Minnesota Revenue Department offered this equation: For every 10 percent increase in the price of cigarettes, sales fall 4.5 percent.

On average, cigarettes cost $1.90 a pack, including the 24-cent federal tax and state taxes that range from Virginia's 2.5 cents to Massachusetts' 51 cents.

New York state is fairly typical. Tobacco revenues slid from $606 million in fiscal 1991 to $596 million in fiscal 1992. This fiscal year, they're expected to be $557 million.

In Arizona, the decline was reversed by a 1990 increase to 18 cents per pack. Revenues in fiscal 1992 were $52.5 million, up from $51.8 million in 1991.

Yet this steady, if diminishing cash flow, remains attractive to lawmakers, and even presidents.

President Clinton has said he may propose higher taxes on tobacco products to help pay for his national health-insurance plan. Like other advocates of this idea, he suggested it's only fair that smokers pay more.

Hillary Rodham Clinton, his wife and the architect of health-care-reform proposals, reiterated this in a recent interview.

The Clintons weren't the first to latch onto this idea. Former President Carter has endorsed a $2 federal excise tax on cigarettes sought by the American Cancer Society, the American Medical Association and the American Heart Association.

The more than $30 billion it would raise, he said in a Feb. 21 letter to *The New York Times*, "could be put to good use paying for health-care reform, childhood-immunization efforts and other high priorities."

The idea of tying tobacco taxes to health care is spreading.

In Congress, there's a bill that would raise the federal cigarette tax to $1 a pack and put most of the money collected into health care.

But tax experts say it won't work.

"It's just not going to raise enough revenue, which is a fairly serious problem," said Hal Hovey, a former budget director for both Ohio and Illinois who now puts out two newsletters, *State Budget & Tax News* and *State Policy Reports*.

Source: Associated Press, "Tobacco Tax a Bad Source of Revenue, Experts Say," *Arizona Republic*, March 19, 1993, p. A16. Copyright © 1993. Reprinted with permission of Associated Press.

Commentary

Twenty years ago, 45 percent of the population of the United States smoked; today just 24 percent of the population smokes, and smokers are feeling increasingly put-upon. Now taxes as high as $2 per pack are being discussed as a way to help pay for the Clinton administration's health-care reforms. If imposed, these taxes would more than double the price of a pack of cigarettes. Such a high tax ought to raise billions of dollars for the government: If 40 billion packs of cigarettes are purchased each year, then $80 billion of tax revenues should be obtained on an activity most Americans find distasteful. Why, then, is there a debate about the effectiveness of the "sin" tax?

The debate centers on the price elasticity of demand for cigarettes. If the demand for cigarettes is perfectly inelastic, then a tax imposed on the cigarettes will not affect the quantity demanded and the revenues raised will be substantial, in the range of $40 to $80 billion. It is unlikely that the demand for cigarettes is perfectly inelastic, however. In fact, the Minnesota Revenue Department found that for every 10 percent increase in the price of cigarettes, sales fell 4.5 percent. If the Minnesota data are correct, then at current prices, the price elasticity of demand is .45. However, if the price is doubled (raised 100 percent) rather than raised just 10 percent, sales may decline by much more than 45 percent: The price elasticity of demand rises as we move up the straight-line demand curve in the following figure.

As the price is raised, the revenue generated rises until the price elasticity of demand reaches the unity point. Beyond that point, the revenue actually declines as the price increases. Suppose that the current price is $2 per pack. A price increase of $1 (50 percent) would move us to the price of $3, and revenue would increase. But a 100 percent rise would move us to a price of $4, leading to a revenue decline. Whether revenues increase or decrease depends on the price elasticity of demand.

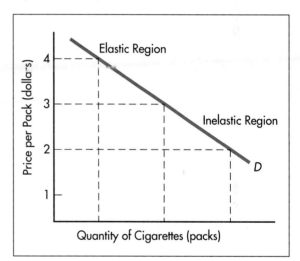

8

Supply: The Costs of Doing Business

FUNDAMENTAL QUESTIONS

1. What is the law of diminishing marginal returns?
2. How do economic costs and profit differ from accounting costs and profit?
3. What accounts for the shapes of the cost curves?
4. Is large always better than small?

In the previous two chapters we discussed demand. In this chapter we begin our analysis of supply. We focus on the firm, for it is firms who supply goods and services. Many issues face the manager of a firm. What size should the firm be? How much should the firm supply? Should it carry inventories or produce only as it sells? All these questions depend on the costs of the alternatives. To understand supply, then, is to understand the costs of doing business.

In many industries, firms must be quite large to compete effectively. The size of the average new supermarket jumped 58 percent in the last decade, and the number of items carried more than doubled, as noted in Figure 1. Midsize corporate law firms—generally those with 15 to 100 lawyers—found that they were too small to survive in the late 1980s, and over 35 percent of them merged into larger firms or disappeared.

In some industries increased size means increased efficiency; in others size is a problem. Large firms can become cumbersome and inefficient.

Sears, for example, had trouble throughout the 1980s. It attempted to alter its image by upscaling its products. When that failed, it then attempted to become known as a price-discounter. Sears struggled with both images, partly because it had become so large. It has terminated its catalogue and closed over 100 retail outlets in an attempt to increase its profitability. Sears is far from alone in downsizing. Exxon, Burroughs, ITT, and Gulf & Western, Inc. have attempted to sell off parts of their businesses in order to decrease their size, Federated Department Stores filed for bankruptcy in January 1990 following its acquisitions of Bloomingdale's, Stern's, and Bon Marché, and Macy's filed bankruptcy in 1992 in order to reorganize with fewer stores in its chain.

As we shall discuss in this chapter, the best size for a firm depends on the size of the market the firm is supplying—that is, on the demand for the firm's output and on the costs of doing business. We shall also consider how managers determine the quantities of output they want to produce or offer for sale and the resources necessary to provide those quantities, and why in some industries a firm must be large to be successful, while in others large size is a detriment.

1. FIRMS AND BUSINESS

A business firm is a business organization controlled by a single management. The terms *company, enterprise*, and *business* are used interchangeably

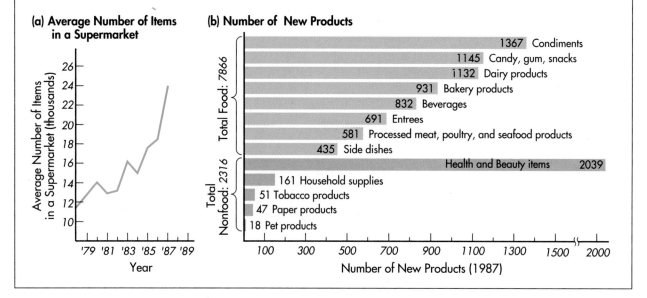

Figure 1
The Growth of Supermarkets
During the 1980s, the size of the average new supermarket grew by 58 percent. This size jump is partly explained by increased consumer demand for more items, as well as consumers' desire for the convenience of one-stop shopping. Supermarkets can carry flowers, wine, and drugs as easily as food and with lower marginal costs. Figure 1(a) shows the sharp increase in the average number of items sold in a supermarket during the second half of the decade. Figure 1(b) charts the number of new food and nonfood products added to supermarkets in 1987. Sources: J. Tooley and M. Knight, "One of This and That . . .," *U.S. News & World Report,* June 20, 1988. Data from Gorman's *New Product News.*

with *firm.* Recall from Chapter 4 that firms can be organized as sole proprietorships, partnerships, or corporations and can be national or multinational companies. In our discussion of the costs of doing business, we use *firm* to refer to all types of business organizations. We distinguish between types of firms only when absolutely necessary. Thus, we speak of a firm as a business organization that brings together the different resources—land, labor, capital, and entrepreneurial ability—to produce a product or service. The term *produce* is also used broadly; it refers not only to manufacturing but also to the retailer who buys goods from a wholesaler and offers the goods to the customers.

The organizational structure of most firms looks like a pyramid. At the top is the president, chief executive officer (CEO), or chairman of the board. Moving down from the top, we may find several vice presidents, several assistant vice presidents, and so on through middle management. At the base of the pyramid is the pool of employees—the people who put the product together or provide the service. In our discussion of the firm, we use *manager* to refer to the person—specifically, the CEO—hired by the entrepreneur or owner to run the firm. We use *employees* to refer to everyone else.

1.a. The Relationship Between Output and Resources

The simplest circular flow diagram from Chapter 4 is reproduced here as Figure 2. It shows that money flows from the household sector to the business sector in payment for goods and services. The flow of money from the house-

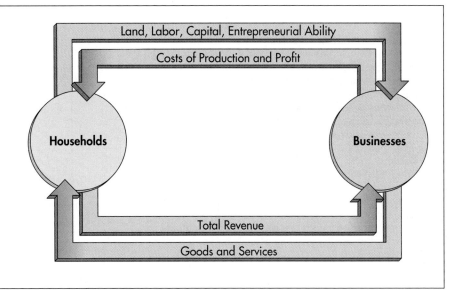

Figure 2
The Circular Flow
The flow of goods and services and money between the household and business sectors is pictured. Businesses sell goods and services to households. The money received is total revenue. The difference between total revenue and the payment for land, labor, and capital is profit. The resources —land, labor, capital, and entrepreneurial ability—flow from the household to the business sector. The payment for these resources flows from the business sector to the household sector.

hold sector to the business sector is the firm's total revenue. In turn, money flows from the business sector to households as payment for the use of their resources—land, labor, capital, and entrepreneurial ability. After the owners of land, labor, and capital have been paid, the entrepreneur receives what is left. Clearly, the amount received by the entrepreneur depends on the output produced by the firm and the quantities of land, labor, and capital used by the firm to produce the output. Entrepreneurs want to produce output at the lowest possible cost. Doing so requires an entrepreneur to compare all combinations of resources (inputs) that can be used to produce output and select the least-cost combination.

Let's use a hypothetical firm, Pacific Western Airlines (PWA), to discuss the relationship between inputs and output. Suppose that PWA has 100 planes, each with a capacity of 300 passengers. On average, in the airline industry, for every hour a jet spends in the air, it spends more than 12 hours on the ground in maintenance. The managers must decide how many mechanics to employ to keep planes flying and in safe condition.

The number of passenger-miles that result when PWA employs alternative numbers of mechanics is shown in the table in Figure 3. Data in the first two columns of the table are plotted in Figure 3(a) as the total-physical-product curve. The **total physical product (TPP)** is the maximum output that can be produced when successive units of a *variable* resource are added to *fixed* amounts of other resources. In other words, the TPP curve shows what a firm could produce in the *short run* employing various quantities of the variable resource.

Recall from the previous chapter that the short run is a period of time just short enough that the quantity of one or more resources cannot be altered. For the airline, the short run might be a year or less because it takes at least a year to obtain an additional airplane. For a basket maker, the short run could be just a day because it might take only a day to obtain additional straw. The TPP curve in Figure 3(a) is a short-run curve because the only variable resource is the number of mechanics; all other resources are fixed.

Columns 1 and 2 of the table in Figure 3 and the total-physical-product

total physical product (TPP): the maximum output that can be produced when successive units of a variable resource are added to fixed amounts of other resources

Figure 3
The *TPP, MPP,* and *APP* Curves

The table provides plotting data for the other sections of Figure 3. Figure 3(a) shows the total-physical-product (*TPP*) curve, which indicates the maximum output that can be produced by combining increasing quantities of one resource with fixed quantities of other resources. The *TPP* curve rises as additional units of the variable resource are added, and it reaches a maximum with the seventh mechanic. The eighth mechanic causes output to decline.

Figure 3(b) shows the marginal-physical-product (*MPP*) curve. The MPP is the additional output generated by an additional mechanic. The first two mechanics add increasing amounts of output, but then each additional mechanic adds less and less to total output until finally the eighth mechanic actually causes the MPP to be negative.

Figure 3(c) shows the marginal-physical-product (*MPP*) and the average-physical-product (*APP*) curves. The average output, or output per mechanic, rises as long as the MPP is greater than the APP. The average output declines as long as the last mechanic added generates less output than each mechanic was, on average, generating before that last mechanic was hired.

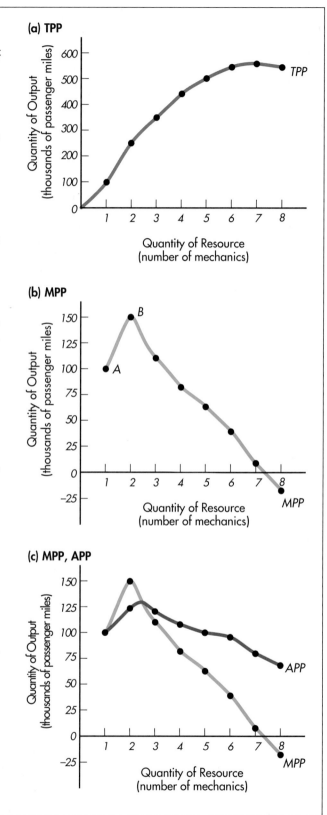

(a) TPP

(b) MPP

(c) MPP, APP

(1) Number of Mechanics	(2) Total Physical Product (TPP)[a]	(3) Marginal Physical Product (MPP)[b]	(4) Average Physical Product (APP)[c]
0	0		0
1	100	100/1 = 100	100/1 = 100
2	250	150/1 = 150	250/2 = 125
3	360	110/1 = 110	360/3 = 120
4	440	80/1 = 80	440/4 = 110
5	500	60/1 = 60	500/5 = 100
6	540	40/1 = 40	540/6 = 90
7	550	10/1 = 10	550/7 = 78.6
8	540	−10/1 = −10	540/8 = 67.5

[a]Output (TPP) is measured in thousands of passenger-miles per week.
[b]MPP = change in output/change in number of mechanics
[c]APP = total output/number of mechanics

Entrepreneurs combine quantities of land, labor, and capital to produce goods and service in the most profitable way. Technological improvements help entrepreneurs produce a larger quantity of goods and services at lower cost, thereby increasing profitability. Here, an Egyptian woman supervises several automatic sewing machines. One woman can produce the same quantity with the automatic machines 100 times faster than when the sewing was done by hand. Employing more people may speed up production; eventually, however, employing more people would not speed up production and could actually retard production as the workers interfere with each other's tasks.

curve of Figure 3(a) show that *total* output increases with each additional mechanic hired until the seventh mechanic is hired. With the eighth mechanic, output declines. In this example, if 7 or fewer mechanics are working, room is adequate, although perhaps not comfortable. Space is totally inadequate when the eighth mechanic tries to join the others. The mechanics interfere with one another, and the total output (TPP) falls.

The additional output produced by an additional unit of the variable resource is called the **marginal physical product (MPP)**.

$$MPP = \frac{\text{change in total physical product}}{\text{change in quantity of variable resource}}$$

As additional mechanics are hired—while the number of planes, the amount of hangar space, and the quantities of tools and other resources are held constant—the additional output generated by each new mechanic (the MPP) initially increases but eventually decreases because of the law of diminishing marginal returns. According to the **law of diminishing marginal returns**, when successive equal amounts of a variable resource (such as labor) are combined with a fixed amount of another resource (such as land or space), marginal increases in output that can be attributed to each additional unit of the variable resource will eventually decline.

marginal physical product (MPP):
the additional quantity that is produced when one additional unit of a resource is used in combination with the same quantities of all other resources

law of diminishing marginal returns:
when successive equal amounts of a variable resource are combined with a fixed amount of another resource, marginal increases in output that can be attributed to each additional unit of the variable resource will eventually decline

I.b. Diminishing Marginal Returns

What is the law of diminishing marginal returns?

Diminishing marginal returns are not unique to the airline industry. In every instance where increasing amounts of one resource are combined with fixed amounts of other resources, the additional output that can be produced initially increases but eventually decreases.

For instance, diminishing marginal returns limit the effort to improve passenger safety during collisions by installing air bags in the dashboards of cars. The air bags open on impact to keep the driver and front-seat passengers from hitting the steering wheel and dashboard. The first air bag added to a car increases protection considerably. The second adds an element of safety, particularly for the front-seat passenger. But additional air bags would provide very little additional protection and eventually would lessen protection as they interfered with each other. As successive units of the variable resource, air bags, are placed on the fixed resource, the car, the additional amount of protection provided by the air bags declines.

The law of diminishing marginal returns also applies to studying. On a typical day, during the first hour you study a subject you probably get a great deal of information. During the second hour you may also learn a large amount of new material, but eventually another hour of studying will produce no benefits and could be counterproductive.

Diminishing marginal returns occur because the efficiency of variable resources depends on the quantity of the fixed resources. If the airline mechanics must stand around waiting for tools or for room to work on the jet engines, then an additional mechanic will allow few, if any, additional passenger-miles to be flown. The limited capacity of the fixed resources—the number of planes, tools, and hangar space—causes the efficiency of the variable resource—the mechanics—to decline.

The effect of the law of diminishing marginal returns is evident in column 3 of the table in Figure 3 and in the marginal-physical-product curve shown in Figure 3(b). The first mechanic increases total output from 0 to 100. The change in total output is 100 and the change in the number of mechanics is 1. Thus, the MPP is 100/1, which is plotted as point *A* in Figure 3(b). Increasing the number of mechanics from 1 to 2 increases total output to 250. The change in output is 150 and the change in the number of mechanics is 1. The MPP is 150/1, plotted as point *B* in Figure 3(b). Total output rises until the eighth mechanic is hired, but the *additional*, or *marginal*, output that is generated by one more mechanic, the MPP, declines when the third mechanic is hired.

average physical product (APP):
output per unit of resource

The **average physical product (APP)** is the total output divided by the quantity of variable resources used to produce that output, or the output per unit of resource. When the last unit hired adds more than the average, the average will rise; when the last unit hired adds less than the average, the average will fall. This is evident in Figure 3(c), where the APP, listed in column 4 of the table in Figure 3, is plotted along with the MPP. APP rises as long as MPP is above APP. APP falls when MPP is below APP.

1.b.1. Average and Marginal Average and marginal relationships behave the same way with respect to each other no matter whether they refer to physical product, cost, utility, grade points, or anything else. For instance, think of the grade point average (GPA) that you get each semester as your *marginal* GPA and your cumulative, or overall, GPA as your *average* GPA. You can see the relation between marginal and average by considering what will happen to your cumulative GPA if this semester's GPA is less than your cumulative GPA. Suppose your GPA this semester is 3.0 for 16 hours of classes and your cumulative GPA, not including this semester, is 3.5 for 48 hours of classes. Your marginal (this semester's) GPA will be less than your average GPA. Thus, when your marginal GPA is added to your average GPA, the average GPA falls, from 3.5 to 3.375. *As long as the marginal is less than the average, the average falls.* If your GPA this semester is 4.0 instead of 3.0, your average GPA will rise from 3.5 to 3.625. *As long as the marginal is greater than the average, the average rises.*

Part II / Product Market Basics

If the average is falling when marginal is below average and rising when marginal is above average, then marginal and average can be the same only when the average is neither rising nor falling. If your GPA this semester is 3.5 and your cumulative GPA up to this semester was 3.5, then your new GPA will be 3.5. Average and marginal are the same when the average is constant. This occurs only when the average curve is at its maximum or minimum point. You can see in Figure 3(c) that the *MPP* curve cuts the *APP* curve (*MPP* = *APP*) at the maximum point of the *APP*.

RECAP

1. According to the law of diminishing marginal returns, as successive units of a variable resource are added to the fixed resources, the additional output produced will initially rise but will eventually decline.
2. Diminishing marginal returns occur because the efficiency of variable resources depends on the quantity of the fixed resources.
3. As long as the marginal is less than the average, the average falls. As long as the marginal is greater than the average, the average rises.

2. REVENUE, COSTS, AND PROFIT

How do economic costs and profit differ from accounting costs and profit?

The *TPP* and *MPP* curves show a firm's manager the technological possibilities for efficiently combining resources to produce output. For instance, a manager might be confronted with several different technologically efficient combinations of resources that can produce the same output. Table 1 shows such a situation. Combinations A, B, C, and D produce the same level of output. Which of the four combinations should be used? The answer depends on the costs of the four production processes. The manager will choose the *least-cost combination*.

2.a. Opportunity Cost and Economic Profit

Economists view revenue, costs, and profit differently from most other people because economists take opportunity costs into account. Consider a medical

TABLE I
Alternative Production Processes

Combination	Mechanics	Planes	Tools	Total Output
A	7	100	50	100
B	9	100	30	100
C	6	60	50	100
D	7	60	40	100

doctor (M.D.) organized as a sole proprietorship. The doctor earns $500,000 of total revenue each year. Profit is the difference between total revenue and total costs. With costs totaling $250,000 per year, the doctor has a profit of $250,000 per year. Let's call this profit *accounting profit*. To be of use to the economist, this accounting profit figure must be adjusted to include the opportunity cost of the doctor's time. If the doctor could have earned $200,000 working for another organization, such as a group of doctors, then the doctor's *economic profit* is $50,000, not $250,000. **Economic profit** is the difference between total revenue and total cost when total cost includes opportunity costs.

economic profit:
total revenue less total costs including opportunity costs

Employment in another organization may not be the only opportunity that the doctor has forgone in order to be a sole proprietor. If the money the doctor has put into the business could have been invested in another business or deposited in a bank and allowed to earn interest, the return or interest on that money is the **opportunity cost of capital**.

opportunity cost of capital:
the forgone return on the entrepreneur's funds used in business

Suppose that a dentist has used $400,000 of her own money to purchase equipment and supplies to get her dental practice started. If the dentist could have earned 10 percent per year on this $400,000, then her opportunity cost of capital is $40,000 per year.

Economic profit can be negative even if accounting profit is positive. A lawyer whose revenue is $200,000 per year and whose direct costs are $100,000 per year has an accounting profit of $100,000. If the lawyer's opportunity costs are $150,000, the lawyer has a negative economic profit of $50,000 even though accounting profit is $100,000.

Economic profit is total revenue less total costs including the cost of resources that the entrepreneur already owns. Resources already owned by the entrepreneur usually include the entrepreneur's labor and the entrepreneur's money that is used in the business.

2.b. Economic and Accounting Costs

Let's now look at economic and accounting costs and profit in a large corporation. Table 2 is an income statement for our hypothetical firm, Pacific Western Airlines (PWA). The gross sales (total revenue) are $200,000,000 for the year. *Explicit* total costs are $100,000,000 and include employee expenses

TABLE 2
Income Statement for Pacific Western Airlines

Revenues:	
Net sales and operating revenues	$200,000,000
Operating expenses:	
Employee expenses	$ 90,000,000
Materials, building, land, marketing	$ 10,000,000
Total costs	$100,000,000
Net income before income taxes	$100,000,000
Taxes	$ 10,000,000
Net income (profit)	$ 90,000,000

and the cost of materials, buildings, land, and marketing. Total revenue less explicit costs leaves $100,000,000, which is net income, or profit before taxes. Taxes are $10,000,000, so the after-tax profit is $90,000,000.

The costs listed in the income statement are referred to as *explicit* to distinguish between *economic costs* and other uses of the terms *cost* and *profit*. Explicit costs are the direct, or out-of-pocket, expenses of hiring workers, buying equipment, paying rent, and so on. **Economic costs** include those explicit costs but also include the full opportunity costs of the resources that the producer does not buy or hire but already owns, such as the returns forgone when personal funds are used in a business and the value of the owner's labor. These costs are sometimes referred to as *implicit costs*.

economic costs:
total costs including explicit costs and the full opportunity costs of the resources that the producer does not buy or hire but already owns

Economists alter the standard or most commonly used measure of profit—accounting profit—because they are attempting to understand why owners make the choices they do, and choices involve opportunity costs. PWA's reported accounting profit of $90,000,000 is the basis of statements provided to banks or investors. PWA's economic profit would be some figure less than $90,000,000 because the opportunity costs would have to be subtracted. Although, the economic profit is not printed on a public statement, it is extremely important for understanding business decision-making. It signals whether the business makes sense and explains why new businesses are begun while others fold. If economic profit is positive, the owners are more than covering their opportunity costs. This means that the owners could do nothing else and be better off. On the other hand, if economic profit is negative, the owners would be better off pursuing another opportunity.

RECAP

1. Accounting profits are total revenues less explicit costs.
2. Economic profits are total revenues less explicit costs and the opportunity costs of the resources already owned by the producer.

3. COST SCHEDULES AND COST CURVES

Having considered the process of turning resources into output and having defined *economic costs* and *profit*, we are ready to look more closely at the costs of doing business. Keep in mind that in economics the term *costs* means opportunity costs and includes resources used in production but previously paid for or owned.

3.a. An Example of Costs

Let's examine the costs of doing business for our hypothetical company, Pacific Western Airlines. Let's suppose that the costs of transporting passengers each week are shown in the table in Figure 4. Column 1 lists the total quantity (Q) of output produced (measured in hundred-million passenger-miles). Notice that we have listed the data in Figure 4 by equal increments of output, from 1 to 2 to 3 and so on (hundred-millions of passenger-miles) because we want to focus on the relationship between output and costs.

Column 2 lists the **total fixed costs (TFC)**, costs that must be paid whether the firm produces or not. Fixed costs are $10,000—this is what must

total fixed costs (TFC):
costs that must be paid whether the firm produces or not

Overhead

An article in the May 18, 1992, *Business Week* entitled "Can Corporate America Get Out from Under Its Overhead?" pointed out that throughout the 1980s corporations reduced labor costs by laying off millions of hourly workers. The dollar's fall, on top of cost-cutting, has helped lower U.S. unit labor costs by 42 percent against those of America's major trading partners since 1985. Now, experts say, "The problem is overhead, chiefly plump white-collar bureaucracies." Many U.S. companies *still* can't compete with their international rivals because of overhead, which equaled 26 percent of sales for U.S. companies, as opposed to 21 percent for Western European companies and 18 percent for Japanese companies.

Economists classify costs as fixed or variable. Fixed costs do not change as the volume of production changes. Variable costs, on the other hand, depend on the volume of production. In business,

costs are classified into overhead and direct operating costs. Overhead costs are those that are not directly attributable to the production process. They include such items as taxes, insurance premiums, managerial or administrative salaries, paperwork, the cost of electricity not used in the production process, and others. Overhead costs can be either fixed or variable. Insurance premiums, taxes, and managerial salaries are fixed costs. They must be paid regardless of how much is produced. Electricity used to operate the production process is a variable cost, increasing as the quantity of output produced is increased.

Statements like "We need to spread the overhead" sound somewhat like the concept of declining average fixed costs—fixed cost per unit of output declines as output rises. But overhead may also include variable costs. Thus, the need to "spread the overhead" refers to reducing the total costs

that are not directly attributable to the production process. The more a firm can keep its overhead costs the same and increase its volume of production, the more that overhead costs look and act like fixed costs. The higher the percentage of overhead costs that are fixed, the more closely related the economists' and the businessperson's classifications will be. But the two are not—and are not meant to be—the same.

The different classifications provide different information. The economist is interested in the decision to produce, how much to produce, and whether to produce at all. This is the information provided by fixed and variable costs. The businessperson is interested in attributing costs to different activities, that is, in determining whether the business is running as cost-efficiently as it can. The classification of costs into direct and overhead provides this information.

total variable costs (TVC):
costs that rise or fall as production rises or falls

total costs (TC):
the sum of total variable and total fixed costs

be paid whether 1 or 1 billion passenger-miles are produced. The fixed costs in this example might represent the weekly portion of the annual payment for the planes, which are the resource whose quantity is fixed. Column 3 lists the **total variable costs (TVC)**, costs that rise or fall as production rises or falls. The costs of resources such as employees, fuel, water, and meals reflect Pacific Western's success in attracting passengers. **Total costs (TC)**, the sum of total variable and total fixed costs, are listed in column 4. (Note that although the distinction between variable and fixed costs is important to economists, many businesspeople focus more on overhead and direct costs. The relation between these concepts is discussed in the Economic Insight "Overhead.")

The total cost curves are plotted in Figure 4(a). The total-fixed-cost curve (*TFC*) is a horizontal line that intersects the vertical axis at the dollar amount of the fixed costs, $10,000. The total-variable-cost curve (*TVC*) begins at zero and rises as output rises. Total costs are found by adding total fixed costs to total variable costs at each level of output: $TC = TFC + TVC$. Thus, the vertical distance between the *TVC* curve and the *TC* curve is the total fixed costs, $10,000.

Figure 4
The Cost Curves

The table provides plotting data for the other sections of Figure 4. Figure 4(a) shows total costs (TC), total variable costs (TVC), and total fixed costs (TFC). The total-fixed-cost curve is a horizontal line because fixed costs do not vary as output changes. Total variable costs rise as output rises; total costs, the sum of total variable and total fixed costs, rise as output rises. The distance between total costs and total variable costs is total fixed costs.

Figure 4(b) shows the average fixed, average variable, average total, and marginal costs. Average fixed costs (AFC) decline steadily from the first unit of output.

Fixed costs are spread over more units of output. Average variable costs (AVC) initially decline but then rise as output rises. Average total costs (ATC), the sum of average fixed and average variable costs, decline and then rise as output rises. The distance between the ATC and AVC curves is AFC. The ATC and AVC curves approach each other as output rises because average fixed costs are decreasing. As long as the marginal cost is less than the average variable or average total costs, average costs fall; when the marginal cost is greater than the average variable or average total costs, the AVC and ATC curves rise. The MC curve crosses the AVC curve at its minimum point, point A, and crosses the ATC curve at its minimum, point B.

(1) Total Output (Q)[a]	(2) Total Fixed Costs (TFC)[b]	(3) Total Variable Costs (TVC)[b]	(4) Total Costs (TC)[b]	(5) Average Fixed Costs (AFC)[c]	(6) Average Variable Costs (AVC)[c]	(7) Average Total Costs (ATC)[c]	(8) Marginal Costs (MC)[c]	
0	$10	$ 0	$10					
1	10	10	20	$10	$10	$20	$10	
2	10	18	28	5	9	14	8	
3	10	25	35	3.33	8.33	11.6	7	
4	10	30	40	2.5	7.5	10	5	
5	10	35	45	2	7	9	5	
6	10	42	52	1.66	7	8.66	7	Point A
7	10	50.6	60.6	1.44	7.2	8.6	8.6	Point B
8	10	60	70	1.25	7.5	8.75	9.4	
9	10	80	90	1.1	8.8	10	20	

[a]Total output is measured in hundred-million passenger-miles.
[b]TFC, TVC, and TC are measured in thousands of dollars.
[c]AFC, AVC, ATC, and MC are measured in thousands of dollars per hundred-million passenger-miles.

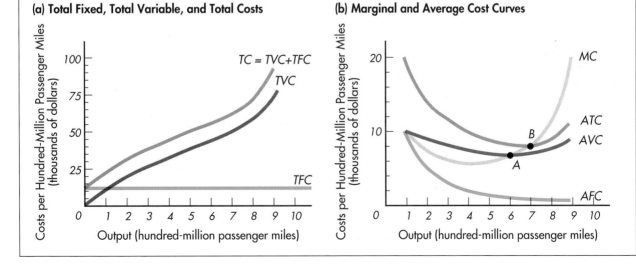

(a) Total Fixed, Total Variable, and Total Costs

(b) Marginal and Average Cost Curves

Average costs—average total, average fixed, and average variable—are derived by dividing the corresponding total costs by the number of passenger-miles that are produced. The average-cost curves are shown in Figure 4(b). *Average fixed costs* (AFC) decline as output rises because the total fixed cost, $10,000, is divided by more and more output. *Average variable costs* (AVC) and *average total costs* (ATC) first decline and then rise. The reason for this pattern is the law of diminishing marginal returns. To transport more passengers, Pacific Western needs more of the variable resources, such as mechanics and fuel. The first few additional resources will increase output a great deal, but eventually the fixed resource becomes restrictive. Increasingly more of the variable resources are needed to increase output. The *AVC* curve reaches a minimum at the 500 to 600 million passenger-mile levels. The *ATC* curve lies above the *AVC* curve by the amount of the average fixed costs. Average total costs decline until the 700 million passenger-mile point and then rise.

marginal costs (MC):
the additional costs of producing one more unit of output

The MC curve intersects the AVC curve at the minimum point of the AVC curve; the MC curve intersects the ATC curve at the minimum point of the ATC curve.

Marginal costs (MC), the additional costs that come from producing an additional unit of output, are listed in column 8 of the table in Figure 4. Marginal costs fall and then rise, just as do average variable and average total costs. The *MC* curve begins below the *AVC* and *ATC* curves and declines until the 500 million passenger-mile point, where it begins to climb. The *MC* curve passes through the *AVC* curve at the minimum value of the *AVC* curve and then continues rising until it passes through the *ATC* curve at the minimum point of the *ATC* curve. The marginal-cost curve intersects the average-cost curves at the minimum points of the average-cost curves. The Economic Insight "Glossary of Costs" summarizes the cost classifications.

3.a.1. The Relationship Between Marginal and Average

The relationship between marginal and average noted in section 1.b.1. is evident in Figure 4(b); the average-total-cost and average-variable-cost curves slope down when the marginal-cost curve lies below them and slope up when the marginal-cost curve lies above them. Average variable costs are falling between output levels 0 and 5. Marginal costs are less than average variable costs in this output range. Between output levels 7 and 9, average variable costs are rising. Marginal costs are greater than average variable costs in this output range. Average variable and marginal costs are the same at the minimum point of the average-variable-cost curve, point *A* in Figure 4(b). The same relationship holds between the average-total-cost and marginal-cost curves. The only point at which the two are equal is the minimum of the average-total-cost curve, point *B*.

3.b. The U Shape of the Cost Curves

short-run average total cost (SRATC):
the lowest-cost combination of resources with which each level of output is produced when the quantity of at least one resource is fixed

The cost curves shown in Figure 4 are called *short-run cost curves* because they exist during time periods when the quantity of at least one of the resources is fixed. Note that the **short-run average-total-cost (SRATC)**, average-variable-cost (AVC), and marginal-cost (MC) curves are U-shaped (see Figure 4). This U shape is due to the law of diminishing marginal returns. When the quantity of at least one of the resources is fixed, each additional unit of a variable resource initially increases output by more than the previous unit but eventually increases output by less than the previous unit. The first mechanic may increase output by 100 and the second by 150, but

Glossary of Costs

1. **Total fixed costs (TFC)** are costs that do not vary as the quantity of goods produced varies. An example of a fixed cost is the rent on a building. Rent has to be paid whether or not the firm makes or sells any goods.

2. **Average fixed costs (AFC)** are total fixed costs divided by the quantity produced:

$$AFC = \frac{TFC}{Q}$$

3. **Total variable costs (TVC)** are costs that change as the quantity of goods produced changes. The cost of materials is usually variable. For instance, the cost of leather for making boots or cloth for manufacturing clothing changes as the quantity produced changes. The fuel required to fly planes will increase as more passengers are transported.

4. **Average variable costs (AVC)** are total variable costs divided by the quantity produced:

$$AVC = \frac{TVC}{Q}$$

5. **Total costs (TC)** are the sum of fixed and variable costs:

$$TC = TFC + TVC$$

6. **Average total costs (ATC)** are total costs divided by the total quantity of the good that is produced, Q:

$$ATC = \frac{TC}{Q}$$

7. **Marginal costs (MC)** are the additional costs that come from producing an additional unit of output:

$$MC = \frac{\text{change in } TC}{\text{change in } Q}$$

What accounts for the shapes of the cost curves?

the third increases output by only 110, the fourth by 80, and so on. Because each mechanic costs the same, each additional unit of output becomes increasingly more costly.

3.b.1. The Link from Physical Product Curves to Costs The physical product curves show the relationship between quantities of inputs (resources, factors of production) and quantities of output. These curves and relationships seem to have nothing to do with money and costs, but that appearance is deceiving. The physical product relationships form the basis of the cost relationships with which firms must deal. The relationship between production and costs is illustrated in Figure 5. The TPP of Figure 3(a) is reproduced in Figure 5(a). The number of mechanics employed each week is measured on the horizontal axis, and the resulting output from employing each quantity of mechanics is measured in thousands of passenger-miles per week along the vertical axis.

Suppose that each mechanic costs $1,000 per week. By multiplying the measurements along the horizontal axis by $1,000, the horizontal axis can be converted into costs, as shown in Figure 5(b). Now switch the axes so that quantity is measured on the horizontal axis and costs are measured on the vertical axis, as shown in Figure 5(c); you can trace the points from A, B, etc., to A', B', etc. Figure 5(c) is a cost curve; in fact, it is the total-variable-cost curve, showing the relationship between the quantity of output produced and the total variable cost of producing that output. Notice how the curve has the same shape as the *TVC* curve in Figure 4(a). You can now see that the shape of the total-variable-cost curve is taken directly from the shape of the *TPP* curve.

Figure 5
The Link Between Production and Costs

The *TPP* of Figure 3(a) is reproduced in Figure 5(a). The number of mechanics is measured on the horizontal axis and the resulting output from employing each quantity of mechanics is measured in thousands of passenger-miles along the vertical axis. Each mechanic costs $1,000 per week. Multiplying the measurements along the horizontal axis by $1,000, the horizontal axis is converted into costs, as shown in Figure 5(b). Switching the axes so that quantity is measured on the horizontal axis and costs are measured on the vertical axis, results in Figure 5(c). Figure 5(c) is the total-variable-cost curve, showing the relationship between the quantity of output produced and the total variable cost of producing that output.

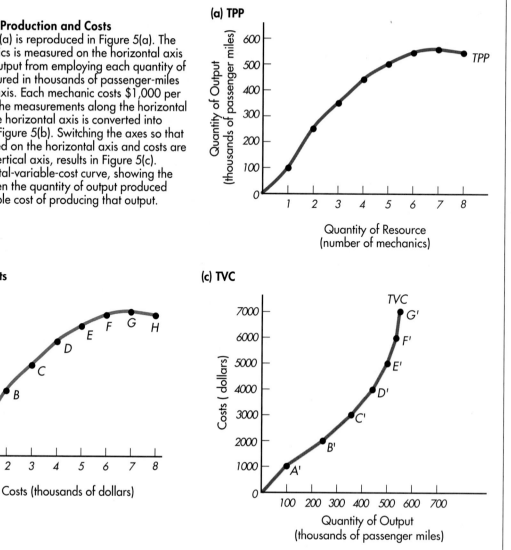

Figure 6 further illustrates how the physical product relationships define the cost relationships. In Figure 6 we have taken the data from Figure 3, converted them to dollars, and plotted the resulting numbers. Column 1 in the table of Figure 6 is the same as column 1 in the table of Figure 3, the number of mechanics. Column 2 in the table of Figure 6 is the quantity of output produced; column 3 is the cost per mechanic per week (assumed to be $1,000); column 4 is the total variable cost, the cost per mechanic times the number of mechanics. Column 5 is the total fixed cost, the cost of the fixed resources ($2,000); and column 6 is the total cost, the sum of total variable and total fixed costs. In columns 7–9, the total costs are converted into average costs. Column 7 is the average variable cost, defined as the total variable cost divided by the total quantity; column 8 is the average fixed cost, defined as the total fixed cost divided by the total quantity; and column 9 is the average total cost, defined as the average total cost divided by the total quantity. The

Figure 6
Another Look at the Link Between Production and Costs

In Figure 6(a) the total cost, total variable cost, and total fixed cost data are plotted. In Figure 6(b) the average and marginal cost data are plotted. Keep in mind that the curves have come directly from the physical product relationships of Figure 3. Thus, the shapes of the cost curves are related to the shapes of the physical product curves. Notice, for instance, that the average and marginal cost curves are U-shaped while the average and marginal physical product curves are "hump-shaped." The U-shape and the hump shape result from the marginal physical product curve. Also notice that the MC curve cuts the minimum point, or bottom, of the AVC and ATC curves; the MPP curve cuts the maximum point, or top, of the APP curve.

(1) Number of Mechanics	(2) TPP or Quantity	(3) Weekly Cost per Mechanic	(4) Total Variable Cost (TVC)	(5) Total Fixed Cost (TFC)	(6) Total Cost (TC)	(7) Average Variable Cost (AVC)	(8) Average Fixed Cost (AFC)	(9) Average Total Cost (ATC)	(10) Marginal Cost (MC)
0	0	$1,000	$ 0	$2,000	$2,000				
1	100	1,000	1,000	2,000	3,000	$10	$20	$30	$10
2	250	1,000	2,000	2,000	4,000	8	8	16	6.7
3	360	1,000	3,000	2,000	5,000	8.3	5.6	13.9	9.1
4	440	1,000	4,000	2,000	6,000	9.1	4.5	13.6	12.5
5	500	1,000	5,000	2,000	7,000	10	4	14	16.7
6	540	1,000	6,000	2,000	8,000	11.1	3.7	14.8	25
7	550	1,000	7,000	2,000	9,000	12.7	3.6	16.4	100

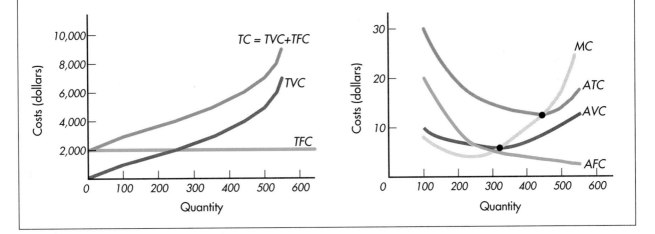

(a) Total Fixed, Total Variable, and Total Costs

(b) Marginal and Average Cost Curves

last column is the change in total cost divided by the change in total output, which is the marginal cost, MC.

In Figure 6(a) the total cost, total variable cost, and total fixed cost data are plotted. In Figure 6(b) the average and marginal cost data are plotted. Keep in mind that the curves have come directly from the physical product relationships of Figure 3. Thus, the shapes of the cost curves are defined by the shapes of the physical product curves. Notice, for instance, that the average and marginal cost curves of Figure 6 are U-shaped while the average and marginal physical product curves of Figure 3 are "hump-shaped." The U shape is the result of the same factor that leads to the hump-shaped product curves, diminishing marginal physical product. Also notice that the *MC* curve cuts the minimum point, or bottom, of the *ATC* and *AFC* curves, while the *MPP* curve cuts the maximum point, or top, of the *APP* curve.

RECAP

1. Fixed costs are costs that cannot be varied during the period under consideration. Variable costs vary as output varies. Hence, total fixed costs are constant, while total variable costs rise as output rises.

2. Total costs include both variable and fixed costs.

3. Average total cost is total cost per unit of output—total cost divided by the number of units of output produced.

4. Average fixed costs decline as output rises because the fixed costs are spread over more units. Average variable costs decline and then rise as output increases.

5. Marginal cost is the change in cost divided by the change in output.

6. The reason for the U shape of the average-variable-cost curve is the initially increasing and then decreasing efficiency of production as more and more variable resources are combined with the fixed resources. More and more workers or more and more materials are combined with the fixed size of the manufacturing plant. The U shape of short-run cost curves is due to diminishing marginal returns.

7. The marginal-cost curve intersects the average-variable-cost curve at the minimum point of the average-variable-cost curve, and it intersects the average-total-cost curve at the minimum point of the average-total-cost curve.

4. THE LONG RUN

A firm can choose to relocate, build a new plant, or purchase additional planes only in the long run, or planning stage. A manager can choose any size of plant or building and any combination of other resources when laying out the firm's plans because all resources are variable in the long run. In essence, during the long run the manager compares all short-run situations.

4.a. Economies of Scale and Long-Run Cost Curves

Figure 7(a) shows several short-run cost curves along which a firm could produce. Each short-run cost curve is drawn for a particular quantity of the capital resource (a particular plant size, number of planes, hangars, etc.). Once the quantity of the capital resource is selected, the firm brings together different combinations of the other resources with the fixed capital resource. If a small quantity of the capital resource is selected, the firm might operate along $SRATC_1$. If the firm selects a slightly larger quantity of the capital resource, then it will be able to operate anywhere along $SRATC_2$. With a still larger quantity, the firm can operate along $SRATC_3$, $SRATC_4$, $SRATC_5$, or some other short-run average-total-cost curve.

Figure 7
The Short-Run and Long-Run Average-Cost Curves
The long-run average-cost curve represents the lowest costs of producing any level of output when all resources are variable. Short-run average-cost curves represent the lowest costs of producing any level of output in the short run, when at least one of the resources is fixed. Figure 7(a) shows the possible *SRATC* curves facing a firm. Figure 7(b) shows the *LRATC* curve, which connects the minimum cost of producing each level of output. Notice that the *SRATC* curves need not indicate the lowest costs of producing in the long run. If the short run is characterized by $SRATC_3$, then quantity Q_4 can be produced at point *C*. But if some of the fixed resources are allowed to change, managers can shift to $SRATC_4$ and produce at point *D*.

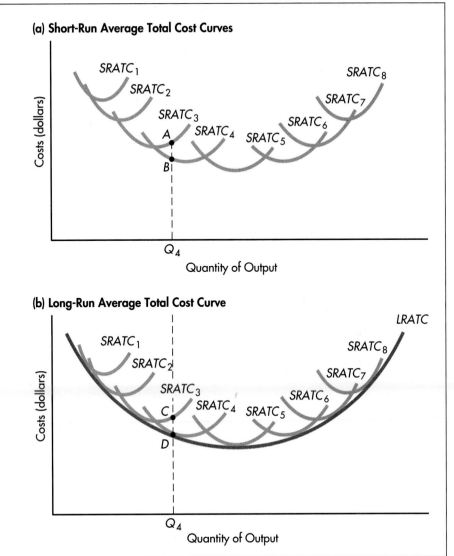

(a) Short-Run Average Total Cost Curves

(b) Long-Run Average Total Cost Curve

In the long run, the firm can choose any of the *SRATC* curves. All it needs to do is choose the level of output it wants to produce and then select the least-cost combination of resources with which to reach that level. Least-cost combinations are represented in Figure 7(b) by a curve that just touches each *SRATC* curve. This curve is the **long-run average-total-cost** curve (**LRATC**—the lowest cost per unit of output for every level of output when all resources are variable). If the firm had chosen to acquire or use a quantity of fixed resources indicated by $SRATC_3$ in Figure 7(b), then it could produce Q_4 only at point *C*. Only by increasing its quantity of fixed resources could the firm produce at point *D* on $SRATC_4$.

You can see in Figure 7(b) that the long-run average-total-cost curve does *not* connect the minimum points of each of the short-run average-cost curves ($SRATC_1$, $SRATC_2$, etc.). The reason is that the minimum point of a short-run average-total-cost curve is not necessarily the lowest-cost method of producing a given level of output. For instance, point *A*, on $SRATC_3$ in Figure 7(a),

long-run average total cost (LRATC):
the lowest-cost combination of resources with which each level of output is produced when all resources are variable

is much higher than point *B* on $SRATC_4$, but output level Q_4 could be produced at either *A* or *B*. When the quantities of all resources can be varied, the choices open to the manager are much greater than when only one or a few of the resources are variable.

The U shape tends to characterize both the long-run average-total-cost and short-run average-total-cost curves. This common shape has different causes, however. The U shape of short-run cost curves is the result of diminishing marginal returns. As increasing quantities of some resources are combined with a fixed quantity of other resources, costs initially decrease but eventually increase. For example, have you ever walked into a restaurant where several tables are empty, yet the host tells you nothing is currently available and a 15-minute wait is necessary? The restaurant is responding to diminishing marginal returns. There are not enough waiters or waitresses to handle all of the available resources. If all tables were used, customers would receive poor service and the restaurant would lose future business. By reducing the number of tables (the variable resource), the waiters and waitresses (the fixed resource) can be more productive and fewer customers will be dissatisfied.

When managers add increasing amounts of a variable resource to a fixed quantity of another resource, they eventually run into diminishing marginal returns. If the quantities of all resources could be changed, diminishing marginal returns would not occur. As Pacific Western increases the number of mechanics, the company also increases the number of planes, hangars, and tools so that the mechanics do not interfere with one another. Remember that the long run is a period of time just long enough that the quantities of all resources can be altered. It is often referred to as the *planning period* because firms forecast and plan their sales before deciding how much space or how many planes they will need.

The long-run average-total-cost curve gets its shape from economies and diseconomies of scale. When the quantities of all resources can be varied, diminishing marginal returns do not occur. For other reasons, the cost per unit of output initially declines and eventually increases as output rises. If producing each unit of output becomes less costly as the amount of output produced rises, there are **economies of scale**—unit costs decrease as the quantity of production increases and all resources are variable. If the cost per unit rises as output rises, there are **diseconomies of scale**—unit costs increase as the quantity of production increases and all resources are variable. Economies of scale account for the downward-sloping portion of the long-run average-cost curve. Diseconomies of scale account for the upward-sloping portion.

If the cost per unit of output is constant as output rises, there are **constant returns to scale**. Figures 8(a), 8(b), and 8(c) show three possible shapes of a long-run average-cost curve. Figure 8(a) is the usual U shape, indicating that economies of scale are followed by constant returns to scale and then diseconomies of scale. Figure 8(b) is a curve indicating only economies of scale. Figure 8(c) is a curve indicating only constant returns to scale. Each of these long-run average-total-cost curves would connect several short-run average-total-cost curves, as shown in Figures 8(d), 8(e), and 8(f).

4.b. The Reasons for Economies and Diseconomies of Scale

Firms that can specialize more as they grow larger may be able to realize economies of scale. Specialization of marketing, sales, pricing, and research,

economies of scale:
the decrease of unit costs as the quantity of production increases and all resources are variable

diseconomies of scale:
the increase of unit costs as the quantity of production increases and all resources are variable

constant returns to scale:
unit costs that remain constant as the quantity of production is increased and all resources are variable

Part II/Product Market Basics

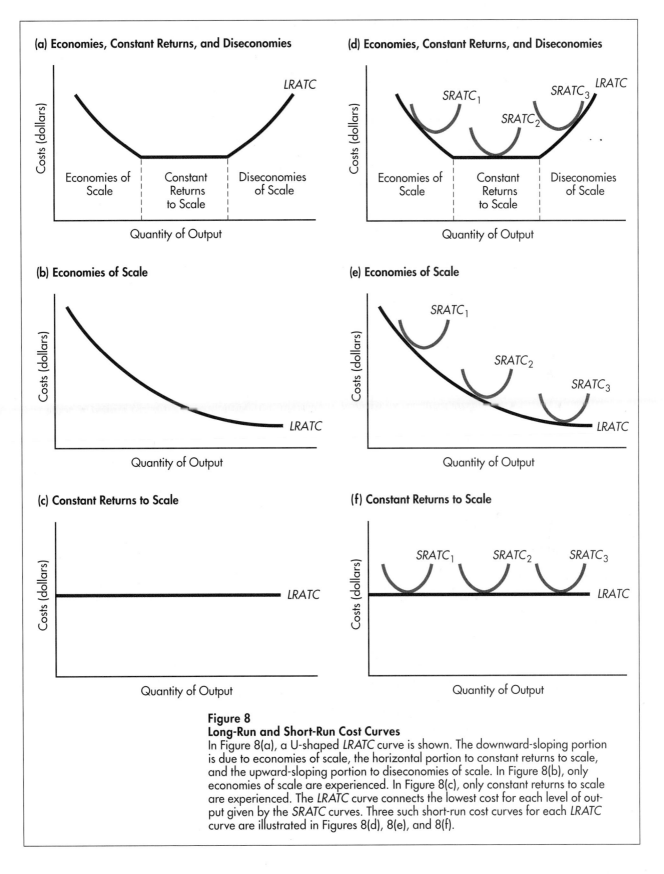

Figure 8
Long-Run and Short-Run Cost Curves
In Figure 8(a), a U-shaped *LRATC* curve is shown. The downward-sloping portion is due to economies of scale, the horizontal portion to constant returns to scale, and the upward-sloping portion to diseconomies of scale. In Figure 8(b), only economies of scale are experienced. In Figure 8(c), only constant returns to scale are experienced. The *LRATC* curve connects the lowest cost for each level of output given by the *SRATC* curves. Three such short-run cost curves for each *LRATC* curve are illustrated in Figures 8(d), 8(e), and 8(f).

for example, allows scientists to focus on their research while others focus on marketing and still others focus on sales and on pricing.

Economies of scale may also result from the use of large machines, which are often more efficient than small ones. Large blast furnaces can produce more than twice as much steel per hour as smaller furnaces, but they do not cost twice as much to build or operate. Large electrical-power generators are more efficient (more output per quantity of resource) than small ones.

Size, however, does not automatically improve efficiency. The specialization that comes with large size often requires the addition of specialized managers. A 10 percent increase in the number of employees may require an increase greater than 10 percent in the number of managers. A manager to supervise the other managers is needed. Paperwork increases. Meetings are held more often. The amount of time and labor that are not devoted to producing output grows. In addition, it becomes increasingly difficult for the CEO to coordinate the activities of each division head and for the division heads to communicate with one another. In this way, size can cause diseconomies of scale.

4.c. The Minimum Efficient Scale

The law of diminishing marginal returns applies to every resource, every firm, and every industry. Whether there are economies of scale, diseconomies of scale, constant returns to scale, or some combination of these depends on the industry under consideration. No law dictates that an industry will have economies of scale eventually followed by diseconomies of scale, although that seems to be the typical pattern. Theoretically, it is possible for an industry to experience only diseconomies of scale, only economies of scale, or only constant returns to scale.

Most industries experience both economies and diseconomies of scale. For example, Mrs. Fields' Cookies trains the managers of all Mrs. Fields' outlets at its headquarters in Park City, Utah. The training period is referred to as Cookie College. By spreading the cost of Cookie College over more than 700 outlets, Mrs. Fields' Cookies is able to achieve economies of scale. However, the company faces some diseconomies because the cookie dough is produced at one location and distributed to the outlets in premixed packages. The dough factory can be large, but the distribution of dough produces diseconomies of scale that worsen as outlets are opened farther and farther away from the factory.

minimum efficient scale (MES):
the minimum point of the long-run average-cost curve; the output level at which the cost per unit of output is the lowest

If the long-run average-total-cost curve reaches a minimum, the level of output at which the minimum occurs is called the **minimum efficient scale (MES)**. Table 3 lists the MES for several manufacturing industries. You can see that the MES varies from industry to industry; it is significantly smaller, for instance, in the production of shoes than it is in the production of cigarettes. A shoe is made by stretching leather around a mold, sewing the leather, and fitting and attaching the soles and insoles. The process requires one worker to operate just two or three machines at a time. Thus, increasing the quantity of shoes made per hour requires more building space, more workers, more leather, and more machines. The cost per shoe declines for the first few shoes made per hour, but rises thereafter. Cigarettes, on the other hand, can be rolled in a machine that can produce several thousand per hour. Producing 100 cigarettes an hour is more costly per cigarette than producing 100,000 per hour.

TABLE 3
Minimum Efficient Scale as a Percentage of the Industry's U.S. Output

Industry	Minimum Efficient Scale
Turbogenerators	23.0
Refrigerators	13.0
Home laundry equipment	11.0
Man-made fiber	11.1
Aircraft	10.0
Synthetic rubber	7.2
Cigarettes	6.6
Transformers	4.9
Paperboard	4.4
Tires and inner tubes	3.8
Blast furnaces and steel	2.7
Detergents	2.4
Storage batteries	1.9
Petroleum refining	1.8
Cement	1.7
Glass containers	1.5
Ball and roller bearings	1.4
Paints and varnishes	1.4
Beer	1.1
Flour mills	0.7
Machine tools	0.3
Cotton textiles	0.2
Shoes	0.2

Sources: F. M. Scherer, A. Beckenstein, E. Kaufer, and R. D. Murphy, *The Economics of Multi-Plant Operation* (Cambridge, Mass.: Harvard University Press, 1975), Ch. 3; C. F. Pratton, *Economies of Scale in Manufacturing Industries* (New York: Cambridge University Press, 1971); L. W. Weiss, "Optimal Plant Size and the Extent of Suboptimal Capacity," in *Essays on Industrial Organization in Honor of Joe S. Bain*, edited by R. T. Masson and P. D. Qualls (Cambridge, Mass.: Ballinger, 1976), pp. 124–141.

4.d. Large Scale Is Not Always Best

Is large always better than small?

Economies of scale result in lower average costs of production as the volume of production increases. It might seem, then, that a firm equal in size to the MES would always have an advantage over smaller firms, but that isn't necessarily so. Efficiency and specialization are limited by the size of the market. If demand is not sufficient to buy all of the output produced at the MES, then producing that much output would not make sense.

Consider the case of the small, developing country, where the domestic market for manufactured goods is quite limited. The most modern technology for an industry may involve a size that exceeds the reasonable market in the country. Sri Lanka, for example, sought assistance from the former Soviet Union to establish a steel mill. The smallest plant the Soviets operated had a capacity of 60,000 tons of steel a year, but total demand in Sri Lanka

Is Small Always Beautiful?

Small firms are often supported and subsidized by developing countries in the belief that these firms use more labor per unit of capital than large firms and thus better make use of the abundant labor the countries have. The belief is often mistaken. Size is not a good indicator of efficiency. The efficiency of small firms is dependent on the same factors that influence efficiency in large firms—the nature of the industry, the array of available technologies, the framework of prices and incentives, and the competitive environment.

Where government policies are biased heavily in favor of small firms, there is a substantial risk that small firms that use resources inefficiently will be established. India is an example. The government has encouraged village industries that use traditional techniques in the production of soap, cloth, and other items, and more than 800 products, mainly chemicals and light engineering goods, are allowed to be produced by small firms only. The result has not been beneficial to the country. In the textile industry, for example, a requirement that more labor-intensive looms be used in mills has led to a lower output and higher price than would have occurred without the requirement. Similarly, in the sugar industry, the government's restriction of the size of sugar-refining mills has led to higher prices and fewer jobs than would have been the case otherwise. The government's restrictions on the expansion of labor engineering firms have fostered the rapid growth of small engineering firms that lack the technical capacity for producing high-quality goods or adopting new technology.

Evidence from other countries also suggests that small may not always be beautiful. In the Republic of Korea, for example, small firms employing fewer than 50 workers were the most efficient in only 32 of 139 industries. And in Colombia, the larger metalworking firms were more efficient than the smaller firms. In contrast, in Sierra Leone the smaller firms were the more efficient.

Source: From *The World Development Report 1990* by The World Bank. Copyright © 1990 by the International Bank for Reconstruction and Development/The World Bank.

was only 35,000 tons a year. As a result, the mill set up by the Soviets could be used to only about 58 percent of its capacity. At that rate of output, the mill operated inefficiently. Copying the plans of an industrial country resulted in a minimum efficient scale that was too large for the developing country. As a result of their smaller size, domestic markets of developing countries are often better served by relatively old-fashioned methods of production than by the most up-to-date methods of production. An illustration is provided in the Economic Insight "Is Small Always Beautiful?"

Since markets in different countries may not support the minimum efficient scale available with the most modern plant, you might wonder why nations don't specialize in industries where they can achieve a minimum efficient scale that is competitive with the most efficient producers and buy from other countries the products for which the domestic market is too small to support competitive production. In fact, there is some evidence that scale economies help determine the pattern of trade across countries. Countries that can achieve an efficient scale of production in an industry like steel or autos sell products to countries that are unable to produce sufficient scale economies. The problem with this scenario is that many countries do not allow certain goods and services to be purchased from other countries, and as a result, local firms are the only sources of these goods and services. This means that the small size of the domestic market in many countries prolongs the use of traditional methods of production.

RECAP

1. Most industries are characterized by U-shaped long-run average-cost curves.

2. The long-run average-total-cost curve gets its U shape from economies and diseconomies of scale, unlike the short-run cost curves, which get their U shape from diminishing marginal returns.

3. The minimum efficient scale (MES) is the size of a firm that is at the minimum point of a long-run average-cost curve.

4. The MES varies from industry to industry. Some industries, like the electric-power industry, have large economies of scale and a large MES. Other industries, like the fast-food industry, have a relatively small MES.

5. Economies of scale may result from specialization and technology. Diseconomies of scale may occur because coordination and communication become more difficult as size increases.

6. In some cases, the market is not large enough to allow firms to produce at the MES. This is often the case in small nations.

SUMMARY

1. A firm is a business organization that brings together land, labor, capital, and entrepreneurial ability to produce a product or service. §1

2. The short run is a period of time just short enough that the quantity of at least one of the resources cannot be altered. §1.a

3. The total-physical-product curve is a picture of the short-run relationship between resources (inputs) and output when one resource is variable. §1.a

▲▼ **What is the law of diminishing marginal returns?**

4. According to the law of diminishing marginal returns, when successive equal amounts of a variable resource are combined with a fixed amount of another resource, there will be a point beyond which the extra or marginal product that can be attributed to each additional unit of the variable resource will decline. §1.a

▲▼ **How do economic costs and profit differ from accounting costs and profit?**

5. Economic profit is total revenue less economic costs. §2.a

6. Economic costs include explicit costs and the opportunity costs of the resources that the pro-

ducer does not hire or buy but instead already owns. §2.b

7. Fixed costs are costs that do not vary as the quantity of goods produced varies. §3.a

8. Total variable costs rise as the quantity of goods produced rises. §3.a

9. Total costs are the sum of fixed and variable costs. §3.a

10. Average total costs are the costs per unit of output—total costs divided by the quantity of output produced. §3.a

11. Average costs fall when marginal costs are less than average and rise when marginal costs are greater than average. §3.a.1

▲▼ **What accounts for the shapes of the cost curves?**

12. The U shape of short-run average-total-cost curves is due to the law of diminishing marginal returns. §3.b

13. The U shape of long-run average-total-cost curves is due to economies and diseconomies of scale. §4.a

14. Economies of scale result when increases in output lead to decreases in unit costs and the quantities of all resources are variable. §4.a

15. Diseconomies of scale result when increases in output lead to increases in unit costs and the quantities of all resources are variable. §4.a

16. Constant returns to scale occur when increases in output lead to no changes in unit costs and the quantities of all resources are variable. §4.a

17. The minimum efficient scale (MES) occurs at the minimum point of the long-run average-total-cost curve. §4.c

▲▼ *Is large always better than small?*

18. Large scale is not always best. The best size depends on the structure of costs and the extent of the market. §4.d

KEY TERMS

total physical product (TPP) §1.a

marginal physical product (MPP) §1.a

law of diminishing marginal returns §1.a

average physical product (APP) §1.b

economic profit §2.a

opportunity cost of capital §2.a

economic costs §2.b

total fixed costs (TFC) §3.a

total variable costs (TVC) §3.a

total costs (TC) §3.a

marginal costs (MC) §3.a
  (see Economic Insight "Glossary of Costs")

average fixed costs (AFC) §3.a
  (see Economic Insight "Glossary of Costs")

average variable costs (AVC) §3.a
  (see Economic Insight "Glossary of Costs")

average total costs (ATC) §3.a
  (see Economic Insight "Glossary of Costs")

short-run average total cost (SRATC) §3.b

long-run average total cost (LRATC) §4.a

economies of scale §4.a

diseconomies of scale §4.a

constant returns to scale §4.a

minimum efficient scale (MES) §4.c

EXERCISES

1. Can accounting profit be positive and economic profit negative? Can accounting profit be negative and economic profit positive? Explain.

2. Use the following information to calculate accounting profit and economic profit.

Sales $100
Employee expenses $40
Inventory expenses $20
Value of owner's labor in any other enterprise $40

3. Use the following information to list the total fixed costs, total variable costs, average fixed costs, average variable costs, average total costs, and marginal costs.

Output	Costs	TFC	TVC	AFC	AVC	ATC	MC
0	$100						
1	150						
2	225						
3	230						
4	300						
5	400						

4. Use the following table to answer the questions listed below.

Output	Cost	TFC	TVC	AFC	AVC	ATC	MC
0	$ 20						
10	40						
20	60						
30	90						
40	120						
50	180						
60	280						

a. List the total fixed costs, total variable costs, average fixed costs, average variable costs, average total costs, and marginal costs.

b. Plot each of the cost curves.

c. At what quantity of output does marginal cost equal average total cost and average variable cost?

5. Describe some conditions that might cause large firms to experience inefficiencies that small firms would not experience.

6. What is the minimum efficient scale? Why would different industries have different minimum efficient scales?

7. Describe the relation between marginal and average costs. Describe the relation between marginal and average fixed costs and between marginal and average variable costs.

8. President Clinton appointed an executive from Salomon Brothers investment banking company to a position in his administration. The executive had to sacrifice a million-dollar salary to accept a government position paying only $100,000 per year. What are the executive's opportunity costs? Are the costs different in the short run and the long run?

9. Explain why the short-run marginal-cost curve must intersect the short-run average-total-cost and average-variable-cost curves at their minimum points. Why doesn't the marginal-cost curve also intersect the average-fixed-cost curve at its minimum point?

10. Explain the relationship between the shapes of the production curves and the cost curves. Specifically, compare the marginal-physical-product curve and the marginal-cost curve, and the average-physical-product curve and the average-total-cost curve.

11. Consider a firm with a fixed-size production facility as described by its existing cost curves.

a. Explain what would happen to those cost curves if a mandatory health insurance program is imposed on all firms.

b. What would happen to the cost curves if the plan required the firm to provide a health insurance program for each employee worth 10 percent of the employee's salary?

c. How would that plan compare to one that requires each firm to provide a $100,000 group program that would cover all employees in the firm no matter the number of employees?

12. Explain the fallacy of the following statement: "You made a real blunder. The $600 you paid for repairs is worth more than the car."

13. Explain the statement "We had to increase our volume to spread the overhead."

14. Three college students are considering operating a tutoring business in economics. This business would require that they give up their current jobs at the student recreation center, which pay $6,000 per year. A fully equipped facility can be leased at a cost of $8,000 per year. Additional costs are $1,000 a year for insurance and $.50 per person per hour for materials and supplies. Their services would be priced at $10 per hour per person.

a. What is the accounting cost? (It varies according to the number of students. Look at the costs of 100 students and then 1,000 students.)

b. What is the economic cost? (Again, this varies according to the number of students. Choose 100 and then 1,000 students.)

c. What are fixed costs?

d. What are variable costs?

e. What is the marginal cost?

f. How many students would it take to break even on an economic cost basis?

15. Express Mail offers overnight delivery to customers. It is attempting to come to some conclusion on whether to expand its facilities or not. Currently its fixed costs are $2 million per month and its variable costs are $2 per package. It charges $12 per package and has a monthly volume of 2 million packages. If it expands, its fixed costs will rise by $1 million and its variable costs will fall to $1.50 per package. Should it expand?

Agencies Say Change May Increase Demand for Temporary Workers

GASTONIA—"Busy" best describes what it's like in the two offices for temporary workers that Darlene Edge manages in Gastonia and Lincolnton.

Even so, she's anticipating an even brisker pace now that President Clinton has signed the family and medical leave bill.

The law grants employees working at companies with 50 or more workers up to 12 weeks unpaid leave annually for births or serious family illnesses. The bill takes affect Aug. 5.

Edge hopes companies will hire temporary workers to fill in for the absent employee.

"We're busy right now and have been for the past two to three weeks—especially because I think the economy is on an upswing," says Edge, general manager for Universal Temporaries of Gastonia & Lincolnton Inc.

"I really feel like it is going to open up more for us," she says.

Other area temporary agencies see it as a possible boon for their business, too.

Especially because Gaston and Lincoln counties have a textile and light industrial labor market that lends itself to seeking help from temporary agencies, they say.

"Hey, this can't help but be a boost to our agencies," says Fredia Hamrick, district manager of the Manpower Temporary Services offices in Shelby and Gastonia.

Manpower, an international company, has 800 offices in the United States, Hamrick says.

Many mills and industries request temporary workers already, Edge says.

"I'd say 80 percent of our business is industrial," Edge says. "And we do a lot of textile."

However, the anticipated increase in calls may not play out for temporary agencies everywhere.

"In general, we are not foreseeing a huge influx in business in response to the bill," says Barb Schryver, information specialist for Manpower Temporary Services at its corporate office in Milwaukee.

Wisconsin has a family leave law that provides two weeks unpaid

leave every year for medical reasons and six unpaid weeks annually for adoption or birth of a child.

"I don't think we'll see tons of people coming forward needing to use the bill," she says.

That's because such a small segment of the work force is covered by its provisions, she says. The Labor Department estimates 5 percent of U.S. employers have 50 or more workers.

Also, several states, unlike North Carolina, already have some sort of law that grants family leave for births, adoption and family emergencies.

"Filling in for emergencies of this type—caring for elderly parents or a pregnancy—have always been a part of our business and companies have always known we're here," says Schryver.

Source: Suzanne Jeffries, "Agencies Say Change May Increase Demand for Temporary Workers," *Charlotte Observer*, Feb. 14, 1993, p. 1. Copyright © 1993 by The Charlotte Observer. Reprinted by permission.

Commentary

Will the Family and Medical Leave Act increase the demand for temporary employees? One reason it might, according to the article, is that firms will need to hire temporary employees to fill in when permanent employees take the leaves of absence defined by the act. Another reason could be that firms will use temporary rather than permanent employees in order to avoid providing the mandated twelve weeks of unpaid leave. Whether either effect occurs depends on whether employees choose to take the unpaid leaves and whether firms find that the leaves increase the cost of doing business.

The cost of doing business is the cost of land, labor, capital, and entrepreneurial ability. Typically, these costs are examined in the short run, a period of time in which the quantity of all resources except labor are fixed. The average total- and variable-cost curves and the marginal-cost curve derive their U shape from the effect of adding an increasing quantity of labor to fixed quantities of land and capital—the result is diminishing marginal returns.

How might the Family and Medical Leave Act affect the costs of doing business for the firm? Assume that a firm with more than fifty employees has cost curves similar to those drawn in the accompanying figure. Prior to the Family and Medical Leave Act, the firm had short-run average- and marginal-cost curves labeled MC_b and $SRATC_b$, where the subscript b means "before the law." The firm chose to produce 250,000 units of its product at an average cost of $5 per unit. Suppose that the Family and Medical Leave Act imposes a cost of $1,000 per employee per year. This cost is a combination of having to provide additional training to all employees so that remaining employees can cover for an employee who takes the unpaid leave of absence and of having to use a temporary worker who is not trained as well as the permanent employee. Suppose further that both fixed and variable costs are affected. Fixed costs rise because the firm must create and maintain training programs and facilities for such programs. Variable costs rise because it is more likely that with more output and thus more employees, more will take the unpaid leave of absence.

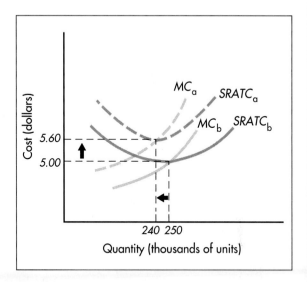

The fixed-cost increase of, say, $75,000 is equivalent to a $.30 per unit cost increase for 250,000 units. The variable-costs increase of, say, $75,000 on a volume of 250,000 is also a $.30 per unit cost increase. (For smaller quantities the variable-cost increase is less than $75,000 and for larger quantities the variable-cost increase is greater than $75,000.) Thus the $SRATC$ curve shifts up by $.60 on a volume of 250,000 (to $SRATC_a$). The subscript a represents *after* the Act is implemented.

The firm can produce any quantity it wants, but it will be at a higher cost after the act than before the act. If the Family and Medical Leave Act does increase costs as illustrated, then the firm must decide how much to produce and how to produce. A firm that is attempting to produce with the lowest possible costs will have to decide whether to use more temporary employees, use more temporary employees and fewer permanent employees, or use fewer employees altogether. Which option the firm will choose will depend on which one allows the firm to earn the greatest profit. According to the diagram, the lowest possible costs would occur at a volume of 240,000 units after the act, a reduction of 10,000 units.

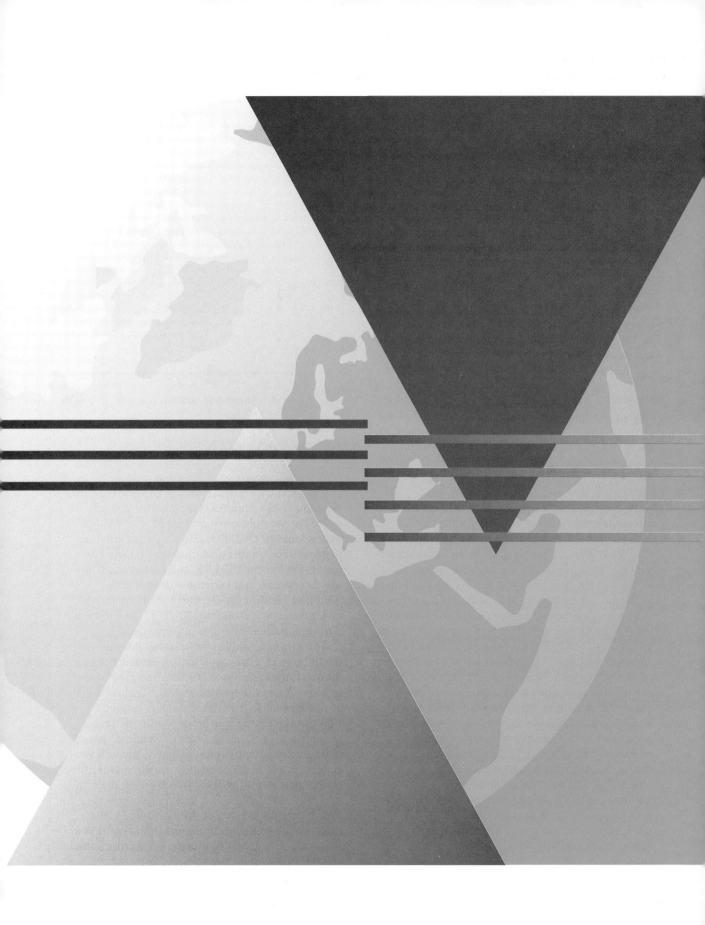

III

Product Markets

9

An Overview of Product Markets and Profit Maximization

FUNDAMENTAL QUESTIONS

1. How do firms maximize profit?
2. How do firms decide how much to supply?
3. What is a market structure?
4. What are price takers?
5. What are price makers?
6. What does the marginal-revenue curve of a firm in each market structure look like?

In the previous three chapters, we first examined demand, then elasticities, and then turned to supply, or the costs of doing business. In this chapter, we put demand and supply together. Unfortunately, this is not as easy as it sounds. There are nearly six million business establishments in the United States alone. And they each face different demands and different costs. As a result, they behave differently. A brewery might spend hundreds of millions of dollars each year to tell you that "This Bud's for you" or that "Not any lite will do." An individual farmer, in contrast, is not likely to spend money to differentiate his or her oats or wheat from other farmers' oats and wheat. Different airlines almost always offer identical fares on the same routes, whereas Kodak sets the prices of its photofinishing chemicals and paper some 15 percent above the prices set by Trebla, Hunt, and Mitsubishi. The price of Bayer aspirin is nearly double the price of generic aspirin. Some firms (such as Sharper Image) offer the first available version of a product at high prices. Other firms (Nordstrom, for instance) offer great service. Still others (like Kmart) don't worry much about service and don't try to be the first to offer a product, but do offer low prices on everything.

PREVIEW

A list of differences among firms could fill many pages. This diversity makes generalization difficult: it is hard to understand why individual firms behave as they do. We know that firms must respond to their customers, that is, to demand. But how firms respond depends on their producing and selling environments: how many competitors or close substitutes there are; how easy it is for them to switch from the production of one product to another; how easy it is for new competitors to start up a business; or, in general, on the factors that influence demand and supply elasticities. Without some means of simplification, we'd have to consider hundreds of thousands of specific cases every time we wanted to discuss the supply side of a market. The simplification economists have devised is a classification scheme based on producing and selling environments. There are four possible environments, or what are called market structures: *perfect competition*, *monopoly*, *monopolistic competition*, and *oligopoly*. The following three chapters examine these market-structure models in detail. In this chapter we introduce the models and look at some of the ways that firms behave.

I. PROFIT MAXIMIZATION

The assumption that consumers behave so as to maximize utility allows economists to describe consumer behavior in a consistent and logical man-

ner. Similarly, the assumption that firms behave so as to maximize profit allows economists to describe firm behavior in a consistent and logical manner. Profit maximization is a simplifying assumption. It does not describe exactly how every firm behaves, but it provides a theory about firm behavior that can be used to examine real-life circumstances.

The profit-maximization assumption does not apply to some firms even in theory. Some firms are explicitly not for profit; they are organized to provide a service, such as education or health care, regardless of whether a profit is made. Public enterprises such as government agencies, public colleges and universities, and some hospitals do not attempt to maximize profits. Objectives other than profit dominate and describe the behavior of these "not-for-profit" firms. Nevertheless, for most firms most of the time, profit maximization appropriately describes their operating behavior.

1.a. Profit

zero economic profit (normal profit):
total revenue equals the sum of direct and opportunity costs

positive economic profit (above-normal profit):
total revenue exceeds the sum of direct and opportunity costs

When a firm has a zero economic profit, its owners are earning sufficient revenue to pay all direct costs and just cover the owner's opportunity costs.

When a firm has above-normal profit, the firm's revenues pay for direct costs and provide the owners more than their opportunity costs.

A negative economic profit means a firm's owners would be better off using their time and money in another activity.

Profit is revenue less costs. *Economic profit* is the difference between total revenue and total costs including opportunity costs, as you learned in the previous chapter. If a firm is making an economic profit, its revenues are enough to pay all of its direct costs and its opportunity costs as well. Economic profit is zero when total revenue equals direct costs plus opportunity costs. Since opportunity cost is the value of the best forgone alternative, if a firm earns a **zero economic profit**, the owners of the firm could not use their time or money better in any other business. A zero economic profit is called a **normal profit** or **normal accounting profit**. If a firm earns a **positive economic profit,** then the owners of the firm are earning more than they could in any other business. Thus, positive economic profit is referred to as **above-normal profit**, or **above-normal accounting profit**.

Accounting profit does not include opportunity costs. Thus, accounting profit could be positive and economic profit negative. A firm could report to its shareholders that it had a profitable year and yet it could have negative economic profit because its revenues were not covering the owner's opportunity costs, or the opportunity costs of the owner's money used in the business. In such a case, the owners would be better off putting their time and money into other activities.

Total revenue is price times quantity sold, $P \times Q$. A demand curve gives price and quantity combinations that are available to a firm. Three demand curves are drawn in Figure 1: a perfectly elastic demand curve in Figure 1(a), the downward-sloping straight-line demand curve in Figure 1(b), and a perfectly inelastic demand curve in Figure 1(c). Below each demand curve is the corresponding total-revenue curve.

With the perfectly elastic demand curve of Figure 1(a), as quantity is increased, total revenue rises. Price is constant at P_1, so $P_1 \times Q$ continues to rise as Q rises. Total revenue is a straight, upward-sloping line starting at the origin.

Along the downward-sloping straight-line demand curve of Figure 1(b), both P and Q change. As we move down a straight-line downward-sloping demand curve, revenue initially rises (in the price-elastic region) and then declines (in the price-inelastic region). This is shown in the lower half of Figure 1(b).

With the perfectly inelastic demand curve, Figure 1(c), quantity is a constant, Q_1, determined by the amount that the buyers must have. Total revenue then depends on what price is, $P \times Q_1$. As price rises, total revenue rises.

Figure 1
Demand and Total Revenue

Figure 1(a) shows a perfectly elastic demand curve at price P_1. The total-revenue curve drawn below 1(a) shows that revenue rises as the quantity produced and sold rises, $P_1 \times Q$. Figure 1(b) shows a typical downward-sloping demand curve. Below it is the total-revenue curve. Total revenue rises as price is decreased in the elastic region; total revenue reaches a maximum at the unit-elastic point; total revenue falls as price is decreased in the inelastic region. Figure 1(c) is a perfectly inelastic demand curve. The total revenue is the fixed quantity, Q_1, multiplied by the price. The higher the price, the higher total revenue.

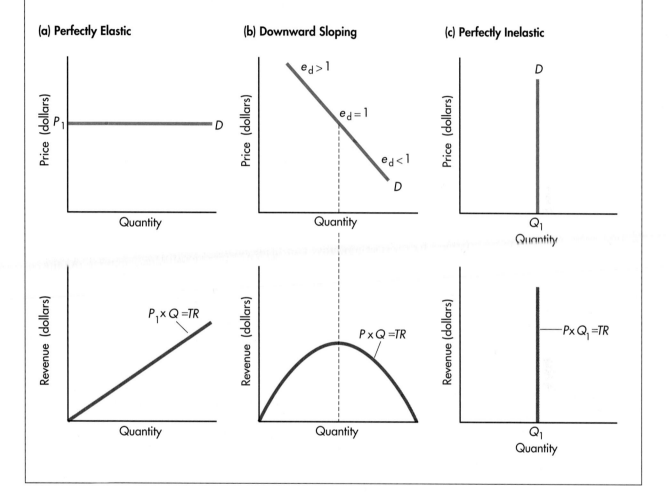

Recall from the previous chapter, "Supply: The Costs of Doing Business," that total costs rise relatively slowly at low levels of production but then as diminishing marginal returns set in, total costs rise more and more rapidly. This is shown in Figure 2.

In Figure 3, the total-revenue and total-cost curves are placed together. The firm wants to maximize profit, or find the quantity at which total revenue exceeds total costs by the greatest amount. In Figure 3(a) you can see that profit is maximized at quantity Q^*; in Figure 3(b), profit is maximized at quantity Q^{**}; and in Figure 3(c), profit rises as price rises (until demand no longer exists). Keep in mind that profit refers to economic profit.

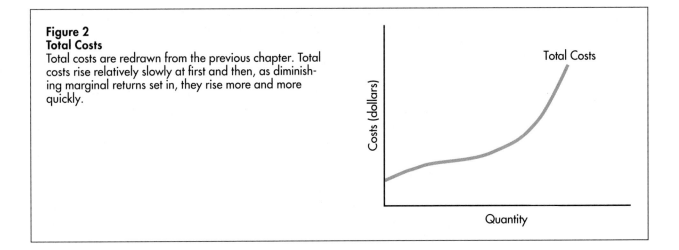

Figure 2
Total Costs
Total costs are redrawn from the previous chapter. Total costs rise relatively slowly at first and then, as diminishing marginal returns set in, they rise more and more quickly.

I.b. Firm Behavior and Price Elasticity of Demand

Figures 3(a), (b), and (c) give you some idea of the different behaviors we might expect of firms. The firms facing perfectly elastic demand curves have no discretion over price; their goods must have the same price as their competitors' goods. These firms choose how much to produce and, as profit-maximizing firms, produce the quantity where total revenue exceeds total cost by the greatest amount. The firms facing a downward-sloping straight-line demand curve choose both price and quantity. The firms will choose the combination of price and quantity that maximizes profit. Firms facing perfectly inelastic demand select only the price to charge for their products since

Figure 3
Total Profit
In Figure 3(a) the total-revenue curve from the perfectly elastic demand curve and the total-cost curve are placed together. The profit-maximizing point is Q^*. In Figure 3(b) the total-revenue curve from the downward-sloping demand curve and the total-cost curve are put together. The profit-maximizing point is shown as Q^{**}, which is not the revenue-maximizing point. In Figure 3(c) the total-revenue curve of the perfectly inelastic demand curve is placed together with the total-cost curve. Total profit rises as price rises.

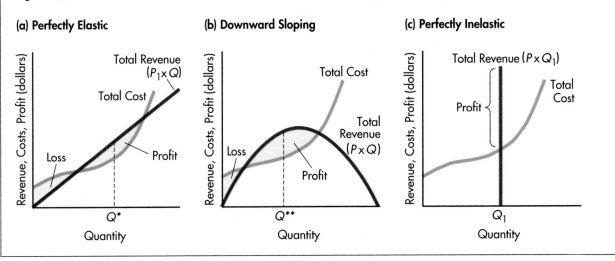

(a) Perfectly Elastic

(b) Downward Sloping

(c) Perfectly Inelastic

quantity is defined or determined by how much consumers want (or need). At least up to some price where consumers cannot purchase the good, the higher the price the greater the profit.

You can see how firms might prefer to face the most inelastic demand curves possible. Thus, we might expect firms to try to influence the elasticity of demand. How might a firm make the demand for its product more inelastic? Since the price elasticity of demand depends on the availability of substitutes, along with the importance of the product in the buyer's total budget and the period of time under consideration, a firm might attempt to reduce the price elasticity of demand for its product by reducing the availability of substitutes. One strategy some firms take is to differentiate their products from those of competitors. For instance, Procter & Gamble might alter the ingredients of its detergent All to make it different from Tide, or Quaker might make sure that the taste or appearance of its raisin bran cereal is different from the raisin bran cereal of General Mills. Anything that successfully distinguishes or differentiates products will reduce the price elasticity of demand because it reduces the number of "close" substitutes.

It may not be possible for a firm to differentiate its product, however. Kyrene Scrap Metal is a firm that collects discarded appliances and other metal items and processes them into scrap metal to sell to steel manufacturers. Kyrene Scrap Metal cannot differentiate its scrap from scrap supplied by other scrap metal firms; scrap is scrap to the steel manufacturers. Similarly, it may not be possible for Old MacDonald to differentiate his wheat from wheat grown on another farm. The selling environments of the scrap metal company and the individual wheat farm are very different from that of Procter & Gamble.

1.c. Firm Behavior and Price Elasticity of Supply

A firm's producing and selling environment does not depend solely on the demand for its product. It also depends on the costs of producing and selling. The cost curves we derived in the previous chapter represent the cost curves of nearly any firm. Granted, fixed costs are larger for airline companies than desktop publishers, but the relationship of the cost curves to each other and the general shapes of the curves are approximately the same for airlines and desktop publishers.

If there are huge fixed costs in a particular line of business, such as airlines, then entrepreneurs might be reluctant to start up in that business. As a result, existing firms in that business do not have to fear immediate new competition in response to price changes or product differentiation strategies. If existing firms can make above-normal profits, they may be able to keep their above-normal profits for a long period of time because new competition will not immediately arise. Conversely, if fixed costs are very low, such as in desktop publishing, a small profit increase for a firm would induce a multitude of entrepreneurs to start up competing businesses. For these firms, above-normal profits would not last long. Thus, we might expect firms to attempt to increase the fixed costs necessary to begin a new business or to somehow make it difficult for new firms to enter their line of business. In this way, firms might be able to retain above-normal profits for a longer period of time.

Imagine if you were the only producer of a product that consumers really needed (desperately wanted)—say, a life-saving pharmaceutical. Your profit

For decades electric utility companies have been thought of as natural monopolies. As a result of the huge economies of scale in the transmission and distribution of electricity, governments have regulated the utilities, attempting to force them to provide the service and the quantity of electricity desired by the public at a cost equal to average total costs. In the past ten years or so, technology has changed the electric utility industry. Regulators have allowed competitors to arise by allowing small producers of electricity to use the utility's transmission lines and to sell the electricity generated whenever the producer has generated more electricity than personally needed. Some customers can purchase electricity from different suppliers. Is electricity generation and distribution a natural monopoly or has it become more of an oligopoly?

potential would be huge. Thus, we might expect firms to attempt to become the sole suppliers of necessary goods and services. For instance, if a firm could exploit economies of scale and thus be able to produce at a lower average cost than any other firm, it might become the only producer of a good. Or, perhaps a firm could get a law passed that gave it the exclusive rights to supply a good. Being the only producer of a good or service people desperately want could mean above-normal profits for a long time.

RECAP

1. The assumption that firms behave so as to maximize profit allows economists to describe firm behavior in a consistent, logical way.
2. Profit is maximized at the level of output where total revenue exceeds total costs by the greatest amount.
3. Firm behavior depends on the factors that affect the price elasticities of demand and supply.

2. MARGINAL REVENUE AND MARGINAL COST

A market consists of demand and supply: buyers and sellers of a well-defined good or service. To understand how markets function we examine individual buyers (consumers) and individual sellers (firms). In the chapter, "Consumer Choice," we looked at the individual buyer's purchasing decisions. Here we begin to examine the individual firm's production and selling decisions.

2.a. Demand and Cost Curves

How do firms decide how much to supply?

A firm's decision to supply a good or service depends on expected profit. An entrepreneur or manager of a firm looks at the demand for the firm's product and at its costs of doing business and determines whether a profit potential exists. To analyze the firm's decisions, we must put the demand for the firm's product together with the firm's costs.

Consider Figure 4, in which the average-total and marginal-cost curves, derived in the previous chapter, are drawn along with a downward-sloping demand curve. (Alternatively, the demand curve could be horizontal or vertical.) The demand curve and the cost curves characterize the environment in which the firm is producing and selling.

With the downward-sloping demand curve, the firm knows that total revenue first rises and then declines as price is lowered down along the demand curve. Maximum revenue is the point where the price elasticity of demand is 1. But this point is not necessarily the profit-maximizing point. How do we find the profit-maximizing point?

Profit is the difference between total revenue and total costs. Consider the profit the firm shown in Figure 4 earns at price P_1 selling output Q_1. Total revenue is price times quantity, or $P_1 \times Q_1$, the rectangle $ABCD$. At price P_1 total cost is given by $ABEF$, found by determining the average total cost (cost per unit of output) at price P_1 and multiplying that by the quantity produced, Q_1. Profit at quantity Q_1, then, is the difference between the rectangle $ABCD$ and the rectangle $ABEF$. Profit at Q_1, is given by: $ABCD - ABEF = FECD$.

The profit given by the rectangle $FECD$ in Figure 4 is the profit the firm would earn by producing and selling quantity Q_1. The area $FECD$ is not necessarily the maximum profit—the firm might earn more producing more or less than Q_1. To find the quantity at which profit is maximized, we could compare total revenue and total cost for each output level. There is an easier way, however: to find the quantity of output at which profit is a maximum, simply compare marginal cost and marginal revenue.

Supply rule: produce and offer for sale the quantity at which marginal revenue equals marginal cost (MR = MC).

Figure 4
Revenue, Cost, and Profit
In Figure 4 the demand curve is drawn along with the average-total and marginal-cost curves. A point of output, Q_1, is arbitrarily chosen to illustrate what total costs, total revenue, and total profit would be at that output point. The price, P_1, is given by the demand curve, tracing Q_1 up to the demand curve. Total revenue, $P_1 \times Q_1$, is given by the rectangle labeled $ABCD$. The total costs are given by seeing how much it costs per unit of output to produce Q_1. That quantity, BE, multiplied by the total quantity AB, provides the total cost area, $ABEF$. Total profit is total revenue minus total costs, $ABCD - ABEF = FECD$.

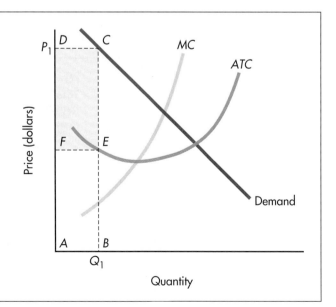

2.b. Profit Maximum: Marginal Revenue Equals Marginal Cost

Profit is maximized at the output level where marginal revenue and marginal cost are equal (MR = MC).

Marginal cost is the additional cost of producing one more unit of output. *Marginal revenue* is the additional revenue obtained from selling one more unit of output. If the production of one more unit of output increases costs less than it increases revenue—that is, if marginal cost is less than marginal revenue—then producing (and selling) that unit will increase profit. Conversely, if the production of one more unit costs more than the revenue obtained from the sale of the unit, then producing that unit will decrease profit. When marginal revenue is greater than marginal cost, producing more will increase profit. Conversely, when marginal revenue is less than marginal cost, producing more will lower profit. Thus, *profit is at a maximum when marginal revenue equals marginal cost.*

The profit-maximizing rule, $MR = MC$, is illustrated in Table 1, which lists output, total revenue, total cost, marginal revenue, marginal cost, and profit for an individual firm selling custom-made mountain bicycles. The first column is the total quantity (Q) of bikes produced. In column 2 is the total revenue (TR) generated by selling each quantity, and in column 3 is the total cost (TC) of producing each quantity. Fixed costs, the costs the firm encounters even when it produces nothing, amount to $1,000, as listed in column 3, line 1. Marginal revenue (MR), the change in total revenue that comes with the production of an additional bike, is listed in the fourth column. The marginal revenue of the first bike produced is the change in revenue that the firm receives for increasing its production and sales from zero to 1 unit; the marginal revenue of the first unit is listed in the row of bike number 1. The marginal revenue of the second bike produced is the change in revenue that the firm receives for increasing its production and sales from 1 to 2 bikes; the marginal revenue of that second bike is listed in the row of bike number 2. Marginal cost (MC), the additional cost of producing an additional bike, is listed in column 5. The marginal cost of the first bike is the additional cost of producing the first bike; the marginal cost of the second bike is the increase

TABLE I
Profit Maximization

(1) Total Output (Q)	(2) Total Revenue (TR)	(3) Total Cost (TC)	(4) Marginal Revenue (MR)	(5) Marginal Cost (MC)	(6) Profit (TR − TC)
0	$ 0	$1,000			$−1,000
1	1,700	2,000	$1,700	$1,000	− 300
2	3,300	2,800	1,600	800	500
3	4,800	3,500	1,500	700	1,300
4	6,200	4,000	1,400	500	2,200
5	7,500	4,500	1,300	500	3,000
6	8,700	5,200	1,200	700	3,500
7	9,800	6,000	1,100	800	3,800
8	10,800	7,000	1,000	1,000	3,800
9	11,700	9,000	900	2,000	2,700

in costs that result from increasing production from 1 to 2 bikes. Total profit, the difference between total revenue and total cost ($TR - TC$), is listed in the last column.

The first bike costs $2,000 to produce ($1,000 of fixed costs and $1,000 of variable costs); the marginal cost (additional cost) of the first bike is $1,000. When sold, the bike brings in $1,700 in revenue, so the marginal revenue is $1,700. Since marginal revenue is greater than marginal cost, the firm is better off producing that first bike than not producing it.

The second bike costs an additional $800 (column 5) to produce and brings in an additional $1,600 (column 4) in revenue. With the second bike, marginal revenue exceeds marginal cost. Thus the firm is better off producing 2 bikes than none or one.

Profit continues to rise as production rises until the eighth bike is produced. The marginal cost of producing the seventh bike is $800, and the marginal revenue from selling the seventh bike is $1,100. The marginal cost of producing the eighth bike is $1,000, and the marginal revenue from selling that eighth bike is also $1,000. The marginal cost of producing the ninth bike, $2,000, exceeds the marginal revenue obtained from the ninth bike, $900. Profit declines if the ninth bike is produced. The firm increases profit by producing the seventh bike and reduces profit by producing the ninth bike. Thus, the firm can maximize profit by producing eight bikes, the quantity at which marginal revenue and marginal cost are equal.[1]

2.b.1. The Marginal-Revenue Curve The example of the mountain bikes shows us that the only thing we need to add to Figure 1 to be able to point out the profit-maximizing point is the marginal-revenue curve. Drawing the marginal-revenue curve is really quite simple. The first step is to recognize that the demand curve is also the average-revenue curve; it shows the revenue per unit. Thus, the marginal-revenue curve and the demand curve are related to each other in the same way any average and marginal curves are related. That is, when the average is declining, the marginal is also declining and lies below the average. Thus, when the demand curve is downward-sloping, the marginal-revenue curve is also downward-sloping but lies below the demand curve.

The steeper the demand curve, the steeper the marginal-revenue curve; the marginal-revenue curve for a perfectly inelastic demand curve is the same vertical line as the demand curve. The flatter the demand curve, the flatter the marginal-revenue curve; the marginal-revenue curve for the perfectly elastic demand curve is the same as the demand curve. In between these two extremes, the marginal-revenue curve lies below the demand curve and slopes down.

For the downward-sloping demand curve, we can be more specific in drawing the marginal-revenue curve than to simply note that it slopes down and lies below the demand curve. Recall that the marginal-revenue curve is positive as long as total revenue is rising and is negative as total revenue

---

[1]You might notice that profit is at the maximum level for quantities of 7 and 8 bikes. This occurs because we are dealing with integers, 1, 2, 3, etc., when discussing output. There would be a unique quantity for which profit is at its maximum level if we could divide the quantities into small units instead of having to deal with integers. That unique quantity would be where $MR = MC$. Thus, we always choose the quantity at which marginal revenue and marginal cost are the same as the profit-maximizing quantity.

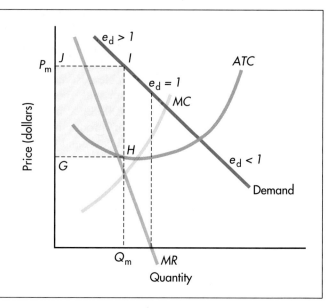

Figure 5
Profit Maximum with MR = MC
The demand, ATC, and MC curves from Figure 4 are redrawn. In addition, the MR curve is added. MR is drawn by recognizing that demand is average revenue, and since average revenue is falling, marginal revenue must also be falling and lie below average. In addition, marginal revenue crosses the horizontal axis at the output level where the price elasticity of demand is unity. Profit is then found where $MR = MC$. This is quantity Q_m and price P_m. Total profit is the rectangle $GHIJ$.

declines. Since total revenue rises in the price-elastic region of the demand curve, marginal revenue is positive in that region. Total revenue reaches its peak at the unit-elastic point of the demand curve and then turns down; marginal revenue is zero at the unit-elastic point. And total revenue declines in the inelastic region of the demand curve, so marginal revenue must be negative in the inelastic region. Thus, the marginal-revenue curve slopes down and crosses the horizontal axis at the quantity where the demand curve is unit-elastic.

In Figure 5 we have redrawn Figure 4 and added the marginal-revenue curve. Now we can easily find the profit-maximizing point. It is the point at which $MR = MC$. In Figure 5, the profit-maximizing point is given by price P_m and the quantity Q_m, and total profit is given by the rectangle $GHIJ$.

Both Figures 3 and 5 allow us to find the profit-maximizing point, but Figure 5 provides more information than Figure 3 does, as it allows us to view demand, marginal revenue, and average and marginal costs. Economists rely heavily on diagrams like Figure 5 to analyze business behavior; the demand curve may be different depending on the price elasticity of demand, or the position of the cost curves might be different depending on cost conditions, but in general, Figure 5 provides a useful and powerful framework of analysis for understanding business behavior.

RECAP

1. The average- and marginal-cost curves and the demand and marginal-revenue curves together characterize the producing and selling environments of a firm.

2. The demand curve is also the average-revenue curve. Thus, the marginal-revenue and demand curves are related to each other, as are any average

and marginal curves. When demand declines, marginal revenue declines and lies below demand.

3. The profit-maximizing rule is to produce where marginal revenue equals marginal cost.

3. SELLING ENVIRONMENTS OR MARKET STRUCTURE

Kyrene Scrap Metal, as mentioned earlier, is a processor of scrap metal; the employees collect used appliances, junked autos, and other scrap metals, and then the metal is processed and offered to steel-manufacturing plants. The demand curve for scrap metal is nearly perfectly elastic; if Kyrene Scrap Metal attempts to increase the price per ton of its metal, the steel-manufacturing plants turn to other scrap collectors. Although Kyrene Scrap Metal has no control over the price of its scrap metal, having to price at whatever all other scrap metals are priced, it does determine the quantity of metal it processes. And the quantity it processes is given by the point where marginal revenue and marginal cost are equal.

Burroughs-Wellcome is the only producer of AZT, for many years the only drug authorized by the FDA to inhibit the emergence of AIDS in those who were found to be HIV positive. Burroughs-Wellcome thus faced an almost perfectly inelastic demand for AZT; buyers had no alternative pharmaceuticals to turn to when the price of AZT rose. Burroughs-Wellcome set a very high price on AZT, approximately $10,000 for a year's supply.

Kyrene Scrap Metal and Burroughs-Wellcome face very different demand curves and thus behave differently. Kyrene Scrap Metal really has no choice over the price to charge for its metal. Burroughs-Wellcome, on the other hand, sets the price of AZT.

In contrast, The Gap clothing firm faces a demand curve that is neither perfectly elastic nor perfectly inelastic. Although it chooses to manufacture a quantity of clothing given by where marginal cost and marginal revenue are equal, The Gap must attempt to convince customers that its clothing is different and better than the lines offered by J. Crew, Limited, Benetton, or others. Neither Kyrene Scrap Metal nor Burroughs-Wellcome has any incentive to advertise, but The Gap devotes considerable resources toward advertising. It wants to convince customers not to switch to the other clothing lines whenever the price of one of the lines is reduced.

Southwest Airlines has been able to differentiate its service from that of other airline companies. But, unlike The Gap, which behaves somewhat independently of all other clothing retailers, anytime Southwest changes fares or alters its service, it has to take into account how America West and other airlines will respond. If Southwest reduces fares and all other airlines follow, Southwest's profits decline. If Southwest introduces a new service and all other airlines follow suit, the new service gains Southwest nothing. Thus, Southwest Airlines is particularly sensitive to the actions its competitors might take.

In just these four firms, we see a wide range of behaviors. Whereas all four firms attempt to maximize profits, and thus operate where $MR = MC$, each differs with respect to its allocation of resources to advertising and its control over the prices of its products. The four differ because they produce and sell in different types of markets.

3.a. Characteristics of the Market Structures

What is a market structure?

Economists analyzing the behavior of firms assume that firms can be classified into one of four market-structure models. Once a market structure is defined, economists can then examine the behavior of firms within it. A market structure is a *model*—a simplification of reality. Few if any industries fit neatly into one market structure or another. Economists use the four models to describe how firms might behave under certain conditions. They can then modify the models to improve their understanding of how firms behave in real life.

The market structure in which a firm produces and sells its product is defined by three characteristics:

- the number of firms that make up the market
- the ease with which new firms may enter the market and begin producing the good or service
- the degree to which the products produced by the firms are different

In some industries, such as agriculture, there are millions of individual firms. In others, such as in the photofinishing supplies industry, there are very few firms. It is relatively easy and inexpensive to enter the desktop publishing business, but it is much more costly and difficult to start a new airline. In some industries entry is strictly prohibited. It is illegal, for example, for any firm other than the U.S. Postal Service to deliver certain classes of mail in the United States.

In some industries, the products offered by each seller are virtually identical; in other industries, each product is slightly different. **Differentiated products** are perceived by consumers as having characteristics that products offered by other sellers do not have. **Standardized or nondifferentiated products** are perceived by consumers as being identical.

differentiated products:
products that consumers perceive to be different from one another

standardized or nondifferentiated products:
products that consumers perceive to be identical

3.b. Market-Structure Models

Table 2 summarizes the characteristics of the four market structures discussed in this section. Though it is not stated in the table, it is commonly assumed that consumers and firms have perfect information about prices and other decisions made by a firm. In other words, it is assumed that consumers and firms know the prices, locations, and products of all firms in the market in each market-structure model. Other than this common assumption, the characteristics that define each market structure are listed in the table. The name of the market structure is listed in column 1 of the table. The table lists the number of firms, the entry conditions, and the product type of the firms in each market structure, as well as the kind of price and promotion strategies a firm is likely to follow.

3.b.1. Perfect Competition Perfect competition is a market structure characterized by a very large number of firms, so large that whatever any *one* firm does has no effect on the market; firms that produce an identical (standardized or nondifferentiated) product; and easy entry. Because of the large number of firms, consumers have many choices of where to purchase the good or service, and there is no cost to the consumer of going to a different store. Because the product is standardized, consumers do not prefer one store to another or one brand to another. In fact, there are no brands—only identical,

TABLE 2
Summary of Market Structures and Predicted Behavior

| Market Structure | Characteristics | | | Behavior | |
	Number of Firms	Entry Condition	Product Type	Price Strategy	Promotion Strategy
Perfect competition	Very large number	Easy	Standardized	Price taker	None
Monopoly	One	No entry possible	Only one product	Price maker	Little
Monopolistic competition	Large number	Easy	Differentiated	Price maker	Large amount
Oligopoly	Few	Impeded	Standardized or differentiated	Interdependent	Little or large amount

generic products. For instance, wheat from one farm is no different than wheat from another farm; scrap metal from one firm is no different than scrap metal from another firm.

Easy entry means a firm cannot earn more than a normal profit. Above-normal profit attracts entrepreneurs who also want to earn more than their opportunity costs. With more firms and more production, the price of the good is driven down and economic profit is reduced. Entry continues until no one is earning more than a normal profit. At this point, firms in the industry cannot do better leaving the industry, and firms outside cannot do better entering. An equilibrium where there is neither entry nor exit is reached at zero economic, or normal, profit.

Perfectly competitive firms sell their goods at the price prevailing in the market. They cannot set a price that is above the market price, and they will not set a lower price because they can sell at the market price *all* they produce. The perfectly competitive firm is just one among very many—for instance, 1 farm among 2 million farms. Thus, a 10 percent or even a 50 percent increase in its output will have no effect on the total quantity produced in the market. About 300 billion tons of oats are grown each year by 2 million farms—each farm produces 150,000 tons. A 66 percent production increase by one farm (a 100,000-ton increase) is only a 0.03 percent increase in the market supply. It is very unlikely that such a small increase in quantity supplied would affect the market price.

What are price takers?

price taker:
a firm that is unable to set a price that differs from the market price without losing profit

Because each farm is such a small part of the total market, each farmer expects to sell at the *market price* everything produced on his or her farm. A reduction in quantity does not bring a higher price, and an increase in quantity does not require a lower price. For this reason, the perfectly competitive firm is called a **price taker**. It takes the price determined in the market as its price. A firm in perfect competition is the only firm that is a price taker.

The demand curve confronting the individual firm in a perfectly competitive market is perfectly elastic—a horizontal line at the market price. Figure 6(a) shows the market for oats, measured in billions of pounds of oats produced annually in the United States. The price determined by *market* demand and supply is $.50 per pound. Individual producers in a perfectly

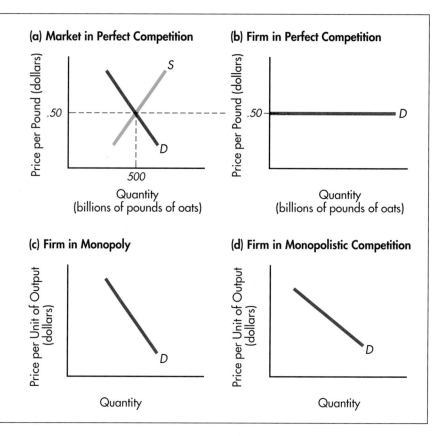

Figure 6
The Demand Curve Facing an Individual Firm
Figure 6(a) shows the market for oats. The price, determined by market demand and supply, defines the demand curve faced by a perfectly competitive firm. The demand curve is a horizontal line at the market price, as shown in Figure 6(b).

Figure 6(c) shows the market demand, which is the demand curve faced by the monopoly firm. The firm is the only supplier and thus faces the entire market demand.

Figure 6(d) shows the downward-sloping demand curve faced by the firm in monopolistic competition. The curve slopes downward because of the differentiated nature of the products in the industry.

competitive market know that they could sell all they want to sell at that $.50 per pound price. Each producer is such a small portion of the market, 1 of 2 million farms producing oats, that whether he or she produces a little or a lot will not affect the market supply and thus the market price. In addition, because each is such a small part of the market and the oats produced on one farm are no different from the oats produced on the other 1,999,999 farms, no producer can charge a price that is higher than the market price, as shown in Figure 6(b). Faced with a price increase, buyers (grain silo owners) would immediately purchase from the other farms. Thus, 1 farm among the 2 million that produce oats views demand as a horizontal line at the current market price.

The individual firm in perfect competition does not advertise. By definition the firm can't differentiate its product, and it can't increase the demand for its product independent of the other firms in the market.

3.b.2. Monopoly Monopoly is a market structure in which there is just one firm and entry by other firms is not possible. Because there is only one firm, consumers have only one place to buy the good, and there are no close substitutes. Because entry is impossible, even if the firm earns above-normal returns, no new firms can compete for those returns. As a result, the firm in a monopoly can earn positive (above-normal) economic profit over a long period of time.

A monopoly may come into existence because of economies of scale: the larger the firm, the lower the cost per unit of output produced by the firm. In

natural monopoly:
a monopoly that emerges because of economies of scale

the case of economies of scale, a large firm can supply the product at a lower cost per unit than a smaller firm could. As a result, the larger firm can underprice smaller firms and force them out of the market. The large firm then becomes the only supplier. A monopoly that emerges because of economies of scale is called a **natural monopoly**. Electric utilities are often said to be natural monopolies because of the huge economies of scale that exist in the generation of electricity.

A second type of monopoly arises as the result of laws that restrict entry. The U.S. Postal Service is a monopoly supplier of mail delivery. By law, no other firm can provide mail delivery. The Federal Reserve Bank is a monopoly supplier of U.S. currency. By law, no other firm can supply U.S. dollars. In the fifteenth through the seventeenth centuries governments raised revenue by granting monopolies to special interest groups in return for some of their profits. Christopher Columbus was granted a monopoly from Queen Isabella of Spain; the Hudson Bay Company was granted a monopoly by the English monarchy; most of the explorers and trading ships of the time had been granted monopoly charters. As you can see in the Economic Insight "Cable TV," that policy continues today. Patents provide a government-created monopoly. Burroughs-Wellcome was granted a patent on AZT and thus was, by law, the only supplier of the drug for a period of seventeen years.

For more than a hundred years, it has been argued that a monopoly may result from unfair and anticompetitive practices engaged in by firms, known as the *monopolization of a market*. Many economists argue that no such thing as monopolization occurs, that tactics designed to monopolize a market are simply intense forms of competition. Regardless of the arguments, hundreds of firms have been accused of monopolization and taken to court. A famous case involved the Rockefellers. John D. and William Rockefeller organized Standard of Ohio in 1870 and by 1872 owned all but three or four of the approximately forty-five oil refineries in Cleveland. Standard Oil of Ohio and its successor, Standard Oil of New Jersey, were accused of attempting to create a monopoly in the retail gas market because, by controlling 90 to 95 percent of oil refining, Standard Oil could increase the price of gasoline to competitors and drive them out of business. Another famous case resulted when Alcoa was accused of creating a monopoly because it controlled an ingredient necessary to produce aluminum.[2] And today, Microsoft is being accused of monopolization and anticompetitive actions in the computer software business.

People often refer to a business as being a monopoly even though many firms nationwide or worldwide supply the product. Universities, hotels, cable TV companies, newspapers, and electric utilities have all been called monopolies at one time or another. They are not monopolies according to the strict definition of being the only firm providing a good or service, but they may be "local" monopolies. A hotel may be the only supplier within the center of the city, and entry by others is virtually impossible. There may be only one major newspaper in a city, and entry is very difficult. One cable TV company may be the only supplier within a city or a portion of a city, and competition is not allowed by law.

---

[2]Stuart B. Bruchey, *The Wealth of the Nation: An Economic History of the United States* (New York: Harper & Row Publishers), 1988, p. 126; Irwin M. Stelzer, *Selected Antitrust Cases: Landmark Decisions* (Homewood, IL: Richard D. Irwin), 1981, pp. 3–90.

Cable TV

Government-created monopolies are not in short supply. One of the most publicized recent instances of government-created monopoly involves cable television. With a handful of exceptions, the roughly 9,000 cable franchises in the United States meet the definition of a monopoly. These firms are granted permission to run the cable business by local governments, who pass out such monopolies and fiercely defend them. The franchise fees that local governments charge cable operators rise with the revenues and total hundreds of millions of dollars annually.

Defenders argue that cable television is one of those businesses, like a utility, that works best as a monopoly. Given the expense and

street disruption required to lay cable to every home in an area, putting in more than one system would be a waste of resources and an annoyance for residents. Operators argue that in some places competition was tried, but it failed, leaving a monopoly anyway. They conclude that "it's simply not viable to have two franchises in one area."

Since a federal law deregulating local government control over cable prices was enacted in 1984, cable television companies have been free to charge whatever they like for basic service. Because most areas that have cable television are served by only one company, many people claim that there is no direct competition to restrain prices, and

thus the customer pays for the monopoly. Nicholas Miller, a partner in the law firm of Miller, Young & Holbrook, which represents many municipalities on cable issues, said in a recent *New York Times* interview that "in a monopoly situation, they are pricing like monopolies." As a result of the price increases, the cable TV industry was reregulated in 1992.

Sources: Geraldine Fabrikant, "In Cable TV a Free Rein Raises Prices," *New York Times*, Dec. 11, 1988, p. 46; John R. Emshwiller, "Prying Open the Cable-TV Monopolies," *Wall Street Journal*, Aug. 10, 1989, p. B1; "FCC Chairman Sikes Criticizes Rising Cable TV Rates, Abuses," *Investors Daily*, March 5, 1990, p. 31.

What are price makers?

price maker, price setter, price searcher:
a firm that sets the price of the product it sells

The demand curve facing the single firm in a monopoly is the market demand because the firm is the only supplier in the market. Figure 6(c) shows the demand curve facing the firm in a monopoly. Being the only producer, the firm in a monopoly must carefully consider what price to charge. Unlike a price increase in a perfectly competitive market, a price increase in a monopoly will not drive every customer to another producer. But if the price is too high, revenue will decline as consumers decide to forgo the product supplied by that one firm. A firm operating in any market but perfect competition is not a price taker. Economists have used different names to refer to a firm that is not a price taker, sometimes using **price maker**, other times **price setter**, and still other times **price searcher**. All three terms are meant to imply the same thing: that the firm determines the quantity it produces and the price at which it sells the products.

The firm in a monopoly market structure may advertise in an attempt to increase the market demand (to shift the demand curve out), but advertising and promotion are likely to be low-priority items. For instance, a local electric utility may promote the all-electric home or advertise energy-efficient electric air conditioners or heating systems, but the utility's advertising budget is likely to be a very small portion of its overall budget.

3.b.3. Monopolistic Competition A monopolistically competitive market structure is characterized by a large number of firms, easy entry, and differentiated products. Many agricultural products provide good examples of non-differentiated products—milk is milk and oats are oats. But beer, detergents, cereal, and soft drinks provide examples of differentiated products—Coke is not Pepsi and Cheerios are not Wheaties. Each brand is to some degree different from the others. Sam Adams beer differs from Budweiser, Miller, and Moosehead. Tide detergent differs from All, Clorox, and Fab.

Product differentiation distinguishes a perfectly competitive market from a monopolistically competitive market (in both entry is easy and there are a large number of firms). When a firm enters a perfectly competitive market, it produces an identical product—more scrap metal or more wheat, for example. When a new firm enters a monopolistically competitive market, it produces a slightly different product. For instance, all major breweries produce several lines of beer, and competition often takes the form of a new line such as Coors's Keystone. Keystone is the first Coors entry into a key category of the beer market called popular-priced. Anheuser-Busch, Miller, and Stroh each have several lines of beers in this market category, including Busch, Milwaukee's Best, and Old Milwaukee. The soft-drink industry also competes by introducing new lines of products. In 1990, the Coca-Cola Company introduced PowerAde as a fountain product in convenience stores to directly compete with Quaker Oats's Gatorade, and the Pepsi-Cola Company quickly followed with Mountain Dew Sport.

Even though there are many firms in a monopolistically competitive market structure, the demand curve faced by *any one firm* slopes downward, as in Figure 6(d). Because each product is slightly different from all other products, each firm is like a mini-monopoly—the only producer of that specific product. The downward slope reflects the differentiated nature of the products: the products are not perfect substitutes (identical goods) as in the case of perfect competition. Thus, the firm in monopolistic competition is a price maker. As the price of Sam Adams beer is increased, everything else held constant, consumers switch to other beers or to other beverages, and the quantity demanded of Sam Adams beer falls, but not to zero, as would be the case in perfect competition. As the price of Tide increases, everything else held constant, the quantity demanded of Tide falls, but not to zero.

The greater the differentiation among products, the less elastic the demand, so the degree to which the quantity demanded changes as price changes depends on the degree to which the products are substitutes. Thus, a firm in monopolistic competition wants to differentiate its products from its competitors' products as much as possible, and advertising and marketing strategies become very important. (See the Economic Insight "Taste Tests.")

3.b.4. **Oligopoly** In an oligopoly, there are few firms—more than one, but few enough so that each firm alone can affect the market. Auto producers constitute one oligopoly, steelmakers another. Entry into an oligopoly is more difficult than entry into a perfectly competitive or monopolistically competitive market, but in contrast to monopoly, entry can occur. The products offered by the firms in an oligopoly may be differentiated or nondifferentiated. Buicks differ from Fords and Nissans. However, the steel produced by USX is no different from the steel produced by Bethlehem Steel.

Because an oligopoly consists of just a few firms, each firm, or oligopolist, must take the actions of the others into account. Oligopolistic firms are *interdependent*, and this interdependence distinguishes oligopoly from the other market structures. An oligopolist that is trying to decide whether to lower the price of its product must consider whether its competitors will follow suit. If one firm lowers its price and the competitors do follow suit, none of the firms

Taste Tests

If you pay attention to commercials, you may be able to identify some attempts to create differentiated products. Taste tests are a common approach. Suppose consumers strolling through a grocery store are asked whether they prefer Coke or Pepsi. If they say Coke, they are asked to take a taste test. They are given a small white cup with one brand of soft drink in it. Then they are given a second cup containing another brand. They indicate whether they prefer the first or the second. The result, Pepsi might claim, is that more than half of all Coke drinkers preferred Pepsi in a taste test.

At first the results of this test may sound quite convincing. But if most consumers are unable to differentiate between the products in blind taste tests, then it is likely that 50 percent of any group of consumers will choose one of the products and 50 percent the other. Realizing this, the testing company ensures that only the consumers who say they prefer the competitor's product will be asked to participate in the taste test. Coke can, and has, turned the tables by asking those who claim to prefer Pepsi to participate in a test.

In which market structure would such taste tests matter? Clearly not in perfect competition, since products are identical. It is in the market structure of monopolistic competition that we find most efforts to differentiate products.

in the oligopoly will be able to increase their sales much. However, if the competitors do not follow suit, the sales of the now lower-priced firm may rise substantially. For instance, as an airline is deciding whether to raise or lower fares, it must consider whether the other airlines will follow suit.

The oligopolist faces a downward-sloping demand curve, but the shape of the curve depends on the behavior of competitors. Oligopoly is the most complicated of the market-structure models to examine because there are so many behaviors firms might display. Because of its diversity, many economists describe oligopoly as the most realistic of the market-structure models.

3.c. Comparisons of the Market Structures

What does the marginal-revenue curve of a firm in each market structure look like?

The characteristics of the four market structures are noted in the left side of Table 2, and the predicted behavior of each of the market structures is summarized in the right side of the table. Possible pricing strategies include being a price taker or a price maker, or, in the case of oligopoly, being interdependent. The promotion strategy refers to whether advertising or marketing is likely to occur in the market. For instance, there would be no advertising or marketing in a perfectly competitive market. The demand curves faced by a firm in each of the market structures (except oligopoly, where the shape of the demand curve varies depending on how firms interact) are shown in Figure 6. The demand curves are all downward-sloping except for the firm in perfect competition, whose demand curve is perfectly elastic. The marginal-revenue curve of all firms but perfect competitors slope down and lie below the demand curve. For the perfect competitive firm, the demand and marginal revenue curves are the same.

As you use the market structure models to study the behavior of firms, keep in mind that they are *models*—simplifications of reality—that provide a framework for discussing the behavior of firms in the real world. They do not, themselves, necessarily describe the real world. It is not easy to assign real-life firms and industries to one of the four market structures. An indus-

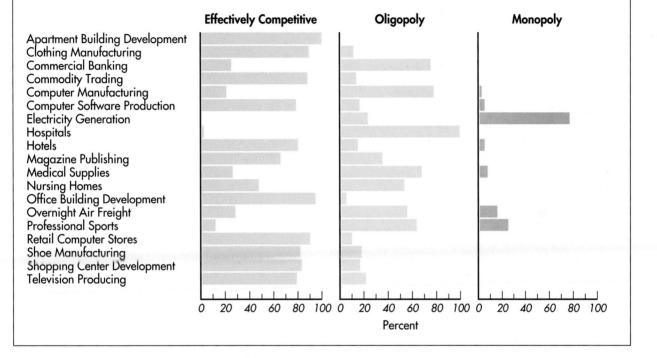

Figure 7
Opinions Can Vary in Classifying Industries According to Market Structure
The chart shows how twenty economists classified a sampling of industries according to three categories: "effectively competitive," "monopoly," and "oligopoly." In only a few instances was there widespread agreement, such as "Apartment building development," "Hospitals," and "Office building development." The difference of opinion suggests that real-life industries do not often fit any one of the four market-structure categories exactly. Source: John J. Siegfried, "Could a Score of Industrial Organization Economists Agree on Competition?" *Review of Industrial Organization*, vol. 3, no. 4 (Fall 1988), pp. 139–148. Used by permission of the *Review of Industrial Organization*.

try is likely to have characteristics of more than one structure. Consider the soft-drink industry. There are many brands (a characteristic of monopolistic competition), yet Pepsi and Coca-Cola account for about 60 percent of the total market (a characteristic of oligopoly). Consider farming. There are millions of farmers (a characteristic of perfect competition), but starting a farming operation can be very expensive (a characteristic of oligopoly).

A few years ago, twenty economists were asked to classify several industries into three groups: (1) effectively competitive (perfect or monopolistic competitors), (2) monopoly, and (3) oligopoly. The results are shown in Figure 7. The economists agreed in only a few instances.

RECAP

1. Economists have identified four market structures: perfect competition, monopoly, monopolistic competition, and oligopoly.

2. Perfect competition is a market structure in which many firms are producing a nondifferentiated product and entry is easy.

3. Monopoly is a market structure in which only one firm supplies the product and entry cannot occur.

4. Monopolistic competition is a market structure in which many firms are producing differentiated products and entry is easy.

5. Oligopoly is a market structure in which a few firms are producing either standardized or differentiated products and entry is possible but not easy. The distinguishing characteristic of oligopoly is that the firms are interdependent.

SUMMARY

▲▼ How do firms maximize profit?

1. The basic assumption about the behavior of firms is that firms maximize profit. Although some firms may deviate from profit maximization, the assumption of profit maximization is a useful simplification of reality. §1

2. Profit is maximized at the output level where total revenue exceeds total costs by the greatest amount. §1.a

3. Firms facing perfectly elastic demand curves have no discretion over price; firms facing perfectly inelastic demand select only the price, since quantity is determined by consumers. §1.b

▲▼ How do firms decide how much to supply?

4. The supply rule for all firms is to supply the quantity at which the firm's marginal revenue and marginal cost are equal. §2.b

▲▼ What is a market structure?

5. A market structure is a model of the producing and selling environments in which firms operate. The three characteristics that define market structure are number of firms, the ease of entry, and whether the products are differentiated. §3.a

6. A perfectly competitive market is a market in which a very large number of firms are producing an identical product and entry is easy. §3.b.1

7. A monopoly is a market in which there is only one firm and entry by others cannot occur. §3.b.2

8. A monopolistically competitive market is a market in which a large number of firms are producing differentiated products and entry is easy. §3.b.3

9. The demand curve facing a monopolistically competitive firm is downward-sloping because of the differentiated nature of the products offered by the firm. §3.b.3

10. An oligopoly is a market in which a few firms are producing either differentiated or nondifferentiated products and entry is possible but not easy. The distinguishing characteristic of an oligopoly is that the firms are interdependent. §3.b.4

11. The demand curve facing a firm in an oligopoly is downward-sloping. The elasticity depends on the actions and reactions to price changes by fellow oligopolists in the industry. §3.b.4

▲▼ What are price takers?

12. The demand curve facing a perfectly competitive firm is a horizontal line at the market price. The firm takes the price determined in its market as its price. §3.b.1

▲▼ What are price makers?

13. The demand curve facing a firm in a monopoly is the market demand curve because the firm is the only supplier. The firm determines the quantity it produces and the price at which it sells the products; it is a price maker. §3.b.2

▲▼ What does the marginal-revenue curve of a firm in each market structure look like?

14. The marginal-revenue curve for all firms except those in perfect competition is downward-sloping and lies below the demand curve. The marginal-revenue curve for the perfectly competitive firm is the same as the demand curve, a horizontal or perfectly elastic curve. §3.c

KEY TERMS

zero economic profit (normal profit) §1.a
positive economic profit (above-normal profit) §1.a
differentiated products §3.a
standardized or nondifferentiated products §3.a

price taker §3.b.1
natural monopoly §3.b.2
price maker (price setter, price searcher) §3.b.2

EXERCISES

1. Why is the assumption of a very large number of firms important to the definition of perfect competition?

2. Which type of market characterizes most businesses operating in the United States today?

3. Since a firm in monopoly has no competitors producing close substitutes, does the monopolist set exorbitantly high prices?

4. Advertising to create brand preferences is most common in what market structures?

5. Draw a perfectly elastic demand curve on top of a standard U-shaped average-total-cost curve. Now add in the marginal-cost and marginal-revenue curves. Find the profit-maximizing point, $MR = MC$. Indicate the firm's total revenues and total cost.

6. Give ten examples of differentiated products. Then list as many nondifferentiated products as you can.

7. Describe profit maximization in terms of marginal revenue and marginal cost.

8. Use the information below to calculate total revenue, marginal revenue, and marginal cost. Indicate the profit-maximizing level of output. If the price was $3 and fixed costs were $5, what would variable costs be? At what level of output would the firm produce?

Output	Price	Total Costs	Total Revenue ($P \times Q$)
1	$5	$10	
2	5	12	
3	5	15	
4	5	19	
5	5	24	
6	5	30	
7	5	45	

9. If agriculture is an example of perfect competition, why are there so many brands of dairy products at the grocery store?

10. Using demand curves, illustrate the effect of product differentiation on the part of haircutters.

11. Why might society prefer perfect competition over monopoly?

12. Try to classify the following firms into one of the four market-structure models. Explain your choice.

   a. Rowena's Gourmet Foods (produces and sells a line of specialty foods)

   b. Shasta Pool Company (swimming pool and spa building)

   c. Merck (pharmaceutical)

   d. America West Airlines

   e. UDC Homebuilders

   f. Legal Seafoods (restaurant chain)

13. Draw two sets of cost curves. For the first set, assume fixed costs are huge and there are large economies of scale (large MES). For the second set, assume fixed costs are small and the economies of scale are small (small MES). Now, on each set of cost curves place a downward-sloping demand curve. Find the profit-maximizing point in each case.

14. "Neither geography nor laboratory technology can restrain the cultivation of illicit drugs. Poppy, coca, and cannabis can be grown almost anywhere, and the ability to refine them or to produce synthetic drugs is widely available." Based on this statement, in what market structure would you classify illicit drugs? Explain.

The Poor Pay More for Food in New York, Survey Finds

City grocery stores are exacting a steep toll on the have-nots.

An unusually detailed report by a New York City agency shows that prices are highest in the areas where the customers are least able to afford it—in impoverished inner-city neighborhoods, where shoppers pay significantly more but get inferior foodstuffs and poor service. Far fewer supermarkets do business in poor areas, and those that do are smaller and poorly stocked, compared with stores in middle-class areas.

That picture is particularly clear in the tiny grocers known as bodegas, which dot inner-city streets and are the source of sustenance for 60% to 70% of residents in some areas even though the shops often don't stock fresh meat or fish. Eggs are typically unrefrigerated, despite the risk of spoilage. Lettuce—often wilted—frequently sells at $1.19 a head vs. 59 cents for a fresh head in a Waldbaum's on Staten Island.

The scant number of supermarkets that can be found in poor areas are cramped, typically only one-third to one-fifth the size of the average supermarket in better-heeled areas, the study finds. The inner-city stores, spanning 4,000 to 9,000 square feet compared with 20,000 to 30,000 feet in middle-class areas, don't churn adequate sales volume to keep prices down through economies of scale.

The city report echoes conditions found elsewhere in the U.S. In Baltimore and Hartford, Conn., surveys in the mid-1980s also found the poor pay more. The New York findings provide new ammunition for the long-standing complaints of community leaders.

But the study is drawing a mixed response, as some activists complain that the city is belatedly looking at the problem and question whether any corrective measures will be all that effective—or lasting—in their impact.

"What's unfortunate is that this mammoth problem, which has been well known for decades by inner-city residents, is just beginning to get attention by government and the American mainstream," says Norma Goodwin, president of Health-Watch, a New York–based organization that promotes health in minority communities. "Things won't change until neighborhoods change," adds Madie McLean, who teaches nutrition to Harlem residents under the U.S. government's Expanded Food and Nutrition program. "What clout do poor people on welfare have?"

The report by the city's Department of Consumer Affairs shows that New York's low-income shoppers, on average, pay 8.8% more—or at least $350 more each year for a family of four that can ill afford it—than shoppers in middle-class areas pay for the same basket of groceries.

For instance, the agency found that an A&P in blighted Harlem was charging 13% more for the same basket of goods as an A&P in middle-class Queens. A spokesman for the **Great Atlantic & Pacific Tea Co.** declined to comment.

Moreover, small, independently owned supermarkets and mom-and-pop bodegas don't have enough room to carry high-margin items such as film or beauty aids, which large supermarket operators routinely use to offset the price breaks they give customers on food staples. The tiny outlets boast no scanner systems or other high-technology equipment that maximize sales per foot, and they seldom accept product coupons. Nor can they compete with the bulk purchasing power and sales volume of large chains.

City officials touted the report, which took almost a year to complete and entails 140 interviews and price surveys of 21 products in 60 stores in various neighborhoods, as the most comprehensive analysis of food shopping in New York's low-income areas that has ever been conducted.

Source: Reprinted by permission of The Wall Street Journal, © 1991 Dow Jones & Company, Inc. All Rights Reserved Worldwide.

Commentary

Inner-city residents pay more for food than those living in the suburbs, but inner-city residents have lower incomes, on average, than residents of the suburbs. Why would inner-city residents be willing and able to pay more for food? Wouldn't their demand for food be less because of their lower incomes?

In fact, the demand for food by residents of the inner city is less price-elastic than the demand for food by residents of the suburbs because inner-city dwellers have fewer alternatives. They cannot hop on a bus and travel to the suburbs to go grocery shopping—to do so would cost them more than their savings. There are fewer stores in the inner city than in the suburbs, so inner-city consumers have fewer choices. Thus, the demand is more inelastic for inner-city residents than for suburban residents.

A single grocery store facing two sets of customers with different price elasticities of demand would charge each a different price. Those with the less-elastic demand would pay higher prices than those with the more-elastic demand. Since a single store does not have two sets of customers but instead different stores deal with different kinds of customers, how can the different prices be explained? The explanation requires us to look at supply as well as demand.

On the supply side, the type of industry must be identified. Is the grocery business a perfectly competitive business, a monopolistically competitive business, an oligopoly, or a monopoly? If it is a perfectly competitive business, the first brief appearance of an above-normal profit will induce entry of identical firms offering identical products and the competing away of that above-normal profit. But perfect competition does not seem to describe the grocery business since firms and products are not identical. Oligopoly and monopoly do not seem to describe the grocery business either since there are many firms supplying the product. Thus, it would seem that the grocery business is most accurately described as a monopolistically competitive business.

If the grocery business is monopolistically competitive, then above-normal profit should bring

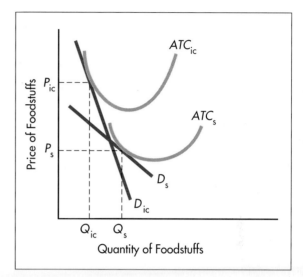

quick entry with a differentiated product—a larger store, more selection, different foods—and the reduction of profit to normal levels. Since firms are not rushing to the inner city we must conclude that the inner-city firms are not earning above-normal profit even though they are charging higher prices. This could only occur if the costs of doing business are higher in the inner city than in the suburbs.

Consider the figure showing the cost curves for an inner-city store, ATC_{ic}, and for a suburban store, ATC_s. The higher costs in the inner city include the higher cost of land, the higher cost of security, higher taxes and more costly environmental controls, and the higher costs of insurance. In addition, because land is more expensive and large spaces difficult to find in the inner city, the store cannot achieve economies of scale. All these factors lead to a higher cost of doing business in the inner city than in the suburb. Notice that the inner-city firm is smaller, produces only Q_{ic}, has higher costs (ATC_{ic} is above ATC_s), charges a higher price (P_{ic} is above P_s), and still earns only a normal profit.

The article does point out that some supermarkets are considering a move into the inner city because they have "saturated" the suburbs—meaning that the suburbs are providing only normal profits. Entry in the inner city will occur only if the firms believe above-normal profits are available.

10

Perfect Competition

FUNDAMENTAL
QUESTIONS

1. What is perfect competition?
2. What does the demand curve facing the individual firm look like, and why?
3. How does the firm maximize profit in the short run?
4. At what point does a firm decide to suspend operations?
5. When will a firm shut down permanently?
6. What is the break-even price?
7. What is the firm's supply curve in the short run?
8. What is the firm's supply curve in the long run?
9. What is the long-run market supply curve?
10. What are the long-run equilibrium results of a perfectly competitive market?

A griculture is often used as a real-life example of the perfectly competitive market structure, and indeed, many individual farmers are *price takers*, unable to affect the price of the product. Agriculture is a worldwide industry consisting of hundreds of millions of individual producers. To enter the industry in the low-income developing countries, all one needs is a small plot of land, seed, and access to water and tools. In the developed industrial nations, however, the average farm exceeds 400 acres and relies on combines and tractors costing several hundred thousand dollars, as well as on fertilizers and other materials. Nonetheless, the product is indistinguishable, and each individual firm is a very small part of the entire market. The grain from one farm is indistinguishable from that from another farm, and no single farm is able to increase the price of its grain and still sell the grain.

PREVIEW

Another market that closely resembles the model of perfect competition is the market for scrap metal. Scrap metal is junk that is crushed and then melted in open-hearth furnaces to produce new steel. Discarded bicycles, automobiles, refrigerators, and washing machines have value as scrap metal. The metal is essentially nondifferentiated. A scrap-metal processor doesn't care which junk is offered—a ton of scrap is a ton of scrap. It is not particularly difficult to enter the business. If you have a truck and a winch, you can travel around and gather scrap metal to sell to junk dealers or scrap processors. There are nearly 2,000 scrap processors throughout the United States. They collect the scrap and then separate it into grades or types of scrap to sell to steel manufacturers. The steel manufacturers do not care where the Number 1 grade scrap comes from. One seller of Number 1 grade is no different than another seller of Number 1 grade.

Even an industry like oil transport has some of the characteristics of the perfectly competitive model. One supertanker transporting oil is just like another. It is not easy or costless to enter the industry, but it is not too difficult. You must convince an international banker or broker to provide more than $100 million per tanker, but once you have overcome the hurdle of financing, entry is not blocked. Nearly 1,000 firms ranging in size from one supertanker to twenty-five supertankers offer their services to the oil refineries. The oil companies do not care from whom they buy the oil. One shipload is identical to another. Thus, the supertankers are price takers.

The model of perfect competition is not simply an exercise in theory that has no practical basis. Understanding how the firm in a perfectly competitive market structure behaves can provide clues to many real-life situations. In this chapter we use these real-life industries to illustrate many of the concepts and outcomes of the model of a perfectly competitive market. As you read, keep in mind that no industry fits the model perfectly, that it is indeed a *model*.

I. THE PERFECTLY COMPETITIVE FIRM IN THE SHORT RUN

We begin our analysis of perfect competition by taking the viewpoint of an individual farmer who is currently in business, having already procured the necessary land, tools, equipment, and employees to operate a farm. After we discuss how much the individual farmer decides to produce and how the price of the farmer's produce is determined, we discuss the entry and the exit processes. We examine how someone begins a business and how someone leaves or exits the business. We then alter our perspective and look at the market as a whole. Let's start our discussion by reviewing the characteristics of a perfectly competitive market.

I.a. The Definition of Perfect Competition

What is perfect competition?

Perfect competition is a model of firm behavior when many firms produce identical products and entry is easy.

A market that is perfectly competitive exhibits the following characteristics:

1. There are many sellers. No one firm can have an influence on market price. Each firm is such a minute part of the total market that however much the firm produces—nothing at all, as much as it can, or some amount in between—it will have no effect on the market price.

2. The products sold by the firms in the industry are identical. The product sold by one firm can be substituted perfectly for the product sold by any other firm in the industry. Products are not differentiated by packaging, advertising, or quality.

3. Entry is easy and there are many potential entrants. There are no huge economies of scale relative to the size of the market. Laws do not require producers to obtain licenses or pay for the privilege of producing. Other firms cannot take actions to keep someone from entering the business. Firms can stop producing and can sell or liquidate the business without difficulty.

4. Buyers and sellers have perfect information. Buyers know the price and quantity at each firm. Each firm knows what the other firms are charging and how they are behaving.

I.b. The Demand Curve of the Individual Firm

What does the demand curve facing the individual firm look like, and why?

A firm in a perfectly competitive market structure is said to be a *price taker* because the price of the product is determined by market demand and supply, and the individual firm simply has to accept that price. In 1992 the world market price of corn was about $1 per bushel, and nearly 20 billion bushels worldwide were produced. Approximately 46 percent of all the corn harvested in the world comes from the United States. Nevertheless, the average farm in the United States produces an extremely small percentage of the total quantity harvested each year.

What would occur if one U.S. farmer decided to set the price of corn at $1.20 per bushel when the market price was $1 per bushel? According to the model of a perfectly competitive market, no one would purchase the higher-priced corn because the identical product could be obtained without difficulty elsewhere for $1 per bushel. In this instance, what the model predicts is what actually occurs in the real-world corn market. The grain silo owner who buys the farmers' grain would simply pass on that farm's grain and move to the next truckful of grain at $1 per bushel. By setting a price above the market price, the individual farmer may sell nothing.

Is an individual farmer likely to set a price of $.80 per bushel when the market price is $1 per bushel? Not in a perfectly competitive market. All of the produce from a single farm can be sold at the market price. Why would a farmer sell at $.80 per bushel when he or she can get $1 per bushel? The individual farm is a price taker because it cannot charge more than the market price and it will not charge less.

The individual firm in a perfectly competitive industry is a price taker because it cannot charge more than the market price and it will not charge less.

You could think of price takers as being the sellers in a big auction. The potential buyers bid against each other for the product until a price is determined. The product is then sold at that price. The seller has no control over the price, as discussed in the Economic Insight "Setting Prices with Auctions."

Market demand and supply are shown in Figure 1(a). The demand curve of a single firm is shown in Figure 1(b). The horizontal line at the market price is the demand curve faced by an individual firm in a perfectly competitive market structure. It shows that the individual firm is a price taker—that the demand curve is perfectly elastic. The question facing the individual firm in a perfectly competitive industry is how much to produce, not what price to charge.

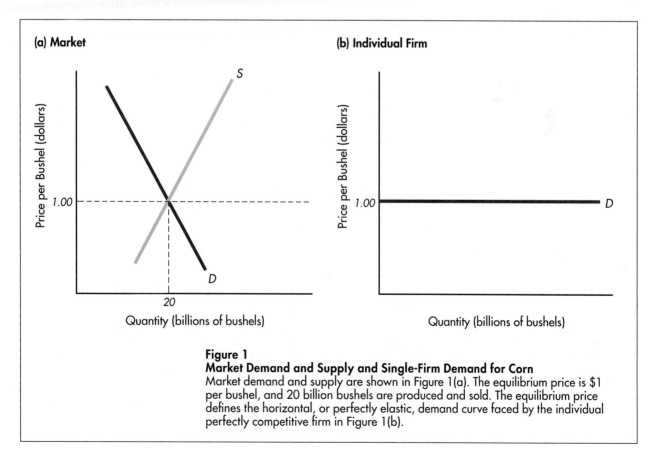

Figure 1
Market Demand and Supply and Single-Firm Demand for Corn
Market demand and supply are shown in Figure 1(a). The equilibrium price is $1 per bushel, and 20 billion bushels are produced and sold. The equilibrium price defines the horizontal, or perfectly elastic, demand curve faced by the individual perfectly competitive firm in Figure 1(b).

l.c. Profit Maximization

How does the firm maximize profit in the short run?

How much should a firm produce? It should produce the quantity at which it will maximize profit. Let's continue to consider an individual corn producer as an example of a perfectly competitive firm maximizing profit. The revenues and costs faced by this farm producing corn in the United States are listed in the table in Figure 2. Total output—number of bushels of corn (Q)—is listed in column 1. The market price (P), $1 per bushel, is listed in the second column. Total revenue (TR) is shown in the third column. Total revenue is equal to price multiplied by total output: $TR = P \times Q$. Total cost (TC) is shown in the fourth column. (You can see that even at a zero output level there is a cost of $1. This is the fixed cost—the land rent and the mortgages on a house and equipment that have to be paid even when no corn is harvested.) Total profit is shown in column 5. It is the difference between total revenue and total costs ($TR - TC$).

As we learned in the last chapter, the profit-maximizing level of output can be determined by comparing marginal revenue (MR), in column 6, to marginal cost (MC), in column 7. *Marginal revenue* is the change in total revenue divided by the change in quantity:

$$MR = \frac{\text{change in total revenue}}{\text{change in quantity of output}} = \frac{\Delta TR}{\Delta Q}$$

Since the demand curve facing the individual firm in perfect competition is perfectly elastic, each additional bushel sells for the same price, in this case, $1. Thus, marginal revenue is a constant $1, the same as price. Recall from the previous chapter that the marginal-revenue curve and the demand curve are the same when demand is perfectly elastic.

Marginal cost is the change in total cost divided by the change in quantity:

$$MC = \frac{\text{change in total cost}}{\text{change in quantity of output}} = \frac{\Delta TC}{\Delta Q}$$

The marginal-cost and marginal-revenue curves are shown in Figure 2. Marginal cost is less than marginal revenue until production reaches 9 bushels. With the tenth and successive bushels, marginal cost exceeds marginal revenue.

Profit maximization occurs at the output level where MR = MC.

We know that profit is maximized when $MR = MC$. Profit rises when the revenue brought in by the sale of one more unit (one more bushel) is greater than the cost of producing that unit. Conversely, if the cost of producing one more unit is greater than the amount of revenue brought in by selling that unit, profit declines with the production of that unit. Only when marginal revenue and marginal cost are the same is profit at a maximum.[1]

---

[1]Marginal revenue and marginal cost could be equal at small levels of production and sales, such as with the first bushel, but profit would definitely not be at its greatest level. The reason is that marginal cost is falling with the first unit of production—the marginal cost of the second unit is less than the marginal cost of the first unit. Since marginal revenue is the same for both the first and second units, profit actually rises as quantity increases. Profit maximization requires that marginal revenue equal marginal cost *and that marginal cost be rising*. Since marginal revenue and marginal cost are the same for the ninth bushel and marginal cost is rising, the ninth bushel is the profit-maximizing level of output.

Figure 2
Profit Maximization
The profit-maximization point for a single firm is shown for a price of $1 per bushel. Marginal revenue and marginal cost are equal at the profit-maximization point, 9 bushels. At quantities less than 9 bushels, marginal revenue exceeds marginal cost, so increased production would raise profits. At quantities greater than 9, marginal revenue is less than marginal cost, so reduced production would increase profits. The point at which profit is maximized is shown by the highlighted row in the table. The profit per unit is the difference between the price line and the average-total-cost curve at the profit-maximizing quantity. Total profit ($1.14) is the rectangle ABCD, an area that is equal to the profit per unit times the number of units.

Total Output (Q)	Price (P)	Total Revenue (TR)	Total Cost (TC)	Total Profit (TR − TC)	Marginal Revenue (MR)	Marginal Cost (MC)	Average Total Cost (ATC)
0	$1	$ 0	$ 1.00	$−1.00			
1	1	1	2.00	−1.00	$1	$1.00	$2.00
2	1	2	2.80	−.80	1	.80	1.40
3	1	3	3.50	−.50	1	.70	1.1667
4	1	4	4.00	0.00	1	.50	1.00
5	1	5	4.50	.50	1	.50	.90
6	1	6	5.20	.80	1	.70	.8667
7	1	7	6.00	1.00	1	.80	.8571
8	1	8	6.86	1.14	1	.86	.8575
9	1	9	7.86	1.14	1	1.00	.8733
10	1	10	9.36	.64	1	1.50	.936
11	1	11	12.00	−1.00	1	2.64	1.09

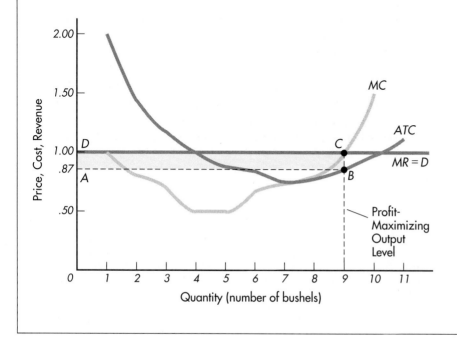

Setting Prices with Auctions

Perfect competition has often been described as a giant auction where prices and quantities supplied and demanded are determined. The reason for thinking of the perfectly competitive market structure as an auction is that an auction conjures up an image of free and unfettered buying and selling—a bunch of price takers. The auctioneer calls out a price and sees what buyers and sellers want to do. If the quantity demanded is greater than the quantity supplied at that price, the auctioneer increases the price and tries again. Only when the quantities demanded and supplied are the same does the auctioneer stop and allow buyers to buy and sellers to sell.

Auctions are used to sell a wide range of objects, from art works to drilling rights to government contracts. Very frequently, the U.S. Treasury sells billions of dollars of Treasury bonds with an auction. One of the earliest reports of an auction is by the ancient Greek historian Herodotus, who described the bidding of men for wives in Babylon around 500 B.C. In ancient Rome, auctions were used in commercial trade, and Romans in financial straits used them to liquidate property.

Auctions are not all alike.

Actually, the word itself is something of a misnomer. *Auctio* means "to increase," but not all auctions involve calling out higher and higher bids. In *oral auctions*, bidders hear one another's bids as they are made and can make counteroffers; each bidder knows how many others are bidding. In *sealed-bid auctions*, bidders simultaneously submit one or more bids to the seller without revealing their bids to one another.

The most common types of oral auctions are the English and the Dutch auctions. The auctioneer in an English auction raises the price until only one bidder remains, and that bidder wins the good at the price that was bid. The auctioneer in a Dutch auction (used to sell tulip bulbs in Holland and fish in Israel) calls out a high price and then continuously lowers the price until some bidder stops the bidding and claims the good at that price.

Most people think of an auction as generating identical prices for identical items no matter when the specific item is sold during the auction. Auctions seem to produce some results that do not mesh with this view, however. A few economists have discovered that in some auctions identical items are sold for different prices; of two

identical items, the one sold later in the auction will have a lower price than the one sold earlier in the auction. This has been called a price anomaly because it seems contradictory to the theory of perfect competition—identical goods should have identical prices. Yet, in wine auctions, real estate auctions, and auctions involving agricultural products, identical items seem to sell for different prices merely because of their place in the auction. To date, the reasons for the price anomaly have not been determined.

Sources: Loretta J. Mester, "Going, Going, Gone: Setting Prices with Auctions," *Business Review* (March–April 1988), pp. 3–13; Orley Ashenfelter and David Genesove, "Testing for Price Anomalies in Real Estate Auctions," *American Economic Review.* (May 1992); Penny Burns, "Experience and Decision Making: A Comparison of Students and Businessmen in a Simulated Progressive Auction," vol. 3 of *Research in Experimental Economics* (Greenwich, Conn.: JAI Press, Inc., 1985); Paul Milgrom, "Auctions and Bidding: A Primer," *Journal of Economic Perspectives*, vol. 3, no. 3 (Summer 1989), pp. 3–22; Orley Ashenfelter, "How Auctions Work for Wine and Art," *Journal of Economic Perspectives*, vol. 3, no. 3 (Summer 1989), pp. 23–36.

1.d. Short-Run Profits and Losses

At what point does a firm decide to suspend operations?

With a price of $1 per bushel, the individual farm maximizes profit by producing 9 bushels. We can illustrate how much profit the individual firm in perfect competition earns, or whether it makes a loss, by calculating total costs at the quantity where $MR = MC$ and comparing that with total revenue.

In Figure 2, the price per bushel of $1 exceeds the cost per bushel (average total cost, $.8733) by the distance *BC* ($.1267) when 9 bushels are produced. This amount ($.1267) is the profit per bushel. The total profit is the rectangle *ABCD* (highlighted in the table).

MR = MC is the profit-maximizing or loss-minimizing output
level.

Figure 3 illustrates what occurs to the individual firm in a perfectly competitive market as the market price changes. The only curve in Figure 3 that
changes as a result of the price change is the perfectly elastic demand curve
(which is also the price line and the marginal-revenue curve). Let's assume
that the market price changes to $.70 per bushel so that the individual farm's
demand curve shifts down. Whether the firm is making a profit or not is
determined by finding the new quantity at which the new marginal-revenue
curve, MR_2, equals the marginal-cost curve, at point F, and then tracing a
vertical line from point F to the ATC curve at point G. The distance FG is the

Figure 3
Loss Minimization
In Figure 3 the price changed
from $1 per bushel to $.70 per
bushel. The profit-maximization,
or loss-minimization, point is the
level of output where $MR = MC$.
If, at this output level, the price is
less than the corresponding
average-cost curve, the firm
makes a loss. At a price of $.70
per bushel, a loss is incurred—
the loss-minimizing level of output is 6 bushels, as shown by
the highlighted bar in the table.
The total loss is the rectangle
$EFGH$.

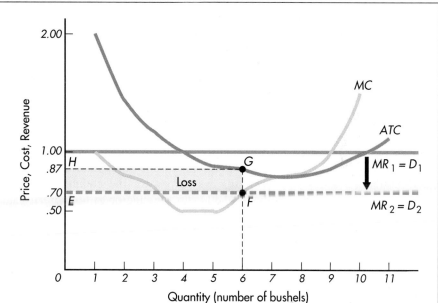

Total Output (Q)	Price (P)	Total Revenue (TR)	Total Cost (TC)	Total Profit (TR − TC)	Marginal Revenue (MR)	Marginal Cost (MC)	Average Total Cost (ATC)
0	$.70	$0	$1.00	$−1.00			
1	.70	.70	2.00	−1.30	$.70	$1.00	$2.00
2	.70	1.40	2.80	−1.40	.70	.80	1.40
3	.70	2.10	3.50	−1.40	.70	.70	1.1667
4	.70	2.80	4.00	−1.20	.70	.50	1.00
5	.70	3.50	4.50	−1.00	.70	.50	.90
6	.70	4.20	5.20	−1.00	.70	.70	.8667
7	.70	4.90	6.00	−1.10	.70	.80	.8571
8	.70	5.60	6.86	−1.26	.70	.86	.8575
9	.70	6.30	7.86	−1.56	.70	1.00	.8733
10	.70	7.00	9.36	−2.36	.70	1.50	.936
11	.70	7.70	12.00	−4.30	.70	2.64	1.09

profit or loss per unit of output. If the demand curve is above the *ATC* curve at that point, the firm is making a profit. If the *ATC* curve exceeds the price line, as is the case in Figure 3, the firm is suffering a loss.

A profit cannot be made as long as the price is less than the average-cost curve, because the cost per bushel (*ATC*) exceeds the revenue per bushel (price). At a price of $.70 per bushel, marginal revenue and marginal cost are equal as the sixth bushel is produced (see Figure 3 and the highlighted bar in the table), but the average total cost is greater than the price. The cost per bushel (*ATC*) is $.8667, which is higher than the price or revenue per bushel of $.70. Thus, the firm makes a loss, shown as the rectangle *EFGH* in Figure 3.

Recall that an economic loss means that opportunity costs are not being covered by revenues; that is, the owners could do better in another line of business. An economic loss means that a firm is confronted with the choice of whether to continue producing, shut down temporarily, or shut down permanently. The decision depends on which alternative has the lowest opportunity cost.

I.e. Short-Run Break-Even and Shutdown Prices

When will a firm shut down permanently?

In the short run, certain costs, such as rent on land and equipment, must be paid whether or not any output is produced. These are the firm's fixed costs. If a firm has purchased equipment and buildings but does not produce, the firm still has to pay for the equipment and buildings. Thus, the decision about whether to produce or to temporarily suspend operations depends on which option promises the lesser costs. In order to continue producing in the short run, the firm must earn sufficient revenue to pay all of the *variable* costs (the costs that change as output changes), because then the excess of revenue over variable costs will enable the firm to pay some of its fixed costs. If all of the variable costs cannot be paid for out of revenue, then the firm should suspend operations temporarily because by continuing to produce, the firm must pay its fixed costs as well as those variable costs in excess of revenue.

Does suspending operations mean quitting the business altogether—shutting down permanently? It may, but it need not. The decision depends on the long-term outlook. If the long-term outlook indicates that revenue will exceed costs, then production is warranted. However, if the outlook is for continued low prices and the inability to cover costs, a firm would be better off quitting the business altogether.

To see how producing at a loss can at times be better than not producing at all, let's return to the individual farm in Figure 4. At a price of $.70 per bushel, the output at which *MR = MC* is 6 bushels, as shown by the highlighted bar in the table. At 6 bushels, total revenue is $4.20 and total cost is $5.20. The farm loses $1 by producing 6 bushels. The question is whether to produce at all. If production is stopped, the fixed cost of $1 must still be paid. Thus, the farmer is indifferent between producing 6 bushels and losing $1 or shutting down and losing $1. Should the price be less than the minimum point of the average-variable-cost curve (*AVC*), as would occur at any price less than *P* = $.70 per bushel, the farm is not earning enough to cover its variable costs (see Figure 4 and accompanying table). By continuing to produce, the farm will lose more than it would lose if it suspended operations or shut down until the outlook improved. The minimum point of the average-variable-cost curve is the **shutdown price**. If the market price is less than the

shutdown price:
the minimum point of the average-variable-cost curve

Figure 4
Shutdown Price

When the firm is making a loss, it must decide whether to continue producing or suspend operations and not produce. The decision depends on which alternative has higher costs. When the price is equal to or greater than the minimum point of the average-variable-cost curve, $.70, the firm is earning sufficient revenue to pay for all of the variable costs. When the price is less than the minimum point of the average-variable-cost curve, the firm is not covering all of its variable costs. In that case the firm is better off shutting down its operations. For this reason, the minimum point of the *AVC* curve is called the *shutdown price*. The *break-even price* is the minimum point of the *ATC* curve because at that point all costs are being paid.

Total Output (Q)	Price (P)	Total Revenue (TR)	Total Cost (TC)	Total Profit (TR − TC)	Marginal Revenue (MR)	Marginal Cost (MC)	Average Total Cost (ATC)	Average Variable Cost (AVC)
0	$.70	$0	$1.00	$−1.00				
1	.70	.70	2.00	−1.30	$.70	$1.00	$2.00	$1.00
2	.70	1.40	2.80	−1.40	.70	.80	1.40	.90
3	.70	2.10	3.50	−1.40	.70	.70	1.1667	.833
4	.70	2.80	4.00	−1.20	.70	.50	1.00	.75
5	.70	3.50	4.50	−1.00	.70	.50	.90	.70
6	.70	4.20	5.20	−1.00	.70	.70	.8667	.70
7	.70	4.90	6.00	−1.10	.70	.80	.8571	.714
8	.70	5.60	6.86	−1.26	.70	.86	.8575	.7325
9	.70	6.30	7.86	−1.56	.70	1.00	.8733	.7622
10	.70	7.00	9.36	−2.36	.70	1.50	.936	.836
11	.70	7.70	12.00	−4.30	.70	2.64	1.09	1.00

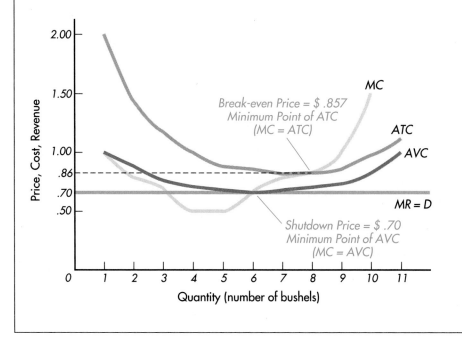

minimum point of the *AVC* curve, then the firm will incur fewer losses if it does not produce than if it continues to produce in the short run.

At prices above the minimum point of the average-variable-cost curve, the excess of revenue over variable cost means that some fixed costs can be paid. A firm is better off producing than shutting down because by producing it is able to earn enough revenue to pay all the variable costs and some of the fixed costs. If the firm does not produce, it will still have to pay all of the fixed costs. When the price equals the minimum point of the average-total-cost curve, the firm is earning just enough revenue to pay for all of its costs, fixed and variable. This point is called the **break-even price**. At the break-even price, economic profit is zero—all costs are being covered, including opportunity costs. Because costs include the opportunity costs of the resources already owned by the entrepreneur—his or her own labor and capital—zero economic profit means that the entrepreneur could not do better in another activity. Zero economic profit is normal profit, the profit just sufficient to keep the entrepreneur in this line of business.

break-even price:
a price that is equal to the minimum point of the average-total-cost curve

The shutdown price is the price that is equal to the minimum point of the *AVC* curve. The break-even price is the price that is equal to the minimum point of the *ATC* curve.

In the examples just discussed, the firm continues to operate at a loss because variable costs are being covered and the long-term outlook is favorable. Many firms decide to operate for a while at a loss, then suspend operations temporarily, and finally shut down permanently. A firm will shut down permanently if all costs cannot be covered in the long run. In the long run, the minimum point of the *ATC* curve is the permanent shutdown point. Price must exceed the minimum point of the *ATC* curve in the long run if the firm is to remain in business. Of the 80,000 businesses that shut down permanently in 1992, most went through a period in which they continued to operate even though variable costs were not being covered by revenue.

1.f. The Firm's Supply Curve in the Short Run

As long as revenue equals or exceeds variable costs, an individual firm will produce the quantity at which marginal revenue and marginal cost are equal. This means that the individual firm's supply curve is the portion of the *MC* curve that lies above the *AVC* curve. An individual firm's supply curve shows the quantity that a firm will produce and offer for sale at each price. When the price is less than the minimum point of the *AVC* curve, a firm incurs fewer losses from not producing than from producing. The firm thus produces and supplies nothing, and there is no supply curve. When the price is greater than the minimum point of the *AVC* curve, the firm will produce and offer for sale the quantity yielded at the point where the *MC* curve and the *MR* line intersect for each price. The supply curve is thus the *MC* curve. The portion of the *MC* curve lying above the minimum point of the *AVC* curve is the individual firm's supply curve in the short run.

In our example of an individual farm illustrated in Figure 4, nothing is produced at a price of $.50 per bushel. At $.70 per bushel, the farm produces 6 bushels in the short run; at $1 per bushel, the farm produces 9 bushels. The higher the price, the greater the quantity produced and offered for sale.

A firm may continue to produce and offer its products for sale even if it is earning a negative economic profit, as long as it earns enough revenue to pay its variable costs and expects revenue to grow enough to pay all costs eventu-

ally. If the business does not improve and losses continue to pile up, the firm will shut down permanently. In the long run, the firm must be able to earn enough revenue to pay all of its costs. If it does not, the business will not continue to operate. If the firm does earn enough to pay its costs, the firm will produce and offer for sale the quantity of output yielded at the point where $MR = MC$. This means that the firm's supply curve is the portion of its MC curve that lies above the minimum point of the ATC curve.

RECAP

1. The firm maximizes profit or minimizes losses by producing at the output level at which MR and MC are equal.

2. In order to remain in business, the firm must earn sufficient revenue to pay for all of its variable costs. The shutdown price is the price that is just equal to the minimum point of the AVC curve.

3. The firm's break-even price is the price that is just equal to the minimum point of the ATC curve.

4. The portion of the marginal-cost curve lying above the minimum point of the AVC curve is the firm's short-run supply curve.

5. The portion of the marginal-cost curve lying above the minimum point of the ATC curve is the firm's long-run supply curve.

2. THE LONG RUN

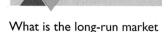

What is the long-run market supply curve?

Exit and entry are long-run phenomena.

In the short run, at least one of the resources cannot be altered. This means that new firms cannot be organized and begin producing. Thus the supply of firms in an industry is fixed in the short run. In the long run, of course, all quantities of resources can be changed. Buildings can be built or purchased and machinery accumulated and placed into production. New firms may arise as entrepreneurs not currently in the industry see that they could earn more than they are currently earning and decide to expand into new businesses. Entrepreneurs who were operating in a different line of business put up their own money or organize a group of investors to finance a new business. In 1907, Henry Ford left the Edison Illuminating Company and began the Henry Ford Automobile Company. Steven Jobs and Steve Wozniak gave up positions with Atari and Hewlett-Packard to begin Apple Computer. Estée Lauder gave up acting and began a cosmetics firm. Mary Kay Ash gave up a successful selling job with Stanley Products to begin Mary Kay Cosmetics.

Entry and exit can both occur in the long run. An entrepreneur who is operating a particular business but not covering his or her opportunity costs will quit producing. 3M Corporation gave up the production of photofinishing chemicals and paper. Bricklin quit the automobile business. Eastern, Braniff, and several non-United States airlines got out of the airline business. Drexel Burnham Lambert got out of the stock-trading business.

On average, 4.5 percent of the total number of farms go out of business each year, and more than half of them file for bankruptcy. The numbers leaving the business increased substantially in the 1980s as the costs of doing business rose and agricultural prices fell. On average, 6.5 percent of existing farms left the agricultural industry each year in the 1980s.

How does exit occur? Entrepreneurs may sell their businesses and move to another industry, or they may use the bankruptcy laws to exit the industry. A sole proprietor or partnership may file Chapter 13 personal bankruptcy; a corporation may file Chapter 7 bankruptcy or a Chapter 11 reorganization; a farmer may file Chapter 12. All of these special sections of the law describe the way creditors are paid off and the firm is dismantled. In the United States nearly 80,000 businesses filed for bankruptcy each year between 1990 and 1992.

Every year, new businesses in all types of industries are begun while others cease to exist. From the mid-1970s to the present, the average birthrate for all industries (the percent of total businesses that begin during a year) has been just over 11.2 percent, and the average death rate (the percent of total businesses that disappear during a year) has been 9.6 percent. The total number of businesses has grown by about 1.6 percent per year since the mid-1970s.

2.a. The Market Supply Curve and Exit and Entry

The short-run *market* supply curve is the horizontal sum of the short-run supply curves of all firms currently operating in a particular business. It is short-run because the quantity of at least one of the inputs—typically the amount of land or the quantity of capital—is fixed. In the long run, however, all inputs are variable. Thus, an existing firm can expand, construct new buildings, purchase new equipment, and hire more workers; an existing firm can also liquidate the business, selling the buildings and equipment and laying off workers. Furthermore, new businesses can spring up.

When additional firms enter the industry and begin producing the product, the market supply curve shifts out.

When firms leave the industry, the market supply curve shifts in.

Recall from Chapter 3 that the market supply curve shifts when the number of suppliers changes. In the corn-producing business, when new farms enter the market, the total quantity of corn supplied at each price increases. In other words, entry causes the market supply curve to shift out to the right.

Conversely, exit means fewer producers and lower quantities supplied at each price and a leftward or inward shift of the market supply curve. Suppose some existing farms are not covering their costs and believe the future is not bright enough to warrant continued production. As a result, they shut down their operations and sell their equipment and land. As the number of farms in the industry declines, everything else held constant, the market supply curve shifts to the left—as long as those remaining in the business produce the same quantity, or less, as they did before the farms exited.

2.b. Normal Profit in the Long Run

One of the principal characteristics of the perfectly competitive market structure is that entry and exit can occur easily. Thus, entry and exit occur whenever firms are earning more or less than a *normal profit* (zero economic profit). When a normal profit is being earned there is no entry or exit. This condition is the long-run equilibrium.

The process of establishing the long-run position is shown in Figure 5. The market demand and supply curves for corn are shown in Figure 5(a), and the cost and revenue curves for a representative firm in the industry are shown in Figure 5(b). Let's assume that the market price is $1. Let's also assume that at $1 per bushel, the demand curve facing the individual farm (the price line) is equal to the minimum point of the *ATC* curve. The quantity produced is 9 bushels. The individual farm and the industry are in equilibrium. There is no

Figure 5
Economic Profit in the Long Run

Market demand and supply determine the price and the demand curve faced by the single perfectly competitive firm. At a price of $1 per bushel, the individual farm is earning normal profit. After an agricultural disaster in Russia increases the demand for U.S. corn, the price rises to $1.50. At $1.50 per bushel, the single farm makes a profit equal to the yellow rectangle. Above-normal profits induce new farms to begin raising corn and existing farms to increase their production.

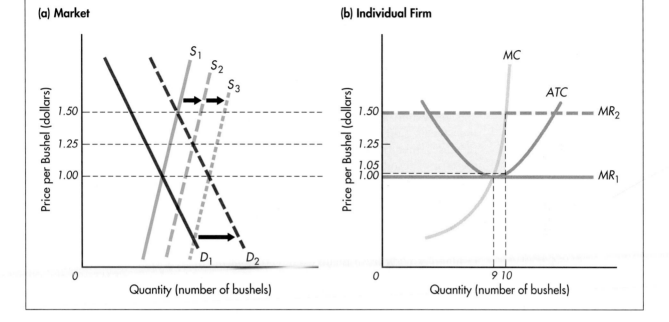

(a) Market

(b) Individual Firm

reason for entry or exit to occur, and no reason for individual farms to change their scale of operation.

To illustrate how the process of reaching the long-run equilibrium occurs in the perfectly competitive market structure, let's begin with the market in equilibrium at $S_1 = D_1$. Then let's suppose a major agricultural disaster strikes Russia and Russia turns to the United States to buy agricultural products. As a result of the increased Russian demand, the total demand for U.S. corn increases, as shown by the rightward shift of the demand curve to D_2 in Figure 5(a). In the short run, the market price rises to $1.50 per bushel, where the new market demand curve intersects the initial market supply curve, S_1. This raises the demand curve for the individual farm to the horizontal line at $1.50 per bushel. In the short run, the individual farms in the industry increase production (by adding variable inputs) from 9 bushels to 10 bushels, the point in Figure 5(b) where $MC = MR_2 = \$1.50$, and earn economic profit of the amount shown by the yellow rectangle.

The above-normal profit attracts others to the farming business. The result of the new entry and expansion is a rightward shift of the market supply curve. How far does the market supply curve shift? It shifts until the market price is low enough that firms in the industry earn normal profit. Let us suppose that the costs of doing business do not rise as the market expands. Then, if the market supply curve shifts to S_2, the new market price, $1.25, is less than the former price of $1.50 but still high enough for firms to earn above-normal profits. These profits are sufficient inducement for more firms to enter, causing the supply curve to shift farther right. The supply curve continues to shift until there is no incentive for additional firms to enter—that is, until firms are earning the normal profit, where price is equal to the minimum *ATC*, shown as S_3 in Figure 5(a).

Whether the long-run adjustment stops at a price that is above, equal to, or below the original price depends on whether the industry is an increasing-, constant-, or decreasing-cost industry, as discussed in the next section. In any case, when the adjustment stops, firms are just earning the normal profit.

In the long run, perfectly competitive firms earn normal profits.

2.c. Constant-, Increasing-, and Decreasing-Cost Industries

constant-cost industry:
an industry that can expand without affecting the prices of the resources it purchases

increasing-cost industry:
an industry in which the cost of resources rises when the industry expands

decreasing-cost industry:
an industry in which the cost of resources declines as the industry expands

As new operations are begun and as existing firms expand, the quantity of resources—land, labor, water, fuel, equipment, and so on—used in production will rise as well. If the additional use of resources from the expansion and entry into a business does not change the cost of resources, then the industry is said to be a **constant-cost industry**. If the cost of resources increases, then the industry is said to be an **increasing-cost industry**. And if the cost of resources declines due to the expansion of the industry, then the industry is known as a **decreasing-cost industry**. (The Economic Insight "Focus on Terminology" provides a clarification of some of the terms we have used to describe firms and industries.)

The fresh-fish business may be described as a constant-cost industry. Many fish are now farmed rather than caught in natural waters. Trout farms in Idaho provide fresh Idaho trout; catfish farms in Nebraska provide much of the catfish found in restaurants; shrimp farms in Louisiana and Hawaii provide some of the shrimp available in supermarkets; and farms along the U.S. coasts are used to raise shellfish. When the demand for fish rises, new farms start up and existing farms expand their artificial lakes and supply a larger quantity of eggs and feed. The price of the water, feed, and eggs does not increase as a result of the increased demand for fish, because the fish farms use such a small portion of total water and feed that they have almost no impact on the prices of those items.

Let's suppose that the market for fish is in equilibrium at a price of $4 per pound and that the demand for fish increases because of a discovery about the health benefits of eating fish. This is illustrated in Figure 6(a); on the left side is the industry demand and supply curves and on the right side is a single, representative firm. Because of the increase in demand, existing firms earn an above-normal profit. Entry occurs, causing the market supply curve to shift out. In a constant-cost industry, the short-run market supply curve shifts out until the market price returns to the original level, $4 per pound, but at the larger quantity, point *B*. The long-run market supply curve is obtained by combining the equilibrium points, *A* and *B*; it is the horizontal line, S^{LR}.

When the entry and expansion taking place in an industry raise the prices of resources used, the industry is said to be an *increasing-cost industry*. The scrap-metal industry displays the characteristics of a perfectly competitive market structure with increasing costs. Millions of tons of scrap metal are available annually as Americans discard cars, refrigerators, bicycles, and washing machines. Junk and scrap collectors find these discards and take them to processors. When the demand for metal rises, the demand for junk rises. The scrap collectors must travel farther, search harder, and spend more time finding junk. As a result, the costs rise. The increased resource costs

Figure 6
Constant-, Increasing-, and Decreasing-Cost Industries

In Figure 6(a), a constant-cost industry—fish farming—is shown on the left, and a representative firm in that industry is shown on the right. When firms in the industry are earning above-normal profit, new firms enter. The increased production means that the market supply curve shifts out. Fish farms use just a small amount of the total quantities of water and feed, so the cost of these resources does not change. The combination of equilibrium points—all points where firms are earning normal profits—traces out a horizontal curve, the long-run supply curve, S^{LR}. In Figure 6(b), an increasing-cost industry—scrap metal—is shown on the left, and a representative firm in that industry is shown on the right. As expansion of the industry takes place, obtaining a given quantity of scrap becomes increasingly costly. The new equilibrium occurs at a higher price than the original. The combination of equilibrium points traces out an upward-sloping long-run supply curve, S^{LR}. In Figure 6(c), a decreasing-cost industry—consumer electronics (VCRs)—is shown on the left, and a representative firm in the industry is shown on the right. As expansion of the industry occurs, resource costs decline. The long-run supply curve is the downward-sloping curve, S^{LR}. The curve slopes down because the firm's cost curves fall.

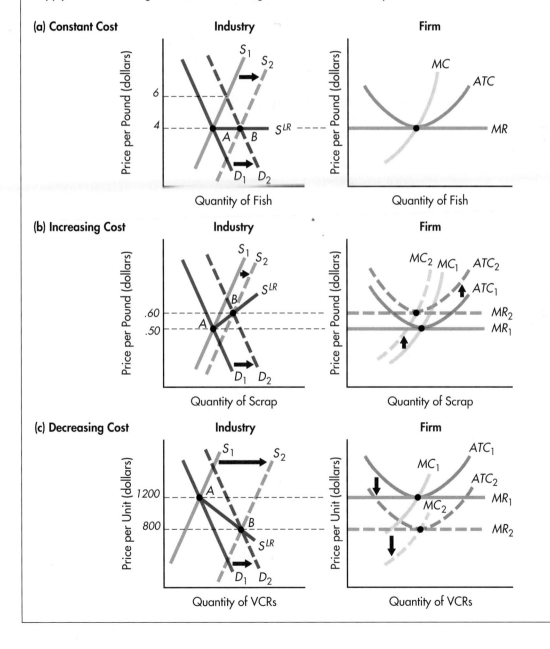

Focus on Terminology

Several terms and concepts used in the last couple of chapters sound sufficiently alike that they could be confused:

- The law of *diminishing marginal returns*

- Economies and diseconomies of scale

- Constant returns to scale

- Increasing-, decreasing-, and constant-cost industries

Let's take a moment to clarify these terms and concepts.

The *law of diminishing marginal returns* applies only to the short run. It describes the additional output that is produced when additional units of a variable input are combined with a particular quantity of a fixed input.

Economies and diseconomies of scale and *increasing-, constant-, and decreasing-cost industries* are con-cepts that apply to the long run. Economies and diseconomies of scale refer to an individual firm. Increasing, decreasing, and constant costs refer to an entire industry.

Economies and diseconomies of scale describe what happens to a firm's costs as the firm increases production and no other firms influence it. The shape of the firm's long-run average-cost curve is determined by the extent to which the firm experiences economies and diseconomies of scale.

The concepts of increasing-, constant-, and decreasing-cost industries describe what happens in an entire industry when the industry changes its production quantities. If an entire industry expands, thereby causing resource or input costs to change, the costs to each individual firm change as well. When the costs increase, the industry is called an *increasing-cost* industry. When the costs decrease, the industry is a *decreasing-cost* industry. When costs do not change, the industry is a *constant-cost* industry. When the input costs change, the individual firm's cost curves shift. Contrast this to the case of economies and disecon-omies of scale, where we are talk-ing about a single firm moving up and down one cost curve—the long-run average-total-cost curve. To summarize:

- Diminishing marginal returns is a short-run concept.

- Economies and diseconomies of scale and constant returns to scale are long-run concepts applicable to an individual firm.

- Constant-cost, increasing-cost, and decreasing-cost industries are long-run concepts applicable to an entire industry.

---

mean that each individual firm faces higher costs; each firm's cost curves shift up, as shown in the right side of Figure 6(b). Because each firm now has higher costs, each is willing and able to produce and offer for sale a smaller quantity of output at each price than would have occurred had costs not changed. This means that although the expansion and entry cause the market supply curve to shift out, it does not shift as far as it would if the industry were a constant-cost industry. The new long-run equilibrium price for scrap steel rises from $.50 per pound to $.60 per pound, and the long-run market supply curve slopes up, as shown by curve S^{LR} in the left side of Figure 6(b).

When the price of inputs decreases as an industry expands, the industry is said to be a *decreasing-cost industry*. Consumer electronics presents good examples of decreasing-cost industries, although perhaps not perfectly com-petitive industries. When the first videocassette recorder (VCR) was offered for sale in the 1950s, its price exceeded $1,200. Expansion in the industry led to innovations and efficiencies as well as to additional supplies of the plastics and metals used in VCRs. As a result, the price of the resources used in the production of VCRs actually declined.

If the expansion of existing firms and new entry lead to a reduction in resource costs, the individual firm's *ATC* and *MC* curves shift down, as in the shift from ATC_1 to ATC_2 in the right side of Figure 6(c). Even without an increase in the number of firms offering goods, the lower resource costs would cause the market supply curve to shift out. Coupled with new firms and with existing firms producing more is the lower cost of producing. Thus, the market supply curve in a decreasing-cost industry shifts out more in response to the initial demand increase than does the market supply curve in a constant-cost or increasing-cost industry. The result is that the price of the product declines. Shown in Figure 6(c), the price of the VCR declines from $1,200 to $800 because of the increased demand for VCRs. The long-run market supply curve in the decreasing-cost industry is S^{LR}, a downward-sloping curve shown in the left side of Figure 6(c).

In sum, the long-run market supply curve in a perfectly competitive industry can be perfectly horizontal (constant costs), upward-sloping (increasing costs), or downward-sloping (decreasing costs).

2.d. The Predictions of the Model of Perfect Competition

According to the model of perfect competition, whenever above-normal profits are earned by existing firms, entry occurs until a normal profit is earned by all firms. Conversely, whenever economic losses occur, exit takes place until a normal profit is made by all remaining firms.

In the past decade, U.S. consumers have dramatically switched their consumption from beef to fish. The doubling of the amount of fish consumed has led to an expansion of the fish-producing industry. Most fish consumed are not caught in oceans or rivers but are grown on farms, such as this one in Caldwell, Idaho. As demand rises, prices rise, and existing producers earn above-normal profits. Entry is relatively easy in the industry, so new farms are built and existing farms expand. The expansion and icreased demand for fish tanks, pumps, fresh or salt water, and fish food do not drive the prices of these items up because the industry is a constant-cost industry. As a result, the expansion of the industry continues until the price of the fish is the same as it was prior to the demand increase.

Perfect competition results in economic efficiency.

It is so important to keep in mind the distinctions between economic and accounting terms that we repeatedly remind you of them. A *zero economic profit* is a *normal accounting profit*, or just *normal profit*. It is the profit just sufficient to keep an entrepreneur in a particular line of business, the point where revenue exactly equals direct costs plus opportunity costs. Entrepreneurs earning a normal profit are earning enough to cover their opportunity costs—they could not do better by changing—but are not earning more than their opportunity costs. A *loss* refers to a situation where revenue is not sufficient to pay all of the direct costs and opportunity costs. A firm can earn a positive accounting profit and yet be experiencing a loss, not earning a normal profit.

The long-run equilibrium position of the perfectly competitive market structure shows firms producing at the minimum point of their long-run average-total-cost curves. If the price is above the minimum point of the *ATC* curve, then firms are earning above-normal profit and entry will occur. If the price is less than the minimum of the *ATC* curve, exit will occur. Only when price equals the minimum point of the *ATC* curve will neither entry nor exit take place.

Producing at the minimum of the *ATC* curve means that firms are producing with the lowest possible costs. They could not alter the way they produce and produce less expensively. They could not alter the resources they use and produce less expensively.

Firms produce at a level where marginal cost and marginal revenue are the same. Since marginal revenue and price are the same in a perfectly competitive market, firms produce where marginal cost equals price. This means that firms are employing resources until the marginal cost to them of producing the last unit of a good just equals the price of the last unit. Moreover, since price is equal to marginal cost, consumers are paying a price that is as low as it can get; the price just covers the marginal cost of producing that good or service. There is no waste—no one could be made better off without making someone else worse off. Economists refer to this result as **economic efficiency**.

economic efficiency:
when the price of a good or service just covers the marginal cost of producing that good or service and people are getting the goods they want

2.d.1. Producer Surplus *Efficiency* is the term economists give to the situation where firms are producing with as little cost as they can (minimum point of the *ATC* curve) and consumers are getting the products they desire at a price that is equal to the marginal cost of producing those goods. To say that a competitive market is efficient is to say that all market participants get the greatest benefits possible from market exchange.[2]

How do we measure the benefits of the market? In the chapter on consumer choice, we discussed the concept of consumer surplus, indicating that it is a measure of the difference between what consumers would be willing to

---

[2]Economists have classified efficiency into several categories. *Productive* efficiency refers to the firm using the least-cost combination of resources to produce any output level. This output level may not be the goods consumers want, however. *Allocative* efficiency is the term given to the situation where firms are producing the goods consumers most want and consumers are paying a price just equal to the marginal cost of producing the goods. Allocative efficiency may occur when firms are not producing at their most efficient level. Economic efficiency exists when both productive and allocative efficiency occurs.

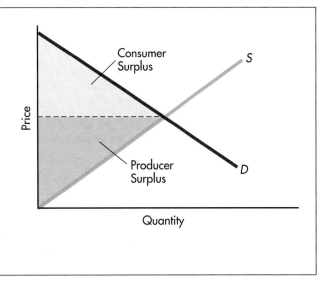

Figure 7
Producer and Consumer Surplus
Since the firm is willing to sell the product at the marginal cost and since the firm receives the market price, the difference between the two is a bonus to the firm, a bonus of market exchange. This bonus is producer surplus. Figure 7 illustrates total producer surplus in a competitive market, the sum of the producer surplus received by each firm in the market. Producer surplus is the area below the price line and above the supply curve. Also pictured is total consumer surplus. Recall that consumer surplus is the difference between what the consumer would be willing to pay for a good, the demand curve, and the price actually paid. The sum of producer and consumer surplus represents the total benefits that come from exchange in a market: benefits that accrue to the consumer plus those that accrue to the firm.

producer surplus:
the difference between the price firms would have been willing to accept for their products and the price they actually receive

pay for a product and the price they actually have to pay to buy the product. Consumer surplus is a measure of the benefits consumers receive from market exchange. A similar measure exists for the firm. It is called **producer surplus**. Producer surplus indicates the difference between the price firms would have been willing to accept for their products and the price they actually receive.

Since the firm is willing to sell the product at the marginal cost and since the firm receives the market price, the difference between the two is a bonus to the firm, a bonus resulting from market exchange. This bonus is producer surplus.

Consumer surplus = Area above equilibrium price and below the demand curve

Producer surplus = Area below equilibrium price and above the supply curve

Figure 7 illustrates consumer and producer surplus in a competitive market. The sum of producer and consumer surplus represents the total benefits that come from exchange in a market: benefits that accrue to the consumer plus those that accrue to the firm.

The primary result of perfect competition is that things just do not get any better: total consumer and producer surplus is at a maximum. Any interference with the market exchange reduces the total surplus. Consider rent control on apartments, for instance. The market for rental apartments is pictured in Figure 8. As shown in Figure 8, the market solution would yield a monthly rent of $400. The consumer surplus would be the area *ABC*; the producer surplus would be the area *ABD*. Now, suppose the city imposes a rent control at $300 per month. The producer surplus changes to area *EFD* while the consumer surplus changes to *EFHC*. Clearly the total surplus has been reduced. The question policymakers must decide is whether the additional benefits to consumers offset the losses to producers. In those cities imposing rent controls, the answer must be yes.

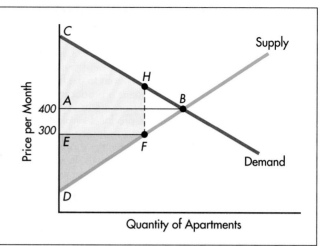

Figure 8
Rent Control and Market Efficiency
The market for rental apartments is pictured in this graph; the market solution would yield a monthly rent of $400. The consumer surplus would be the area *ABC*; the producer surplus would be the area *ABD*. Now, suppose the city imposes rent control at $300 per month. The producer surplus changes to area *EFD* while the consumer surplus changes to *EFHC*. The total surplus has been reduced by the rent control.

RECAP

1. Entry occurs when firms are earning above-normal profit or positive economic profit.

2. A temporary shutdown occurs when firms are not covering their variable costs in the short run. In the long run, exit occurs when firms are not covering all costs.

3. The short-run market supply curve is the horizontal sum of the supply curves of all individual firms in the industry.

4. The long-run market supply curve shows the quantities supplied at each price by all firms in the industry after exit and entry occur.

5. The long-run market supply curve slopes up in increasing-cost industries, down in decreasing-cost industries, and is a horizontal line in constant-cost industries.

6. In a perfectly competitive market, firms produce goods at the least cost, and consumers purchase the goods they most desire at a price that is equal to the marginal cost of producing the good. There is no waste—no one could be made better off without making someone else worse off. Economists refer to this result as economic efficiency.

7. Producer surplus is the benefits the firm receives for engaging in market exchange; it is the difference between the price the firm would be willing to sell its goods for and the price the firm actually receives.

8. Consumer surplus is the area below the demand curve and above the equilibrium price; producer surplus is the area above the supply curve and below the equilibrium price.

SUMMARY

▲▼ *What is perfect competition?*

1. Perfect competition is a market structure in which there are many firms that are producing an identical product and where entry and exit are easy. §1.a

▲▼ **What does the demand curve facing the individual firm look like, and why?**

2. The demand curve of the individual firm is a horizontal line at the market price. Each firm is a price taker. §1.b

▲▼ **How does the firm maximize profit in the short run?**

3. The individual firm maximizes profit by producing at the point where $MR = MC$. §1.c

▲▼ **At what point does a firm decide to suspend operations?**

4. A firm will shut down operations temporarily if price does not exceed the minimum point of the average-variable-cost curve. §1.d

▲▼ **When will a firm shut down permanently?**

5. A firm will shut down operations permanently if price does not exceed the minimum point of the average-total-cost curve in the long run. §1.e

▲▼ **What is the break-even price?**

6. The firm breaks even when revenue and cost are equal—when the demand curve (price) just equals the minimum point of the average-total-cost curve. §1.e

▲▼ **What is the firm's supply curve in the short run?**

7. The firm's short-run supply curve is the portion of its marginal-cost curve that lies above the minimum point of the average-variable-cost curve. §1.f

▲▼ **What is the firm's supply curve in the long run?**

8. The firm produces at the point where marginal cost equals marginal revenue, as long as marginal revenue exceeds the minimum point of the average-total-cost curve. Thus, the firm's long-run supply curve is the portion of its marginal-cost curve that lies above the minimum point of the average-total-cost curve. §1.f

▲▼ **What is the long-run market supply curve?**

9. The market supply curve is the horizontal sum of the supply curves of the individual firms in an industry. In the long run, if these firms are earning above-normal profit, new firms enter the industry, and the market supply curve shifts to the right. If firms are earning negative economic profit, existing firms exit the industry, and the market supply curve shifts to the left. The movement from one equilibrium position to another traces out the long-run market supply curve. §2.a

10. Entry occurs when firms earn above-normal profit. Exit occurs when a firm's revenues are not sufficient to pay all direct and opportunity costs. An industry is in equilibrium when firms are earning a normal profit. §2.b

11. If resource costs rise as an industry expands, the industry is called an *increasing-cost* industry. If resource costs fall as an industry expands, the industry is a *decreasing-cost* industry. If resource costs do not change as an industry expands, the industry is a *constant-cost* industry. §2.c

12. The long-run market supply curve slopes up in an increasing-cost industry, down in a decreasing-cost industry, and is a horizontal line in a constant-cost industry. §2.c

▲▼ **What are the long-run equilibrium results of a perfectly competitive market?**

13. In the long run, all firms operating in perfect competition will earn a normal profit by producing at the lowest possible cost, and all consumers will buy the goods and services they most want at a price equal to the marginal cost of producing the goods and services. §2.d

14. Economic efficiency is the result of perfect competition. §2.d

15. Producer surplus is the difference between what a firm would be willing to produce and sell a good for and the price the firm actually receives for the good. Consumer surplus is the difference between what an individual would be willing to pay for a good and what the individual actually has to pay. Total consumer and producer surplus is at a maximum in a perfectly competitive market. §2.d.1

KEY TERMS

shutdown price §1.e

break-even price §1.e

constant-cost industry §2.c

increasing-cost industry §2.c

decreasing-cost industry §2.c

economic efficiency §2.d

producer surplus §2.d.1

EXERCISES

1. Cost figures for a hypothetical firm are given in the following table. Use them to answer the questions below. The firm is selling in a perfectly competitive market.

Out-put	Fixed Cost	AFC	Variable Cost	AVC	Total Cost	ATC	MC
1	$50		$ 30				
2	50		50				
3	50		80				
4	50		120				
5	50		170				

a. Fill in the blank columns.

b. What is the minimum price needed by the firm to break even?

c. What is the shutdown price?

d. At a price of $40, what output level would the firm produce? What would its profits be?

2. Label the curves in the following graph.

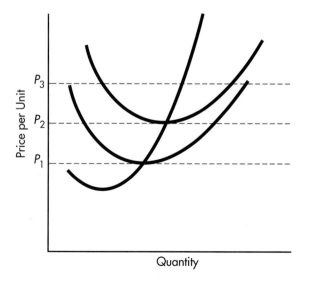

Quantity

a. At each market price, P_1, P_2, and P_3, what output level would the firm produce?

b. What profit would be earned if the market price was P_1?

c. What are the shutdown and break-even prices?

3. Why might a firm continue to produce in the short run even though the market price is less than its average total cost?

4. Explain why the demand curve facing the individual firm in a perfectly competitive industry is a horizontal line.

5. Explain what occurs in the long run in a constant-cost industry, an increasing-cost industry, and a decreasing-cost industry when the market demand declines (shifts in).

6. What can you expect from an industry in perfect competition in the long run? What will price be? What quantity will be produced? What will be the relation between marginal cost, average cost, and price?

7. Assume that the market for illegal drugs is an example of a perfectly competitive market structure. Describe what the perfectly competitive market model predicts for illegal drugs in the long run. What is likely to be the impact of the U.S. government's war on drugs in the short run? In the long run?

8. If no real-life industry meets the conditions of the perfectly competitive model exactly, why do we study perfect competition? What is the relevance of the model to the decision by Estée Lauder to switch careers? Why might it shed some light on pollution, acid rain, and other social problems?

9. Using the model of perfect competition, explain what it means to say, "Too much electricity is generated," or "Too little education is produced." Would the firm be producing at the bottom of the *ATC* curve?

10. Private swimming pools can be dangerous. There are serious accidents each year in those areas of the United States where backyard pools are common. Should pools be banned? In other words, should the market for swimming pools be eliminated? Answer this in terms of producer and consumer surplus.

11. Discuss whether the following are examples of perfectly competitive industries.

    a. The U.S. stock market

    b. The automobile industry

    c. The consumer electronics market

    d. The market for college students

12. Macy's was making millions of dollars in profits when it declared bankruptcy. Explain Macy's decision.

13. Entry and exit of firms occur in the long run but not the short run. Why? What is meant by the long run and the short run? Would you say that entry is more or less difficult than exit?

14. Use the following data to answer the questions below.

Price	Quantity Supplied	Quantity Demanded
$20	30	0
18	25	5
16	20	10
14	15	15
12	10	20
10	5	25
8	0	30

a. What is the equilibrium price and quantity?

b. Draw the demand and supply curves. If this represents perfect competition, are the curves individual-firm or market curves? How is the quantity supplied derived?

c. Show the consumer surplus. Show the producer surplus.

d. Suppose that a price ceiling of $12 was imposed. How would this change the consumer and producer surplus? Suppose a price floor of $16 was imposed. How would this change the consumer and producer surplus?

e. Suppose this is an increasing-cost industry and the existing firms are earning above-normal profits. What will occur?

15. Explain the following statement: "The market can better determine the value of polluting than the politicians. Rather than assign an emission fee to a polluting firm, simply allow firms to purchase the rights to pollute."

Food Marketers Show a Taste for Video Growth

CHICAGO—Video rental and sales in the supermarket industry have, in the last several years, gone from an afterthought to a major money-maker. That was the consensus of video suppliers, fixturing companies, and manufacturers at the Food Marketing Institute's annual Supermarket Industry Convention, held May 2–6 at McCormick Place here.

"Video is no longer a loss leader in supermarkets," said Stewart Gershenbaum, VP of the Midwest division for JD Store Equipment of Lombard, Ill. "The change has accrued over the last three years. Before, supermarkets weren't marketing video the way they should—all the space they'd devote to video was 20 feet of wall. Now they're operating 5,000-square-foot, and larger, video sections." The St. Louis-based Schnucks supermarket chain, for instance, said Gershenbaum, "has a store-within-a-store setup, and it's the biggest video entity in St. Louis."

"You'll still find grocery stores with the 20-foot wall," he said, "but a relatively large chain will add a video staff and create their own department, headed up by a nonfood video coordinator." . . .

Executives of Selectrak Family Video of Hillside, Ill., which leases video management programs to 200 stores across the country, reported an increase in rental revenues this past year—a testament, they say, to the increasing viability of video in supermarkets. "Unlike the rest of the industry, which reports flat rentals, ours continue to rise," said marketing coordinator Tamara Sokolec.

Selectrak provides fixtures, racking, custom computer setups, and free marketing support to its clients. "Over the last year, we've put a great deal of effort into marketing," said Sokolec, who attributed Selectrak's rental increase to that stepped-up marketing effort.

Selectrak does "target certain titles for sell-through," noted Sokolec, "but rental is still the biggest part of the business. We target three to four sell-through titles a year. Moms with kids are our primary customers." The Selectrak program tends to work best, said Sokolec, in rural areas more so than urban, where there is "less dense competition."

For many supermarkets, video rental vending machines are the way to go. Michael Malet, president of Lakeland, Fla.-based Keyosk Corp. (headquartered in Irvine, Calif.), said 200–300 supermarkets around the country use Keyosk's Video Rental Center vending machines. Typical clients are "stores which don't have the space for a video section, or which don't want to hire extra staff for a video section," he said.

According to Malet, one major California supermarket chain, Hughes Markets, has switched from staffed video centers to Keyosk vending machines over the last year. "The machines are simple to operate and to service," Malet noted. "Our field people don't need to be technicians."

Companies that deal exclusively in sell-through report significant numbers in the supermarket arena, as well as those involved in rental. "We've doubled our supermarket business over the last couple of years," said David Sutton, president of Front Row Entertainment of Edison, N.J., which manufactures and distributes budget sell-through video.

"The programs we offer are lucrative for supermarkets," Sutton continued. "Our titles are $3.99–$8.99, with full exchange privileges, and we offer 30–60-day promotions."

Cabin Fever Entertainment, a video manufacturer based in Greenwich, Conn., made its first FMI appearance this year. "Supermarkets are a growing business for video companies," said national sales director Dick Zima, who said Cabin Fever's 80-title product line has become available in supermarkets just during the past year.

Zima said Cabin Fever has been "utilizing parent company U.S. Tobacco's accounts to expand into supermarkets. There's a huge potential consumer base."

Source: Moira McCormick, "Food Marketers Show a Taste for Video Growth," *Billboard*, May 23, 1992, p. 49. © 1992 BPI Communications used by permission of Billboard.

Commentary

Video-rental stores have become a staple of the American retail landscape. Their widespread proliferation has increased the number of outlets available to consumers, but owners of these video stores are beginning to realize only meager profits. The rapid growth in the number of video-rental stores suggests an ease of entry that characterizes a perfectly competitive industry. Having video-rental outlets on virtually every corner means there are a large number of sellers. The rising interest in offering video rentals by supermarkets increases the number of sellers even further. And, with the new ways to display videos, the space required to open a video-rental outlet has diminished considerably, allowing even more entry into the industry. All of these facts imply that each video-rental store is a price-taker and can be analyzed according to the model of a firm in an industry that is perfectly competitive.

The graph on the left depicts the demand and supply curves for the video-rental market, and the graph on the right illustrates the corresponding cost and marginal-revenue curves for a typical video rental store. The market supply and demand curves labeled S_1 and D_1 represent the situation a few years ago, when video store owners realized above-normal profit. The rental price of $4 that resulted from the intersection of S_1 and D_1 (at point e_1 in the graph on the left) allowed the typical video store to enjoy a profit (represented by the rectangle $ABCD$ in the graph on the right). This profit occurred because the point at which marginal revenue intersected marginal cost was above the average-total-cost curve.

Everyone wants to get in on a good thing, however, and the presence of above-normal profit led to market entry. New video-rental stores opened and existing supermarkets expanded their video offerings. This led to an outward shift of the market-supply curve to S_2. The new market-supply curve intersects demand at the lower price of $3 per rental (point e_2 in the graph on the left). At this price, the marginal revenue of the typical firm crosses the marginal-cost curve at the bottom of the average-total-cost curve (point F in the graph on the right). The price each firm receives from the video rentals is lower than the initial price, and firms no longer make economic profits.

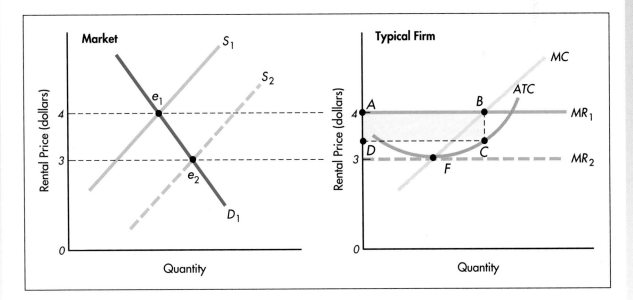

11

Monopoly

FUNDAMENTAL QUESTIONS

1. What is monopoly?
2. How is a monopoly created?
3. What does the demand curve for a monopoly firm look like, and why?
4. Why would someone want to have a monopoly in some business or activity?
5. Under what conditions will a monopolist charge different customers different prices for the same product?
6. How do the predictions of the models of perfect competition and monopoly differ?

I n 1986, Burroughs Wellcome Company announced the first breakthrough in the treatment of AIDS: the life-prolonging drug AZT. In 1989 the company was accused of "reaping unseemly profits from AIDS patients and federally funded medicaid by keeping the price of AZT at a level that makes it one of the most expensive drugs ever sold."[1] Many people were outraged by what was referred to as Burroughs Wellcome's monopolistic practices.

What is a monopoly? Why does the word conjure up dastardly images? If Burroughs Wellcome is earning an above-normal profit, why won't other pharmaceutical firms enter the business of providing AZT and thus drive the profit down to the normal level? The purpose of this chapter is to answer these questions.

In the previous chapter, we examined the model of perfect competition. You learned that perfect competition results in consumers getting what they want at the lowest possible prices and firms operating at the lowest cost. The

PREVIEW

model of monopoly provides a stark contrast: the prediction that comes from it is *inefficiency*. In fact, a comparison of the predictions that come from the models of perfect competition and monopoly provides a set of theoretical bookends to the behavior of all firms. Virtually every real-life action on the part of a firm can be described as a combination of the characteristics of perfect competition and monopoly.

I. THE MARKET STRUCTURE OF MONOPOLY

What is monopoly?

Perhaps the source is the Parker Brothers' board game Monopoly, or maybe there is some other explanation, but there are widespread beliefs about monopoly that demand our attention. One such belief is captured in the Preview regarding the Burroughs Wellcome Company: that a monopolist can earn unseemly profits by charging outrageously high prices. Another is that a monopolist does not have to respond in any way to customer desires. And a third is that it is impossible for a monopolist to make a loss. We'll discuss these beliefs in this chapter. We begin by defining what a monopolist is.

---

[1]Marilyn Chase, "Burroughs Wellcome Reaps Profits, Outrage from Its AIDS Drug," *Wall Street Journal*, Sept. 15, 1989, pp. 1, A9.

I.a. Market Definition

monopoly:
a market structure in which there is a single supplier of a product

monopoly firm (monopolist):
a single supplier of a product for which there are no close substitutes

Monopoly is a market structure in which there is a single supplier of a product. A **monopoly firm (monopolist)** may be large or small, but whatever its size, it must be the *only supplier* of the product. In addition, a monopoly firm must sell a product for which there are *no close substitutes*. The greater the number of close substitutes for a firm's products, the less likely it is that the firm has a monopoly. As a child you probably played with bricks known as Legos, the product of a Danish family-owned company. Lego has such a strong market position that it has been said to have a monopoly of construction toys. Is Lego a monopoly firm? There may not be any other plastic bricks, but there are other construction toys. Erector sets and Tinker Toys come to mind as possible substitutes for Legos. More generally, in the overall market for children's toys, Lego is far from a monopoly firm. There are many close substitutes. A monopoly firm produces a product for which there are no close substitutes.

If Lego is not a monopoly firm, then what is? You purchase products from monopoly firms every day, perhaps without realizing it. When you mail a letter, you are purchasing the services of a monopoly firm, the U.S. Postal Service. Congress created the U.S. Postal Service to provide first-class mail service. No other firm is allowed to provide that service. The currency you use is issued and its quantity is controlled by a government entity known as the Federal Reserve. It is illegal for any organization or individual other than the Federal Reserve to issue currency. When you turn on the lights, the heat, or the air conditioning, you are using electricity produced by a public utility, a monopoly firm. Either you purchase electricity from that firm or you don't purchase electricity. In cans of coffee, packages of medicine, shoes, and many other goods, you will often find a capsule that looks like a little barrel. This capsule draws moisture out of packages and maintains freshness. For two decades, the capsules contained desiccant clay, a special clay found only in a small mine in New Mexico. The mine was owned by a single family. That family had a monopoly on desiccant clay. All these examples are monopoly firms because they are the sole suppliers of products for which there are no close substitutes.

I.b. The Creation of Monopolies

How is a monopoly created?

barrier to entry:
anything that impedes the ability of firms to begin a new business in an industry in which existing firms are earning above-normal profit

Burroughs Wellcome's profits doubled in the three years following the introduction of AZT. Burroughs Wellcome was a monopoly supplier of AZT, and it was earning above-normal profits. But if a product is valuable and the owners are getting rich from selling it, won't others develop substitutes and also enjoy the fruits of the market? Yes, unless something impedes entry. The name given to that something is **barrier to entry**. There are three general classes of barriers to entry:

- natural barriers, such as economies of scale
- actions on the part of firms that create barriers to entry
- governmentally created barriers

I.b.I. Economies of Scale Economies of scale can be a barrier to entry. There are very large economies of scale in the generation of electricity. The larger the generating plant, the lower the cost per kilowatt-hour of electricity produced. A large generating plant can produce each unit of electricity much less expensively than several small generating plants. Size thus constitutes a barrier to entry since to be able to enter and compete with existing large-scale public utilities, a firm needs to be large so that it can produce each kilowatt-hour as inexpensively as the large-scale plants.

1.b.2. Actions by Firms   Entry is barred when one firm owns an essential resource. The owners of the desiccant clay mine in New Mexico had a monopoly position because they owned the essential resource, clay. Inventions and discoveries are essential resources at least until others come up with close substitutes. The creation of high fixed costs can impede entry.

1.b.3. Government   Barriers to entry are often created by governments. The U.S. government issues patents, which provide a firm a monopoly on certain products, inventions, or discoveries for a period of seventeen years. Such is the case with the Burroughs Wellcome monopoly. The company was granted a patent on AZT and thus was, by law, the only supplier of the drug. Domestic government policy also restricts entry into many industries. The federal government issues broadcast licenses for radio and television and grants airlines landing rights at certain airports. City governments limit the number of taxi companies that can operate, the number of cable television companies that can provide service, and the number of garbage collection firms that can provide service. State and local governments issue liquor licenses and restrict the number of electric utility companies. These are just a few of the government-created monopolies in the United States.

1.c. Types of Monopolies

natural monopoly:
a monopoly that arises from economies of scale

The word *monopoly* is often associated with other terms such as *natural monopoly*, *local monopoly*, *regulated monopoly*, and *monopoly power*. A **natural monopoly** is a firm that has become a monopoly because of economies of scale and demand conditions. The adjective *natural* indicates that the monopoly arises from cost and demand conditions, not from government action. If costs decline as the quantity produced rises, only very large producers will be able to stay in business. Their lower costs will enable them to force smaller producers, who have higher costs, out of business. Large producers can underprice smaller producers, as illustrated in Figure 1. The larger firm, operating along ATC_2, can set a price anywhere between P_1 and P_2 and thereby drive the smaller firm, operating along ATC_1, out of business. If

Figure 1
Economies of Scale
A large firm producing along ATC_2 can produce output much less expensively per unit than a small firm operating along ATC_1. The large firm, therefore, can set a price that is below the minimum point of the small firm's average-total-cost curve yet still earn profit. Any price between P_1 and P_2 will provide a profit for the large firm and a loss for the small firm.

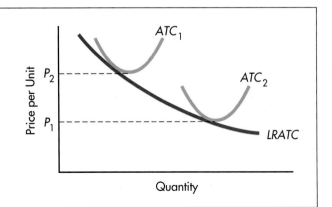

Public utilities are regulated monopolies in the United States and are government-run enterprises in other parts of the world. In France, the telephone company is a government enterprise and it's the only firm offering telephone services in the country. A French college student is calling home using the phone company's card, Telecarte. In the United States, the student would have a choice as to several telephone services, AT&T or MCI for instance, as well as the mobile phone services.

the market can support only one producer or if the long-run average-total-cost curve continually slopes downward, the monopoly that results is said to be *natural*.

A **local monopoly** is a firm that has a monopoly within a specific geographic area. An electric utility is the sole supplier of electricity in a municipality or local area. A taxicab company may have a monopoly for service to the airport or within a city. Cable TV companies may have monopolies within municipalities. An airline may have a monopoly over some routes.

A **regulated monopoly** is a monopolist whose prices and production rates are controlled by a government entity. Electric utility companies are regulated monopolies. A state corporation or utility commission sets its rates, determines the costs to be allowed in the production of electricity, and restricts entry by other firms.

Monopoly power is market power, the ability to set prices. It exists whenever the demand curve facing the producer is downward-sloping. Monopolies exercise monopoly power, but so do all firms except those operating in perfectly competitive markets. A firm that has monopoly power is a price maker rather than a price taker.

local monopoly:
a monopoly that exists in a limited geographic area

regulated monopoly:
a monopoly firm whose behavior is monitored and prescribed by a government entity

monopoly power:
market power, the ability to set prices

RECAP

1. A monopoly firm is the sole supplier of a product for which there are no close substitutes.

2. A monopoly firm remains the sole supplier because of barriers to entry.

3. Barriers to entry may be economic, such as economies of scale or due to the exclusive ownership of an essential resource, or they may be created by government policy.

4. A natural monopoly is a monopoly that results through economies of scale. A regulated monopoly is a monopoly whose pricing and produc-

tion are controlled by the government. A local monopoly is a firm that has a monopoly in a specific geographic region.

5. Monopoly power, or market power, is the ability to set prices.

2. THE DEMAND CURVE FACING A MONOPOLY FIRM

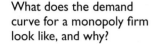

What does the demand curve for a monopoly firm look like, and why?

In any market, the industry demand curve is a downward-sloping line because of the law of demand. Although the industry demand curve is downward-sloping, the demand curve facing an individual firm in a perfectly competitive market is a horizontal line at the market price. This is not the case for the monopoly firm. Because a monopoly firm is the sole producer, it *is* the industry, so its demand curve is the industry demand curve.

2.a. Marginal Revenue

The demand curve facing the monopoly firm is the industry demand curve.

In the early 1990s, a small U.S. company introduced a wireless VCR that could operate from more than one television set and didn't even have to be placed in the same room as the television. For a few years, this company had a monopoly on the wireless VCR. Let's consider the pricing and output decisions of the firm, using hypothetical cost and revenue data.

Suppose a wireless VCR sells for $1,500, and at that price the firm is selling 5 VCRs per day, as shown in Figure 2. If the monopoly firm wants to sell more, it must move down the demand curve. Why? Because of the law of demand. People will do without the wireless VCR rather than pay more than they think it's worth. As the price declines, sales increase. The table in Figure 2 shows that if the monopoly firm lowers the price to $1,350 per unit from $1,400, it will sell 8 VCRs per day instead of 7.

Figure 2
Demand Curve for a Monopolist
As the VCR price is reduced, the quantity demanded increases. But because the price is reduced on all quantities sold, not just on the last unit sold, marginal revenue declines faster than price.

Quantity per Day	Price	Total Revenue	Marginal Revenue
1	$1,700	$ 1,700	$1,700
2	1,650	3,300	1,600
3	1,600	4,800	1,500
4	1,550	6,200	1,400
5	1,500	7,500	1,300
6	1,450	8,700	1,200
7	1,400	9,800	1,100
8	1,350	10,800	1,000
9	1,300	11,700	900

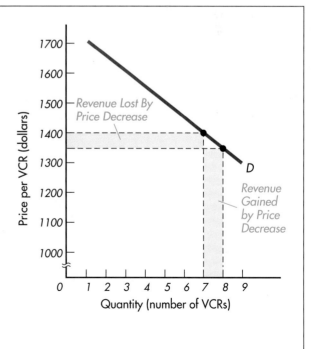

What is the firm's marginal revenue? To find marginal revenue, the total revenue earned at $1,400 per VCR must be compared to the total revenue earned at $1,350 per VCR—the change in total revenue must be calculated. At $1,400 apiece, 7 VCRs are sold each day and total revenue each day is

$$\$1,400 \text{ per VCR} \times 7 \text{ VCRs} = \$9,800$$

At $1,350 apiece, 8 VCRs are sold and total revenue is

$$\$1,350 \text{ per VCR} \times 8 \text{ VCRs} = \$10,800$$

The difference, change in total revenue, is $1,000. Thus, marginal revenue is

$$\frac{\Delta TR}{\Delta Q} = \frac{\$1,000}{1 \text{ VCR}} = \$1,000$$

The change in revenue is the difference between the increased revenue due to increased quantity sold, the yellow area in Figure 2, and the decreased revenue due to a lower price, the blue area in Figure 2.

The price is $1,350 per VCR, but marginal revenue is $1,000 per VCR. Price and marginal revenue are not the same for a monopoly firm. This is a fundamental difference between a monopoly and a perfect competitor. For a perfect competitor, price and marginal revenue are the same.

Marginal revenue is less than price for a monopoly firm.

Marginal revenue is less than price and declines as output rises because the monopolist must lower the price in order to sell more units. When the price of a VCR is $1,400, the firm sells 7 VCRs. When the price is dropped to $1,350, the firm sells 8 units. The firm does not sell the first 7 VCRs for $1,400 and the eighth one for $1,350. It might lose business if it tried to do that. The customer who purchased the good at $1,350 could sell the product for $1,375 to a customer about to pay $1,400, and the firm would lose the $1,400 sale. Customers who would have paid $1,400 could decide to wait until they too can get the $1,350 price. As long as customers know about the prices paid by other customers and as long as the firm cannot easily distinguish among customers, the monopoly firm is not able to charge a different price for each additional unit. All units are sold at the same price, and in order to sell additional units, the monopolist must lower the price on all units. As a result, marginal revenue and price are not the same.

2.a.1. Marginal and Average Revenue   Recall from the chapter "Elasticity: Demand and Supply" that whenever the marginal is greater than the average, the average rises, and whenever the marginal is less than the average, the average falls. Average revenue is calculated by dividing total revenue by the number of units of output sold.

$$AR = \frac{P \times Q}{Q} = P$$

At a price of $1,500 per VCR, average revenue is

$$\frac{\$7,500}{5} = \$1,500$$

Average revenue at a price of $1,450 per VCR is

$$\frac{\$8,700}{6} = \$1,450$$

Average revenue is the same as price; in fact, *the average-revenue curve is the demand curve.* Because of the law of demand, where quantity demanded

Figure 3
Downward-Sloping Demand Curve and Revenue
The straight-line downward-sloping demand curve in Figure 3(a) shows that the price elasticity of demand becomes more inelastic as we move down the curve. In the elastic region, revenue increases as price is lowered, as shown in Figure 3(b); in the inelastic region, revenue decreases as price is lowered. The revenue-maximizing point, the top of the curve in Figure 3(b), occurs where the demand curve is unit-elastic, shown in Figure 3(a).

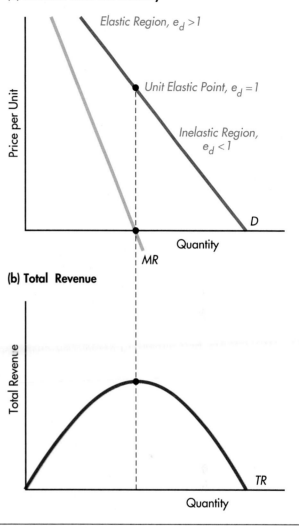

(a) Demand and Price Elasticity

Elastic Region, $e_d > 1$

Unit Elastic Point, $e_d = 1$

Inelastic Region, $e_d < 1$

Price per Unit

Quantity

D

MR

(b) Total Revenue

Total Revenue

Quantity

TR

rises as price falls, average revenue (price) always falls as output rises (the demand curve slopes downward). Because average revenue falls as output rises, marginal revenue must always be less than average revenue. For the monopolist (or any firm facing a downward-sloping demand curve), marginal revenue always declines as output increases, and the marginal-revenue curve always lies below the demand curve.

Also recall from previous chapters that the marginal revenue curve is positive in the elastic region of the demand curve $(e_d > 1)$, is zero at the output level where the demand curve is unit-elastic $(e_d = 1)$, and is negative in the inelastic portion of the demand curve $(e_d < 1)$.[2] This is illustrated in Figure 3 (repeated from the chapter "Elasticity: Demand and Supply").

---

[2]The slope of the demand curve is one-half the slope of the marginal-revenue curve. Consider the demand formula $P = a - bQ$; total revenue is $PQ = aQ - bQ^2$, so marginal revenue is $MR = a - 2bQ$.

1. The demand curve facing a monopoly firm is the industry demand curve.
2. For the monopoly firm, price is greater than marginal revenue. For the perfectly competitive firm, price and marginal revenue are equal.
3. As price declines, total revenue increases in the elastic portion of the demand curve, reaches a maximum at the unit-elastic point, and declines in the inelastic portion.
4. The marginal-revenue curve of the monopoly firm lies below the demand curve.
5. For both the perfectly competitive firm and the monopoly firm, price = average revenue = demand.

3. PROFIT MAXIMIZATION

The objective of the monopoly firm is to maximize profit. Where does the monopolist choose to produce, and what price does it set? Recall from the chapter "An Overview of Product Markets and Profit Maximization," that all profit-maximizing firms produce at the point where marginal revenue equals marginal cost.

3.a. What Price to Charge?

A schedule of revenues and costs for the wireless VCR producer accompanies Figure 4. Total revenue (TR) is listed in column 3; total cost (TC), in column 4. Total profit ($TR - TC$), shown in column 5, is the difference between the entries in column 3 and those in column 4. Marginal revenue (MR) is listed in column 6, marginal cost (MC) in column 7, and average total cost (ATC) in column 8.

The quantity of output to be produced is the quantity that corresponds to the point where $MR = MC$. How high a price will the market bear at that quantity? The market is willing and able to purchase the quantity given by $MR = MC$ at the corresponding price on the demand curve. As shown in Figure 4(a), the price is found by drawing a vertical line from the point where $MR = MC$ up to the demand curve and then extending a horizontal line over to the vertical axis. That price is $1,350 when output is 8.

3.b. Monopoly Profit and Loss

Why would someone want to have a monopoly in some business or activity?

The profit that the monopoly firm generates by selling 8 VCRs at a price of $1,350 is shown in Figure 4(a) as the colored rectangle. The vertical distance between the ATC curve and the demand curve, multiplied by the quantity sold, yields total profit.

Just like any other firm, a monopoly firm could experience a loss. A monopoly supplier of sharpeners for disposable razor blades probably would not be very successful, and the U.S. Postal Service has failed to make a profit in five of the last ten years. Unless price exceeds average costs, the firm loses money. A monopolist producing at a loss is shown in Figure 4(b)—the price is less than the average total cost.

Like a perfectly competitive firm, a monopolist will suspend operations in the short run if its price does not exceed the average variable cost at the

Figure 4
Profit Maximization for the VCR Producer
The data listed in the table are plotted in Figure 4(a).
The firm produces where MR = MC, 8 units; charges a
price given by the demand curve directly above the
production of 8 units, a price of $1,350 per VCR; and
earns a profit (yellow rectangle). In Figure 4(b), the firm
is shown to be operating at a loss (blue rectangle). It
produces output Q at price P, but the average total cost
exceeds the price.

(1) Total Output (Q)	(2) Price (P)	(3) Total Revenue (TR)	(4) Total Cost (TC)	(5) Total Profit (TR − TC)	(6) Marginal Revenue (MR)	(7) Marginal Cost (MC)	(8) Average Total Cost (ATC)
0	$1,750	$ 0	$1,000	$−1,000			
1	1,700	1,700	2,000	−300	$1,700	$1,000	$2,000
2	1,650	3,300	2,800	500	1,600	800	1,400
3	1,600	4,800	3,500	1,300	1,500	700	1,167
4	1,550	6,200	4,000	2,200	1,400	500	1,000
5	1,500	7,500	4,500	3,000	1,300	500	900
6	1,450	8,700	5,200	3,500	1,200	700	867
7	1,400	9,800	6,000	3,800	1,100	800	857
8	1,350	10,800	7,000	3,800	1,000	1,000	875
9	1,300	11,700	9,000	2,700	900	2,000	1,000

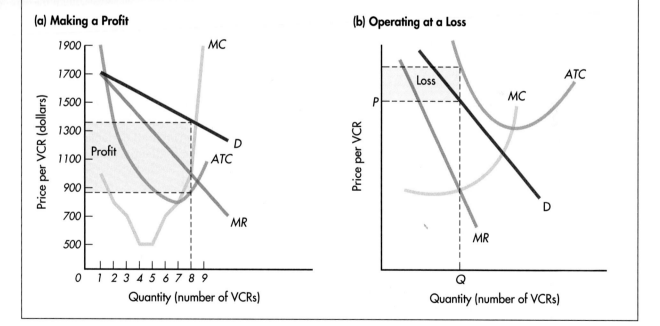

(a) Making a Profit

(b) Operating at a Loss

A monopolist can earn above-normal profit in the long run.

quantity the firm produces. And, like a perfectly competitive firm, a monopolist will shut down permanently if revenue is not likely to equal or exceed all costs in the long run (unless the government subsidizes the firm, as it does in the case of the U.S. Postal Service). In contrast, however, if a monopolist makes a profit, barriers to entry will keep other firms out of the industry. As a result, the monopolist can earn above-normal profits in the long run.

3.c. **Monopoly Myths**

There are a few myths about monopoly that we have debunked here. The first myth is that a monopolist can charge any price it wants and will reap unseemly profits by continually increasing the price. We know that a monopolist maximizes profit by producing the quantity that equates marginal revenue and marginal cost. We also know that a monopolist can only price and sell the quantities given by the demand curve. If the demand curve is very inelastic, as would be the case for a life-saving pharmaceutical, then the price the monopolist will charge will be high. Conversely, if demand is very price-elastic, the monopolist will experience losses by charging exorbitant prices. A second myth is that a monopolist is not sensitive to customers. The monopolist can stay in business only if it earns at least a normal profit. Ignoring customers, producing a good no one will purchase, setting prices that all customers think are exorbitant, and providing terrible service or products customers do not want will not allow a firm to remain in business for long. The monopolist faces a demand curve for its product and must search for a price and quantity that are dictated by that demand curve. The third myth is that the monopolist cannot make a loss. A monopolist is no different than any other firm in that it has costs of doing business and it must earn sufficient revenues to pay those costs. If the monopolist sets too high a price or provides a product few want, revenues may be less than costs and losses may result.

RECAP

1. Profit is maximized at the output level where $MR = MC$.
2. The price charged by the monopoly firm is the point on the demand curve that corresponds to the quantity where $MR = MC$.
3. A monopoly firm can make profits or experience losses. A monopoly firm can earn above-normal profit in the long run.
4. The monopoly firm will shut down in the short run if all variable costs aren't covered. It will shut down in the long run if all costs aren't covered.

4. PRICE DISCRIMINATION

Up to now we have assumed that the monopolist charges all customers the same price. Under certain conditions, a firm operating in markets that are not perfectly competitive can increase profits by charging different customers different prices. This is called *price discrimination*. The objective of the firm is to charge each customer exactly what each is willing to pay and in this way extract the total consumer surplus.

4.a. **Necessary Conditions for Price Discrimination**

You read in Section 2.a that the monopoly firm has to sell all of its products at a uniform price; otherwise, one customer could sell to another, thereby reducing the monopoly firm's profits. However, if customers do not come

Under what conditions
would a monopolist charge
different customers different
prices for the same product?

into contact with each other or are somehow separated by the firm, the firm may be able to charge each customer the exact price that he or she is willing to pay. By doing this, the firm is able to collect a great deal more of the consumer surplus than it would receive if it charged all customers the same price. Although a firm does not have to be a monopolist to price-discriminate, the monopolist can more easily separate customers than the oligopolist or monopolistic competitor.

When different customers are charged different prices for the same product or when customers are charged different prices for different quantities of the same product, price discrimination is occurring. Price discrimination occurs when price changes result not from cost changes but from the firm's attempt to extract more of the consumer surplus. Certain conditions are necessary for price discrimination to occur:

- The firm cannot be a price taker (perfect competitor).

- The firm must be able to separate customers according to price elasticities of demand.

- The firm must be able to prevent resale of the product.

4.b. Examples of Price Discrimination

Examples of price discrimination are not hard to find. Senior citizens often pay a lower price than the general population at movie theaters, drugstores, and golf courses. It is relatively easy to identify senior citizens and to ensure that they do not resell their tickets to the general population.

Tuition at state schools is different for in-state and out-of-state residents. It is not difficult to find out where a student resides, and it is very easy to ensure that in-state students do not sell their place to out-of-state students.

Airlines discriminate between business passengers and others. Passengers who do not fly at the busiest times, who purchase tickets in advance, and who can stay at their destination longer than a day pay lower fares than business passengers, who cannot make advance reservations and who must travel during rush hours. It is relatively easy for the airlines to separate business from nonbusiness passengers and to ensure that the latter do not sell their tickets to the former.

Electric utilities practice a form of price discrimination by charging different rates for different quantities of electricity used. The rate declines as the quantity purchased increases. A customer might pay $.07 per kilowatt-hour for the first 100 kilowatt-hours, $.06 for the next 100, and so on. Many utility companies have different rate structures for different classes of customers as well. Businesses pay less per kilowatt-hour than households.

Grocery coupons, mail-in rebates, trading stamps, and other discount strategies are also price discrimination techniques. Shoppers who are willing to spend time cutting out coupons and presenting them receive a lower price than those not willing to spend that time. Shoppers are separated by the amount of time they are willing to devote to coupon clipping. Another illustration of price discrimination is provided in the Economic Insight "Price Discrimination Affects Independent Pharmacists."

4.c. The Theory of Price Discrimination

How does price discrimination work? Suppose there are two classes of buyers for movie tickets, senior citizens and everybody else, and each class has a different elasticity of demand. The two classes are shown in Figure 5. Profit is maximized when $MR = MC$. Because the same firm is providing the goods in two submarkets, MC is the same for senior citizens and the general public, but the demand curves differ. Because the demand curves of the two groups differ, there are two MR curves: MR_{sc} for senior citizens, in Figure 5(a), and MR_{gp} for the general population, in Figure 5(b). Profit is maximized when $MR_{sc} = MC$ and when $MR_{gp} = MC$. The price is found by drawing a vertical line from the quantities where $MR = MC$ up to the respective demand curves, D_{sc} and D_{gp}.

Notice that the price to the general population, P_{gp}, is higher than the price to the senior citizens, P_{sc}. The reason is that the senior citizens' demand curve is more elastic than the demand curve of the general population. Senior citizens are more sensitive to price than is the general population, so to attract more of their business, the merchant has to offer them a lower price.

By discriminating, a monopoly firm makes greater profits than it would make by charging both groups the same price. If both groups were charged the same price, P_{gp}, the monopoly firm would lose sales to senior citizens who found the price too high, Q_{sc} to Q_2. And if both groups were charged P_{sc}, so few additional sales to the general population would be made that revenues would fall.

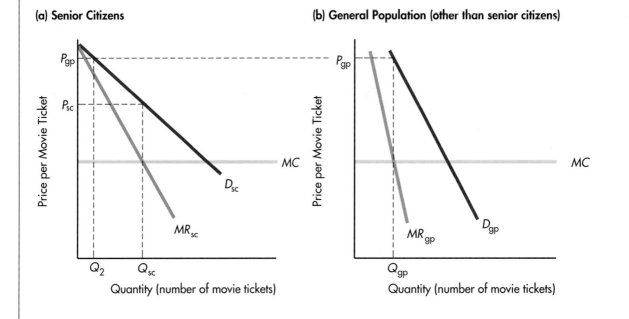

Figure 5
Price Discrimination
There are two classes of buyers for the same product. Figure 5(a) shows the elasticity of demand for senior citizens. Figure 5(b) shows the elasticity of demand for the general population. The demand of the senior citizens is more elastic than that of the general population. As a result, faced with the same marginal cost, the firm charges senior citizens a lower price than it charges the rest of the population. The quantity sold to senior citizens is Q_{sc}, the intersection between MC and MR_{sc}, and the price charged is P_{sc}. The quantity sold to the general population is Q_{gp}, and the price charged is P_{gp}.

(a) Senior Citizens

(b) General Population (other than senior citizens)

Price Discrimination Affects Independent Pharmacists

Price discrimination occurs at the wholesale level as well as at the retail level. For instance, the drugstore from which you purchase your medicine is the subject of price discrimination by pharmaceutical firms. For the independent pharmacy, price discrimination can mean real financial problems. Richard E. Beck had run a pharmacy for thirteen years before finally shutting it down. He claimed that he couldn't continue because even though he was selling drugs at his cost, his prices were among the highest in town due to discriminatory pricing on the part of the pharmaceutical firms.

Pharmaceutical firms separate customers into as many as eight classes: retailers, wholesalers, chain warehouses, mail order companies, nursing homes, health maintenance organizations (HMOs), hospitals, and physicians. The price elasticities of demand differ among the classes, so the pharmaceutical firms

are able to charge different prices. Hospitals usually pay the lowest prices and retailers the highest. One brand-name manufacturer charges some hospital pharmacies $4.99 for 100 tablets of a tranquilizer while retail pharmacies pay $40, eight times more, for the same amount of the product. Next to hospitals, the mail order outfits obtain the lowest prices. The American Association of Retired Persons (AARP) has created a huge business with its ability to obtain pharmaceuticals at low prices. Because AARP is able to purchase the pharmaceuticals at a lower price, AARP retail prices through mail order are as much as 30 percent less than even the average wholesale price. AARP benefits from its low overhead, its ability to buy generics and multisource patented drugs on a bid basis (which retail druggists cannot do) and its ability to purchase in large volumes.

Because mail order organiza-

tions, HMOs, doctors, and hospitals are all able to purchase pharmaceuticals at lower prices than either chains or independent retailers, retailers are looking for ways to reduce their disadvantage. One approach taken by retailers has been to form co-ops in order to purchase in large volume and thereby obtain the lower prices offered to the other customers of the pharmaceutical firms. Another approach has been to call for government regulation of mail order pharmacies.

Sources: Robert McCarthy, "Mail Order Continues to Grow," *American Druggist,* March 1988, pp. 37–40, and "Buying Co-Ops: Hanging Tough," *American Druggist,* March 1988, pp. 43–46; Stanley Siegelman, "The Growing Threat of AARP," *American Druggist,* Jan. 1990, pp. 27–36; B. J. Spalding, "Pharmacists Fight Discriminatory Pricing," *American Druggist,* April 1989, pp. 25–28.

4.d. Dumping

dumping:
setting a higher price on goods sold domestically than on goods sold in foreign markets

Price discrimination is a strategy used by many firms that sell their products in different countries. A derogatory name for this policy is **dumping**. Dumping occurs when an identical good is sold to foreign buyers for a lower price than is charged to domestic buyers. International dumping is a controversial issue. Producers in a country facing foreign competitors are likely to appeal to their domestic government for protection from the foreign goods being dumped in their market. Typically, the appeal for government assistance is based on the argument that the dumping firms are practicing **predatory dumping**—dumping intended to drive rival firms out of business. A successful predator firm raises prices after the rival is driven from the market.

predatory dumping:
dumping to drive competitors out of business

Canadian electronics manufacturers might accuse Japanese firms of dumping if the Japanese firms are selling electronics in Canada for less than they charge in Japan. The Canadian manufacturers may appeal to the Canadian government, asserting that the Japanese firms are engaged in predatory dumping to drive the Canadian firms out of business and warning that the Japanese firms will then raise the price of electronics products in Canada without fear of competition by the domestic Canadian firms. Claims of predatory dumping are often emotional and stir up the nationalistic sympathy of the rest of the domestic economy.

The U.S. government frequently responds to charges of dumping brought against foreign firms by U.S. industry. The government has pursued claims of predatory dumping against South African manufacturers of steel plate in 1984; German, Italian, and French winemakers in 1985; Japanese manufacturers of semiconductors in 1985 and 1987; Singapore typewriters in 1993; and nineteen steel-producing nations, also in 1993.

One famous case involved Sony Corporation of Japan. In the United States, Sony was selling Japanese-made TV sets for $180 while charging buyers in Japan $333 for the same model. U.S. television producers claimed that Sony was dumping TV sets in the U.S. market and seriously damaging U.S. television manufacturers. (Although U.S. producers disliked the low price of Japanese competitors, U.S. consumers benefited.) The U.S. government threatened to place high tariffs on Japanese television sets entering the United States unless Japan raised the price of Japanese televisions sold in the United States. The threat worked, and the price of Japanese TVs exported to the United States increased.[3]

Charges of predatory dumping make good news stories, but it is also true that dumping is to be expected when producers with the ability to set prices (as is the case for firms operating in markets that are not perfectly competitive) face segmented markets that have different price elasticities of demand. Conceptually, dumping is no different from what happens when a car dealer charges one buyer a higher price than another for the same car. If both buyers were aware of the range of prices at which the dealer would sell the car, or if both buyers had exactly the same price elasticity of demand, they would pay exactly the same price.

The Japanese electronics manufacturer realizes that the electronics market in Japan is separate from the electronics market in Canada or the United States. If the price elasticity of demand for electronics is different in each country, the Japanese manufacturer will maximize profit by charging a different price in each country.

RECAP

1. Price discrimination occurs when a firm charges different customers different prices for the same product or charges different prices for different quantities of the same product.

2. Three conditions are necessary for price discrimination to occur: (a) the firm must have some market power; (b) the firm must be able to separate customers according to price elasticities of demand; and (c) the firm must be able to prevent resale of the product.

3. Dumping is setting a higher price on goods sold in the domestic market than on goods sold in the foreign market. Dumping is another name for price discrimination in sales to customers that occurs in different countries.

---

[3]"Japan TV Set Makers Pressured by U.S. to Alter Prices or Face Antidumping Fee," *Wall Street Journal,* Aug. 31, 1970, p. 6; "U.S. Acts to End Dumping of TV Sets by Japanese," *New York Times,* Aug. 29, 1970, p. 1.

How do the predictions of the models of perfect competition and monopoly differ?

The perfectly competitive market structure results in economic efficiency because price is equal to marginal cost and firms are producing at the bottom of the average-total-cost curve. The monopoly market structure does not yield efficiency.

5.a. Costs of Monopoly: Inefficiency

In the long run, the perfectly competitive firm operates at the minimum point of the long-run average-total-cost curve and the firm's price is equal to its marginal cost. Profit is the normal level. A monopolist does not operate at the minimum point of the average-total-cost curve and does not set price equal to marginal cost. Because entry does not occur, a monopoly firm may earn above-normal profit in the long run.

Figure 6(a) shows a perfectly competitive market. The market demand curve is D; the market supply curve is S. The market price determined by the intersection of D and S is P_{pc}. At P_{pc} the perfectly competitive market produces Q_{pc}. Consumers are able to enjoy the consumer surplus indicated by the triangle $P_{pc}BA$, by purchasing the quantity Q_{pc} at the price P_{pc}. Firms

Figure 6
Monopoly and Perfect Competition Compared
Figure 6(a) shows a perfectly competitive industry; it produces at the point where industry demand, D, and industry supply, S, intersect. The quantity produced by the industry is Q_{pc}; the price charged is P_{pc}. Consumer surplus is the triangle $P_{pc}BA$. Figure 6(b) shows what happens if the industry is monopolized. The single firm faces the industry demand curve, D, and has the marginal-revenue curve MR. The intersection of the mar-

ginal-cost curve and the marginal-revenue curve Indicates the quantity that will be produced, Q_m. The price charged for Q_m is P_m. Thus, the monopoly firm produces less and charges more than the perfectly competitive industry. Consumer surplus, shown as the triangle P_mCA, is smaller in the monopoly industry. The area $P_{pc}ECP_m$ is the consumer surplus in perfect competition that is transferred from consumer to producer. The producer surplus is area $OFCP_m$. The deadweight loss is the area CFB.

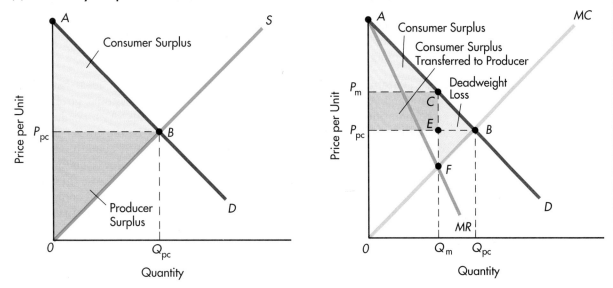

(a) The Perfectly Competitive Market

(b) Monopoly

receive the producer surplus indicated by triangle OBP_{pc} by producing the quantity Q_{pc} and selling that quantity at price P_{pc}.

Let's assume that all of the firms in a perfectly competitive industry are merged into a single monopoly firm and that the monopolist does not close or alter plants and does not achieve any economies of scale. In other words, what would occur if a perfectly competitive industry is transformed into a monopoly—just one firm determines price and quantity produced? The industry demand curve becomes the monopoly firm's demand curve, and the industry supply curve becomes the monopoly firm's marginal-cost curve. This is illustrated in Figure 6(b).

The monopoly firm restricts quantity produced to Q_m where $MR = MC$, and charges a price P_m as indicated on the demand curve shown in Figure 6(b). *The monopoly firm thus produces a lower quantity than does the perfectly competitive industry, Q_m compared to Q_{pc}, and sells that smaller quantity at a higher price, P_m compared to P_{pc}.* In addition, the consumer surplus in monopoly is the triangle $P_m CA$, which is smaller than the consumer surplus under perfect competition, $P_{pc}BA$. The rectangle $P_{pc}ECP_m$ is part of consumer surplus in perfect competition. In monopoly, that part of consumer surplus is transferred to the firm. The total producer surplus is area $OFCP_m$.

Thus, firms are better off (more producer surplus) while consumers are worse off (less consumer surplus) under monopoly compared to perfect competition. Consumers are worse off by area $P_{pc}BCP_m$ and firms are better off by area $P_{pc}ECP_m$ less area EFB. The triangle CFB is lost by both consumers and firms and goes to no one. This loss is the reduction in consumer surplus and producer surplus that is not transferred to the monopoly firm or to anyone else; it is called a **deadweight loss**. If a monopoly firm can produce output at the same cost as the perfectly competitive industry, there is a loss to society in going from perfect competition to monopoly; that loss is called deadweight loss. (The tradeoff between producers and consumers in perfect competition and monopoly is explored in the Economic Insight "How New York's Taxicab Monopoly Was Broken.")

deadweight loss:
the reduction of consumer surplus without a corresponding increase in profit when a perfectly competitive firm is monopolized

5.b. The Deadweight Loss May Be Overstated

The deadweight loss just described may, in reality, be overstated. A monopolist may face the potential of rivals if profit gets too high or may have to worry about government intervention.

5.b.1. Potential Competition The Lego family has lost legal battles in Britain and America to protect itself from imitations. Without government protection, the family is constantly fearful of new rivals. As a result, Legos are not priced as high, and more are sold than might be the case if the firm did not fear entry. The lower the price relative to what it could be, the less the deadweight loss. Monopoly firms may keep the price lower and produce more output than is suggested by the theory of monopoly because these firms fear that if their profit is too high, it could bring about entry and competition in the future. The fear of potential entry is called **potential competition**.

potential competition:
possible entry or rivalry capable of forcing existing producers to behave as if the competition actually existed

5.b.2. Government Intervention Another constant fear for the monopoly firm is that the government will intervene. Since the 1930s, the governments of most of the developed nations have scrutinized business operations in an

How New York's Taxicab Monopoly Was Broken

New York City requires a license, or medallion, to operate a taxi, as do most other municipalities in the United States. Under New York City law, anyone who wants to offer taxi service must buy the right to do so from some other operator in the form of a medallion originally issued by the city. Since medallions are limited in number, the holders of the medallion—the yellow taxicabs—have a monopoly.

The number of medallions in New York City remained fixed at 11,787 for nearly half a century. During this time, the value of a medallion—reflecting the profits that can be earned—rose from $10 in 1937 to $105,000 in 1986. These increasingly valuable medallions gave rise to a push to increase the number of medallions in New York City. When the existing medallion holders fought the push, entry began in other ways. Livery cars, black cars with radio phones that are supposed to respond only when called, have proliferated, for example. While drivers of the yellow medallion cabs cruise the streets and pick up any passengers who hail them, the drivers of the black nonmedallion livery cars have authorization to respond only to customers who have ordered the cabs in advance by phone or other means. The yellow-cab owners, who once had a monopoly by virtue of their 11,787 medallions, complain that the influx of non-medallion cabs has decreased revenue for them and their drivers. They claim that the nonmedallion cars are illegally picking up passengers on city streets. The taxi industry in New York City now finds itself awash in cabs and is not sure what to do.

The monopolists are experiencing a declining profit while passengers are reaping the benefits. Customers can negotiate prices with limousines and liveries; corporate customers are negotiating frequent-use discounts with the black cars and limousines. Some neighborhood livery companies are offering special fares to elderly people and to churchgoers on Sundays.

Sources: Winston Williams, "Owners Bewail Flood of Cabs in New York," *New York Times*, April 10, 1989, p. E1; Robert O. Boorstin, "Taxicab Regulation from Many Directions," *New York Times*, Nov. 24, 1986, p. E6; "New York City Looks at Taxi Regulation," *Regulation*, March/April 1982, p. 11.

attempt to discourage the formation of monopolies. Many proposed mergers have been prohibited because of the fear that monopoly might result. The activities of large firms are watched especially closely. This pressure may lessen the deadweight losses of monopoly.

5.b.3. Economies of Scale Underlying the preceding comparison of perfect competition and monopoly is the assumption that cost conditions will not change. However, it seems unrealistic to assume that the acquisition or merger of many firms would not change the cost structure in the industry. If there are economies of scale, the large-scale firm will be able to produce the product at a lower cost per unit than the many smaller firms. As a result, the deadweight losses imposed on society by a monopoly firm may be diminished.

5.c. The Deadweight Losses May Be Understated

The deadweight losses imposed by monopoly firms may be smaller than suggested by the comparison of perfect competition and monopoly, but it is also possible that they could actually be larger than the comparison suggests. The monopoly could operate less efficiently, and resources could be taken away from productive activities and devoted to maintaining a monopoly.

5.c.1. Higher Costs and X-Inefficiency

As you have learned, a monopoly firm does not operate at the minimum point on the average-total-cost curve, but a perfectly competitive firm does. Thus, the monopolist not only imposes a deadweight loss but also produces at a higher cost per unit than does the perfectly competitive firm. The high cost may go even higher if the monopolist becomes inefficient because of a lack of competition or potential competition.

Many monopolies are created and maintained by the government. The resulting monopoly firms do not have to worry about potential competition or government intervention. Monopoly firms may not feel the need to operate efficiently because they face no competition from entering firms. Many economists have argued that because monopoly firms have no fear of competition, they operate less efficiently than would competitive firms producing the same output. The inefficiency that occurs in the absence of fear of entry and rivalry is called **X-inefficiency**. X-inefficiency is represented by an upward shift of the average-total-cost curve.

The greater X-inefficiency is, the greater the cost to society when a perfectly competitive industry is monopolized. As the average costs of production rise because of X-inefficiency, consumer surplus falls without a corresponding increase in the monopolist's profit. The additional loss in consumer surplus due to X-inefficiency is an increase in deadweight losses.

5.c.2. Rent Seeking

Monopolists devote significant resources to preserving their monopoly positions. Liquor licenses are valuable because they bestow a local monopoly on the recipients. Similarly, radio and television broadcasting rights provide above-normal profits to the holders of those rights. To protect their above-normal profits and ensure political support for their monopoly positions, the owners provide significant amounts of money to lobbyists, lawyers, and political action committees (PACs). Activities that are undertaken simply to create a transfer from one group to another are known as **rent seeking**. Rent-seeking expenditures do not add to productive activity. A lawyer working to take $100 from the consumer and give it to the monopoly firm is giving up some other productive activity. The opportunity cost of the lawyer's time is a deadweight loss to society.

Lobbying expenditures are quite large. In early 1990, the *Wall Street Journal* identified the lawmakers who received the most money from PACs, which are the lobbying arms of businesses, labor, and special-interest groups. In the Senate, John D. Rockefeller IV led the list with $830,000; in the House, Glen Browder led the group with $444,000.[4] The PAC contributions flow to senators and representatives who are in positions that enable them to help maintain monopoly as a market power. For instance, PAC contributions by AT&T went to members of the congressional commercial, judiciary, and tax-writing committees that oversee telephone issues; and the PAC created by RJR Nabisco, a tobacco company, focused on committees that deal with smoking issues.

The potential for rent seeking is indicated in Figure 7 as the above-normal profit, the rectangle *EBCF*. It would be worthwhile for the owners of the monopoly firm to devote resources up to the amount of their profit in order to maintain their monopoly. Any profit that remains in excess of the amount

X-inefficiency:
the tendency of a firm not faced with competition to become inefficient

rent seeking:
the use of resources simply to transfer wealth from one group to another without increasing production or total wealth

---

[4]Jill Abramson and Brooks Jackson, "Debate Over PAC Money Hits Close to Home as Lawmakers Tackle Campaign-Finance Bill," *Wall Street Journal*, March 7, 1990, p. A2.

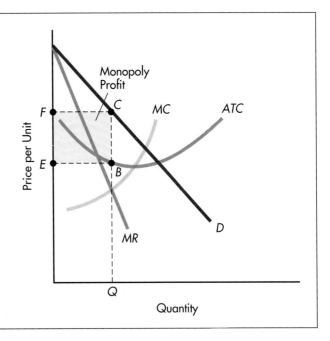

Figure 7
Rent Seeking
A monopoly firm earns an above-normal profit. The managers of the firm are willing to expend all of the profit to retain the monopoly. The amount of the profit used to maintain the monopoly is rent seeking.

spent on rent seeking would still be above-normal profit to the owners. When profit, *EBCF* in Figure 7, is used to pay for the nonproductive lobbying activities, it becomes part of the deadweight loss.

5.c.3. Innovation If a monopoly firm tends to be more or less innovative than a perfectly competitive firm would be, the costs imposed on society by the monopoly may be smaller or larger than the comparison with perfect competition suggests. If profits that can be obtained with a successful invention are quickly competed away, there might be less incentive to innovate than there would be if above-normal profits could exist for a number of years. This argument forms the basis of patent laws. A patent confers a monopoly on a firm or individual for a certain product or part for seventeen years.

The counterargument is that entrepreneurs are always looking for ways to earn additional profit and protect against additional losses. If an entrepreneur is unwilling to spend money for research and development, competitors will quickly put the firm out of business because they will innovate and be able to produce products less expensively or produce better products than the firm that fails to innovate.

5.d. Supply and the Monopoly Firm

For the firm in perfect competition, the supply curve is that portion of the marginal-cost curve that lies above the average-cost curve, and the market supply curve is the sum of all the individual firms' supply curves. The supply curve for the firm selling in any of the other market structures is not as straightforward to derive and, therefore, neither is the market supply curve. The reason is that firms selling in market structures other than perfect competition are price makers rather than price takers. This means that the hypothetical experiment of varying the price of a product and seeing how the firm selling that product reacts makes no sense.

In the case of the monopolist, the firm supplies a quantity determined by setting marginal revenue equal to marginal cost, but it also sets the price to go along with this quantity. Varying the price will not change the decision rule since the firm will choose to produce its profit-maximizing output level and set the price accordingly. There is, therefore, only one quantity and price at which the monopolist will operate. There is a supply point, not a supply curve. Moreover, because the monopolist is the only firm in the market, its supply curve (or supply point) is also the market supply curve (or point).

The complications of the price makers do not alter the supply rule: a firm will produce and offer for sale a quantity that equates marginal revenue and marginal cost. This supply rule applies to all firms, regardless of the market structure in which the firm operates.

5.e. Regulation

Monopoly is inefficient; perfect competition, efficient. This comparison between monopoly and perfect competition has provided the basis for attempting to make monopolies behave more like perfectly competitive firms. Most natural monopolies are regulated by some level of government. In particular, the prices or rates that public utilities such as telephone companies, natural gas companies, and electricity suppliers can charge is determined by a federal, state, or local regulatory commission or board.

Figure 8 shows the demand, marginal-revenue, and long-run average-cost and marginal-cost curves for a natural monopoly. The huge economies of scale means it would be inefficient to have many small firms supply the product. Yet, producing at $MR = MC$ and setting a price of P_m from the demand curve yield too little output and too much profit for the firm, in comparison to the perfectly competitive result. In addition, since price is greater than marginal cost, resources are not being allocated efficiently. In fact, too few

Figure 8
Natural Monopoly and Regulation
The demand, marginal-revenue, and long-run average-cost and marginal-cost curves for a natural monopoly are shown. The huge economies of scale means it would be inefficient to have many small firms supply the product. Yet, producing at $MR = MC$ and setting a price of P_m from the demand curve yields too small an output and too much profit for the firm, in comparison to the perfectly competitive result. Too few resources are devoted to this product—too few because if more was produced, MC would equal price. To achieve allocative efficiency (giving consumers the goods they most want), the regulatory agency must attempt to have the monopolist set a price equal to marginal cost. This price would be P_r. The monopolist would then produce at quantity Q_r. The problem with the regulated price P_r is that the revenues do not cover average costs. The fair-rate-of-return price is set to allow the monopolist a normal profit. The price corresponding to the normal profit is one where demand and average total costs are equal, P_f.

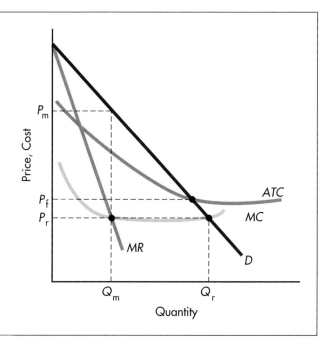

resources are devoted to this product—too few because if more was produced, MC would equal price. Can regulation solve this problem?

If the objective of the regulatory commission is to achieve allocative efficiency (giving consumers the goods they most want), it must attempt to have the monopolist set a price equal to marginal cost. This price would be P_r in Figure 8. The monopolist would then produce at quantity Q_r.

The problem with the regulated price P_r is that the regulated firm could actually make a loss. You can see in Figure 8 that revenues do not cover average costs. Figure 8 illustrates a fairly common situation with the public utilities because the costs of the public utility companies are large. Most public utilities must acquire sufficient resources (generating capacity or telephone-linking capacity, for example) to supply the *peak* demands. But because the peak periods are only a small portion of daily sales, the revenue generated overall is not sufficient to pay for the total resource required. For instance, air conditioning is used most heavily during the 5 P.M. to 9 P.M. time period during the months of the summer. To meet the demands during this peak period, the electric company has to acquire nearly double the generating capacity it would need to satisfy only the nonpeak demand. Thus, the regulated price equal to marginal cost is not sufficient to provide the revenue to pay for the large costs.

fair rate of return:
a price that allows a monopoly firm to earn a normal profit

Regulatory commissions quickly moved away from setting price equal to marginal cost and have allowed for a **fair rate of return**. The fair-rate-of-return price is set to allow the monopolist a normal profit. The price corresponding to the normal profit is one where demand and average total costs are equal, P_f.

When price is set in order to achieve the most efficient allocation of resources (P = MC), the regulated firm is likely to suffer losses. Survival of the firm would then require subsidies from the public. On the other hand, the fair-return price (P = ATC) allows the monopolist to cover costs, but it does not solve the misallocation of resources problem since price is greater than marginal cost. Other issues in regulation are discussed in the chapter "Government Policy Toward Business."

RECAP

1. A monopoly firm produces a smaller quantity and charges a higher price than a perfectly competitive industry if the two industries have identical costs.

2. The consumer surplus is smaller if an industry is operated by a monopoly firm than it is if an industry is operated by perfectly competitive firms. Profits are larger in the monopoly case.

3. The costs to society that result when a perfectly competitive industry becomes a monopoly are a reduction of consumer surplus as well as producer surplus that is not transferred to anyone. This loss is called a *deadweight loss.*

4. The deadweight loss imposed by monopoly firms may be overstated because the monopoly fears that entry or government intervention could occur.

5. The deadweight loss imposed by monopoly firms may be understated if monopoly firms tend to operate inefficiently and devote resources to maintaining their monopoly positions.

6. If a monopoly firm is more innovative than perfectly competitive firms, the deadweight loss of monopoly will be smaller than indicated by a direct comparison of the pricing and output decisions of the two. Conversely, if the monopoly firm is less innovative, the deadweight loss will be larger.

SUMMARY

▲▼ What is monopoly?

1. Monopoly is a market structure in which there is a single supplier of a product. A monopoly firm, or monopolist, is the only supplier of a product for which there are no close substitutes. §1.a

▲▼ How is a monopoly created?

2. Natural barriers to entry (such as economies of scale), barriers erected by firms in the industry, and barriers erected by government may create monopolies. §§1.b, 1.b.1, 1.b.2, 1.b.3

3. The term *monopoly* is often associated with natural monopoly, local monopoly, regulated monopoly, and monopoly power. §1.c

▲▼ What does the demand curve for a monopoly firm look like, and why?

4. Because a monopolist is the only producer of a good or service, the demand curve facing a monopoly firm is the industry demand curve. §2

5. Price and marginal revenue are not the same for a monopoly firm. §2.a

6. The average-revenue curve is the demand curve. §2.a.1

7. A monopoly firm maximizes profit by producing the quantity of output yielded at the point where marginal revenue and marginal cost are equal. §3.a

8. A monopoly firm sets a price that is on the demand curve and that corresponds to the point where marginal revenue and marginal cost are equal. §3.a

▲▼ Why would someone want to have a monopoly in some business or activity?

9. A monopoly firm can make above-normal or normal profit or even a loss. If it makes above-normal profit, entry by other firms does not occur and the monopoly firm can earn above-normal profit in the long run. Exit occurs if the monopoly firm cannot cover costs in the long run. §3.b

▲▼ Under what conditions would a monopolist charge different customers different prices for the same product?

10. Price discrimination occurs when the firm is not a price taker, can separate customers according to their price elasticities of demand for the firm's product, and can prevent resale of the product. §4.a

11. *Dumping* is a derogatory name given to the price discrimination used by firms selling in more than one nation. §4.d

▲▼ How do the predictions of the models of perfect competition and monopoly differ?

12. A comparison of monopoly and perfectly competitive firms implies that monopoly imposes costs on society. These costs include less output being produced and that output being sold at a higher price. §5.a

13. The deadweight losses of monopoly may not be as large as the comparison with perfect competition suggests if (a) monopoly firms are more innovative; (b) the threat of potential competition or of government intervention causes the monopoly firm to lower price and increase quantity; or (c) the monopoly firm operates more efficiently than would a perfectly competitive firm. §5.b

14. The deadweight losses of monopoly may be larger than the comparison with perfect competition suggests if (a) the monopoly firm operates inefficiently because of a lack of competition; (b) rent seeking occurs; or (c) the monopolist is less innovative than the perfect competitor. §5.c

15. Because monopoly is inefficient and perfect competition efficient, governments have attempted to regulate the natural monopolies to make them more like perfect competitors. The huge economies of scale rule out breaking the natural monopolies up into small firms. Instead, price has been set at a fair rate of return, $P = ATC$. §5.e

KEY TERMS

monopoly §1.a

monopoly firm (monopolist) §1.a

barrier to entry §1.b

natural monopoly §1.c

local monopoly §1.c

regulated monopoly §1.c

monopoly power §1.c

dumping §4.d

predatory dumping §4.d

deadweight loss §5.a

potential competition §5.b.1

X-inefficiency §5.c.1

rent seeking §5.c.2

fair rate of return §5.e

EXERCISES

1. About 85 percent of the soup sold in the United States is Campbell's brand. Is Campbell Soup Company a monopoly firm?

2. Price discrimination is practiced by movie theaters, motels, golf courses, drugstores, and universities. Are they monopolies? If not, how can they carry out price discrimination?

3. Why is it necessary for the seller to be able to keep customers from reselling the product in order for price discrimination to occur? There are many products for which you get a discount for purchasing large quantities. For instance, most liquor stores will provide a discount on wine if you purchase a case. Is this price discrimination? If so, what is to keep one customer from purchasing cases of wine and then reselling single bottles at a price above the case price but below the liquor store's single-bottle price?

4. Many people have claimed that there is no good for which substitutes are not available. If so, does this mean there is no such thing as monopoly?

5. Suppose that at a price of $6 per unit, quantity demanded is 12 units. Calculate the quantity demanded when the marginal revenue is $6 per unit. (*Hint*: The price elasticity of demand is unity at the midpoint of the demand curve.)

6. In the figure below, if the monopoly firm faces ATC_1, which rectangle measures total profit? If the monopoly firm faces ATC_2, what is total profit? What information would you need in order to know whether the monopoly firm will shut down or continue producing in the short run? In the long run?

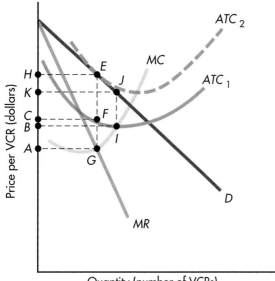

Price per VCR (dollars) — vertical axis

Quantity (number of VCRs) — horizontal axis

7. In recent years, U.S. car manufacturers have charged lower car prices in western states in an effort to offset the competition by the Japanese cars. This two-tier pricing scheme has upset many car dealers in the eastern states. Many have called it discriminatory and illegal.

a. What conditions are necessary for this pricing scheme to be profitable to the U.S. companies?

b. Is this pricing scheme the same as dumping?

8. Consider the following demand schedule. Does it apply to a perfectly competitive firm? Compute marginal and average revenue.

Price	Quantity
100	1
95	2
88	3
80	4
70	5
55	6
40	7
22	8

9. Suppose the marginal cost of producing the good in question 8 is a constant $10 per unit of output. What quantity of output will the firm produce?

10. Do you agree or disagree with this statement: "A monopoly firm will charge an exorbitant price for its product." Explain your answer.

11. Do you agree or disagree with this statement: "A monopoly firm will run a much less safe business than a perfect competitor." Explain your answer.

12. The pistachio nut growers of California petitioned the U.S. government to restrict the flow of Iranian pistachios because of dumping. Iranian pistachios were being sold in the United States at a price that was lower than it cost to produce the California variety of nuts. If you were an economist with the U.S. government, would you support the petition of the California growers?

13. State colleges and universities have two levels of tuition or fees. The less expensive is for residents of the state, the more expensive for nonresidents. Assume the universities are profit-maximizing monopolists and explain their pricing policy. Now, explain why the colleges and universities give student aid and scholarships.

14. Several electric utilities are providing customers with a choice of billing procedures. Customers can select a "time-of-day" meter that registers electrical usage throughout the day, or they can select a regular meter that registers total usage at the end of the day. With the time-of-day meter, the utility is able to charge customers a much higher rate for peak usage than for nonpeak usage. The regular meter users pay the same rate for electrical usage no matter when it is used. Why would the electrical utility want customers to choose the time-of-day meter?

15. Suppose that a firm has a monopoly on a good with the following demand schedule:

Price	Quantity
$10	0
9	1
8	2
7	3
6	4
5	5
4	6
3	7
2	8
1	9
0	10

a. What price and quantity will the monopolist produce at if the marginal cost is a constant $4?

b. Calculate the deadweight loss from having the monopolist produce, rather than a perfect competitor.

c. What price would the regulatory commission set if it wanted to achieve maximum efficiency?

d. What price would the regulatory commission set if it wanted to allow a normal profit?

Drugs Earned Excess Profits

President Clinton's campaign to rein in prescription-drug costs got a boost yesterday with the release of a major federal study that says drug prices could be cut and the industry could still remain very profitable.

The study by the Office of Technology Assessment says that individual drugs earned millions more for their investors than was needed to pay off research and development costs.

In studying the drugs that came on the market from 1981 to 1983, the OTA concluded that each drug made at least $36 million more for its investors, after taxes, than was needed to pay off the costs to develop it.

"This surplus return amounts to about 4.3 percent of the price of each drug over its product life," it said.

The industry's profitability is 2 to 3 percentage points greater than for comparable industries, even after factoring in the risks of new-drug development, the report said.

The report, which examined the industry's research and development costs, risks and rewards, shows that the industry has considerable pricing power because the U.S. market doesn't work to keep costs in check for most American patients.

"The market for prescription drugs is broken," said Judith L. Wagner, the study's director.

The *Inquirer*, in a five-part series published in December, detailed how consumers have little control over what drugs they buy and how much they pay. The choice of drug is made by a doctor, who often has little knowledge of the cost and is influenced by the drug industry's sales tactics, The Inquirer reported.

The series also said that pharmaceutical companies spend more on drug promotion and advertising than on research and development—although the companies cite high R&D costs as the reason for their high prices.

Wagner also pinned blame for drug costs on doctors, who assume that insurance companies will pay for most drugs they prescribe.

The industry yesterday echoed an oft-stated response to the OTA report: Any restrictions on its profits will hurt the chances of conquering diseases, from cancer to Alzheimer's.

"Reform of the U.S. health-care system should not discourage . . . innovations, and if it does, it may bring with it very substantial long-term costs to our society," said Bob Allnutt, executive vice president of the Pharmaceutical Manufacturers Association.

The OTA study, however, said it could not determine "whether today's level of pharmaceutical R&D is unquestionably worth its cost to society."

The OTA cited a European study that said more than half of all drugs launched in the U.S. market between 1975 and 1989 offered no medical advantage over existing drugs.

Consequently, said Rep. Henry Waxman (D., Calif.), who chairs the House Health and Environment subcommittee, which requested the study, U.S.-based drug companies spend about $4 billion a year—or roughly half of their total 1992 research budget—on research that duplicates existing medicines.

He asserted that the report showed that drug companies could reduce drug prices and still come up with new breakthrough medicines. To bring drug prices down, he said, Congress should focus on redundant research, promotion budgets and excess profits, which he said cost the nation's health-care system $2 billion in 1991.

The cuts would not prevent the drug companies from earning "handsome profits," Waxman said.

The PMA took issue with many of the report's conclusions, saying that figures on drugs first marketed a decade ago don't apply to drugs coming out in the future.

Allnutt also said the OTA used an economic model for its measure of excess profitability that was based on certain assumptions, such as the importance of sales abroad and capital for new plants.

"Alternative, and still reasonable, assumptions applied to the OTA economic model would provide quite different results than those reported," he said.

Source: Reprinted with permission from *The Philadelphia Inquirer*.

Philadelphia Inquirer/February 26, 1993

Commentary

What is a fair profit for a firm that develops a new drug? Firms will not undertake risky research projects unless they can be reasonably assured of a profit if the research is successful; they must be able to earn normal economic profits. But because the discovery of a new drug can lead to above-normal profit, there is an incentive for pharmaceutical firms to find new drugs. Incentive also exists for competing firms to use the findings from one firm's research to produce the new drug themselves. This drives down the economic profits to the firm that undertook the original research. In fact, since the copycats do not have to bear the research costs of the firm that actually discovers the drug, their costs are lower and a normal profit to them will not allow the original firm to earn a profit. Unless there are barriers to entry, economic profits will eventually disappear for the firm that actually discovers the drug. The barriers to entry in the pharmaceutical industry are minimal since the defection of just a few key people with knowledge of the process of producing the drug or the independent development of the necessary technology is all that is needed for other firms to produce a newly developed drug. As a result, pharmaceutical companies have few incentives to undertake costly and risky research projects. Instead, they are better off waiting for others to develop the drugs and then producing similar drugs based on the original research.

This argument is used to justify the patent system. A patent gives a firm a monopoly on a drug for a period of seventeen years. Patents on new drugs are an attempt to reward research through the creation of monopoly power. The pricing, or monopoly, power given to a firm through the granting of a patent allows the firm to profit by restricting supply and thus forcing the price to rise above the level that would be found in a perfectly competitive industry.

Should pharmaceutical companies be allowed to earn above-normal profits? It is very difficult to come to a definitive answer. Since the high profit on individual drugs may offset the losses on research that does not turn out. The government study cannot say whether the excess profit is sufficient to induce more rapid development of new drugs or whether a lower profit would lead to exit from the industry and the discovery and development of fewer new drugs.

12

Monopolistic Competition and Oligopoly

FUNDAMENTAL QUESTIONS

1. What is monopolistic competition?
2. What behavior is most common in monopolistic competition?
3. What is oligopoly?
4. In what form does rivalry occur in an oligopoly?
5. Why does cooperation among rivals occur most often in oligopolies?

ow often have you read or heard that some firm is offering a new product: McDonald's brings out the McBLT; Acura expands its line to include the Vigor; Procter & Gamble offers another detergent . . . the list goes on. These are examples of *nonprice competition*. Rather than reducing the price to attract additional customers, the producers use advertising, packaging, color, location, safety features, quality, and size to offer slightly different products. Nonprice competition is a common characteristic of many firms in the real world, but it is not explained by the theory of perfect competition. A monopolist might use nonprice means to discriminate among its customers, but a monopolist is the only producer of a product; clearly breakfast foods, soft drinks, beer, automobiles, and many other industries are not monopolies. To understand much of firm behavior, one or more of the characteristics of perfect competition and monopoly must be altered. The result of these alterations is the models of monopolistic competition and oligopoly.

PREVIEW

The first model discussed here, *monopolistic competition*, captures many real-world characteristics of competition—brand-name proliferation, product differentiation, advertising, marketing, and packaging—that do not occur in the theory of perfect competition. In a monopolistically competitive market, many firms are producing a slightly different product.

In some industries, however, one large firm dominates. The dominant firm is not a monopoly, but it is not just one among many either. For example, in photofinishing supplies, many agree that Kodak dominates all others. In soup, Campbell Soup Company is a leader. In children's construction toys, Lego is very strong. In other industries, such as steel, tobacco, beer, and athletic shoes, two or three firms dominate. In still other industries, such as automobiles and consumer electronics, eight to ten firms account for the lion's share of the market. Oligopoly, like monopolistic competition, allows for nonprice competition but, unlike monopolistic competition, includes only a few firms.

In this chapter we discuss monopolistic competition and oligopoly. We begin with monopolistic competition and then turn to oligopoly in Section 2.

I. MONOPOLISTIC COMPETITION

What is monopolistic competition?

Monopolistic competition is a market structure in which (1) there are a large number of firms, (2) the products produced by the firms are differentiated, and (3) entry and exit occur easily. The definitions of *monopolistic competi-*

tion and *perfect competition* overlap. In both structures, there are a large number of firms. The difference is that each firm in monopolistic competition produces a product that is slightly different from all other products, whereas in perfect competition the products are standardized. The definition of *monopolistic competition* also overlaps with that of *monopoly*. Because each firm in monopolistic competition produces a unique product, each has a "mini" monopoly over its product. Thus, like a monopolist, the firm in a monopolistically competitive market structure has a downward-sloping demand curve; for a monopolistically competitive firm, marginal revenue is below the demand curve and price is greater than marginal cost. What distinguishes monopolistic competition from monopoly is ease of entry. Anytime firms in monopolistic competition are earning above-normal profit, new firms enter and entry continues until firms are earning normal profit. In monopoly, a firm can earn above-normal profit in the long run. Table 1 summarizes differences among perfect competition, monopoly, and monopolistic competition.

1.a. Profits and Entry

Suppose you are an executive with Adolph Coors Company and your firm is producing just one beer, Coors. Your firm's product is recognized for its cool, light taste and sales are good, but other breweries have introduced several new beers. Anheuser-Busch has expanded its market share by introducing a premium beer called Michelob, a lower-priced beer called Busch, a low-calorie beer called Bud Lite, and a nonalcoholic beer. The introduction of these beers has affected the sales of Coors beer; the demand curve for Coors beer has shifted in. How does your firm respond?

You could lower the price of Coors, and this would increase the quantity demanded. This strategy might attract some of the Busch crowd and even some of the Bud customers, but it would not attract many of the Michelob drinkers. You could advertise that Coors has always been low in calories. But that claim might offend current Coors drinkers who never worry about calories. Your best response is to introduce your own new products: Coors Gold (premium), Coors Light (low-calorie), Keystone (lower priced), and Pale Ale

TABLE 1
Summary of Perfect Competition, Monopoly, and Monopolistic Competition

	Perfect Competition	Monopoly	Monopolistic Competition
Number of Firms	Many	One	Many
Type of Product	Undifferentiated	One	Differentiated
Entry Conditions	Easy	Difficult or impossible	Easy
Demand Curve for Firm	Horizontal (perfectly elastic)	Downward-sloping	Downward-sloping
Price and Marginal Cost	$MC = P$	$MC < P$	$MC < P$
Long-run Profit	Zero	Yes	Zero

Monopolistic competitors and some oligopolies offer differentiated products. Cigarettes are differentiated with advertising, size, packaging, and taste. One of the more successful advertising campaigns in recent years has been Joe Camel, the hip, race-car driving, sports-enthusiastic camel shown on the billboard. This particular billboard also shows another aspect of the monopolistically competitive strategy, apppealing to a market segment. Located in a Spanish-speaking area of San Antonio, Texas, this billboard is directed toward the Spanish-speaking citizens. The same billboard, in English, is located a few miles away.

Monopolistically competitive firms produce differentiated products.

(nonalcoholic). In this way you can meet the other breweries head-on. You might even be able to gain market share.

Firms in monopolistic competition tend to use product differentiation more than price to compete. They attempt to provide a product for each market niche. Even though the total market might not be expanding, they divide the market into smaller and smaller segments by introducing variations of products. You can think of a market demand curve for beer, but within that market there are many niches and many demand curves. In fact, there are separate demand curves for each product—for Coors, for Coors Gold, for Coors Light, and for Keystone, as well as for Bud, for Bud Lite, for Busch, and for Michelob. Each individual demand curve is quite price-elastic because of the existence of many close substitutes.

When a new product is introduced, the demand curve for all closely related products shifts in toward the origin because less of the total market is available for each product. What can firms do to offset this effect? Each firm must accept the reduced demand and attempt to increase the demand for its product lines by introducing new products or new variations of existing products. New products are introduced as long as there are above-normal profits.

1.a.1. In the Short Run The demand curve faced by a monopolistically competitive firm is downward-sloping. This means that if a monopolistically competitive firm wants to sell more of one of its products, it must lower the price of that product. Figure 1(a) shows the cost and revenue curves of a monopolistically competitive firm providing a single product in the short run. As with all profit-maximizing firms, production occurs at the quantity where $MR = MC$. The price the firm charges, P_1, is given by the demand curve at the quantity where $MR = MC$. Price P_1 is above average total cost, as indicated by the distance AB. Thus, the firm is earning above-normal profit, shown as the rectangle $CBAP_1$.

If the firms in a monopolistically competitive market are earning normal profit, the marginal-revenue and marginal-cost curves for each firm intersect at quantity Q_1 in Figure 1(b), and the price is P_1. The price is the same as the

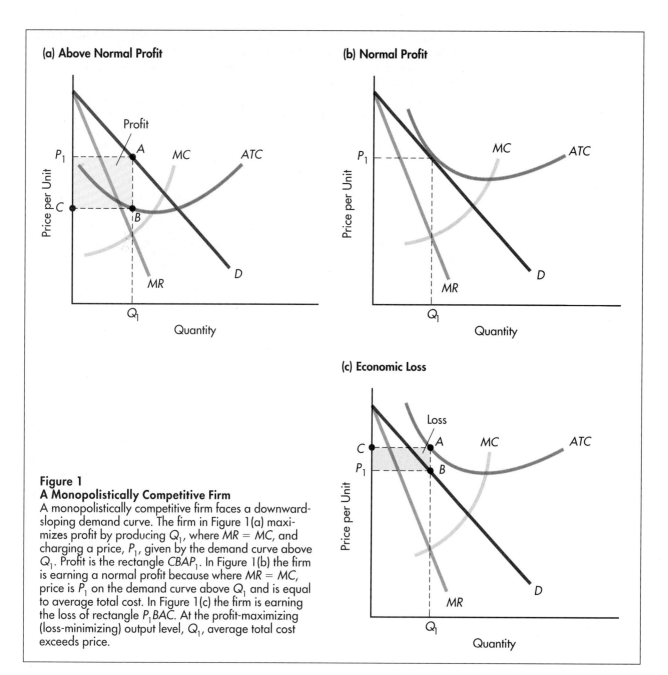

(a) Above Normal Profit

(b) Normal Profit

(c) Economic Loss

Figure 1
A Monopolistically Competitive Firm
A monopolistically competitive firm faces a downward-sloping demand curve. The firm in Figure 1(a) maximizes profit by producing Q_1, where $MR = MC$, and charging a price, P_1, given by the demand curve above Q_1. Profit is the rectangle $CBAP_1$. In Figure 1(b) the firm is earning a normal profit because where $MR = MC$, price is P_1 on the demand curve above Q_1 and is equal to average total cost. In Figure 1(c) the firm is earning the loss of rectangle P_1BAC. At the profit-maximizing (loss-minimizing) output level, Q_1, average total cost exceeds price.

average total cost at Q_1, so a normal profit is obtained. If the firm is earning a loss, then the average-total-cost curve lies above the demand curve at the quantity produced, as shown in Figure 1(c). At Q_1, the firm is earning a loss, the rectangle P_1BAC. The firm must decide whether to temporarily suspend production of that product or continue producing because the outlook is favorable. The decision depends on whether revenue exceeds variable costs.

I.a.2. In the Long Run Whenever existing firms in a market structure without barriers to entry are earning above-normal profit, new firms enter the business and, in some cases, existing firms expand until all firms are earning the normal profit. In a perfectly competitive industry, the new firms supply a product that is identical to the product being supplied by existing firms. *In a monopolistically competitive industry, entering firms produce a close substitute, not an identical or standardized product.*

As the introduction of new products by new or existing firms occurs, the demand curves for existing products keep shifting in until a normal profit is earned. As each new product is introduced, the demand curves for the existing, slightly differentiated products shift in. For each firm and each product, the demand curve shifts in, as shown in Figure 2, until it just touches the average-total-cost curve at the price charged and output produced, Q_2 and P_2. When profit is at the normal level, expansion and entry cease.

When firms are earning a loss on a product and the long-run outlook is for continued losses, the firms will stop producing that product. Exit means that fewer differentiated products are produced, and the demand curves for the remaining products shift out. This continues until firms are earning normal profits.

I.b. Monopolistic Competition vs. Perfect Competition

Figure 3 shows both a perfectly competitive firm in long-run equilibrium and a monopolistically competitive firm in long-run equilibrium. The perfectly competitive firm, shown as the horizontal demand and marginal-revenue curve, $MR_{pc} = D_{pc}$, produces at the minimum point of the long-run average-total-cost curve at Q_{pc}; and the price, marginal cost, marginal revenue, and average total costs are P_{pc}. The long-run equilibrium for a monopolistically competitive firm is shown with the demand curve D_{mc} and marginal-revenue curve MR_{mc}. The monopolistically competitive firm produces at Q_{mc}, where $MR_{mc} = MC$, and charges a price determined by drawing a vertical line up from the point where $MR_{mc} = MC$ to the demand curve. That price is just equal to the point where the long-run average-total-cost curve touches the

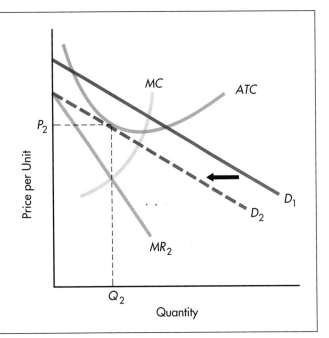

Figure 2
Entry and Normal Profit
In the long run, the firm in monopolistic competition earns a normal profit. Entry shifts the firm's demand curve in from D_1 to D_2. Entry, which takes the form of a differentiated product, continues to occur as long as above-normal profits exist. When the demand curve just touches the average-total-cost curve, as at P_2 and Q_2, profit is at the normal level.

Figure 3
Perfect and Monopolistic Competition Compared

The perfectly competitive firm produces at the point where the price line, the horizontal MR curve, intersects the MC curve. This is the bottom of the ATC curve in the long run, quantity Q_{pc} at price P_{pc}. The monopolistically competitive firm also produces where MR = MC. The downward-sloping demand curve faced by the monopolistically competitive firm means that the quantity produced, Q_{mc}, is less than the quantity produced by the perfectly competitive firm, Q_{pc}. The price charged by the monopolistically competitive firm is also higher than that charged by the perfectly competitive firm, P_{mc} versus P_{pc}. In both cases, however, the firms earn only a normal profit.

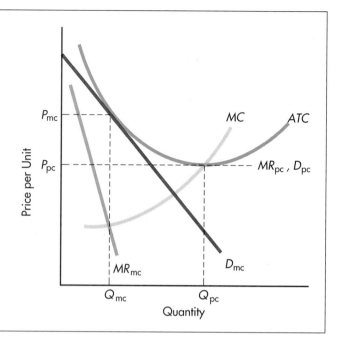

Monopolistically competitive firms produce less and charge a higher price than perfectly competitive firms.

demand curve, P_{mc}. In other words, at Q_{mc} the monopolistically competitive firm is just earning the normal profit.

The difference between a perfectly competitive firm and a monopolistically competitive firm is clear in Figure 3. Because of the downward-sloping demand curve facing the monopolistically competitive firm, the firm does not produce at the minimum point of the long-run average-total-cost curve, Q_{pc}. Instead, it produces a smaller quantity of output, Q_{mc}, at a higher price, P_{mc}. The difference between P_{mc} and P_{pc} is the additional amount consumers pay for the privilege of having differentiated products. If consumers placed no value on product choice—if they desired generic products—they would not pay anything extra for product differentiation, and the monopolistically competitive firm would not exist.

Monopolistic competition does not yield economic efficiency because consumers are willing and able to pay for variety.

Even though price does not equal marginal cost and the monopolistically competitive firm does not operate at the minimum point of the average-total-cost curve, the firm does earn normal profit in the long run. And although the monopolistically competitive firm does not strictly meet the conditions of economic efficiency (since price is not equal to marginal cost), the inefficiency is not due to the firm's ability to restrict quantity and increase price but instead results directly from consumers' desire for variety. It is hard to argue that society is worse off with monopolistic competition than it is with perfect competition since the difference is due solely to consumer desires. Yet, variety is costly and critics of market economies argue that the cost is not worthwhile. Would the world be a better place if we had a simpler array of products to choose from, if there was a simple generic product—one type of automobile, say—for everyone?

Not everyone is willing to pay for the variety nor has to pay for it. Variety is a luxury good; the income elasticity of demand is greater than one. This fact is an important element in the pricing strategies of manufacturers. For instance, consider the array of automobiles offered by Toyota, General Motors, Nissan, Honda, Ford, and Chrysler. Toyota has the Camry, the Land

Cruiser, the 4Runner, and the Lexus line, among others. Each of these cars incorporates a variety of specialized features that are the result of expensive research and development by the Toyota company. The research and development costs are essentially fixed costs. How can a manufacturer recoup these fixed costs? One way is to provide a huge array of options on every automobile. This strategy seems to be common for the relatively lower-priced automobile lines—those ranging below $25,000. You see this if, for instance, you go to a Jeep dealer; you not only find several models of Jeep, but the combinations of options are remarkable. Moreover, the options are expensive, clearly higher-priced than their marginal costs. This strategy is a means to have those who desire variety pay for the research and development costs. Another strategy is to provide all options as standard features. This is the approach taken by the Lexus, Acura, Infiniti, and other expensive automobile lines. The approach appears to be a response to price elasticity of demand; consumers of luxury automobiles are less sensitive to price than are consumers of nonluxury automobiles. Several thousand dollars of options on a nonluxury automobile would drive many customers away, but the same options on a luxury automobile will not affect the customer decision. In both cases, the consumer has the choice of whether to purchase the options or not; variety is up to the customer.

1.c. Nonprice Competition

A firm in a monopolistically competitive market structure attempts to differentiate its product from the products offered by its rivals. Successful product differentiation reduces the price elasticity of demand. The demand curve, shown as the rotation from D_1 to D_2 in Figure 4(a), becomes steeper.

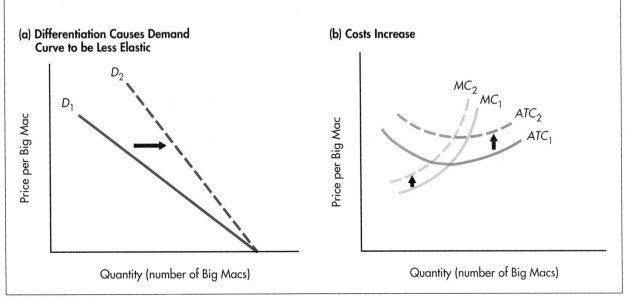

Figure 4
Advertising, Prices, and Profits
A successful differentiation program will reduce the price elasticity of demand, shown as a steeper demand curve, D_2, compared to D_1 in Figure 4(a). The successful differentiation enables the firm to charge a higher price. Advertising is expensive and can cause the cost curves to shift up as well, as shown in Figure 4(b). The combination of higher costs and a more inelastic demand curve can mean greater, the same, or lower profit.

(a) Differentiation Causes Demand Curve to be Less Elastic

Price per Big Mac

D_2
D_1

Quantity (number of Big Macs)

(b) Costs Increase

Price per Big Mac

MC_2
MC_1
ATC_2
ATC_1

Quantity (number of Big Macs)

What behavior is most common in monopolistic competition?

McDonald's, for example, has successfully used advertising to differentiate its product. Figure 4(a) shows that a successful differentiation program increases the steepness of the demand curve and may shift it outward, from D_1 to D_2, and successful differentiation could lead to higher profits. Advertising increases costs, however. Suppose McDonald's Corporation spends about 10 cents to advertise each hamburger it sells. If that expenditure rises to 15 cents, then the average-total-cost curve shifts up, as shown in Figure 4(b). Because costs rise and the demand curve becomes steeper and shifts out, the effect on profit depends on the size of changes in the cost and demand curves. A successful advertising campaign is one that causes profit to rise. But costs could increase so much as a result of the advertising program that profit does not increase. Each firm has to determine the effects of a differentiation program on demand and on costs or, ultimately, on profit.

Numerous characteristics may serve to differentiate products: quality, color, style, safety features, taste, packaging, purchase terms, warranties, and guarantees. A firm might change its hours of operation—for example, a supermarket might offer service 24 hours a day—to call attention to itself. Firms can also use location to differentiate their products. A firm may locate where traffic is heavy and the cost to the consumer of making a trip to the firm is minimal. If location is used for differentiation, however, why do fast-food restaurants tend to group together? Where you find a McDonald's you usually find a Taco Bell or a Wendy's nearby. The model of monopolistic competition explains this behavior. Suppose that five identical consumers—A, B, C, D, and E—are spread out along a line as shown in Figure 5. Consumer C is the median consumer, residing equidistantly from consumers B and D and equidistantly from consumers A and E. Assume that the five consumers care about the costs incurred in getting to a fast-food restaurant and are indifferent between the food offered. McDonald's is the first fast-food provider to open near these five consumers. Where does it locate? It locates as close to consumer C as possible because that location minimizes the total distance of all five consumers from McDonald's.

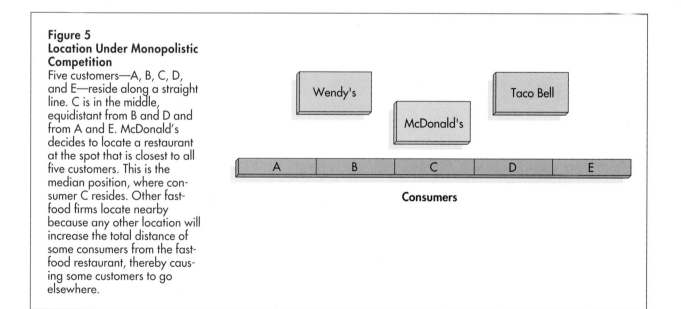

Figure 5
Location Under Monopolistic Competition
Five customers—A, B, C, D, and E—reside along a straight line. C is in the middle, equidistant from B and D and from A and E. McDonald's decides to locate a restaurant at the spot that is closest to all five customers. This is the median position, where consumer C resides. Other fast-food firms locate nearby because any other location will increase the total distance of some consumers from the fast-food restaurant, thereby causing some customers to go elsewhere.

Taco Bell wants to open in the same area. If it locates near consumer D, then Taco Bell will pull customers D and E from McDonald's but will have no chance to attract A, B, or C. Conversely, if it locates near consumer A, only A will go to Taco Bell. Only if Taco Bell locates next door to McDonald's will it have a chance to gather a larger market share than McDonald's. As other fast-food firms enter, they too will locate close to McDonald's.

A prediction that comes from the theory of monopolistic competition is that an innovation or successful differentiation in any area—style, quality, location—leads initially to above-normal profit but eventually brings in copycats that drive profit back down to the normal level. In a monopolistically competitive market structure, innovation and above-normal profit for one firm are followed by entry and normal profit. Differentiation and above-normal profit then occur again. They induce entry, which again drives profit back to the normal level. The cycle continues until product differentiation no longer brings above-normal profit.

RECAP

1. The market structure called *monopolistic competition* is an industry in which many sellers produce a differentiated product and entry is easy.

2. In the short run, a firm in monopolistic competition can earn above-normal profit.

3. In the long run, a firm in a monopolistically competitive market structure will produce at a higher cost and lower output than will a firm in a perfectly competitive market structure. In both market structures, firms earn only a normal profit.

4. Monopolistic competitors may engage more in nonprice competition than in price differentiation.

2. OLIGOPOLY AND INTERDEPENDENCE

What is oligopoly?

Oligopoly is a market structure characterized by (1) few firms, (2) either standardized or differentiated products, and (3) difficult entry. Oligopoly may take many forms. It may consist of one dominant firm coexisting with many smaller firms or a group of giant firms (two or more) that dominate the industry coexisting with other small firms. Whatever the number of firms, the characteristic that describes oligopoly is *interdependence*; an individual firm in an oligopoly does not decide what to do without considering what the other firms in the industry will do. When a large firm in an oligopoly changes its behavior, the demand curves of the other firms are affected significantly.

In monopolistically competitive and perfectly competitive markets, what one firm does affects each of the other firms so slightly that each firm essentially ignores the others. Each firm in an oligopoly, however, must closely watch the actions of the other firms because the action of one can dramatically affect the others. This interdependence among firms leads to actions

In the United States, the airline industry is best characterized as an oligopoly. There are few firms offering a similar service; each firm must take into account the actions of the other firms when setting fares, routes, and other aspects of the service. In many nations, the airline industry is either a government enterprise or is regulated by the government. For instance, China allows only selected airlines to land in its territory. Dragon Air, a Hong Kong airline, is one airline allowed into China. Thus, part of the reason Dragon Air is allowed into China is the close ties between Hong Kong and China; and, with the upcoming Chinese takeover of Hong Kong, all aspects of the Hong Kong economy are being carefully scrutinized by Chinese officials.

not found in the other market structures, such as advertising campaigns directed toward a specific rival, cartels and collusion, cost-plus pricing, most-favored-customer pricing, and other behaviors.

2.a. Why Do Oligopolies Exist?

Market structures are defined by demand and cost conditions. In the case of oligopoly, the cost conditions must be such that entry is difficult and that a few firms are necessary to supply the market. Such a case is illustrated in Figure 6, where the average-total-cost curve is an elongated U shape. The minimum efficient scale can be anywhere in the range from Q_a to Q_c. Thus, one firm of size Q_c and another, or several other firms, of much smaller size

Figure 6
Market Size and MES
Market structures are defined by demand and cost conditions. Figure 6 shows a case where oligopoly might be likely to arise. The average-total-cost curve is an elongated U shape, so the minimum efficient scale can be anywhere in the range from Q_a to Q_c. Thus, one firm of size Q_c and another, or several other firms, of much smaller size could coexist to supply the market (produce enough to satisfy demand). Another structure would be just a few firms of size Q_a supplying the entire market.

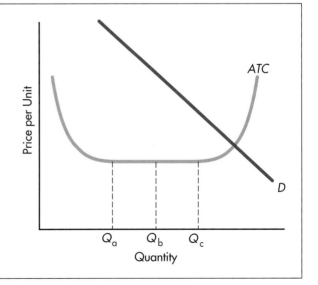

could coexist to supply the market, as is the case in photofinishing supplies. Another structure would be just a few firms of size Q_a supplying the entire market. This illustrates the situation facing the steel, auto, and airline industries.

In addition to cost and demand conditions that require more than one firm to supply the market, oligopoly requires fixed costs that are sufficiently large that entry is difficult. If huge capital expenditures are necessary to operate a business, a firm contemplating entering the industry must consider whether it can obtain the financing and whether the fixed costs are recoverable if it exits the industry. For example, the factories, furnaces, warehouses, and buildings necessary to operate in the steel-producing industry require a huge expenditure. A large percentage of the fixed costs are *sunk*, or nonrecoverable, because the equipment, furnaces, and buildings are not useful in other industries. A few years ago, USX (formerly United States Steel) was thinking about giving up its steel-manufacturing business. To leave the industry would mean abandoning much of its capital but still having to carry the fixed costs for several years after terminating its steel production. Thus, USX decided to remain in the business, at least for a while.

2.b. Oligopoly and Strategic Behavior

In what form does rivalry occur in an oligopoly?

strategic behavior:
the behavior that occurs when what is best for A depends on what B does, and what is best for B depends on what A does

game theory:
a description of oligopolistic behavior as a series of strategic moves and countermoves

Game theory can illustrate ways in which oligopolistic firms interact. Game theory considers each firm a participant in a game where the winners are the firms with the greatest profit.

Oligopolies are interdependent; each firm in an oligopoly takes into account and reacts to what its rivals are doing. Anything can and does occur under oligopoly. Rivalry is very intense in some cases; in others, means have been devised to live and let live. Because of the great variety of behavior possible under oligopoly, economists have been unable to agree on a single description of how oligopolistic firms behave. The only uniform description of the behavior of oligopolistic firms is *strategic*.

Strategic behavior occurs when what is best for A depends on what B does and what is best for B depends on what A does. It is much like a card game—bridge, say—where strategies are designed depending on the cards the players are dealt. Underbidding, overbidding, bluffing, deceit, and other strategies are carried out. In fact, the analogy between games and firm behavior in oligopoly is so strong that economists have applied **game theory** to their analyses of oligopoly. Game theory, developed in the 1940s by John von Neumann and Oskar Morgenstern, describes oligopolistic behavior as a series of strategic moves and countermoves. In this section we briefly discuss some of the theories of oligopolistic behavior.

2.b.1. The Kinked Demand Curve All firms know the law of demand. Thus, they know that sales will rise if price is lowered because people will purchase more of all goods (the income effect) and will substitute away from the more expensive goods to purchase more of the less expensive goods (the substitution effect). But the firms in an oligopoly may not know the shape of the demand curve for their product because the shape depends on how the rivals react to one another. They have to predict how their competitors will respond to a price change in order to know what their demand curve looks like.

Let's consider the auto industry. Suppose General Motors' costs have fallen (its marginal-cost curve has shifted down) and the company is deciding whether to lower the prices on its cars. If GM did not have to consider how the other car companies would respond, it would simply lower the price in order to be sure that the new *MC* curve intersected the *MR* curve, as illustrated in Figure 7(a). But GM suspects that the demand and marginal-revenue curves in Figure 7(a) do not represent its true market situation. GM believes that if it lowers the prices on its cars from their current level of P_1, the other auto companies will follow suit. If they also lower the price on their cars, the substitution effect for the GM cars does not occur; sales of GM cars might increase a little but only because of the income effect. In other words, GM does not capture the market as indicated in Figure 7(b) by D_1 but instead finds the quantity demanded increasing along D_2 (below price P_1). GM also suspects that should it increase the price of its cars, none of the other auto companies would raise theirs. In this case, the price increase would mean substantially reduced sales because of both the income and substitution effects. The quantity demanded decreases, as indicated along D_1. Consequently, the demand curve for GM is a combination of D_1 and D_2. It is D_1 above P_1 and D_2 below P_1, a demand curve with a *kink*.

Figure 7
The Kinked Demand Curve
If competitors follow price changes, the demand curve faced by an oligopolistic firm is the curve D_1 in Figures 7(a) and 7(b). If competitors do not follow price changes, the demand curve faced by the firm is D_2 in 7(b). If competitors match price decreases but not price increases, then the firm faces a combination of the two demand curves. If competitors do not follow a price increase, then above the current price, P_1, the relevant demand curve is D_1. If competitors do follow a price decrease, then below price P_1 the relevant demand

curve is D_2. The demand curve is the shaded combinations of the two demand curves; it has a kink at the current price. The resulting marginal-revenue curve is also a combination of the two marginal-revenue curves. The marginal-revenue curve is MR_1 to the left of the kink in the demand curve and MR_2 to the right of the kink. Between the two marginal-revenue curves is a gap. The firm produces where $MR = MC$. If the MC curve intersects the MR curve in the gap, the resulting price is P_1 and the resulting quantity produced is Q_1. If costs fall, as represented by a downward shift of MC_1 to MC_2, the price and quantity produced do not change.

(a) Competitors Follow Price Changes

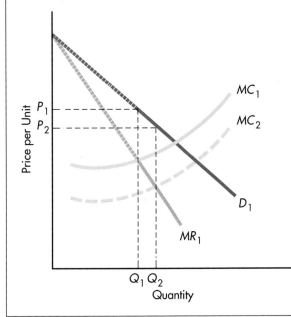

(b) Competitors Do Not Follow Price Changes

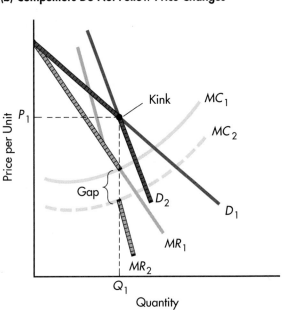

What should GM do? It should price where $MR = MC$. But the resulting marginal-revenue curve is given by a combination of MR_1 and MR_2. MR_1 slopes down gently until reaching the quantity associated with the kink. As we move below the kink, MR_2 becomes the appropriate marginal-revenue curve. Thus, the shaded portions of the two marginal-revenue curves combine to give the firm's marginal-revenue curve. Notice how GM's marginal-cost curves, MC_1 and MC_2, intersect the combined MR curves at the same price and quantity, P_1 and Q_1. Thus, GM's strategy is to do nothing: *not* to change price even though costs have changed.

The firms in an oligopoly might avoid price competition altogether and devote resources to nonprice competition. Even with nonprice competition, however, strategic behavior comes into play, as noted in the next section.

2.b.2. Dominant Strategy
Consider the situation where firms must decide whether to devote more resources to advertising. When a firm in any given industry advertises its product, its demand increases for two reasons. First, people who had not used that type of product before learn about it, and some will buy it. Second, other people who already consume a different brand of the same product may switch brands. The first effect boosts sales for the industry as a whole, while the second redistributes existing sales within the industry.

Consider the cigarette industry as an example and assume that the matrix in Figure 8 illustrates the possible actions that two firms might undertake and the results of those actions. The top left rectangle represents the payoffs, or results, if both A and B advertise; the bottom left is where A advertises but B does not; the top right is the payoffs when B advertises but A does not; and the bottom right is the payoffs if neither advertises. If firm A can earn higher profits by advertising than by not advertising, whether or not firm B advertises, then firm A will surely advertise. This is referred to as a **dominant strategy**—a strategy that produces the best results no matter what strategy the opposing player follows. Firm A compares the left side of the matrix to the right side and sees that it earns more by advertising no matter what firm B does. If B advertises and A advertises, then A earns seventy, but if A does not advertise it earns forty. If B does not advertise, then A earns 100 by advertising and only eighty by not advertising. The dominant strategy for

dominant strategy:
a strategy that produces better results no matter what strategy the opposing firm follows

---

Figure 8
Dominant Strategy Game
Figure 8 illustrates the dominant strategy game. The dominant strategy for firm A is to advertise. No matter what firm B does, firm A is better off advertising. If firm B does not advertise, firm A earns 80 not advertising and 100 advertising. If firm B does advertise, firm A earns 40 not advertising and 70 advertising. Similarly, firm B is better off advertising no matter what firm A does. Both A and B have dominant strategies—advertise.

	Firm A	
	Advertise	Not Advertise
Firm B — Advertise	Firm A 70 / Firm B 80	Firm A 40 / Firm B 100
Firm B — Not Advertise	Firm A 100 / Firm B 50	Firm A 80 / Firm B 90

The Prisoner's Dilemma

Strategic behavior characterizes oligopoly. Perhaps the most well known example of strategic behavior occurs in what is called the prisoner's dilemma.

Two people have been arrested for a crime, but the evidence against them is weak. The sheriff keeps the prisoners separated and offers each a special deal. If one prisoner confesses, that prisoner can go free as long as only he confesses, and the other prisoner will get ten or more years in prison. If both prisoners confess, each will receive a reduced sentence of two years in jail. The prisoners know that if neither confesses, they will be cleared of all but a minor charge and will serve only two days in jail. The problem is they do not know what deal the other is offered or if the other will take the deal.

The options available to the two prisoners are shown in the four cells of the figure. Prisoner B's options are shown along the horizontal direction and prisoner A's along the vertical direction. In the upper left cell is the result if both

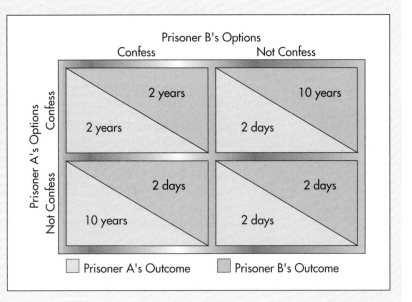

prisoners confess. In the lower left is the result if prisoner A does not confess but prisoner B does; in the upper right cell is the result of A confessing but prisoner B not confessing; and in the lower right cell is the result when neither prisoner confesses. The dominant strategy for both prisoners is to confess and to receive two years of jail time.

If the prisoners had been loyal to each other, each would have received a much smaller penalty. Because both chose to confess, each is worse off than would have been the case if each had known what the other was doing. Yet, in the context of the interdependence of the decisions, each made the best choice.

firm A is to advertise. And according to Figure 8, the dominant strategy for firm B also is to advertise. Firm B will earn eighty by advertising and fifty by not advertising if A advertises. Firm B will earn 100 advertising, but only ninety not advertising if A does not advertise. But notice that both firms would be better off if neither advertised; firm A would earn eighty instead of seventy, and firm B would earn ninety instead of eighty. Yet, the firms cannot afford to *not* advertise because they would lose more if the other firm advertised and they didn't. This situation is known as the prisoner's dilemma; see the Economic Insight "The Prisoner's Dilemma" for a fuller description.

None of the cigarette manufacturers wants to do much advertising, for example. Yet strategic behavior suggests that they must. Firm A advertises, so firm B does also. Each ups the advertising ante. How can this expensive advertising competition be controlled? Each firm alone has no incentive to do it, since unilateral action will mean a significant loss of market share. But if they can ban advertising together, or if the government passes a law banning cigarette advertising, all of the cigarette companies will be better off. In fact, a ban on cigarette advertising on television has been in effect since January 1, 1971. The ban was intended by the government as a means of reducing cigarette smoking—of helping the consumer. Yet who does this ban really benefit?

2.b.3. Nondominant Strategy

There are many situations in which not every firm has a dominant strategy. Suppose that the payoffs for the two cigarette firms are such that firm A is better off advertising no matter what firm B does, but firm B is better off advertising only if firm A advertises. Then, in contrast to the prisoner's dilemma, the best strategy for firm B depends on the particular strategy chosen by firm A. Firm B does not have a dominant strategy.

Suppose the options to both firms are as illustrated in Figure 9 rather than Figure 8. Firm B chooses to advertise if firm A advertises (80 versus 60) and chooses not to advertise if firm A does not advertise (60 versus 50). Even though firm B does not have a dominant strategy, we can indicate what is likely to happen. Firm B is able to predict that firm A will advertise because that is a dominant strategy for firm A. Since firm B knows this, it knows that its own best strategy is also to advertise.

2.b.4. Sequential Games

The strategic situations we have considered so far have been ones in which both players must pick their strategies simultaneously. Each player had to choose a strategy knowing only the incentives facing the opponent, not the opponent's actual choice of strategy. But in many situations, one firm moves first, and the other is then able to choose a strategy based on the first firm's choice; this is known as a **sequential game**.

For years Volvo has been known as the safest automobile on the road. This status enables Volvo to command significantly higher prices than otherwise-similar automobiles can get. Now suppose that Chrysler is considering whether to build an even safer car. Chrysler knows that the firm known for producing the safest car will be able to earn a large profit but also fears the consequences if Volvo counters by building an even safer car.

Suppose that the situation facing Volvo and Chrysler is as illustrated in Figure 10. Both firms start at point A, where Chrysler must decide whether to enter with a car safer than those Volvo produces. If it does not, Volvo will receive a payoff of 120 and Chrysler a payoff of 0, as noted by point C. If

sequential game:
a situation in which one firm moves first and then the other is able to choose a strategy based on the first firm's choice

Figure 9
Non-dominant Strategy Game
The game indicated in Figure 8 is changed so that firm B does not have a dominant strategy. If firm A does not advertise, firm B earns 60 not advertising and 50 advertising; if firm A does advertise, firm B earns 60 not advertising and 80 advertising. Thus, what firm B does depends on what firm A does.

	Firm A	
	Advertise	Not Advertise
Firm B Advertise	Firm A 70 / Firm B 80	Firm A 40 / Firm B 50
Firm B Not Advertise	Firm A 100 / Firm B 60	Firm A 60 / Firm B 60

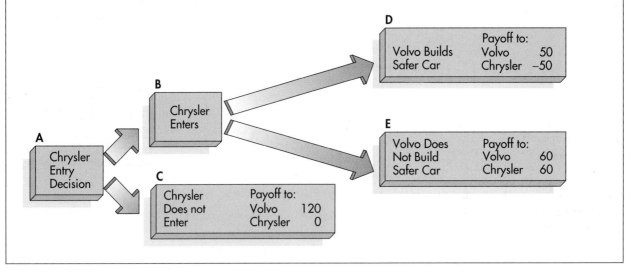

Figure 10
Sequential Game

The game starts at point A, where Chrysler must decide whether to enter with a safer car. If it does not, Volvo will receive a payoff of 120, Chrysler a payoff of 0. If Chrysler enters, however, the game moves to point B, where Volvo must decide whether to build an even safer car. Suppose that if Volvo builds the safer car, its payoff will be 50 while Chrysler will earn a payoff of −50, and that if Volvo does not build the safer car, its payoff will be 60 while Chrysler will get a payoff of 60. Chrysler knows the payoffs facing Volvo and concludes that the best option open to Volvo is not to produce the safer car.

Chrysler enters, however, they move to point B, where Volvo must decide whether to build an even safer car. The payoff to Volvo for building the even safer car is 50, but if Volvo does not build the safer car, its payoff will be 60. Volvo does not want Chrysler to enter, but Chrysler knows the payoffs facing Volvo and can conclude that the best option open to Volvo is not to produce the safer car. Thus, Chrysler builds the safer car and Volvo does not counter.

2.b.5. Contestable Markets and Strategic Deterrence Strategic behavior may mean more than reacting to rivals' actions. It may mean undertaking action in order to *prevent* certain behavior by rivals. This is called **strategic deterrence**. For instance, under certain conditions oligopolies and even monopolies will behave much like perfectly competitive firms and may, as a result, not earn above-normal profit. The conditions under which this will occur are when there are no sunk, or unrecoverable, costs associated with entry and exit. As an example, consider the difference between a wide-bodied aircraft and a new automobile manufacturing plant. Although a wide-bodied aircraft can cost more than $50 million, this may not be a sunk cost. If, when a firm wants to leave the airline market, it can sell or lease the aircraft to another airline, the $50 million is not sunk. Compare this to an automobile manufacturing plant. Once built, if there is no other use for the plant, the resources that are put into the plant are sunk.

Some economists claim that it is not actual entry but the *potential* of entry that matters. If the potential of entry is high, a market is said to be contestable. According to the theory of **contestable markets**, where the threat of entry is credible, incumbent firms are simply not free to charge prices significantly above cost. Even if entry is not easy in a contestable market, the threat

strategic deterrence:
undertaking action to prevent certain behavior by rivals

contestable market:
a market where the potential of entry is high

of entry will ensure that firms earn normal profits. Huge fixed costs and large exit costs are impediments to the functioning of the theory of contestable markets only if the costs are sunk. Because of these costs, firms already in an oligopoly are not likely to fear the potential entrance of new firms. Thus, a firm may want to create a situation where potential entrants would face considerable sunk costs.

Reconsider the example illustrated in Figure 10 and assume that before Volvo had originally built its manufacturing plant and production lines, it had the option of adding a step in the production process that would enable it to build the safest car. Adding this production step at the time the original manufacturing plant was constructed is 10 units, but reduces the cost of building the safest car at any time by 20 units. If Volvo had installed this extra step in the manufacturing plant, the sequential game between it and Chrysler would then be as illustrated in Figure 11.

Volvo's payoff at point D is now 60, 10 units higher than if it had not installed the production step (Volvo saves 20 on building costs, but the production step costs 10). Despite the small changes in payoffs, the presence of the production step alters the outcome. This time Chrysler can predict that if it enters with a safer car, Volvo will bring on-line its extra step and build an even safer car, which means that Chrysler will lose a great deal of money, a payoff of −50. As a result, Chrysler will not find it worthwhile to enter this market, and the market solution is point C.

As illustrated by this strategic situation, firms in an oligopoly can earn above-normal profits for a long period of time if the profits are insufficient to induce a quick entry followed by a quick exit by firms currently outside the industry.

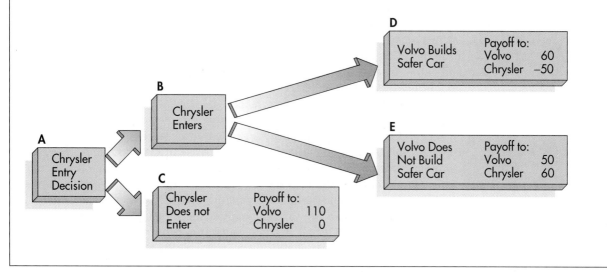

Figure 11
Strategic Deterrence
Volvo's payoff at point D is now 60 (it saves 20 on building costs but pays the 10-unit cost of the production step). Its payoffs at C and E are each 10 units less than in Figure 10 (reflecting the cost of the production step). Despite the small changes in payoffs, the presence of the production step alters the outcome of the game. This time Chrysler can predict that if it enters with a safer car, Volvo will bring on-line its extra step and build an even safer car, which means that Chrysler will receive a payoff of −50. As a result, Chrysler will not find it worthwhile to enter this market, and the game will end at point C.

2.c. Cooperation

Why does cooperation among rivals occur most often in oligopolies?

If the firms in an oligopoly could come to some cooperative agreement, they could all be better off. For instance, Volvo and Chrysler might spend no additional money and agree to share the market; the cigarette companies, discussed with Figures 8 and 9, might agree not to advertise. In each of these cases, the firms would earn greater profits. Cooperation is an integral part of oligopoly because there are only a few firms. The firms can communicate easier than the many firms in a perfectly competitive or monopolistically competitive industry.

2.c.1. Price-Leadership Oligopoly One way for firms to communicate is to allow one firm to be the leader in changes in price or advertising activities. Once the leader makes a change, the others duplicate what the leader does. This action enables all firms to know exactly what the rivals will do. It eliminates a kink in the demand curve because both price increases and price decreases will be followed, and it avoids the situation where excessive expenses are made on advertising or other activities. This type of oligopoly is called a *price-leadership oligopoly*.

The steel industry in the 1960s is an example of a dominant-firm price-leadership oligopoly. For many years, steel producers allowed United States Steel to set prices for the entire industry. The cooperation of the steel companies probably led to higher profits than would have occurred with rivalry. However, the absence of rivalry is said to be one reason for the decline of the steel industry in the United States. Price leadership removed the need for the firms to compete by maintaining and upgrading equipment and materials and by developing new technologies. As a result, foreign firms that chose not to behave as price followers emerged as more sophisticated producers of steel than U.S. firms.

For many years airlines also relied on a price leader. In many cases the price leader in the airlines was not the dominant airline, but instead one of the weaker or new airlines. In recent years, airlines have communicated less through a price leader and more through their computerized reservation system, according to the Justice Department (see the Economic Insight "Price Fixing and the Airlines").

2.c.2. Collusion, Cartels, and Other Cooperative Mechanisms Acting jointly allows firms to earn more profits than if they act independently or against each other. To avoid the destruction of strategic behavior, the few firms in an oligopoly can collude, or come to some agreement about price and output levels. Typically these agreements provide the members of the oligopoly higher profits and thus raise prices to consumers. Collusion, which leads to secret cooperative agreements, is illegal in the United States, although it is acceptable in many other nations.

cartel:
an organization of independent firms whose purpose is to control and limit production and maintain or increase prices and profits

A **cartel** is an organization of independent firms whose purpose is to control and limit production and maintain or increase prices and profits. A cartel can result from either formal or informal agreement among members. Like collusion, cartels are illegal in the United States. International cartels, however, are common, as noted in the Economic Insight "International Cartels." The cartel most people are familiar with is the Organization of Petroleum Exporting Countries (OPEC), a group of nations rather than a group of independent firms. During the 1970s, OPEC was able to coordinate oil produc-

Price Fixing and the Airlines

It is illegal in the United States for firms to agree on prices, that is, to fix prices. But the fact that cooperation can result in higher profits than strategic competition has induced firms to undertake questionable and even illegal ways to communicate with each other. The Department of Justice announced in December 1992 that it believes major airlines are fixing prices. The Justice Department claimed that the airlines violated price-fixing laws by sharing plans for fare changes through a computer system.

According to the Justice Department, investigators are trying to determine whether the airlines have created secret electronic codes in a computerized clearinghouse called the Airline Tariff Publishers Inc, which the airlines own and use. According to the Justice Department, these secret codes were signals of price changes.

tion in such a way that it drove the market price of crude oil from $1.10 a barrel to $32 a barrel. For nearly eight years, each member of OPEC agreed to produce a certain, limited amount of crude oil as designated by the OPEC production committee. Then in the early 1980s, the cartel began to fall apart as individual members began to cheat on the agreement. Members began to produce more than their allocation in an attempt to increase profit. As each member of the cartel did this, the price of oil fell, reaching $12 per barrel in 1988. Oil prices rose again in 1990 when Iraq invaded Kuwait, causing widespread damage to Kuwait's oil fields. But, as repairs have been made to Kuwait's oil wells, it has increased production and oil prices have dropped.

Production quotas are not easy to maintain among different firms or different nations. Most cartels do not last very long because the members chisel on the agreements. If each producer thinks that it can increase its own production, and thus its profits, without affecting what the other producers do, all producers end up producing more than their assigned amounts; the price of the product declines and the cartel falls apart.

Economists have identified certain conditions that make it likely that a cartel will be stable. A cartel is likely to remain in force when

- there are few firms in the industry
- there are significant barriers to entry
- an identical product is produced
- there are few opportunities to keep actions secret
- there are no legal barriers to sharing agreements

The fact that sharing is possible, however, does not mean that successful sharing will occur. The incentive to cheat remains. There must be an ability to punish the cheaters if a cartel is to stick together. Typically a central authority or a dominant member of the cartel will enforce the rules of the cartel. In OPEC, the enforcer has been Saudi Arabia because it has the greatest supply of oil. In other cartels, a governing board acts as the enforcer. Even though cartels are illegal in the United States, a few have been sanctioned by the government. The National Collegiate Athletic Association (NCAA) is a cartel of colleges and universities. It sets rules of behavior and

International Cartels

OPEC, the most well known of the international cartels, has existed for nearly twenty-one years, but its membership is now drifting away and its effectiveness has been severely limited since the mid-1970s. OPEC is far from the only international cartel, however. The following list indicates some of the cartels formed to control the production of various products internationally since the late 1800s. The duration refers to the length of time the cartel operated. For instance, seven different sugar cartels have been formed, varying in duration from two to five years. However, there has been only one bauxite cartel. It lasted ten years.

Cartels are typically short-lived because cheating is simply too great a temptation to resist. But some cartels, like OPEC, coffee, or bauxite, do last a fairly long time. Why? Perhaps some are better able to monitor the behavior of members. In addition, the success of the cartel probably depends on whether the member firms believe their profits are higher with than without the cartel.

Source: Jaime Marquez, "Life Expectancy of International Cartels: An Empirical Analysis," International Finance Discussion Papers, Dec. 1992, Board of Governors of the Federal Reserve System.

Cartel	Duration
Sugar	Seven cartels have existed beginning in 1926. The longest lasted 5 years.
Coffee	Three cartels have existed. Beginning in 1905, the longest lasted 18 years.
Tea	Three cartels have existed: 1933–1943; 1950–1955; and 1973–1979.
Copper	Four cartels: 1888–1890; 1918–1922; 1926–1932; and 1935–1939.
Zinc	Two cartels: 1928–1929 and 1931–1935.
Bauxite	Only one cartel: 1974–1984.
Tin	One cartel that lasted 25 years.

enforces those rules through a governing board. Member schools are placed on probation or their programs are dismantled when they violate the agreement. The citrus cartel, composed of citrus growers in California and Arizona, enforces its actions through its governing board. Sunkist Growers Inc., a cooperative of many growers, represents more than half of the California and Arizona production and also plays an important role in enforcing the rules of the cartel.

2.c.3. Facilitating Practices Several actions by oligopolistic firms can contribute to cooperation and collusion even though the firms do not formally agree to cooperate. Such actions are called **facilitating practices**. Pricing policies can leave the impression that firms are explicitly fixing prices, or cooperating, when in fact they are merely following the same strategies. For instance, the use of **cost-plus/markup pricing** tends to bring about similar if not identical pricing behavior among rival firms. If firms set prices by determining the average cost of an item and adding a 50 percent markup to the cost they would be cost-plus pricing. If all firms face the same cost curves, then all firms will set the same prices. If costs decrease, then all firms will lower prices the same amount and at virtually the same time. Such pricing behavior is common in the grocery business.

facilitating practices:
actions by oligopolistic firms that can contribute to cooperation and collusion even though the firms do not formally agree to cooperate

cost-plus/markup pricing:
a pricing policy that leads to similar if not identical pricing behavior among rival firms

most-favored customer (MFC):
a customer who receives a guarantee of the lowest price and all product features for a certain period of time

Another practice that leads to implicit cooperation is the most-favored-customer policy. Often the time between purchase and delivery of a product is quite long. To avoid the possibility that customer A purchases a product at one price and then learns that customer B purchased the product at a lower price or benefited from product features unavailable to customer A, a producer will guarantee that customer A will receive the lowest price and all features for a certain period of time. Customer A is thus a **most-favored customer (MFC)**.

The most-favored-customer policy actually gives firms an incentive not to lower prices even in the face of reduced demand. A firm that lowers the price of its product must then give rebates to all most-favored customers, which forces all other firms with most-favored-customer policies to do the same. In addition, the MFC allows a firm to collect information on what its rivals are doing. Customers will return products for a rebate when another firm offers the same product for a lower price.

Consider the behavior of firms that produced antiknock additives for gasoline from 1974 to 1979. Lead-based antiknock compounds had been used in the refining of gasoline since the 1920s. From the 1920s until 1948, the Ethyl Corporation was the sole domestic producer of the compounds. In 1948, Du Pont entered the industry. PPG Industries followed in 1961, and Nalco in 1964. Beginning in 1973, the demand for lead-based antiknock compounds decreased dramatically. However, because each company had most-favored-customer clauses, high prices were maintained even as demand for the product declined.

A most-favored-customer policy discourages price decreases because it requires producers to lower prices retroactively with rebates. If all rivals provide all buyers with most-favored-customer clauses, a high price is likely to be stabilized in the industry.

RECAP

1. Oligopoly is a market structure in which there are so few firms that each must take into account what the others do, entry is difficult, and either undifferentiated or differentiated products are produced.

2. Interdependence and strategic behavior characterize an oligopolistic firm.

3. The shape of the demand curve and the marginal-revenue curve facing an oligopolist depends on how rival firms react to changes in price and product.

4. The kinked demand curve is one example of how oligopolistic firms might react to price changes. The kink occurs because rivals follow price cuts but not price increases.

5. Game theory provides a convenient way to describe behavior by oligopolistic firms. Such behavior includes the dominant strategy, as represented by the prisoner's dilemma; the nondominant strategy; and sequential decision-making. In all of these games, the importance of the interdependence of firms is clear.

TABLE 2
Summary of Perfect Competition, Monopoly, Monopolistic Competition, and Oligopoly

	Perfect Competition	*Monopoly*	*Monopolistic Competition*	*Oligopoly*
Number of Firms	Many	One	Many	Few
Type of Product	Undifferentiated	One	Differentiated	Undifferentiated or differentiated
Entry Conditions	Easy	Difficult or impossible	Easy	Difficult
Demand Curve for Firm	Horizontal (perfectly elastic)	Downward-sloping	Downward-sloping	Downward-sloping
Price and Marginal Cost	MC = P	MC < P	MC < P	MC < P
Long-run Profit	Zero	Yes	Zero	Depends on whether entry occurs

6. Strategic deterrence may be used to prevent rivals from entering contestable markets.

7. In a price-leadership oligopoly, one firm determines the price and quantity, knowing that all other firms will follow suit. The price leader is usually the dominant firm in the industry.

8. Oligopolistic firms have incentives to cooperate. Collusion, making a secret cooperative agreement, is illegal in the United States. Cartels, also illegal in the United States, rest on explicit cooperation achieved through formal agreement.

9. Facilitating practices implicitly encourage cooperation in an industry.

3. SUMMARY OF MARKET STRUCTURES

We have now discussed in some detail each of the four market structures. Table 2 summarizes the characteristics and the main predictions yielded by each model. The model of perfect competition predicts that firms will produce at a point where price and marginal cost are the same (at the bottom of the average-total-cost curve) and profit will be zero in the long run. The model of monopoly predicts that price will exceed marginal cost and that the firm can earn positive economic profit in the long run. With monopolistic competition, price will exceed marginal cost and the firm will not produce at the bottom point of the average-total-cost curve, but this is due to the consumer's desire for product differentiation. In the long run, the firm in monopolistic competition will earn a normal profit. In oligopoly, a firm may be able to earn above-normal profit for a long time—as long as entry can be restricted. In oligopoly, price exceeds marginal cost, and the firm does not operate at the bottom of the average-total-cost curve.

SUMMARY

▲▼ **What is monopolistic competition?**

1. Monopolistic competition is a market structure in which many firms are producing a slightly different product and entry is easy. §1

2. Monopolistically competitive firms will earn a normal profit in the long run. §1.a.2

▲▼ **What behavior is most common in monopolistic competition?**

3. Entry occurs in monopolistically competitive industries through the introduction of a slightly different product. §1.a

4. A monopolistically competitive firm will produce less output and charge a higher price than an identical perfectly competitive firm, if demand and costs are assumed to be the same. §1.b

▲▼ **What is oligopoly?**

5. Oligopoly is a market structure in which a few large firms produce identical or slightly different products and entry is difficult but not impossible. §2

▲▼ **In what form does rivalry occur in an oligopoly?**

6. Strategic behavior characterizes oligopoly. Each oligopolist must watch the actions of other oligopolists in the industry. §2.b

7. The kinked demand curve results when firms follow a price decrease but do not follow a price increase. §2.b.1

8. Strategic behavior can be illustrated using game theory. A dominant strategy is when the strategy that makes the firm best off does not depend on what rivals do. A nondominant strategy occurs when a firm's behavior or strategy varies, depending on what its rivals do. §§2.b.2, 2.b.3

9. A sequential game illustrates the situation where one firm selects a strategy before another firm does. §2.b.4

▲▼ **Why does cooperation among rivals occur most often in oligopolies?**

10. The small number of firms in oligopoly and the interdependence of these firms creates the situation where the firms are better off if they cooperate (as in the prisoner's dilemma). §§2.b.2, 2.c

11. Price leadership is another type of strategic behavior. One firm determines price for the entire industry. All other firms follow the leader in increasing and decreasing prices. The dominant firm in the industry is most likely to be the price leader. §2.c.1

12. Practices like collusion and cartels minimize profit-reducing rivalry and ensure cooperation. Both are illegal in the United States but acceptable in many other nations. §2.c.2

13. Cost-plus pricing ensures that firms with the same costs will charge the same prices. The most-favored-customer policy guarantees a customer that the price he or she paid for a product will not be lowered for another customer. Cost-plus pricing and the most-favored-customer policy are facilitating practices. §2.c.3

KEY TERMS

strategic behavior §2.b

game theory §2.b

dominant strategy §2.b.2

sequential game §2.b.4

strategic deterrence §2.b.5

contestable market §2.b.5

cartel §2.c.2

facilitating practices §2.c.3

cost-plus/markup pricing §2.c.3

most-favored customer (MFC) §2.c.3

EXERCISES

1. Disney, Universal, and MGM, among others, have movie studios in Hollywood. Each of these major studios also has one or several subsidiary studios. Disney, for example, has Touchstone. What market structure best describes these movie production companies? Why would each studio have subsidiary studios? Consider the movies that have come out under Disney and those under Touchstone. Are they different?

2. Suppose that Disney was experiencing above-normal profits for its production of *The Little Mermaid*, *Beauty and the Beast*, and *Aladdin*. If Disney was a member of a monopolistically competitive industry, what would you predict would occur over time to its demand curve (the demand curve for Disney movies)? Suppose that Disney was a member of an oligopoly. How would this change your answer?

3. Why is the monopolistically competitive industry said to be inefficient? Suppose that you counted the higher price the consumer pays for the monopolistically competitive firm's product as part of consumer surplus. Would that change the conclusion regarding the efficiency of monopolistic competition?

4. Why might some people claim that the break-fast cereal industry is monopolistically competitive but the automobile industry is an oligopoly? In both cases, about eight to ten firms dominate the industry.

5. The graph that follows shows an individual firm in long-run equilibrium. What market structure is this firm operating in? Explain. Compare the long-run quantity and price to those of a perfectly competitive firm. What accounts for the difference? Why, or why not? Is the equilibrium price greater than, equal to, or less than marginal cost?

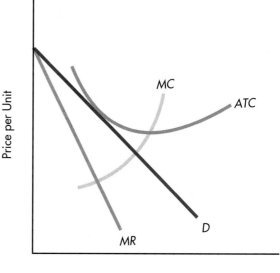

6. Explain what is meant by strategic behavior. How does the kinked demand curve describe strategic behavior?

7. What is the cost to a firm in an oligopoly that fails to take rivals' actions into account? Suppose the firm operates along demand curve D_1, shown below, as if no firms will follow its lead in price cuts or price rises. In fact, however, other firms do follow the price cuts and the true demand curve below price P_1 lies below D_1. If the firm sets a price lower than P_1, what happens?

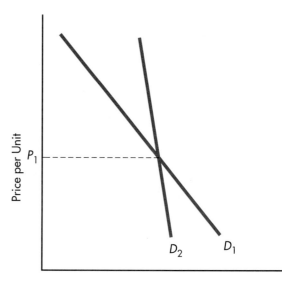

8. Suppose the following demand schedule exists for a firm in monopolistic competition. Suppose the marginal cost is a constant $70. How much will the firm produce? Is this a long- or short-run situation? Suppose the firm is earning above-normal profit. What will occur to this demand schedule?

Price	Quantity
100	1
95	2
88	3
80	4
70	5
55	6
40	7
22	8

9. The cement industry is an example of an undifferentiated oligopoly. The automobile industry is a differentiated oligopoly. Which of these two is most likely to advertise? Why?

10. The South American cocaine industry consists of several "families" who obtain the raw material, refine it, and distribute it to the United States. There are only about three large "families," but there are several small families. What market structure does the industry most closely resemble? What predictions based on the market-structure models can be made about the cocaine business? How do you explain the lack of wars among the families?

11. The NCAA is described as a cartel. In what way is it a cartel? What is the product being produced? How does the cartel stay together?

12. Almost every town has at least one funeral home even if the number of deaths could not possibly keep the funeral home busy. What market structure does the funeral home best exemplify? Use the firm's demand and cost curves and long-run equilibrium position to explain the fact that the funeral home can handle more business than it has. (*Hint*: Is the firm operating at the bottom of the average-total-cost curve?)

13. The payoff matrix below shows the profit two firms earn if both advertise, neither advertises, or one advertises while the other does not. Profits are reported in millions of dollars. Does either firm have a dominant strategy?

Firm 1

	Advertise	Not Advertise
Advertise	Firm 1 earns profit of 100 Firm 2 earns profit of 20	Firm 1 earns profit of 50 Firm 2 earns profit of 70

Firm 2

Not Advertise	Firm 1 earns profit of 0 Firm 2 earns profit of 10	Firm 1 earns profit of 20 Firm 2 earns profit of 60

14. Using the payoff matrix below, answer the following questions. The payoff matrix indicates the profit outcome that corresponds to each firm's pricing strategy.

a. Firms A and B are members of an oligopoly.

Firm A's Price

		$20	$15
Firm B's Price	**$20**	Firm A earns $40 profit Firm B earns $37 profit	Firm A earns $35 profit Firm B earns $39 profit
	$15	Firm A earns $49 profit Firm B earns $30 profit	Firm A earns $38 profit Firm B earns $35 profit

Explain the interdependence that exists in oligopolies using the payoff matrix facing the two firms.

b. Assuming that the firms cooperate, what is the solution to the problem facing the firms?

c. Given your answer to b, explain why cooperation would be mutually beneficial.

d. Given your answer to c, explain why one of the firms might cheat on a cooperative arrangement.

Japanese Conglomerates Offer Firms Mighty Clout

They have been called the "corporate equivalent of blood brotherhood." They are the keiretsus, and they give Japanese computer companies a financial and manufacturing clout that no American company can begin to match.

The word is vague, meaning roughly an "economic or corporate group." Their history is rooted in the zaibatsus, powerful family-based conglomerates that dominated Japan's economy beginning in 1868. During the American occupation following World War II, zaibatsus were blamed for helping start the war and were broken up.

But they formed again into keiretsus, many almost identical to their outlawed ancestors. Today there are two main kinds of keiretsus:—Conglomerates with companies involved in many different industries but centered on a major bank. The six big ones cluster around Sumitomo, Mitsubishi, Mitsui, Dai Ichi Kangyo, Fuji and Sanwa banks, which are the six biggest banks in the world. The Dai

Ichi keiretsu, the biggest, has sales five times as great as General Motors or Exxon, the mightiest U.S. corporations. The Sumitomo keiretsu includes companies involved in computers, metals, steel, glass, coal, real estate, beer, consumer electronics, life insurance and much else.—Companies grouped around a major manufacturer and often supplying that manufacturer. Toyota and Hitachi are leading examples.

The two forms often are linked. Toyota Motors is linked to the Mitsui group and Nissan is linked to Fuyo, the Fuji bank's keiretsu.

There's more to the keiretsu than their size. Their keys are their focus on a bank, their interlocking ownerships and their close commercial ties.

The banks own part of the companies, which American banks can't do. More important, the banks are a steady source of long-term capital, with no pressure to repay.

Do the banks also cut interest rates for their keiretsu fellows?

"Nobody knows," says California investment banker Pierre Lamond, "and you'll never find out."

Even more important are the interlocking ownerships. Each keiretsu member owns a bit—up to 5 percent—of the other members, on the understanding that they will never sell. This, together with minority ownerships by other Japanese institutions, means that up to 80 percent of keiretsu shares are owned by friends and partners of the management.

These shares are never traded and cannot be bought by outsiders—especially foreigners.

The close commercial ties mean the keiretsu companies buy from and sell to one another. American companies have spent years trying to break down this time-hardened loyalty. Most fail.

Altogether, the keiretsus control about 30 percent of Japan's economy.

Source: By: R.C. Longworth © Copyrighted May 17, 1992, Chicago Tribune Company, all rights reserved, used with permission.

Commentary

Firms can earn above-normal or monopoly profits by restricting entry. One means of restricting entry is for the existing firms to band together to form a cartel. Such activity has not been allowed in the United States because of the belief that cartels restrict quantity and raise prices. But in Japan, cartels are accepted in the form of the keiretsus. These cartels consist of firms from different industry groups that come together to create large conglomerates. There are both product and financial ties among the members of each keiretsu: One member will purchase supplies from another member before purchasing them from a nonmember firm, and members must obtain their financing from the member bank. The member banks, and other member firms, will purchase and hold the equity (shares of stock) of the member firm as well.

The article suggests that although the keiretsus might limit competition, they might also lead to lower costs. The article specifically mentions the advantage of having the financial institution in each keiretsu, which lowers the costs to member firms of acquiring financial capital.

Is it possible that the keiretsus can perform better for the industries and for consumers than more direct competition can? If the keiretsu members share profits, can their providing loans at below-market interest rates increase total profits? Can the sale of supplies by one member firm to another at below-market prices increase the profits of the keiretsu?

Suppose one firm has two divisions, one that raises cattle and one that sells hamburgers. Can this firm increase its profits by having its first division sell the cattle to the second division at a low price? The answer is no—the firm loses potential profits by selling the cattle at below-market prices when it could be selling to competitors at a higher price. If the firm is able to sell its hamburgers at a low price because it buys the beef at a low price, perhaps it can run others out of business and earn monopoly profits that way. However, unless it can somehow restrict entry once it runs competitors out of business, that strategy will not increase its profits either.

As long as the market works, that is, as long as customers have complete information about the market and firms can enter an industry that experiences above-normal profits, the keiretsus cannot create more efficiencies for consumers and greater profits for firms. Only if there is some type of market imperfection or market failure that the keiretsus are able to overcome can they benefit industry without harming consumers. A market imperfection might be the result of a bank not knowing details about firms. In such a case, banks have to charge higher interest rates than if they knew these details. Perhaps the financial community and stockholders who are members of a keiretsu know more about the other firms in the keiretsu and thus are able to provide funds or goods at lower prices because of this knowledge. Another possible benefit of the keiretsu could be that it confers special name recognition on all member firms. Perhaps the huge size of the keiretsus (only six in all of Japan) provides special brand-name confidence to all member firms and thus increases the demand for all products produced by the keiretsu members over what would occur if they were all independent firms.

Although these factors could exist, evidence does not seem to indicate that they do exist. Without evidence indicating the cause of cost savings, it is difficult to see how the keiretsus benefits firms and consumers. It is far more likely that it benefits member firms at the expense of consumers.

13

The Economics
of Information:
A Real-World Analysis

FUNDAMENTAL QUESTIONS

1. How much information is the optimal amount?
2. How do people acquire information?
3. What real-world observations are the result of relaxing the assumption of perfect information?

When the Infiniti automobile was introduced in the 1980s, a series of television ads showed fields of grain blowing in the wind, ocean waves breaking on a beautiful beach, mountains, and other scenes apparently having nothing to do with an automobile. The car did not even appear in these ads. This and many other examples indicate that a great deal of consumer and firm behavior is not easily explained by the market-structure models we have discussed so far. Much advertising provides no explicit information, offering instead images, feelings, or attitudes to associate with a product or a firm. Many firms make substantial expenditures on what seem to be nonproductive items; they spend many times more on a building that is architecturally unique than would be necessary to purchase a functional, standard building; they spend many times more on insignias and symbols representing the firm than a simple listing of the firm's name would cost. These firms seem to create a much higher overhead than would be necessary to sell their products. Many firms provide extensive warranties or guarantees, or give cash rebates when they could offer the product at a lower price instead. Some people purchase items with high prices even when lower-priced products with equal quality are available. Some people work at jobs that pay less than they could earn elsewhere; some people are paid more than the value they contribute to the firm. People sometimes cheat, and firms sometimes behave fraudulently. All these and many more examples do not seem to be accounted for by the models of market structure.

Under perfect competition, consumers purchase products at the lowest possible price; there is no advertising, no excessive overhead, and no warranties or guarantees. Under monopoly, people purchase a single product and advertising is virtually nonexistent. With monopolistic competition and oligopoly, advertising may occur, but the advertising provides information only. Consumers purchase different products because the products are, in fact, physically different. With oligopoly, firms behave with their rivals in mind, but no firm, according to these market-structure models, deceives or cheats customers, and individuals are neither dishonest nor deceitful. How, then, do we explain our everyday observations to the contrary?

The problem is that our models have assumed that consumers and firms have perfect information, and the real world does not fit that model. Consumers and firms do *not* have perfect information and usually have to make decisions under varying degrees of uncertainty. You will find that studying firm and consumer behavior under conditions of imperfect knowledge helps you understand brand-name creation, product warranties, the structure of insurance policies, expenditures on sunk (unrecoverable) costs, conspicuous consumption, and other behaviors that do not seem logical in the context of our market-structure models.

I. THE OPTIMAL AMOUNT OF INFORMATION

How much information is the optimal amount?

Information is a scarce good and obtaining it is costly. To search out the best price or verify a warranty, for example, a consumer must forgo other activities. Because there is an opportunity cost to obtaining information, few consumers are likely to have perfect information about price or quality.

The initial stages of gathering information are not typically all that costly. You collect information from the newspaper or from friends or colleagues during normal conversation. The next step of gathering information is more costly. Perhaps you go to the library and examine the consumer magazines for their ratings of products, or you purchase these magazines. You then follow up with calls to manufacturers, to the Better Business Bureau, and to other agencies designed to provide information on products. The additional cost of each additional piece of information rises. At the same time, the marginal utility you get from gathering information declines as additional information is acquired. The first pieces of information are very beneficial: You learn about the product and about others' experiences with the product. The trip to the library provides more information. Further excursions seeking information provide less additional utility, however. (See the Economic Insight "Cognitive Abilities.") As you get more and more information, the marginal cost of collecting it rises very rapidly, and the marginal utility of the additional information is very low. Thus, with the marginal cost of information-gathering rising and the marginal utility of information-gathering falling, the marginal utility per dollar of expenditure on gathering information declines as additional information is collected (diminishing marginal utility). This is shown in Figure 1(a) as the declining curve MU_I/P_I.

You learned in earlier chapters that consumer equilibrium is reached when the marginal utility per dollar of expenditure on an item is equal to the marginal utility per dollar of expenditure on all other items. Suppose that the marginal utility per dollar of expenditure on all other items is the upward-sloping line labeled MU_N/P_N in Figure 1(a). It slopes up because as more information is acquired, and thus fewer other goods and services, the marginal utility of those other goods rises (diminishing marginal utility). Consumer equilibrium occurs when the MU_I/P_I curve intersects the MU_N/P_N line.

It is virtually inconceivable that consumer equilibrium would occur at a point where the consumer has perfect information. Most likely the equilibrium point occurs when the consumer has far less than 100 percent of the information, as illustrated in Figure 1. This means that making decisions with imperfect knowledge and uncertainty is rational. It would simply be too costly to have complete information about everything when information is not free. It would be irrational to seek perfect information.

The optimal amount of information is the amount that equates the marginal cost of acquiring information to the marginal benefit.

Figure 1(a) is more commonly drawn as shown in Figure 1(b) where the marginal costs and marginal benefits of information-gathering are compared. In Figure 1(b), the marginal cost of information-gathering is the upward-sloping curve MC and marginal benefit of information-gathering is the down-

Figure 1
The Optimal Amount of Information

Figure 1(a) illustrates the consumer equilibrium point. The additional cost of each additional piece of information rises—in other words, the marginal cost of information-gathering rises. At the same time, the marginal utility of information-gathering declines as additional information is acquired. Thus, the ratio of the marginal utility per dollar of expenditure on information declines as additional information is gathered. Consumer equilibrium occurs when the ratios of marginal utility per dollar of expenditure on any good or activity are equal. The consumer's optimization point lies where the consumer has far less than 100 percent of the information. This point is also illustrated in Figure 1(b), where the marginal benefits of acquiring information are equated to the marginal costs of acquiring information.

(a) Marginal Utility

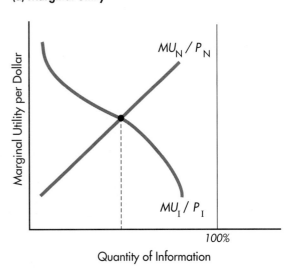

(b) Marginal Costs and Benefits

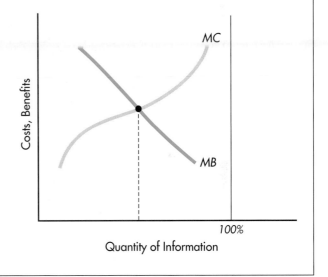

ward-sloping curve *MB*. The marginal costs reflect the sum of the direct and opportunity costs of devoting additional resources to information-gathering. The marginal benefit curve measures the marginal utility of making better-informed decisions, avoiding costly mistakes, and simply feeling better about a decision. The intersection of the marginal-benefit and marginal-cost curves indicates the optimal amount of information, an amount less than 100 percent of the information.

The optimal amount of information collected applies to the firm as well as to the individual. A profit-maximizing firm will gather information up to the point where the marginal cost of additional information just equals the mar-

Information is valuable and it's often costly to obtain. The assumption of perfect competition allows us to simplify; but in reality few consumers know everything about the items they purchase. In this picture, a woman is comparison shopping for cars. She has purchased a *Consumer Report* magazine that compares several sedans and she is taking several trips to local car dealers. Although well-informed by the time she makes her purchase, she still will not have perfect information. At some point, it is not worth the extra time and expense necessary to learn a little more about the cars.

asymmetric information: when participants to an economic transaction have different information about the transaction

ginal benefit of acquiring additional information. The firm, like the individual, will not have perfect information. Moreover, not all economic participants necessarily have the same information. Some consumers seek more information than others, and businesses may have different information than consumers. These situations are called **asymmetric information**.

RECAP

1. The assumption of perfect information does not capture the real world wherein information is costly to acquire.

2. The optimal amount of information is acquired when the marginal utility of additional information per dollar of expenditure is equal to the marginal utility of devoting one dollar of expenditure to any other good or activity. It is also the point where the marginal benefit and marginal cost of additional information are equal.

2. THE ACQUISITION OF INFORMATION: COMMUNICATION AND SIGNALING

How do people acquire information?

Since information is costly to acquire, consumers and firms do not have complete, or perfect, information. As a result, they need to choose among ways to obtain information. The models of the market structures discussed in previous chapters suggest how firms and individuals acquire information: they find the method that provides the greatest revenues at the lowest costs—that is, they acquire the information in the most efficient manner possible. Firms provide the information consumers want and are willing to pay for as long as there is a profit in providing that information. Consumers purchase informa-

Cognitive Abilities

For decades, psychologists have studied how people process information, that is, what their cognitive abilities and limitations are. Without perfect information, people may make decisions that seem irrational, or they may use simple rules of thumb (called *heuristics*) that would seem to make no sense if they had perfect information. For instance, psychologists have found that often consider *out-of-pocket expenses* to be losses while looking at *opportunity costs* as forgone gains. What this means is that people consider the out-of-pocket expenses to be more important than opportunity costs. For example, receiving a $2,000 cash rebate on a $20,000 automobile may be seen as a better deal than buying the same automobile for $18,000. When the consumer pays $20,000, the $2,000 price difference would be a forgone opportunity. The $2,000 rebate, on the other hand, is an in-the-pocket gain. People like to segregate gains. They want the price of the car and the price of the rebate to be separate.

Psychologists have also found that people tend to place more value on large gains combined with small losses than on a smaller gain even when the net amount gained is the same. For instance, most consumers would prefer to win $100 on a radio call-in show the same day they ruin an $80 pair of slacks than to win $20, everything else the same. The gain is the same, $20, but most people choose the larger win. People like to offset a small loss with a larger gain than to simply have the gain be smaller. Marketing managers have found also that people find losses less painful when combined than when experienced separately. A $12,000 swimming pool seems less expensive when included in the $200,000 house price than if purchased separately from the house.

Another interesting situation involves sunk costs. An experiment by economist Richard Thaler had a local pizza parlor offer an all-you-can-eat lunch for $3. He randomly selected half the tables to receive their admission charges back before eating; the other half had to pay the $3. The amount each group ate was different. Surprisingly, the group that received the refunds ate significantly *less* than the other group. Yet the marginal cost of each slice was the same for the two groups; the $3 was simply a sunk cost. Behavior should have been the same.

Many families have swimming pools in their backyards. Often people say that they feel bad when no one in the family uses the pool during a day. Yet the pool is a sunk cost; increased or decreased use means nothing as far as that sunk cost goes. When informed of this, people usually alter their opinion.

Sources. Amos Tversky and Daniel Kahneman, "The Framing of Decisions and the Psychology of Choice," *Science* (1981), pp. 453–458; and "Judgment Under Uncertainty: Heuristics and Biases," *Science* (1974), pp. 1124–1131; R. Thaler, "Toward a Positive Theory of Consumer Choice," *Journal of Economic Behavior*, 1980; and "Mental Accounting and Consumer Choice," *Marketing Science*, vol. 4 (1985); Robert H. Frank, *Microeconomics and Behavior* (New York: McGraw-Hill, 1991), pp. 226–244.

tion up to the point where the marginal utility per dollar of expenditure on information is equal to the marginal utility per dollar of expenditure on any other good.

2.a. Information as a Product

Information has value. If an entrepreneur can provide information to those demanding the information at a lower price than can be obtained elsewhere, the entrepreneur can make a profit providing that information. Similarly, if a firm can provide better information, or less costly information, about its product than its competitors can, then that firm will earn higher profits. A firm will provide information through signals that consumers can use to differentiate company products.

Recognition, reliability, and public confidence are valuable commodities to a firm. Firms may devote considerable sums of money to advertising and location, even an entire building, in order to make a statement to consumers: "we are here, we are stable, we are reliable, and we will be here in the future." The NBC building in Chicago is one of the more distinctive buildings in the Chicago skyline. To ensure that the public associates the building with the company, NBC's peacock adorns the top of the building.

2.b. Brand Names

A firm can provide information to consumers by creating brand names. A brand name is a product that consumers associate with a specific firm: Vidal Sassoon hair care products, Gloria Vanderbilt clothes, Bayer aspirin, McDonald's, and Nike, rather than the names shampoo, jeans, aspirin, fast food, and athletic shoes. If consumers had perfect information, producers would have no incentive to create brand names or to differentiate products other than by actual physical characteristics. But when products are physically identical and consumers know that, how can economic theory explain why the products have different names? It is also difficult to explain why advertising focuses on image and attitude. What information about the Infiniti automobile was given by television advertising showing fields of grain, ocean waves, and mountains but not the car itself? The answer is, of course, that consumers do *not* have perfect information, and thus brand names serve as *signals*—indications of the quality of the product or of the firm producing and selling the product. The brand name is also such a signal; it provides some degree of information to consumers.

Consider the case of sidewalk vendors who sell neckties on the streets of any large city. If such a "firm" tells customers that it will guarantee the quality of its ties, customers will certainly question the validity of the guarantee since if the firm decides to go out of business, it can do so with virtually no losses. It has no headquarters, no brand name, no costly capital equipment, no loyal customers to worry about—indeed, no sunk, or unrecoverable, costs of any kind. In short, a firm with no obvious stake in the future has a difficult time persuading potential customers it will make good on its promises.

The incentives are different for a firm that has devoted significant resources to items that have no liquidation value, such as advertising campaigns or specific capital expenditures like McDonald's golden arches. These firms will do everything they can to remain in business. And buyers, knowing that, can place greater trust in the promise of a high-quality product.

Businesses, then, purchase advertising time and space on television, on radio, and in the newspapers. They construct elaborate signs, build fancy storefronts, and attempt to locate in places where they are visible and accessible. They also package their products in carefully designed boxes and wrappings. All of these expenditures are intended to convince people that their products, identified by brand names, mean something. These expenditures are sunk costs, but they indicate to the consumer that the firm is here to stay, that its products are backed by the existence of the firm.

Many people claim that marketing and advertising create phony or artificial distinctions among products and that the benefits conferred by brand names are illusory. These critics note that there may be no difference between Tide laundry detergent and the generic detergent sold under the grocery store's label, that Ralph Lauren's Polo brand shirts may be constructed of exactly the same fabric and knit design as several less-expensive brands, and that aspirin is aspirin whether or not it is Bayer.

Consumers are nonetheless often willing to pay a higher price for a brand-name product than for a similar product without a brand name because the brand name signals something valuable. Consumers who purchase brand-name pharmaceuticals because they believe the brand name has some value may be right even if a brand-name pharmaceutical and a generic product are chemically identical. Drug companies that spend a great deal of money to create brand names may be less likely to create shoddy or dangerous products than firms that do not offer brand names. When President Clinton was describing the cause of high health care costs, he blamed the drug companies. Supporting his contention, a congressional study pointed out that drug firms spend $10 billion per year on marketing and advertising, $2 billion more than they spend on developing new drugs. But this expenditure may be what is necessary to provide the information consumers want—the sunk costs necessary to provide quality assurance to consumers.[1]

2.c. Guarantees

Another way to inform consumers of the quality of the product is to provide a guarantee against product defects. Guarantees are difficult to fake. A low-quality product would break down frequently, making the guarantee quite costly for the firm. Thus, the higher the quality of the product, the better the guarantee offered by the firm.

In addition to providing information about quality, guarantees force competitors to disclose information about the relative quality of their product. Once the highest-quality product appears with its guarantee, consumers have

---

[1]Sommer, Constance, "Drug firms' 'Excess Profit': $2 Billion Yearly," *Los Angeles Times*, Feb. 26, 1993.

some information about the quality of that product—and also about the quality of all remaining products. They know that products without guarantees are not of the highest quality. Without other information about a product that has no guarantee, consumers might assume the quality of that product to be no better than the average quality of all such products. This places the producer of the second-best product in a difficult position. If it continues to offer no guarantee, consumers will think its product is worse than it really is, but its guarantee cannot match that of the highest-quality product. Thus, the producer of the second-best product must offer a guarantee of its own, but the terms of its guarantee cannot be quite as good as those for the best product.

With the introduction of the guarantee on the highest-quality product, the competitive process is set in motion and in the end all producers must either offer guarantees or live with the knowledge that consumers rank their products lower in quality. The terms of the guarantees will in general be less liberal the lower a product's quality. Producers clearly do not want to announce their low-quality levels by offering stingy warranty coverage, but failure to offer something makes consumers think the quality level is even lower than it is.

RECAP

1. Firms will provide information if they can obtain a profit by doing so, and consumers have incentives to obtain information up to a point.
2. Often the least expensive means of providing information is through signals, indicators of information like brand names and guarantees.

3. ADVERSE SELECTION AND MORAL HAZARD

In some transactions, signals are not economically viable—they can be easily faked or there is no incentive for participants to provide full disclosure. Such circumstances arise under adverse selection and moral hazard.

3.a. Adverse Selection

What real-world observations are the result of relaxing the assumption of perfect information?

adverse selection:
the situation that occurs when higher-quality consumers or producers are driven out of the market because unobservable qualities are misvalued

When you purchase a used car, you are probably unsure of the car's quality. You could hire a mechanic to look at the car before you buy it, but because that procedure is quite expensive, you may choose to forgo it. Most people assume that cars offered for sale by private individuals are defective in some way, and they are not willing to pay top dollar because they expect that the car will need expensive repairs. As a result of asymmetric information, people who do have high-quality used cars for sale cannot obtain the high price they deserve.

Adverse selection occurs when unobservable qualities are misvalued because of a lack of information. People with high-quality used cars are most likely to trade their cars in to a dealer, leaving lower-quality used cars for sale by nondealers. The result of adverse selection is that low-quality consumers or producers drive higher-quality consumers or producers out of the market.

Adverse selection occurs in many markets. Banks do not always know which people applying for loans will default and which will pay on time.

How can a bank distinguish among loan applicants? If the bank increases the interest rate in an attempt to drive high-risk applicants out of the market, adverse selection increases. As the bank raises the interest rate on loans, high-risk applicants continue to apply for loans but high-quality applicants do not. As a result, only high-risk applicants remain in the market. What is the bank to do?

Adverse selection occurs in insurance markets as well. People purchase automobile or health insurance even if they are excellent drivers and enjoy good health. As the cost of insurance rises, the good drivers and healthy people might reduce their coverage while the poor drivers and unhealthy people maintain their coverage. As a result, high-risk applicants take the place of more desirable low-risk applicants in the market for insurance. What is the insurance company to do?

3.a.1. Down Payments and Deductibles Adverse selection gives rise to certain types of behavior that would not exist if information were free. It explains why loan companies require down payments, and why insurance companies require copayments or deductibles. Rather than increasing interest rates to eliminate high-risk applicants, a bank might request a higher down payment. Since only people who expect to pay off the loan and who have sufficient wealth or income to pay off the loan are willing to provide the down payment, adverse selection is reduced. The bank gets the borrower to devote sunk (unrecoverable) costs to the loan. Similarly, by requiring that a borrower provide collateral (a house or car or some other asset), a bank can separate high-risk from low-risk applicants. And an insurance company may require a policyholder to carry a deductible—the policyholder agrees to pay the first $300, say, of damage to his or her car. When an insurance company reduces the insurance charge and increases the deductible, good drivers and healthy people are more willing to purchase insurance, and poor drivers and less healthy people are less willing.

3.a.2. Statistical Discrimination Because of the problem of adverse selection, firms are under pressure to get all the information they possibly can about potential buyers and employees. These pressures often translate into the phenomenon of **statistical discrimination**, whereby group attributes are incorrectly applied to individuals. In insurance markets, for example, two people will often pay different premiums even though their driving records are identical. For instance, males between the ages of eighteen and twenty-five pay higher rates than females of the same age and higher rates than the rest of the male population. Similarly, employers will often pay different wages to otherwise identical members of groups. For instance, before the practice became illegal, males were paid more than females for the same job.

Employers must try to predict the potential productivity of job applicants, but rarely do they know what a worker's actual productivity will be. Often the only information available when they hire someone is information that may be imperfectly related to productivity in general and may not apply to a particular person at all. Reliance on indicators of productivity such as education, experience, age, and test scores may keep some very good people from getting a job and may result in the hiring of some unproductive people. This is statistical discrimination.

Statistical discrimination may help explain the earnings disparities between men and women. Childless women earn substantially less than men simply because women bear children. Many childless women did not know

statistical discrimination: when group attributes are incorrectly applied to individuals

that they would be childless, and the subjects they studied in school as well as the jobs they took upon leaving school probably did not differ much from those of other women. Similarly, prospective employers were unlikely to know which young women would have children and which would not. This uncertainty affected employers' willingness to provide training opportunities or to make other investments in job-related human capital. Because the odds are great that a woman will leave a job for some period of time to have a child, simply being a woman provides a signal to a firm. As a result of this signal, the wage offered a man might be higher than that offered a woman, or the job offered a man might contain better training than the one offered a woman. This difference occurs simply because the odds are better that the man will not choose to leave the job for a period of time.

The law that states that job interviewers cannot inquire about the marital or family status of the interviewee solves little because of the incentive for interviewees to voluntarily disclose information. Consider a job candidate who has no intention of leaving her job to raise a family or who may be unable to have children. That candidate has an incentive to provide the information to the interviewer. This, of course, places other interviewees in the position of having to provide some information or having the interviewer assume they all will have the average tendency to leave the job at some stage.

3.b. Moral Hazard

moral hazard:
when people alter their behavior from what was anticipated when a transaction was made

When information is costly to obtain, monitoring the behavior of the other party in an exchange may be difficult. When verification of trades or contracts is difficult and when people can change their behavior from what was anticipated when a trade or contract was made, a **moral hazard** exists.

People who discover that they have a serious illness and then purchase health insurance are taking advantage of the insurance company's lack of information and creating a moral hazard. A person who drives much less carefully after obtaining car insurance is creating a moral hazard. A person who takes less care to be healthy after obtaining health insurance is creating a moral hazard. A doctor who gives patient care short shrift because he or she has malpractice insurance is creating a moral hazard.

Sometimes moral hazard can be reduced when the person or firm creating the moral hazard and the person or firm being taken advantage of share in the costs. This is another reason why insurance companies require a deductible, so that the company and the customer share in expenses and risks. You are more likely to drive carefully and safeguard your health if you have to pay some of the costs of an accident or illness.

Sometimes, however, it is impossible to distinguish those who create a moral hazard from those who do not. How can an insurance company ensure that a doctor will not commit medical malpractice? It cannot, and as a result doctors in some small towns and in certain specialties (such as obstetrics) cannot even purchase malpractice insurance. What can a doctor do to prove to an insurance company that he or she is not a medical malpractice risk? Very little. Purchasing an expensive sign or building a reputation for quality care does not alter the possibility that the doctor might change his or her behavior after obtaining insurance. Some physicians have responded to the situation by entering a group practice. Group practice refers to the situation where a group of physicians, each with different specialties, organizes into one firm. The firm is then insured because the members of the firm are sharing the risk. The riskiest members must provide some compensation to the less risky members of the group, say through profit-sharing arrangements. Through the risk-sharing, the statistical discrimination is reduced.

3.b.1. Excessive CEO Salaries   Frederick Taylor, the father of scientific management, understood the principle of moral hazard in employment back in 1929 when he wrote that it would be difficult to find a competent worker who does not devote a considerable amount of time to studying just how slowly he can work and still convince his employer that he is going at a good pace.[2] This is not to say that workers are incompetent or unethical, but simply that they have an incentive to *shirk* on the job. Shirking means not doing what you are assigned to do or doing less than your share of the task. Many institutions (customs, habits, rites) have evolved to reduce this moral hazard problem inside firms.

During the period from 1990 to 1993, when most people were experiencing slow or no income growth, there were many critics of the very high pay received by CEOs (chief executive officers) of companies, especially companies that were not performing well. It is possible, however, that the high pay played a role other than to reward the productivity of the CEO; perhaps it was a signal providing information to all employees. If employees see that a firm pays its top executives very high salaries, then employees may work harder in order to be in line for promotions.

Evidence that the pay scale does affect performance is provided by golf tournaments.[3] The average performance in professional golf tournaments varies with the payoff structure of the tournaments. As a whole, players perform better in those tournaments having the greatest first-place payoff and the greatest difference between first and second, second and third, and so on down the line. The contest is more intense because of the added incentives to perform well. Similarly, those firms having the greatest CEO pay and the greatest differential between the pay of top executives and other employees may find the overall productivity of all employees to be higher than firms having a more equal salary distribution.

3.b.2. Efficiency Wages   Figure 2 shows a labor market and indicates the demand for and supply of workers at each wage rate. The equilibrium wage is determined at W_e. Suppose the labor market depicted in Figure 2 is a manufacturing line, where it is difficult to tell exactly how much work any one employee is doing. Then workers have an incentive to shirk on the job and to rely on other workers to pick up the slack. There is a moral hazard problem in this labor market: a worker may be hired and paid according to expected productivity but then change his or her behavior and become dishonest or lazy. If discovered, the shirking worker is fired. But since the dismissed worker can find another job at the equilibrium wage, there is little disciplinary action resulting from the firing—little incentive for other workers not to shirk.

---

[2]Frederick Taylor, *The Principles of Scientific Management* (New York: Harper, 1929).
[3]Ehrenberg, Ronald G. and Bognamo, Michael L., "Do Tournaments Have Incentive Effects?" *Journal of Political Economy*, 98 (December 1990) pp. 1307–34.

Figure 2
Efficiency Wages
Figure 2 illustrates a labor market with the demand for and the supply of workers at each wage rate. The equilibrium wage is determined at W_e. There is a moral hazard problem in this labor market: the worker is hired and paid according to expected productivity but then changes his or her behavior and becomes dishonest or lazy. If discovered, the shirking worker is fired. But since the dismissed worker can find another job at the equilibrium wage, little disciplinary effect on the remaining workers results from the firing. Employers know that this situation creates an incentive for all workers to shirk, so ways to offset the shirking are devised. A firm that cannot identify whether an employee is contributing more than his or her share or is shirking and allowing other members of the team to carry his or her share might pay a wage that exceeds the equilibrium wage. This is called an efficiency wage. The high, or efficiency, wage, W_h, reduces employment from equilibrium Q_e to Q_h. Now, dismissed employees will be at least temporarily unemployed, raising their costs of shirking.

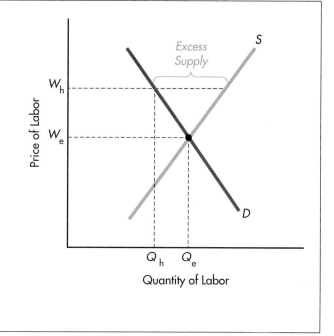

efficiency wages:
wages that are higher than equilibrium wages in order to elicit a certain type of behavior

Employers know that this situation creates an incentive for *all* workers to shirk. They thus devise means to offset the shirking. A firm may attempt to build a reputation as a great firm to work for, one that does not lay off workers even during recessions. Then if fired, the worker loses a job that has benefits not matched by the next job. Another approach is to pay **efficiency wages**. A firm that cannot identify whether an employee is contributing more than his or her share or is shirking and allowing other members of the team to carry his or her share might pay a wage that exceeds the equilibrium wage—called an efficiency wage. By paying an efficiency wage, the firm retains its high-quality, highly trained workers. An employee might fear that being identified as a shirker will lead to losing a job that provides higher compensation than is available elsewhere.

If all firms pay wages that exceed the equilibrium wage, then dismissal will not harm employees if the dismissed people can find other jobs relatively easily. However, as noted in Figure 2, the high, or efficiency, wage, W_h, reduces employment from equilibrium Q_e to Q_h. In this case, dismissed employees will be at least temporarily unemployed, raising their costs of shirking.

RECAP

1. Adverse selection occurs when low-quality consumers or producers force higher-quality consumers or producers out of the market.

2. Moral hazard exists when people alter their behavior in an unanticipated way after an agreement or contract has been defined.

4. THE OPTIMAL AMOUNT OF FRAUD

If consumers and firms had complete, or perfect, information they would have no incentive to cheat, to act fraudulently, or to deceive others. In fact, they could not deceive others because everyone would have perfect information. But with the imperfect, or incomplete, information that characterizes the real world, some firms act fraudulently and some individuals cheat in order to gain more profits or income. Incidents of fraudulent behavior are reported often: we hear of Salomon Brothers cheating in the U.S. government bond market, of Michael Milkin selling junk bonds, of Charles Keating deceiving his savings and loan customers, of Congress's misuse of banking and mailing privileges, of improper actions for pay or favors, and so on. And we know individuals who cheat in class, who shoplift, or who engage in unethical behavior. We have just finished talking about moral hazard, which is, very simply, cheating or fraudulent behavior. Employees shirk on the job and people alter their behavior when insured; these are also examples of cheating. These behaviors would not occur if everyone had perfect information.

We can use the framework of Figure 1(b), as shown in Figure 3, to illustrate why cheating occurs. Given the ethics and laws of a society, there are certain costs to cheating. It is likely that the marginal costs of cheating rise—the initial unethical event is likely to go undetected, but as additional events occur, the likelihood of detection and punishment rises. Thus, the marginal-cost curve slopes up. The marginal-benefit curve of cheating slopes down as the additional profit or income acquired as a result of increasing amounts of unethical behavior declines. The optimal amount of fraud or cheating is given by the intersection of the marginal-cost and marginal-benefit curves.

The optimal amount of fraud is neither 100 percent fraudulent behavior nor 100 percent nonfraudulent behavior. In a world of imperfect information, a certain amount of cheating will occur. The greater the marginal costs of

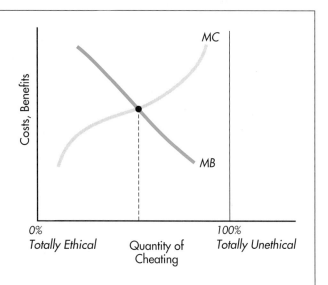

Figure 3
The Optimal Amount of Cheating
The marginal costs and marginal benefits of fraud or cheating are illustrated. The marginal costs rise as the probability of detection and the opportunity cost of lost reputation rises. The marginal benefits decline as additional cheating occurs. The optimal amount of cheating occurs where marginal costs and marginal benefits are equal, $MC = MB$. The optimal amount is neither 100 percent fraud nor 100 percent free of fraud.

cheating, however, the less cheating that will occur. For instance, it is likely that if the professor leaves the room during an exam, more cheating will occur than if the professor and several other monitors remain in the room during the exam. This example suggests that to reduce cheating, the punishment, if detection occurs, must be credible and severe. Another example: the governments of many countries have announced that they will not bargain with terrorists, even when hostages have been taken and their lives threatened. This policy is designed to prevent terrorism because if the potential terrorists know that governments will not negotiate with them, they have no incentive to participate in the terrorist acts. However, if the threat is not credible—if one or more governments do negotiate—then the amount of terrorist activity will rise. Parents face the same dilemma each day with their children. Their threats to ground the kids, or to give them "a punishment you won't forget," work to reduce the undesired activity only if the threats are credible.

We have discussed some of the mechanisms that have developed to reduce the moral hazard problem. In addition to these we could add increased policing or monitoring of activities. Sometimes the idea is to prevent inappropriate behavior by catching it before it occurs. For example, U.S. corporations are not allowed to publish financial statements until the statements are verified by independent accounting firms (auditors), and automobile insurance firms require more than one estimate on the repair of damaged autos. In other cases, an attempt is made to reduce the chance that inappropriate behavior will go undetected. Workers often have to punch in and out on a time clock. Cash rewards are often provided for whistle blowers, to induce employees to monitor the behavior of other employees.

There are, however, situations where monitoring is too expensive. In these cases we might find an incentive contract, such as when the CEO of a firm is given a bonus based on the performance of the firm, or when employees are paid according to the output of their department or unit. Another means to reduce moral hazard is the posting of performance bonds. A performance bond is a sum of money someone must offer to another to ensure that an action will be performed. Failure to perform this action results in forfeiture of the money. For instance, when someone is accused of a crime, that person may be released from jail after the posting of a bond. The bond is an attempt to ensure a certain behavior, the return of the accused person for trial. A performance bond is often required by employers to ensure the behavior of employees. For instance, you see independent contractors advertise that they are bonded; baby-sitting firms also indicate that their employees are bonded. These firms may require bonds from their employees and the firms will post a performance bond with an insurance company or an industry or government organization.

RECAP

1. Fraud and cheating will occur in a market economy. The amount depends on the marginal costs and marginal benefits of cheating or fraudulent behavior.

2. Certain behaviors arise to offset cheating: deductibles and copayments that reduce moral hazard; auditors; multiple estimates of costs; whistle blowers; incentive contracts and performance bonds.

5. A SUMMARY OF MARKET STRUCTURE AND BEHAVIOR UNDER UNCERTAINTY

The four models of market structure discussed so far explain many but not all market behaviors. The behaviors not explained are those that arise when information is costly to obtain.

The model of perfect competition assumes that entry is easy and that there are a large number of firms. This model cannot explain advertising, product differentiation, or many other real-world events. It does, however, provide a picture of how the market system functions and how efficiency is obtained. The model of monopolistic competition accounts for the existence of advertising that provides information to consumers but not for image advertising. If information were widely and freely available, a firm would derive no value from an advertisement suggesting that product A provides a better feeling than product B because all consumers would already know which product produces which feeling. Similarly, expenditures to create brand names, incentive contracts, performance bonds, and other institutions that exist in the real world arise because of imperfect information. Monopolistically competitive firms have to use these means to differentiate their products.

The market model of monopoly explains the existence of a sole supplier, price discrimination, and the regulation of natural monopolies, but fails to describe why firms behave in anticompetitive or fraudulent ways to achieve a monopoly. And oligopoly accounts for strategic behavior and strategic deterrence, but does not describe why guarantees or performance bonds exist. With imperfect information we might expect some cases where firms act so as to acquire above-normal profit in fraudulent, or what are often referred to as anticompetitive, ways.

When the assumption of perfect information is relaxed, we must deal with consumers and firms that are making decisions under uncertainty. As we have described, they will employ many behaviors intended to communicate information at a low cost and to acquire information. But they will not acquire perfect information. As a result, they must select a strategy, or course of action, based on the information at hand and the expectations of what others will do. Depending on the marginal costs and benefits, individuals and firms will engage in some fraudulent or unethical behaviors such as shirking or misleading advertising. And depending on the marginal costs and benefits, institutions will evolve to offset these behaviors. Guarantees, performance bonds, image advertising, pay scales, and other real-world events can be explained using the models of market structure along with costly information.

RECAP

1. The assumption that information is costless in the market-structure models means that some real-world observations cannot be explained. Such observations include the collateral required to secure loans, the deductibles required on insurance, the existence of image advertising, and the importance of brand names. The assumption that information is costly to obtain allows economists to explain these real-world observations within the market-structure models of competition, monopoly, and oligopoly.

SUMMARY

▲▼ How much information is the optimal amount?

1. The optimal amount of information is the amount at which the marginal utility per dollar of expenditure on acquiring additional information is equal to the marginal utility per dollar of expenditure on any other good or activity. The optimal amount of information can also be represented as the point where the marginal costs and marginal benefits of acquiring additional information are equal. §1

▲▼ How do people acquire information?

2. Information has value. Thus, entrepreneurs will provide some information. §2.a

3. Firms attempt to provide signals that portray information about products or services. Such signals include brand names, advertising expenditures, and other sunk costs. §2.b

▲▼ What real-world observations are the result of relaxing the assumption of perfect information?

4. Brand names, image advertising, copayments, down payments, warranties, guarantees, efficiency wages, wage structures within a firm,

performance bonds, and forms of statistical discrimination all result because of imperfect information. §all sections

5. Adverse selection occurs when low-quality consumers or producers force higher-quality consumers or producers out of the market. §3.a

6. Adverse selection results in down payments, deductibles, and other business practices that would make no sense in a world of perfect information. §3.a.1

7. Statistical discrimination exists when the attributes of a group are attributed incorrectly to an individual. §3.a.2

8. Moral hazard exists when people alter their behavior in an unanticipated way after an agreement or contract has been defined. §3.b

9. Efficiency wages are wages that are above the equilibrium wage with the objective of attracting the best employees and minimizing shirking. §3.b.2

10. The optimal amount of fraud or cheating occurs when the marginal costs and marginal benefits of cheating are equal. §4

KEY TERMS

asymmetric information §1
adverse selection §3.a
statistical discrimination §3.a.2

moral hazard §3.b
efficiency wages §3.b.2

EXERCISES

1. Using the marginal-utility-per-dollar-of-expenditure curve, explain why the assumption of perfect information is not realistic. Do the same using the marginal costs and marginal benefits of acquiring information curves. How much information will the rational consumer acquire?

2. What would occur if any maker of aspirin could put a Bayer Aspirin label on its product? Why must a signal between rivals be costly to fake and involve extensive sunk costs?

3. Explain why image advertising provides information.

4. Several studies have shown that when brakes and headlights were first placed on cars, more accidents involving pedestrians occurred. Similarly, the requirement of seatbelts and power-assisted and automatic braking systems have led to an increased incidence of pedestrian-automobile accidents. Explain how this is a moral hazard situation.

5. Explain why a law restricting the information that can be acquired during an interview might not be effective.

6. What is statistical discrimination? Why does it arise? What form might statistical discrimination take in the real estate industry in terms of housing sales by geographic region?

7. What is the basis for believing that a priest is less likely to cheat in a game of cards than a used-car salesperson?

8. Explain why an insurance company lowers the cost of the insurance as the deductible on the policy rises.

9. Suppose faculty were paid on the basis of the performance of their students—the more students learned, the higher the faculty member's reward. Suppose also that to ensure that students performed as well as possible, the professor required students to provide a performance bond. Would this result in better performance? Explain why or why not.

10. Suppose you purchase some electronic equipment from a discount store in your city. The salesperson offers you an extended warranty on your equipment that is backed by the store. Does this warranty provide information to you? Do you purchase the warranty?

11. The economist Milton Friedman once said that the only ethical thing we need to demand from businesses is that they maximize profit. Some business professors have claimed that markets are unethical and are deeply disturbed by Friedman's statement. Explain what Friedman meant, using the model of perfect competition and perfect information. Does his statement lose any credibility when costly information is assumed instead of perfect information?

12. One definition of ethics is efficiency. Another is the absence of any unethical behavior. Using the idea that information is costly to acquire, describe what ethical behavior is according to the economic efficiency standard.

13. Explain what will happen to the insurance company that charges males ages eighteen to twenty-five the same rate as all other customers.

14. According to some, J.C. Penney was the first store to use odd-lot pricing, that is, pricing at $6.99 rather than $7.00. Supposedly, Penney did this to minimize cheating on the part of his employees. Can you explain his strategy?

15. Shoplifting accounts for about 10 percent of the costs of goods sold retail. In more and more stores, items are attached to the goods that unless taken off will sound an alarm when the item is taken from the store. Explain, using the marginal-cost and marginal-benefit curves of Figure 3, how this policy might reduce shoplifting.

Profits, Risks Sustain Credit Card Rates

To explain why banks have kept their credit card rates high while other interest rates have fallen, one need look no further than the banks' balance sheets—and at consumers' behavior.

As the recession took hold, banks began suffering huge losses from business and commercial real estate loan defaults. Since credit card operations were among banks' most profitable operations, banks had tremendous incentive to keep card rates high to offset those losses.

At the same time, analysts say consumers have remained remarkably quiet about the fact that credit card rates have been far higher than other rates. In fact, until the last year the number of credit cards in circulation continued to grow.

The banks' practice of borrowing money at one rate and lending it back out at a higher rate is called playing the spread. It also is the basic theory of banking and is why banks are in business.

On the short term, banks borrow from a variety of sources.

Usually banks pay rates tied to the rate charged by the Federal Reserve Bank, the nation's central bank and chief monetary policy maker. This rate is called the Fed Funds rate. Since January 1990, the Fed Funds rate has dropped from 8.23 percent to 3.73 percent, a decline of 55 percent.

Another source of money for banks is consumers' deposits. As the Fed Funds rate has dropped, banks have lowered the rates they pay consumers for these deposits. The rate for one-year certificates of deposit, for instance, has fallen 48 percent during the same period, from 7.94 percent to 4.15 percent.

Banks have been lending this money out at rates that have not declined to the same degree.

The prime rate, the rate banks charge their most creditworthy business customers for loans, has fallen 36 percent, from 10.11 in January 1990 to 6.5 percent now.

Auto loans have dropped 16 percent, to 9.89 percent.

Mortgage loans, which are tied more to the bond market than the Federal Reserve bank, have fallen 10.6 percent in that same two-year period, from 9.9 percent to 8.85 percent.

And credit card rates have actually risen during that time, from 18.6 percent to 18.63 percent.

David Bowers, head of the finance department at Case Western Reserve University's Weatherhead School of Management, makes this point in regards to the numbers.

Bankers "are supposed to earn as much as they can wherever they can, otherwise the stockholders should fire them."

Bowers puts part of the blame for the high rates on consumers— they're bad shoppers. Instead of switching to cards with lower rates, they have kept their high-rate cards.

He also points out that some people are lousy credit risks and should pay higher interest rates because of it.

But the spread doesn't translate into pure profit. Bookkeeping costs are high and so are losses from those who don't pay, said banking analyst Paul Markey of Dean Witter Reynolds Inc. in New York.

"People would like to think it's all profit, but that just isn't the case," Markey said.

As the fast-growing credit card industry extended credit to more people, it took on more risk, Markey said—and more bad risks.

In the last 10 years, the number of bank credit cards in customers' wallets grew by 219 percent to 263.2 million. But debt on those cards grew even faster—285 percent, to $234 billion.

The growth apparently has been too much.

In the past few years, credit card delinquencies have increased from 2 percent of outstanding debt to around 5 percent, Markey said. Personal bankruptcies grew fourfold during the period to 872,438 in 1991.

Source: Stuart Brown, "Profits, Risks Sustain Credit Card Rates," *Akron Beacon Journal*, May 18, 1992, p. D1. Reprinted by permission of the Akron Beacon Journal. © 1993 Akron Beacon Journal.

Akron Beacon Journal/May 18, 1992

Commentary

Over the past couple of years, interest rates on Treasury bills, commercial loans, certificates of deposit, and other money and capital market instruments have declined substantially. Between May 1989 and March 1993, the prime rate charged by commercial banks dropped from 11.5 percent to about 6 percent, and the interest rate on large-denomination six-month CDs fell from around 9 percent to about 3 percent.

The typical credit card borrower, however, has seen no corresponding decline in card interest rates. Although there is substantial diversity in card rates, the average remains stubbornly high, at about 17 percent. This recent stickiness of credit card rates repeats a familiar story. During several episodes in the 1980s, when other interest rates rose or fell, credit card rates changed little.

This feature of the credit card market is all the more intriguing considering the structure of that industry. The credit card industry consists of many firms offering an identical product, and entry is very easy. This sounds like the market structure model of perfect competition. Ordinarily, such a market structure leads to competitive performance, whereby price is equal to marginal cost, and firms earn a normal profit. Why, then, do credit card rates remain so high?

The explanation requires that we relax the assumption that firms have perfect information about consumers. In fact, credit-issuing firms do *not* have very good information about consumers. They cannot differentiate those customers who will repay the loans immediately, thereby not incurring any interest charges, from those who will repay the loans on a deferred basis, incurring interest charges, from those who will not repay the loans at all. The firms thus incur a risk that the customer will default each time they issue a credit card. This risk of default is an additional cost of doing business, a cost that would not exist in the model of perfect competition. The higher cost is illustrated in the accompanying figure as *ATC + risks*. If competition drives the price down to the point of zero economic profit,

then the higher risks mean a higher price, P_{risks} compared to P. This is what has occurred over the past two to three years.

Suppose a credit card company lowered the rates on its cards. This would attract more customers, but it would also cause the company to operate below its average-cost curve, that is, to operate at a loss. If the company raises its rates, it creates additional costs for itself. The higher rates do not drive away those customers who repay their loans immediately because they do not pay interest charges anyway. The higher rates do not drive the defaulters away because they are not going to pay the rates no matter what their level. Only the desirable customers, those who repay but incur interest costs, are driven away. This is a problem of adverse selection, whereby higher prices attract poorer customers and raise the costs of doing business. Thus, the credit card company is essentially a price-taker, taking the market-determined price as its price. And the price is the one that generates a normal profit. The price is high because costs are high and as bad risk rises and costs rise, the market-determined price rises as well.

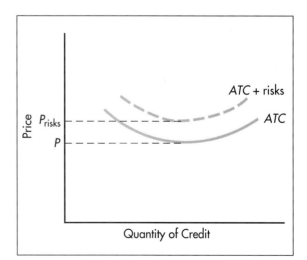

14

Government Policy Toward Business

FUNDAMENTAL QUESTIONS

1. Why does the government intervene in business activity?
2. What is antitrust policy?
3. What is the difference between economic regulation and social regulation?
4. Why have governments deregulated and privatized certain lines of business?

I n the 1960s, computers were sold or leased as complete systems, combinations of central processing units and peripherals—tape drives, disk drives, programs, and other components. A Control Data disk drive did not provide direct competition for an IBM disk drive because the Control Data unit would not work with the IBM central processing unit and software. In the late 1960s, however, several companies developed tape and disk drives that were compatible with the IBM units. This allowed the companies to sell these peripherals in direct competition with IBM, forcing IBM to respond to competition on each piece of equipment as well as on the entire system. IBM's ability to control price and output in the peripherals market was reduced, but, because the peripheral companies could not produce a compatible central processing unit, IBM retained the ability to control price and output in the systems market. IBM dropped the price of its peripherals to the point where the other firms could not compete and retained its higher price on the central processing unit. A lawsuit was filed against IBM, charging anticompetitive behavior. The trial concluded that IBM was not acting in an anticompetitive manner.

In February 1986, Coca-Cola Company declared its intention to purchase the Dr Pepper Company and merge the operations of the two companies. Just a few weeks earlier, Pepsi-Co had announced its intention to purchase the Seven-Up Company, a subsidiary of Philip Morris. These two mergers would have meant the consolidation of the first and fourth and the second and third largest sellers of concentrate for carbonated soft drinks in the United States. Government policymakers determined that these mergers would be anticompetitive and did not allow them.

Cable TV prices rose by nearly twice the rate of inflation in the early 1980s. Complaints that cable TV was a monopoly and acted as such in charging excessively high rates convinced Congress to place cable TV under the control of government policymakers.

Smoking has been linked to cancer and other diseases for several decades. Recently, secondhand smoke has been tied to cancer in nonsmoking spouses of smokers. The state of California decided to protect nonsmokers who work or recreate in close proximity to smokers by banning smoking in all public buildings.

These are examples of government intervention in the affairs of business. In this chapter we look at how the government intervenes in business activity and discuss antitrust policy, economic regulation, and social regulation. We begin with a brief discussion of why the government intervenes in business activity. In the chapters "Market Failure and Environmental Policy" and "Collective Decisionmaking: The Theory of Public Choice" we explore government's role in the economy in more detail.

1. GOVERNMENT AND THE PRIVATE SECTOR

The two main approaches the government uses to intervene in the activities of business are *antitrust policy* and *regulation*. Antitrust policy is an attempt to ensure that businesses compete "fairly." Guidelines of behavior and accepted types of behavior are defined and firms that do not comply are sued. *Economic regulation* involves a more active role for government. It ranges from prescribing the pricing and output behavior of specific industries to the case where the government actually runs and operates the business. Another form of government intervention in business activities is social regulation. *Social regulation*, which applies generally across all businesses, involves health and safety standards for products and the workplace, and standards for protecting the environment.

1.a. Theories of Why the Government Intervenes in Business Activity

Why does the government intervene in business activity?

public interest theory:
the government intervenes in business activity to benefit the general public

capture theory:
the government intervenes in business activity to transfer wealth from one group to another; to benefit a special interest

Why does the government intervene in the affairs of business? One explanation for why the government pursues antitrust action and prescribes rules and regulations is based on the idea that the government's intervention in the economy is for the public good. This is called the **public interest theory** of government intervention. According to this theory, the government carries out antitrust policy, regulates nuclear power, airlines, new pharmaceuticals, workplace safety, product safety, and the environment because the public's well-being depends on the government's actions. Without such intervention, according to this theory, unsafe drugs would be foisted off on an unwary public and unsafe nuclear power plants would be built. It is argued that the government must intervene in agriculture, trucking, airlines, and other industries to protect the public from competition that could destroy these industries. Moreover, the government must prevent large firms from destroying small ones. According to the public interest theory, if the government did not intervene, the public would face many more monopolists.

In opposition to the public interest theory of government is the argument that antitrust and regulation are simply means to transfer wealth from one sector of the economy to another. This theory is called the **capture theory** of government intervention. According to the capture theory, special interests, not the public, receive the benefits of antitrust policy and regulation. For instance, according to the capture theory, the antitrust suit against IBM was an attempt to secure benefits for rival firms, not the general public; the group in charge of trucking regulations is composed of spokesmen from the trucking industry so that the regulations benefit truckers, not the general public; and the agency in charge of regulating nuclear power involves executives from the nuclear power industry, thereby ensuring that the regulations benefit the industry, not necessarily the general public. The capture theory claims that government intervention in business activities is like asking the fox to guard the henhouse.

How could Congress and the regulatory agencies create laws and regulations favorable to a special interest group at the expense of the general pub-

Transportation—via air, bus, or truck—is either a nationalized industry (government enterprise) or regulated in most countries. In Mexico City, Mexico, the bus service from the airport is a government enterprise. The quantity demanded for the service often far exceeds the quantity supplied, as waiting passengers stand in line for the next available bus. The shortage of buses during peak hours was further increased by recent regulations limiting the amount of driving people can do with personal automobiles. The inability to use cars meant that more people had to rely on the government bus lines.

lic? The primary reason is that as a member of the general public you do not have as much concern over some activity that affects a special interest group as you would as a member of that special interest group. For instance, consider regulation that is favorable toward an industry group and unfavorable toward consumers. As a consumer you do not specialize in hiring moving companies, traveling by bus or air, or studying pharmaceuticals. You merely purchase the products that are offered. The industries concerned do specialize in these areas and thus lobby intensely to guide the legislation and regulations that impact the industry. Another factor is that the legislation and regulations do not come with a label spelling out exactly who is benefited or harmed. Laws and rules that end up favoring special interest groups may have been originally intended to benefit, or have been presented as benefiting, the general public. For example, regulation of airport taxis occurred because of the claim that too many consumers were being "ripped off." Thus, the taxi fares were fixed by law. This regulation reduced price competition, restricted entry, and provided stable revenue for the taxi firms—all to their benefit, not the benefit of the general public. Similarly, legislation to increase the safety of new pharmaceuticals through years of testing may benefit the pharmaceutical firms at the expense of consumers, since the process of testing restricts entry and allows above-normal profits for a longer period of time.

With the opposing views of government activity in mind, let's turn to a discussion of antitrust policy and regulation. Antitrust policy began in the late 1800s; the main statutes of antitrust law were passed in 1890 and 1914. Economic regulation came about primarily during the Great Depression; most regulatory agencies were created during the period from 1930 to 1940. Social regulation has come about primarily since 1970.

1.b. Size and Influence

Government policy focuses on the large firm. Government regulations often apply only to large businesses and antitrust policies are typically directed toward large firms. The basis for the focus on large firms comes from the four market-structure models—perfect competition, monopolistic competition, oligopoly, and monopoly.

When considered as a whole, the four market-structure models suggest that the fewer the number of firms controlling the production in an industry, the greater the chance of collusive activity and other behavior designed to monopolize a market. And under monopoly and oligopoly, it is likely that consumers pay more and firms produce less and earn greater profit than if the firms are small, perfect competitors. To have an idea whether these are serious problems, it is necessary to know how prevalent oligopolies and monopolies are, relative to perfectly competitive markets. Measures of size and influence are intended to provide information about market structures.

1.b.1. Measures of Size and Influence

The most commonly used measure of size and influence is called the **Herfindahl index**. The Herfindahl index is a measure of **concentration**—the degree to which a few firms control the output and pricing decisions in a market.[1] The Herfindahl index of concentration is defined as the sum of the squared market shares of each firm in the industry:

$$\text{Herfindahl index} = (S_1)^2 + (S_2)^2 + \ldots + (S_n)^2$$

where S refers to the market share of the firm, the subscripts refer to the firms, and there are n firms. The higher the Herfindahl index number, the more concentrated the industry.

An industry in which each of five firms has 20 percent of the market would have a Herfindahl index value of 2,000:

$$(20)^2 + (20)^2 + (20)^2 + (20)^2 + (20)^2 = 2,000$$

If the largest firm had 88 percent of the market and each of the others 3 percent, the Herfindahl index value would be 7,780:

$$(88)^2 + (3)^2 + (3)^2 + (3)^2 + (3)^2 = 7,780$$

The higher number indicates a much more concentrated market. As you can see from these examples, the Herfindahl index takes into account the size distribution of the firms in an industry. The idea is that an industry in which there is one dominant firm will be quite different from one in which there are several firms of equal size. The Herfindahl indexes for a few industries are shown in Table 1.

In 1982, the Justice Department issued guidelines on market concentration and competition to inform businesses where the government would be especially likely to scrutinize activities. It stated that industries with Herfindahl indexes below 1,000 are considered *highly competitive*; those with indexes between 1,000 and 1,800 are *moderately competitive*; and those with indexes above 1,800 are *highly concentrated*.

1.c. Concentration in the United States

To the extent that concentration reflects oligopolistic or monopolistic behavior, prices and profits in concentrated markets should be higher than in non-

Herfindahl index:
a measure of concentration calculated as the sum of the squares of the market share of each firm in an industry

concentration:
the degree to which a few firms control the output and pricing decisions in a market

---

[1]The four-firm concentration ratio is another commonly used measured of concentration, but it has come under criticism because it does not account for the size distribution of firms. It merely divides the total output of the four largest firms by the total market output.

TABLE 1
Concentration Measures for Selected Industries

Industry	Number of Firms	Herfindahl Index
Aircraft	108	1,358
Soaps and other detergents	642	1,306
Blast furnaces and steel mills	1,787	650
Petroleum refining	282	380
Sawmills	2,430	113
Women's dresses	5,489	24

Source: U.S. Department of Commerce, "Concentration Ratios in Manufacturing," *1982 Census of Manufacturers* (Washington, D.C.: U.S. Government Printing Office, April 1986), MC82-S7.

concentrated markets. Many studies of this proposition have been carried out. The evidence does indeed show a positive relationship between prices and concentration levels, higher accounting profit in concentrated than in non-concentrated industries, and higher profit rates (profit as a percent of assets) for large firms. However, this is not necessarily evidence of the abuse of power or the result of anticompetitive behavior. Those industries in which economies of scale exist may also be higher-cost industries and thus have higher prices without higher profit. Also, recalling the difference between accounting and economic profit, we recognize that higher accounting profit is not necessarily evidence of above-normal profit. Moreover, larger firms may be able to achieve efficiencies and thus earn higher accounting profit than smaller firms. In sum, although evidence supports the notion that large firms are different from small firms and that firms in concentrated markets behave differently from firms in nonconcentrated markets, economists have not been able to demonstrate that concentration means inefficiency, higher costs for consumers, and above-normal profit for firms. (Whether there is a trend toward increased concentration in the U.S. economy is discussed in the Economic Insight "The Aggregate Picture.") Nonetheless, large firms in concentrated markets have long been the focus of government attention.

RECAP

1. Two opposing theories suggest why the government intervenes in business activities, the public interest theory and the capture theory. According to the public interest theory, intervention occurs to benefit the general public. According to the capture theory, intervention occurs to benefit a special interest group.

2. Government policy toward big business involves two areas: antitrust and regulation.

3. The Herfindahl index is a measure of the degree to which a few firms dominate a market. It is the sum of the squares of the sizes of firms in the market.

The Aggregate Picture

The figure shows the percentage of total U.S. manufacturing assets controlled by the largest U.S. manufacturing firms beginning in 1925. Different conclusions can be drawn from this figure. First, one-half of all assets in the manufacturing sector are controlled by the largest one hundred firms; of course, this means that nearly one-half are controlled by smaller firms. Second, there appears to be a slight upward trend in the percentage of assets controlled by the largest firms in the United States. This picture is slightly misleading, however, since it does not include the foreign situation. Throughout most of the period following World War II, overseas investments grew more rapidly for the one hundred largest manufacturers than for their smaller peers. In 1990, U.S. manufacturing corporations derived about 20 percent of their total sales revenues from foreign operations. In addition, the one hundred largest manufacturers diversified into nonmanufacturing ventures more aggressively than did the smaller firms. This meant that while the largest firms grew, the proportion of manufacturing assets they held in domestic activities did not. Thus, the conclusion concern-

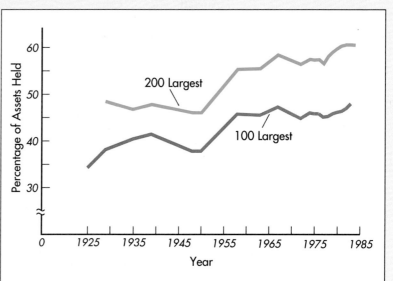

Sources: U.S. Department of Commerce, Bureau of the Census, *Statistical Abstract of the United States, 1986* (Washington, D.C.: U.S. Government Printing Office, 1986); F. M. Scherer and David Ross, *Industrial Market Structure and Economic Performance,* 3d ed. (Boston: Houghton Mifflin, 1990), p. 62.

ing concentration trends in manufacturing depends on whether we look only at domestic manufacturing activities or include the overseas and nonmanufacturing activities.

Including nonfinancial enterprises other than manufacturing alters the aggregate picture as well. Although manufacturing may have become slightly more concen-

trated, other sectors of the economy—for instance, the service industries such as banking and life insurance, retail trade, and transportation—became relatively less concentrated. The overall economy has not become more concentrated as a result; aggregate concentration appears not to have changed much in the past several decades.

2. ANTITRUST POLICY

What is antitrust policy?

In this section we describe antitrust policy and discuss its evolution in the United States (see Figure 1). **Antitrust policy** is the term used to describe government policies and programs designed to control the growth of monopoly and prevent firms from engaging in undesirable practices.

2.a. Antitrust and Business Activities

As noted in Table 2, three laws define the government's approach to antitrust policy—the Sherman, Clayton, and Federal Trade Commission acts. These

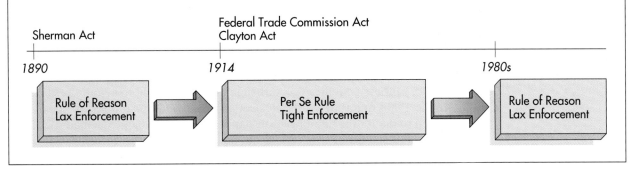

Figure 1
Phases of Antitrust Interpretation
The degree to which antitrust law has been enforced has varied over the years. With the Sherman Act of 1890, the government formally began antitrust policy.

But enforcement was lax, based on a rule of reason, until about 1914. Between 1914 and the early 1980s, strict enforcement based on a per se rule was used. With the Reagan and Bush administrations, enforcement was relaxed again to the rule-of-reason standard.

antitrust policy:
government policies and programs designed to control the growth of monopoly and enhance competition

antitrust laws are intended to limit the creation and behavior of *trusts*, or combinations of independent firms. Today we refer to the process of combining firms as *mergers* and the resulting firms as large firms, or corporations. Antitrust policy limits what these large firms can do. For instance, the firms cannot together decide to fix prices; they cannot restrict competition; and they cannot combine or become trusts if the resulting firm would have too great an influence in the market.

2.b. Interpretation

The government tries to distinguish beneficial from harmful business practices by focusing on *unreasonable* monopolistic activities. What is unreasonable? The answer has varied as the interpretation of the statutes by the courts

TABLE 2
Antitrust Acts

Sherman Antitrust Act (1890)

Section 1 outlaws contracts and conspiracies in restraint of trade.
Section 2 forbids monopolization and attempts to monopolize.

Clayton Antitrust Act (1914)

Section 2, as amended by the Robinson-Patman Act (1936), bans price discrimination that substantially lessens competition or injures particular competitors.
Section 3 prohibits certain practices that might keep other firms from entering an industry or competing with an existing firm.
Section 7, as amended by the Celler-Kefauver Act (1950), outlaws mergers that substantially lessen competition.

Federal Trade Commission Act (1914)

Section 5, as amended by the Wheeler-Lea Act (1938), prohibits unfair methods of competition and unfair or deceptive acts.

---

and government authorities has changed. There have been three distinct phases of antitrust policy in the United States. The first began with passage of the Sherman Antitrust Act in 1890 and lasted until about 1914. In this period, litigation was infrequent. The courts used a **rule of reason** to judge firms' actions: being a monopoly or attempting to monopolize was not in itself illegal; to be illegal, an action had to be unreasonable in a competitive sense, and the anticompetitive effects had to be demonstrated.

The second phase of antitrust policy began in 1914 with the passage of the Clayton Antitrust Act and the Federal Trade Commission Act. Operating under these two acts, the courts used the **per se rule** to judge firms' actions: activities that were potentially monopolizing tactics were illegal; the mere existence of these activities was sufficient evidence to lead to a guilty verdict.

In the 1980s and through the Reagan and Bush administrations, the courts returned to the looser rule-of-reason standard. The only tactic deemed illegal was price fixing. Rival firms could not determine prices by agreement; they had to allow prices to be set by demand and supply.

The government's policy toward mergers depends on the effect of the merger on the Herfindahl index. As mentioned earlier, the Justice Department has made it clear that attempts by firms to merge within an industry that has a Herfindahl index greater than 1,800 will be questioned seriously. A merger that increases the Herfindahl index by 50 points will also be scrutinized.

rule of reason:
to be illegal an action must be unreasonable in a competitive sense, and the anticompetitive effects must be demonstrated

per se rule:
actions that could be anti-competitive are intrinsically illegal

2.c. Procedures

Action against alleged violators of the antitrust statutes may be initiated by the U.S. Department of Justice, by the Federal Trade Commission (FTC), or by private plaintiffs. The Justice Department focuses on the Sherman Antitrust Act. The FTC focuses on the Federal Trade Commission and Clayton Antitrust acts. Private plaintiffs (consumers and businesses) may sue on the basis of any of the statutes except the Federal Trade Commission Act. Since 1941, the FTC and the Justice Department together have filed nearly 2,800 cases, and since 1970, private suits have far outnumbered those filed by the Justice Department and the FTC combined.

2.d. Remedies

Private plaintiffs who prove their injuries can receive compensation up to three times the damages caused by the action. The Justice Department and the FTC do not obtain treble damages but can impose substantial penalties. They can force firms to break up through dissolution or divestiture, and criminal actions can be filed by the Justice Department for violations of the Sherman Act. A guilty finding can result in fines and prison sentences.

2.e. Demonstration of Antitrust Violations

Price fixing is by definition illegal—there is no justification for it. Other aspects of the antitrust statutes are not as clear-cut and are, therefore, difficult to prove. For instance, Section 2 of the Sherman Act outlaws "monopolization" but does not forbid monopolies. Monopoly itself is allowed. *To monopolize* or *to attempt to monopolize* constitutes a violation. If the firm attempts to preserve its monopoly by activities that restrict entry, then the firm may be guilty of a Section 2 violation.

The first step in enforcing an antitrust policy is to define market concentration. Using the Herfindahl index to gauge the extent to which a few firms dominate a market sounds simple, but it is not. Before the concentration of an industry can be calculated, there must be some definition of the market. In a $100 billion market, an $80 billion firm would have an 80 percent market share. But in a $1,000 billion market, an $80 billion firm would have only an 8 percent market share. The Herfindahl index for the former would exceed 2,000, but for the latter it would be less than 1,000. Obviously, antitrust plaintiffs (those accusing a firm of attempting to monopolize a market) would want the market defined as narrowly as possible so that the alleged monopolizer would be seen to have a large market share. Conversely, defendants (those accused of monopolization) would argue for broadly defined markets in order to give the appearance that they possess a very small market share; an example is described in the Economic Insight "Coca-Cola and Dr Pepper," which discusses the attempt by Coca-Cola to purchase Dr Pepper that was described in this chapter's Preview.

Policymakers who tend to look on government actions as explainable by the capture theory would tend to support the rule-of-reason standard; those supporting the public interest theory might be more likely to support the per se rule.

When the market and market shares have been defined, the next task is to establish intent. The ease or difficulty with which intent can be established depends on whether the per se rule or the rule-of-reason standard is being used. This depends, respectively, on whether the president and his administration tend to look at government activity as being in the public interest or as being captured by a special interest group.

2.f. Concentration and Business Policy from a Global Perspective

Concentration measures and the Justice Department guidelines are often defined for production only within the United States; this can present a misleading picture. For instance, the Herfindahl index in the United States for automobiles is very high, but if it took foreign competition into account, it would be significantly lower. In Sweden, two cars are produced, Volvo and Saab, and the Herfindahl index is greater than 5,000. That figure is also misleading, however, for Volvo and Saab account for only about 30 percent of all automobiles sold in Sweden. An appropriate policy measure must take into account all close substitutes whether domestically produced or not. In addition, it must account for firms producing in more than one nation, the multinationals. The Herfindahl index may not provide a good indication of the competitive situation prevailing in an industry if it does not account for these factors or for the different ways that governments treat their businesses—actions that are legal in one country may be illegal in another, for instance. Governments also restrict the imports of some goods and services, thereby affecting the number of substitutes available to domestic consumers.

Compared to other countries, the United States is quite restrictive in terms of allowing certain types of business behavior and quite unrestrictive in placing limits on the importation of goods and services. When the per se rule was emerging in the United States during the 1920s and 1930s, most European nations had no antitrust laws at all, and cartels flourished. Today, many nations support cartels and cooperative behavior that is illegal in the United States. Some of these same nations are very restrictive in the importation of goods. Japan, for instance, allows, even supports, systems of cartels domestically while severely limiting the inflow of foreign-produced goods and services.

At least part of the explanation for the differences among nations lies in

Coca-Cola and Dr Pepper

A recent attempt by Coca-Cola Company to purchase Dr Pepper Company illustrates the problem of defining markets.* Coca-Cola, Dr Pepper, PepsiCo, and Seven-Up are usually identified as producers of carbonated soft drinks (CSD). These firms provide bottlers with the concentrate that is used to make the drinks. The principal question in the analysis of the merger was whether CSD was the appropriate market in which to assess the competitive consequences of the merger, or whether the market should be more widely defined—perhaps to encompass all potable liquids (fruit juices, milk, coffee, tea, etc.). The market definition was determined through interviews with CSD company executives. The executives indi-

cated that they believed their primary competitors were other CSD producers. They maintained that they fashioned their pricing and marketing strategies with other CSD producers in mind—not, as claimed by the defendant, by considering how the sellers of all potable drinks would react. The interviews also revealed that many CSD industry executives thought they could collectively raise the retail prices of carbonated soft drinks by as much as 10 percent with no fear of consumers switching to other beverages. That argument had implications for the definition of the market. If sellers can collectively raise the price by 10 percent without causing consumers to switch to other products, then those sellers represent

the lion's share of the market. However, if consumers switch as a result of the price increase, then the market must be more broadly defined to include the substitutes consumers move to.

In the Coca-Cola case, the narrow definition of the market prevailed, and the merger was not allowed because the combination of Coca-Cola and Dr Pepper would have resulted in too great a level of concentration.

*See Lawrence J. White, "Application of the Merger Guidelines: The Proposed Merger of Coca-Cola and Dr Pepper," in *The Antitrust Revolution*, edited by John E. Kwoka, Jr., and Lawrence J. White (Glenview, Ill.: Scott, Foresman, 1989), pp. 80–98.

the growth and development of the various countries following World War II. The economies of Europe and Japan were severely damaged by the war. As the losers, Germany and Japan were occupied and their laws rewritten by the occupying forces. Thus, their antitrust laws resemble those of the United States. However, because Europe and Japan were not concerned with large business but instead with businesses that were too small to compete in the world markets, the antitrust laws were never enforced. Businesses had to be large enough to achieve economies of scale, and for several decades it seemed that only U.S. firms were of sufficient size. Hence, while the United States was worrying about large businesses becoming too powerful, other countries were attempting to increase the sizes of their businesses. Only since the 1970s have the European countries begun to institute and enforce antitrust laws along the lines the United States has followed since the 1940s. Currently, every Western industrialized nation has some kind of antitrust law, but only the United States has a per se rule against price fixing.

The differences across nations have led many in the United States to call for a new approach to antitrust activity in the United States, one called **industrial policy**. Industrial policy refers to the government being actively involved in determining the structure of industry. Government would select certain industries to be high-growth areas, would offer low-interest loans or subsidies to these industries, and would provide protection from international competition in order for the industries to mature. As we discussed in the

industrial policy:
government direction and involvement in defining an economy's industrial structure

chapter "Elasticity: Demand and Supply," Japan's Ministry of International Trade and Industry (MITI) has performed these functions in that country, and the success of the Japanese economy is part of the reason many people believe the United States should have a similar industrial policy.

Calls for industrial policy in the United States have recently been made by, among others, Ross Perot, one of the 1992 presidential candidates, and President Clinton. They agree that since cartels and collusion are common in other countries, the United States must also support cartels and collusion in order to be able to compete with these other countries.

Industrial policy looks attractive to policymakers because of Japan's economy. Japan's policy, though, has had failures as well.

Critics of industrial policy point out that the free market (without government intervention) will determine what people want and will produce what people want in the most efficient manner; a government agency cannot do any better. These critics further point out that Japanese consumers pay higher prices as a result of the industrial policy in Japan. They note that shipbuilding, aluminum smelting, and petrochemicals were also industries favored by MITI and these industries have done very poorly. And they point to the huge success of Soichiro Honda, who led his company into the auto industry in defiance of MITI, as proof of the limitations of industrial policy. They argue that an industrial policy simply strengthens the ability of special interests to capture the government for the benefit of these special interests.

RECAP

1. Antitrust policy in the United States is based on the Sherman, Clayton, and Federal Trade Commission acts.

2. The enforcement of antitrust policy has evolved through three phases. The first followed the Sherman Act in 1890 and extended to 1914. During this period, the rule-of-reason standard dictated policy. The second phase started with the Clayton and Federal Trade Commission acts in 1914 and lasted through the 1970s. During this period, the per se rule dictated policy. In the 1980s, most practices were considered to be part of the competitive process.

3. Antitrust policy encompasses business actions such as pricing, advertising, restraint of trade, supplier relationships, and mergers.

4. If two or more rivals combine, it is called a merger.

5. Antitrust policy in the United States is stricter than it is in other nations.

6. Industrial policy refers to an industrial structure defined and determined by government actions.

3. REGULATION

What is the difference between economic regulation and social regulation?

The intent of antitrust policy is to enhance the competitive environment—to create a "level playing field" on which firms may compete. When the competitive environment cannot be enhanced, such as in the case with a natural monopoly where cost conditions lead to a sole supplier, then regulation is used to ensure that price and output are more beneficial for consumers than the levels the monopolist would set without government influence.

Regulation of natural monopolies is far from the only type of government regulation that occurs, however. Regulation of industries that are not natural monopolies is also widespread in the United States. This regulation has a number of different rationales, ranging from the protection of the health and safety of the general public to the health of a particular industry.

economic regulation:
the prescription of price and output for a specific industry

social regulation:
the prescribing of health, safety, performance, and environmental standards that apply across several industries

There are two categories of regulations, economic and social regulation. **Economic regulation** refers to the prescribing of prices and output levels for both natural monopolies and industries that are not natural monopolies. Economic regulation is specific, applying to a particular industry or line of business. **Social regulation** refers to prescribed performance standards, workplace health and safety standards, emission levels, and a variety of output and job standards that apply across several industries.

3.a. Regulation of Industries That Are Not Natural Monopolies

Let's briefly look at the historical reasons for the regulation of transportation and the airwaves. These industries provide good examples of the rationales for economic regulation. We will then discuss social regulation.

3.a.1. Transportation and Destructive Competition

For both railroads and air transport, equipment is extremely expensive and operating costs are relatively quite small—in other words, marginal costs are very low relative to fixed costs. This could mean that firms entering the industry have to set price equal to marginal cost to meet competition, but this is not high enough for them to be able to pay for their total costs—they might be covering their variable costs but not their huge fixed costs. Thus, competition between the firms could lead to the failure of the entire industry. In such cases, the government has often restricted entry, allowing only one firm or a few firms to provide a product. Restricting entry, however, allows existing firms to earn above-normal or monopoly profit. This monopoly profit provides a reason for the government to regulate the firms much as it would a natural monopoly.

The government has been involved in the railroad industry since its inception. Land was provided for construction, loans were provided for development, and transportation rates were defined in many cases. When technological change lowered the costs of some services and brought trucking in as a direct competitor to the railroad, the regulatory net spread from railroads into trucking. Trucking was regulated not because of self-destructive competition or because it was a natural monopoly, but because years of regulation had put railroads at a disadvantage relative to trucking. The Interstate Commerce Commission (ICC) was given jurisdiction over railroads in the last quarter of the nineteenth century. Trucking came under its umbrella in 1935.

Like railroads, the argument for regulating airlines was to create orderly growth and avoid self-destructive competition. From the mid-1930s to the mid-1970s, the Civil Aeronautics Authority and its successor, the Civil Aeronautics Board (CAB), controlled entry into airline markets by establishing boundaries between carriers. Each carrier was further restricted to specific routes. For example, United Air Lines was authorized to serve north-south routes on the West Coast, and Delta and Eastern served such routes on the East Coast.

3.a.2. Airwaves and Private Property Rights

In some cases the resource used to supply a product is available to anyone, so free entry and use could consume the resource and destroy the industry. For instance, if just anyone could broadcast radio or TV signals on any of the airwaves, the main broadcast spectrum could become so crowded that a clear signal could not be obtained. The problem is that there are no clear *private property rights* to the airwaves (no one owns a specific airwave frequency), and in the absence of specific property rights, chaos could result if government did not step in. Limiting entry and assigning airwave frequencies (assigning property rights) may create order, but it also creates a monopoly situation. The existence of the resulting monopoly then lends itself to regulation along the lines of a natural monopoly.

Television and broadcasting rights are granted by the Federal Communications Commission (FCC). Until 1982, the FCC also regulated the telecommunications industry, controlling entry and some prices. The purpose of telecommunication regulation was to make high-quality service available to everyone in the country at reasonable prices and to control the natural monopoly held by AT&T.

3.b. Deregulation in the United States

Why have governments deregulated and privatized certain lines of business?

Whether or not the initial rationale justified regulation, the results were disastrous. Over time it became evident that many regulated companies lacked incentives to keep costs under control and to be responsive to consumer demands. The airlines competed in terms of schedules, movies, food, and size of aircraft because the CAB did not allow price competition. Nonprice competition led to a much more rapid increase in the number of flights and expansion of aircraft capacity than were demanded by passengers. As a result, the load factor (the average percentage of seats filled) fell to less than 50 percent in the early 1970s.

Price competition among truckers was also stifled by regulation. The ICC had a complex rate schedule and restrictions affecting whether trucks could be full or less than full and the routes trucks could take. As a result, by the mid-1970s, 36 percent of all truck-miles were logged by empty trucks.

These problems initiated a change in federal government regulatory policy. In some industries, particularly those in which natural monopolies did not exist, the regulatory apparatus was partially dismantled. Trucking was deregulated in 1980. Trucks can now haul what they want, where they want, at rates set by the trucking companies. In air transportation, deregulation meant the end of government control of entry and prices. Deregulation of route authority and fares was completed by 1982, and the CAB was disbanded.

Much of the telecommunications industry was deregulated in 1982, when an antitrust suit against AT&T, filed by the Department of Justice in 1974, was finally settled. As part of the settlement, AT&T agreed to divest itself of the local portions of the twenty-two Bell operating companies. They were restructured into seven separate regulated monopolies. The seven new operating firms are excluded from long-distance service and from manufacturing terminal equipment. AT&T continues to provide long-distance service and telephone equipment, but other suppliers may compete in both spheres, and customers can choose any supplier they wish.

Although regulation leads to problems, not everyone agrees that deregulation is the solution. For instance, many claim that because of deregulation airlines are now less safe.[2] Similar arguments about service and safety apply to other industries that have been deregulated. Cable TV, in fact, was *re*regulated in 1992 because of the public outcry stemming from the price rises during the unregulated period. In short, the move toward deregulation that occurred in several industries during the 1980s has not won unanimous support. Opposing those who want to return to a regulation environment are people who argue that airline safety has indeed improved and that cable TV prices are higher because consumers get more channels and better programming for their money than they did under regulation.

3.c. Social Regulation

Although economists debate the costs and benefits of regulation, the amount of regulation has grown steadily since the Great Depression. Most of this growth has been due to social regulation rather than economic regulation. Although deregulation has occurred in industries faced with economic regulation, social regulation has increased for all industries.

Social regulation is concerned with the conditions under which goods and services are produced and the impact of these goods on the public. The following government agencies are concerned with social regulation:

- The Occupational Safety and Health Administration (OSHA), which is concerned with protecting workers against injuries and illnesses associated with their jobs

- The Consumer Product Safety Commission (CPSC), which specifies minimum standards for safety of products

- The Food and Drug Administration (FDA), which is concerned with the safety and effectiveness of food, drugs, and cosmetics

- The Equal Employment Opportunity Commission (EEOC), which focuses on the hiring, promotion, and discharge of workers

- The Environmental Protection Agency (EPA), which is concerned with air, water, and noise pollution

Social regulation is often applied across all industries. For instance, while the ICC focuses on trucking and railroads, the EPA enforces emission standards related to all businesses.

Social regulation has grown since the early 1970s. The number of rules and regulations and the number of people employed to administer them have increased. The staff of the EPA, for instance, increased by 23 percent and its budget increased by 31 percent between 1988 and 1992. Most of the arguments made in support of social regulation are buttressed by the public interest theory. Over 10,000 workers died in job-related accidents in the United States in 1992. Air pollution is an increasing problem in many cities, leading

---

[2]See, for example, Richard B. McKenzie and William F. Shughart II, "Deregulation and Air Travel Safety," *Regulation*, nos. 3 and 4, 1987, pp. 42–47; Judith Valente, "Some Airlines Narrow Their Safety Margins Seeking to Cut Costs," *Wall Street Journal*, Sept. 19, 1988, p. 1; and "Happiness Is a Cheap Seat," *The Economist*, Feb. 4, 1989, p. 68; and Nancy L. Rose, "Fear of Flying? Economic Analyses of Airline Safety," *Journal of Economic Perspectives*, Spring 1992, pp. 75–94.

to cancer and other diseases, which in turn mean increased demands on health-care agencies. Hundreds of children are killed each year as a result of poorly designed toys. Unfair discharges from jobs and discrimination against minorities occur frequently. It is argued that without government regulation, these events would be much more serious and would impose tremendous costs on society.

There are costs to the regulation, however. It is expensive to administer the agencies and enforce the rules and regulations. Currently, the annual administrative costs of federal regulatory activities exceed $13 billion.[3] Most of this expense is paid by taxpayers. The costs of complying with the rules and regulations, which are imposed on businesses, shift their cost curves up. These compliance costs are estimated to be nearly twenty times the administrative costs. Thus, in 1992, the total compliance costs of federal regulatory activities may have been as high as $260 billion. The new clean-air law will cost business an estimated $25 billion a year in addition to the $32 billion that companies already have been spending each year. The new disabilities law is estimated to cost $20 billion each year.[4]

Added to the direct costs of regulations are the opportunity costs. For instance, the lengthy FDA process for approving new biotechnology has stymied advances in agriculture. Regulatory restrictions on the telecommunications industry has resulted in the United States lagging behind Japan in the development of fiber optics and high-definition television. The Nutrition Labeling and Education Act of 1990, which requires most food products to have labels listing specified nutrients and the amounts contained in each product, discourages businesses from introducing new products. The specialty-food association estimates that the cost of complying with the law will be $6,000 per product. The total cost imposed on the U.S. economy from federal government regulations is estimated to be more than $400 billion a year. According to the capture theory, these costs on the general public benefit a few special interest groups.

Whether an action should be undertaken can be determined by comparing the costs of a certain action to the benefits of that action.

There are both enormous costs and enormous benefits to social regulation. Which view is most valid, the public interest or the capture theory? To answer this question we need to compare the costs and benefits of the regulations. But this is a difficult position. It requires us to answer such questions as: Does the saving of one life justify a million-dollar expenditure? How about $2 million or $100 million? These are the issues that the debate is concerned with. Many economists suggest that we should look at these tradeoffs (dollars per life) but that we must not forget how the competitive market works. If labeling is desired by the public, won't the public voluntarily pay the higher price for it? Why, then, is regulation necessary unless it is to benefit some special interest group? If seat belts and antilock braking systems are desired by the public, won't the public voluntarily pay the price to have these safety systems? Why, if the market would ensure that what the public desires is produced at the lowest possible cost, is it necessary for the government to intervene in the economy and impose regulatory costs of $400 billion or more each year? The debate over social and economic regulation is explored further in the chapters "Market Failure and Environmental Policy" and "Collective Decisionmaking: The Theory of Public Choice."

---

[3]David Warner, "How Do Federal Rules Affect You?" *Nation's Business*, May 1992, p. 56.
[4]David Warner, "Regulations' Staggering Costs," *Nation's Business*, June 1992, p. 50.

3.d. Regulation and Deregulation in Other Countries

privatization:
transferring a publicly owned enterprise to private ownership

contracting out:
the process of enlisting private firms to perform certain government functions

In most European nations, nationalization has been the traditional solution to the natural monopoly rather than regulation. Nationalization is where the government takes over and operates an industry. Deregulation in the United States is privatization in other nations. **Privatization** is the transfer of public-sector activities to the private sector. Privatization may take one of three forms: *wholesale privatization*, in which an entire publicly owned firm is transferred to private ownership; **contracting out**, in which a specific aspect of a government operation is carried out by a private firm; and *auctioning*, in which the rights to operate a government enterprise go to the highest private-sector bidder.

In contracting out, a private firm is paid to perform some activities usually carried out by the government, such as street cleaning, emissions testing, and garbage collection.

The auctioning process is now occurring in many of the Eastern European countries that were formerly under Soviet domination. The potential monopoly profits are competed away by the auction so that only the most efficient producers will be able to supply the good or service. This approach has been used as well in the United States in local broadcasting and transportation and is under scrutiny for prisons, as discussed in the Economic Insight "Privatizing Prisons."

3.e. Multinationals and International Regulation

International regulation arose primarily in response to the growth of *multinationals*, large firms that operate in several different countries. These firms raised concerns over national sovereignty. In cases where the gross domestic product (GDP) of the nation was smaller or not much larger than the sales of the multinational company, the nation feared it would be held hostage to a monopoly firm. A wave of nationalizations and entry restrictions arose in the less-developed countries during the 1960s and 1970s. The conclusion quickly reached by governments was that international action was needed to deal with an international phenomenon such as multinational corporations. The attempt to set up rules of the game, guidelines, standards, and norms of behavior and conduct led to the increased emphasis on regulation at the international level. Because there is no global authority to enforce these rules, and because the interests of countries are so diverse, the international community in most cases settled for something less than regulation. Usually codes containing guidelines are issued as resolutions or declarations of governments rather than as international treaties. They carry moral rather than legal force.

RECAP

1. The stated reason for regulation of industries such as railroads, trucking, and air transport was the potential for self-destructive competition. The stated reason for regulating airwaves was the lack of private property rights.

2. Since the mid-1970s, deregulation has occurred in airlines, trucking, railroads, and communications.

Privatizing Prisons

Prisons and jails have been operated as government enterprises for so long that it is difficult to think of a private firm earning an economic profit by running a prison. Yet some firms insist that they can save taxpayers millions of dollars a year by running prisons more efficiently than government agencies do.

Correctional systems in 39 states contract out a few activities and services: medical and mental health treatment, construction, education, drug treatment, staff training, vocational training, and counseling. The vast majority of programs, however, are still provided by the state. Actual management of prisons for the most part remains in the hands of the government.

Private prison entrepreneurs are in business to make a profit and will operate their facilities as efficiently as possible. Does this mean poor care and maltreatment of inmates? It cannot, for the private firms will have to balance their desire to cut costs with their need for long-term contracts. Furthermore, many of the companies seeking private prison contracts want to operate facilities in several states. Reputations for poor treatment and poor supervision will mean fewer contracts.

The debate over standards and treatment has obscured the question of whether private management will produce major reductions in prison costs. In addition, there are not many experiences to draw from. To date, private operators have been successful in winning contracts for the detention of juvenile offenders and illegal aliens, but not for adult prison inmates. And the jury is still out on the cost-saving effects of privatizing the juvenile and immigration detention facilities. The Immigration and Naturalization Service, for example, reports savings of only about 6 percent from its use of privately operated detention centers.

Nevertheless, the debate over privatization is picking up steam as the cost of housing inmates rises and the penalties for criminal activities are more strictly enforced. Many cities that had abandoned the prison business, turning it over to counties or states, are now being taxed at heavier and heavier rates by the counties and states. Costs per prisoner per day exceed $40 in many cases, and the cities are wondering whether to get back into the prison business or to contract out the business to private entrepreneurs, who say they can get the job done for $10 per prisoner per day.

Sources: Charles R. Ring, "Private Prisons Need a Fair Trial," *Wall Street Journal*, May 8, 1987, p. 20; John A. Jones, "Corrections Corp. Leads in Business of Privatizing Prisons," *Investor's Daily*, March 3, 1990, p. 34; "Try Privatization" (editorial), *Arizona Republic*, March 22, 1990, p. A12.

3. Social regulation deals with workplace safety, product safety, the environment, and other aspects of doing business; it applies to all industries.

4. In other countries, nationalization occurred instead of regulation. In those countries, deregulation means privatization.

5. Although deregulation has been the trend since the early 1980s within developed nations, regulation by international agencies is increasing.

SUMMARY

▲▼ Why does the government intervene in business activity?

1. The public interest theory of regulation asserts that regulation is necessary to protect the public interest. The capture theory of regulation claims that regulation benefits only those who are regulated. §1.a

2. The Herfindahl index is used to measure size and influence; industries with a Herfindahl index above 1,800 are considered highly concentrated. §1.b.1

What is antitrust policy?

3. Antitrust policy is an attempt to enhance competition by restricting certain activities that could be anticompetitive. §2

4. The antitrust statutes include Sections 1 and 2 of the Sherman Antitrust Act, which forbids conspiracies and monopolization; Sections 2, 3, and 7 of the Clayton Antitrust Act, which prohibits anticompetitive pricing and nonprice restraints; and Section 5 of the Federal Trade Commission Act, which prohibits deceptive and unfair acts. §2.a, Table 2

5. The antitrust statutes have undergone three phases of interpretation. In the early years, a rule of reason prevailed; acts had to be unreasonable to be a violation of the statutes. Between 1914 and 1980, a per se rule applied more often. Under this policy, the mere existence of actions that could be used anticompetitively was a violation. Since the early 1980s, the interpretations have returned to the rule-of-reason standard. §2.b

6. Antitrust laws are more rigorously enforced in the United States than elsewhere. This has led to many calls for a U.S. industrial policy. §2.f

What is the difference between economic regulation and social regulation?

7. Economic regulation refers to the prescription of price and output for a particular industry. Social regulation refers to the setting of health and safety standards for products and the workplace, and environmental and operating procedures for all industries. §3

8. Some industries are regulated not because they are natural monopolies but because the government wants to limit entry in order to protect an industry from self-destructive competition and from the formation of a monopoly. Examples include airlines and railroads. §3.a

9. Some industries are regulated to prevent chaos because of the lack of private property rights. §3.a.2

Why have governments deregulated and privatized certain lines of business?

10. By the 1970s, it became apparent that regulation had caused some severe problems. A period of deregulation began in the United States. §3.b

11. Social regulation has increased even as economic regulation has decreased. §3.c

12. Deregulation in other developed countries took the form of privatization: the selling, auctioning, or contracting out of a government enterprise to private interests. §3.d

KEY TERMS

public interest theory §1.a

capture theory §1.a

Herfindahl index §1.b.1

concentration §1.b.1

antitrust policy §2

rule of reason §2.b

per se rule §2.b

industrial policy §2.f

economic regulation §3

social regulation §3

privatization §3.d

contracting out §3.d

EXERCISES

1. Using demand and cost curves, demonstrate why a typical monopolistically competitive firm might want to create a barrier to entry.

2. Using the demand and cost curves of an individual firm in oligopoly, demonstrate what the effects of each of the following are:

   a. The Clean Air Act

   b. The Nutrition and Labeling Act

   c. A ban on smoking inside the workplace

   d. A sales tax

3. What is self-destructive competition? How does a natural monopoly differ from a firm that has large fixed costs and relatively small marginal costs?

4. Kodak has developed an important brand name through its advertising, innovation, and product quality and service. Suppose Kodak sets up a network of exclusive dealerships, and one of the dealers decides to carry Fuji and Mitsubishi as well as Kodak products. If Kodak terminates the dealership, is it acting in a pro- or anticompetitive manner?

5. Explain why auctioning broadcast licenses might be more efficient than having the FCC assign licenses on some basis designed by the FCC.

6. Which of the three types of government policies—antitrust, social regulation, economic regulation—is the basis for each of the following?

   a. Beautician education standards

   b. Certified Public Accounting requirements

   c. Liquor licensing

   d. Justice Department guidelines

   e. The Clean Air Act

   f. The Nutrition and Labeling Act

7. Provide the arguments for and against each of the rules or regulations listed in question 6 using the public interest theory and the capture theory.

8. In the chapter "Monopoly," we discussed the Burroughs Wellcome monopoly on the AIDS drug AZT. As an active member of an AIDS prevention organization, argue that regulation by the FDA has been harmful. As an executive of Burroughs Wellcome, argue that the FDA regulation has been beneficial.

9. Many airline executives are calling for reregulation. Why might an executive of an airline prefer to operate under a regulated environment?

10. Suppose the Herfindahl index for domestic production of televisions is 5,000. Does this imply a very competitive or a noncompetitive environment?

11. Discuss the claim that social regulation is unnecessary. Does the claim depend on whether the industrial structure of an industry is composed primarily of perfect competition or primarily of oligopoly?

12. Suppose a monopolist is practicing price discrimination and a lawsuit against the monopolist forces an end to the practice. Is it possible that the result is a loss in efficiency? Explain.

13. Explain how the Justice Department ban on the alleged price fixing on the part of universities might be harmful to students.

14. Explain the often-heard statement that "There ought to be a law" in terms of the public interest theory and the capture theory of government intervention in business activity. For instance, suppose a consumer hires Bekins moving company to transfer him from California to Utah and Bekins damages $3,000 worth of furniture and refuses to compensate the consumer. The consumer in frustration says, "There ought to be a law."

15. "The Japanese are beating us at every step. We must act as they do. We must allow and encourage cooperation among firms and we must develop partnerships between business and government. The first place we should begin is with the aerospace industry. Let's use the government to transfer the resources no longer employed in aerospace to nondefense industries such as the environment and health." Evaluate this industrial policy.

Economically Speaking

A Lesson in Free-Market Economics

PRINCETON—Collusion and free agency are part of the everyday language of professional sports.

Now they're becoming part of the lexicon of academia.

Alleging antitrust violations, the U.S. Justice Department filed suit in Philadelphia last year to block Ivy League schools and the Massachusetts Institute of Technology from fixing uniform financial-aid offers to students accepted at more than one of the prestigious schools.

Reluctantly, the schools gave in.

Constans Salcedo, an 18-year-old Texan, is one of thousands who has benefited since. He enrolled at Princeton this year after receiving $7,000 more in aid than either Columbia University or another prominent East Coast school offered.

"I'd always wanted to go to Princeton," he said. "The financial-aid offer confirmed it."

There are lots of Constans Salcedos this year, students who have become academic free agents, eagerly taking advantage of a sort of bidding war among colleges.

A year ago, there would have been no difference in the offers. Traditionally, each spring, officials from 23 schools, including the eight that make up the Ivy League, would meet to set the financial-aid offers that would go to about 10,000 students who each year are accepted at more than one of the schools. The schools were known as the Overlap Group.

The offers never varied. A student who was accepted at both Princeton and the University of Pennsylvania, for example, would receive the same amount of financial aid from each school. . . .

The schools, which deny any wrongdoing, defend the annual meetings, saying they help lower costs by preventing a bidding war for students.

The suit alleged that Princeton, Penn and the six other schools in the Ivy League, as well as MIT, violated federal antitrust laws. Saying that the legal costs of disputing the allegations in court were too high, the Ivy League universities shortly thereafter signed a consent decree agreeing to discontinue the annual "overlap meeting." The settlement in effect stopped the Ivy League schools—and the other colleges that attended the meetings—from collectively setting student aid. . . .

The Justice Department thinks college tuition will rise more slowly as a result of the settlement. But college administrators lobbying Congress to reverse the change say that while the brightest students will profit, others will suffer. . . .

In the future, college officials say, the new rules could lead to a more intense bidding war for the brightest students, regardless of financial need. That would force universities to offer less aid to needier students, they add.

"The additional moneys provided to one student are moneys that are not available to meet the needs of another student, maybe another minority student or another student disadvantaged in some way," said Robert Durkee, a vice president at Princeton who oversees the school's relations with the federal government.

"I think there was an agenda (by Justice Department lawyers) to reverse the commitment to need-based aid" in order "to provide aid to students from families like themselves," Durkee said.

Robert Bloch, the Justice Department lawyer who headed the investigation, denies that. As he sees it, in the 35 years that the Overlap Group collectively set financial aid offers, it simply deprived many students of higher offers they might otherwise have received.

He even thinks the settlement might force colleges to keep tuition increases to a minimum, to attract students.

"The rate of increase in tuitions was astronomical before," he said, "and it's not altogether clear that colleges couldn't be more cost-conscious." . . .

MIT, a member of the Overlap Group, did not sign the consent decree and is contesting the Justice Department's accusations in a trial to be held in U.S. District Court in Philadelphia in April. . . .

Source: Jonathan D. Rockoff, "A Lesson in Free-Market Economics," *Philadelphia Inquirer*, Feb. 7, 1992, p. A01.

Commentary

D id it shock you to learn that the Antitrust Division of the U.S. Department of Justice recently investigated alleged price fixing among twenty-three prestigious East Coast colleges and universities, including MIT, Brown, Columbia, Cornell, Dartmouth, Harvard, the University of Pennsylvania, Princeton, Yale, Amherst, Barnard, Bowdoin, Bryn Mawr, Colby, Mount Holyoke, Middlebury, Smith, Trinity, Tufts, Vassar, Wesleyan, and Williams? In May 1991, the department formally charged these colleges with price fixing on scholarship aid.

The existence of meetings in which schools agreed on financial-aid offers suggests the restriction of competition through collusion. Even though tuition prices were not discussed at these meetings, setting financial-aid awards determined the price of students' education. What are the consequences of collusion for students and for schools? In the figure, the perfectly competitive outcome occurs where the marginal-cost curve intersects the demand curve, with the price P_1 and the quantity Q_1. The monopoly outcome, which the collusive schools collectively enforce, occurs at the higher price, P_2 and the lower quantity, Q_2. The amount of the schools' gain due to collusion is the area P_1ABP_2 minus the area CFA. The loss in consumer surplus is the area P_1FBP_2. Thus, collusion benefits sellers and harms consumers.

The benefits to sellers in the case described in the article are even more pronounced. The most profitable outcome for a monopolist is to offer a different price to each consumer and to have each price represent just the amount that the individual consumer is willing to pay. If a monopolist can do this successfully, it will capture all of the consumer surplus and obtain the entire area under the demand curve. In terms of the graph, the schools' gain will be P_1FP_3 and there will be no consumer surplus. For this outcome to occur, it is necessary that sellers know the amount each consumer is willing to pay. With financial-aid forms, colleges have this information. Another necessary condition for price discrimination is that consumers not resell the product among themselves. It is impossible to resell education, so this condition is also met.

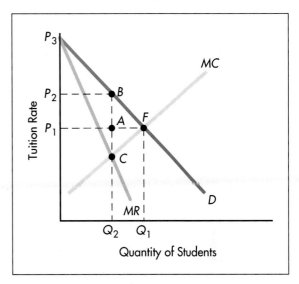

The extent of a cartel's monopoly power depends on whether there are close substitutes for that cartel's product. Though students often have the option of attending a number of colleges, to a certain extent, these twenty-three schools may enjoy some market power relative to a wide range of other schools because of the prestige associated with a degree from an Ivy League school. This means that these schools can set prices above those of other schools and still have an excess demand for their services.

What will be the effects of greater competition for students? The schools that used to meet to agree on financial-aid awards will now be forced to offer a greater supply of financial aid. Students who are in great demand by a number of schools will attract larger financial-aid packages. Whether students who are less in demand will also benefit is not clear. If the marginal cost of admitting these students is low, then competition for them will drive up the financial aid they are offered. If, on the other hand, the marginal cost exceeds the amount these students would pay, these less attractive applicants may find less financial aid offered to them.

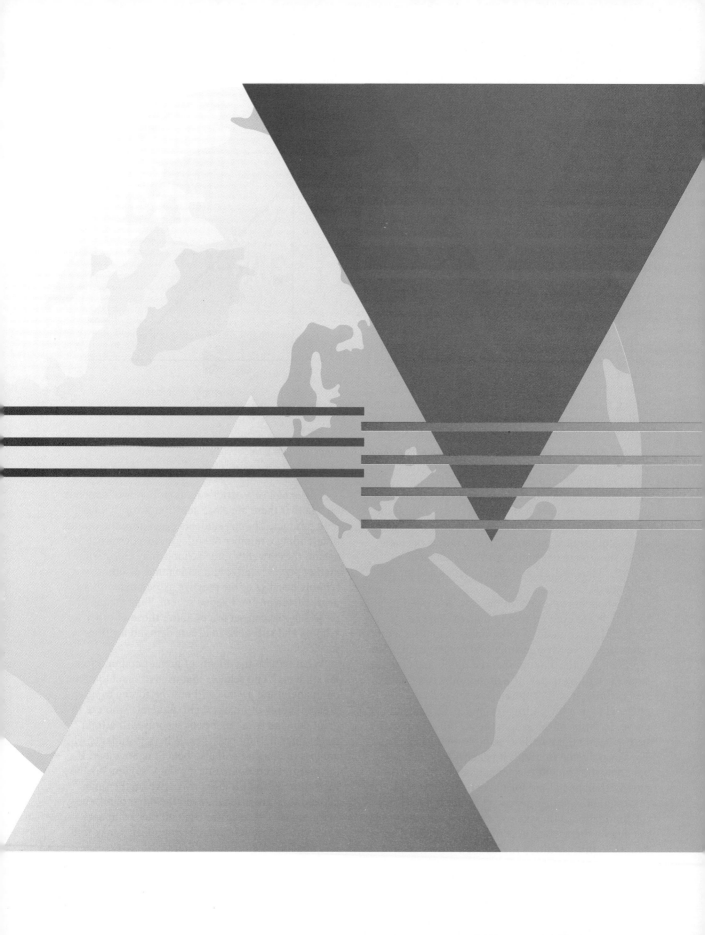

IV

Resource Markets

15

An Overview of Resource Markets

FUNDAMENTAL QUESTIONS

1. Who are the buyers and sellers of resources?
2. How are resource prices determined?
3. How does a firm allocate its expenditures among the various resources?

D ownsizing or streamlining companies through the elimination of middle-management positions has become a widespread practice in the United States. The American Management Association surveyed 1,100 U.S. companies in 1991 and 1992 and reported that although middle managers comprised only 5 to 8 percent of all workers, they represented 17 percent of all layoffs.[1] In addition, many companies have decided that the only way they will survive in the global economy is by reducing the cost of labor and increasing the automation of their production processes—in other words, by substituting capital for labor, or what some refer to as robotics. It has been estimated that over half a million jobs in the United States will be taken over by some 200,000 industrial robots by 1995, and virtually half of all manufacturing jobs will be replaced with robots by 2010.[2]

PREVIEW

Firms are in business to make profits: we have learned how they attempt to differentiate their products, restrict entry, and otherwise behave so as to increase their profits. And we've seen that the type of behavior they undertake depends on the market structure in which they operate. But profit is not just the revenue obtained from selling products. The costs of running the business must be subtracted from that revenue to arrive at the profit figure. Firms attempt to use those combinations of resources that enable them to produce their products at the lowest cost.

Which combinations of resources are most profitable? The answer does not depend solely on what the firms want. It depends also on the resource markets. It is in the resource markets that the demand for and supply of resources determines the prices and the quantities of those resources. Firms are the demanders of resources, and the resource owners are the suppliers. To understand why firms lay off middle managers, use more robotics, provide training for employees, purchase less fuel, locate offices in other nations, or expand the size of their buildings, it is necessary to understand how the resource markets function, to know what demand and supply look like and how they interact. This chapter provides an overview of the resource markets. Since there are four broad categories of resources—land, labor, capital, and entrepreneurial ability—there are four resource markets. The properties that are

---

[1]Tom H. Woods, "Riding the Restructuring Roller Coaster," *Business Forum*, Summer 1992, p. 3.
[2]William B. Rose, Ross L. Fink, and Robert K. Robinson, "Technological Displacement: Who Is Responsible for Retraining the Displaced?" *Industrial Management*, July/Aug. 1992, pp. 12–15.

common to each of these markets and a description of how the markets work are presented. You will see how the prices of resources and the quantities demanded are determined. You will also discover how a firm allocates its spending among different resources in order to maximize profit.

1. BUYERS AND SELLERS OF RESOURCES

Who are the buyers and sellers of resources?

residual claimants:
entrepreneurs who acquire profit, or the revenue remaining after all other resources have been paid

There are four general classes of resources (*factors of production*, or *inputs*) and thus four resource markets: land, labor, capital, and entrepreneurial ability. The price and quantity of each resource are determined in its resource market. Rent and the quantity of land used are determined in the land market. The wage rate and the number of people employed are determined in the labor market. The interest rate and the quantity of capital used are determined in the capital market. Profit is a residual, left from revenue after all costs (including opportunity costs) have been paid. The entrepreneur claims that residual, and for that reason, owners or entrepreneurs are often referred to as **residual claimants**.

1.a. The Resource Markets

To understand the four resource markets, you need to realize that the roles of firms and households are reversed from what they are in the product markets. Figure 1 is the circular flow diagram you saw in Chapter 4. It illustrates the roles of firms and households in the product and resource markets. The product market is represented by the top lines in the figure. Households buy goods and services from firms, as shown by the line going from firms to households; and firms sell goods and services and receive revenue, as shown by the line going from households to firms. The resource market is represented by the bottom half of the diagram in Figure 1. Households are the sellers of resources, and firms are the buyers of resources. Households sell resources, as shown by the line going from households to firms; and firms

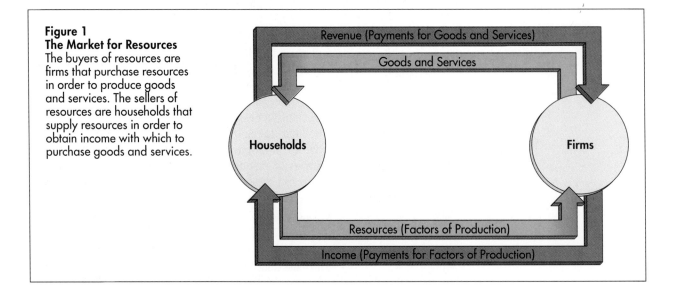

Figure 1
The Market for Resources
The buyers of resources are firms that purchase resources in order to produce goods and services. The sellers of resources are households that supply resources in order to obtain income with which to purchase goods and services.

Revenue (Payments for Goods and Services)

Goods and Services

Households

Firms

Resources (Factors of Production)

Income (Payments for Factors of Production)

pay households income, as shown by the line going from firms to households.

Resources are wanted not for themselves but for what they produce. A firm uses resources in order to produce goods and services. Thus, the demand for a resource by a firm depends on the demand for the goods and services that the firm produces. For this reason, the demand for resources is often called a **derived demand**: an automobile manufacturer uses land, labor, capital, and entrepreneurial ability to produce cars; a retail T-shirt store uses land, labor, capital, and entrepreneurial ability to sell T-shirts; a farmer uses land, labor, capital, and entrepreneurial ability to produce agricultural products.

derived demand:
demand stemming from what a resource can produce, not demand for the resource itself

Households supply resources in order to earn income. By offering to work, individuals supply their labor; by purchasing stocks, bonds, and other financial capital, households supply firms with the ability to acquire capital; by offering their land and the minerals, trees, and other natural resources associated with it, households supply land; and by offering to take the risk of business and produce goods and services, households offer their entrepreneurial ability.

RECAP

1. Resources are classified into four types: land, labor, capital, and entrepreneurial ability.
2. The price of each type of resource—rent, wages, interest, and profits— and the quantity of each resource used are determined in the resource markets.
3. The buyers of resources are firms; the suppliers are households.

2. THE MARKET DEMAND FOR AND SUPPLY OF RESOURCES

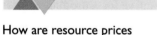

How are resource prices determined?

Firms demand resources and households supply resources. Except for this reversal in buyers and sellers, the supply and demand curves for resource markets look just like the supply and demand curves for product markets. The market demand curve slopes downward and the market supply curve upward. In resource markets, as in product markets, equilibrium defines the price and quantity. Changes in demand or supply cause the equilibrium price and quantity to change.

2.a. Market Demand

A firm chooses inputs in order to maximize profits.

The demand curve for a resource slopes down, as shown in Figure 2, because as the price of the resource falls, everything else held constant, producers are more *willing* and more *able* to use (to purchase or rent) that resource. If the price of the resource falls, that resource becomes relatively less expensive than other resources that the firm could use. Firms will substitute this now relatively less expensive resource for other now relatively more expensive resources. Thus substitution occurs in production just as it does in consumption. Construction firms switch from copper tubing to plastic pipe as copper becomes relatively more expensive than plastic. Firms move from Manhattan to Dallas as land in Manhattan becomes relatively more expensive than land

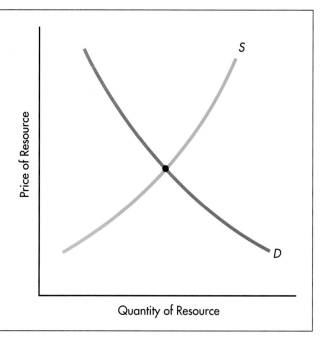

Figure 2
Resource Market Demand and Market Supply
The demand curve for a resource slopes down, reflecting the inverse relation between the price of the resource and the quantity demanded. The supply curve of a resource slopes up, reflecting the direct relation between the price of the resource and the quantity supplied. Equilibrium occurs where the two curves intersect; the quantities demanded and supplied are the same at the equilibrium price. If the resource price is greater than the equilibrium price, a surplus of the resource arises and drives the price back down to equilibrium. If the resource price is less than the equilibrium price, a shortage occurs and forces the price back up to equilibrium.

in Dallas. Economists may be hired to teach finance, management, and even accounting classes as the wages of professionals in those other fields rise relative to the wages of economists.

A lower price for a resource also increases a firm's *ability* to hire that resource. At a lower price, everything else held constant, firms can purchase more resources for the same total cost. If the price of a machine drops by 50 percent, the firm can buy two machines at the old cost of one. This means not that the firm will buy two machines but that it is able to buy the second machine. Thus, the demand curve for a resource slopes down because of income and substitution effects just as the demand curve for a product slopes down because of income and substitution effects, as you learned in the chapter on consumer choice.

2.a.1. The Elasticity of Resource Demand The amount by which firms will alter their use of a resource when the price of that resource changes is measured by the price elasticity of resource demand. The price elasticity of the demand for a resource, e_r, is defined in exactly the same way as the price elasticity of demand—as the percentage change in the quantity demanded of a resource divided by the percentage change in the price of the resource:

$$e_r = \frac{\text{percentage change in quantity demanded of resource } j}{\text{percentage change in price of resource } j}$$

If the price of lumber rises by 10 percent and the quantity demanded falls by 5 percent, the price elasticity of demand for lumber is .5. If the rental rate of office space falls by 5 percent and the quantity demanded increases by 20 percent, the price elasticity of demand for office space is 4. The price elasticity of demand for a resource depends on the

■ price elasticity of demand for the product the resource is used to produce

■ proportion of total costs constituted by the resource

- number of substitutes for the resource
- time period under consideration

Price elasticity of the product The price elasticity of demand for a resource depends on the price elasticity of demand for the product the resource is being used to produce. For instance, if the price elasticity of demand for newspapers is very high and the price of newspapers increases, the quantity demanded of newspapers will fall by a "great deal." As a result, a similarly "great deal" fewer resources are needed. Suppose then that the price of one of these resources, ink, rises. If the higher ink cost leads to a rise in the price of newspapers, then the quantity of newspapers demanded will decline by a significant amount and cause the quantity of ink purchased to decline by a significant amount. Everything else the same, we can say that the larger the price elasticity of demand for a product, the larger the price elasticity of demand for resources used to produce that product. The reverse is true as well.

Proportion of total costs The larger one resource's proportion of the total costs of producing a good, the higher the price elasticity of demand for that resource. If airplanes constitute 60 percent of the total costs of running an airline, the price elasticity of demand for airplanes will be high. A small increase in the price of an airplane will tend to raise the airline's costs significantly, and this is likely to increase the price of tickets. The higher price for tickets will reduce the quantity demanded and thereby reduce the number of airplanes demanded.

Number of substitutes The number of substitutes for a resource affects the price elasticity of demand for a resource. For instance, if copper tubing, plastic tubing, steel tubing, or corrugated aluminum tubing can be used in construction equally well, the price elasticity of demand for any one of these types of tubing will be relatively high. Even a small increase in copper tubing would cause firms to switch immediately to other types of tubing.

Time period The time period is also important in determining the price elasticity of demand. The longer the period of time under consideration, the greater the price elasticity of demand for a resource. A longer period of time enables firms to discover other substitutes and to move relatively immobile resources into or out of use.

The price elasticity of resource demand varies according to the four factors just mentioned. The price elasticity of resource demand also varies along a straight-line resource demand curve, going from elastic to inelastic as we move down the demand curve, just as is the case with a product demand curve (see the chapter on demand and supply elasticities).

2.a.2. Shifts in the Demand for a Resource The demand curve for a resource will shift when one of the *nonprice* determinants of demand changes. Nonprice determinants of demand for a resource include the

- prices of the product the resource is used to produce
- productivity of a resource
- number of buyers of the resource
- prices of related resources
- quantities of other resources

Entrepreneurs must combine land, labor, and capital to produce the goods and services they hope to sell for a profit. Leo Lindy's on Broadway in New York City had to spend more on very specific capital, this neon-lighted sign, than if the deli was located off-Broadway since it is competing for the attention of theater goers. The specific capital provides benefits to the firm in that it provides information to consumers about the stability of the firm and the type of sevice provided by the firm. Consumers can choose between the deli with the neon sign or a dark bistro down the street.

Price of product When the price of copper rises, the demand for copper miners increases—the demand curve shifts out to the right. Mining firms hire more workers at each wage rate in order to produce more copper and earn the higher revenues.

Productivity When a resource becomes more productive—that is, when each unit of the resource can produce more output—the firm will use more of the resource. For instance, if new printing presses are able to produce twice as much in the same amount of time as existing presses, the demand for new printing presses will rise. The demand curve for printing presses will shift out to the right.

Number of buyers When new firms enter an industry, they require resources. The demand curve for resources will shift out to the right. For instance, when Wal-Mart builds a store in a small town, it must hire workers and acquire land, capital, buildings, and other supplies. The demand for workers, for capital, for land, and for the other supplies increases with the entry of Wal-Mart—the demand curves shift out to the right.

Substitutes A change in the price of substitute resources will affect the demand for a resource. For instance, if labor and machines are substitutes in the production of iron ore, then when the price of labor rises, the demand for machines increases—the demand curve for machines shifts out to the right. Conversely, if copper and plastic are substitutes in construction, then when the price of plastic declines, the demand for copper decreases—the demand curve for copper shifts in.

Quantity of other resources A restaurant using only 10 of its 60 tables requires only one waiter. If the other 50 tables are also used, the restaurant needs more waiters. With a bigger pot and more soil, the quantity of flowers grown with each additional amount of fertilizer applied will be larger than it would be with a smaller pot and less soil. More capital tends to increase the demand for labor; more land tends to increase the demand for tractors. In other words, the demand for a resource depends on how many of the other resources are available.

2.b. Market Supply

A household supplies resources in order to maximize utility.

Individuals act so as to maximize their utility. They receive utility when they consume goods and services, but they need income to purchase the goods and services. To acquire income, households must sell the services of their resources. They must give up some of their leisure time and go to work or offer their other resources in order to acquire income. The quantity of resources that are supplied depends on the wages, rents, interest, and profits offered for those resources. If, while everything else is held constant, people can get higher wages, they will offer to work more hours; if they can obtain more rent for their land, they will offer more of their land for use, and so on. The quantity supplied of a resource rises as the price of the resource rises.

2.b.1. The Elasticity of Resource Supply The amount by which resource owners alter the quantity they offer for use when the price of the resource changes is measured by the price elasticity of resource supply, e^s_r. The price elasticity of supply for a resource is defined as the percentage change in the quantity supplied divided by the percentage change in the price of a resource:

$$e^s_r = \frac{\text{percentage change in quantity of resource supplied}}{\text{percentage change in price of resource}}$$

The price elasticity of resource supply depends on the number of substitute uses for a resource and the time period under consideration. Some resources have no substitutes. For instance, there are few if any substitutes for a rocket scientist; as a result, the price elasticity of supply for the rocket scientist is very low. Typically, the longer the period under consideration, the more likely that substitutes for a resource can be discovered. Given a few years, even an economist could be trained to be a rocket scientist. For a month or two, the quantity of oil that can be pulled from the ground is relatively fixed; given a year or so, new wells can be drilled and new supplies discovered. The price elasticity of resource supply increases as the time period increases.

economic rent:
the portion of earnings above transfer earnings

transfer earnings:
the portion of total earnings required to keep a resource in its current use

When a resource has a perfectly inelastic supply curve, its pay or earnings is called **economic rent**. If a resource has a perfectly elastic supply curve, its pay or earnings is called **transfer earnings**. For upward-sloping supply curves, resource earnings consist of both transfer earnings and economic rent. Transfer earnings is what a resource could earn in its best alternative use (its opportunity cost). It is the amount that must be paid to get the resource to "transfer" to another use. Economic rent is earnings in excess of transfer earnings. It is the portion of a resource's earnings that is not necessary to keep the resource in its current use. A movie star can earn more than $1 million per movie but probably could not earn that kind of income in another occupation. Thus, the greatest share of the earnings of the movie star is economic rent.

There are two different meanings for the term *rent* in economics. The most common meaning refers to the payment for the use of something, as distinguished from payment for ownership. In this sense, you purchase a house but rent an apartment; you buy a car from Chrysler but rent cars from Avis. The second use of the term *rent* is to mean payment for the use of something that is in fixed—that is, perfectly inelastic—supply. The total quantity of land is fixed; payment to land is economic rent.

2.b.2. Shifts in the Supply of a Resource
The supply of a resource will change—increase or decrease at every price—if

- tastes change
- the number of suppliers changes
- the prices of other uses of the resource change

Suppose it suddenly becomes more prestigious to be a lawyer. The supply of people entering law schools will increase—the supply curve of lawyers will shift up or out to the right. The shift will occur because of a change in tastes (more prestige), not because of a change in the wage rate of lawyers.

An increase in the number of suppliers means that the supply curve shifts out to the right. For instance, discovery of oil in a country that is not currently an oil producer would mean an increase in the supply of oil—at each price a greater quantity of oil would be supplied. Immigration increases the supply of labor. More producers of bulldozers increase the supply of bulldozers.

The supply curve of a resource will shift if the price of related resources changes. If the wage rate of professionals in finance rises, economists and others may offer their services in the finance market. The supply curve of finance professionals will shift out. If the rental rate of land used for production of wheat rises, everything else held constant, land currently used to produce alfalfa will be switched over to wheat—the supply curve of land used in the production of wheat will shift out to the right.

2.c. Equilibrium

The intersection between the market demand and supply curves determines the price and quantity of a resource. If the demand curve shifts out, everything else held constant, the price rises; if the supply curve shifts out, everything else held constant, the price decreases. If the price rises above the equilibrium price, then a surplus exists and the price is forced back to equilibrium; if the price falls below the equilibrium level, then a shortage arises and the price is forced back up to equilibrium.

2.c.1. Price Ceilings and Floors
A resource market will move toward its equilibrium price and quantity as long as nothing interferes with the market adjustment. There are many instances where floors or ceilings are placed on the resource price, however. Consider the impact of a price floor in the labor market and a price ceiling in the steel market.

Figure 3(a) shows a labor market, with the quantity of labor in hours along the horizontal axis and the hourly wage rate along the vertical axis. The equilibrium wage determined in the market would be $W_e = \$3.50$. The government has imposed a minimum wage at $4.50 per hour, however, so that the actual wage paid is $W_m = \$4.50$, a price floor. At the minimum wage, the quantity of hours that people are willing and able to work is Q_s, while the quantity of hours that firms are willing and able to pay for is Q_d. The difference between Q_s and Q_d is the number of hours that people would like to work but for which there is no work.

A price ceiling works in just the opposite way of the price floor. The price ceiling creates a shortage. For instance, suppose the government requires for-

Figure 3
Price Ceilings and Price Floors

Figure 3(a) is a labor market showing the quantity of labor in hours along the horizontal axis and the hourly wage rate along the vertical axis. The equilibrium wage determined in the market would be $W_e = \$3.50$, but because a minimum wage at $4.50 per hour has been imposed, the actual wage paid is $W_m = \$4.50$, a wage floor. At the minimum wage, the quantity of hours that people are willing and able to work is Q_s, while the

quantity of hours that firms are willing and able to pay for is Q_d. The difference between Q_s and Q_d is the number of hours that people would like to work but for which there is no work.

Figure 3(b) represents the market for steel. The equilibrium price is P_e, but because the government has implemented a program whereby foreign steel producers cannot sell their steel for more than P_m, the equilibrium price plays no role. A shortage is created equal to Q_d less Q_s.

(a) Labor Market

(b) Steel Market

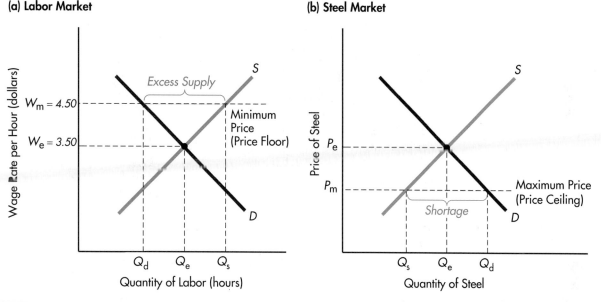

eign steel producers to sell their steel to U.S. manufacturers for no more than P_m in Figure 3(b). The quantity of steel demanded rises from Q_s to Q_d, whereas the quantity that the steel suppliers are willing to provide for sale at P_m is Q_s. The difference between Q_d and Q_s represents the shortage of steel.

RECAP

1. Firms purchase resources in such a way that they maximize profits. Households sell resources in order to maximize utility.

2. Transfer earnings is the portion of total earnings required to keep a resource in its current use.

3. Economic rent is earnings in excess of transfer earnings.

4. Equilibrium in a resource market defines the price (wages, rent, interest, profit) of that resource as long as the price and quantity are free to adjust. Price ceilings lead to shortages; price floors lead to surpluses.

3. HOW FIRMS DECIDE WHAT RESOURCES TO BUY

How does a firm allocate its expenditures among the various resources?

The market demand for a resource consists of the demands of each firm willing and able to pay for a resource. An electric utility firm in Iowa demands engineers, as does a construction firm in Minnesota. The market demand for engineers consists of demands of the Iowa utility and the Minnesota construction firm. Each firm's demand depends on separate and distinct factors, however. The electric utility firm hires more engineers to modernize its plant; the construction firm hires more engineers to fulfill its contracts with the state government to build bridges. Yet all firms have the same decision-making process for hiring or acquiring resources.

3.a. Individual Firm Demand: Marginal Revenue Product

How do you decide how much you are willing to pay for something? Don't you decide how much it is worth to you? This is what businesses do when they decide how much to pay a worker or to pay for a machine. A firm uses the quantity of each resource that will enable the firm to maximize profit. Firms maximize profit when they operate at the level where marginal revenue (MR) equals marginal cost (MC). Thus, firms acquire additional resources until MR = MC. If the acquisition of a resource will raise the firm's revenues more than it will increase its costs—that is, if MR will be greater than MC—the firm will hire the resource. Conversely, if the acquisition of a resource will raise costs more than it will raise revenue—that is, if MR will be less than MC—then the firm will not hire the resource.

A firm will purchase the services of another unit of a resource if that additional unit adds more to the firm's revenue than it costs. Recall from the chapter on the costs of doing business that the additional output an extra unit

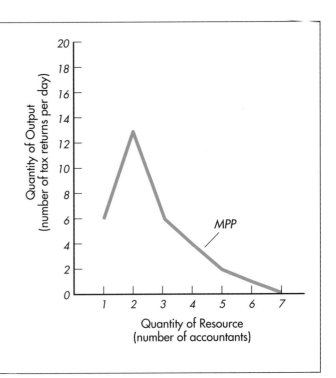

Figure 4
The *MPP* Curve
The value of a resource to a firm depends on the additional output that the resource produces. This additional output is the marginal physical product of the resource. The marginal physical product of accountants measured in number of tax returns per day is listed in the table. The marginal physical product is drawn as a curve in the graph.

(1) Number of Accountants	(2) Number of Tax Returns per Day	(3) *MPP*
1	6	6
2	19	13
3	25	6
4	29	4
5	31	2
6	32	1
7	32	0

Part IV/Resource Markets

of a resource produces is called the marginal physical product (MPP) of that resource. The MPP of tax accountants for a CPA firm is the number of tax returns that additional tax accountant can complete; the MPP is listed in column 3 of the table in Figure 4, and the MPP curve is drawn in the accompanying graph. The MPP curve initially rises and then declines according to the law of diminishing marginal returns.

The value of this additional output to the firm is the additional revenue the output generates—the marginal revenue. Multiplying marginal physical product by marginal revenue yields the value of an additional unit of a resource to the firm, which is called the **marginal revenue product (MRP)**:

marginal revenue product (MRP):
the value of the additional output that an extra unit of a resource can produce, MPP × MR; the value to the firm of an additional resource

$$MRP = MPP \times MR$$

The MRP of a resource, such as labor, is a measure of how much the additional output generated by the last worker is worth to the firm. The marginal-revenue-product curve is drawn in Figure 5. The information from Figure 4 is listed in columns 1–3 of Figure 5. Marginal revenue is calculated in column 6 of the

(1) Number of Accountants	(2) Number of Tax Returns per Day	(3) MPP	(4) Output Price (per tax return)	(5) Total Revenue	(6) Marginal Revenue	(7) MRP (MPP × MR)
1	6	6	$100	$ 600	$100	$ 600
2	19	13	100	1,900	100	1,300
3	25	6	100	2,500	100	600
4	29	4	100	2,900	100	400
5	31	2	100	3,100	100	200
6	32	1	100	3,200	100	100
7	32	0	100	3,200	0	0

Figure 5
The Marginal Revenue Product
The marginal physical product multiplied by the marginal revenue yields the marginal revenue product. The *MPP* curve from Figure 4 is multiplied by the marginal revenue and plotted in Figure 5 as the *MRP* curve. The information from Figure 4 is listed in columns 1–3 of Figure 5. The output price is listed in column 4, the total revenue, P × Q, is listed in column 5, and marginal revenue is calculated in column 6. Multiplying column 6 by column 3 yields the *MRP*, listed in column 7.

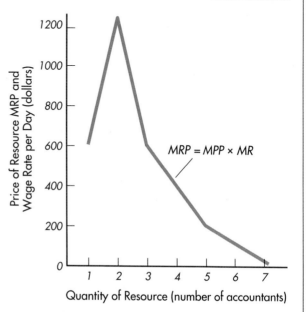

Chapter 15 / An Overview of Resource Markets

387

table in Figure 5 and multiplied by the MPP to arrive at the MRP in column 7. You can see that after rising initially, the MRP curve slopes downward.

3.b. Marginal Factor Costs

The MRP measures the value of an additional resource to a firm. To determine the quantity of a resource that a firm will hire, the firm must know the cost of each additional unit of the resource. The cost of an additional unit of a resource depends on whether the firm is purchasing resources in a market with many suppliers or in a market with one or only a few suppliers.

3.b.1. Hiring Resources in a Perfectly Competitive Market
If the firm is purchasing resources in a market where there is a very large number of suppliers of an identical resource—a perfectly competitive resource market—the price of each additional unit of the resource to the firm is constant. Why? Because no seller is large enough to individually change the price. A firm can hire as much of the resource as it wants without affecting either the quantity available or the price of that resource. This situation is shown in Figures 6(a) and 6(b) for the market for accountants. The market wage is defined by the market demand and market supply, as shown in Figure 6(a), and that wage translates to a horizontal supply curve for the individual firm, as shown in Figure 6(b).

Let's assume that the market wage for accountants is $150 per day. The firm can hire as many accountants as it wants at $150 per day without influ-

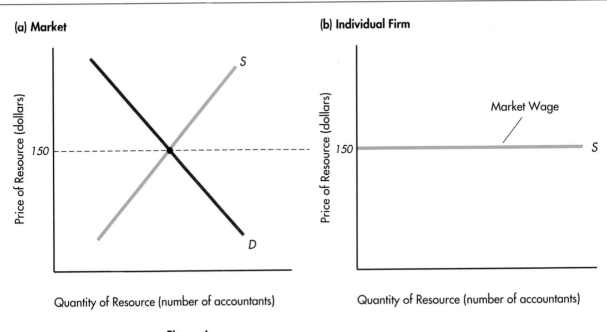

Figure 6
The Perfectly Competitive Resource Market and the Individual Firm
The demand for and supply of a resource determine the price of the resource, as shown in Figure 6(a). This market price is the price the individual firm must pay to obtain any units of the resource. As shown in Figure 6(b), the individual firm is a price taker.

encing the price. How many accountants will the firm hire? It will hire additional accountants as long as the additional revenue brought in by the last accountant hired is no less than the additional cost of that accountant.

Let's use the information in Figure 7, which combines Figures 5 and 6, to see how many accountants the firm would hire. The first accountant hired has a marginal revenue product of $600 per day and costs $150 per day. It is profitable to hire her. A second accountant, bringing in an additional $1,300 per day and costing $150 per day, is also profitable. The third accountant brings in $600 per day, the fourth $400 per day, the fifth $200 per day, the sixth $100 per day, and the seventh nothing. Thus, the third, fourth, and fifth are profitable, but the sixth and seventh aren't. At $150 per day, the firm hires five accountants. You can see in the graph that the marginal revenue product lies above the wage rate until after the fifth accountant is hired.

The firm hires additional accountants until MRP is equal to the cost to the firm of another accountant. Remember, the MRP is the value of the additional resource to the firm; thus, the firm wants to be sure that the value of a resource exceeds its costs. The cost of an additional unit of a resource is the **marginal factor cost (MFC)**, also known as the *marginal resource cost* or *marginal input cost*. The marginal factor cost for accountants is listed as column 3 in Figure 7.

The firm hires additional accountants until the marginal revenue product equals the marginal factor cost, MRP = MFC. This is a general rule; it holds whether the firm sells its output in a perfectly competitive, monopoly, monopolistically competitive, or oligopoly market; and it holds for all resources, not just accountants.

marginal factor cost (MFC): the additional cost of an additional unit of a resource

Resources will be employed up to the point at which MRP = MFC.

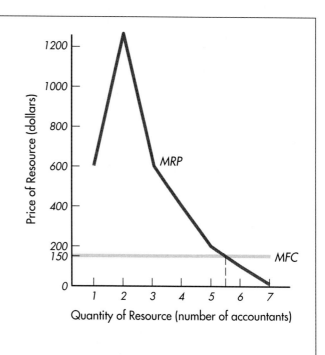

Figure 7
The Employment of Resources
The marginal revenue product and the marginal factor cost (wage rate) together indicate the number of accountants the individual firm would hire. The MRP and the MFC for an individual firm are listed in the table. The *MRP* curve and the *MFC* curve are shown in the graph. The marginal revenue product exceeds the marginal factor cost (wage rate) until after the fifth accountant is hired. The firm will not hire more than five, for then the costs would exceed the additional revenue produced by the last accountant hired.

(1) Number of Accountants	(2) MRP	(3) MFC (wage per day)
1	$ 600	$150
2	1,300	150
3	600	150
4	400	150
5	200	150
6	100	150
7	0	150

monopsonist:
a firm that is the only buyer
of a resource

3.b.2. Hiring Resources as a Monopoly Buyer

If only one firm is bidding for a resource or a product, that firm is called a **monopsonist**. In the early days of mining in the United States it was not uncommon for firms to create entire towns in order to attract a readily available supply of labor. The sole provider of jobs in the town was the mining company. Thus, when the company hired labor, it affected the prices of all workers, not just the worker it recently hired. In the 1970s along the Alaskan pipeline, and in the 1980s in foreign countries where U.S. firms were hired to carry out specialized engineering projects or massive construction jobs, small towns dependent on a single U.S. firm were created. There are cases where a monopsony exists even though a company town was not created. For instance, many universities in small communities are monopsonistic employers—they are the primary employer in the town. When these universities hire a mechanic, they affect the wage rates of all mechanics in the town. Other examples of monopsonies are discussed in the Economic Insight "The Company Town."

A monopoly firm will pay resources less than their marginal revenue products. Suppose, for example, that a large semiconductor firm in a small town is the primary employer in the town and that the firm is in the process of hiring accountants. As shown in Figure 8 (see table), at a wage of $25 per day only 1 person is willing and able to work. If the firm pays $50 per day, it can hire 2 accountants. However, the firm isn't able to hire the first at $25 and the second at $50; it must pay both $50. Otherwise, the first will quit and then be rehired at $50 per day (only 2 were willing and able to work for $50). As a result, the total cost (called *total factor cost*) of two accountants is $100, not $75, and the additional, or marginal, factor cost is $75 rather than the $50 wage of the second accountant. If the firm offers $150 per day, it can hire 4 accountants; its total factor cost will be $600 and its marginal factor cost $300. This is shown in columns 8, 9, and 10 of the table. Column 8 is the wage per day, 9 is the total factor cost (column 1 times column 8), and 10 is the marginal factor cost.

The graph in Figure 8 shows the marginal factor cost and the supply curve of accountants in the small town. The *MFC* curve is plotted from data in column 10 of the table, and the supply curve is plotted from data in column 8. For a monopsonist, the *MFC* curve lies above the supply curve. The reason is that the cost of each additional accountant to the firm is the additional accountant's wage *plus* the additional wages paid to all of the other accountants.

The rising marginal factor cost means that the accountants would be paid less than their marginal revenue product. The firm would hire 4 accountants since the fifth accountant costs the firm $400 (MFC) but brings in only $200 (MRP). The fourth accountant produces $400 of additional revenue for the firm (MRP), costs the firm an additional $300 (MFC), but is paid only $150.

As long as resource services are purchased by other than a monopsonist, they are paid their marginal revenue products. A monopsonist pays less than the marginal revenue product.

A firm buying in a perfectly competitive resource market will pay the marginal revenue product; a monopsonistic firm will pay less than the marginal revenue product.

3.c. Hiring When There Is More Than One Resource

To this point we've examined the firm's hiring decision for one resource, everything else, including the quantities of all other resources, held constant. However, a firm uses several resources and makes hiring decisions regarding

(1) Number of Accountants	(2) Number of Tax Returns per Day	(3) MPP	(4) Product Price (per tax return)	(5) Total Revenue	(6) MR	(7) MRP	(8) Wage per Day	(9) Total Factor Cost of Accountants	(10) MFC
1	6	6	$100	$ 600	$100	$ 600	$ 25	$ 25	$ 25
2	19	13	100	1,900	100	1,300	50	100	75
3	25	6	100	2,500	100	600	100	300	200
4	29	4	100	2,900	100	400	150	600	300
5	31	2	100	3,100	100	200	200	1,000	400
6	32	1	100	3,200	100	100	250	1,500	500
7	32	0	100	3,200	100	0	300	2,100	600

Note: Marginal revenue is the change in total revenue divided by the change in output. In this case, it is the change in total revenue divided by the change in the number of tax returns produced.

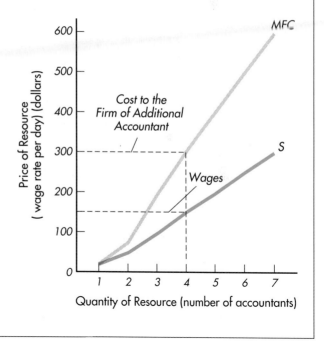

Figure 8
The Monopsonist
When the firm is a monopsonistic buyer of resources, it faces a marginal factor cost curve that lies above the supply curve. Each time the firm purchases a unit of the resource, the price of all units of the resource is driven up. As a result, the cost of one additional unit of the resource exceeds the price that must be paid for that additional unit of the resource. This is shown in columns 8 through 10 of the table; columns 8 and 10 are plotted in the graph. The firm hires resources until the marginal revenue product and marginal factor cost are equal. The firm pays resources the price given by the supply curve at the quantity determined by MFC = MRP. Thus, the resource receives less than its marginal revenue product.

most of them all the time. How does the firm decide what combinations of resources to use? Like the consumer deciding what combinations of goods and services to purchase, the firm will ensure that the benefits of spending one more dollar are the same no matter which resource the firm chooses to spend that dollar on.

You may recall that the consumer maximizes utility when the marginal utility per dollar of expenditure is the same on all goods and services purchased:

$$MU_{cake}/P_{cake} = MU_{coffee}/P_{coffee} = \ldots = MU_n/P_n$$

The Company Town

Early in his career, Milton Friedman, the Nobel Prize–winning economist, served as an instructor for the navy. His assignment was in Hershey, Pennsylvania, where he stayed at the Hershey Hotel, on the corner of Cocoa Avenue and Chocolate Boulevard, across the street from the Hershey Junior College, down the street from the Hershey Department Store. Friedman describes Hershey as a benevolent company town, but not all company towns that arose in the early 1900s were so benevolent. Workers who were employed in factories or mines located far from large cities were often required to live in company housing and buy their food and other supplies at company stores. The prices many paid at the company store were very high, because the stores were local monopolies.

By the 1940s, most company towns and stores had disappeared, but a few still exist today. Documented and undocumented aliens who work in the agricultural areas of the Southwest often must pay their employers for their sleeping quarters, their food and drinks, and other items. The workers are paid in kind rather than cash and often end up owing more to the company store than they receive in wages.

Sources: Andrew Gulliford, *Boomtown Blues: Colorado Oil Shale, 1885–1985* (Boulder: University Press of Colorado, 1990); Dennis Farney, "Price of Progress," *Wall Street Journal*, April 3, 1990, pp. 1, A14; Milton Friedman, "The Folly of Buying Health Care at the Company Store," *Wall Street Journal*, Feb. 3, 1993, p. A14.

A similar rule holds for the firm attempting to purchase resource services in order to maximize profit and minimize costs. The firm will be maximizing profit when its marginal revenue product per dollar of expenditure on all resources is the same:

$$MRP_{land}/MFC_{land} = MRP_{labor}/MFC_{labor} = \ldots = MRP_n/MFC_n$$

The last dollar spent on resources must yield the same marginal revenue product no matter which resource the dollar is spent on.

As long as the marginal factor cost of a resource is less than its marginal revenue product, the firm will increase profit by hiring more of the resource. If a dollar spent on labor yields less marginal revenue product than a dollar spent on capital, the firm will increase profit more by purchasing the capital than if it purchases the labor.[3]

If a resource is very expensive relative to other resources, then the expensive resource must generate a significantly larger marginal revenue product than the other resources. For instance, for a firm to remain in Manhattan, it must generate a significantly larger marginal revenue product than could be obtained in Dallas or elsewhere, because rents are so much higher in Manhattan. The price of land in Tokyo is so high that its use requires a very high marginal revenue product.

A firm will streamline its work force when the last dollar of expenditures on labor generates less marginal revenue product than if that dollar were

---

[3]This equimarginal rule can also be written as $MPP_{land}/MFC_{land} = MPP_{labor}/MFC_{labor} = \ldots$ since $MRP = MFC$ or $MRP/MFC = 1$ and since $MRP = MPP \times MR$, $MPP/MFC = 1/MR$ for all resources.

spent on another resource; a firm will streamline by reducing its middle management if the last dollar spent on middle management generates less return (lower MRP) than if that dollar were spent on other labor or another resource. During the early 1990s, many U.S. firms decided that their expenditures on middle management particularly, but also on their entire labor force, were not generating the same return that expenditures on other resources would yield. As a result, firms reduced their work force; they dismissed many middle-management employees. The media referred to this process as streamlining, but it was part of the ongoing process by firms to ensure that the last dollar of expenditure on each resource generated the same MRP.

A firm in equilibrium in terms of allocating its expenditures among resources will alter the allocation only if the cost of one of the resources rises relative to the others. For instance, if government-mandated medical or other benefits mean that labor costs rise while everything else remains constant, then firms will tend to hire less labor and use more of other resources. (This issue is discussed further in the Economic Insight "Labor Regulations and Employment.") Everything else the same, if the costs of doing business in the United States rise, firms will locate offices or plants in other countries.

3.d. Product Market Structures and Resource Demand

Firms purchase the types and quantities of resource services that allow them to maximize profit; each firm equates the MRP per dollar of expenditure on all resource services used. The MRP depends on the market structure in which the firm sells its output. A perfectly competitive firm produces more output and sells that output at a lower price than a firm operating in any other market, everything else the same. Since the perfectly competitive firm produces more output, it must use more resources. Thus, everything else the same, the demand curve for a resource by a perfectly competitive firm will lie above the demand curve for a resource by a firm selling in monopoly, oligopoly, or monopolistically competitive markets.

For the perfectly competitive firm, price and marginal revenue are the same, P = MR. Thus, the marginal revenue product, MRP = MR × MPP, for the perfectly competitive firm can be written as P × MPP. Sometimes this is called the value of the marginal product, VMP, to distinguish it from the marginal revenue product.

$$MRP = MR \times MPP$$

$$VMP = P \times MPP$$

The demand for a resource by a single firm is the MRP of that resource, no matter whether it sells its goods and services as a monopolist or as a perfect competitor (for the perfectly competitive firm, VMP = MRP, so that MRP is its resource demand as well). However, since for the firms not selling in a perfectly competitive market, price is greater than marginal revenue, VMP would be greater than MRP, which indicates that the perfectly competitive firm's demand curve for a resource lies above (or is greater than) the demand curve for a resource by a monopoly firm, oligopoly firm, or monopolistically competitive firm.

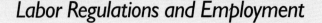

ECONOMIC INSIGHT

Labor Regulations and Employment

Firms must contribute to workers' compensation programs, which provide medical benefits and cash transfers to workers injured on the job; in some cases, stress is an acceptable basis for providing workers' compensation. The Clinton administration recently proposed legislation to require all firms to provide health insurance to their employees. The Family Leave Act implemented in 1993 provides for up to a twelve-week period per year for employees to leave their jobs without pay in order to take care of family matters and then to return to their jobs without penalty. How do these rules, regulations, and programs affect the resource market for labor?

If these programs are additional costs of using labor services, then firms will find that the ratios of their marginal revenue product per dollar of expenditure on labor and on all other resources are not equal; the ratio for labor will have been reduced. As a result, firms must find ways to reduce labor costs or use less labor. Firms can reduce labor costs if they find ways

to avoid paying workers' compensation or health insurance or allowing workers to take unpaid leaves of absence. Firms have discovered that temporary and part-time workers do not have to be provided these benefits. The *Wall Street Journal* recently reported that temporary employment grew ten times faster than overall employment in the United States between 1982 and 1990, and that temporary and part-time workers now make up about 25 percent of the work force. By turning to temporary agencies, smaller employers may be exempted from providing worker benefits. For instance, the family leave provisions apply only to firms with fifty or more permanent employees. Thus, a firm with sixty permanent employees must provide the benefit of family leave; by making eleven or more of these employees temporary, the firm does not have to provide the benefit of family leave. Moreover, firms do not have to provide workers' compensation or health and medical benefits for temporary employees.* Another way that firms can

reduce labor costs is to pay the mandatory benefits but reduce the compensation provided workers. About 85 percent of the costs of workers' compensation are passed on to employees through lower wages.** In this sense, the MFC of the workers is increased much less than the workers' compensation costs, so the ratio of MRP/MFC falls only a little relative to that of other resources. For workers whose wages are near the minimum wage, the costs cannot be shifted to them, so their MRP/MFC ratio will decline relatively more. Finally, if labor costs cannot be reduced, employment will fall as firms allocate their expenditures to other resources and away from labor.

*Clare Ansberry, "Hired Out," *Wall Street Journal*, March 11, 1993, p. A1.

**Jonathan Gruber and Alan Krueger, "The Incidence of Mandated Employer-Provided Insurance: Lessons from Workers' Compensation Insurance," NBER Working Paper No. 3557, Feb. 1991.

3.e. A Look Ahead

In the following chapters, we will examine aspects of the resource markets. In the labor market we discuss why different people receive different wages, why firms treat employees the way they do, the impact of labor laws, and the causes and results of discrimination. In the land market we'll look at problems of the environment and why the government is such a large player in the natural resources area. We will discuss the capital market and examine why firms carry out research and development and purchase robotics. Selling resource services creates income, so we'll examine who has income and why.

We'll look at the health-care market and examine why the United States is spending so much more on health care than other nations. These and other aspects of the resource markets will be examined within the framework discussed in this chapter.

RECAP

1. The MRP of a resource is a measure of how much the additional output generated by the last unit of the resource is worth to the firm.

2. Resources are hired up to the point at which MRP = MFC.

3. In a perfectly competitive resource market, resources are paid an amount equal to their marginal revenue product. In a monopsonistic resource market, resources are paid less than their marginal revenue product.

4. A firm will allocate its budget on resources up to the point that the last dollar spent yields an equal marginal revenue product no matter on which resource the dollar is spent.

5. A perfectly competitive firm will hire and acquire more resources than firms selling in monopoly, oligopoly, or monopolistically competitive product markets, everything else the same.

SUMMARY

▲▼ Who are the buyers and sellers of resources?

1. The term *resource markets* refers to the buyers and sellers of four classes of resources: land, labor, capital, and entrepreneurial ability. §1

2. The buyers of resources are firms that purchase resources in order to produce goods and services. §1.a

3. The sellers of resources are households that supply resources in order to obtain income with which to purchase goods and services. §1.a.

▲▼ How are resource prices determined?

4. Equilibrium in each resource market defines the rate of pay of the resource and the quantity used. §2

5. The rate of pay of a resource consists of two parts: transfer earnings and economic rent. Transfer earnings is the rate of pay necessary to keep a resource in its current use. Economic rent is the excess of pay above transfer earnings. §2.b

6. A single firm's demand for a resource is the downward-sloping portion of the marginal-revenue-product curve for that resource. §3.a

7. A firm purchasing resources in a perfectly competitive resource market will hire resources up to the point that MRP = MFC. A firm that is one of only a few buyers or the only buyer of a particular resource (a monopsonist) will face a marginal-factor-cost curve that is above the supply curve for that resource. As a result, the resource is paid less than its marginal revenue product. §§3.b.1, 3.b.2

▲▼ How does a firm allocate its expenditures among the various resources?

8. A firm will allocate its budget on resources in such a way that the last dollar spent will yield the same marginal revenue product no matter on which resource the dollar is spent. §3.c

KEY TERMS

residual claimants §1
derived demand §1.a
economic rent §2.b.1
transfer earnings §2.b.1

marginal revenue product (MRP) §3.a
marginal factor cost (MFC) §3.b.1
monopsonist §3.b.2

EXERCISES

1. What does it mean to say that the demand for resources is a derived demand? Is the demand for all goods and services a derived demand?

2. Using the information in the table, calculate the marginal revenue product (MRP = MPP × MR).

3. Using the data in question 2, determine how many units of resources the firm will want to acquire.

Units of Resources	Total Output	Output Price	Resource Price
1	10	$5	$10
2	25	5	10
3	35	5	10
4	40	5	10
5	40	5	10

4. Suppose the output price falls from $5 to $4 to $3 to $1 in question 2. How would that change your answers to questions 2 and 3?

5. Using the data in question 2, calculate the marginal factor cost.

6. Suppose the resource price rises from $10 to $12 to $14 to $18 to $20 as resource units go from 1 to 5. How would that change your answer to question 5? How would it change your answer to question 3?

7. Using question 6, calculate the transfer earnings and economic rent of the third unit of the resource when four units of the resource are employed. Do the same calculations when only three units of the resource are employed. How do you account for the different answers?

8. Do resources earn their marginal revenue products? Demonstrate under what conditions the answer is *yes*.

9. What is a monopsonist? How does a monopsonist differ from a monopolist?

10. Supposedly Larry Bird once said that he would play basketball for $10,000 per year. Yet he was paid over $1 million per year. If the quote is correct, how much was Bird's transfer earnings? How much was his economic rent?

11. In 1989 the Japanese spent more than $14 billion to buy 322 foreign companies, half of them in the United States, and $100 billion to buy foreign stocks and bonds. Why was Japanese money flowing so heavily out of Japan and into other parts of the world?

12. Early in her journalistic career, Gloria Steinem posed as a Playboy Bunny to examine the inside of a Playboy Club. Steinem discovered that the Bunnies had to purchase their costumes from the club, pay for the cleaning, purchase their food from the club, and so on. This "company store" exploited the employees (the Bunnies), according to Steinem. Explain what Steinem meant by exploitation.

13. Explain the idea behind the lyrics "You load 16 tons, and what do you get? You get another day older and deeper in debt. Saint Peter, don't you call me, 'cause I can't go. I owe my soul to the company store."

14. The Burroughs Wellcome Company had a monopoly on AZT, a pharmaceutical that delayed the onset of AIDS after someone had become HIV positive. The demand for that pharmaceutical was virtually perfectly price-inelastic. Explain how that might affect the demand for employees by the Burroughs Wellcome Company.

Economically Speaking

Trade Pact May Be Good for Business, Bad for Labor

LOUISVILLE—Kentucky might lose some jobs but gain others from the North American Free Trade Agreement with Mexico and Canada.

Workers in low-skilled manufacturing jobs, such as those in the apparel industry, are particularly vulnerable to having their jobs exported, because their Mexican counterparts are paid much lower wages.

But those with more highly skilled jobs could benefit as it becomes easier for companies to sell U.S.-made products in Mexico.

The agreement, if approved, would eliminate tariffs and reduce other restrictions on goods flowing across the U.S., Canadian and Mexican borders over the next 15 years.

Most area businesses contacted yesterday said they weren't familiar with details of the agreement, but they generally favored opening those markets.

Kentucky's labor unions generally oppose the agreement, however. Union leaders fear the agreement will tempt more businesses to move plants to Mexico in search of cheaper labor and fewer health, safety and environmental restrictions.

"There just seems to be a lack of concern and of loyalty to workers in American businesses," said Lisa Wallace, spokeswoman for the Kentucky State AFL-CIO.

She said Kentucky garment workers are especially at risk of losing jobs.

Rep. Chris Perkins, D-Ky., expressed similar fears.

The 7th District congressman, an opponent of the trade agreement, said in Washington yesterday that it jeopardizes the jobs of the 5,000 to 6,000 Eastern Kentuckians who work in the apparel industry.

Larry Martin of the American Apparel Manufacturers Association said: "I can't deny that some jobs are going to move to Mexico. How many I don't know."

With Mexican workers earning only about 50 cents an hour, it is difficult for U.S. workers to compete, he said.

Joe Medalie of Fruit of the Loom in Bowling Green, Ky., said that although some jobs might be lost to Mexico, the agreement should boost sales of U.S.-made garments south of the border.

"We look on the agreement favorably because there's a strong market in Mexico for our product," Medalie said.

Ford Motor Co.'s truck plants in the Louisville area also might benefit from the agreement. Stiff tariffs prevent Ford from selling any Explorer sport-utility vehicles in Mexico. But the agreement eliminates those tariffs.

"People down there have been crying for Explorers," said Joe Eby, executive director of Ford's corporate-strategy unit.

Companies already doing a lot of business in Mexico don't expect the agreement to make much difference for them. General Electric, for example, builds gas stoves at a plant south of the border. For that reason, company spokesman Jim Allen doesn't expect the agreement to affect production at Louisville's Appliance Park.

Several other companies with area ties, such as United Parcel Service, Cummins Engine Co., Ford and General Motors Corp., also have operations in Mexico.

Schnadig Corp., which makes end tables and coffee tables at its Henderson, Ky., plant, is in the process of moving work to Mexico.

Jim Waters, vice president of employee relations, confirmed that Schnadig is contracting with a company that manufactures tables in Mexico, and will reduce the number of jobs at its Henderson plant from 80 to about 25. It once employed 180 people.

Waters said workers at Henderson earn an average $6.50 an hour, plus benefits worth about $3.25 an hour. That's too high for Schnadig to compete with manufacturing costs in Taiwan, Honduras and Mexico, he said.

Source: *Louisville Courier-Journal*, Aug. 13, 1992, p. C1. Copyright © 1992. Courier-Journal & Louisville Times Co. Reprinted with permission.

Louisville Courier-Journal/August 13, 1992

Commentary

Trade barriers such as tariffs restrict the flow of goods and resources. The North American Free Trade Agreement (NAFTA) has been a controversial issue in the United States because there will be winners and losers as a result of the agreement.

The figure on the left shows a labor market for semiskilled or unskilled workers wherein the marginal-revenue-product curve is independent of country. The labor costs are different in the United States and Mexico however, as illustrated by the MFC_{US} and MFC_{MEX} curves. The MFC curve for the U.S. workers is higher than the MFC curve for the Mexican workers, resulting in higher U.S. wages, W_{US} compared to W_{MEX}.

Elimination of the trade barriers will permit goods to flow across the borders. The Mexican products produced by lower-paid Mexican workers will flow north to sell next to the U.S. products made by higher-paid U.S. workers. With lower-priced Mexican substitutes available, the demand for the U.S. products will decline. If the demand for the U.S. goods falls, the demand for the U.S. workers who make these products will decline as well. At the same time, the demand for Mexican products and the workers who make those products will rise. The MRP curve for U.S. workers will shift down to MRP_{US} and that for Mexican workers will shift up to MRP_{MEX}.

In the figure on the right, the U.S. MRP curve lies above the Mexican MRP curve because of the higher skills of the U.S. worker. Trade barriers mean that Mexican consumers are not allowed to purchase the products made by the higher-skilled U.S. workers. The free trade agreement will allow Mexican consumers to purchase the higher-quality U.S. products. The demand for higher-skilled U.S. workers will rise (to MRP_{US}') and the demand for the Mexican workers making those products competing with the higher-quality U.S. products will fall (to MRP_{MEX}'). As a result, the wages for the higher-skilled U.S. workers will rise.

Higher-skilled U.S. workers will gain and lower-skilled U.S. workers lose due to the free trade agreement.

The relatively unskilled U.S. workers who must compete with the much larger pool of unskilled workers from Mexico will be hurt because their wages will decline. The skilled workers in the United States will experience rising wages as their products are purchased by Mexican consumers. Consumers in both countries are sure to gain. Firms will experience lower total costs, output prices will decline, and a wider variety of goods will be available.

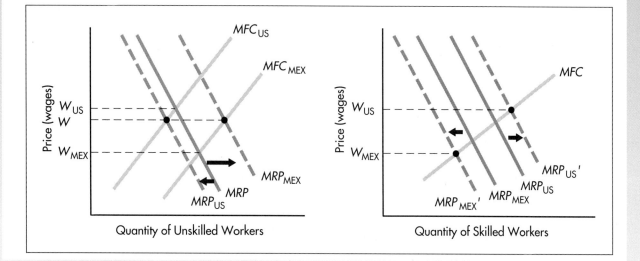

16

The Labor Market: Wage Differentials and Personnel Practices

FUNDAMENTAL
    QUESTIONS

1. Are people willing to work more for higher wages?

2. What are compensating wage differentials?

3. Why might wages be higher for people with more human capital than for those with less human capital?

4. Why do older workers tend to earn more than younger workers?

5. What is the explanation for widespread personnel practices that appear to contradict economic theory?

O lder workers tend to earn higher wages than younger workers; males earn more than females; whites earn more than blacks and Hispanics; and unionized workers earn more than nonunionized workers. Yet, as you learned in the previous chapter, a worker will be paid his or her marginal revenue product (except in a monopsonistic firm). Does this mean that older workers are more productive than younger ones, males more productive than females, whites more productive than people of color, and so on, or is there something missing in our theory of the labor market? In this and the next chapter we reexamine the labor market.

I. THE SUPPLY OF LABOR

PREVIEW

The supply of labor comes from individual households. Each member of a household must determine whether to give up a certain number of hours each day to work. That decision is the individual's labor supply decision and is called the *labor-leisure tradeoff*.

I.a. Individual Labor Supply: Labor-Leisure Tradeoff

There are only twenty-four hours in a day, and people have to decide how to allocate this scarce time. They really have only two options: they can spend their time (1) working for pay, or (2) not working. *Any* time spent not working is called *leisure time*. Leisure

Are people willing to work more for higher wages?

People can allocate their time to work or leisure.

time includes being a "couch potato," serving as a volunteer coach for your daughter's first-grade soccer team, volunteering to serve food at St. Jude's food bank, or participating in any other activity except working at a paying job. People want leisure time. Although most people enjoy aspects of their jobs, most would rather have more leisure time and less work time. However, people must purchase the desired good, leisure, by forgoing the wages they could earn by working. As wages increase, the cost of leisure time increases, causing people to purchase less leisure. Purchasing less leisure means working more.

The number of hours that people are willing and able to work rises as the wage rate rises, at least until people say, "I have enough income; perhaps I'll enjoy a little more leisure." When the price of leisure increases—in other words, when the wage rate increases—people choose to work more. But, as the wage rate increases, some people choose to enjoy more leisure time. They now have more income with which they can purchase all goods and services, including leisure time. Thus, a wage increase has two opposing effects: one leads to increased hours of work and one leads to decreased hours. This means that the quantity of labor supplied may rise or fall as the wage rate rises.

The labor supply curve shown in Figure 1 is what the labor supply curve for an individual usually looks like. It rises as the wage rate rises until the wage is sufficiently high that people begin to choose more leisure; then the curve begins to turn backward. This is called the **backward-bending labor supply curve**.

backward-bending labor supply curve:
a labor supply curve indicating that a person is willing and able to work more hours as the wage rate increases until, at some sufficiently high wage rate, the person chooses to work fewer hours

I.a.I. Do People Really Trade Off Labor and Leisure?   As discussed in the Economic Insight "The Overworked American?" not all economists agree with the idea that people trade off work and leisure. There is no doubt that few have the luxury of deciding each minute whether to work or take leisure time. Some might be able to choose between part-time and full-time work, but full-time work usually means eight hours a day, and part-time work typically means lower-quality jobs and much less pay per hour than the full-time job. Most people, then, are unable to choose how much to work on a day-to-day basis depending on their preferences for leisure that day. But over a month, a year, or several years, people do choose to put in more or less time on the job. Some people choose occupations that enable them more flexibility; many prefer to be self-employed in order to be able to choose whether to put in more or less time on the job. People can also *moonlight*, work an additional job or put in extra hours after the full-time job is completed.

I.b. From Individual to Market Supply

labor force participation:
entering the work force

When you enter the labor market, you offer various levels of services at various wage rates. The decision about whether to offer your labor services for employment is a decision about **labor force participation**, joining the work force in the United States. People over the age of sixteen who are actively seeking a job are said to be members of the labor force. These are the people who have chosen to offer their labor services for employment at specific wage

Figure 1
The Individual's Labor Supply Curve
As the wage rate rises, people are willing and able to supply more labor, at least up to some high wage rate. A higher wage rate means that the opportunity cost of leisure time increases so that people will purchase less leisure (will work more). Conversely, as the wage rate rises and people's incomes rise, more of all goods are purchased, including leisure time. As a result, fewer hours are supplied for work. Which of these opposing effects is larger determines whether the labor supply curve slopes upward or downward. The most commonly shaped labor supply curve is one that slopes upward until the wage rate reaches some high level and then, as people choose more leisure time, begins to bend backward.

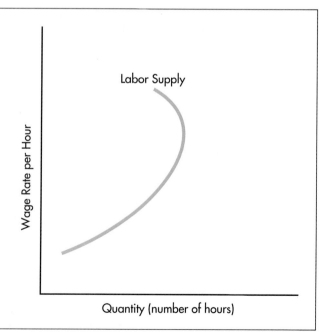

Figure 2
The Labor Market Supply Curve
Figure 2(a) shows the labor market supply curve obtained by adding the individual labor supply curves of Figures 2(b) and 2(c). Figure 2(a) indicates that as the wage rate rises, the number of hours each person is willing and able to work increases, at least up to some high wage rate, and the number of people willing and able to supply hours of work increases.

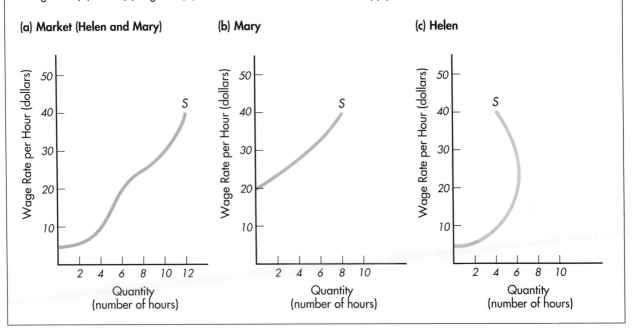

(a) Market (Helen and Mary) (b) Mary (c) Helen

rates. As the wage rate increases, the number of people participating in the labor force increases.

Figure 2(a) shows the labor *market* supply curve. It consists of the horizontal sum of all individual labor supply curves, such as the sum of the individual labor supply curves shown in Figures 2(b) and 2(c). If the labor supply curve for each individual slopes upward, then the market supply curve, the sum of each individual supply curve, slopes upward. Even if the individual labor supply curve bends backward at some high wage, it is unlikely that all of the curves will bend backward at the same wage. Not everyone has the same tradeoffs between labor and leisure; not all offer to work at the same wage rate; not all want the same kind of job. As the wage rate rises, some people who chose not to participate in the labor market at lower wages are induced to offer their services for employment at a higher wage. You can see in Figure 2(b) that Mary chooses not to enter the labor force at wages below $20 per hour. Helen, in Figure 2(c), enters the labor force for any wage above $5 per hour. Thus, the labor market supply curve slopes up because the number of people willing and able to work rises as the wage rate rises and because the number of hours that each person is willing and able to work rises as the wage rate rises, at least up to some high wage rate.

1.c. Equilibrium

The labor market consists of the labor demand and labor supply curves. We've just discussed labor supply. Labor demand is based on the firms' marginal revenue product curves, as discussed in the previous chapter. The inter-

The Overworked American?

The average employed person in America is now on the job an additional 163 hours, or the equivalent of an extra month a year, as compared to 1969.[1] What accounts for the increased hours devoted to work and thus the fewer hours devoted to leisure? The view of most economists is that people choose to work more in order to acquire more income. People trade off leisure for more work and thus more income.

Not all economists agree with the view that people can trade off work and leisure. Many argue that individuals have no choice, that leisure time is simply being squeezed out by the necessity of working and the demands of firms. A group of economists known as *institutionalists* argue that the modern industrial state does not give workers the flexibility economists seem to imply in their labor demand and labor supply model. The institutional economists argue that firms set the hours they require of their employees and employees must accept them or accept significantly lower standards

of living. They point to studies that have asked people about their work habits and found that people did not have a choice of hours; they had a choice of either no job or a job at hours that were not those they would choose.[2] In a popular book, *The Overworked American: The Unexpected Decline of Leisure*, author Juliet Schor argues that consumer-workers become indoctrinated by firms into consuming, which requires more income and thus more hours devoted to work. According to Schor, workers can't really trade off work and leisure but if they could, their indoctrination to consume constrains them; they must work more and more to be able to consume more and more.[3]

The economists opposing the institutionalists' view point out that workers can change occupations or jobs because hours worked vary considerably from occupation to occupation and that workers can also moonlight (work extra jobs or hours) or retire in order to alter their hours.[4] They also point to surveys where it was found that

people preferred their current number of hours and pay to working fewer hours at the same rate of pay or more hours at the same rate of pay.[5] Like most issues in economics, unanimity of opinion over this issue does not exist.

[1] Juliet B. Schor, *The Overworked American: The Unexpected Decline of Leisure* (New York: Basic Books, 1991).

[2] Shulamit Kahn and Kevin Lang, "Constraints on the Choice of Work Hours: Agency vs. Specific-Capital," *National Bureau of Economic Research Working Paper 2238*, May 1987, p. 14; Robert Moffit, "The Tobit Model, Hours of Work, and Institutional Constraints," *Review of Economics and Statistics* 64, August 1982, pp. 510–515.

[3] Schor, op.cit.

[4] Joseph Altonji and Christina H. Paxson, "Labor Supply Preferences, Hours Constraints, and Hour-Wage Tradeoffs," *Journal of Labor Economics* 6, No. 2, 1988, pp. 254–276.

[5] Susan E. Shank, "Preferred Hours of Work and Corresponding Earnings," *Monthly Labor Review* (November 1986), p. 41, table 1.

section of the labor demand and labor supply curves determines the equilibrium wage, W_e, and the quantity of hours people work at this equilibrium wage, Q_e, as shown in Figure 3.

The labor market pictured in Figure 3 suggests that as long as workers are the same and jobs are the same, there will be one equilibrium wage. In fact, workers are not the same, jobs are not the same, and wages are definitely not the same. College-educated people earn more than people with only a high school education, and people with a high school education earn more than those with only a grammar school education. Older workers earn more than younger workers. Men earn more than women. Whites earn more than nonwhites. Unionized workers tend to earn more than nonunionized workers.

The labor market model also suggests that workers will be paid their marginal revenue products. The more productive a worker is, the higher his or her compensation will be, and vice versa. This relationship does not always

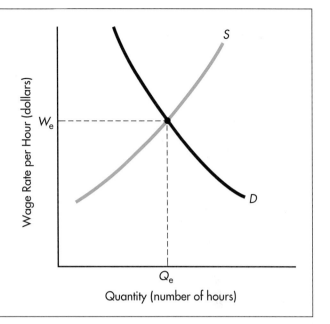

Figure 3
Labor Market Equilibrium
If all workers are identical to firms—that is, if a firm doesn't care whether it hires Bob, Ray, Kate, or Allie—and if all firms and jobs are the same to workers—that is, if a worker doesn't care whether a job is with IBM or Ted's Hot Dog Stand—then one demand curve and one supply curve define the labor market. The intersection of the two curves is the labor market equilibrium at which the wage rate is determined.

hold in the real world, however. There are large salary differences for people with similar levels of productivity, and people who are vastly different in terms of productivity are paid the same. Some explanations for these wage differentials are given in the remainder of this chapter.

RECAP

1. An increase in the wage rate causes workers to increase the hours they are willing and able to work and reduce the hours of leisure; at the same time, the wage increase also means that income is higher and more leisure can be purchased. This causes the individual labor supply curve to be backward-bending.

2. The labor market supply curve slopes upward because as the wage rate rises, more people are willing and able to work and people are willing and able to work more hours.

3. Equilibrium in the labor market defines the wage rate and the quantity of hours people work at that wage.

2. WAGE DIFFERENTIALS

If people were identical, if jobs were identical, and if information was perfect, there would be no wage differentials.

If all workers are the same to a firm—that is, if a firm doesn't care whether it hires Bob, Ray, Kate, or Allie—and if all firms and jobs are the same to workers—that is, if IBM is no different from Ted's Hot Dog Stand to individual workers—then the one demand for labor and the one supply of labor define the one equilibrium wage. However, if firms do differentiate among workers and if workers do differentiate among firms and jobs, then there is more than one labor market and more than one equilibrium wage level. In this case, wages may differ from job to job and from person to person. The reasons for wage differences include compensating wage differentials and differences in individual levels of productivity.

2.a. Compensating Wage Differentials

What are compensating wage differentials?

compensating wage differentials:
wage differences that make up for the higher risk or poorer working conditions of one job over another

Some jobs are quite unpleasant because they are located in undesirable locations or are dangerous or unhealthy. In most market economies, enough people voluntarily choose to work in unpleasant jobs that the jobs get filled. People choose to work in unpleasant occupations because of **compensating wage differentials**—wage differences that make up for the high risk or poor working conditions of a job. Workers mine coal, clean sewers, and weld steel beams fifty stories off the ground because, compared to alternative jobs for which they could qualify, these jobs pay well.

Figure 4 illustrates the concept of compensating differentials. There are two labor markets, one for a risky occupation and one for a less risky occupation. At each wage rate, fewer people are willing and able to work in the risky occupation than in the less risky occupation. Thus, if the demand curves were identical, the supply curve of the risky occupation would be above (to the left of) the supply curve of the less risky occupation. As a result, the equilibrium wage rate is higher in the risky occupation ($10) than

Figure 4
Compensating Wage Differentials
Figure 4(a) shows the market for a risky occupation. Figure 4(b) shows the market for a less risky occupation. At each wage rate, fewer people are willing and able to work in the risky occupation than in the less risky occupation. Thus, the supply curve of the risky occupation is higher (supply is less) than the supply curve of the less risky occupation. As a result, the wage in the

risky occupation ($10 per hour) is higher than the wage ($5 per hour) in the less risky occupation. The differential ($10 − $5 = $5) is an equilibrium differential—the amount necessary to induce enough people to fill the jobs. If the differential were any higher, more people would flow to the risky occupation, driving wages there down and wages in the less risky occupation up. If the differential were any lower, shortages would prevail in the risky occupation, driving wages there up.

(a) Risky Occupation

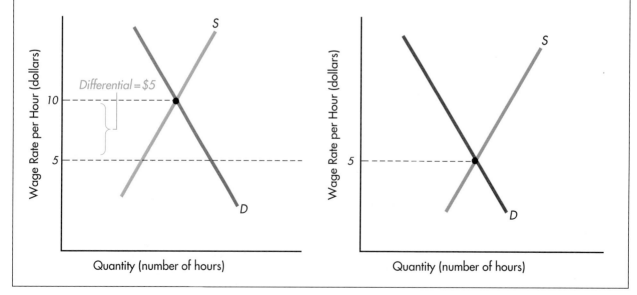

(b) Less Risky Occupation

Quantity (number of hours)

Some jobs are more dangerous than others; as a result, fewer people would be willing to work in the dangerous job if it paid the same as a less-dangerous job. To induce enough people to work as oil-well fire fighters in the hot deserts of Kuwait, the Red Adair Company offers very high wages. Some of the employees earned more in two months than many employees in less-risky jobs earn in a year.

in the less risky occupation ($5). The difference between the wage in the risky occupation ($10 per hour) and the wage in the less risky occupation ($5 per hour) is an *equilibrium differential*—the compensation a worker receives for undertaking the greater risk.

Commercial deep-sea divers are exposed to the dangers of drowning and several physiological disorders as a result of compression and decompression. They choose this job because they earn about 90 percent more than the average high school graduate. Coal miners in West Virginia or in the United Kingdom are exposed to coal dust, black lung disease, and cave-ins. They choose to work in the mines because the pay is twice what they could earn elsewhere. Wage differentials ensure that deep-sea diving jobs, coal-mining jobs, and other risky occupations are filled.

Any characteristic that distinguishes one job from another may result in a compensating wage differential. A job that requires a great deal of travel and time away from home usually pays more than a comparable job without the travel requirements because most people find extensive travel and time away from home to be costly. If people were indifferent between extensive travel and no travel, there would be no compensating wage differential.

2.b. Human Capital

Why might wages be higher for people with more human capital than for those with less human capital?

People differ with respect to their training and abilities. These differences influence the level of wages for two reasons: (1) skilled workers have higher marginal productivity than unskilled workers, and (2) the supply of skilled workers is smaller than the supply of unskilled workers because it takes time and money to acquire training and education. Because of greater productivity and smaller supply, then, skilled labor will generate higher wages than less skilled labor. For instance, in Figure 5, the skilled-labor market generates a wage of $15 per hour, and the unskilled-labor market generates a wage of $8 per hour. The difference exists because the demand for skilled labor relative to the supply of skilled labor is greater than the demand for unskilled labor relative to the supply of unskilled labor.

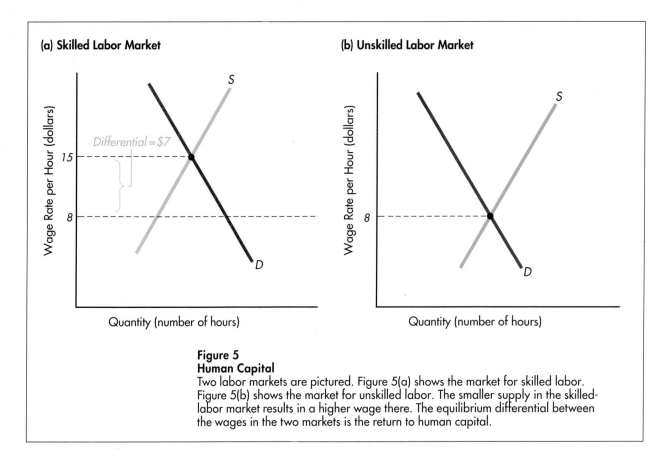

(a) Skilled Labor Market

Wage Rate per Hour (dollars)

Differential = $7

15

8

S

D

Quantity (number of hours)

(b) Unskilled Labor Market

Wage Rate per Hour (dollars)

8

S

D

Quantity (number of hours)

Figure 5
Human Capital
Two labor markets are pictured. Figure 5(a) shows the market for skilled labor. Figure 5(b) shows the market for unskilled labor. The smaller supply in the skilled-labor market results in a higher wage there. The equilibrium differential between the wages in the two markets is the return to human capital.

human capital:
skills and training acquired through education and on-the-job training

The expectation of higher income induces people to acquire **human capital**—skills and training acquired through education and job experience. People go to college or vocational school or enter training programs because they expect the training to increase their future income. When people purchase human capital, they are said to be *investing in human capital*. Like investments in real capital (machines and equipment), education and training are purchased in order to generate output and income in the future.

2.b.1. Investment in Human Capital Individuals who go to college or obtain special training expect the costs of going to college or obtaining the training to be more than offset by the income and other benefits they will obtain in the future. Individuals who acquire human capital reap the rewards of that human capital over time. Figure 6(a) is an example of what the income profiles of workers with college degrees and workers without college degrees might look like. We might expect income of the worker without the degree to increase rapidly from the early working years until the worker gets to be about fifty; then income might rise more slowly, until the worker moves into retirement age. Until around age thirty, the worker without the college degree clearly enjoys more income than the college-educated worker. The shaded areas represent estimated income lost to the college-educated worker while he or she is attending classes and then gaining work experience. It may take several years after entering the labor market for a college-degree recipient to achieve and then surpass the income level of a worker without a degree, but on average a college-educated person does earn more than some-

**Figure 6
Income Profiles and
Educational Level**
Income rises rapidly until age
fifty, then rises more slowly
until retirement. Figure 6 compares the income earned by
the worker without a degree
with the income earned by a
college graduate. Figure 6(a)
suggests what the actual pattern looks like. Initially, the college graduate gives up
substantial income in the form
of direct costs and forgone
earnings to go to college.
Eventually, however, the
income of the college graduate
exceeds that of the high
school-educated worker.
Figure 6(b) illustrates the
actual disparities between college-educated and non-college-educated individuals.
Source: *Statistical Abstract of the
United States*, 1992, p. 450, table
723; *Economic Report of the
President*, 1992, p. 101.

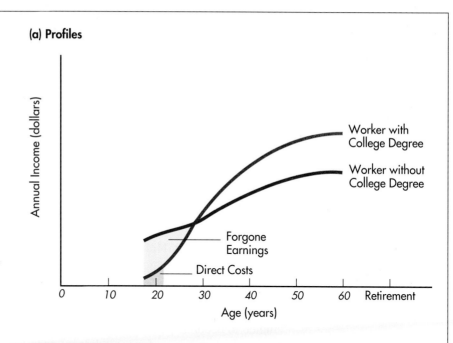

(a) Profiles

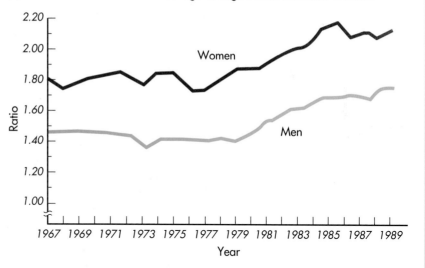

(b) Ratio of Median Incomes of College-to High-School-Educated Workers

one without a college education, as shown in Figure 6(b). Figure 6(b) shows
the ratios of the median incomes of college- to high-school-educated male
and female workers. As mentioned in Chapter 1, college-educated people
earn more over their lifetimes than people without a college degree.

The decision about whether to attend college depends on whether the benefits exceed the costs.[1] Over the course of a lifetime, will the income and

---

[1]In the chapter "Capital, Land, and Entrepreneurial Ability" we discuss the concept of
present value, which is the value today of benefits or costs that occur in the future. A person compares the present value of the benefits of college to the present value of the costs
of college in deciding whether to attend college.

other benefits of a college degree offset the loss of income during the early years? Individuals who answer *yes* choose to attend college. This economic model of the decision to attend college does not suggest that every high school senior carries out a series of calculations regarding the expected costs and benefits of attending college. What it does suggest is that these people behave *as if* they carried out these calculations. As we discussed in Chapter 1, for many high school students, the decision to attend college was made long before they were in high school—there simply was no other alternative considered. For many, it was taken for granted by all friends and family members that college followed high school. This is the pattern for many families. Such patterns do not occur by accident. There is a reason why so many young adults go to college, and the economic model of labor suggests what that reason is: college-educated people have better-paying jobs and jobs with greater benefits and security than non–college-educated people.

2.b.2. Choice of a Major If you decide to attend college, you must then decide what field to major in. Your decision depends on the opportunity costs you face. If your opportunity costs of devoting a great deal of time to a job are high, you will choose to major in a field that is not overly time-consuming. For instance, for several years after college, men and women who have studied to become medical doctors, lawyers, and accountants face long training periods and very long workdays, and they have to devote significant amounts of time each year to staying abreast of new developments in their profession. If you think that you are not likely to undertake and complete a four- or five-year apprenticeship after college in order to reap the rewards from your expenditure of time and money, then it would be very costly for you to be a premed student or to major in accounting or law. Your choice of a college major and an occupation reflects the opportunity costs you face. The greater the opportunity costs of any one occupation, the smaller the number of people who will select that occupation, everything else the same. For instance, it takes more time, money, and effort to become a medical doctor than to become a teacher in the K-12 schools. For this reason, many more people would choose to become teachers than doctors. As a result, a wage differential between the two fields exists that is sufficient to compensate them for the extra opportunity costs of the medical career.

2.b.3. Changing Careers It is estimated that one in three people in the United States labor force today will change careers at least once during their work lives. People choose a major and thus a career on the basis of information they have at their disposal, family influences, and other related factors. People acquire additional information once involved in their occupation, and sometimes their tastes change. They decide to embark on another career path. Who will make such a change? What types of occupations might see more changes?

Relying on the labor market model, we can suggest some answers to these questions. There might be a temptation to say that those who devoted the most effort, time, and money to their first occupation would be the least likely to change. But it is the marginal cost that matters; the effort, time, and money devoted to that first career are gone whether one remains in the first occupation or moves to another. In the words of the chapter on monopolistic competition and oligopoly, these are sunk, or unrecoverable, costs. Thus, we would expect people who have the greatest expected net gains to make a change. Those who see they are in dead-end positions or in occupations whose outlook for future income increases is not as good as other occupations would be more likely to move to a new career. We might expect people not to remain in or enter those professions where the marginal costs of remaining in the profession are high. For instance, those occupations that require continuous time and/or financial commitments if their members are to remain productive, such as the high-tech occupations, the hard sciences, engineering, accounting, or law, might lose relatively more people to areas that do not require similar time and money expenditures, such as management and administration.

2.c. Wage Differentials That Do Not Fit Neatly into the Labor Market Model

Wages vary with the amount of general or specific training a worker has received, with job characteristics, and with age or experience. These factors, which give rise to wage differentials, may be considered mechanisms for allocating labor in a freely functioning labor market in which wages reflect a worker's marginal revenue product. As we'll see in the next section and in the next chapter, though, there are also several instances where pay scales do not reflect marginal revenue products.

RECAP

1. Compensating wage differentials are wage differences that make up for the higher risk or poorer working conditions of one job over another. Risky jobs pay more than risk-free jobs, and unpleasant jobs pay more than pleasant jobs.

2. Human capital is the education, training, and experience embodied in an individual.

3. An individual's choice of an occupation reflects a tradeoff between expected opportunity costs and expected benefits. An individual is likely to choose an occupation in which expected benefits outweigh expected opportunity costs.

3. REAL-WORLD PERSONNEL PRACTICES

You may recognize that in a world of perfect information and costless movement of resources, workers would be paid their marginal revenue products (as long as they were not in a monopsony market), and compensating wage differentials would explain all earnings differences. In a world where individuals and firms have less than perfect information and where resources cannot transfer across markets costlessly, however, there often is no way to know exactly what a person's marginal revenue product is. It is too costly, if not impossible, to measure each individual's contribution to the revenues of the firm. As a result, policies regarding employees that tend to mimic the results of perfect information in a setting of imperfect information emerge. In this section we consider a few of these common practices.

personnel practices:
a firm's policies toward its employees

Personnel practices are the policies firms use for hiring, paying, and promoting employees, and assigning employees to tasks. At first glance, many personnel practices do not correspond to our model of the labor market. As discussed in the Economic Insight "Different Approaches to Pay and

Different Approaches to Pay and Incentives

The Lincoln Electric Company has had a policy of paying employees for their output since the 1930s. Lincoln's factory workers are paid "piece rates" rather than hourly wages or salaries. The faster an employee works and the more output produced, the higher the employee's pay. Employees are not paid for coffee breaks, lunch breaks, or holidays. They are paid solely on the basis of the output they produce. Over the years pay rates have changed as technology or work methods changed. The workers are also eligible for yearly bonuses that have on average doubled their earnings. The distribution of bonuses is based on merit ratings of the workers on such factors as their dependability, quality, output, ideas, and cooperativeness. The name of the worker who produced a machine is stenciled on the machine. If a quality problem is discovered, the worker responsible must correct it on his or her own time. Also, the worker's bonus is reduced.

Lincoln has a policy of permanent, or lifetime, employment. After two years with the firm, a worker is guaranteed at least 30 hours' work a week. In fact, Lincoln has had no layoffs for over 40 years.

Contrast the Lincoln experience with an experiment at Du Pont. E.I. Du Pont de Nemours and Company instituted a plan for its 20,000 employees in the fibers division in which employees put some of their annual wage and salary increases in a "pool" that would be at risk of loss or subject to huge gains. Bonuses to the pool were to be paid on how the division performed relative to an earnings target. Just meeting the target would mean the employees got their money back. If earnings exceeded target, employees would get at least twice their money back. If the division achieved only 80 percent of target they would lose the money they had put in the pool. Du Pont was trying to find out whether tying pay to group performance would have any positive effects. In the first year, employees received $19 million more in bonuses than they would have gotten without the pool plan. However, when business slowed in 1990, employees complained about their coworkers, and morale fell so low that the pool plan was rescinded.

As with the Du Pont case, there are instances where a direct tie between pay and performance can be determined. Consider the medical arena where the recent move toward managed health-care systems has, in some cases, involved incentive pay for doctors. Many health maintenance organizations (HMOs), such as FHP International, Cigna, New York Life Insurance, and AvMed-Santa Fe, are paying bonuses to doctors on the basis of the patients' sense of quality. Critics do not like the idea, arguing that patients do not really know the quality of a doctor. In addition, some experiments with the idea have made it difficult for the doctors to work together in a collegial way. Dr. Gene Lindsay of the Harvard Community Health Plan said, "We had doctors almost getting into fistfights over what amounted to a $500 bonus." Other HMOs, however, are finding the practice of incentive pay very productive. According to a report in the *Wall Street Journal*, the incentive-pay idea works very well for the HMOs that deal with independent practitioners, as opposed to HMOs that have their own full-time physicians on staff. "That's because pay differentials—even tiny ones—are more likely to heat up rivalries among staff doctors."

Sources: "Here Come Richer, Riskier Pay Plans," *Fortune* (Dec. 19, 1988), pp. 50–58; Paul Milgrom and John Roberts, *Economics, Organization and Management* (Englewood Cliffs, N.J.: Prentice-Hall, 1992), pp. 393, 417; "Du Pont Plan Linking Pay to Fibers Profit Unravels," *Wall Street Journal*, Oct. 25, 1990, p. B1; George Anders, "More Managed Health-Care Systems Use Incentive Pay to Reward 'Best' Doctors," *Wall Street Journal*, Feb. 9, 1993, p. B1.

Incentives," some firms link pay directly to marginal revenue product while others seem to have no link between pay and MRP. It is common for firms to pay more senior workers more than less senior workers even though the more senior workers are not necessarily more productive. Another widespread practice, until the federal government in 1981 said it was illegal, was mandatory retirement. If older workers are not more productive than younger ones, why pay the older ones more? If they are more productive, then why terminate their employment at some age? A common practice that has come under a great deal of criticism in recent years is to provide chief executive officers (CEOs) with salaries and bonuses that far exceed the salaries and bonuses of the next person in charge. Why pay the CEO such a high salary when many other people could do just as good a job at much less pay? Corporations also spend enormous amounts to relocate middle- and upper-level managers on a fairly regular basis. Why uproot families and sever relationships, causing stress, bad will, and difficulties for those employees the firms most favor? And why not pay more attention to the individuals? Corporations often pay according to job classifications rather than tie the pay to individuals. For instance, a secretary 1 might earn less than a secretary 2 regardless of who the people in those positions are. Let us see if we can discover any reasons for these seemingly irrational behaviors.

3.a. Age Earnings and Age Productivity Profiles

Why do older workers tend to earn more than younger workers?

age-earnings profile:
a representation of the earnings a worker will receive at each age

In the past forty years, the age-earnings profile for any given worker has tended to look like the curve labeled "compensation" in Figure 7. The **age-earnings profile** is a representation of the earnings a worker will receive at each age. The age-earnings profile shown in Figure 7 is upward-sloping because earnings continue to rise throughout most of an individual's work life.

3.a.1. General Human Capital One explanation for the upward-sloping age-earnings profile is that workers acquire on-the-job training. If this training, or human capital, is portable—can be taken by the worker to any job— then the firm is helping the worker by giving him or her the opportunity to acquire on-the-job training. The firm will pay the worker for his or her marginal revenue product, and if that increases over time as the worker acquires more training, then wages will increase over time. In this case, firms and workers are indifferent about job separations; the firm can acquire another

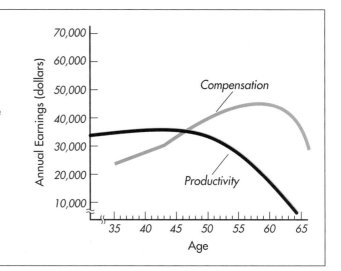

Figure 7
Age-Earnings and Age-Productivity Profiles
The curve labeled "productivity" represents the age-productivity profile of an average worker. Productivity rises until about age forty-five and then declines. The "compensation" curve is the age-earnings profile of an average worker. Earnings continue to increase until late in the worker's life. A comparison of the age-earnings and age-productivity profiles shows that workers can expect to earn less than their current marginal revenue products during the early years of their work lives but more than their current marginal revenue products during their later work lives.

worker and begin the on-the-job training, and the worker can acquire another job and apply his or her human capital to the new job.

3.a.2. Firm-Specific Human Capital Firm-specific training refers to skills that are applicable only on one job or in one firm. Many skills acquired by an employee of Daimler-Benz's automobile manufacturing division can be used only in that division. They are of no use even in other automobile manufacturing firms. If the on-the-job training is firm-specific, the training acquired by the worker is permanently lost if the employment relationship with a given firm is severed. Premature job terminations and separations can be costly to both parties: the firm loses the trained employee, and the worker may find it difficult to transfer skills to another job. To ensure against these losses, both worker and firm are willing to contribute to the payment for the training. The worker contributes by receiving wages that are less than his or her marginal revenue product during the years prior to acquiring the on-the-job training, and the firm contributes by paying the worker more than his or her marginal revenue product after the worker has acquired the on-the-job training.

Whether the on-the-job training is firm-specific or not, in order to explain the upward-sloping age-earnings profile, workers have to become continually more productive over time. The problem is that the facts show that productivity does not continually rise. The curve labeled "productivity" in Figure 7 illustrates the level of productivity of an individual over that individual's work life. The "productivity" curve is called an **age-productivity profile**; productivity rises until the worker is about age forty-five and then declines.

age-productivity profile:
the level of an individual's productivity over his or her work life

Workers are paid less than their marginal revenue products during early years with a firm and more than their MRP during later years.

A comparison of the age-earnings and age-productivity profiles shows that workers are paid less than their current marginal revenue products during their early work lives and more than their current marginal revenue products during their later work lives—yet productivity does not continually rise. What are the implications of such a relationship? For one thing, workers are induced to remain with a given firm. A worker who has been paid less than current marginal revenue product in his or her early years will not want to leave the job before recouping the difference between productivity and earnings.

The compensation scheme indicated by Figure 7 can motivate workers to increase productivity over their lifetimes. If a worker is always paid a value equal to his or her current marginal product, there is little cost to quitting or losing a job. The worker can go to another firm at a rate of pay equal to the marginal product. But with a steep age-earnings profile, the closer a worker is to retirement, the greater the cost of losing a job. The worker loses the premium of compensation in excess of current marginal product. Thus, workers have smaller and smaller incentives to slack off or shirk as they get older. Workers know that they will collect an excess above current marginal revenue product if they work to a certain age.

This compensation scheme means that firms could be stuck with workers for a very long time after the workers' productivity levels fall below their compensation levels. How can firms resolve this problem? **Mandatory retirement** was a policy that prevented employees from working after they reached a certain age. Mandatory retirement thus ensured that workers did not remain with a firm too long. Why didn't firms simply terminate workers at the stage when compensation began to exceed productivity? A firm did not want to be known as an "early terminator" for fear that it would be able to

mandatory retirement:
a policy that prevents employees from working after a certain age

attract only low-productivity employees. Thus, the age-productivity-compensation scheme of Figure 7, coupled with mandatory retirement, seemed to have the result of increasing employee productivity.

Congressional action in 1981 eliminated mandatory retirement. Congress acted in response to pressure from older citizens, who viewed mandatory retirement, which forced them out of their jobs, as a penalty. If mandatory retirement allowed firms to use the age-productivity-compensation scheme of Figure 7 to increase worker productivity over the worker's lifetime, what took the place of mandatory retirement?

The lifting of such rules, while protecting workers' rights to continue at the same job past the age of sixty-five, does not ensure that workers will actually remain on the job. Pension plans exert economic pressure on individuals to leave their jobs or even leave the labor force. A pension that can be taken at a given age provides workers with the option of leaving their jobs and accepting payments at that age. Thus, generous pensions may fulfill the role played by mandatory retirement. In fact, most pension plans are set up to encourage retirement at a particular age; extending work life beyond that age results in incremental decreases in the returns from the pension plans.

3.b. CEO Pay Packages

Chief executive officers (CEOs) commonly earn salaries and bonuses that far exceed the salaries and bonuses of the next person in charge. Steven Ross, the Time Warner boss, gathered $74.8 million in bonuses in 1990 even as *Time* magazine laid off employees. J.F. O'Reilly of H.J. Heinz pulled in $74.8 million in total compensation in 1991 although Heinz had a rather average year. Leon C. Hirsch of U.S. Surgical Corporation collected $169.8 million from stock options as the price of the company's stock rose during 1991. General Motors's former chairman, Roger Smith, receives a $1.2 million annual pension even though GM lost both market share and money during Smith's tenure. In the mid-1970s, CEOs earned about 34 times the pay of the average working person; by the late 1980s they earned 109 times that average. According to the *Business Week* annual survey, the total compensation of the CEOs in the largest 365 corporations grew 212 percent during the 1980s, four times more than the growth in pay of the average factory worker and three times more than the earnings per share of stock. Why would competitive firms reward their CEOs so highly?

One answer is that the market for CEOs has failed in that the owners of firms and the managers of the firms are different groups of people. The owners, thousands of shareholders, exert little influence over the day-to-day activities of the manager and have little influence over the manager's pay. Another is that CEO pay is the result of a conspiracy involving other CEOs and friends of the CEO who, as members of the compensation board of a firm, fail to listen to investors or look to the firm's performance and simply provide the types of compensation they also want to receive. Although some evidence of both of these explanations has been found, it is not very convincing. An alternative explanation to the market failure or conspiracy arguments claims that CEO pay makes sense from an economic efficiency basis. This explanation is built on an analogy with contests or tournaments.

In a tournament, the larger the first prize, and the larger the difference between the first prize and all other prizes, the more productive are the contestants. Thus, if we consider the labor market as a contest where the first

High executive salaries could be the result of a tournament where the executive has won first prize; the pay increases the incentive for all employees to work harder and better.

prize is the CEO position, a large first prize induces more effort and higher productivity from all contestants. An extremely high pay package for the CEO induces that individual, and all employees (current and future), to exert extra efforts during their working lives.

3.c. Frequent Relocation of Managers

Any of you with parents, relatives, or friends employed by a large corporation have probably experienced several geographic moves. Typically the moves bring little in extra compensation but impose large costs on the family in the sense that ties are broken and children uprooted and transplanted. Why would firms expose their employees to such difficult experiences? The tournament view of labor markets provides an answer.

It is possible that the hierarchy within the headquarters location may not provide sufficient "tournaments" to ensure that the best people emerge as winners. The contests are spread geographically in order to provide sufficient opportunities for evaluating workers in various settings. So workers are rotated through various geographic locations to allow more complete evaluations to occur.

An alternative explanation is that geographic moves result in temporary productivity boosts. When a manager has been in a position for a significant length of time, procedures and practices become accepted and commonplace. There is little questioning of the approaches and little examination of whether more efficient or less costly methods are available. Limiting the exposure of teams of workers to the same manager may provide the opportunity for the teams to seek the most efficient means to accomplish the tasks. In addition, long-term relationships tend to provide biases in the relationship between the manager and selected workers. One worker may be a favorite of the manager due to an early experience. That worker may begin to shirk without retribution from the manager. Changing managers on a periodic basis will ensure that such behavior is temporary.

3.d. Team Production, Job Rating, and Firm-Size Effects

Have you ever been assigned a group project in one of your classes—a project that you and several other students working together must complete? For some this is a positive learning experience. For others it is an opportunity to discover firsthand what shirking is. Some team members invariably do not work as hard as others. Yet all members of the group receive the same grade, the grade of the project. Because the teacher is unable to differentiate the contributions of each individual group member, some members can slack off or shirk their responsibility without jeopardizing their rewards as long as other members complete the task.

There are many jobs in which the manager has the same problem of identifying the individual contributions or marginal products of employees. When teams handle a production process, a means of dividing compensation among team members must be determined. The most common approach is through a system of job categories. Job categories define responsibilities and specify compensation. All positions within a firm are ranked according to attributes such as responsibilities, pressure, and time requirements, and each position carries a different compensation level.

For example, suppose that there are three levels of secretarial positions, 1, 2, and 3. Also, suppose that a secretary at level 1 has fewer responsibilities than a secretary at level 2, and that a secretary at level 2 has fewer responsibilities than a secretary at level 3. Finally, suppose that the salary range for the level 1 position is $10,000 to $15,000 per year, the range for the level 2 position is $13,000 to $17,000, and the range for the level 3 position is $15,000 to $21,000.

On average, level 2 secretaries earn more than level 1 secretaries. Also, on average, level 2 secretaries are not as productive as level 3 secretaries but are more productive than level 1 secretaries in the sense that they have fewer or more responsibilities. By assigning compensation to classes and giving classes different responsibilities, compensation based on marginal revenue product is approximated.

Another curious aspect of pay scales in firms is that someone working in a small firm receives less compensation than if that person had the same job and same responsibilities in a large firm. Why should this be if there are no productivity differences? The most credible explanation is that the larger firm has to pay more to offset the fact that monitoring of individual performances is more difficult in a larger firm. By paying more, the larger firm is likely to get the better workers, who are more wary of losing their job and thus shirk less than if they were working with a smaller firm. Thus, in many large firms you will find higher average pay than in smaller firms but a more uniform pay scale based on job categories rather than a pay scale based on merit or productivity.

3.e. The Economics of Superstars

superstar effect:
the situation where people with small differences in abilities or productivity receive vastly different levels of compensation

Sometimes it appears that small differences in ability translate into huge differences in compensation. We saw how this phenomenon occurs in firms at the CEO level. It occurs in other situations as well, particularly in sports enterprises, which gave rise to its name—the **superstar effect**. Consider that the playing ability of the top ten tennis players or golfers is not much better than the playing ability of the players ranked between 40 and 50. Nonetheless, the compensation differences are incredibly large. The average income of the top ten tennis players and golfers is in the millions, while that of the lower-ranked ten players is in the thousands. If their productivity differences are so small, why are their compensation differences so large?

One explanation might be the limited time of those watching tennis or golf tournaments. Since most consumers have limited time, they choose to follow the top players. A tennis match between the 40th and 41st players might be nearly as good as that between the first and second. Yet, given the limited time to allocate between the two, nearly everyone would choose to watch the first and second players. At golf tournaments, huge throngs surround the top players, while lesser-known players play the game without the attention of adoring fans. These differences mean that the demand for the top players is huge relative to the demand for the lesser-ranked players. The sports franchises (the owners of the New York Yankees, for example) or the firms selling tickets to sporting events will be able to earn significantly higher prices if the ranked players are included in the activity; the marginal revenue product of the top-ranked players is thus much higher than that of the lesser-ranked players.

The superstar effect occurs outside of sports. You might, for example, observe two lawyers of relatively equal ability earning significantly different fees, or two economic consultants with apparently similar abilities earning vastly different consulting fees. When there is an "all-or-nothing" result in the market, the superstar effect might occur. Consider, for instance, the economist who offers advice to lawyers in cases involving firm behavior. A lawsuit filed against a firm might mean billions of dollars won or lost. Even if there are very small differences between economists, if the better economist means a win, then the better economist will receive huge compensation relative to the lesser economist. A $40 billion victory means that the marginal revenue product of the better economist is significantly greater than the marginal revenue product of the lesser economist, who has a $40 billion loss.

3.f. The Labor Market Model and Reality

What is the explanation for widespread personnel practices that appear to contradict economic theory?

Personnel practices that seem to be contradictory to the theory of the labor market under perfect information do not seem quite so strange when the real world of imperfect information is considered. These practices ensure that, as much as possible, resources are paid their marginal revenue products. If the practices are successful in one firm, other firms mimic them, thereby eventually leading to similar personnel practices across firms. When we observe widely followed practices that seem to be contradictory to our economic models, we must look closely into the practices to see if they are indeed contradictory. Rather than reject the models or turn to limited explanations, it is likely that we can find explanations for the practices that correspond to the logic of the economic model. Thus, wage scales within firms that are more uniform than productivity levels, huge differences between CEO pay and the pay of others in a firm, geographic moves on a regular basis, and wide differences in compensation accompanying small differences in productivity make sense in the context of the economic model of labor when imperfect information is considered or when all-or-nothing events occur.

RECAP

1. Under perfect information and in perfectly competitive markets, workers are paid their marginal revenue products. In the real world, this often does not occur. Instead, personnel practices arise that replicate the results of the competitive market under perfect information.

2. Personnel practices that appear to contradict economic theory include rising age-earnings profiles relative to age-productivity profiles, mandatory retirement, excessive pay for CEOs, and frequent transfers within a firm.

3. The general explanation for many of the personnel practices that firms engage in rests on the inability to monitor individual actions. To minimize shirking and increase productivity, pay scales tend to benefit the more senior employee. Mandatory retirement plans solved the problem of separation of senior worker and firm in the context of a rising age-earnings profile. CEOs are paid huge amounts because they are the winners of a series of contests or tournaments that are aimed at raising the performance of all employees. Frequent transfers tend to provide many mini-tournaments and induce short-term productivity boosts. And job

categories tend to minimize the problems of assigning marginal products in a setting of team production.

4. Superstar effects occur when there is an all-or-nothing aspect to the market and result in cases where individuals with small productivity differences receive vastly different compensation.

SUMMARY

▲▼ Are people willing to work more for higher wages?

1. The individual labor supply curve is backward-bending because at some high wage, people choose to enjoy more leisure rather than to earn additional income. §1.a

▲▼ What are compensating wage differentials?

2. Equilibrium in the labor market defines the wage and quantity of hours worked. If all workers and all jobs were identical, then one wage would prevail. There are differential wages, however, because jobs and workers differ. §1.c

3. A compensating wage differential exists when a higher wage is determined in one labor market than in another due to differences in job characteristics. §2.a

▲▼ Why might wages be higher for people with more human capital than for those with less human capital?

4. Human capital is the training, education, and skills people acquire. Human capital increases productivity. Because acquiring human capital takes time and money, the necessity of obtaining human capital for some jobs reduces the supply of labor to those jobs. §2.b

▲▼ Why do older workers tend to earn more than younger workers?

5. Older workers earn more than younger workers because of on-the-job experience and seniority. Older workers may also earn more than younger workers because firms pay older workers more in order not to lose the training and skills they have invested in these workers. In addition, a firm may use the higher wage for more senior workers to induce younger workers to be more productive. §3.a

▲▼ What is the explanation for widespread personnel practices that appear to contradict economic theory?

6. Firms operating under imperfect information cannot know each employee's marginal product and cannot perfectly monitor the performance of each employee. As a result, personnel practices that tend to mimic the results of the competitive market under perfect information (pay equal to MRP) arise. Examples of such practices include rising age-earnings profiles, pension plans, very high executive salaries, frequent transfers within a firm, and compensation tied to job categories. §3

KEY TERMS

backward-bending labor supply curve §1.a
labor force participation §1.b
compensating wage differentials §2.a
human capital §2.b
personnel practices §3

age-earnings profile §3.a
age-productivity profile §3.a.2
mandatory retirement §3.a.2
superstar effect §3.e

EXERCISES

1. What could account for a backward-bending labor supply curve?

2. What is human capital? How does a training program such as Mrs. Fields Cookie College affect human capital? Is a college degree considered to be human capital?

3. Define equilibrium in the labor market. Illustrate equilibrium on a graph. Illustrate the situation in which there are two types of labor, skilled and unskilled.

4. Describe how people choose a major in college. If someone majors in English literature knowing that the starting salary for English literature graduates is much lower than the starting salary for accountants, is the English literature major irrational?

5. Motorola, a U.S. electronics firm, requires that a very extensive process be followed before an employee who has been with the firm for ten years can be terminated or laid off. The division head must discuss the dismissal with the employee; the vice president of the division must discuss the dismissal; and the president of the firm must discuss the dismissal. What is the purpose of such a practice?

6. Explain why a large firm might be expected to have different methods of payment to employees than a smaller firm. Which would be more likely to have the higher pay scales? Which would be more likely to have across-the-board pay raises rather than differential pay raises based on productivity?

7. Explain the following real-world observations: the existence of seniority rules (first in, last out); higher pay than marginal revenue product during later years and lower pay than marginal revenue product during early years; management trainee programs for newly hired college graduates; a willingness on the part of firms to pay more for a college graduate even though the firms readily admit that the classes a student takes in college provide few marketable skills.

8. A study in 1990 indicated that at that time only 13 U.S. firms with more than 1,000 employees had explicit policies never to institute a general layoff: Delta Air Lines, Digital Equipment, Federal Express, IBM, S.C. Johnson, Lincoln Electric, Mazda, Motorola, National Steel, New United Motor, Nissan, Nucor, and Xerox. Why do you think that so few firms have adopted such a policy? After huge losses in 1992, IBM altered its policies and implemented large layoffs. What factors went into IBM's decision?

9. A 1989 study found that workers who were laid off generally received lower wages once they found new jobs. Workers who had been in their previous jobs only a short period of time suffered relatively smaller losses than those who had been with the employer for a longer period. How would you explain this?

10. A 1980 study found that the average worker with forty years' experience with a firm could retire with a pension of $79,000. If the same worker had retired ten years earlier, the pension would have been twice as much, $160,000. What would be the effects of such a policy? Why would firms institute such a policy?

11. In the 1980s and early 1990s, the U.S. airline industry went through a major shakeup. Many airlines went bankrupt and others expanded. Thousands of airline pilots lost their jobs with the bankrupt airlines. The expanding airlines, meanwhile, hired thousands of new pilots. The pilots hired by the expanding airlines, however, were those who had the least experience. The senior pilots from the bankrupt airlines could not get new jobs. Many claimed that this was a wasteful policy, one that the government should stop. How might you defend the practice?

12. The probability of a worker being fired from or quitting a job declines the longer the worker has been with a firm. How would you account for this?

13. It is a common practice in technology-based companies such as Hewlett-Packard, Unisys, and Sun Electronics for employees to experience lateral moves—moves to other locations or other parts of the company that carry no increase in compensation or responsibility. Why would these firms participate in such practices?

14. It is a common practice in the largest multinational companies for employees to experience assignments of three to five years in locations outside the United States. Why would a firm uproot a family and set it down in a new culture and society?

15. Suppose you are in charge of designing employee policies for a firm where failure has huge costs and success only normal benefits. For example, your firm inspects nuclear power plants or ensures the safety of airlines, buses, and trains. How would you recruit, promote, and pay employees?

Workers Are Forced to Take More Jobs with Few Benefits

Lou Capozzola worked 10 years at *Sports Illustrated*, jetting from Super Bowls to the Olympics as a lighting specialist. He was on the road 180 days a year, working 15- to 20-hour days.

In February 1990 he was called into his boss's office and informed that his job was being eliminated, but that he could continue as an independent contractor. His base pay would be about halved to $20,000. His overtime pay would be cut by as much as two-thirds. And he could forget about his $20,000-a-year benefit package, including medical coverage.

Then he was asked to leave town on assignment. "They say 'We value you and your skills. We're just going to pull the rug out from under your feet because we want to save $20,000,'" he says.

In spite of the low pay and benefits, he agreed to stay on. He was the sole supporter of a wife and two children. "What could I do? They offered me some form of employment, I had to take it," he says.

This is the 1990s workplace. After spending years at one company, more American office and factory employees are getting transplanted overnight to a temporary or subcontracting nether world. They do the same work at the same desk for less pay and with no health insurance or pension benefits.

Others are farmed out to an employment agency, which puts them on its payroll to save the mother company paperwork and cost.

"They [the companies] feel 'Let some one else have those headaches,'" says Robert Lefcort, chief operating officer of Labor World in Boca Raton, Fla., a franchiser of temporary-help offices. "By using us, they don't have to deal with the costs of injuries, drug screening, workers' compensation and unemployment claims."

Temporary-help employment grew 10 times faster than overall employment between 1982 and 1990. In 1992, temporary jobs accounted for about two-thirds of new private-sector jobs. And the big rise in new jobs this January came almost entirely from temporary and part-time jobs. When taken together, temporary, contract and part-time workers now make up about 25% of the work force.

That percentage could grow with the recently passed family-leave bill, which forces firms with more than 50 workers to provide extra benefits. By turning to temporary agencies, smaller employers may fall below the magic number and be exempt from providing those benefits. And while many people, especially women with young children, prefer the freedom of a temporary job, an increasing number are forced into it.

For better or worse, contingent workers—a term encompassing temporary and part-time help, contract laborers and leased employees—are the medium for a corporate America preaching a message of flexibility and cost cutting. Increased global and domestic competition is prompting companies to cultivate a just-in-time, bare-bones and cheaper work force. Contingent workers cost an estimated 20% to 40% less than core employees.

Cost is why Time Warner Inc., the parent of *Sports Illustrated*, changed Mr. Capozzola's status. It made more economic sense to have independent contractors on call around the country than to have a staff employee flying all over and accumulating heavy overtime.

Peter Costiglio, vice president for communications for Time Inc., says, "We looked at the job and our needs and felt we could do it more cost effectively on a contractual basis." An arbitrator agreed with the magazine's cost argument and denied Mr. Capozzola's reinstatement.

A company using contract labor "may save money," Mr. Capozzola says, "but it's always on the little guy's back."

Source: Clare Ansberry, "Workers Are Forced to Take More Jobs with Few Benefits," *Wall Street Journal*, March 11, 1993, p. A1.

Commentary

According to the article, Lou Capozzola's salary was cut in half in February 1990. Had he become one-half as valuable over night? The article also quotes Lou expressing his opinion that as the sole supporter of a wife and two children he had no choice but to take the company's offer. As useful as our demand/supply model is, it does not seem to account for Lou Capozzola's experience.

Let's attempt to maintain some objectivity, even as we sympathize with Mr. Capozzola, and see if we can understand what is going on. Time Inc., like any firm, operates to maximize profit. To maximize profit, the firm must offer consumers a product they want at a price they are willing to pay. Since other firms are competing with Time Inc, and *Sports Illustrated*, Time Inc. must offer the highest quality at the lowest price. If another firm can offer the same product at a lower price, Time Inc. will lose business. Thus, the firm is always on the lookout for ways to reduce costs without harming the quality of the product. The article notes that using contract labor can cost as much as 40 percent less than using full-time or permanent labor.

In the figure, the lower costs of contract labor in the labor market are represented as W_c and the higher costs of permanent labor are represented as W_p. Everything else the same, that is, with the same MRP, the firm will hire contract labor over permanent labor. For instance, the firm would be willing to hire Q_p workers at the cost of W_p. If the firm had a choice of whether to pay W_p or W_c, it would choose the lower cost, W_c. Indeed, the firm could increase employment out to Q_c.

We can understand the employment decision from the firm's perspective, which our simple labor market diagram illustrates. What about from the employee's perspective? Consider the plight illustrated by Mr. Capozzola's statement that even though the contract position paid only half his former salary, at least he had a job. What if Mr. Capozzola had quit that job and attempted to offer his services elsewhere?

Suppose there are two labor markets, one for contract labor and one for permanent labor. Suppose that fewer people are willing and able to

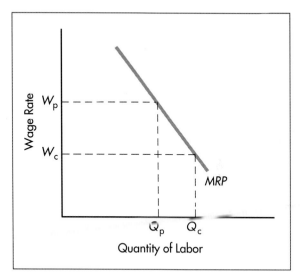

work as a contract employee than are willing to work as a permanent employee. Then, everything else the same, the contract employee's wages will rise and the permanent employee's will decline until an equilibrium differential is reached. The compensating wage differential between the two labor markets, $W_p - W_c$, illustrates the amount that will just equate the demand and supply in each market. If Mr. Capozzola decided not to accept the contract labor, he would offer his services only in the permanent labor market. If he and several others did the same, the wage in the contract market would have to rise and that in the permanent market fall, until a new set of equilibriums is reached.

From what we can discern from the article, Mr. Capozzola must have felt that during the time he would be looking for a permanent job, he would not be drawing enough income to support his family. This was unacceptable to him. In addition, he might have known that all such positions were being converted to contract labor and that there were no or very few permanent positions around that could use his experience and abilities. In this case, he had the choice of remaining in the job but earning less or of retraining and looking for a position in another occupation. Although either would mean a different standard of living, the choice does fit in the model of the labor market.

17

Wage Differentials: Race, Gender, Age, and Unionization

FUNDAMENTAL QUESTIONS

1. What accounts for earnings disparities between males and females and between whites and nonwhites?

2. Are discrimination and freely functioning markets compatible?

3. What government policies have been implemented to reduce wage differentials?

4. Have unions been able to increase the wages of union members relative to the wages of nonunionized workers?

5. What effects do government policies and programs such as minimum wages and the Family and Medical Leave Act have on the labor market?

I
n the United States in 1990, the average black male worker earned only 74 percent of what the average white male worker earned. This ratio was 8 to 10 percentage points higher than it had been in the mid-1960s, when the average black worker earned about 65 percent of what the average white male worker earned. White female weekly wages were about 58 percent of average white male weekly wages in 1976, 59 percent in 1980, and 70 percent in 1990. In 1990, male Hispanics had incomes averaging only 69 percent of those of white males. The average union member earned more than the average nonunion member, somewhere between 10 and 20 percent more in 1990.[1]

The discussion in the previous two chapters suggests that workers receive compensation equal to their marginal revenue products. The economic model of the labor market also suggests that discrimination on the basis of race, sex, or age should not exist. How then do we explain why minorities and women earn significantly less than white males in the U.S. labor market? Moreover, why do union members earn more than nonunion members? These differentials call for a further investigation of the labor market. The purpose of this chapter is to carry out that investigation.

PREVIEW

I. DISCRIMINATION

The United States is not alone in having differentials based on race and sex. In fact, there seem to be differentials among certain groups in nearly every country. Studies have found that "colored" workers in

What accounts for earnings disparities between males and females and between whites and nonwhites?

Britain earn only about 60 percent of white workers' incomes. There are differentials in Israel between the Oriental-Sephardic Jews and Ashkenazic Jews and in other nations between different groups based on color or religion. And in all countries women earn less than men. The Scandinavian countries, France, Australia, and New Zealand have female-to-male hourly pay ratios of 80 to 90 percent while other countries in Western Europe have pay ratios of 65 to 75 percent.[2]

I.a. Definition of Discrimination

Is discrimination present when there is prejudice or just when prejudice has harmful results? Consider a firm with two branch offices. One office employs only blacks; the other, only whites. Workers in both branches are paid the

---

[1]*Bureau of Labor Statistics*, 1990.

[2]Francine D. Blau and Lawrence M. Kahn, "The Gender Earnings Gap: Some International Evidence," NBER Working Paper No. 4224, December 1992.

same wages and have the same opportunities for advancement. Is discrimination occurring?

Is a firm that provides extensive training to employees discriminating when it prefers to hire young workers who are likely to stay with the firm long enough for it to recoup the training costs? Is an economics department that has no black faculty members guilty of discrimination if black economists constitute only 1 percent of the profession? Would your answer change if the department could show that it advertised job openings widely and made the same offers to blacks and whites? Clearly, discrimination is a difficult subject to define and measure.

From an economist's viewpoint, a worker's value in the labor market depends on the factors affecting the marginal revenue product. When a factor that is unrelated to marginal revenue product acquires a positive or negative value in the labor market, **discrimination** is occurring. In Figure 1, if D_M is the demand for males and D_F is the demand for females, and males and females have identical marginal revenue products, then the resulting wage differences can be attributed to discrimination. Race, gender, age, physical handicaps, religion, sexual preference, and ethnic heritage may be factors that take on positive or negative values in the labor market and yet are unrelated to marginal revenue products.

discrimination:
when factors unrelated to marginal revenue product affect the wages or jobs that are obtained

1.b. Theories of Discrimination

Are discrimination and freely functioning markets compatible?

Wage differentials due to race or gender pose a theoretical problem for economists because the labor market model attributes differences in wages to demand and supply differences that depend on productivity and the labor-leisure tradeoff. How can economists account for different pay scales for men and women, or for one race versus another, in the absence of marginal productivity differences between sexes or races? They identify discrimination as

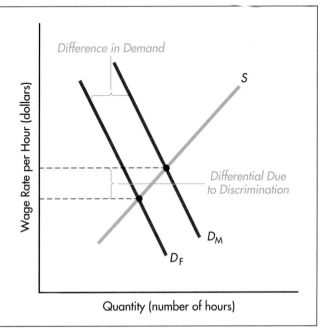

Figure 1
Discrimination
D_M is the demand for males and D_F the demand for females. The two groups of workers are identical except in gender. The greater demand and the higher wage rate for males, even though males and females are equally productive, are due to discrimination.

the cause of the differences even though they find discrimination difficult to rationalize because it is costly to those who discriminate.

In the freely functioning labor market, there is a profit to be made in *not* discriminating; therefore, discrimination should not exist. But, because discrimination does exist, economists have attempted to find plausible explanations for it. They have identified two sources of labor market discrimination. The first is *personal prejudice*: employers, fellow employees, or customers dislike associating with workers of a given race or sex. The second is statistical discrimination: employers project certain perceived group characteristics onto individuals. Economists tend to argue that personal prejudice is not consistent with a market economy, but have acknowledged that statistical discrimination can coexist within a market economy.

I.b.I. Personal Prejudice

Certain groups in a society could be precluded from higher-paying jobs or from jobs that provide valuable human capital by personal prejudice on the part of employers, fellow workers, or customers.

Employer prejudice If two workers have identical marginal revenue products and one worker is less expensive than the other, firms will want to hire the lower-cost worker. Otherwise, profits will be lower than they need to be. Suppose white males and others are identically productive, but managers prefer white males. Then the white males will be more expensive than women and minorities, and hiring white males will lower profits.

Under what conditions will lower profits as a result of personal prejudice be acceptable? Perhaps a monopoly firm can forgo some of its monopoly profit in order to satisfy the manager's personal prejudices (see the discussion of X-inefficiency in the chapter on monopoly), or perhaps firms that do not maximize profits can indulge in personal preferences. However, for profit-maximizing firms selling their goods in the market structures of perfect competition, monopolistic competition, or oligopoly, personal prejudice will mean a loss of profit unless all rivals also discriminate. Could firms form a cartel to discriminate? Recall from the discussion of oligopoly that cartels do not last long—there is an incentive to cheat—unless an entity like the government sanctions and enforces the cartel.

In the United States, well-meaning legislation intended to protect women actually created a situation in which women were denied access to training and education and thus were not able to gain the human capital necessary to compete for high-skill, high-paying jobs. Until the 1960s, women were barred from jobs because of legislation that attempted to protect them from heavy labor or injury. In reality, this legislation precluded women from obtaining certain kinds of human capital. Without the human capital, a generation or more of women were unable to obtain many high-paying jobs. For another example, see the Economic Insight "South Africa's Labor Policy."

Worker prejudice Workers may not want to associate with other races or sexes. White males may resist taking orders from females or sharing responsibility with a member of a minority group. White male workers who have these discriminatory preferences will tend to quit employers who employ women or minorities on a nondiscriminatory basis.

The worker prejudice explanation of discrimination assumes that white males are willing to accept lower-paying positions to avoid working with anyone other than a white male. Such discrimination is costly to those who discriminate.

Discrimination might occur as employers attempt to hire only certain kinds of workers, as employees attempt to work only with certain kinds of coworkers, or as customers attempt to purchase goods and services from certain kinds of workers.

Discrimination is costly in that less productive employees or more expensive but not more productive employees are used.

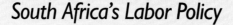
South Africa's Labor Policy

One way to establish barriers is to use government power to serve the interests of special groups at the expense of others. Sometimes the use of government authority is blatantly discriminatory—witness South Africa's Colour Bar Act of 1911, which authorized the establishment of a maximum ratio of African to white employees in that country's mines.

During World War I nonwhites in South Africa were able to make inroads into jobs previously held by whites. Immediately after the war,

however, the whites reestablished their dominant positions with government help. The Wage Act of 1925, passed in the name of preventing sweatshops and encouraging industrial efficiency, set up a wage board that had the power to establish wages in various non-union jobs. By setting relatively high wages for the skilled trades in which whites were employed, incumbent white artisans were able to keep nonwhites out of these jobs while appearing to adhere to high-sounding principles. The so-

called "civilized labour policy" was built upon the economic reality that social background and inferior educational facilities prevented nonwhites from attaining the skill levels of whites. The only hope nonwhites had of securing jobs held by whites was to offer their services in these occupations at lower wages. The "civilized labour policy" prevented this.

Source: W. H. Hutt, *The Economics of the Colour Bar* (London: Andre Deutsch, 1964).

Consumer prejudice   Customers may prefer to be served by white males in some situations and by minorities or women in others. If their preferences for white males extend to high-paying jobs such as physician and lawyer and their preferences for women and minorities are confined to lower-paying jobs like maid, nurse, and flight attendant, then women and minorities will be forced into occupations that work to their disadvantage.

The consumer prejudice explanation of discrimination assumes that consumers are willing to pay higher prices to be served by white males. In certain circumstances and during certain periods of time, this may be so; but over wide geographic areas or across different nations and over long periods of time, consumer prejudice does not appear to be a very likely explanation of discrimination.

statistical discrimination: discrimination that results when an indicator of group performance is incorrectly applied to an individual member of the group

1.b.2. Statistical Discrimination   Discrimination not related to personal prejudices can occur because of a lack of information. Statistical discrimination was discussed in the chapter on the economics of information as one way that firms and individuals deal with a lack of information. Employers must try to predict the potential productivity of job applicants, but rarely do they know what a worker's actual productivity will be. Often, the only information available when they hire someone is information that may be imperfectly related to productivity in general and may not apply to a particular person at all. Reliance on indicators of productivity such as education, experience, age, and test scores may keep some very good people from getting a job and may result in the hiring of some unproductive people.

Suppose two types of workers apply for a word-processing job: those who can process 80 words per minute and those who can process only 40 words per minute. The problem is that these actual productivities are unknown to the employer. The employer can observe only the results of a five-minute word-processing test given to all applicants. How can the employer decide who is lucky or unlucky on the test and who can actually process 80 words per minute? Suppose the employer discovers that applicants from a particular vocational college, the DeVat School, are taught to perform well on pre-employment tests but their overall performance as employees is the same as that of the rest of the applicants—some do well and some do not. The employer might decide to reject all applicants from DeVat because the good and bad ones can't be differentiated. Is the employer discriminating against DeVat? The answer is *yes*. The employer is using statistical discrimination.

Let's extend this example to race and gender. Suppose that, on average, minorities with a high school education are discovered to be less productive than white males with a high school education because of differences in the quality of the schools they attend. An employer using this information when making a hiring decision might prefer to hire a white male. Statistical discrimination can cause a systematic preference for one group over another even if some individuals in each group have the same measured characteristics.

1.c. Occupational Segregation

crowding:
forcing a group into certain kinds of occupations

occupational segregation:
the separation of jobs by sex

Statistical discrimination and imperfect information can lead to **crowding**—forcing women and minorities into occupations where they are unable to obtain the human capital necessary to compete for high-paying jobs. Today, even in the industrial nations, some occupations are considered "women's jobs" and different occupations are considered "men's jobs." This separation of jobs by sex is called **occupational segregation**.

There is a substantial amount of occupational segregation in the United States and other industrialized nations.[3] One reason for occupational segregation is differences in the human capital acquired by males and females. Much of the human capital portion of the discrepancy between men and women is due to childbearing. Data suggest that marriage and children handicap women's efforts to earn as much as men. Many women leave the labor market during pregnancy, at childbirth, or when their children are young. These child-related interruptions are damaging to subsequent earnings because three out of four births occur to women before the age of thirty, the period in which men are gaining the training and experience that lead to higher earnings later in life. Second, even when mothers stay in the labor force, responsibility for children frequently constrains their choice of job: they accept lower wages in exchange for shorter or more flexible hours, location near home, limited out-of-town travel, and the like. Third, women have a disproportionate responsibility for child care and often have to make sacrifices that men do not make. For instance, when a young child is present, women are more likely than men to be absent from work, even when the men and women have equal levels of education and wages.

Perhaps most important of all, because most female children are expected to be mothers, they have been less likely than male children to acquire marketable human capital while in school. In the past, this difference was reflected in the choice of a curriculum in primary and secondary schools, in

---

[3]Victor R. Fuchs, "Women's Quest for Economic Equality," *Journal of Economic Perspectives* 3, no. 1 (Winter 1989), pp. 25–42, suggests that about half the occupations in the United States are gender-biased, or "crowded." The ratios vary among the other industrialized nations, some having more and some having less occupational segregation. See Blau and Kahn, op. cit.

a college major, and in the reluctance of females to pursue graduate school training or to undergo the long hours and other rigors characteristic of apprenticeships in medicine, law, business, and other financially rewarding occupations. Females were channeled into languages, typing, and home economics, while males were channeled into mechanical drawing, shop, chemistry, and physics. This situation is changing, but the remnants of the past continue to influence the market. Since the late 1970s, about half of all law school classes and about one-third of medical school classes have been female. Nonetheless, mostly females major in languages, literature, education, and home economics, while mostly males major in physics, mathematics, chemistry, and engineering.

If new female entrants into the labor force have human capital equal to the human capital of new male entrants and thus greater than the human capital of females already in the labor force, then the average human capital and wages of females will rise. But even while the wage gap between males and females is decreasing, a gap will continue to exist because the average male in the labor force has more marketable human capital than the average female. The average rate of pay of males will continue to exceed that of females.

Statistical discrimination has a role in earnings disparities between men and women as well. As noted in the chapter on the economics of information, childless women earn less than men simply because it is the women who bear children. The human capital (training, education) women acquire will often be different, and less marketable, than that acquired by men. This occurs because many childless women did not know that they would be childless, and the subjects they studied in school as well as the jobs they took upon leaving school did not provide the marketable training that most men received. Also, prospective employers were unlikely to know which young women would have children and which would not, which would leave their jobs and which would not, and this affected the employers' willingness to provide training opportunities or to make other investments in job-related human capital. Because the odds are great that a woman will leave a job for some period of time to have a child, simply being a woman provides a signal to a firm. As a result of this signal, the wage offered a man might be higher than that offered a woman, or the job offered a man might contain better training than the one offered a woman.

Uncertainty about children does not end quickly for women or their employers. Even women who are childless at age thirty have a 1 in 4 chance of having at least one child by the time they are thirty-five. If females came into the world with a sign announcing the number of children that they would ultimately bear, the relationship between women's earnings and their number of children would be much stronger than the one we observe.

I.d. Immigration

While the less marketable human capital that women acquire can account for at least some of the differences between the wages of women and men, immigration accounts for some of the differences between the wages of whites and nonwhites. Immigration increases the supply of labor—causing an outward shift of the labor supply curve, as shown in Figure 2. The equilibrium wage rate is driven down from $10 an hour to $8 an hour. Not all workers are hurt by the immigration, however. If most of the immigrants are unskilled, then

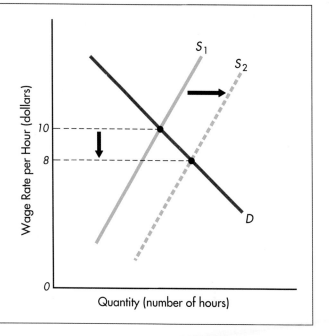

Figure 2
Immigration and the Labor Market
Immigration means an increased supply of labor. The labor supply curve shifts out from S_1 to S_2. The wage rate declines as a result, from $10 to $8, and employment rises.

the wage rate is driven down only in the unskilled-labor market. The skilled labor does not feel the effects of immigration.

As can be seen in Figure 3, immigration was quite high in the 1970s and 1980s. It did not exceed the rate between 1900 and 1920, but it was second only to the influx in that twenty-year period. Between 1901 and 1910, 8.8 million immigrants arrived in the United States, the all-time record for a single decade. Between 1911 and 1920, 5.7 million more immigrants came to the United States.

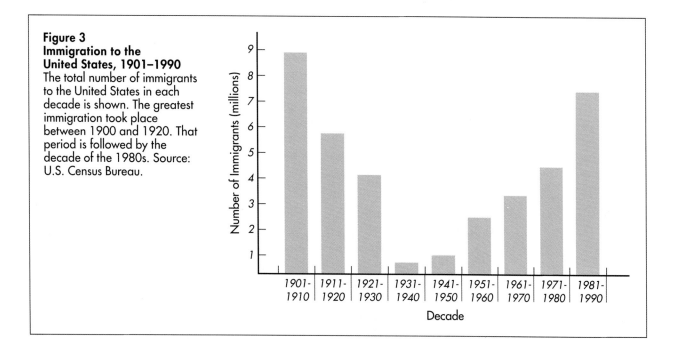

Figure 3
Immigration to the United States, 1901–1990
The total number of immigrants to the United States in each decade is shown. The greatest immigration took place between 1900 and 1920. That period is followed by the decade of the 1980s. Source: U.S. Census Bureau.

In the early 1900s, immigrants came primarily from Europe. In the 1970s, the flow of people from Europe declined by 0.5 million and the flow from Latin America increased sharply. Almost 1.3 million immigrants came from Mexico alone, and another 0.5 million came from the West Indies. Immigration from Asia also increased significantly. In 1980 almost 1.8 million new U.S. residents were from Asia, mostly from the Philippines, South Korea, and Vietnam. Rather than entering the United States along the northern Atlantic seaboard and settling in the eastern and northern states, as European immigrants had done, the new immigrants entered across the southern and western borders and settled in relatively large numbers in the South and West. California alone accounts for more than 25 percent of the foreign-born population in the United States, and California, New York, and Florida have one-half of this population.

As is true of migrants in general, the new immigrants tend to be relatively young, primarily ages twenty to forty-nine. During the late 1960s and early 1970s, many immigrants to the United States were relatively skilled individuals from low-income countries. More than 22 percent of the immigrants had four or more years of college education, whereas in 1980 only 16.2 percent of U.S. residents had attended college for four or more years. Among immigrants twenty-five years old and over, 6.9 percent from Latin America and 37.4 percent from Asia had at least four years of college. Since 1975, skilled immigration to the United States from both low- and high-income countries has remained close to the levels of the early 1970s, but there has been a dramatic growth in the immigration of the unskilled. A large number, 12.8 percent, have less than five years of elementary school education. (The comparable figure for U.S. residents is 3.6 percent.)

This pattern of immigration has had two major effects on the labor market in the United States. First, it has tended to widen the earnings gap between Hispanics and whites, since most of the unskilled immigrants are coming from Latin America and their primary language is Spanish. As a result, Hispanics in the United States must continue to assimilate increasing numbers of the unskilled, who must learn English as well as attempt to acquire marketable skills. As one generation (usually the second) acquires education and training, its average earnings rise. But as new immigrants continue to arrive, average earnings of all Hispanics fall.

The second impact of recent immigration has been to widen the earnings gap between skilled and unskilled workers. More unskilled workers than skilled workers are immigrating to the United States. As a result, the supply of unskilled labor is increasing and wages in the unskilled-labor market are falling without affecting wages in the skilled-labor market. Hence, the wage gap between the two sectors is widening.

RECAP

1. Discrimination occurs when factors unrelated to marginal physical product acquire a positive or negative value in the labor market.

2. Earnings disparities may exist for a number of reasons, including personal prejudice, statistical discrimination, and human capital differentials. Human capital differentials may exist because of occupational

choice, statistical discrimination, and unequal opportunities to acquire human capital.

3. There are two general classes of discrimination theories: prejudice theory and statistical theory. Prejudice theories claim that employers, workers, and consumers express their personal prejudices by, respectively, earning lower profits, accepting lower wages, and paying higher prices. Statistical discrimination theory asserts that firms have imperfect information and must rely on general indicators of marginal physical product to pay wages and hire people and that reliance on these general indicators may create a pattern of discrimination.

4. Occupational segregation is the separation of jobs by sex. Some jobs are filled primarily by women, and other jobs are filled primarily by men.

5. In recent years, immigrants to the United States have included increasing numbers of unskilled people from Latin America. The impact of their arrival on the labor market has been to widen the earnings gap between Hispanics and whites and between the skilled and unskilled.

2. WAGE DIFFERENTIALS AND GOVERNMENT POLICIES

What government policies have been implemented to reduce wage differentials?

Not until the 1960s did wage disparities and employment practices become a major public policy issue in the United States. In 1963 the Equal Pay Act outlawed separate pay scales for men and women performing similar jobs, and Title VII of the 1964 Civil Rights Act prohibited all forms of discrimination in employment.

2.a. Antidiscrimination Laws

Since the 1930s, about thirty states have enacted fair employment practice laws prohibiting discrimination in employment on the basis of race, creed, color, or national origin. Under state fair employment practice legislation, it is normally illegal for an organization to refuse employment, to discharge employees, or to discriminate in compensation or other terms of employment because of race.

These state laws did not apply to women, however. In fact, prior to the 1960s, sex discrimination was officially sanctioned by so-called protective labor laws, which limited the total hours that women were allowed to work and prohibited them from working at night, lifting heavy objects, and working during pregnancy.

With the Civil Rights Act of 1964, however, it became unlawful for any employer to discriminate on the basis of race, color, religion, sex, or national origin. Unions also were forbidden from excluding anyone on the basis of those five categories. Historically, it had been very difficult for racial minorities to obtain admission into unions representing workers in the skilled trades. This exclusion prevented minorities from obtaining the human capital necessary to compete for higher-paying jobs.

The Civil Rights Act applied only to actions after the effective date of July 1, 1965. It also permitted exceptions in cases where religion, sex, or national origin is a bona fide occupational qualification reasonably necessary to the normal operation of a business. This qualification might apply to certain jobs in religious organizations, for example. In addition, the act permits an employer to differentiate wages and other employment conditions on the basis of a bona fide seniority system, provided that such differences are not the result of an intention to discriminate. As a result of these exceptions, the Civil Rights Act has had neither as large nor as quick an impact on wage and job differentials as many had anticipated. It has, however, led to a clearer definition of discrimination.

Two standards, or tests, of discrimination have evolved from court cases: disparate treatment and disparate impact. **Disparate treatment** means treating individuals differently because of their race, sex, color, religion, or national origin. The difficulty created by this standard is that personnel policies that appear to be neutral because they ignore race, gender, and so on, may nevertheless continue the effects of past discrimination. For instance, a seniority system that fires first the last person hired will protect those who were historically favored in hiring and training practices. Alternatively, a standard of hiring by word of mouth will perpetuate past discrimination if current employees are primarily of one race or sex.

The concern with perpetuating past discrimination led to the second standard, **disparate impact**. Under this standard it is the result of different treatment, not the motivation, that matters. Thus, statistical discrimination is illegal under the impact standard even though it is not illegal under the treatment standard.

disparate treatment:
treatment of individuals differently because of their race, sex, color, religion, or national origin

disparate impact:
an impact that differs according to race, sex, color, religion, or national origin, regardless of the motivation

2.b. Comparable Worth

comparable worth:
the idea that pay ought to be determined by job characteristics rather than by supply and demand and that jobs with comparable requirements should receive comparable wages

The persistent wage gap between men and women in particular, but also between white males and minorities, has prompted well-meaning reformers to seek a new remedy for eliminating the gap—laws requiring companies to offer equal pay for jobs of comparable worth. **Comparable worth** is a catchword for the idea that pay ought to be determined by job characteristics rather than by supply and demand and that jobs with comparable requirements should receive comparable wages.

To identify jobs of comparable worth, employers would be required to evaluate all of the different jobs in their firms, answering questions such as these: What level of formal education is needed? How much training is necessary? Is previous experience needed? What skills are required? How much supervision is required? Is the work dangerous? Are working conditions unpleasant? By assigning point values to answers, employers could create job classifications based on job characteristics and could pay comparable wages for jobs with comparable "scores." A firm employing secretaries and steelworkers, for example, would determine the wages for these jobs by assessing job characteristics. If the assessment shows secretaries' work to be comparable to that of steelworkers, then the firm would pay secretaries and steelworkers comparable wages.

Proponents of comparable worth claim that market-determined wages are inappropriate because of the market's inability to assess marginal products as a result of statistical discrimination, team production, and personal prejudice. They argue that mandating a comparable worth system would minimize wage differentials that are due to statistical discrimination and occupational segregation, and they charge that a freely functioning market will continue to misallocate pay.

Opponents of comparable worth argue that interference with the functioning of the labor market will lead to shortages in some occupations and excess supplies in others. For instance, Figure 4 shows two markets for university professors, a market for computer science professors and a market for English professors. The supply and demand conditions in each market determine a wage for English professors that is less than the wage for computer science professors. The wage differential exists even though professors in both disciplines are required to have a Ph.D. and have essentially the same responsibilities.

Advocates of comparable worth would say that the two groups of professors should earn the same wage, the wage of the computer science professors, W_{CS}. But at this wage there would be a surplus of English professors, $QE_2 - QE_1$. The higher wage would cause the university to reduce the number of English professors it employs, from QE to QE_1. The net effect of comparable worth would be to reduce the number of English professors employed but to increase the wages of those who are employed. The policy would also have a detrimental effect in the future. The wage would send the incorrect signal to

Figure 4
Comparable Worth
Two markets are shown, a market for computer science professors and a market for English professors. Demand and supply conditions determine that the wages for computer science professors are higher than the wages for English professors. Proponents of comparable worth might argue that the wages of both groups of professors should be equal to the higher wages of computer science professors since the requirements and responsibilities of the two jobs are virtually identical. However, the effect of imposing a higher wage in the market for English professors, W_{CS}, is to create a surplus of English professors, $QE_2 - QE_1$. In addition, the higher wage sends the signal to current college students that majoring in English will generate the same expected income as majoring in computer science. Students who might have studied computer science turn to English. In the future, an excess of English professors remains and even grows while the number of computer science professors shrinks.

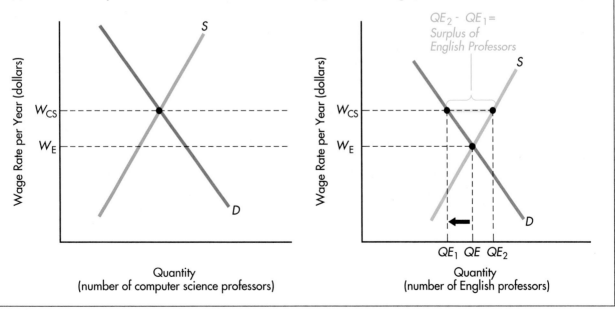

(a) Market for Computer Science Professors

(b) Market for English Professors

Law firms can be challenging or interesting or exciting or frustrating or difficult places to work, depending on one's view. Law firms have been known to hire people at the junior ranks, work these people seventy or so hours a week, and pay them little. If, after three or four years, these people have successfully completed the arduous time, they may become partners in the firm. Law firms typically pay partners more than their marginal revenue product and junior employees less than their marginal revenue product. The pay structure induces the junior employees to work hard and be productive so they too can reap the rewards of partnership eventually. Not all lawyers are attracted by the potential benefits of partnership. For instance, this attorney chose to forgo the high income of a partnership in a private law firm to serve the community from which she came. She chose to use her training in the Mexican American Legal Defense Fund.

current college students. It would tell students to remain in English instead of forgoing English for computer science.

Comparable worth has not fared well in the U.S. courtroom. On the whole, U.S. federal courts have not accepted the notion that unequal pay for comparable jobs violates existing employment discrimination law. Perhaps not surprisingly, therefore, the concept has made little headway in the private sector. Greater success has occurred in the public sector at the local and state levels. In Colorado Springs, San Jose, and Los Angeles, and in Iowa, Michigan, New York, and Minnesota, pay adjustments have been made on the basis of comparable worth. More than two-thirds of the state governments have begun studies to determine whether compensation of state workers reflects the worth of their jobs. Why has comparable worth had more success in the government sector? State governments suffer from the problem of team production, and if personal prejudice is to occur, it is more likely to occur in nonprofit organizations such as government where firms do not employ to the profit-maximizing point where MFC = MRP. Thus, it is in the state, local, and federal governments that comparable worth can be an effective policy. Comparable worth was adapted nationwide in Australia in the early 1970s and aspects of it have arisen in parts of the United Kingdom.

RECAP

1. The first national antidiscrimination law was the Civil Rights Act of 1964. It forbade firms from discriminating on the basis of sex, race, color, religion, or national origin.

2. Two tests of discrimination have evolved from court cases. According to the disparate treatment standard, it is illegal to intentionally treat individuals differently because of their race, sex, color, religion, or national origin. According to the disparate impact standard, it is the result, not the intention, of actions that is illegal.

3. Comparable worth is the idea that jobs should be evaluated on the basis of a number of characteristics and all jobs receiving the same evaluation should receive the same pay regardless of demand and supply conditions. Proponents argue that comparable worth is a solution to a market failure problem. Opponents argue that it will create surpluses and shortages in labor markets.

3. UNIONIZATION AND WAGE DIFFERENTIALS

Have unions been able to increase the wages of union members relative to the wages of nonunionized workers?

Unionized sectors of the U.S. economy earn higher wages than nonunionized sectors. Nevertheless, union membership is declining in the private sector of the U.S. economy. In this section we discuss the role of unions in creating wage differentials.

3.a. Monopsony

Many people argue that unions arise under bad management. In other words, unions arise when workers are being exploited or mistreated by mismanagement. According to this viewpoint, a union is a means to offset a monopsony.

A monopsony is a market situation in which there is just one buyer of a resource. A monopsonistic firm hires additional labor as long as labor's value to the firm exceeds its cost. Yet the labor is not paid its value to the firm. It receives a wage rate that is less than its marginal revenue product. Actually, there are not many situations in which just one firm buys a resource. Most monopsonies occur when several firms join together to form a buyers' cartel. Agricultural firms in California might organize a cooperative to bring itinerant labor from Mexico to harvest crops. The cooperative would send workers to farms as needed. Individual public schools do not hire teachers; instead, school districts comprising several schools employ teachers. In some cities, hospitals have formed an organization that hires all nurses and staff other than doctors and then apportions the workers as needed.

Athletics is a particularly fertile area for the formation of monopsony cartels because the government allows, even supports, the cartel even though cartels are illegal in other businesses. One of the most effective is the NCAA, the National Collegiate Athletic Association. Not long after intercollegiate football became a substantial source of income to colleges, the best football players began to receive large money inducements—wages—to attend certain schools. Some college administrators opposed all money payments to amateur athletes. They believed amateurism has some inherent virtue and wanted to maintain the distinction between college athletics and professional sports.

That belief, coupled with widespread membership in the NCAA, has resulted in a monopsony situation in which student-athletes are paid substantially less than their marginal revenue products. In fact, student-athletes receive no pay. Universities and colleges are prohibited from offering salaries to athletes, from "making work" for them at the school and paying them relatively high wage rates for a job that usually pays much less (for example, paying athletes $30 an hour to reshelve books in the university library), and from offering cars, clothes, trips, and other inducements to attract athletes.

College is not the only place where athletes have faced a cartel. Players in major league baseball, professional basketball, and professional football have all been subject to such cartels. Players in each sport once worked under a system in which a player could deal only with the team that initially signed him. A reserve clause in most players' contracts made the player the exclusive property of the team that first signed him or the team to which he was traded thereafter. According to the clause, if a player refused to accept the wage of the team whose property he was, he could not play for any other team. People hired by a monopsony are paid wages that are less than their marginal revenue product—in other words, they are exploited.

The monopsonist is said to exploit its employees because of the low compensation level relative to the compensation level offered by a competitive firm. Some have argued that this exploitation also means shoddy working conditions, terrible treatment, and very high levels of injuries. There is no doubt that the monopsonist provides a total compensation package (salary, working conditions, and other job-related factors) that is less than the competitive firm (nonmonopsonist) would offer. However, the composition of that compensation depends on what the workers want. For instance, the coal miners in West Virginia may prefer some compensation in the form of safety equipment or filters in the mines. The coal mining firms would be willing to provide that equipment as part of the compensation package for the employees. The amount of safety would not necessarily be less than a competitive firm would provide, but the total compensation package would be. However, the total compensation has to be sufficient to induce workers to become coal miners. The coal miners, while earning less from a monopsonist than from a competitive firm, nevertheless can earn more than they could doing something other than coal mining.

3.b. Bilateral Monopoly

When people are paid wages that are less than their marginal revenue products, they have an incentive to find ways to offset this monopsony power. One approach has been for workers to form what we might call a sellers' cartel, a union. Major league baseball players in the 1960s received only about one-fifth of their estimated net marginal revenue products because of the monopsony situation enjoyed by team owners. In the 1970s, the players formed a union. The result was that salaries soared; in 1977 the average salary rose 40 percent and by 1986 the average was $410,000, up from $51,501 in 1976, the last year of the reserve clause that prohibited players from leaving one team to seek a higher wage with another team.[4]

---

[4]Paul M. Sommers and Noel Quinton, "Pay and Performance in Major League Baseball: The Case of the First Family of Free Agents," *Journal of Human Resources* 17, Summer 1982, p. 227.

bilateral monopoly:
a market in which a monopsonistic buyer of resources faces a monopoly seller of resources

Unions may arise as an offset to monopsony or as an institution that benefits both firms and employees.

A union can enable workers to speak with one voice—to confront the one buyer with just one seller. The result is a **bilateral monopoly**—a monopsony of buyers facing a monopoly of sellers. Figure 5 shows a monopsonistic labor market. The monopsonistic firm wants to hire a quantity of labor, L_1 (500 hours' worth of labor), given by MRP = MFC, and pay a wage rate, W_1 = $15, at which people are willing and able to supply L_1 = 500 hours. Instead of accepting this wage, the union demands a higher wage, W_2 = $20, which is equal to the marginal revenue product. The resulting wage rate may be anywhere between W_1 and W_2. Where it ends up depends partly on which side has the stronger bargaining position, partly on the negotiating skills of the parties, and partly on luck.

3.b.1. Efficiency Bases for Unions

Offsetting the power of the monopsonist is not the only reason for a union. In fact, unions exist in many industries other than monopsonies. A union may serve the purposes of both firms and workers. For instance, a large corporation having many different types of jobs may find negotiating with each and every employee very time consuming and costly. In addition, the firm may have no means to communicate with employees regarding issues such as the performance of the firm and personnel policies the firm is implementing. In such cases, the firm may find it less costly to work with a union. In this way, the firm can communicate with the leaders of the union and allow the union to communicate with workers. The firm can also set wages and working conditions in agreement with the union leaders and have these policies apply to all workers, thus avoiding the costs of negotiating with each employee. Unions may also provide ways that the firm is assured of a supply of skilled labor. The union may require that members have a certain amount of experience or serve an apprenticeship. Also, it and the firm may agree that layoffs occur in a certain order, such as last hired/first fired, and that the callback of employees begins with those

Figure 5
The Monopsonistic Labor Market
In a monopsonistic labor market, the firm hires the quantity given by the equilibrium between the marginal revenue product (*MRP*) and the marginal factor cost (*MFC*), but the firm pays a wage that is less than the marginal revenue product. The wage rate that is equal to marginal revenue product is W_2 ($20). The wage that the monopsonistic firm pays is W_1 ($15). It is found by dropping a vertical line to the supply curve from the point where *MFC* = *MRP*.

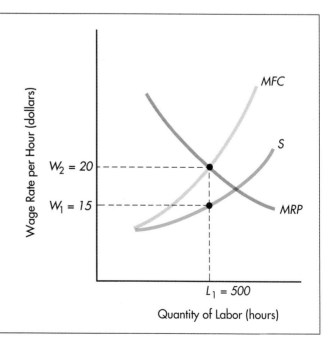

employees last laid off. The firm thus does not have to devote resources to attracting new employees and training those employees; a readily available source of employees will exist.

Unions appear able to reduce the firm's costs more in the manufacturing sectors than in the service sectors. At least the manufacturing sectors are more unionized than are the service sectors. However, as manufacturing has become a smaller proportion of total employment in the United States and services have become a larger proportion, the membership in unions has declined. The only area in which union membership has grown in the last 15 years in the United States has been in the public sector—government employees.

collective bargaining:
the process by which union and management negotiate labor contracts

The process by which unions and firms hammer out a compromise regarding wages or working conditions is called **collective bargaining**. Under collective bargaining, union and management meet to negotiate a mutually agreeable contract specifying wages, working conditions, pension benefits, and other aspects of the job. The resulting contract usually extends over two or three years. Most multiyear agreements contain cost-of-living allowances (COLAs). Such allowances allow for periodic changes in money wages during the life of the agreement, based on changes in the purchasing power as measured by inflation. In some cases where a firm is unprofitable, unions have agreed to wage concessions or cuts for a short period of time, depending on the ability of the firm to reach profitability. In recent years, negotiations have focused more on working conditions and fringe benefits than on wages. Health insurance, child care, and retirement benefits are very important issues.

3.c. Economic Effects of Unions

Unionized sectors of the U.S. economy earn higher wages than nonunion sectors. In 1991, union wages were on average 30 percent higher than nonunion wages. The union-nonunion differential ranges from no difference in the financial services industry to a 75 percent difference in construction. This wage differential could be the result of union members having jobs that require greater skills than nonunion members and the greater age and experience of union workers. However, even if skill differences are taken into consideration, there is a wage differential of about 10 percent.

A union may have an effect on wages through the demand for and/or the supply of labor. The demand for any resource is its marginal revenue product, MPP × MR; thus, an increase in either MPP or MR causes the demand curve to shift. If the union is able to increase the productivity of labor, to raise MPP, the demand for labor rises. Thus a benefit of unionization for a firm may be increased productivity. By providing workers with a direct means to voice their discontent to management and by basing job rights on seniority, unions may reduce workers' discontent and reduce turnover, or quit, rates. Firms with low quit rates have an incentive to provide training or human capital to employees, and human capital is positively related to productivity. The establishment of a seniority system and of formal grievance procedures may enhance productivity by improving workers' morale, motivation, and effort. Studies analyzing the effects of unions on productivity have shown a great deal of variation. Unions have been shown to have raised the productivity of all U.S. manufacturing by about 20 percent. For specific

Unionization in Japan

In the United States companies bargain with several unions representing workers with different skills or jobs. For example, airline mechanics, pilots, stewards, and baggage handlers each have their own union. In contrast, unions in Japan are organized on an enterprise (company or plant) basis. All employees in an enterprise are members of the same union. The enterprise-based structure of Japan is consistent with the practice of large Japanese companies to offer lifetime employment. It is not unusual for Japanese workers to spend their entire work life in a single company. In forming unions, then, Japanese workers have been most concerned with factors that affect the well-being of their company or plant.

Unions in Japan seldom mount large-scale offensives against management. Most contracts in Japan are renegotiated annually. Each spring a *shunto*, or spring wage campaign, is organized by the unions. A target for wage demands is set. Each union is allotted one day to strike by a schedule created by the unions and the firms. At the end of the strike, wage and other issues are resolved by the enterprise, and everyone goes back to work at the new wage.

Sources: Japan Institute of Labor, *Labor Unions and Labor-Management Relations* (Tokyo: Japan Institute of Labor, 1979); Tadashi Mitsufuji and Kiyohiko Hagisawa, "Recent Trends in Collective Bargaining in Japan," *International Labour Review* 105 (1972), pp. 135–153; Robert J. Flanagan, Robert S. Smith, and Ronald G. Ehrenberg, *Labor Economics and Labor Relations* (Glenview, Ill.: Scott, Foresman, 1984), pp. 330–340, 430–434.

industries, however, the effects range from a negative 20 percent to a positive 30 percent.[5]

A union may also be able to reduce the wage elasticity of demand for labor. A lower wage elasticity means that any increase in wages will have a smaller effect on the quantity of labor employed. The lower the wage elasticity, the more likely a union is to push for larger wage advances. In addition, a union may be able to increase the demand for union labor or use political power to influence legislation that benefits the unionized sectors of the economy. In monopsonistic markets a union may affect the supply of labor in order to offset the monopsony power of the resource buyer. In competitive labor markets a union may be able to control the supply of skilled labor.

Suppose Figure 6(a) represents the labor market in the absence of unions. The market demand for and market supply of labor determine a wage rate of $10 and an employment level of L_e. Each individual firm faces a horizontal supply of labor, as shown in Figure 6(b). Now, suppose that a union is able to establish a $20 wage in the industry—$10 more than the current wage. For the individual competitive firm, the higher wage means an upward shift of the marginal-factor-cost curve. This is shown in Figure 6(b) as the shift from $MFC_1 = \$10$ to $MFC_2 = \$20$ and a decline in the quantity of labor employed by the firm. The higher wage means that less labor is employed—L_2 is employed rather than L_1. Since all firms are affected in the same way, the higher wage creates a surplus in the labor market. L_4 workers are willing to work at $20, but only L_3 obtain jobs.

---

[5]See Ronald G. Ehrenberg and Robert S. Smith, *Modern Labor Economics*, 3d ed. (Glenview, Ill.: Scott, Foresman, 1987), p. 487.

Figure 6
Union Effects on the Labor Market

If the labor market is competitive, as shown in Figure 6(a), an increase in the wage from $10 to $20 per hour increases the quantity of people willing and able to work and decreases the quantity of jobs available that pay $20 per hour. The result is a labor surplus. Figure 6(b) shows the individual firm's response to an increase in the hourly wage. The higher marginal-factor-cost curve (MFC_2) intersects the marginal-revenue-product curve (MRP) at a smaller quantity of labor. The firm employs fewer workers.

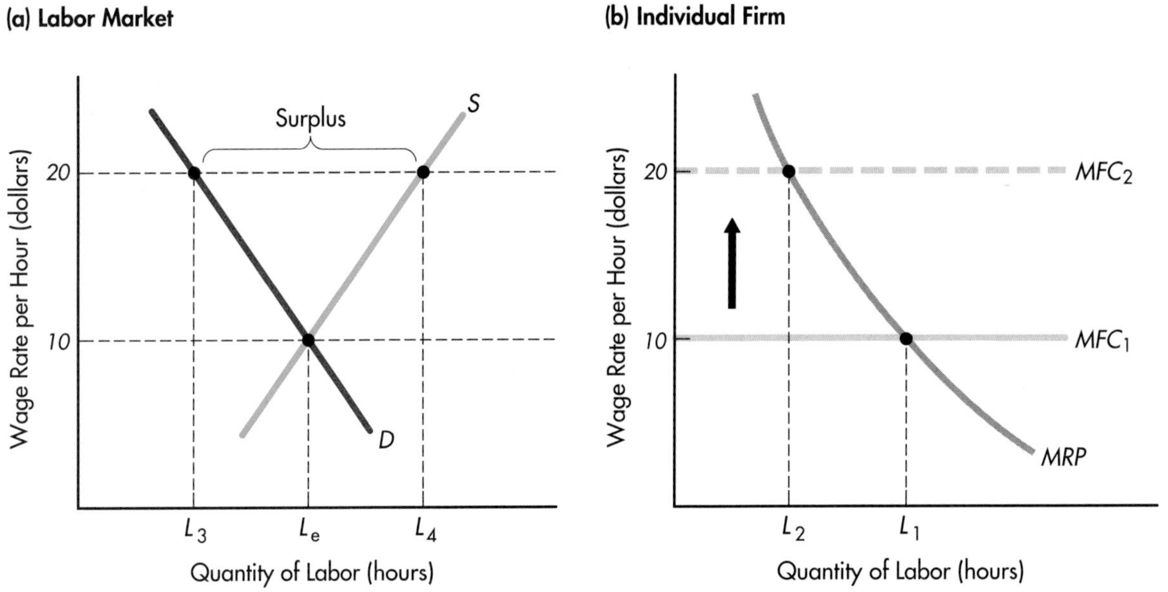

(a) Labor Market

(b) Individual Firm

Two questions arise from this analysis. First, how does a union increase wages in a competitive market? Second, what happens to workers who are unable to get union employment?

3.c.1. How Do Unions Increase Wages?   Unions increase wages by restricting the supply of union labor and by increasing the demand for union labor.

The closed and union shop   If a firm could hire only union workers, called a **closed shop**, the union would be able to restrict the supply of labor by restricting union membership. By contrast, in a **union shop**, a workplace in which employees must join the union within a certain amount of time after obtaining a job, a union is unable to effectively control the supply of labor. This difference between union shops and closed shops is why unions opposed the Taft-Hartley Act in 1947, which outlawed closed shops. Since 1947, unions have not been able to restrict the supply of union labor through union membership.

Immigration restrictions   Restricting immigration has been a common theme throughout the history of organized labor in the United States. In 1869, the first national convention of labor unions proposed excluding Chinese contract labor. Four months later, the first national convention of black unions likewise voted for exclusion. In 1872, the Working Men's party of California forced passage of a new California constitution that forbade the hiring of Chinese workers by any corporation or public body. In 1882,

closed shop:
a workplace in which union membership is a condition of employment

union shop:
a workplace in which all employees must join a union within a specific period of time after they are hired

Congress ended Chinese immigration. Throughout the 1920s and 1930s, the AFL fought to restrict and then to abolish immigration. Unions today strongly oppose the relaxation of immigration restrictions.

Barriers to entering specific occupations   To restrict the supply of labor to a particular profession, unions can require lengthy training programs or apprenticeships, and the government can mandate licensing. The entry of electricians, plumbers, beauticians, and others into their professions is limited by the need to acquire a license in order to practice. The ease or difficulty of obtaining a license reflects how high a barrier to entry is desired. High barriers increase the wage rate and reduce the flow of workers from other occupations to the restricted profession.

Increasing demand   Unions might try to increase the demand for union labor, causing the demand curve to shift out and become more inelastic. If unions can convince consumers to buy only union-made goods and services, the demand for union labor will rise and the wage elasticity of the demand for union labor will fall. Bumper stickers and advertisements urging support for unions ("Look for the union label") are appeals to consumers to purchase goods made in union shops and thus to stimulate the demand for union workers.

If unions can limit the entry of nonunion firms or restrict the sale of output produced by nonunion labor, the demand for union labor will increase and the wage elasticity of demand for union labor will decrease. For this reason, the United Auto Workers has supported legislation restricting the import of autos, and the textile workers' union has supported tariffs or taxes on imported textiles.

Unions may try to safeguard union jobs by opposing the introduction of new technology and by featherbedding. **Featherbedding** is the requirement that more workers than are actually needed be employed. For several years after diesel engines replaced coal-burning engines and made railroad firemen obsolete, the railway union required firemen on each train. Similarly, airlines were required to carry three pilots even after new planes made the third pilot obsolete. The musicians' union used to require that a certain number of musicians be employed for each performance even if the music did not call for that many.

3.c.2. What Happens to Nonunion Labor?   The excess supply of labor forces unions to ration the available jobs among members. One approach is to rely on seniority. Another approach is called *work-spreading*. Under work-spreading, the workweek is shortened so that more people have jobs. Instead of 40 people working 60 hours per week, 60 people work 40 hours per week, for example.

Workers who are rationed out or unable to find union employment look for jobs in the nonunion sector, increasing the supply of labor there and lowering the rate of pay for nonunion workers. Figure 7 shows two labor markets, one for union labor and one for nonunion labor. The same wage initially exists in each market. If the union is able to reduce the supply of union labor, the supply curve in the unionized market shifts in (from S_1 to S_2), driving the union wage up (from W_1 to W_2). Workers unable to obtain employment in the unionized sector ($L_2 - L_1$) move to the nonunion sector (the graph in part [b]). This causes the supply curve in the nonunion sector to shift out (from S_1 to S_2), and the wage rate to be forced down from W_1 to W_2.

featherbedding:
the requirement that more workers than are actually needed be employed

Figure 7
The Economic Effect of Unions
Two labor markets are pictured, one for union labor and one for nonunion labor. Initially the two markets are in equilibrium at the same wage. The union successfully restricts the supply of labor in the unionized mar-

ket, from S_1 to S_2 (part [a]). As a result, the wage rate is driven up. The higher wage means that fewer workers are employed, L_2 instead of L_1. As a result, these workers flow to the nonunion sector (part [b]), increasing supply there from S_1 to S_2 and driving the wage rate down from W_1 to W_2.

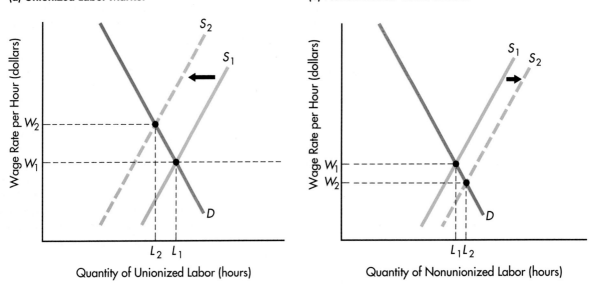

(a) Unionized Labor Market

(b) Nonunionized Labor Market

RECAP

1. Monopsony exists when there is only one buyer of a resource. Most monopsonies arise because buyers form a cartel.

2. Bilateral monopoly exists when a monopsony faces a single seller of a resource. The outcome of negotiations in a bilateral monopoly depends on the relative strengths of buyer and seller.

3. Collective bargaining is the process of negotiating wage and job contracts.

4. Unions can provide benefits to both employers and employees.

5. Union wages tend to be higher than nonunion wages. The reason for the difference may be the ability of unions to affect the demand for and supply of labor.

6. Unions may be able to restrict the supply of labor to the unionized sectors of the economy, thereby driving wages up there and down in the nonunion sectors. The closed shop, now illegal, was one method of reducing the supply of union labor. Restrictions on immigration and barriers to certain occupations may also reduce the supply of labor.

7. Unions may be able to affect the demand for labor by causing it to increase or by reducing the wage elasticity of demand.

4. LABOR MARKET LAWS: MINIMUM WAGES, OCCUPATIONAL SAFETY, AND THE FAMILY AND MEDICAL LEAVE ACT

What effects do government policies and programs such as minimum wages and the Family and Medical Leave Act have on the labor market?

The governments of developed nations have intervened in their labor markets on a regular basis. In most of the European nations, labor market activities are more tightly regulated by the government than they are in the United States. In Germany, for example, all workers are guaranteed thirty days' paid vacation a year. In the United States, minimum wages have been imposed since the late 1930s, rules and regulations regarding job safety have been prescribed by the government since the 1970s, and in 1993, President Clinton enacted the Family and Medical Leave Act, which allows employees in firms of more than fifty workers to take up to twelve weeks of unpaid leave without having their jobs or responsibilities affected. Unions are important advocates of minimum wage laws and health and safety requirements. Why? What impacts do such laws have on the labor market?

4.a. Minimum Wages

A minimum wage is a government policy that requires firms to pay at least a certain wage, the minimum wage. A minimum wage has existed in the United States since 1938 when it was set at $.25 per hour. The minimum wage is currently $4.25 per hour. The arguments in favor of the minimum wage are that a worker must earn at least the minimum wage in order to have a decent standard of living. At $4.25 per hour, 40 hours per week, 52 weeks per year, you would earn $8,840 per year. Currently, the government defines the poverty level of income for a family of four to be about $14,000. (See the chapter "Income Distribution, Poverty, and Government Policy" for more on poverty.) Thus, at the minimum wage, a single wage-earner family would be far below the poverty level. The arguments opposed to minimum wages claim that implementation of such minimums will increase unemployment, particularly among those on the bottom of the economic ladder, the unskilled—teenagers, minorities, and women—and lead to worse cases of poverty. Let's discuss the minimum wage policies and their effects on the labor market.

A minimum wage was adopted as part of the Fair Labor Standards Act of 1938. The act set the first minimum wage at $.25 per hour and provided for it to be increased to $.40 by 1945. Over the years, Congress has amended the act in order to increase the minimum wage (see Figure 8). The rate of increase, however, has not kept up with inflation and the rate of increase in the cost of living. In Figure 8, the legal minimum wage, indicated by the solid line, is adjusted for inflation in the dashed line. The dashed line shows that the purchasing power of the legal minimum wage has in fact changed little since 1938. Not all firms and industries must pay the minimum wage. Some are granted exemptions. Today about 80 percent of all jobs that are not in agriculture are required to pay at least the minimum wage.

In a competitive labor market, a worker's wages are equal to the value of his or her marginal revenue product. A minimum wage set above the equilibrium wage creates a labor surplus (unemployment). If, on the other hand, an employer is a monopsonist, a worker's wage is less than the value of his or her marginal product. In Figure 9(a), setting the minimum wage (W_m) at $15, above the equilibrium wage (W) of $10, creates a labor surplus. Figure 9(b)

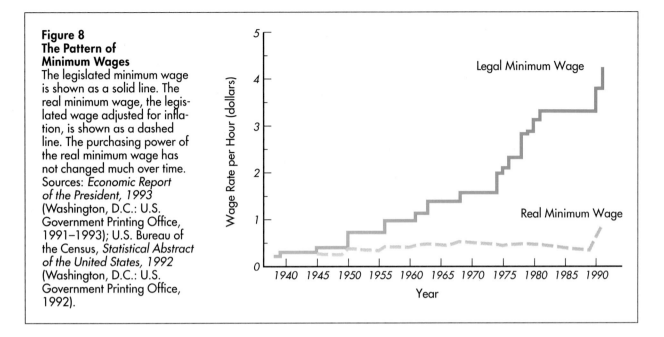

Figure 8
The Pattern of Minimum Wages
The legislated minimum wage is shown as a solid line. The real minimum wage, the legislated wage adjusted for inflation, is shown as a dashed line. The purchasing power of the real minimum wage has not changed much over time. Sources: *Economic Report of the President, 1993* (Washington, D.C.: U.S. Government Printing Office, 1991–1993); U.S. Bureau of the Census, *Statistical Abstract of the United States, 1992* (Washington, D.C.: U.S. Government Printing Office, 1992).

Government attempts to reduce wage differentials may be well-intended but may have adverse consequences for the most unskilled sectors of the labor force.

shows that if an employer is a monopsonist, a worker's wage (W_1) is less than MRP. The imposition of a binding minimum wage set at a level that is less than MRP but greater than the wage rate that the monopsonistic firm wants to pay may actually increase the level of employment. The minimum wage (W_m) of \$15 in Figure 9(b) shows that employment rises from L_1 to L_2.

Thus, in monopsonistic markets a minimum wage benefits all workers, but in nonmonopsonistic markets minimum wages benefit some and harm others. Studies show that the minimum wage adversely affects teenagers and other low-skilled workers, causing increased unemployment among these groups. A 10 percent increase in the minimum wage is estimated to result in a 1 to 3 percent decrease in teenage employment. Allowing a "subminimum" wage for teenagers reduces the job loss. Government policies do allow subminimum wages of about 75 percent of the minimum wage to be paid to teenagers.

Unions are among the strongest proponents of minimum wages. Why? Considering that the unskilled and those most hurt by minimum wages are not union members, the unemployment effects of minimum wages do not harm the union members. In addition, if firms must pay a minimum wage for an unskilled worker or pay a slightly higher wage for a skilled, union worker, the firm may find it worthwhile to pay for the skilled worker. Unions therefore anticipate that the minimum wage will increase the demand for their members and thus increase the wages of their members.

4.b. Occupational Safety

The minimum wage is far from the only government law that affects the labor market. The government also administers health, safety, and working conditions. The Occupational Safety and Health Act (OSHA), enacted in 1970, requires strict safety standards in the workplace. Its goal is "to insure the highest degree of health and safety protection for the employee." The act

Figure 9
The Effect of Minimum Wages

In a competitive labor market, a minimum wage above equilibrium causes a surplus—increases unemployment. This is shown in Figure 9(a). In a monopsonistic market, a minimum wage can increase both the wage and employment rates, as shown in Figure 9(b). The wage rises from $W_1 = \$10$ (the wage rate the monopsonistic firm wants to pay) to $W_m = \$15$, the legal minimum wage; and the quantity of labor employed rises from L_1 to L_2.

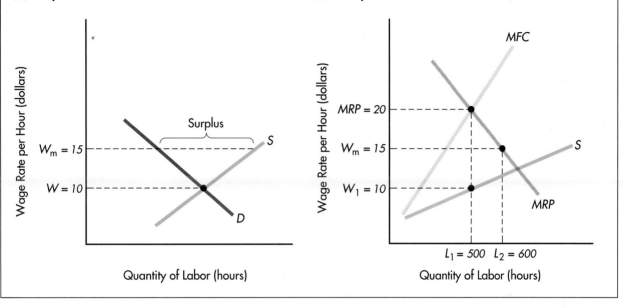

(a) Competitive Labor Market

Wage Rate per Hour (dollars) — Surplus — $W_m = 15$ — $W = 10$ — S — D — Quantity of Labor (hours)

(b) Monopsonistic Labor Market

Wage Rate per Hour (dollars) — MFC — $MRP = 20$ — $W_m = 15$ — $W_1 = 10$ — S — MRP — $L_1 = 500$ $L_2 = 600$ — Quantity of Labor (hours)

would seem to go against the wishes of workers. If a worker is willing to work in a less safe job for additional pay, then by requiring all jobs to have the same safety standards, the act is reducing the income of that worker. Much like the minimum wage, the act increases the costs of doing business to the firm by raising the compensation package offered to employees. This mandated increase will, in competitive markets, reduce employment among the most disadvantaged employees. However, like the minimum wage, the increased safety requirements could theoretically increase employment in the monopsonistic industries in addition to making working conditions better. In this latter case, the question arises as to whether employees would prefer increased pay or increased safety. The act does not allow this choice.

As with minimum wages, unions have been strong proponents of government health and safety requirements based on the belief that the increased costs of employing a worker will shift the demand away from nonunion members toward union members and, as a result, will increase the wages of union members.

Unions have been at the forefront in supporting governmental work-related wages and standards but are not the only proponents. In the case of the recently enacted Family and Medical Leave Act, unions were generally supportive, but the strongest proponents were women's groups. What is the difference between the effects of the other labor laws and the effect of the Family and Medical Leave Act?

4.c. Family and Medical Leave Act

The Family and Medical Leave Act was the first law enacted after Bill Clinton became president. The act requires firms of more than 50 employees to grant an unpaid leave of absence to any employee for a period of up to twelve weeks a year so that the employee can take care of family matters—to care for a new infant or a sick relative. Approximately one-half of all employees in the United States will be affected by the act; they work for firms larger than 50 employees.

The smallest firms were exempted from the act because Congress believed that the act could be a hardship. If a firm has only one employee trained for a specific task, then if that employee takes an unpaid leave, the firm must hire a temporary employee, train that employee, and then terminate the employment of that temporary employee when the permanent employee returns. The firm must either bear the additional expense of cross-training employees, maintain more than one employee trained for a specific task, or undergo the on-the-job training costs of a temporary employee each time a permanent employee requests a leave of absence. Thus, the Family and Medical Leave Act is likely to raise the costs of labor. Congress felt that the large firm could bear those additional costs without a problem while small firms could not and so exempted the small firms.

If labor costs rise, a firm will either hire less labor or attempt to reduce the labor costs. Firms could rely more on temporary employees since temporary employees, those working less than thirty hours a week, are not subject to the act. Bank of America, in fact, announced in February 1993 that from then on it was using only temporary employees for its tellers. Other banks have followed suit. Firms might also lower the wages of employees subject to the leave-of-absence policy, in a sense making the employees pay for at least part of the cost of the Family and Medical Leave Act. This would occur if the demand curve of firms for labor shifted down (the MRP declined) as a result of the act.

It is theoretically possible for the Family and Medical Leave Act to improve productivity. If the idea that a leave of absence could be taken in the case of a family emergency without affecting one's future with a firm raises employee morale and makes employees more productive (increases their MRP), then the act could have a positive effect on all labor. Or, if the act ensures that less occupational segregation occurs as a result of gender, it may induce firms to employ more women, avoid statistical discrimination, and thus increase the productivity of the labor market overall. If this occurs, the wage gap between males and females would decline over time.

The effects of labor market laws are not necessarily what they would seem to be on the surface. While it might appear that minimum wages, health and safety requirements, and family leave policies are nothing but beneficial for workers, in reality different workers are affected differently. As one of the principles of economics suggests, "there is no free lunch." If such laws raise costs to firms, then firms will respond by reducing employment in general; reducing the employment of some particular group of workers; or by reducing the wages of its workers. The laws do benefit some groups, however. Minimum wages clearly benefit those who receive the jobs and are paid the minimum wage, when without the law they would receive even lower wages. Minimum wages may also benefit the higher-skilled workers as firms turn more toward the skilled workers and away from the less-skilled workers.

Health and safety standards will benefit all employees who retain a job and whose pay does not decline as a result of the standards. And the Family and Medical Leave Act may benefit women who take time off to have a child, or men and women who want to reduce the number of hours they work each year without negatively affecting their jobs.

As we have seen, the U.S. government intervenes in the labor market in a big way. How does the U.S. situation compare to that of other industrial nations? Let's look at some of the other nations' labor market policies.

4.d. Labor Policies in Other Industrial Nations

In general, U.S. policies are less restrictive than those in other industrial nations. The United States was the last Western industrial nation to impose a government-mandated leave at the federal level and that occurred only with the 1993 Family and Medical Leave Act. However, unpaid leaves for child-bearing were provided for about 92 percent of all employees in medium and large firms in the United States prior to the implementation of the act. In Sweden, nearly a year of unpaid parental leave after twelve weeks of paid leave is provided. Australia offers one year of unpaid leave; Italy, five months at 80 percent pay; the United Kingdom forty weeks at about 90 percent pay; and Austria, Germany, Hungary, and Norway provide about 15 weeks of paid leave.[6]

There are significant unionization differences among nations as well. The U.S. unionization rates (percentages of workers that are unionized) of 20.5 percent for male and 12.5 percent for female workers are considerably lower than elsewhere. The unionization rates for men range from 35 percent in Germany to 78 percent in Sweden, and from 18 percent in Germany to 80 percent in Sweden for women. Even these statistics are slightly misleading because the wage-setting process in the U.S. unionized sectors differs considerably from those in other nations. In the United States, collective bargaining is decentralized, with plant-specific or at least firm-specific agreements, while in other nations agreements are nationwide.

Other Western industrial nations are more unionized, have less wage disparity, and more occupational segregation than the United States.

The results of these differences are not easy to measure since the composition of the labor forces and the types of industries differ. Nevertheless, there is more wage disparity in the United States than in the other Western industrial nations. There is also less occupational segregation between men and women in the United States than in the other industrial nations. Furthermore, the percentage of employed women in the United States who work part time (less than 35 hours per week) is smaller than in any other country. About 46 percent of Swedish and 53 percent of Norwegian employed women work part time, compared to only 24 percent of U.S. employed women. On the surface, at least, it would appear that the greater involvement of the other nations' government in the labor market might result from higher unionization; that the involvement might lead to more equal wages; and that the involvement might lead to more part time work and more occupational segregation. Are these laws beneficial? The answer you give to this question depends on where you stand.

---

[6] Blau and Kahn, op. cit.

RECAP

1. Federal law requires that certain jobs pay no less than the prescribed minimum wage.
2. Minimum wages cause unemployment in competitive markets and increase employment in monopsonistic markets.
3. Job safety rules affect the labor market in much the same way as minimum wages, benefiting some workers and harming others.
4. The Family and Medical Leave Act requires firms with more than fifty employees to grant unpaid leaves of absence to employees for up to twelve weeks a year so they can take care of family emergencies.

SUMMARY

▲▼ What accounts for earnings disparities between males and females and between whites and nonwhites?

1. Earnings disparities may result from discrimination, occupational choice, human capital differences, educational opportunity differences, age, and immigration. §§1.a, 1.c, 1.d
2. Discrimination occurs when some factor not related to marginal revenue product affects the wage rate someone receives. §1.a

▲▼ Are discrimination and freely functioning markets compatible?

3. There are two general types of discrimination—personal prejudice and statistical discrimination. §1.b
4. Personal prejudice is costly to those who demonstrate the prejudice and should not last in a market economy. For it to last, some restrictions on the functioning of markets must exist. §1.b.1
5. Statistical discrimination is the result of imperfect information and can occur as long as information is imperfect. §1.b.2
6. Occupational segregation exists when some jobs are held mainly by one group in society and other jobs by other groups. A great deal of occupational segregation exists between males and females in the United States. §1.c
7. High rates of immigration in the 1970s and 1980s, particularly of unskilled workers, has widened the earnings gap between Hispanics and whites and between skilled and unskilled workers. §1.d

▲▼ What government policies have been implemented to reduce wage differentials?

8. Comparable worth is an attempt to resolve the problems of wage differentials, occupational segregation, and discrimination. §2.b

▲▼ Have unions been able to increase the wages of union members relative to the wages of nonunionized workers?

9. Bilateral monopoly occurs when a monopoly seller faces a monopsonistic buyer. A monopsonistic firm pays less than the marginal revenue product to resources. §3.b
10. A union attempts to offset the monopsony power of the firm and force the rate of pay up to the marginal revenue product by creating a monopoly of sellers. A union may increase the productivity of the employees. §§3.b, 3.c
11. Unionized sectors of the economy tend to have higher wages than nonunion sectors. Reasons for the difference include the impact of unions in monopsonistic markets, restrictions on the supply of union labor, and increases in the demand for union labor. §§3.c, 3.c.1, 3.c.2

▲▼ What effects do government policies and programs such as minimum wages and the Family and Medical Leave Act have on the labor market?

12. Minimum wages and occupational safety rules benefit some workers and harm others. Low-skilled, new entrants into the labor force are most harmed by minimum wage and occupational safety laws. §§4.a, 4.b

KEY TERMS

discrimination §1.a

statistical discrimination §1.b

crowding §1.c

occupational segregation §1.c

disparate treatment §2.a

disparate impact §2.a

comparable worth §2.b

bilateral monopoly §3.b

collective bargaining §3.b.1

closed shop §3.c.1

union shop §3.c.1

featherbedding §3.c.1

EXERCISES

1. What is the effect of immigration on the labor market? Using the production possibilities curve, illustrate what immigration means for society as a whole. Recall that the PPC is based on the existing quantity and quality of resources. (You may want to review Chapter 2). Immigration is an increase in the quantity of resources; is it an increase in the quality as well?

2. Explain what is meant by discrimination, and explain the difference between personal prejudice and statistical discrimination.

3. Explain why occupational segregation by sex might occur. Can you imagine any society in which you would not expect to find occupational segregation by sex? Explain. Would you expect to find occupational segregation by race in most societies?

4. Why are women's wages only 60 to 80 percent of men's wages, and why has this situation existed for several decades? Now that women are entering college and professional schools in increasing numbers, why doesn't the wage differential disappear?

5. Why do economists say that discrimination is inherently inefficient and therefore will not occur in general?

6. Demonstrate, using two labor markets, what is meant by comparable worth. What problems are created by comparable worth? Under what conditions might comparable worth make economic sense? Explain.

7. Using a perfectly competitive resource market, demonstrate the effect of unionization of the labor force.

8. Using a perfectly competitive resource market, demonstrate the effect of immigration on the labor market.

9. Answer questions 7 and 8 using a monopsonistic labor market.

10. Demonstrate how minimum wages affect the labor market. First use a perfectly competitive labor market, then use a labor market in which the firm is a monopsonist. Do the same for job safety requirements.

11. Why would unions want to limit the number of hours in the workweek?

12. What impact would a mandatory four-week vacation period for all employees have on the economy?

13. There is a great deal of talk in the United States of providing more job flexibility for families. Why is it necessary for the government to provide the flexibility through the Family and Medical Leave Act and other programs? Why doesn't the private market provide this flexibility?

14. Consider the decision of a working woman or man who has young children or elderly relatives to take care of. Explain in terms of the labor supply curve how this person's decision to work is affected by the presence of dependents. What happens to the opportunity cost of working? How is the labor supply curve affected?

Glamor Trade Is under Fire by Workers Who Claim Age Bias

It was Joyce Chorbajian's big break. After more than a dozen years selling advertising for various magazines, she cracked the ranks of management by becoming sales manager for *Inc.* Magazine in March, 1989.

"I thought my dreams had come true," Chorbajian said. She thought the move might eventually lead to "all the things you aspire to when you have a career," including an eventual job as a publisher.

Instead, it led to disaster.

In August, Chorbajian, then 44, was fired. She says she was replaced by two younger women.

Chorbajian filed a lawsuit in federal district court in Manhattan, accusing the Goldhirsh Group, *Inc.*'s Boston-based owner, of discriminating against her on the basis of age.

Allegations such as Chorbajian's reflect a recent wave of age discrimination complaints, particularly in "glamor industries" such as advertising, ad sales and fashion and style-oriented publishing, where many workers say image frequently counts more than skill and experience. . . .

A worker who believes that an employer's action was based on age, rather than a legitimate business reason, such as firing for nonperformance or a layoff due to economic hard times, can sue under the federal Age Discrimination in Employment Act, which protects people over 40, as well as state and local anti-bias laws.

In the past, age discrimination suits often have involved workers in their mid-50s and 60s. But Wilfred F. Rice, a Chicago attorney, says "older workers are becoming younger" these days. A lot of age discrimination suits now involve people in their 40s.

For instance, Sheila Sullivan, 49, a former senior fashion editor at *Harper's Bazaar* magazine, recently filed an age discrimination suit against the Hearst Corp., the publication's owner.

According to a document Sullivan filed in federal district court, she was one of nine people, eight of whom were over 40, fired by the magazine's Elizabeth Tilberis, the magazine's new editor-in-chief. Jeffrey M. Bernbach, the attorney representing both Sullivan and Chorbajian, said several other suits may be filed soon by fired *Harper's Bazaar* editors, almost all of whom, he said, were replaced by younger people.

Tilberis, who is in her 40s and replaced an older editor, "wants a youthful magazine, and to achieve that end, she wants a youthful staff," Bernbach said. "There's nothing wrong with it except that the law makes it illegal to replace older people with younger people simply because of their age."

Charlotte Veal, a spokeswoman for Hearst, said the company doesn't engage in age discrimination and that there won't be more suits. . . .

Experts acknowledge that age has often been something of a handicap in many industries, where experienced workers are replaced with younger people at lower wages. . . .

People who follow these industries say [older] workers are more vulnerable to age discrimination not only because they are frequently paid more than younger colleagues, but also because they are seen as being less willing to take risks in fields that place a high value on fresh ideas. Moreover, they are considered less attractive to clients.

"People on the client side who make the decisions [to select an agency] are usually under 45, and they want to talk to their contemporaries," said Jerry Fields, an advertising industry headhunter who is over 70. He laments what he sees as the industry's age bias, pointing out that many of the most creative and successful people in advertising are over 60.

Gary Hoenig, editor of *News Inc.*, a trade publication for the newspaper industry, and editorial director of *Magazine Week*, another trade publication, said the same forces are at work at style-oriented magazines.

"The heat is on so much to be hip and young and with-it that I think people are often tossed aside," Hoenig said. . . .

Others said advertisers and publishers are in peril of missing one of the fastest-growing and lucrative demographic groups—affluent Americans 55 and older—if they jettison those who might understand that market best. . . .

Source: Reprinted with permission of the Los Angeles Times Syndicate.

Newsday/November 8, 1992

Commentary

Discrimination means that something other than a worker's marginal-revenue product determines his or her wages and working conditions. In the case discussed in the article, something other than the worker's marginal-revenue product determined whether the worker had a job or not. That something was age. Age discrimination, like any other discrimination not based on marginal-revenue products, must come from the firm, the coworker, or the consumer, or must result from statistical discrimination. Otherwise, at least according to economic definitions, discrimination is not occurring.

Age discrimination is costly to a firm: It means that a more productive employee is dismissed and a less productive employee is retained. For a firm to participate in age discrimination, it must either be earning above-normal profit and thus choosing to consume some of its profit in the form of having younger workers, or be a monopoly firm, protected by barriers to entry, in which case it can choose to discriminate without affecting its competitive position. Is it likely that *Inc.* magazine, *Harper's Bazaar,* or other so-called "glamour" industries are protected by barriers to entry? No, entry is not difficult. Thus there is no reason to suspect these firms can afford to participate in discrimination.

As discussed previously, firms often pay younger, inexperienced workers less than their marginal-revenue products and older, experienced workers more than their marginal-revenue products. Such a policy does not lend itself to the routine firing of the more expensive, more experienced workers. Otherwise, no one would ever go to work for those firms, knowing that they would never be paid their marginal-revenue products. If more experienced workers are valuable to a firm, then the firm will do everything it can to retain those experienced workers and everything it can to ensure that the best employees stay with the firm for a long time. Replacing more expensive older workers with less expensive younger workers makes economic sense only if firms do not value experience and retention of good employees and if the older workers generate less revenue for the firm than younger workers. Nonetheless, the article does point out that many age-discrimination lawsuits were filed during the recession of 1990–1992. Many older workers were, in fact, dismissed during this recession. Far more than in previous recessions, firms attempted to cut costs by trimming their work force, particularly in middle management, where most of the workers tend to be between forty-five and fifty-five.

If consumers desire younger workers, then the firm's decision to employ only younger workers could be profitable. The article mentions that the glamour industries are looking to a younger audience, where image, fashion, and style weigh heavily. If older workers mean fewer sales, then the marginal-revenue product of older relative to younger workers declines and either the pay or the employment of older workers will decline relative to younger workers. This is not discrimination according to economics; it is the market defining what it wants. The unfortunate result, if such an event is occurring, is that older workers are paying the price of not being as valuable to the firm as younger workers. For this situation to exist, older workers must be unable to understand the issues of interest to younger consumers. This seems unlikely to be the case for all older workers. Perhaps a few cannot grasp the difference between rap and Barry Manilow, between bell-bottom pants and straight-leg pants, but many can. A policy of dismissing all older workers because some cannot understand the perspective of the young consumers would be a case of statistical discrimination. If the consumer wants the perspective of the younger worker, but if some older workers are able to provide that perspective even though they are older, then those older workers should bear no effects.

Discrimination that results in employment, wages, or working conditions being based not on productivity but on some other factor (age, sex, race, etc.) is illegal. If the dismissed worker can demonstrate to the courts that the dismissal occurred because of discrimination, then the firm will be penalized and the worker compensated. However, if the firm can demonstrate that the dismissal occurred because of job-related performance, then the firm will be exonerated.

18

Capital, Land, and Entrepreneurial Ability

FUNDAMENTAL QUESTIONS

1. What role does saving play in the economy?
2. What is present value?
3. Does economic rent serve the allocative role that other resource prices serve?
4. What is conservation?
5. Why does the entrepreneur receive profit?
6. How are the resource markets tied together?

oes a firm spend $100,000 today to acquire a machine that is expected to generate output for ten years? Do we extract more oil from the ground now, or leave it for future generations? Does an individual obtain a college degree, which may provide benefits throughout life, when the cost of a four-year college education exceeds $100,000? The alternatives faced by these decision-makers are similar to those confronting the employees of an aerospace company in suburban Los Angeles who offered to sell their winning California lottery ticket worth $3 million. The employees were willing to take $1.2 million cash. Three million dollars for only $1.2 million—that sounds like a good deal, but it's not as good as it sounds. A $3 million Lotto ticket is not $3 million: it is a promise that if the winner and the lottery survive twenty years, the winner will receive a check for about $150,000 each year before taxes (about $100,000 after taxes). "You're talking about money then versus money now," claimed one of the ticket holders, who figured that lots of undesirable things could happen in the next twenty years:

the lottery fund could go belly-up, the price of a loaf of bread could rise to $10, or nuclear disaster could make the annual payments worthless.

This issue is typical of a great deal of what occurs in the resource markets—comparing values over time. This chapter discusses the role of time in production and consumption as it examines the remaining resource markets—capital, land, and entrepreneurial ability.

I. CAPITAL

Capital is the resource we refer to when we say that a production process is mechanized or when we talk about the capacity of a factory. Capital is buildings and machinery produced for the purpose of producing goods and services. Human capital is the training and education that people acquire in order to increase their productivity.

I.a. Saving

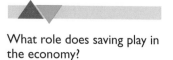

What role does saving play in the economy?

In some less developed countries, farming is done solely by hand; in most nations, however, farming is quite mechanized. No doubt it has occurred to farmers in the less developed countries that they could produce more if they had some capital—for instance, a plow and a horse. Unfortunately, the capital needed to make the switch to a more mechanized operation can be obtained only by sacrificing current consumption. The construction of the plow requires that the farmer spend time away from the planting, care, or harvesting of the crops to build the plow, or she or he can use some of the crops to purchase the plow. Similarly, a horse can be obtained only by accumulating enough crops to purchase the horse; and the care and feeding of the horse, once acquired, would consume some of each year's crops. In order to obtain the capital, the farmer must forgo current consumption of the crops, and this sacrifice could be severe if the farmer's family depends on the crops for sustenance. Nevertheless, if the benefits of the additional production made possible by the plow and horse seem likely to be greater than the forgone consumption, the plow and horse will be acquired.

The process of sacrificing current consumption in order to accumulate capital (plows, horses) with which more output can be produced in the future, and thus more consumption enjoyed in the future, is called roundabout production. It is simply the process of **saving**. With saving, everything produced today is not consumed today. Some output, the amount saved, is used to create more production in the future. If the existing quantities of all resources were used today—if the forests were razed and every bit of timber were used, and if the world's supply of oil were extracted and used—living standards today might be higher but the future would be bleak. Forgoing some current consumption allows households, businesses, and society to obtain capital resources that can be used to increase future production and consumption. Any economy that grows—produces increasing amounts of goods and services and thus generates more income—must save and accumulate significant amounts of capital.

saving:
not consuming all current production

1.b. The Capital Market

The capital market is the channel through which consumers and producers match their future plans with their behavior today. The demand for and supply of capital determine the equilibrium quantity and cost of capital.

1.b.1. Demand for Capital
A firm acquires additional capital as long as the marginal revenue product of the additional capital exceeds the marginal factor cost of that additional capital. When a firm rents capital (where *rent* refers to payment for the use of capital), its calculations are identical to the calculations it made when deciding whether to hire another worker. Suppose a rock-crushing firm rents the trucks it uses to haul crushed rock. The firm will rent another truck only if the rental rate is less than the marginal revenue product generated by the rented truck.

Not all capital is rented, however. Firms also purchase capital: they buy buildings and machines that they might use for several years. And, of course, rental or leasing companies must own the capital that they rent to other firms. To decide how much capital to buy, a firm must compare the prices paid for the building or equipment today with the marginal revenue product generated by the capital over the lifetime of the capital.

The firm's problem is identical to the problem faced by the holders of the winning lottery ticket. To know whether a machine should be purchased, or whether the $3 million payoff over twenty years should be purchased for $1.2 million cash today, it is necessary to compare two values: a purchase price today and a return that occurs over several years. To make this comparison, it is necessary to take into account that people prefer to consume today instead of waiting until tomorrow and that there is a risk that future payoffs will not

What is present value?

present value:
the equivalent value today of
some amount to be received in
the future

future value:
the equivalent value in the
future of some amount received
today

be made or that money in the future will not purchase as much as it does today. The value today of an amount to be paid or received in the future is called the **present value**. The value at a future date of some amount to be paid or received today is called the **future value**.

How can the future and present values be calculated? If you have $100,000 today, you can deposit that $100,000 into an account that will yield the principal (the original amount, $100,000) plus the interest after some period of time. If the interest rate is 9 percent per year, you will get interest earnings of $9,000 after one year:

$$\$100,000 \times .09 = \$9,000$$

Thus, $109,000 one year in the future is the *future value* of $100,000 today at an interest rate of 9 percent, or $100,000 today is the *present value* of $109,000 one year in the future at a 9 percent interest rate. Let's express "one year in the future" as *FV* (future value) and "today" as *PV* (present value). Then we can write

$$FV = PV(1 + \text{interest rate})$$

If we divide both sides by (1 + interest rate), we have

$$PV = FV/(1 + \text{interest rate})$$

Thus, the present value, *PV*, is $100,000:

$$PV = \$109,000/(1.09) = \$100,000$$

Calculating present and future values is simple when you are looking only one year into the future. The calculations become more complicated when you are looking ahead several years. If there is a stream of values, such as with the Lotto ticket paying $100,000 per year for twenty years, you could calculate the present value of each payment and sum all the values to get the present value of the entire stream. Or you could use tables, such as Table 1, that have been constructed to show what the present value of some future amount is or what the future value of some current amount is.

Let's use Table 1 to see what a Lotto ticket that pays $100,000 per year (after taxes) over twenty years is worth today. To calculate the present value of $100,000 per year for twenty years at a specific rate of interest, find the row for 20 periods and then read across the columns until you reach the appropriate interest rate. For instance, at an 8 percent rate of interest, the number indicated is 9.8181. This number is the present value of payments of $1 per period for 20 periods at 8 percent. To get the present value of a stream of payments of $100,000 per year for twenty years at 8 percent, multiply $100,000 times 9.8181. The result is $981,810. You can see from the table that as the interest rate increases, the present value of the money to be received in the future declines. Look at a 10 percent rate of interest and 20 periods in the table; the value indicated is 8.5136, so $100,000 each year for twenty years is worth $851,360 today at a 10 percent rate of interest.

Now let's put this in the context of a firm that is deciding whether to purchase a unit of capital. Suppose an airline is contemplating the purchase of a new wide-body plane that will yield $100,000 per year for twenty years. As seen in Table 1, the present value of the marginal revenue product from the plane is $981,810 at an 8 percent interest rate. If the price of the plane is $900,000, the firm will buy the plane. As the interest rate rises, the present value of the plane's marginal revenue product declines. At a 10 percent inter-

TABLE I
Present Value of an Annuity of $1.00 per Period

Period (n)	Interest (Discount) Rate (i)								
	1%	2%	3%	4%	5%	6%	7%	8%	9%
1	0.9901	0.9804	0.9709	0.9615	0.9524	0.9434	0.9346	0.9259	0.9174
2	1.9704	1.9416	1.9135	1.8861	1.8594	1.8334	1.8080	1.7833	1.7591
3	2.9410	2.8839	2.8286	2.7751	2.7232	2.6730	2.6243	2.5771	2.5313
4	3.9020	3.8077	3.7171	3.6299	3.5460	3.4651	3.3872	3.3121	3.2397
5	4.8534	4.7135	4.5797	4.4518	4.3295	4.2124	4.1002	3.9927	3.8897
6	5.7955	5.6014	5.4172	5.2421	5.0757	4.9173	4.7665	4.6229	4.4859
7	6.7282	6.4720	6.2303	6.0021	5.7864	5.5824	5.3893	5.2064	5.0330
8	7.6517	7.3255	7.0197	6.7327	6.4632	6.2098	5.9713	5.7466	5.5348
9	8.5660	8.1622	7.7861	7.4353	7.1078	6.8017	6.5152	6.2469	5.9952
10	9.4713	8.9826	8.5302	8.1109	7.7217	7.3601	7.0236	6.7101	6.4177
11	10.3676	9.7868	9.2526	8.7605	8.3064	7.8869	7.4987	7.1390	6.8052
12	11.2551	10.5753	9.9540	9.3851	8.8633	8.3838	7.9427	7.5361	7.1607
13	12.1337	11.3484	10.6350	9.9856	9.3936	8.8527	8.3577	7.9038	7.4869
14	13.0037	12.1062	11.2961	10.5631	9.8986	9.2950	8.7455	8.2442	7.7862
15	13.8651	12.8493	11.9379	11.1184	10.3797	9.7122	9.1079	8.5595	8.0607
16	14.7179	13.5777	12.5611	11.6523	10.8378	10.1059	9.4466	8.8514	8.3126
17	15.5623	14.2919	13.1661	12.1657	11.2741	10.4773	9.7632	9.1216	8.5436
18	16.3983	14.9920	13.7535	12.6593	11.6896	10.8276	10.0591	9.3719	8.7556
19	17.2260	15.6785	14.3238	13.1339	12.0853	11.1581	10.3356	9.6036	8.9501
20	18.0456	16.3514	14.8775	13.5903	12.4622	11.4699	10.5940	9.8181	9.1285
21	18.8570	17.0112	15.4150	14.0292	12.8212	11.7641	10.8355	10.0168	9.2922
22	19.6604	17.6580	15.9369	14.4511	13.1630	12.0416	11.0612	10.2007	9.4424
23	20.4558	18.2922	16.4436	14.8568	13.4886	12.3034	11.2722	10.3711	9.5802
24	21.2434	18.9139	16.9355	15.2470	13.7986	12.5504	11.4693	10.5288	9.7066
25	22.0232	19.5235	17.4131	15.6221	14.0939	12.7834	11.6536	10.6748	9.8226

est rate, the present value of the marginal revenue product is $851,360. The airline will not purchase the plane in this case. As the interest rate rises, the quantity of capital purchased declines.

This same relationship holds for households as well. An individual deciding whether to purchase a college education compares the present value of the benefits generated by the degree with the purchase price of the degree. If the purchase price is less than the present value of the benefits, then the person goes to college. At a higher interest rate, the present value of the benefits will not exceed the purchase price. As a result, the human capital will not be purchased.

The market demand for capital is shown in Figure 1(a) as a downward-sloping curve with the quantity of capital measured along the horizontal axis and the price of capital measured along the vertical axis. An increase in the price of capital, say from $80,000 to $100,000 per machine in Figure 1(a), decreases the quantity of capital demanded, from 350,000 to 300,000

Table 1 (cont.)

Period (n)	\multicolumn{11}{c}{Interest (Discount) Rate (i)}
	10%	**12%**	**14%**	**15%**	**16%**	**18%**	**20%**	**24%**	**28%**	**32%**
1	0.9091	0.8929	0.8772	0.8696	0.8621	0.8475	0.8333	0.8065	0.7813	0.7576
2	1.7355	1.6901	1.6467	1.6257	1.6052	1.5656	1.5278	1.4568	1.3916	1.3315
3	2.4869	2.4018	2.3216	2.2832	2.2459	2.1743	2.1065	1.9813	1.8684	1.7663
4	3.1699	3.0373	2.9137	2.8550	2.7982	2.6901	2.5887	2.4043	2.2410	2.0957
5	3.7908	3.6048	3.4331	3.3522	3.2743	3.1272	2.9906	2.7454	2.5320	2.3452
6	4.3553	4.1114	3.8887	3.7845	3.6847	3.4976	3.3255	3.0205	2.7594	2.5342
7	4.8684	4.5638	4.2883	4.1604	4.0386	3.8115	3.6046	3.2423	2.9370	2.6775
8	5.3349	4.9676	4.6389	4.4873	4.3436	4.0776	3.8372	3.4212	3.0758	2.7860
9	5.7590	5.3282	4.9464	4.7716	4.6065	4.3030	4.0310	3.5655	3.1842	2.8681
10	6.1446	5.6502	5.2161	5.0188	4.8332	4.4941	4.1925	3.6819	3.2689	2.9304
11	6.4951	5.9377	5.4527	5.2337	5.0286	4.6560	4.3271	3.7757	3.3351	2.9776
12	6.8137	6.1944	5.6603	5.4206	5.1971	4.7932	4.4392	3.8514	3.3868	3.0133
13	7.1034	6.4235	5.8424	5.5831	5.3423	4.9095	4.5327	3.9124	3.4272	3.0404
14	7.3667	6.6282	6.0021	5.7245	5.4675	5.0081	4.6106	3.9616	3.4587	3.0609
15	7.6061	6.8109	6.1422	5.8474	5.5755	5.0916	4.6755	4.0013	3.4834	3.0764
16	7.8237	6.9740	6.2651	5.9542	5.6685	5.1624	4.7296	4.0333	3.5026	3.0882
17	8.0216	7.1196	6.3729	6.0472	5.7487	5.2223	4.7746	4.0591	3.5177	3.0971
18	8.2014	7.2497	6.4674	6.1280	5.8178	5.2732	4.8122	4.0799	3.5294	3.1039
19	8.3649	7.3658	6.5504	6.1982	5.8775	5.3162	4.8435	4.0967	3.5386	3.1090
20	8.5136	7.4694	6.6231	6.2593	5.9288	5.3527	4.8696	4.1103	3.5458	3.1129
21	8.6487	7.5620	6.6870	6.3125	5.9731	5.3837	4.8913	4.1212	3.5514	3.1158
22	8.7715	7.6446	6.7429	6.3587	6.0113	5.4099	4.9094	4.1300	3.5558	3.1180
23	8.8832	7.7184	6.7921	6.3988	6.0442	5.4321	4.9245	4.1371	3.5592	3.1197
24	8.9847	7.7843	6.8351	6.4338	6.0726	5.4510	4.9371	4.1428	3.5619	3.1210
25	9.0770	7.8431	6.8729	6.4642	6.0971	5.4669	4.9476	4.1474	3.5640	3.1220

machines. This represents the case where, for instance, a farmer will postpone the purchase of a new tractor or buy fewer tractors if the price increases, or an airline will postpone the purchase of a new airplane or purchase fewer airplanes as the price of airplanes increases.

As is the case for any demand curve, the demand curve for capital shifts when one of the nonprice determinants of demand changes. Perhaps the most important nonprice determinant of capital is the interest rate. You have seen how an increase in the interest rate decreases the present value of a future stream of income. In exactly the same manner, a higher interest rate lowers the present value of the marginal revenue product of capital, causing the demand curve for capital to shift in. Each time the interest rate increases, from 10 to 11 to 12 percent, the demand curve for capital shifts in, as shown in Figure 1(b) by the move from $D_1(10\%)$ to $D_2(11\%)$ to $D_3(12\%)$. The number in parentheses next to the demand curves represents the interest rate associated with each demand curve.

Figure 1
The Market Demand for Capital

In Figure 1(a) the demand for capital is shown as a downward-sloping line with the quantity of capital measured on the horizontal axis and the price of capital measured on the vertical axis. As the price of capital changes, say from $80,000 to $100,000 per unit of capital (per machine), the quantity of capital demanded changes, from 350,000 to 300,000 machines. In Figure 1(b) the relationship between the demand for capital and the interest rate is illustrated. As the rate of interest rises, the demand for capital declines—the demand curve shifts in. The interest rate associated with each demand curve is in parentheses beside the curve.

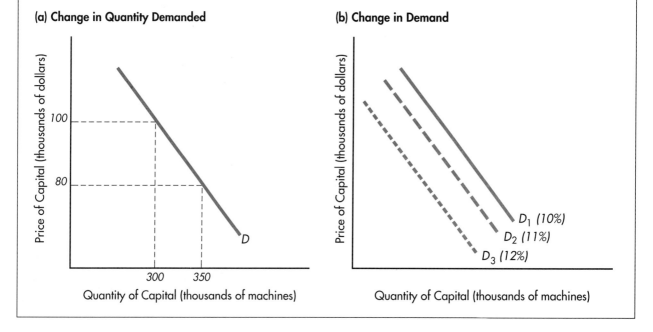

(a) Change in Quantity Demanded

(b) Change in Demand

The demand curve also shifts when any other determinant of demand changes. For instance, if a technological change increases the marginal physical product of capital, everything else held constant, the demand for capital increases. The invention of jet engines increased the demand for airplanes. The invention of small computers increased the overall demand for computers. Expectations and changes in income will also alter the demand for capital. For example, a business that expects strong demand for its goods purchases more capital now, causing the demand curve for capital to shift out.

1.b.2. Supply of Capital Some firms specialize in producing capital. John Deere supplies farm equipment, Boeing supplies airplanes, IBM produces computers, and so on. The quantity of capital supplied by these producers depends on the price of the capital. As the price of capital rises, the quantity that producers are willing and able to offer for sale rises, as shown in Figure 2 by the upward-sloping curve, S.

1.b.3. Equilibrium The demand for and supply of capital determine the price of capital, as well as the quantity produced and purchased. Changes in demand or supply change the equilibrium price and quantity. For example, changes in the interest rate affect the demand for capital and thus the price of capital. If the interest rate rises, the demand for capital decreases and the

Figure 2
The Interest Rate, the Price of Capital, and the
Rate of Return on Capital
The supply of capital is an upward-sloping curve. The
demand for and supply of capital determine the price of
capital as well as the quantity of capital produced and
purchased. The rate of return on capital is the additional annual revenue generated by additional capital,
divided by the purchase price of the capital. As the
interest rate rises, the demand for capital declines (the
demand curve shifts in) and the price of capital
declines. As a result of the lower price, the rate of return
rises.

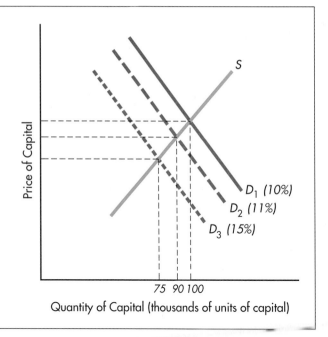

price of capital falls, shown in Figure 2 in the move from D_1(10%) to
D_2(11%) to D_3(15%). At an interest rate of 10 percent, 100,000 units of capital are demanded; at an 11 percent rate of interest, 90,000 units of capital are
demanded; and at a 15 percent rate of interest, 75,000 units of capital are
demanded. As the demand for capital shifts in, the price of capital falls.

Interest is the payment to the owners of capital for use of the capital services. Figure 2 illustrates the relationship among the price of capital, the
interest rate, and the rate of return on capital. The rate of return on capital is
the additional revenue generated by the capital each year (in present-value
terms) divided by the price of the capital. For instance, if a $100,000
machine generates $10,000 of additional revenue each year (in present-value
terms), the rate of return on that machine is 10 percent per year. With a lower
price but the same marginal revenue product, the rate of return on the capital
increases. The $10,000 per year divided by a $90,909 expenditure is an 11
percent-per-year return. Since the demand curve shifts in and the price of
capital decreases each time the interest rate rises, the rate of return on capital
must increase each time the interest rate rises. Similarly, the rate of return on
capital must decrease each time the interest rate declines.

The interest rate represents the opportunity cost of capital, the annual rate
of return available from alternative uses of the funds with which capital is
acquired. A firm contemplating a $100,000 expenditure on a piece of equip-
ment has many alternative uses for that $100,000. One alternative is to place
the funds in an interest-earning account. Thus, the firm must expect to earn a
rate of return on its capital that is at least equal to the interest rate if it is to
purchase the capital in the first place. If the interest rate rises above the
expected rate of return on capital, the demand for capital declines, the price
of capital falls, and the rate of return on capital rises. For example, if the rate
of return on a $100,000 piece of equipment is expected to be 10 percent to a

firm but the interest rate that can be obtained from other uses of the $100,000 has risen to 11 percent, the firm is better off seeking other uses and not purchasing the piece of equipment. As many firms react this way, the demand for capital declines and the price of capital falls. The price continues to decline until the rate of return equals the interest rate, at a price of $90,909, since $10,000/$90,909 = 11 percent. Conversely, if the rate of return on the $100,000 equipment is expected to be 10 percent per year but the interest rate has fallen to 9 percent, the firm is better off purchasing the equipment. Thus, the demand for capital rises, the price of capital rises, and the rate of return on capital falls. The price will continue to rise until the rate of return equals the interest rate, at a price of $111,111, since $10,000/$111,111 = 9 percent.

The rate of return on capital and the interest rate will be equal in the long run. Anytime the two are not equal, the price of capital will change, which in turn causes the rate of return on capital to change.

RECAP

1. Roundabout production is the process of saving and accumulating capital in order to increase production, and thus consumption, in the future.
2. Saving is the act of delaying consumption.
3. The capital market is the channel through which consumers and producers match their plans for the future with their behavior today.
4. Present value is the equivalent value today of some amount to be received in the future. Future value is the equivalent value in the future of some amount received today.
5. The demand for capital is represented by a downward-sloping curve, illustrating that the quantity of capital demanded rises as the price of capital falls.
6. The demand for capital shifts in when the interest rate rises.
7. The supply of capital is represented by an upward-sloping curve, illustrating that the quantity of capital supplied rises as the price of capital rises.
8. The demand for and supply of capital determine the price of capital. An increase in the price of capital lowers the rate of return on capital. Conversely, a decrease in the price of capital raises the rate of return on capital.
9. The rate of interest represents the rate of return on alternative uses of the funds with which capital is purchased. Thus, when the rate of interest rises above the rate of return on capital, the demand for capital declines, the price of capital declines, and the rate of return on capital rises. Conversely, when the rate of interest falls below the rate of return on capital, the demand for capital rises, the price of capital rises, and the rate of return on capital falls.

2. LAND AND NATURAL RESOURCES

Recall from the chapter on resource markets that there are two uses of the term *rent*: payment for the use of something, such as a car or an apartment, and payment for the use of something that is in fixed supply. This latter definition describes the payment to landowners for the use of their land.

2.a. Land Surface and Economic Rent

The aggregate quantity of the land surface—which may have value as a farm, as a pasture, as a city, or in some other use—is fixed. The demand for land depends on the demand for the products and services that the land helps produce, and thus reflects land's marginal revenue product. The demand and supply curves are shown in Figure 3. The demand curve slopes down and the supply curve is perfectly inelastic, the vertical line S, at 2.3 billion acres of land.

The rental rate of land is determined by the point at which the demand curve and the vertical supply curve intersect, $120 per acre in Figure 3. If the demand for land increases, the demand curve shifts out, from MRP_1 to MRP_2, as shown in Figure 3(b), causing the rental rate of land to increase. Because the quantity supplied does not change, the only effect of the demand increase is a rent increase. The rental rate rises from $120 to $200 per acre, and the total payment to landowners rises from $120 per acre times 2.3 billion acres to $200 per acre times 2.3 billion acres. Even with a higher rent, no new land is supplied. The higher rent does not (and cannot) induce owners to increase the quantities of land that are supplied. Pure economic rent does not serve as an incentive to resource owners to increase or decrease quantities supplied.

2.a.1. Different Rents on Different Parcels of Land
The price of land in Tokyo, Japan, is about $1,000 per square foot; land outside of Kearny, Nebraska, sells for about $.02 per square foot. Different parcels of land earn

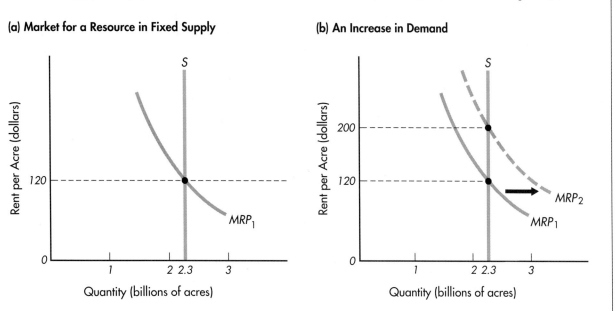

Figure 3
Economic Rent
Figure 3(a) shows the market for a resource in fixed supply—land surface. The fixed supply is illustrated with the vertical supply curve, S, at 2.3 billion acres. The

demand for the land is the marginal-revenue-product curve (MRP_1). The intersection of the demand and supply curves determines the rental rate, $120. An increase in the demand for land causes the rental rate to rise from $120 to $200, as shown in Figure 3(b).

(a) Market for a Resource in Fixed Supply

(b) An Increase in Demand

In the central valley of California, migrant workers pick green peppers by hand then place them on conveyor belts. The desert valley is supplied with water from a man-made canal. As a result of the water and the migrant workers, the California central valley is one of the most productive agricultural areas in the world. The marginal revenue product of the land of farmland has risen considerably as compared to its use as desert land.

widely varying rents because of differences in demand. Demand for the parcel in Tokyo is substantially higher than demand for the parcel in Kearny. Thus, the rental rate and the total rental income in Tokyo are significantly higher than they are in Kearny.

Why is demand for land in Tokyo greater than demand in Kearny? The marginal revenue product of the land in Tokyo is higher. Location is a major determinant of the marginal revenue product of a particular parcel of land. Suppose you can obtain a McDonald's franchise and place it anywhere you want. All you have to do is pay for the land. You would be willing to pay significantly more for a space in the middle of a city than for one in the country, everything else held constant. The sales that can be generated in the city far exceed the sales that can be made in the country. Hence, the city land offers a much higher marginal revenue product than country land. Physical features of the land, such as fertility and mineral content, and the climate of the area in which the parcel is located also increase the marginal revenue product of land.

Does economic rent serve the allocative role that other resource prices serve?

2.a.2. Rent and the Allocation of Land Resource prices serve as an allocating mechanism, ensuring that resources flow to their highest-valued uses. You might think that land rent fails to serve as an allocating mechanism because an increase in the rent on land does not increase the quantity of land supplied. Moreover, pure economic rents do not seem to have anything to do with costs because land surface just exists—it is a gift of nature. You might even say that pure economic rents are unearned windfalls to those who happen to own the land.

Despite appearances—that is, despite the fact that the quantity supplied does not change as economic rents change—economic rents do serve the function of allocating parcels of land to their most productive uses. Think of what a typical large city looks like. Tall buildings are clustered in the city center. As the distance from city center increases, the density and the height of the buildings decrease. Let's assume that the land in a city has only two uses, commercial and residential. As the distance from city center increases, the cost of using the land for commercial purposes increases because transportation and communication are more difficult. The aggregate quantity of land is fixed, but the quantity of commercial land is not fixed. Residential land can be used for commercial purposes (businesses can buy and tear down blocks of houses and construct buildings), and commercial land can be used for residential purposes (abandoned warehouses and factories can be converted into apartments).

The market for the commercial use of the land is shown in Figure 4. The supply of commercial land slopes up because as the rental rate rises, more landowners offer their land to the commercial market, everything else held constant. According to Figure 4(a), at a rental rate of $10 per square foot, 5 million square feet of land are used for commercial purposes and the rest of the land is put to residential uses.

Suppose an increased number of businesses move to the city. The demand curve for commercial property shifts out, and the rental rate of existing commercial space rises. This is shown as the move from MRP_1 to MRP_2 in Figure 4(b). As the rental rate rises, from $10 to $15, a certain amount of land that was residential is shifted into commercial uses. This is shown as the shaded area in Figure 4(b). Thus, rent does serve the allocation role that other resource prices serve. As the rental rate changes, the allocation of land among its uses changes. The market for land defines the payments to landowners, and rental rates on different parcels allocate these parcels to their highest-valued use.

Figure 4
The Allocation of Land Among Uses

Figure 4(a) shows the market for commercial uses of land. The supply curve for commercial land rises as the rental rate rises. As the rental rate of commercial land rises, more people take their land currently used for residential purposes and offer it for commercial uses,

everything else held constant. The intersection of MRP (the marginal revenue product of land in commercial use) and S (the supply of commercial land) determines the rental rate, $10 per square foot. As the demand for land for commercial uses increases, from MRP_1 to MRP_2 in Figure 4(b), the rental rate rises and more land is used for commercial purposes.

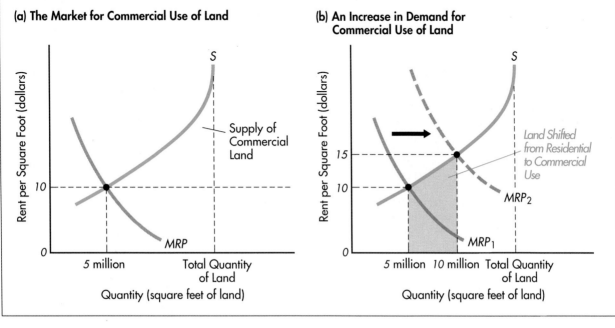

(a) The Market for Commercial Use of Land

(b) An Increase in Demand for Commercial Use of Land

2.b. Natural Resources

nonrenewable (exhaustible) natural resources:
natural resources whose supply is fixed

renewable (nonexhaustible) natural resources:
natural resources whose supply can be replenished

The category of resources we call "land" refers not just to land surface but to everything associated with the land—the natural resources. Natural resources are the nonproduced resources with which a society is endowed. **Nonrenewable (exhaustible) natural resources** can be used only once and cannot be replaced. Examples include coal, natural gas, and oil. **Renewable (nonexhaustible) natural resources** can be used repeatedly without depleting the amount available for future use. Examples include the land, sea, rivers, and lakes. Plants and animals are classified as nonexhaustible natural resources because it is possible for them to renew themselves and thus replace those used in production and consumption activities. The prices of natural resources and the quantities used are determined in the market for natural resources.

2.b.1. The Market for Nonrenewable Resources The market for nonrenewable natural resources consists of the demand for and supply of these resources. Supply depends on the amount of the resource in existence, and the supply curve is perfectly inelastic. Only a fixed amount of oil or coal exists, so the more that is used in any given year, the less that remains for future use. This means that an upward-sloping supply curve exists for a particular period of time, such as a year. The quantity that resource owners are willing to extract and offer for sale during any particular year depends on the price of the resource. The supply curve in Figure 5(a) is upward-sloping to reflect the relationship between the price of the resource today and the amount extracted and offered to users today. Resource owners are willing to extract more of a resource from its natural state and offer it for sale as the price of the resource increases.

As some of the resource is used today, less is available next year. The supply curve of the resource in the future shifts up, as shown in Figure 5(b) by

---

Figure 5
The Market for Nonrenewable Resources
The demand curve slopes down, and the supply curve slopes up. The intersection of demand and supply determines the quantity used today and the price at which the quantity was sold, as shown in Figure 5(a). As quantities are used today, less remains for the future. Because the available quantities come from increasingly more expensive sources, the supply curve shifts up over time, as shown in Figure 5(b). S_1 represents the quantities supplied in 1890 at $1 per barrel, and S_2 represents the quantities supplied today at $17 per barrel. Figure 5(c) shows the effect on the supply of a resource over time as more of the resource is extracted. If 200 billion barrels of crude oil are extracted this year, then next year the extraction of 200 billion barrels will be more difficult—more expensive—than the extraction of 200 billion barrels was this year. S_1 is the supply in 1990, S_2 the supply in 1991, and so on, as more of the resource is used each year.

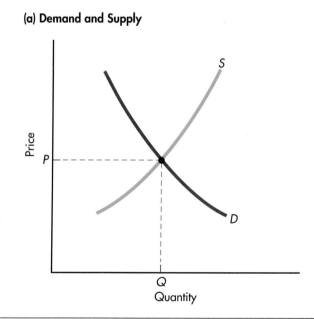

(a) Demand and Supply

the move from S_1 to S_2. The shift occurs because the cost of extracting any quantity of the resource rises as the amount of the resource in existence falls. The first amounts extracted come from the most accessible sources, and each additional quantity then comes from a less accessible source. For instance, in the late 1800s, oil became an important resource. At first, it was extracted with small pumps that gathered up oil seeping out of the ground. The supply curve of oil for that period was S_1. Let's say that a quantity of 200 billion barrels could be extracted and offered for sale at a price of $1 per barrel in 1890. Once that extremely accessible source was gone, wells had to be dug. Over time, wells had to be deeper and be placed in progressively more difficult terrain. From land, to the ocean off California, to the rugged waters off Alaska, to the wicked North Sea, the search for oil has progressed. As more and more is extracted, the marginal cost of extracting any given amount increases, and the supply curve shifts up, from S_1 to S_2 in Figure 5(b). In 1990, 200 billion barrels can no longer be offered for sale at $1 per barrel; the price per barrel must exceed $17.

If 200 billion barrels of crude oil are extracted this year, then in the future the extraction of another 200 billion barrels will be more difficult—more expensive—than the extraction of the 200 billion barrels was this year. This increase is illustrated by an upward shift of the supply curve. Figure 5(c) illustrates how the supply of a nonrenewable resource decreases over time as additional amounts of the resource are used. S_1 is the supply in 1990, S_2 in 1991, S_3 in 1992, and so on, as more of the resource is used each year.

The demand for a nonrenewable natural resource is determined in the same way as the demand for any other resource. It is the marginal revenue product of the resource. Thus, anything that affects the MRP of the nonrenewable resource will affect the demand for that resource.

Equilibrium occurs in the market for a nonrenewable natural resource when the demand and supply curves intersect, as shown in Figure 6. The

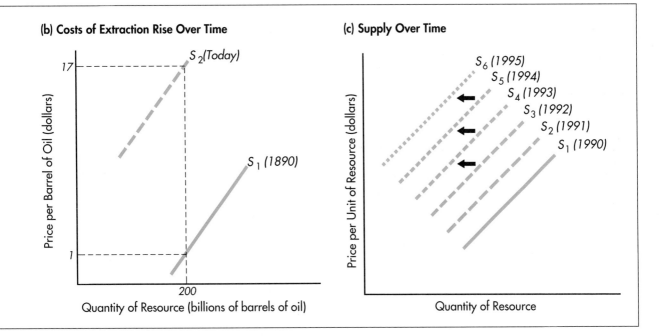

(b) Costs of Extraction Rise Over Time

(c) Supply Over Time

Figure 6
Price Today and in the Future
Equilibrium occurs in the market for an exhaustible natural resource when the demand and supply curves intersect. The equilibrium price, $15, and quantity, 200 billion barrels, represent the price and quantity of the resource used today. Selling the equilibrium quantity of 200 billion barrels today reduces the quantity available tomorrow by 200 billion barrels. With a smaller and probably less accessible quantity, extracting the resource tomorrow is probably going to be more costly than extracting it today. Thus, the supply curve for the resource in the future lies above the supply curve for today, S_2 rather than S_1, if any of the resource is being consumed today. With a higher supply curve, the price is higher, $20 rather than $15. Thus, the price in the future is likely to be higher than the price today.

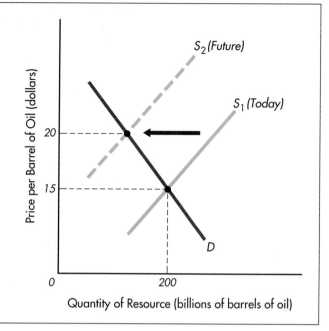

Quantity of Resource (billions of barrels of oil)

equilibrium price, $15, and quantity, 200 billion barrels, represent the price and quantity today. Extracting and selling the equilibrium quantity of 200 billion barrels today reduces the quantity available tomorrow by 200 billion barrels. This means that extracting the resource tomorrow is probably going to be more costly than extracting it today. Thus, the supply curve for the resource in the future lies above the supply curve for today, S_2 rather than S_1, if any of the resource is being consumed today. With a higher supply curve and the same demand, the price is higher, $20 rather than $15. Thus, the price in the future is likely to be higher than the price today if some of the resource is extracted and sold today.

The resource owner must decide whether to extract and sell the resource today or leave it in the ground for future use. Suppose that by extracting and selling the oil that lies below someone's land today, the landowner can make a profit of $10 per barrel after all costs of extraction have been paid. With that $10 the owner could buy stocks or bonds or put the money into a savings account or use it to acquire education or marketable skills. If the interest rate is 10 percent, the owner could realize $11 one year from now from the $10 profit obtained today. Should the oil be extracted today? The answer depends on how much profit the resource owner expects to earn on the oil one year from now, and this depends on what the price of oil and the cost of extraction are one year from now. In other words, the answer depends on whether the present value of extracting and selling the resources exceeds the present value of leaving the resource in the ground.

If the owner expects to obtain a profit of $13 a barrel one year from now, the present value of that $13 at a 10 percent rate of interest is $13/1.1 = $11.82. Clearly, the oil should be left in the ground. If the profit on the oil one year from now is expected to be only $10.50, the present value is $10.50/1.1 = $9.55. In this case, the oil should be extracted and the proceeds used to buy stocks, bonds, or savings accounts. If the profit one year from now is $11 a barrel, the present value is $10; the same whether the oil is extracted today or next year.

As discussed in the first section of the chapter, the present value declines as the interest rate rises. Should the interest rate rise from 10 percent to 15 percent, then the present value of $11.50 one year from now is $10. A profit per barrel exceeding $11.50 next year would be necessary to leave the oil in the ground. As the interest rate rises, more is extracted and sold today and less is left for the future.

Because suppliers and potential suppliers continually calculate whether to extract now or in the future and how much to extract, an equilibrium arises where the present value of profit in the future just equals the value today; for this to occur, the year-to-year rate of increase in the price of the resource must equal the rate of interest on alternative uses of the funds. If the rate of interest is 10 percent a year, everything else held constant, the resource price will rise at a rate of about 10 percent a year.

If the present values of extracting and selling the resources now and of leaving them in the ground until a point in the future are to be equal, then the higher the interest rate, the greater the spread between present and future prices of an exhaustible resource must be. Suppose the interest rate rises above the current rate of return on the nonrenewable resource, oil. The higher interest rate means that producers looking to pump the oil out of the ground will pump more today and purchase stocks, bonds, or savings accounts with the money they get from selling the oil. More extraction means that the supply curve today shifts out and today's price falls. At the same time, the supply curve in the future shifts in (since less will be available in the future) and the future price rises. This will occur until the rate of return on leaving the oil in the ground equals the interest rate—that is, until the present value of pumping the oil and selling it is the same as the present value of the oil left in the ground. A higher interest rate implies the use of more resources today. Conversely, a lower interest rate implies the use of fewer resources today.

2.b.2. The Market for Renewable Resources

Renewable resources, unlike exhaustible or nonrenewable resources, can replenish themselves. Forests and wildlife can reproduce and renew their supplies. The role of the market for renewable resources is to determine a price at which the quantity of the resource used is just sufficient to enable the resource to renew itself at a rate that best satisfies society's wants.

Owners of forest lands could harvest all their trees in one year and reap a huge profit. But if they did so, several years would pass before the trees had grown enough to be cut again. The rate at which the trees are harvested depends on the interest rate. A large harvest one year means fewer trees available in the future and a longer time for renewal to occur. This would suggest a lower price today and a higher price in the future. If the interest rate rises, everything else held constant, owners will want to increase harvesting in order to get more money with which to purchase stocks and bonds. This would mean more trees now and fewer in the future, thereby driving up the price of the trees not cut today. If the interest rate falls, owners will want to harvest fewer trees today. This would mean that today's price will rise and the future price will fall. As was the case with the nonrenewable resources, the market adjusts so that the resources are allocated to their highest-valued use now and in the future. The timing of the use of resources depends on the rate of interest.

In summary, the markets for nonrenewable and renewable resources operate to ensure that current and future wants are satisfied in the least costly manner and that resources are used in their highest-valued alternative now and in the future. When a nonrenewable resource is being rapidly depleted, its future price rises and the present value of using the resource in the future rises so that less of the resource is used today. When a renewable resource is being used at a rate that does not allow the resource to replenish itself, the future price rises and the present value of the future use rises so that less of the resource is used today.

What is conservation?

2.b.3. Conservation The term *conservation* is often used to mean that a resource is not used—it is preserved for the future. And conservation in this sense often carries a positive connotation. We are applauded as we use paper bags rather than plastic ones, drive less, use less electricity and less water, avoid ozone-damaging products, and we are called on to help save the rain forest. Is the positive connotation justified? What does *conservation* mean in the context of the markets for natural resources?

Conservation means the *optimal* rate of use, not the *nonuse* of a resource. The optimal use of a resource is one that is determined in the markets for natural resources. It could imply that *more* of a resource is used today, not less. Though this may at first seem contradictory to the way the term *conservation* is normally used, think about what a policy of not using resources at all today in order to save them for future generations means. It means that less income is created today because the costs of production are higher. Less income means that less is available to allocate to capital goods and future production. This, in turn, means that the economy will grow at a slower rate than it otherwise would have grown, which suggests that future generations will have less wealth than they otherwise would have had. If we ignore the markets for resources and simply dictate that a resource cannot be used today, we may be doing a great disservice to future generations. They will face a much more costly world, one in which the combinations of resources necessary to produce goods and services will be less efficient and in which there will be less wealth.

RECAP

1. Pure economic rent is the payment that a resource in fixed supply receives.
2. Rents serve to allocate a resource in fixed supply to its highest-valued use.
3. Nonrenewable natural resources are natural resources whose supply is fixed. Renewable natural resources are natural resources that can be replenished.
4. The gap between the equilibrium price today and the equilibrium price at some point in the future generates a rate of return on nonrenewable resources that is equal to the interest rate on comparable assets. Changes

in the interest rate lead to different rates of use of nonrenewable resources.

5. The harvest rate of renewable resources is such that the rate of return on the resources is equal to the interest rate on comparable assets.

6. Conservation refers to the optimal rate of use of natural resources, not to the nonuse of these resources. The optimal rate of use is determined in the markets for natural resources.

3. ENTREPRENEURIAL ABILITY

When Pablo Valdez arrived in Florida penniless in the 1980 Mariel boatlift from Cuba, Miami's Cuban community helped him get a job at a Cuban-run real estate firm. He sold $11 million in property during the first year and now employs Cubans at his own two companies. Julie Pellatt, Paula Chiungus, and Katherine Robinson left the Boston office of stockbroker Kidder Peabody & Co. in the fall of 1987 to begin Beacon Hill Nannies Inc. Just two years later, their Beacon Hill organization had revenues exceeding $500,000 and they were contemplating expansion to Los Angeles. These people are **entrepreneurs**, individuals who recognize an opportunity for earning economic profit, acquire and organize the resources for production, and undertake the risk necessary to obtain this profit. They have **entrepreneurial ability**.

entrepreneur:
someone who recognizes an opportunity for earning economic profit and is able to collect and organize the resources and undertake the risk necessary to obtain this profit

entrepreneurial ability:
someone who has the ability to be an entrepreneur

You may hear someone refer to an *intrapreneur*. An intrapreneur is an employee who acts as an entrepreneur within the employee's firm. Unlike an entrepreneur, who starts up a venture, an intrapreneur develops an idea with the full support of the company for which he or she works. William Norris began Control Data in the 1950s, after leaving Sperry-Rand in order to pursue his interest in producing supercomputers. At Control Data, Norris supports the intrapreneurial spirit so that the company does not lose innovative employees to other firms. He formed a separate department dedicated solely to creating the opportunity for existing employees to begin their own businesses within Control Data. Several advances in Control Data have resulted from this encouragement of intrapreneurial ability.

3.a. Entrepreneurs and Profit

Why does the entrepreneur receive profit?

The owners of labor, land, and capital receive wages, rents, and interest; entrepreneurs receive economic profit. What services performed by entrepreneurs enable them to claim profit? One explanation of why the entrepreneur receives profit is that the entrepreneur is paid for being a trader. Another reason is that profit is the entrepreneur's reward for taking risks. The final explanation is that the entrepreneur is paid for being an innovator.

3.a.1. Trader "Buy low and sell high" is the credo of the successful trader. Many believe that the entrepreneur earns a profit by being a trader—by buying resources low and selling products high. The entrepreneur hires the appropriate combinations of resources, organizes resources, and ensures that production takes place. The entrepreneur receives the residual remaining from revenue after land, labor, and capital are paid. The entrepreneur has an incentive to produce a product in the most cost-effective way and to produce a product and sell it at a price consumers will pay. The better the entrepreneurs do this, the higher their profits.

3.a.2. Risk Bearer At least a portion of the economic profit that entrepreneurs receive is payment for their willingness to bear the risk of offering their time, capital, and abilities in a world of uncertainty. All resource owners bear some risk—they may not be paid for their services. The higher the possibility of not getting paid, the more resource owners will demand for their services. Labor suppliers may demand frequent payments—weekly or biweekly—and lenders may require collateral and down payments before they make loans. These additional restrictions can be considered a return for risk bearing, as can a larger payment or a higher interest rate.

Resource owners also bear the risk that the market value of their resources will fall. Resource owners have to be concerned that their resource will lose value. For instance, homeowners bear the risk that their house will lose market value—that it will sell for less than what they paid for it. Owners of human capital bear such risks as well. If you choose an occupation and acquire human capital only to find after several years of schooling that your occupation is paying substantially less than what you had anticipated, you will have experienced a loss in the value of your human capital. To induce people to undertake an activity in which there are risks, a higher wage, rent, or interest must be paid. Everything else the same, the higher the risk, the greater the payment must be to induce people to undertake the activity. This same idea of reward for risk-taking describes how at least a portion of the return to entrepreneurs is determined. People with entrepreneurial ability bear the risk that a new venture will fail and that their entrepreneurial ability will lose value. Profit is a reward for risk-taking.

3.a.3. Innovator An entrepreneur who can produce a good that consumers are willing and able to buy less expensively than others obtains at least short-run profits. If an entrepreneur invents a new product, above-normal profits will exist until entry and imitation occur.

3.b. Profit and the Supply of Entrepreneurs

Only about seven of every ten new firms succeed, as discussed in the Economic Insight "The Road to Success." What induces people to give up an existing job and undertake the risks of running their own business? In addition to the independence or freedom that comes with "being your own boss," it is the potential income that can be obtained. If someone begins a new business and that business generates $100,000 per year, then the owner can sell the business for a value that reflects the present value of this earning stream. The entrepreneur may be able to walk away from the business with a lump sum of money. That lump sum is called the **capitalized value** of the firm and is the present value of the future income stream.

capitalized value:
the present value of an expected future income stream

A business generating $1 million in sales each year that is expected to be successful for five to ten more years could have a capitalized value of between $2 million and $5 million. Thus, the entrepreneur could sell the business and walk away with a substantial lump sum of money instead of continuing to manage the business for the next five to ten years. The greater the potential rewards, everything else held constant, the greater the quantity of people willing to undertake the activity.

Profit influences the allocation of resources among alternative uses. It is the expectation of profit that induces firms (or entrepreneurs) to innovate and to make expenditures on new technologies and on research and development. It is the expectation of profit that induces entrepreneurs to leave one activity

ECONOMIC INSIGHT

The Road to Success

An estimated 38 percent of the men and nearly half of the women in today's work force want to start their own companies. In 1965 there were 204,000 business start-ups in the United States; in the 1990s, that figure has grown to 700,000. But it is neither easy nor necessarily rewarding to start your own business.

For all industries from 1976 to 1985, the birthrate (the number of new businesses divided by the total number of businesses) averaged 11 percent per year. Over the same period, the death rate (the number of businesses that shut their doors divided by the total number of businesses) averaged nearly 9.5 percent per year. By far the greatest number of new businesses are in the services area. The average birthrate exceeded 13 percent in services and was less than 10 percent in manufacturing. Death rates were highest in retail trade and lowest in wholesale trade.

A survey of 2,994 new businesses by American Express Company and the National Federation of Independent Businesses found that 77 percent of new businesses lived to celebrate their third birthday. This is a higher success rate than had been found in earlier surveys. During the 1970s, fewer than half of all new businesses survived five years.

What determines success or failure? It does not seem to matter whether an entrepreneur has prior managerial experience or not; 75 percent of new entrepreneurs with no prior supervisory experience survived three years, and 77 percent of those with extensive managerial experience also survived three years. It seems that a desire to serve the customer is what counts. Of companies saying that better service was the key to their strategy, 82 percent survived. Among companies that competed mainly on price, the survival rate was 70 percent. In addition, hard work and intimate knowledge of the business are required. Only 9 percent of the business owners surviving three years spent more than a quarter of their time supervising employees. "The typical successful entrepreneur spent more time either selling or working directly with customers than on any other aspect of running a new business," said William J. Dennis, a researcher with the National Federation of Independent Businesses. What has made or broken many of the companies is the ability (or inability) to recognize and react to the completely unpredictable, to use enough managerial sense to plan and anticipate, yet know when things are going wrong and be able to find solutions. In other words, the ability to solve problems may be the most important aspect of success, according to a survey by *Inc.* magazine.

Survival does not necessarily mean huge success or growth. Only 37 percent of the new companies increased the number of employees in their first three years; 15 percent actually reduced the number of employees. Growing companies were more likely than others to have outside investors. In addition, the owners of the growing firms had more formal education and were more likely to be acting on a business idea that occurred to them while they were in a previous job.

The financial rewards of being a manager of a large corporation far exceed the rewards of starting and operating your own business. The average pay of the bosses of the 350 largest firms in the United States exceeds $2 million. The average pay to owners of start-ups was only $25,000.

Sources: Leslie Brokaw, "The Truth About Start-Ups," *Inc.*, April 1991, pp. 52–56; Roger Ricklefs, "Road to Success Becomes Less Littered with Failures," *Wall Street Journal*, Oct. 10, 1989, p. B2; Diane Cole, "The Entrepreneur," *Psychology Today* (June 1989), p. 60; U.S. Small Business Administration, Office of Advocacy, Small Business Data Base, USELM file, version 6, March 1987; "The Greed and the Glory of Being Boss," *The Economist*, June 17, 1989, p. 17; *Statistical Abstract of the United States*, 1991.

to carry out another. The production of buggy whips is discarded as the automobile comes along; the production of regular television will be discarded as high-definition television is introduced. It is profit-seeking that leads to the changes: entrepreneurs see the profit potential of the automobile relative to the buggy and the profit potential of high-definition television relative to regular television.

RECAP

1. An entrepreneur is someone who sees an opportunity and acts to take advantage of or make a profit from that opportunity.
2. An intrapreneur serves as an entrepreneur while an employee of a firm.
3. The return to entrepreneurial ability is profits.

4. TYING RESOURCE MARKETS TOGETHER

How are the resource markets tied together?

In this and the previous two chapters, we have been discussing the four broad categories of resources—labor, capital, land, and entrepreneurial ability. We have examined each market somewhat in isolation, but make no mistake about it, the resource markets are linked together; developments in one affect the others. As a general rule, resources flow to their most highly valued use. For instance, if skilled labor is more highly valued than unskilled labor, more resources will flow to the skilled-labor market. If capital used in the service industry provides a greater return than capital used in manufacturing, more capital will flow to the service sector. If high-definition television (HDTV) yields greater profit than regular TV, resources will flow to the HDTV area. As resources flow to their more highly valued use, they flow away from their lower-valued uses.

The value of a use is determined by demand and supply. Businesses demand resource services, allocating their expenditures among resources in order to equate the MRP per dollar of expenditure. Households own the resources and earn income by supplying and selling the services of their resources. Households can consume all of their income today, or they can forgo some consumption and enhance the quality of their resources or acquire more resources with which future income can be created—that is, they can save. Households allocate their income across all goods and services, including future goods and services (that is, saving), according to the rule that the marginal utility per dollar of expenditure on each good and service is the same. A change in the MRP or MFC of a resource will alter the demand for the resource's services; a change in the marginal utility or acquisition price of a resource will alter the supply of resource services.

In each resource market, the demand for resource services (the firm's marginal revenue product) and the supply of resource services offered determine the payment for the use of the resource—the wages, interest, rent, or profit. These payments divided by the purchase price of the resource determine the rate of return of that resource. In present-value terms, a college education costing $100,000 that yields an additional $10,000 per year in salary generates a 10 percent rate of return; a share of stock or a bond that costs $100 and returns $9 per year in interest or dividends generates a 9 percent rate of return; land that has a value of $200,000 and yields a $15,000 profit per year from being farmed has a rate of return of 7.5 percent.

Households can use their savings to enhance the quality of their resource services—to acquire more education or training, for example—or to purchase new or additional resources. Households have a choice of whether to purchase additional education and training, shares of stock or bonds, acres of land or natural resources, or to begin a new business. Which of these households decide to purchase depends on which is expected to yield the greatest rate of return. If college is expected to yield a 10 percent rate of return while all other resources are yielding a 9 percent rate of return and they all have the same risk and generate the same utility, households will purchase more higher education. Their purchases will increase the supply of labor that has a college education and lower the rate of return on the higher education. A college degree that costs $100,000 and generates a return of $10,000 per year has only a 9 percent rate of return if the additional income of the degree falls to $9,000 and the cost of college remains at $100,000.

As households sell assets that are offering lower rates of return and purchase those with higher rates of return, the purchase prices of the assets will change so that the rates of return are equalized. For instance, the rate of return on a college education rose during the 1980s. As a consequence, households reduced their purchases of other resources and spent more on college educations. As a result of more people having acquired college degrees, the return on those degrees will fall, everything else held constant. At the same time, as households reduced their purchases of other resources or sold other resources and spent more on college educations, the rates of return on the other resources rose. All in all, the rates of return on the different resources should equalize over time. When they are not equal, demands and/or supplies will change until they are equal.

RECAP

1. Households own resources and offer them for use to firms. Households choose which resources to own on the basis of expected rate of return.

2. The rate of return is determined by dividing the annual payment for the resource (wages, rent, interest, profit) by the purchase price of the resource. The annual payment is determined in each resource market (labor, land, capital, and entrepreneur) by the demand for and supply of the resource's services.

3. In the long run, rates of return should be equal as households allocate their savings to those resources offering the highest rate of return.

SUMMARY

▲▼ **What role does saving play in the economy?**

1. Saving is the process of using a portion of current production to acquire capital resources so that production can be increased in the future. §1.a

▲▼ **What is present value?**

2. Present value is the equivalent value today of some amount to be received in the future; future value is the equivalent value in the future of some amount received today. §1.b.1

3. The demand for and supply of capital determine the price of capital and the quantity produced and purchased. A change in either demand or supply changes the price and quantity of capital. §1.b.3

4. When the interest rate rises, the demand for capital decreases and the price of capital falls. This, in turn, raises the rate of return on capital. §1.b.3

5. The rate of return on capital and the interest rate tend toward equality. §1.b.3

▲▼ **Does economic rent serve the allocative role that other resource prices serve?**

6. Pure economic rent is payment for the use of a resource that is fixed in supply. §2

7. Rent serves to allocate the fixed resource to its highest-valued use. §2.a.2

▲▼ **What is conservation?**

8. The term *conservation* usually means "not consuming a natural resource to preserve it for the future." §2.b.3

9. The optimal use of natural resources is determined in the markets for renewable and nonrenewable natural resources. The optimal use may not be to save resources for the future and thus may seem contradictory to the customary idea of conservation. §2.b.3

▲▼ **Why does the entrepreneur receive profit?**

10. An entrepreneur is someone who sees an opportunity to earn a profit and acts to take advantage of that opportunity. §3

11. Entrepreneurs receive profit because they are successful traders, they bear risk, or they are innovators. §3.a

12. The incentive for beginning a new business is profit. §3.b

▲▼ **How are the resource markets tied together?**

13. The buyers of resource services are firms; the suppliers are the resource owners, households. Resources flow to their most highly valued uses. As entrepreneurs seek profits, they move resources from unprofitable or less profitable activities to more profitable activities. As households seek to acquire income, they acquire the resources that offer them the greatest income and they offer the resources' services to the areas in which the resources have highest value. §4

14. Rates of return on resources tend to be equal in the long run and will equal the rates of return on alternative uses of household savings, the interest rate. §4

KEY TERMS

saving §1.a

present value §1.b.1

future value §1.b.1

nonrenewable (exhaustible) natural resources §2.b

renewable (nonexhaustible) natural resources §2.b

entrepreneur §3

entrepreneurial ability §3

capitalized value §3.b

EXERCISES

1. What is saving? Would seed be considered the savings of a gardener or farmer? Would expenditures on college be considered part of the savings of a household?

2. Financial capital refers to the stocks, bonds, and other financial instruments businesses use to raise money. What occurs to the present value of financial capital when the interest rate rises, everything else held constant?

3. You purchase a car for $2,000 down and $250 per month for five years. What is your total expenditure on the car? If the sticker price is $12,000, what is your total interest payment?

4. Calculate the present values of the following:

a. $1,000 one year from today at interest rates of 5, 10, and 15 percent

b. $1,000 per year for five years at interest rates of 5, 10, and 15 percent

5. Why are banks more willing to lend to a medical student than to a student in a vocational college?

6. Someone who expects to inherit a huge amount of income tends to be a borrower. Could an entire society expect future income to be much greater than current income and therefore borrow? If so, would the interest rate paid by that society tend to be higher or lower than the rate paid by a society that is not expecting future income growth? What would the change in the interest rate mean for capital accumulation?

7. Data appear to tell us that the saving rate in Japan is nearly three times the rate in the United States. If these data are correct, how might this difference affect the two economies?

8. Suppose the interest rate on a one-year bond in the United States is 10 percent and in Japan the rate is 5 percent on an identical bond.

   a. What do you expect would happen?

   b. Suppose that the yen price of a dollar is 250 ($1 can buy 250 yen) but is expected to change to 225 by the end of the year. What impact does this information have on your answer to part a?

9. If the rate of return on capital is higher than the rates of return on all other assets, what will occur? What happens in the other resource markets as a result?

10. What is the basic economic function of the interest rate? What is the difference between the price of an asset (for instance, a resource) and the interest rate?

11. Explain how a government policy to lower interest rates might influence the natural resource markets.

12. You have savings of $20,000. You are deciding what to do with your savings. You have an opportunity to purchase an education that will mean a 10 percent per year higher salary over your lifetime, a stock that will generate 9 percent per year, and a land investment that is promised to return 20 percent per year. Why are these rates of return different? Which use of your savings would you choose?

13. The entrepreneur receives profit. Explain what this means. How does the entrepreneur function in a perfectly competitive world where economic profits are zero? Explain the impact in all resource markets of a tax on profits.

14. The economic plan unveiled by President Clinton in February 1993 contained higher taxes on the use of nonrenewable resources. What is the likely impact of these taxes? How are the taxes likely to affect saving? Will future generations be better off as a result of the taxes?

15. Entrepreneurs are profit-seekers. They and thus other resources flow to where the profits are or are expected to be. How, then, will a policy to restrict the flow of foreign-produced goods into the United States affect the functioning of the U.S. economy?

Voters Do a Slash-and-Burn on Candidates Supported by Timber-Industry Money

OLYMPIA—TIMBERRR!!! Watch out for crashing political consultants from the forest-products industry.

In an election that turned into a nightmare for Republicans and many of their business allies, few bet heavier and lost bigger than the state's timber giants.

An analysis of public election records shows that timber interests—a list of 20 firms such as Weyerhaeuser and Boise Cascade, along with a handful of top executives—spent $750,000 in campaign contributions on state races. That is three times what the industry gave out in 1988, according to records.

Yet every major candidate they invested in, and virtually every candidate preaching the industry's message that "environmental extremism" was behind the loss of jobs in the woods and mills, was rejected at the polls.

"Shellshocked might be a pretty good word for how we feel," said William Jacobs, executive director of the Washington Forest Protection Association, the industry's chief lobbying group in Olympia.

It's hard to isolate the importance of the timber vote amid the huge Democratic victory last week in the state. Still, environmental leaders were elated.

Jim Pissot, head of the National Audubon Society's state office, said the results showed the industry's message was as "archaic as the flat-Earth theory." Cooperation and results in ending the forest wars, not more polarization, is what interested voters, Pissot claims.

The biggest disappointment for pro-timber forces was the defeat of public lands commissioner candidate Ann Anderson by state Rep. Jennifer Belcher, a strong environmentalist. Anderson, a Republican state senator from Whatcom County, received $325,000 from timber and pulp companies— roughly 40 percent of all her cash.

"The industry seemed intent on some kind of last-gasp, 19th-century effort to make people choose between the environment and jobs," said outgoing Public Lands Commissioner Brian Boyle, a Republican. "People don't like to be told they have to make those choices. They elect us to find solutions." . . .

Nationally, the fight is over how much timber will be harvested from the region's federal forests—a matter that remains tied up in the courts nearly four years after the spotted owl was listed for protection under the Endangered Species Act.

During the race, Republicans used the Endangered Species Act in a sort of populist shorthand: Only those willing to amend the act, they implied, were on the side of traditionally Democratic millworkers and lumberjacks.

"Quite frankly," said Boyle, "the industry is desperately looking for friends."

But in that search, timber companies and Republican politicians misread the public mind, says Steve Gano, a lobbyist for Plum Creek Timber and the manager of McDonald's gubernatorial campaign.

They based their strategy on polls that showed the majority of the public believed protecting jobs should come before protecting the environment. U.S. Sen. Slade Gorton seemed to have tapped that sentiment in his 1988 election, when the Republican wooed Democratic timber communities by bashing Seattle environmentalists.

This year, President Bush made his only campaign visit in the state to a Colville lumber mill, where he told the friendly audience that the Endangered Species Act made owls and salmon more important than families who make their living in the woods.

By contrast, Bill Clinton promised to bring environmentalists and the industry together for a summit to hammer out an agreement on the fate of the region's national forests.

"People in timber country have been promised by Bush and Republicans for four years that they'd come to their rescue. And they never did," says Gano. "They had no reason to believe it this time." . . .

Source: Jim Simon, "Voters Do a Slash-and-Burn on Candidates Supported by Timber-Industry Money Environmentalists Call It a Rejection of 'Jobs or Owls' There," Seattle Times, 11/10/92, p. A1. Copyright © 1992. Reprinted with permission of The Seattle Times.

Seattle Times/November 10, 1992

Commentary

Which is worth more: a job now or the existence of an animal species in the future? Which is worth more: lumber today or a mature forest in the future? These are some questions voters must answer in the Northwest.

Why is this issue of such concern in the political arena? Couldn't it be resolved in the private market-place, just as the allocation of any scarce good would be? In theory, the markets for renewable and nonrenewable resources should define the rates of use of those resources and, simultaneously, the amount of resources left for future use. If, for instance, a private landowner wants to use the resources of the land at a rate that maximizes their present value, he or she must decide whether to cut the trees on the land now or save them until the future. The benefits of cutting the trees now include the income from the lumber. The costs of cutting those trees include not having larger trees in the future and, perhaps, damaging the environment. If the public wants the environment protected, it need only compensate the landowner. Conversely, if the public wants the lumber now, it need only compen-sate the landowner. The answer seems so simple. All we have to do is rely on the private landowner to maximize the present value of his or her future income stream from the use of the land. The landowner will then harvest trees at a rate that max-imizes the present value of the forest. Clear-cutting (the harvesting of every tree in a wide area) is unlikely to occur because that would mean no trees in the future and a lower value for the landowner's resource than if the trees were harvested selectively. Similarly, no harvesting at all is unlikely since the value of the cut trees today would become very high. A balance that maximizes the value of the land and resources will result. Why doesn't this bal-ance occur in the Northwest?

There appear to be two diametrically opposed groups in the battle over the use of the forests: those who are employed cutting the trees and those who wish to protect the environment. If the forests were privately owned, each group could bid for the land use, and the landowner would take the highest bid.

Suppose the market for the trees is illustrated in the accompanying figure, where S_T is the supply

today. The intersection of the demand and supply curves determines the price. Suppose that one group in society prefers that more be available in the future while another group prefers the trees be harvested today. The group preferring that the trees be available in the future must somehow reduce the demand for the trees and thus reduce the price of the trees today. They could do this by making the trees more valuable in the future or by changing tastes.

Why, then, has the issue fallen into the political arena and out of the private market? Because most of the forests are on government land, so there is no private landowner concerned with maximizing the value of the resource. Thus, the two opposing groups have no way to bid for the land use. Instead, they must turn to demonstrations, lobbying, and ultimately, voting to determine whether the trees will be harvested or not.

According to the article, the groups wanting the jobs associated with harvesting of the forests devoted considerable funds to lobbying. Nonetheless, the public decided it wanted the forests to remain unharvested. If this decision meant fewer jobs in forestry, the voters seemed to say, then so be it. What would have been the out-come had the land been privately owned?

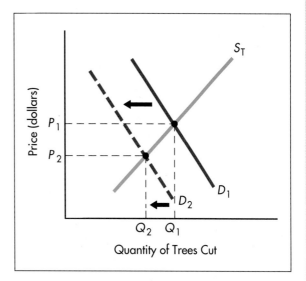

V

Current Issues Involving The Public Sector and The Market Economy

19

The Economics of Aging and Health Care

FUNDAMENTAL QUESTIONS

1. Why is the U.S. population aging?
2. What does it mean to say that there is a market for children?
3. What is social security?
4. What accounts for the increasing percentage of expenditures allocated to health care?

T he population of the United States is aging rapidly. Currently, more than 12 percent of the population is retired—living off pensions, savings, and social security. By the year 2030, 21 percent of the population will be older than sixty-five. The aging of the population is likely to have a dramatic effect on living standards. For instance, the types of goods and services produced will increasingly be influenced by the elderly. In particular, expenditures on health care will continue to rise. Already, people in the United States allocate more than 14 percent of their income to medical care. Is there a limit to how much they are willing to commit? The aging of the population also means that an increasing percentage of people will be retired and a smaller percentage will be producing goods and services and paying taxes. What are the implications for social security and for productivity?

PREVIEW

Why is the population aging? It is a combination of factors: the birthrate has declined and people are living longer than they used to. In the 1950s,

there was 1 birth each year for every 4 people in the population. Today, the rate is 1 birth for every 6 people. Why has the birthrate fallen? In the first section of this chapter we use economic analysis to answer this question. We examine the formation of the family and the decisions to produce children. In the second and third sections we look at the impact of an aging population on retirement and medical care.

I. THE HOUSEHOLD

The average size of the nearly 90 million households in the United States is 2.66 persons. Approximately 63 percent of the population is married, 22 percent single, 7 percent widowed, and 8 percent divorced. Only 28 percent of all households have one income earner; 42 percent have two income earners, and the remaining 30 percent may have none or as many as six income earners.

In 1990 there were nearly 2.6 million marriages, involving 10.5 percent of the population. This rate has not changed in several decades, but people are now marrying at an older age. In 1970 the median age of males marrying for the first time was 22.5; of females, 20.6. In 1990 the median age of males marrying for the first time was nearly 25; of females, 23. Divorce is increasing in frequency. In 1965 the divorce rate was 2.3 percent of the total population. By 1990 it had reached more than 5.0 percent. The number of children per family is declining. It is currently less than 1 per household for middle-income households and just over one for all households.[1]

I.a. Children

What does it mean to say that there is a market for children?

In some societies, households consider children as a resource, labor. In others, a child is the only source of pension benefits for the elderly. The extended family—children, parents, and grandparents living together under one roof—is a means of providing retirement benefits for the elderly. In the developed nations of the West, however, children are neither a source of retirement benefits nor a source of labor; they are a source of utility.

The baby's first smile and first step are things of joy to a parent. Like a painting that hangs on the wall, a child provides continual enjoyment. Children are demanded because of the benefits they embody. The demand curve for children slopes down, as shown in Figure 1, indicating that a decrease in the relative "price" of children (an increase in benefits per child) increases the *quantity demanded.*

Supply reflects the marginal cost of each child. The marginal cost of a child includes the cost of the goods and services consumed by the child and the household work provided by family members because of the child. One child increases daily household work by a spouse not employed outside the home by 3 hours, two children by 5 hours, and three by 5.5 hours. Because the opportunity cost of time differs among households, the cost of rearing children differs as well.

The marginal cost of a child may decline for the first few children before it starts to rise. The first child requires baby clothes, cribs, strollers, car seats, and other resources, including the time required to develop child-care skills. Once these items have been obtained for the first child, they may be available at very little extra cost for the second, third, and so on. The second child can wear "hand-me-downs," sleep in the same crib, ride in the same stroller, and use the same car seat as the first.

The greatest cost of children may be the opportunity cost of the time required for their care, but the marginal cost appears to decline because of economies of scale as the number of children increases. Looking after two children may not require twice as much time as looking after one. Cooking for two children may not take any more time than cooking for one. At some point, the older child (children) can assist in caring for the younger child (children). Of course, the age gap between children is an important determinant of the marginal costs of each child. If the gap is too small, the older child cannot help with the younger. If the gap is too wide, many hand-me-downs will not be useful. There is some age difference between children that is optimal in the sense that costs are minimized.

The supply curve of children may decline initially and then rise if the marginal cost of children declines over the first few children and then rises, or the supply curve may rise slowly at first and then more rapidly as the number of children increases, as shown in Figure 1.

The number of children a household has is determined by the demand for and supply of children.

The number of children a household has is determined by the demand for and supply of children. Impacts on this market, such as religious influences or the different requirements of living in an agrarian society versus those of

---

[1]U.S. Bureau of the Census, *Statistical Abstract of the United States, 1991* (Washington, D.C.: Government Printing Office, 1991).

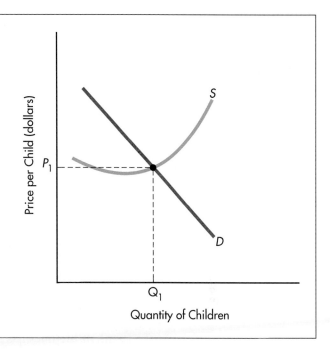

Figure 1
The Market for Children
The figure shows the initial equilibrium in the market for children. The number of children, Q_1, and the price per child, P_1, are determined by the demand for and supply of children. The demand curve for children slopes down, reflecting the law of demand. The supply of children is the marginal cost of each child. The supply curve may decline initially, but eventually it rises.

an urbanized society, are reflected in shifts in the demand for or supply of children. The Second World War had a major impact on the market. By separating men and women, the war virtually destroyed the child market—there was no demand. At the conclusion of the war, there was a pent-up demand for children, and a record number were born between 1946 and 1961. The demand for children that had shifted in from 1940 to 1945 shifted out with a vengeance in 1946. However, once the marginal cost of another child exceeded the marginal benefits of another child, couples quit producing children. Because so many children were produced between 1946 and 1961, there was less demand for additional children after 1961. As a result, a large number of children were produced between 1946 and 1961 but relatively few in the years before and after. This increase in the birthrate is known as a *baby boom*, and the name given to the population born between 1946 and 1961 is *baby boomers*.

The baby boom generation is contributing to the aging of the U.S. population. The baby boomers, who are now in their thirties and forties, constitute half of the adult U.S. population. The baby boom, however, is not the only reason for the aging of the population. A contributing factor is that the number of children being produced has declined.

1.b. Changes in Marriage and the Family

Although the marriage rate has not fallen since the mid-1950s, marriage is changing. Divorce is more prevalent, about double the rate of thirty years ago, and middle- and upper-income families are having fewer children. The primary reason for these developments is the revolutionary change that has taken place in the work force in the last twenty years. Women are entering the work force in record numbers and are acquiring marketable skills. More than one-third of the new lawyers, physicians, and doctoral-degree recipients are women—up from 1 in 16 twenty years ago.

The American family pictured in television shows like "Leave It to Beaver" and "Father Knows Best" comprised four or five people, only one of whom worked outside of the home. Dad went off to his job every morning while Mom and the kids stayed at home. This family was never as common as it was made out to be; even in the 1950s and 1960s, about one-fourth of wives with children held jobs outside of the home. Nevertheless, Mom did have the major responsibilities of caring for the children and homemaking. Within the traditional marriage, specialization has historically meant that the male entered the marketplace and the female remained at home. In the past decade, however, increasing numbers of women have entered the labor force. As a result, children have become more costly; many women have to leave the labor market during pregnancy, at childbirth, or when their children are young.

As we noted in the chapter "Wage Differentials: Race, Gender, Age, and Unionization," having a child has become more costly because the opportunity costs of disrupting their careers have risen as more women have entered the labor force. As a result of the higher costs, they are delaying having children, which necessarily means fewer children. Later childbirth, combined with the large baby boom population, means a steadily aging population.

In addition to the baby boom generation and developments in marriage, the length of lifetimes has risen and thus contributed to the aging of the population. In 1930, those who reached age sixty-five could expect to live to age seventy-five. By 1990, someone age sixty-five could expect to live to age eighty-two.

RECAP

1. The number of children a family has depends on the benefits a child produces and on the costs of a child. The benefits include the utility—pleasure—children provide. The costs include the costs of care and feeding and the time involved in raising children.

2. World War II had a major impact on the supply of children—a large number were born in the postwar years.

3. Because it has become increasingly costly for women to have children during the prime years of human-capital acquisition, the decision to have a child has been delayed. This delay, combined with the increased costs imposed on a woman who has a child, has meant a smaller number of children.

4. The aging of the population is due to the aging of the baby boom generation, the decreased birthrates, and the increased life expectancies.

2. AGING AND SOCIAL SECURITY

Why is the U.S. population aging?

The oldest population of the United States, persons sixty-five years or older, numbered 30 million in 1990 and represented more than 12 percent of the U.S. population, about one in every eight Americans. The oldest group itself is getting older. In 1990, the sixty-five to seventy-four age group was 8 times larger than in 1900, but the seventy-five to eighty-four group was 12 times larger and the eighty-five-plus group was 22 times larger.

The percentage of the U.S. population over age sixty-five is expected to continue to grow. This growth will slow somewhat during the 1990s because of the relatively small number of babies born during the Great Depression of the 1930s, but the most rapid increase ever is expected between the years 2010 and 2030, when the baby boom generation reaches age sixty-five. The pattern of aging is clearly visible in Figure 2, which shows the age of the U.S. population at three points of time, 1970, 1990, and what is anticipated for 2010. The pattern has been described as a python swallowing a pig: the pig represents the baby boom generation working its way up the age scale, the python.

The growth of the older population in the United States has brought several issues to the forefront of political debate. Among them are social security and health care.

2.a. Social Security

What is Social Security?

An aging population means that the concerns of the aged will dominate national concerns. Retirement and security for the aged is one such concern. Old Age, Survivors, and Disability Insurance (OASDI), also known as social security, had been established in 108 countries by the beginning of 1975. Some of the oldest plans are those of Germany (1889), the United Kingdom

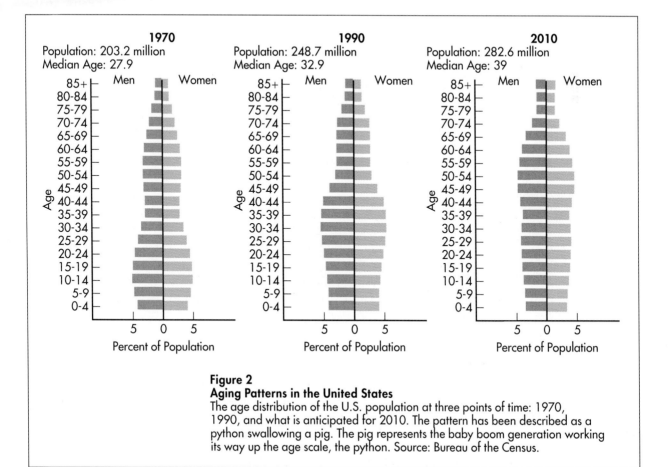

Figure 2
Aging Patterns in the United States
The age distribution of the U.S. population at three points of time: 1970, 1990, and what is anticipated for 2010. The pattern has been described as a python swallowing a pig. The pig represents the baby boom generation working its way up the age scale, the python. Source: Bureau of the Census.

(1908), France (1910), Sweden (1913), and Italy (1919). The United States did not enact a national retirement program until 1935.

The social security system in the United States is financed by a payroll tax, FICA, levied in equal portions on the employer and the employee. From the initial tax of 1 percent of the first $3,000 of wage income paid by both parties in 1935, the tax rate rose to 7.65 percent (or a total 15.3 percent) on the first $57,600 of earnings. In addition, another 1.45 percent of salaries less than $135,000 is withheld for Medicare, the medical program of social security.

2.b. The Viability of Social Security

Social Security was intended to supplement the retirement funds of individuals.

The social security taxes the working population pays today are used to provide benefits for current retirees. As a result, the financial viability of the system depends on the ratio of those working to those retired. The age distribution of the United States population has affected this viability. The consequence is a change in the ratio of workers to social security beneficiaries, as shown in Figure 3. The ratio has declined from 16.5 in 1950 to about 3 today and is expected to decline to 2 by 2030. The situation in the United States is not any different from that in other parts of the world, as noted in the Economic Insight "The World Is Aging." This trend means that the source of social security benefits is getting relatively smaller. The viability of the system depends on whether the trends of recent years continue. If birthrates remain low and if people continue to live longer, then the obligations to people who will retire in twenty-five years will be large relative to the income of the working population at that time. The Social Security Administration estimates that if everything remains as it currently is, then beginning in the year 2030, social security taxes will be insufficient to fund benefits.

The social security tax has risen more rapidly in the past two decades than any other tax. Social security tax revenues were less than 5 percent of personal income in 1960 and currently exceed 11 percent of personal income.

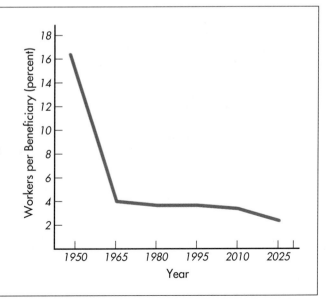

Figure 3
Social Security Viability
The ratio of workers to social security beneficiaries is shown. The ratio has declined from 16.5 in 1950 to about 3 today and is expected to decline to 2 or less by 2030. This trend means that the source of social security benefits is getting relatively smaller. The viability of the system depends on whether the trends of recent years continue. Sources: *Statistical Abstract of the United States, 1991*; Joseph E. Stiglitz, *Economics of the Public Sector* (New York: W.W. Norton, 1986), p. 277; Henry J. Aaron, Barry P. Bosworth, Gary T. Burtless, *Can America Afford to Grow Old?* (Washington, D.C.: Brookings Institution, 1989), p. 38.

The World Is Aging

The United States is not the only country whose population is growing older. Most of the developed nations in the world are experiencing the same aging of their populations. As seen in the accompanying figure, the elderly population constituted about 12 percent in the United States in 1985 but nearly 17 percent in Sweden. Although three-quarters of the world's population resides in developing areas, these areas contain only about 50 percent of the world's elderly. The developed countries are aging because the birthrates in these countries have decreased and life expectancy has increased. Japan's life expectancy of seventy-seven years is the highest among the major countries, but most developed nations approach seventy-five years. In contrast, Bangladesh and some African nations south of the Sahara have life expectancies of forty-nine years.

As longevity has increased and families have had fewer children, the ratio of persons sixty-five and older to persons age twenty to sixty-four has risen in most of the developed countries. These elderly support ratios will rise modestly over the next fifteen years because the large number of people born between 1946 and 1961 will still be in the labor force. But as the large working-age population begins to retire after 2005, the elderly support ratio will rise sharply.

Source: U.S. Department of Commerce, Bureau of the Census, International Population Reports, Series P-95, No. 78, "An Aging World," 1991.

	Elderly Population (Percent)
United States	12.0
Western Europe	
Sweden	16.9
Norway	15.5
United Kingdom	15.1
Denmark	14.9
Germany, former Fed. Rep.	14.5
Austria	14.1
Belgium	13.4
Greece	13.1
Italy	13.0
Luxembourg	12.7
France	12.4
Eastern Europe	
Hungary	12.5
Bulgaria	11.3
Poland	9.4
Other Developed Countries	
Canada	10.4
New Zealand	10.4
Australia	10.1
Japan	10.0
Developing Countries	
Uruguay	10.7
Israel	8.9
Hong Kong	7.6
Singapore	5.2
China	5.1
Brazil	4.3
India	4.3
Mexico	3.5
Indonesia	3.5
Philippines	3.4
Bangladesh	3.1
Guatemala	2.9

■ 80 Years and over
▨ 65 Years and over

The revenues from the personal income tax were 3.4 percent of personal income in 1940 and rose to the current amount of more than 15 percent in the early 1980s. Corporate tax revenues are actually a slightly smaller percentage of personal income now than they were in 1940. Social security expenditures also have risen more rapidly than any other government program. Social security outlays currently constitute 7 percent of GDP, whereas national defense is less than 5.5 percent, and education and training expenditures are less than 1 percent. From 1979 to 1990, national defense expenditures rose 53.6 percent, education and training expenditures rose 0.8 percent, GDP grew 30.2 percent, and social security grew 70.9 percent, adjusted for inflation.

If the system was funded solely by the revenues collected from the social security tax and if those revenues could be used for no other purpose than to provide benefits to social security recipients, then the worries about the system's viability would be much smaller. However, the social security system is included in the federal government's budget, and its revenues are used to pay for general government expenditures. This means that the excess of social security taxes over social security benefits of $60 billion or so in 1990 was used to pay for other government programs; the funds were not deposited in a trust fund and allowed to accumulate for future years.

If the amount paid into the social security system by an individual was equal, on average, to the amount received by that individual in retirement benefits, the worries about the viability of the system would also be less. But people who retired in the 1980s, after working since the age of twenty-one at the minimum wage level will recover all social security taxes paid, including employer and employee shares, in less than 4 years; at the maximum taxable amount each year, the employee would have recovered the total contributions in only 5 years. In the 1990s, the years to recover the total contributions and interest earnings grow to 5 and 7 years. At an age of eighty-two, the average worker who retired at age sixty-five will have received more than twice his and his employer's contributions to social security. Other social security issues are noted in the Economic Insight "Myths About Social Security."

RECAP

1. The U.S. population is aging due to lower birthrates, higher life expectancy, and the impact of the baby boom generation.

2. Social security, otherwise known as Old Age, Survivors, and Disability Insurance, is financed by a tax imposed on employers and employees.

3. Social security is funded by the current working population's contributions being used to provide benefits to the current retirees. As the population ages, the ratio of contributors to beneficiaries declines.

3. HEALTH ECONOMICS

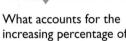

What accounts for the increasing percentage of expenditures allocated to health care?

Spending for health care in the United States exceeds $500 billion. Figure 4 shows that in 1965 health-care expenditures were only 5.9 percent of GDP but were nearly 12.5 percent by 1990. Per capita spending in 1990 was about $2,000, nearly 18 percent of per capita consumption and 14 percent of per capita income. Why have health-care expenditures risen so dramatically?

Figure 4
The Growth of U.S. Health-Care Spending
As a percentage of gross domestic product, health-care expenditures have risen from about 6 percent in 1965 to over 12 percent in 1990. Sources: *Health Care Financing Review* (Health Care Financing Administration, 1991); Office of National Health Statistics, Office of the Actuary; *Economic Report of the President, 1992.*

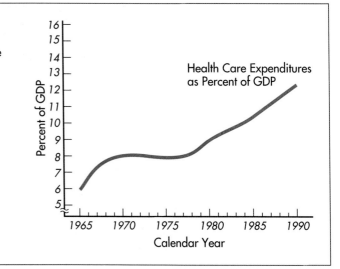

3.a. Overview

Figure 5 shows where the nation's health-care dollar is spent and where the money comes from. Figure 5(a) shows that expenditures for hospital services constitute 39 cents of every dollar, or 39 percent of the nation's health-care bill; nursing home expenditures, 8 percent; spending for physicians' services, 20 percent; and spending for other personal health-care services (dental care, other professional services, drugs and other nondurables, durable medical products, and miscellaneous personal-care services), 21 percent. The remaining 12 percent of national health expenditures goes for medical research, con-

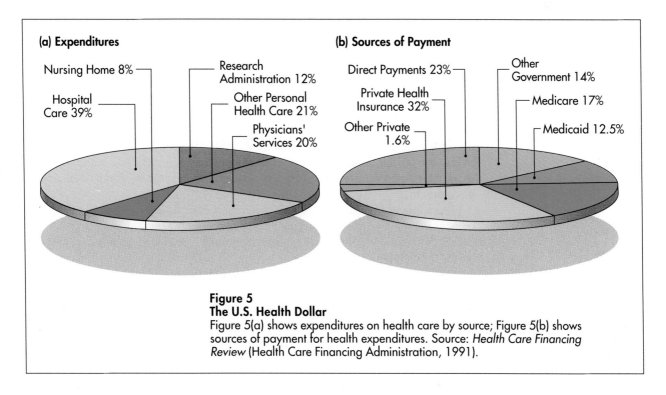

Figure 5
The U.S. Health Dollar
Figure 5(a) shows expenditures on health care by source; Figure 5(b) shows sources of payment for health expenditures. Source: *Health Care Financing Review* (Health Care Financing Administration, 1991).

ECONOMIC INSIGHT

Myths About Social Security

The first recipient of social security in the United States was Ida Mae Fuller in 1940. Her check was for $22.45. By the time she died, shortly after her one hundredth birthday, she had collected about $20,000 in benefits, a large return considering that she had paid in a total of $22.

"We've contributed to that fund all our lives! It's our money! It's not the government's money!" This is one of the most strongly and widely held myths about the social security system. In fact, the typical retiree collects more than twice the amount represented by employer and employee contributions plus interest.

"The benefits of the system are determined by a scientific formula designed to ensure that the fund remains viable." This is another myth about social security. The system of annually adjusting social security benefits as the cost of living increases dates only from 1975, and it came about as the result of political machinations, not foresight. In 1975, the annual benefits were about $7,000. Attempting to hold the line on federal spending, President Nixon proposed a 5 percent increase in social security benefits and threatened a veto of anything higher. Democrats saw an opportunity to embarrass the president. They decided to pass a 10 percent increase and force Nixon to make an unpopular veto. The 10 percent increase was introduced in the Senate, but then rumors that Nixon would double-cross them and sign the bill anyway began circulating. So Congress increased the benefits to 20 percent, knowing that this huge increase would be vetoed. Nixon, however, signed the bill and proudly boasted of how well he had taken care of the elderly. Congress, irritated at being out-flanked, passed the cost-of-living adjustment program to show that it, too, cared about the elderly.

"Social Security ensures that only the elderly poor are cared for." In fact, there are at least a million individuals currently collecting social security benefits who also have incomes exceeding $100,000 per year.

Sources: Jack Anderson, "Why Should I Pay for People Who Don't Need It?" *Parade Magazine*, Feb. 21, 1993, p. 4; Eric Blac, "Social Security: Myths, Facts," *Arizona Republic*, Feb. 21, 1993, p. F1.

---

struction of medical facilities, government public health services, and the administration of private health insurance.

Figure 5(b) shows the sources of payment for these expenditures. Of the $500 billion spent on health care, $293 billion (59 percent) comes from private sources: private insurance and direct payments. Private health insurance, the single largest payer for health care, accounts for 32 cents of every dollar of national health expenditures, or 32 percent. Private direct payments account for 23 percent. Direct payments consist of out-of-pocket payments made by individuals, including copayments and deductibles required by many third-party payers (third-party payers are insurance companies and government).

Government spending on health care (including Medicare and Medicaid) constitutes 43.5 percent of the total; the federal government pays about 70 percent of this. **Medicare**, the largest publicly sponsored health-care program, funds health-care services for more than 32 million aged and disabled enrollees. The Medicare program pays for 17 percent of all national health expenditures. **Medicaid**, a jointly funded federal and state program, finances 12.5 percent of all health care. Other government programs pay for 14 percent.

Health-care spending varies tremendously among various groups in the U.S. population. Figure 6 illustrates how health-care expenditures vary across the economy. If each person spent the same amount on health care, the line

Medicare:
a federal program providing health care for the elderly and disabled

Medicaid:
a joint federal-state program providing long-term health care for the elderly and disabled

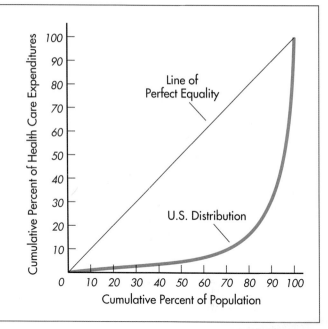

Figure 6
The Inequality of U.S. Health-Care Spending
High-cost users of health care account for most health-care spending. The top 1 percent account for 30 percent of expenditures, the top 5 percent for 55 percent of expenditures. In contrast, the bottom 70 percent account for only 10 percent of health-care expenditures. Source: Steven A. Garfinkel et al., "High-Cost Users of Medical Care," *Health Care Financing Review* (Health Care Financing Administration, Summer 1988), pp. 41–50.

of perfect equality shown in Figure 6 would describe the distribution of spending. In fact, the distribution of health expenditures is heavily skewed. In 1990, the top 1 percent of persons ranked by health-care expenditures accounted for almost 30 percent of total health expenditures, and the top 5 percent incurred 55 percent of all health expenditures. The bottom 50 percent of the population accounted for only 4 percent of all expenditures, and the bottom 70 percent accounted for only 10 percent of costs.

The high-cost segment of the population is older now than it was twenty years ago. In 1970, 32 percent of the highest 1 percent of users were elderly; the percentage of elderly increased to 43.4 in 1980 and continued to rise during the 1980s. Figure 7 shows that the distribution of spending for hospital care and for nursing homes is heavily dominated by the elderly. The top curve in Figure 7 represents the cumulative percentage of the population in each age group. As the age rises from under five to ten to twenty and so on, there are increasing numbers of people. Eventually 100 percent of the population has been accounted for. The bottom curve represents the cumulative percentage of nursing home expenditures accounted for by people in each age group. Similarly, the middle line represents the cumulative percentage of expenditures on hospitals accounted for by each age group.

3.b. The Market for Medical Care

Health care costs have risen because the demand for health care has risen relative to supply.

Rising costs or expenditures mean that the demand for medical care has risen relative to supply (Figure 8). The initial demand for medical care is D_1, and the supply of medical care is S_1. The intersection determines the price of medical care, P_1, and the total expenditures, P_1 times Q_1. An increase in demand relative to supply is shown as the outward shift of the demand curve, from D_1 to D_2. As a result, the price of medical care rises, from P_1 to P_2, as do the total expenditures on medical care, from P_1 times Q_1 to P_2 times Q_2. What accounts for the rising demand relative to supply?

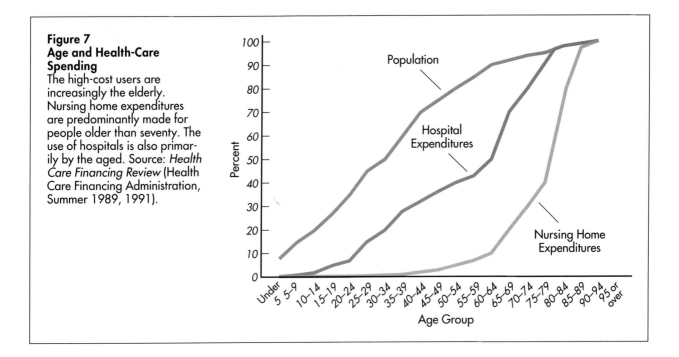

Figure 7
Age and Health-Care Spending
The high-cost users are increasingly the elderly. Nursing home expenditures are predominantly made for people older than seventy. The use of hospitals is also primarily by the aged. Source: *Health Care Financing Review* (Health Care Financing Administration, Summer 1989, 1991).

3.b.1. Demand Increase: The Aging Population The aging of the population stimulates the demand for health care. The elderly consume four times as much health care per capita as the rest of the population. About 90 percent of the expenditures for nursing home care are for persons sixty-five or over, a group that constitutes only 12 percent of the population. The aged (sixty-five or older) currently account for 35 percent of hospital expenditures. In contrast, the young, although they constitute 29 percent of the population, con-

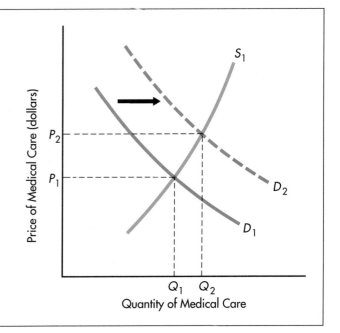

Figure 8
The Market for Medical Care: A Demand Shift
The demand for and supply of health care determine the price of medical care, P_1, and the total expenditures, P_1 times Q_1. Rising health-care expenditures may be due to increased demand. A larger demand, D_2, means a higher price and a greater total quantity of expenditures, P_2 times Q_2.

sume only 11 percent of hospital care. Per capita spending on personal health care for those eighty-five years of age or over is 2.5 times that for people age sixty-five to sixty-nine years. For hospital care, per capita consumption is twice as great for those age eighty-five or over as for those age sixty-five to sixty-nine; for nursing home care, it is 23 times as great.

3.b.2. Demand Increase: The Financing Mechanism

For demand to increase, the aged must be both *willing* to buy medical care and *able* to pay for it. The emergence of Medicare and Medicaid in 1966 gave many elderly the ability. Medicare is a federal program that provides health care for the elderly and disabled. It provides hospital and other medical benefits to 32 million people, of whom 29 million are eligible on the basis of age and 3 million on the basis of disability. Medicaid is a joint state-federal program that provides long-term health care (such as for people living in nursing homes).

The effect of the Medicare and Medicaid programs has been to increase the demand for services and to decrease the price elasticity of demand because payment to physicians and hospitals is geared to cost. Private sources pay for about 59 percent of personal health care for the general population, and Medicare and Medicaid pick up most of the remainder. Private sources, however, pay for 74 percent of care for people under age sixty-five. For the elderly, the private share of spending is only 15 percent for hospital care, 36 percent for physicians' services, and 58 percent for nursing home care.[2] Medicaid spending for those eighty-five or over is seven times the spending for people age sixty-five to sixty-nine and three times greater than the spending for people age seventy-five to seventy-nine. This difference is attributable to the heavy concentration of Medicaid money in nursing home care, which those eighty-five or over use much more than others. Medicare spending for the oldest group is double that for the sixty-five to sixty-nine group.

3.b.3. Demand Increase: New Technologies

New medical technologies provide the very sick with increased opportunities for survival. Everyone wants the latest technology to be used when their life or the lives of their loved ones are at stake. But because these technologies are cost-increasing innovations and because costs are not paid by the users, the increased technology increases demand.

3.b.4. Supply

Even if the demand curve for medical care was not shifting out rapidly, the cost of medical care could be forced up by an upward shift of the supply curve, as shown in Figure 9. The supply curve, composed of the marginal-cost curves of individual suppliers of medical care, shifts up, from S_1 to S_2, if the cost of producing medical care is rising—that is, if resource prices are rising or if diseconomies of scale are being experienced. The three largest resources in the medical industry in terms of total expenditures are hospitals (39 percent), physicians (20 percent), and nursing homes (8 percent).

Hospitals The original function of hospitals was to provide the poor with a place to die. Not until the twentieth century could wealthy individuals who were sick find more comfort, cleanliness, and service in a hospital than in

---

[2]*Health Care Financing Review,* various issues, 1989–1991.

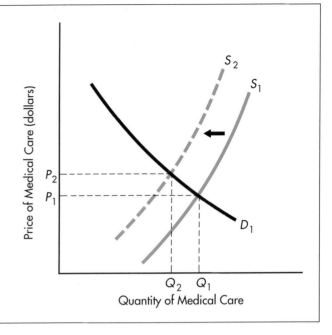

Figure 9
The Market for Medical Care: A Supply Shift
The rising cost of medical care may be caused by an increase in the costs of supplying medical care. The supply curve shifts up, from S_1 to S_2, and the price of medical care rises, from P_1 to P_2.

their own homes. As technological changes in medicine occurred, the function of the hospital changed: the hospital became the doctor's workshop.

The cost of hospital care is attributable in large part to the way current operations and capital purchases are financed. Only a small fraction of the cost of hospital care is paid for directly by patients; the bulk comes from *third parties*, of which the government is the most important. The term *third-party payers* refers to insurance companies and government programs: neither the user (the patient) nor the supplier (the physician or hospital) pays. Until recently, the public-sector, third-party payers made very little effort to question the size of hospital bills. The rate of reimbursement for each hospital was determined primarily by the hospital's costs. Thus, high-cost hospitals were rewarded with higher reimbursement. In 1983, Medicare instituted the prospective payment system, which changed this reimbursement scheme. The **prospective payment system (PPS)** assigns specific reimbursement rates for certain procedures so that high-cost hospitals are reimbursed at the same rate for the same procedure as low-cost hospitals. The result has been to slightly slow the rate of growth of hospital costs and to increase the use of outpatient facilities and at-home care.

prospective payment system (PPS):

the use of a preassigned reimbursement rate by Medicare to reimburse hospitals and physicians

Hospital size is typically measured in numbers of beds; efficiency, in expenditures per case or expenditures per patient-day. To make precise determinations of the effect of size on efficiency is difficult because hospitals that differ in size are likely to differ also with respect to location, kind of patient admitted, services provided, and other characteristics. Hospitals that do not provide a large number of complex services need not be very large to be efficient. But if hospitals do provide a large number of services, it is very inefficient for them to be small. A hospital of 200 beds can efficiently provide most of the basic services needed for routine short-term care. If that hospital grows to 600 beds yet still provides only the same basic services, inefficiencies are likely to develop because of increasing difficulties of administrative control. What is more likely to happen, however, is that specialized services will be introduced—services that could not have been provided at a reasonable cost when the hospital had only 200 beds.

Hospitals have changed dramatically in the past twenty years. The average number of beds per hospital increased by 50 percent. Inpatient days declined by about 10 percent. Lengths of stay declined by about 10 percent, and occupancy rates declined by nearly 20 percent. The problem that more beds per hospital and shorter stays creates for the hospital is that the present occupancy rate is about 66 percent. The minimum efficient scale (MES) of a hospital occurs with an occupancy rate between 80 and 88 percent.

One problem facing hospital administrators is that many key decisions are made by physicians, who typically have little financial stake in keeping hospital costs down. In fact, many have incentives that run counter to cost control in the hospital. For instance, the use of increased diagnostic testing as a defensive measure against malpractice lawsuits raises the costs of each patient. The role of the physician is particularly important with respect to the cost of care, not just because of physicians' fees but because physicians control the total process of care. Typically, the physician is not an employee of the hospital but is a member of the voluntary staff and is referred to as an attending physician. Although not an employee, the physician has primary influence over what happens. The physician decides who is admitted, what is done to and for the patient, and how long the patient stays.

The delivery of hospital care is typically in the hands of health professionals such as pharmacists, nurses, and technicians, who take their instructions from the physician. Although the pharmacy that fills a prescription is usually an independent business and the pharmacist may be more knowledgeable about drugs than the physician, the pharmacist is legally obliged to fill a prescription exactly as written. In many states a pharmacist cannot substitute one brand of the same drug for another, even if the substitution would result in substantial savings for the patient. Only a physician can prescribe drugs. In addition, all tests and surgery are based solely on the physician's judgment.

Physicians Physicians affect the cost of medical care not only through their impacts on the operation of the hospital but also through their fees. Expenditures on physicians' services rose more rapidly than any other medical-care expenditure category in the 1980s. Is the increased cost of physicians due to a shortage of doctors? The answer is not necessarily "yes". From 1966 to 1990, the supply of physicians increased 100 percent while the American population increased only about 25 percent. As a result, the ratio of active physicians per 100,000 people increased substantially, from 169 in 1975 to 233 in 1990.

The factors that have led to rising physicians' fees include an increase in demand relative to the supply of certain types of physicians, the ability of physicians to restrict price competition, and the payment system. The number of physicians per population has risen in many areas of the country. Yet, because the American Medical Association restricts advertising by physicians, consumers are unable to obtain complete information about prices or professional quality, and physicians are less likely to compete through advertising or lower prices. Moreover, the restrictions on advertising enable established physicians to keep new, entering physicians from competing for their customers by charging lower prices.

The payment system influences physicians' fees and the supply of physicians. Over 31 percent of all physicians' fees are set by the government. More than 75 percent are set by third-party providers. The physicians are reimbursed on the basis of procedures and according to specialty. A gynecologist would have to examine 275 women a week to achieve the income earned by one cardiac surgeon doing two operations per week. The rates of return from medical education by specialty are shown in Table 1. You can see that the rate of return varies tremendously among specialties. The payment system has been a windfall (an economic rent) for surgical specialists, anesthesiologists, radiologists, and pathologists and has induced more physicians to specialize in those areas than would have occurred otherwise.

The costs of doing business have risen for physicians. The cost of malpractice insurance, a negligible expense fifteen years ago, has increased about 25 percent a year during the past two decades. Only about 1 percent of health-care expenditures can be directly attributed to malpractice suits, but there are some implicit costs associated with the fear of malpractice suits. The threat of malpractice suits has caused an increase in both the number of tests ordered by physicians and in the quantity of medical equipment purchased by them.

3.c. Alternatives: HMOs and PPOs

health maintenance organization (HMO):
an organization that provides comprehensive medical care to a voluntarily enrolled consumer population in return for a fixed, prepaid amount of money

The increased costs of medical care and the increased supply of physicians have led to new medical-care delivery systems, the health maintenance organization and the preferred provider organization. A **health maintenance organization (HMO)** provides comprehensive medical care, including preventive, diagnostic, outpatient, and hospital services in return for a fixed, prepaid amount of money from the enrollees.

There are four basic types of HMOs: staff, medical group, independent practice associations (IPAs), and networks. *Staff HMOs*, such as the Group Health Cooperative of Puget Sound in Seattle and ANCHOR Health Plan in

TABLE 1
Rates of Return from Medical Education

Specialty	Rate of Return (percent)
Pediatrics	9
General practice/family practice	11
Psychiatry	13
Internal medicine	14
Obstetrics-gynecology	16
Pathology	17
Surgery	19
Radiology	20
Anesthesiology	22
Total, all physicians	16

Sources: Steven R. Eastaugh, *Financing Health Care* (Dover, Mass.: Auburn House Publishing Co., 1987), p. 57; *Statistical Abstract of the United States, 1991*, p. 104.

Health-care costs in the United States have risen nearly 300 percent in the past decade. Part of the reason for these costs has been the increasingly sophisticated and expensive equipment used in diagnoses and treatment. This cat scan provides a picture of the brain; the picture is two dimensional and can be taken from any angle. Even more sophisticated machines provide virtual reality, showing three dimensional pictures of the brain.

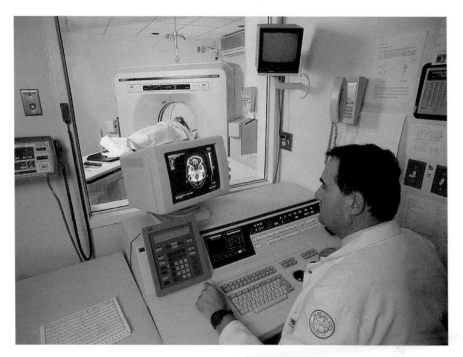

Chicago, hire physicians as salaried employees. *Group HMOs* function as a medical group practice. Several physicians operating as a partnership or corporation contract with HMO management and an insurance plan to provide services and pool and redistribute income according to a predetermined formula. *Independent practice associations* are separate legal entities that contract with individual physicians practicing in a traditional office setting. *Networks* are organizations that franchise operations, in the same way that McDonald's and Pizza Hut are franchised operations. For instance, Blue Cross/Blue Shield is the main company, and local HMOs are franchises of Blue Cross/Blue Shield.

The preferred provider organization is making inroads into the market served by HMOs. A **preferred provider organization (PPO)** is a group of physicians who contract with a firm to provide services at a price discount of 3 to 9 percent in hopes of increasing their volume of business. A general practitioner serves as a member's primary-care provider and refers patients to specialists as needed. Instead of contacting a specialist directly, a patient must be referred to a specialist by the primary-care provider. Specialists are reimbursed out of the fees paid to the PPO plan by the firms that contract with it. The general practitioners have an incentive to reduce total costs because they split a portion of the fixed fees that remain at the end of the year. As a result, the use of specialists and special tests is lower than in health-care plans that permit patients to select the specialists. Many hospitals are organizing PPOs in hopes of better managing hospital utilization and offsetting declining revenues.

Because HMOs and PPOs provide comprehensive coverage, they alter incentives for the patient. Patients who belong to an HMO or PPO are less likely to seek hospitalization for diagnostic work and other care that can be provided on an outpatient basis than are patients whose health insurance coverage is limited to care provided in the hospital. An HMO also alters incen-

preferred provider organization (PPO):
a group of physicians who contract to provide services at a price discount

tives for physicians. Because their income is determined by annual payments, they are not likely to provide or order unnecessary care as a way of boosting their incomes.

3.d. National Comparisons

As per capita national income rises, the proportion of that income that is spent on health grows: a 10 percent increase in gross domestic product (GDP) per capita is associated with a 4.4 percent increase in the share of GDP going for health. (*Gross domestic product*, you will recall, is a measure of the total income created in an economy during one year.) Figure 10 shows the health-to-GDP ratios of the twenty-four members of the Organization for Economic Cooperation and Development (OECD) in 1990. The share of health expenditures in GDP varied from 4.0 percent in Turkey to 12.4 percent in the United States. The average was 7.4 percent. Although the OECD average ratio has stabilized, the U.S. ratio is still increasing, and the gap between the United States and other countries continues to widen.

In 1990, per capita expenditures for health ranged from $197 in Turkey to $2,566 in the United States, as shown in Figure 11. U.S. per capita spending exceeded spending in Canada by 43 percent, France by 86 percent, Germany by 99 percent, and Japan by 124 percent.

Increases in health-care expenditures and the widening gap between the United States and other countries have led to a consideration of how medical care is provided in various countries. The comparison considered most often is between the United States and Canada because the two are neighbors with not too dissimilar economic and political systems and yet very different medical systems.

U.S. and Canadian payment systems differ considerably. In the United States, physicians are paid more for doing more, and the return on their time is higher if they perform a procedure than if they use their cognitive skills. Because procedures often require hospital care, this approach translates into

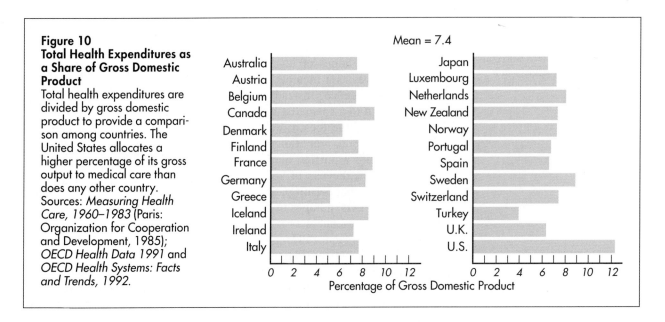

Figure 10
Total Health Expenditures as a Share of Gross Domestic Product
Total health expenditures are divided by gross domestic product to provide a comparison among countries. The United States allocates a higher percentage of its gross output to medical care than does any other country.
Sources: *Measuring Health Care, 1960–1983* (Paris: Organization for Cooperation and Development, 1985); *OECD Health Data 1991* and *OECD Health Systems: Facts and Trends, 1992.*

Mean = 7.4

Percentage of Gross Domestic Product

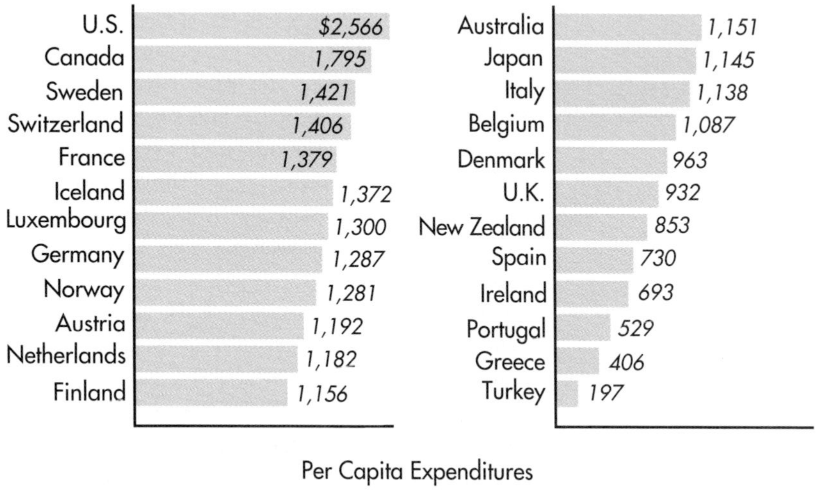

Figure 11
Per Capita Health Spending
The per capita expenditures of several countries are shown. U.S. expenditures are the highest. Sources: *Measuring Health Care, 1960–1983* (Paris: Organization for Cooperation and Development, 1985); *OECD Health Data 1991* and *OECD Health Systems: Facts and Trends, 1992.*

Country	Per Capita Expenditures	Country	Per Capita Expenditures
U.S.	$2,566	Australia	1,151
Canada	1,795	Japan	1,145
Sweden	1,421	Italy	1,138
Switzerland	1,406	Belgium	1,087
France	1,379	Denmark	963
Iceland	1,372	U.K.	932
Luxembourg	1,300	New Zealand	853
Germany	1,287	Spain	730
Norway	1,281	Ireland	693
Austria	1,192	Portugal	529
Netherlands	1,182	Greece	406
Finland	1,156	Turkey	197

Per Capita Expenditures

higher expenditures for hospital care. In Canada, by contrast, physicians operate under a system of fee schedules and overall provincial limits on health spending, and they have no incentive to increase the number of procedures.

Canadian patients are virtually fully insured. There are no deductibles or copayments. Canadian physicians are mostly reimbursed on a fee-for-service basis. Very little use is made of the prepaid group practices that have grown so rapidly in the United States. Government sanctions cause Canadian physicians to limit their use of tests and other procedures. The biggest difference between the U.S. and Canadian systems is that in Canada most of the funds for health care come from a single source. Because hospital budgets are set in advance by the Canadian government, it is very difficult for hospital administrators, physicians, or patients to spend more than has been budgeted. In addition, Canada has a significantly lower ratio of specialists to general practitioners than the United States has. In the United States, the large number of surgeons and other specialists order a large number of procedures and experience a low average workload.

Canadians receive fewer health services than Americans, yet there is no discernible difference in the infant-mortality and life-expectancy statistics of the two nations. Do Americans enjoy the diversity, the extra services, and the choice that they pay extra for even if there are no discernible differences in measures of health? For instance, the average stay in a hospital is shorter in the United States than it is in Canada, but the tests and procedures are more numerous. Would Canadians pay more for a shorter stay and more tests and procedures if they had the choice? If the answer to these questions is *no*, can we say that the system in the United States is less desirable than the system in Canada?

3.e. Do the Laws of Economics Apply to Health Care?

The explosion of health-care costs and the emergence of health care as a central issue in the administration of Bill Clinton has led many people to claim that, or act as if, health care is different, that the laws of economics do not apply to it.[3] People tend to look at health care as a "right," something everyone is entitled to regardless of costs. During the 1993 hearings on health-care reform, Hillary Clinton's task force received nearly 100,000 letters from citizens. Most carried the tone of a letter from Mrs. Milford Gray, 72, who described how Medicare and private insurers paid only a portion of the costs for treatment of her husband's irregular heartbeat. Mrs. Gray stated that she and her husband should not have had to pay for any of the treatment and should have received the best treatment available.[4] What does it mean to say that the laws of economics have been repealed or do not apply in the case of medical care?

Consider first whether there is a market for health care. Is the product, health care, a scarce good? The answer is a clear *yes*; at a zero price more people want health care than there is health care available, the definition of a scarce good. Scarcity means that choices must be made, that there is an opportunity cost for choosing to purchase the scarce good. The choice is made on the basis of rational self-interest. These principles of economics suggest that health care is an economic good and subject to the laws of economics.

The demand curve for medical care looks like any other demand curve; it slopes down because the higher the price, the lower the quantity demanded. The demand curve is probably quite inelastic, but it does slope downward due to diminishing marginal utility. There also is a standard-looking supply curve. Physicians, hospitals, and medical firms offer an increasing quantity of medical care for sale as the price rises. As shown in Figures 8 and 9 and repeated in Figure 12, the demand and supply curves look no different than the curves representing a market in any other economic good.

In Figure 12, the price for medical care is the level at which the demand and supply curves intersect, the point of equilibrium. At price P_1, the quantity of medical care demanded is equal to the quantity supplied. Those people willing and able to pay price P_1 (all those lying along the demand curve from A to B) get the medical care. Those not willing and able to pay the price (all those lying along the demand curve from B to C) do not get the health care.

The problems that arise in the health-care market are due not to a repeal of the laws of economics but instead to the nature of the product. People believe they and others have an inalienable right to medical care, that it is not right to ignore those people making up the demand curve from B to C. As a result, government programs to provide medical insurance have been created. These programs, along with private insurance programs, mean that most of the payments for medical care are made by third parties, as described earlier in this chapter. The third-party payment system allows many of those who would not be willing and able to purchase the health care, those lying along the demand curve from B to C, to be able to purchase the care. This shifts the

"Repealing the laws of economics" in the case of health care means that the demand for and supply of health care do not determine the price or quantity, and not just those willing and able to pay get the care.

[3]David Wessel and Walt Bogdanich, "Laws of Economics Often Don't Apply in Health Care Field," *Wall Street Journal,* Jan. 22, 1992, p. A1; Nora C. O'Malley, "Age-Based Rationing of Health Care: A Descriptive Study of Professional Attitudes," *Health Care Management Review* 16(1), 1991, pp. 83–93; Horace B. Deets, Executive Director, American Association of Retired Persons, "Health Care Is Not a Commodity," Letters to the Editor, *Wall Street Journal*, Nov. 23, 1993.

[4]"'Dear Hillary': Letters Clamor for Health Reform," by Les Bowman, Scripps Howard, April 7, 1993, *Arizona Republic*, p. A1.

Figure 12
Do the Laws of Economics Apply to Health Care?

The price of medical care is the level at which the demand and supply curves intersect, the point of equilibrium. At price P_1, the quantity of medical care demanded is equal to the quantity supplied. Those people willing and able to pay price P_1 (all those lying along demand curve D_1 from A to B) get the medical care. Those not willing and able to pay the price (all those lying along the demand curve from B to C) do not get the health care.

The third-party payment system allows many who would not be willing and able to purchase the health care (those lying along the demand curve from B to C) to be able to purchase the care. This shifts the demand curve out, which drives health-care costs up, as shown by the shift in the demand curve from D_1 to D_2.

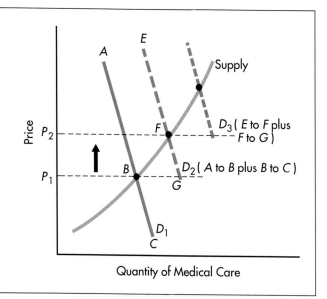

demand curve out, which drives health-care costs up, as shown by the shift from D_1 to D_2 in Figure 12.

The government and private insurance programs thus face ever-rising health-care costs: each new equilibrium means some are unable to afford the care; if their demand is covered, the demand curve shifts out again, to D_3. One attempt to limit these increases in the United States is known as "managed competition."

managed competition:
government intervention in the health-care market to guide competition so that costs are reduced

Managed competition is a general term that includes many possible scenarios. In most cases, it refers to the use of large buying groups to purchase medical care and pharmaceuticals, thereby using monopsony power to force lower prices. The Canadian system, wherein each province has control over the hospital and medical care budgets, is an example of the monopsony approach. The large buyer, the provincial government, purchases services for the citizens in the province. Each citizen alone could not negotiate lower prices, but all citizens together can. This gives the provincial government the power to demand lower prices. In addition to increasing the buyer power of health care consumers, the aim of managed competition is to make employees and employers more cost conscious in their choice of insurance coverage. Employees will purchase their health services not from fee-for-service providers who have no incentive to control costs, but from health maintenance organizations (HMOs) and other forms of managed care who have an incentive to minimize costs. And Medicare will provide payments for HMOs but not for the fee-for-service providers; thus, people may have to forgo their "own" doctor in order to obtain government-provided health care. Along with the idea of managed competition are ways to limit the expenditures by government on health care through "global budgets." A global budget refers to the total amount the government would spend on health care. The budget would be determined by the federal government. It would allocate a set sum to Medicare expenditures, thereby forcing all health care providers to live within the budget. The hope is that this would avoid the problem of the current reimbursement of expenses approach whereby expenditures continue rising because expenses continue rising.

With a limit on expenditures and with managed competition, health care in the United States would change. One result of the government's reform of the health care system will be a different kind of rationing. In markets, including the health care market where prices serve as the allocating device, rationing according to those willing and able to pay results. With managed competition will come other rationing schemes. Non-price rationing (usually referred to as "rationing") of any good occurs when the price system is not allowed to work. In the market for apartments, in the case of interest rates, and in medical care, rationing occurs when a price ceiling is imposed below the equilibrium price. For instance, Figure 13 represents two markets for medical care. Part (a) represents the market for "basic" medical care; part (b) is the market for high technology medical care. The health-care systems of Canada and Europe and the system proposed by many for the United States place a price ceiling in the market for basic medical care and then refuse to provide government payment for the high-technology medical care. The result is a shortage in the market for basic medical care; quantity demanded exceeds quantity supplied at the price ceiling, P_m. With an excess demand, and with a restricted price, something other than price must allocate the basic medical services. Typically it is waiting times, lines, or delays of weeks or months before getting an appointment that works to ration the scarce good.

Figure 13
Rationing
Two markets for medical care are shown. Part (a) represents the market for "basic" medical care; part (b) is the market for high-technology medical care. The health-care systems of Canada and Europe and the system proposed by many for the United States place a price ceiling in the market for basic medical care and then refuse to provide government payment for high-technology medical care. The result is an excess demand in the market for basic medical care: D exceeds S at the price ceiling, P_m. With an excess demand, and with a restricted price, something other than price must allocate the basic medical services.

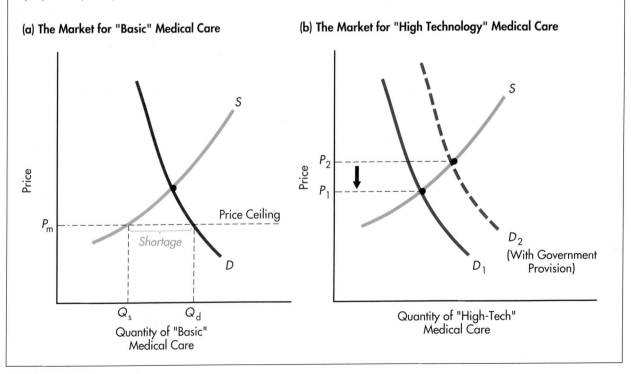

(a) The Market for "Basic" Medical Care

(b) The Market for "High Technology" Medical Care

In the market for the high-technology medical care, the refusal of government to subsidize or pay for services means that the demand for such medical care will be lower and the price lower than would be the case if the government provided those services (compare P_2 with P_1). But, only those willing and able to pay for the high-technology medical care (those represented along D_1 above the price) would get the care; those not willing or able to pay would not get it. The result is that many older people will be unable to get the life-saving, high-tech medical care they need to stay alive. This *age-based rationing* will occur because it is the elderly who constitute the major portion of the demand for high-tech medical care.

Rationing of one kind or another is inevitable with a scarce good. For the vast majority of goods, people have chosen rationing by price. Many people have difficulty applying that same choice to medical care. The question that must be answered is whether rationing by price is better or worse than rationing by some other criterion.

RECAP

1. Health care is the fastest-growing portion of total national expenditures. It is rising primarily because of the rising cost of physician services, nursing homes, and hospital services.

2. The demand for medical care has risen at a very rapid rate. One reason for the increase is the introduction of Medicare and Medicaid and private insurance plans that make demand relatively inelastic. The aging of the population has also increased the demand for medical care.

3. The cost of providing medical care has risen because of increases in hospital costs and physicians' fees. Rising hospital costs are partly a result of the reimbursement plans of third-party providers and partly a result of the control of the operation of hospitals by physicians.

4. Physicians' fees have risen even though the supply of physicians has risen. The demand for medical services does not match the supply; reimbursement methods have led to higher rates of return in certain specialties and thus have drawn an increasing number of physicians to those specialties.

5. In some nations, nearly all medical care is provided by the government; in others, most medical care is purchased by patients. In all, the scarce good, health care, must be rationed, either by price or by some other mechanism.

6. The laws of economics do apply to the medical arena. The difficulty is that people do not like the outcome of those laws.

SUMMARY

▲▼ *Why is the U.S. population aging?*

1. The U.S. population is aging because the number of births has declined while people are living longer than they used to.
§§ Preview, 1.b

▲▼ *What does it mean to say that there is a market for children?*

2. Children are demanded either because they provide utility to the parents or because they are a source of labor and pensions. The benefit

provided by each additional child declines (the demand curve slopes down). The cost of supplying children may decrease for the first few children, but it probably rises thereafter so that the supply curve slopes up. The number of children in a family is determined by demand and supply. The number has declined in recent decades as the cost of children has risen. §1.a

▲▼ **What is social security?**

3. Social security is a government-mandated pension fund. In the United States it is funded by a tax on employer and employee. The current tax collections are used to provide benefits to current retirees. §2.a

▲▼ **What accounts for the increasing percentage of expenditures allocated to health care?**

4. The rapidly rising costs of medical care result from increases in demand relative to supply. §3.a

5. The increasing demand results from the aging of the population and from payment systems that decrease the price elasticity of demand. §§3.b.1, 3.b.2

6. The reduced supply (higher costs of producing medical care) results from inefficiencies in the allocation of physicians among specialties and inefficiencies in the operation and organization of hospitals. §3.b.4

7. The health industry is changing in response to rapidly rising costs. Alternative methods of providing health care have arisen. HMOs and PPOs provide health care at a lower cost. §3.c

8. The percentage of income allocated to health care varies tremendously from country to country. The United States spends more per capita for health care than any other nation. The United States provides medical care through a combination of government programs (Medicare and Medicaid) and private purchases, insurance, and direct payments. Some nations have primarily government-provided systems; others have primarily private systems. §3.d

KEY TERMS

Medicare §3.a
Medicaid §3.a
prospective payment system (PPS) §3.b.4

health maintenance organization (HMO) §3.c
preferred provider organization (PPO) §3.c
managed competition §3.e

EXERCISES

1. Describe the market for children. Then answer the following questions.

   a. What is the demand and what is the supply in this market?

   b. What is the price in this market?

   c. What does the intersection of demand and supply mean? Who are the demanders? Who are the suppliers?

2. Explain the result of a law restricting families to only one child (such as exists in China).

3. What is social security? What is Medicare? What is the economic role of these government policies?

4. Why have medical-care expenditures risen more rapidly than expenditures on any other goods and services?

5. Explain how both the supply of physicians and physicians' fees can increase.

6. Why are there more medical specialists and fewer general practitioners in the United States than in Canada?

7. What is the economic logic of increasing social security benefits?

8. What does it mean to say people have a right to a specific good or service? Why do people believe they have a right to medical care but do not believe they have a right to a 3,000-square-foot house?

9. Suppose the objective of government policy is to increase an economy's growth and raise citizens' standards of living. Explain in this context the roles of retirement, social security, Medicare, and mandatory retirement.

10. Explain why the U.S. system of payment for medical procedures leads to higher health costs than a system of payment for physicians' services.

11. Analyze the following solutions to the problem of social security.

    a. The retirement age is increased to seventy.

    b. The FICA tax is increased.

    c. The income plus social security payments cannot exceed the poverty level.

    d. The total amount of social security benefits received cannot exceed the amount paid in by employer and employee plus the interest earnings on those amounts.

12. Oregon proposed a solution to the health costs problem that was widely criticized. The solution would allow the state to pay only for common medical problems. Special and expensive problems would not be covered. Using the market for medical care, analyze the Oregon plan.

13. What would be the impact of a policy that did away with Medicare and Medicaid and instead provided each individual with the amounts they contributed during their working lives to the Medicare program?

14. Why is a third-party payer a problem? Private insurance companies are third-party payers and yet they want to maximize profit. So wouldn't they ensure that the allocation of dollars was efficient?

15. "We must recognize that health care is not a commodity. Those with more resources should not be able to purchase services while those with less do without. Health care is a social good that should be available to every person without regard to his resources." Evaluate this statement.

Variety of Groups Criticize Oregon Health Care Plan

Oregon's health care rationing plan has plenty of opponents, despite widespread enthusiasm for its goal of extending basic health care to 420,000 Oregonians who have no medical coverage at all.

And those opponents, who range from an anti-abortion Catholic organization to an activist with acquired immune deficiency syndrome, are awaiting with some concern the federal government's decision on whether to approve Oregon's ambitious plan. . . .

Most opponents say they're worried that the plan will deliver something less than is promised. Many complain about the concept of rationing something as vital as health care.

Supporters of the plan say society already rations health care to poor people through manipulation of Medicaid eligibility requirements. When the state has more money to spend on Medicaid, it loosens the requirements, allowing more people to join the Medicaid rolls. When money is tight, the state cinches down those requirements, dropping poor people from Medicaid.

Under the Oregon Health Plan, the medical benefits of needy Oregonians would fluctuate depending on the amount of money available, but no one would lose coverage completely.

At the heart of the program is a prioritized list of 709 medical procedures. State officials say they have enough money to pay for Oregonians to receive the first 587 treatments on the list. But critics fear the list of covered procedures will shrink if the state runs out of health funds, if more people seek medical care more often than is expected or if the state has underestimated costs.

. . . The best-organized opposition in the state comes from the Oregon Catholic Conference.

Spokesman Bob Castagna says the conference fears the new plan would allow more poor women to obtain abortions.

"We don't like the increased number of state-financed abortions," Castagna said. "It's reasonable to assume that, if you increase the number of participants, the number of abortions will go up." . . .

Castagna said that while he doesn't endorse the current Medicaid system, he can't justify replacing it with a system he believes is worse.

"It's inequitable," he said. "In periods of insufficient revenue, you place the burden of balancing the books on the state's poor. The providers aren't asked to contribute anything." . . .

Brad Buvinger, organizing director of Oregon Fair Share, which advocates universal medical care, said the plan "gives the illusion of universal access while protecting the profits of the medical industry. . . . It controls costs through limiting benefits and the freedom to choose physicians."

Buvinger said the grass-roots lobbying group he directs represents 60,000 families statewide on health care and tax issues.

Buvinger complains that the Oregon Health Plan stops short of guaranteeing basic health care. He calls it a "roadblock" to comprehensive health coverage, which would give everyone, rich and poor, equal access to medical care. . . .

Anita Hendrix, project coordinator for the Oregon Human Rights Coalition, said she believed the plan would abandon people who are seriously ill.

She said the coalition, which lobbies for the rights of low-income people, mistrusts the Oregon Health Plan.

"I have heard that they have really overbudgeted," she said. "My concern is that they may cut services if they can't afford what they've planned for."

Hendrix and other critics also are uncomfortable with the formula upon which the priority list was based. Creators of the list tried to calculate the worth of certain medical procedures by combining cost factors, success rates and indicators for the patient's subsequent quality of life.

"I do not think we are advanced enough as a society to decide who should get care and who should not," she said.

Source: Reprinted by permission of *The Oregonian.*

Oregonian/May 13, 1992

Commentary

The article is concerned with the Oregon plan to ration medical treatments. What does rationing mean and why is Oregon proposing to ration health care? The demand curve for medical care looks like any other demand curve; it slopes down because the higher the price, the lower the quantity demanded. There also is a standard looking supply curve; physicians, hospitals, and medical firms offer an increasing quantity of medical care for sale as the price rises.

The state of Oregon has attempted to provide medical care to people who are willing, but unable, to buy it. But, as medical-care costs have risen, the state of Oregon has found that it does not have enough money to pay for every eligible person's medical needs. Yet, it wants to ensure that poor people are provided basic medical needs. Thus, the state has proposed a rationing scheme based on the types of medical treatments.

In reality, rationing of a scarce good always occurs since wants and desires exceed the quantities available. In those cases where the market solves the scarcity problem, it is the price, and thus the willingness and ability to pay, that ration the scarce good. When the price is not allowed to serve as the rationing device some other means is devised. For instance, when a price ceiling is imposed below the equilibrium price, then the quantity demanded will exceed the quantity supplied and some means for allocating the quantity supplied to the larger quantity demanded must be devised. Placing a price ceiling, P_c, below P_1, shows that the quantity of health care demanded, Q_d, exceeds the quantity supplied, Q_s. More people want and, at price P_c, are willing and able to pay for health care than there is care available. Who then gets the care? The answer depends on how health care is rationed.

Under the Oregon plan, a list of 709 medical procedures was drawn up and prioritized. Oregon officials say they have enough money to pay for 587 of the procedures. Anyone needing one of the 587 and not able to pay for it will have the expense covered by the state. Anyone needing the 588th or 600th

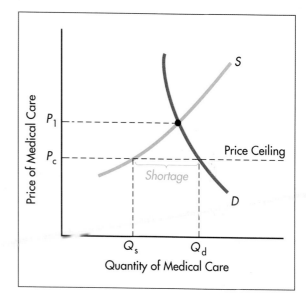

procedure and not able to pay for it will not be able to get the procedure.

The debate over the plan focuses not just on the fact that not everyone will be able to get every procedure, but also over the procedures included in the list of 587. Some groups oppose abortions, one of the 587 procedures. Others believe that procedures used to prolong life for the very aged should not be on the list. Still others do not support the procedures ensuring that very premature babies survive.

The rationing proposal also strikes fear into those who see an ever dwindling list of acceptable procedures. As state revenues decline or as medical procedures get more expensive, the list of 587 may be pared to 580 or 500 or less.

Rationing of one kind or another is inevitable with a scarce good. For the vast majority of goods people have chosen rationing by price. Many people have difficulty applying that same choice to medical care. The question that must be answered is whether rationing by price is better or worse than rationing by some other criterion.

20

Income Distribution, Poverty, and Government Policy

FUNDAMENTAL
QUESTIONS

1. Are incomes distributed equally in the United States?
2. How is poverty measured, and does poverty exist in the United States?
3. Who are the poor?
4. What are the determinants of income?
5. How does the government try to reduce poverty?

Half a million Americans will spend today living on city streets or in temporary shelters, and more than a million will do so over the next year. The trickle of men and "bag ladies" surviving on city streets a decade ago has become a steady stream—men, women, children, white, black, Hispanic, mentally healthy, mentally ill. "Homeless" used to describe people who were transient, poor, socially isolated, and living in the cheap hotels and flophouses on skid row. They had housing, but they didn't have homes. Today, the homeless are "houseless" too.

The homeless today are extraordinarily poor. Single homeless adults have less than $150 in reported monthly income excluding food stamps.[1] At the same time, the wealthiest *one-half of 1 percent* of households own more than 27 percent of the wealth, nearly $3 million per household, whereas the bottom 20 percent get only 5 percent of national income.

Even the poor in this country are better off than the entire populations of other nations. In Bolivia, the average life expectancy is only fifty-three years,

a full twenty years less than in the United States. In Burma, only about one-fourth of the population has access to safe water. In Burundi, less than one-fourth of the urban houses have electricity. In Chad, less than one-third of the children reach the sixth grade. In Ethiopia, the per capita income is $120, sixty times lower than in the United States.

What accounts for the inequality among nations and among households within a nation? Who are the poor and the rich? Is the inequality of incomes something that can or should be corrected? These questions are the topic of this chapter. Previous chapters have discussed how the market system works to ensure that resources flow to their highest-valued uses, that output is produced in the least-cost manner, and that people get what they want at the lowest possible price—in other words, the efficiency of the market system. Efficiency and equity do not necessarily go together, however. Efficiency implies that goods and services are allocated to those with the ability to pay, not necessarily to those with needs. Even something as vital as health care is not provided equally to all (as discussed in the previous chapter)—the rich can get better care than the poor.

---

[1]Gordon Berlin and William McAllister, "Homelessness," *The Brookings Review*, Fall 1993, p. 12.

I. INCOME DISTRIBUTION AND POVERTY

Are incomes distributed equally in the United States?

In a market system, incomes are distributed according to the ownership of resources. Those who own the most highly valued resources have the highest incomes. One consequence of a market system, therefore, is that incomes are distributed unequally.

I.a. A Measure of Income Inequality

Lorenz curve:
a curve measuring the degree of inequality of income distribution within a society

In the United States, as in every country, there are rich and there are poor. If there were no distinctions between rich and poor—that is, if everyone had the same income—then income would be distributed equally. Incomes are not distributed equally, however, and the degree of inequality varies widely from country to country. In order to compare income distributions, economists need a measure of income inequality. The most widely used measure is the **Lorenz curve**, which provides a picture of how income is distributed among members of a population.

Equal incomes among members of a population can be plotted as a 45-degree line that is equidistant from the axes (see Figure 1). The horizontal axis measures the total population in cumulative percentages. As we move along the horizontal axis, we are counting a larger and larger percentage of the population. The numbers end at 100, which designates 100 percent of the population. The vertical axis measures total national income in cumulative percentages. As we move up the vertical axis, the percentage of total national income being counted rises to 100 percent. The 45-degree line splitting the distance between the axes is called the *line of income equality*. At each point

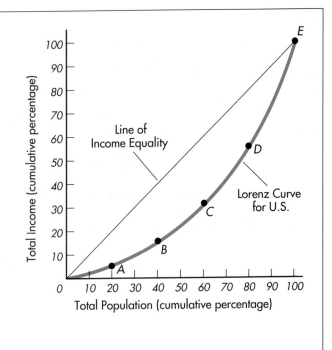

Figure 1
The U.S. Lorenz Curve
   The farther a Lorenz curve lies from the line of income equality, the greater the inequality of the income distribution. The bottom 20 percent of the U.S. population has 4.6 percent of total national income, seen at point A. The second 20 percent accounts for another 10.6 percent of national income, shown as point B, where the bottom 40 percent of the population has 15.2 percent of the national income (4.6 percent owned by the first 20 percent of the population plus the additional 10.6 percent owned by the second 20 percent). The third 20 percent accounts for another 16.5 percent of national income, so point C is plotted at a population of 60 percent and an income of 31.7 percent. The fourth 20 percent accounts for another 23.7 percent of the national income, shown as point D, where 80 percent of the population owns 55.4 percent of the income. The richest 20 percent accounts for the remaining 44.6 percent of national income, shown as point E. With the last 20 percent of the population and the last 44.6 percent of national income, 100 percent of population and 100 percent of national income are accounted for. Point E, therefore, is plotted where both income and population are 100 percent. Source: World Bank, *World Development Report, 1992* (New York: Oxford University Press), Table 30.

on the line, the percentage of total population and the percentage of total national income are equal. The line of income equality indicates that 10 percent of the population earns 10 percent of the income, 20 percent of the population earns 20 percent of the income, and so on, until we see that 90 percent of the population earns 90 percent of the income and 100 percent of the population earns 100 percent of the income.

Points off the line of income equality indicate an income distribution that is unequal. Figure 1 shows the line of income equality and a curve that bows down below the income-equality line. The bowed curve is a Lorenz curve. The Lorenz curve in Figure 1 is for the United States. The bottom 20 percent of the population has 4.6 percent of total national income, seen at point *A*. The second 20 percent accounts for another 10.6 percent of national income, shown as point *B*, so the bottom 40 percent of the population has 15.2 percent of the national income (4.6 percent owned by the first 20 percent of the population plus the additional 10.6 percent owned by the second 20 percent). The third 20 percent accounts for another 16.5 percent of national income, so point *C* is plotted at a population of 60 percent and an income of 31.7 percent. The fourth 20 percent accounts for another 23.7 percent of the national income, shown as point *D*, where 80 percent of the population owns 55.4 percent of the income. The richest 20 percent accounts for the remaining 44.6 percent of national income, shown as point *E*, With the last 20 percent of the population and the last 44.6 percent of national income, 100 percent of population and 100 percent of national income are accounted for. Point *E*, therefore, is plotted where both income and population are 100 percent.[2]

The farther the Lorenz curve bows down, away from the line of income equality, the greater the inequality of the distribution of income. In Chapter 4 it was noted that on average, in developed countries, the richest 20 percent of households receive about 40 percent of household income and the poorest 20 percent receive only about 5 or 6 percent of household income. That distribution, however, is much more equal than the distribution found in less developed countries. The most unequal distribution of income is found in less developed countries: the richest 20 percent of the population receives more than 50 percent of total household income, and the poorest 20 percent receives less than 4 percent of total household income—although, as discussed in the Economic Insight "Income Inequality in the Former Soviet Union," the income distribution in nonmarket economies is difficult to measure. Figure 2 shows two Lorenz curves, one for the United States and one for Mexico. The curve for Mexico bows down far below the curve for the United States, indicating the greater inequality in Mexico.

I.b. Income Distribution Among Nations

Incomes differ greatly from one nation to another as well as within nations. The per capita annual income in Mexico is $2,470, while in the United States it exceeds $21,990. Mexico's income distribution is less equal than in the

---

[2]A Lorenz curve for wealth could also be shown. It would bow down below the Lorenz curve for income, indicating that wealth is more unequally distributed than income. Since data on the distribution of wealth are difficult and costly to obtain, the latest information available is for 1973. Thus, it is not included with the income data. Wealth and income are different and should be kept distinct. *Wealth* refers to nonhuman capital. *Income* refers to payments for human and nonhuman capital and for other resources. Wealth is the stock of assets. Income is the flow of earnings that results from the stock of assets.

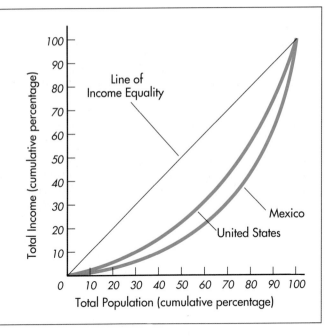

Figure 2
Lorenz Curves for Mexico and the United States
Based on data for the United States and Mexico, the two Lorenz curves show that total national income in Mexico is distributed among Mexican citizens much more unequally than total national income in the United States is distributed among citizens of the United States. Source: World Bank, *World Development Report, 1992* (New York: Oxford University Press), Table 30.

United States, but income levels in Mexico are also significantly lower than in the United States. Figure 3 shows the per capita incomes of several countries. The figure illustrates how great the differences in per capita income are. The Economic Insight "Economic Development and Happiness" suggests that the feeling of well-being of a population generally depends on the levels of per capita income.

The distribution of total world income among nations is very unequal, as shown in Figure 4. Three-fourths of the world's population lives in developing countries, but the income earned by the people in these countries—the

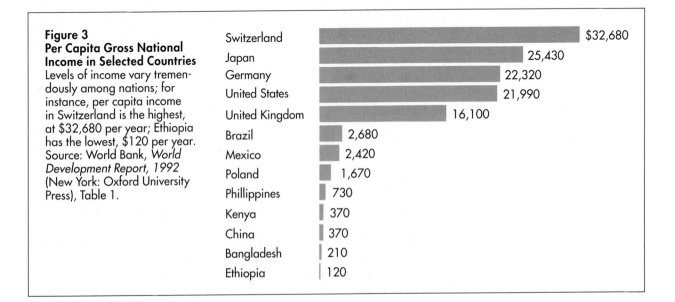

Figure 3
Per Capita Gross National Income in Selected Countries
Levels of income vary tremendously among nations; for instance, per capita income in Switzerland is the highest, at $32,680 per year; Ethiopia has the lowest, $120 per year. Source: World Bank, *World Development Report, 1992* (New York: Oxford University Press), Table 1.

Switzerland	$32,680
Japan	25,430
Germany	22,320
United States	21,990
United Kingdom	16,100
Brazil	2,680
Mexico	2,420
Poland	1,670
Phillippines	730
Kenya	370
China	370
Bangladesh	210
Ethiopia	120

Figure 4
World Lorenz Curve
The Lorenz curve is typically used to illustrate the income distribution within countries. In this figure a Lorenz curve is drawn to compare how world income is distributed across countries. The bottom 90 percent of the world's population, residing in the less developed countries, accounts for 20 percent of the world's income, shown as point A. The richest 10 percent of the population, residing in the developed countries, accounts for 80 percent of total income, shown as point B. Source: World Bank, *World Development Report, 1992* (New York: Oxford University Press), Table 30.

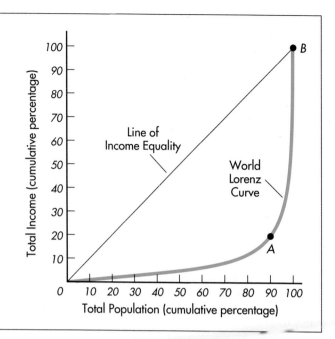

lowest 90 percent of the population in terms of income—is only about 20 percent of the total world income, shown as point A. The richest countries, earning nearly 80 percent of total world income, have only 10 percent of the world's population, the difference between A and B.

1.c. Measuring Poverty

How is poverty measured, and does poverty exist in the United States?

A Lorenz curve does not indicate who the poor are or what their quality of life is. It is a relative measure. On the other hand, an absolute measure such as per capita income does not necessarily indicate how people feel about their income status nor whether they enjoy good health and a decent standard of living. Those who are comfortable in one country could be impoverished in another. The poverty level in the United States would represent a substantial increase in living standards in many other nations. Yet members of a poor family in the United States would probably not feel less poor if they knew that their income level exceeds the median income in other countries.

1.d. The Definition of Poverty

If income or per capita income is to be used as a measure of poverty, then the proper definition of *income* must be used. Economists can measure income before any government intervention affecting the distribution of income, after accounting for government cash transfers, or after accounting for government cash transfers and assistance like food or shelter.

The first of these measurements indicates what people would earn from the market system in the absence of government intervention. To obtain a good measure of this income figure is virtually impossible because the government is such an important part of the economic system in almost all countries, including the United States. The U.S. government transfers over $400 billion annually from taxpayers to various groups.

Income Inequality in the Former Soviet Union

One of the arguments used in support of socialism is income equality. Under socialism, a significant amount of the private sector is replaced by the government sector, and the inequity that exists in market systems is supposed to be eradicated. Income distribution in the socialist countries, thus, was always a question of major interest. Unfortunately, the data necessary to measure the distribution of income are not widely available. Nevertheless, scholars have been able to provide a picture of income distribution in the former Soviet Union—and that picture is *not* one of equality. The general consensus is that the distribution of income in the former Soviet Union was less equal than in Sweden or Norway and more like that of the United Kingdom.

The U.S.S.R. suffered from a chronic shortage of consumer goods throughout its history. This meant that Soviet citizens with high incomes did not necessarily enjoy access to the consumer goods that did exist. On the other hand, those with relatively modest incomes often enjoyed high standards of living because they were allowed access to the goods and services

provided to only a few by the government.

A small percentage of the Soviet population lived in a way that would be classified as middle class by Western Europe or the United States: owning a house or apartment, appliances, furniture, a car, and perhaps a summer cabin or residence. The percentage of the U.S. population with this living standard lies somewhere between 50 and 70 percent. Only 11 percent of the Soviet population enjoyed this kind of living standard prior to the dissolution of the union. As in other countries, there was a group of superrich in the Soviet Union who lived extremely well, with several residences, cars, and other goods. This group consisted primarily of the political elite, high-ranking scientists, athletes, artists, and diplomats.

A study by the Soviet agency Pravda found that families of local party and state officials in one of the central Russian regions consumed between 56 percent and 100 percent of all the high-quality food in their region even though they represented less than 1 percent of the population. These inequities were not offset by gener-

ous transfers to the unfortunate either. Welfare expenditures accounted for only 20 percent of Soviet GNP compared to over 28 percent in the United States. Moreover, the Soviet welfare system benefited the Soviet elite. They enjoyed the best of the free health care, the best of the subsidized recreation facilities, and the best free schools and colleges. The wealthy class was able to take advantage of retirement benefits as well; the average state pension was only 84 rubles a month, while retired members of the elite received pensions of up to 500 rubles a month.

In 1987, the wealth of the lucky 75,000 belonging to the elite was somewhere between 100 and 1,000 times greater than the wealth of the poorest pensioners.

Sources: Andrei Kuteinikov, "Soviet Society—Much More Unequal Than U.S.," *Wall Street Journal*, Jan. 26, 1990, p. A14; Abram Bergson, *Planning and Performance in Socialist Economies* (Boston: Unwin Hyman, 1989), pp. 55–102; Peter J. D. Wiles, *Distribution of Income: East and West* (New York: American Elsevier, 1974).

cash transfers:
money allocated away from one group in society to another

in-kind transfers:
the allocation of goods and services from one group in society to another

Poverty statistics published by the federal government are based on incomes that include earnings from cash transfers but often not in-kind transfers. **Cash transfers** are unearned funds given to certain sectors of the population. They include social security retirement benefits, disability pensions, and unemployment compensation to those who are temporarily out of work. **In-kind transfers**, or noncash transfers, are services or products provided to certain sectors of society. They include food purchased with food stamps and medical services provided under Medicaid. Although economists agree that these in-kind transfers increase the economic well-being of those who receive them, there is much debate over how they should be accounted for and the extent to which they should be added to money income for the purpose of defining *poverty*. For example, the official poverty rate measure

TABLE I

Average Income Poverty Cutoffs for a Nonfarm Family of Four in the United States, 1959–1992

Year	Poverty Level	Year	Poverty Level
1959	$2,973	1982	$ 9,862
1960	3,022	1983	10,178
1966	3,317	1984	10,609
1969	3,743	1985	10,989
1970	3,968	1986	11,203
1975	5,500	1987	11,611
1976	5,815	1988	12,090
1977	6,191	1989	12,675
1978	6,662	1990	13,359
1979	7,412	1991	13,924
1980	8,414	1992	13,950
1981	9,287		

Sources: U.S. Bureau of the Census, *Current Population Reports*, series P-60, no. 174 (Washington, D.C.: U.S. Government Printing Office, 1992); *Social Security Bulletin*, Spring 1992.

does not account for in-kind transfers. If it did, the 1990 rate of 13.5 percent of the U.S. population who are in poverty would have been 11.0 percent.[3]

The U.S. government uses after-transfers income to measure poverty, but does not include all such transfers. It adds market earnings, the cash equivalent of noncash transfers, and cash transfers to calculate family incomes. But it does not include food stamps, aid to families with dependent children (AFDC), or housing subsidies. In sum, the poverty measure is arbitrary. It is an arbitrary level of income, and income is an arbitrary measure of the ability to purchase necessities.

Table 1 lists the average poverty levels of income for a nonfarm family of four since 1959. Families with incomes above the cutoffs would be above the poverty level, in the eyes of the federal government.

Where does the arbitrary poverty income level come from? A 1955 study found that the average family in the United States spent about one-third of its income on food, so when the government decided to begin measuring poverty in the 1960s, it calculated the cost to purchase a meal that met a predetermined nutritional standard and multiplied that cost by 3. That is where it drew the poverty line. Since then, the official poverty-line income has been adjusted for inflation each year. In 1992, a family of four whose income, measured as noted above, fell below $13,950 was defined as being in poverty.

1.e. Poverty Distribution and Economic Trends

How many Americans fall below the poverty line? In 1992, more than 36 million U.S. residents received incomes that were lower than the cutoff. As

---
[3]*Economic Report of the President, 1992*, p. 143.

Incomes are unequally distributed in every nation. In less developed nations, the distinction between rich and poor is greater than in the industrial nations, although the per capita income is significantly less in the LDCs. For instance, although the per capita income in Nigeria is only seven percent of the per capita income in the United States, the wealthy in Lagos, Nigeria live very well, with large houses, servants, expensive clothes, and other accouterments of wealth. During the 1970s, many Nigerians became very wealthy as the price of oil surged and Nigerian oil production rose. Economic crisis and the collapse of oil prices since the late 1970s has led to a decline in Nigeria that wiped out the gains of the previous twenty years.

The health of the economy is a primary determinant of the incidence of poverty.

large as this number is, the incidence of poverty in the United States has declined since 1960, when poverty information was first collected. Figure 5 compares the number of people living in poverty and the percentage of the total population living in poverty for each year from 1960 to 1991. From 1960 to the late 1970s, the incidence of poverty declined rapidly. From the late 1970s until the early 1980s, the incidence of poverty rose; it then began to decline again after 1982. Small upswings in the incidence of poverty occurred in 1968 and 1974, and a large rise occurred between 1978 and 1982. The poverty rate then fell until 1990, when the U.S. once again dipped into recession.

A major factor accounting for the incidence of poverty is the health of the economy. The economy grew at a fairly sustained rate between 1960 and 1969 and from 1982 through 1990. During both growth periods, the poverty rate fell.

People are made better off by economic growth. Economic stagnation and recession throw the relatively poor out of their jobs and into poverty. Economic growth increases the number of jobs and draws people out of poverty and into the mainstream of economic progress.

Four recent recessions have had important impacts on the numbers of people thrown into poverty. The recession of 1969–1970 was relatively mild. Between 1969 and 1971, the unemployment rate rose from 3.4 to 5.8 percent, and the total number of people unemployed rose from 2,832,000 to 5,016,000. This recession halted the decline in poverty rates for two years. When the economy once again began to expand, the poverty rates dropped. The 1974 recession brought on another bout of unemployment that threw people into poverty. The 1974 recession was relatively serious, causing the unemployment rate to rise to 8.3 percent by 1975 and the number of unemployed to rise to 7,929,000. Once again, however, the poverty rate declined as the economy picked up after 1975. The recession of 1980–1982 threw the economy off track again. In 1979, the total number of people unemployed

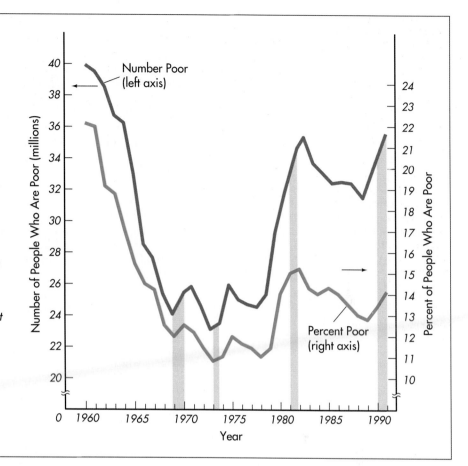

Figure 5
The Trends of Poverty Incidence
The number of people classified as living in poverty is measured on the left vertical axis. The percentage of the population classified as living in poverty is measured on the right vertical axis. The number and the percentage declined steadily throughout the 1960s, rose during the recessions of 1969, 1974, 1981, and 1990 and fell during the economic growth between 1982 and 1990. Sources: U.S. Bureau of the Census, *Current Population Reports*, series P-60, no. 161 (Washington, D.C.: U.S. Government Printing Office, 1988, 1991); *Economic Report of the President, 1992.*

was 6,137,000; by 1982, a whopping 10,717,000 were without jobs. As the economy came out of this recession, the poverty rate began to decline, and it continued to decline as the economy grew throughout the 1980s. However, the poverty rate rose as the economy fell into recession in 1990 and struggled into 1992. The poverty rate of 14.2 percent in 1991 was the highest level in nearly three decades; the number of people living in poverty grew to 35.7 million, the highest since 1964.[4]

RECAP

1. The Lorenz curve shows the degree to which incomes are distributed equally in a society.

2. The Lorenz curve bows down below the line of equality for all nations. It is less bowed for developed nations than for less developed countries, because income is more equally distributed in developed than in less developed nations.

[4]U.S. Bureau of the Census, *Statistical Abstract of the United States, 1991* (Washington, D.C.: U.S. Government Printing Office, 1991).

Economic Development and Happiness

A nation's standard of living influences the attitudes of the nation's population toward life in general, although it is not the only factor. Year after year, the Danes, Swiss, Irish, and Dutch feel happier and more satisfied with life than do the French, Greeks, Italians, and Germans. Regardless of whether they are German-, French-, or Italian-speaking, the Swiss rank very high on life satisfaction— much higher than their German, French, and Italian neighbors. People in the Scandinavian countries generally are both prosperous and happy. However, the link between national affluence and well-being isn't consistent. Germans, for instance, average more than double the per capita income of the Irish, but the Irish are happier. Similarly, although the developed nations all had higher per capita incomes than the Mexicans, the Mexicans stated a higher satisfaction with life than the populations of many of the developed nations. The overall pattern does show that wealthier nations tend to show higher levels of life satisfaction than poorer ones, but income and wealth are not the only factors influencing happiness. Related to wealth is the type of government under which citizens live. The most prosperous nations have enjoyed stable democratic governments, and there is a link between a history of stable democracy and national well-being. The thirteen nations that have maintained democratic institutions continuously since 1920 all enjoy higher life satisfaction levels than do the eleven nations whose democracies developed after World War II.

Sources: Ronald Inglehart, *Culture Shift in Advanced Industrial Society* (Princeton: Princeton University Press, 1990); David G. Myers, *The Pursuit of Happiness* (New York: William Morrow and Company, Inc., 1992).

3. There are two ways to measure poverty: with an absolute measure and with a relative measure. The Lorenz curve is a relative measure. Per capita income is an absolute measure.

4. Per capita income is used by the U.S. government to define poverty. Income after cash and in-kind transfers is per capita income.

5. Recessions increase the incidence of poverty; economic growth reduces the incidence of poverty.

2. THE POOR

Who are the poor?

Poverty is not a condition that randomly strikes women and men and white, black, and Hispanic families equally. Nor does it strike the educated and well trained in the same way it strikes the uneducated. The incidence of poverty itself is unequally distributed among sectors of the society.

2.a. Temporary and Permanent Poverty

If those who are poor at any one time are poor only temporarily, then their plight is only temporary. If people in poverty are able to improve their situation while others slip into poverty temporarily, the problem of poverty for society is not as serious as it is if poverty is a permanent condition once a person has slipped into it.

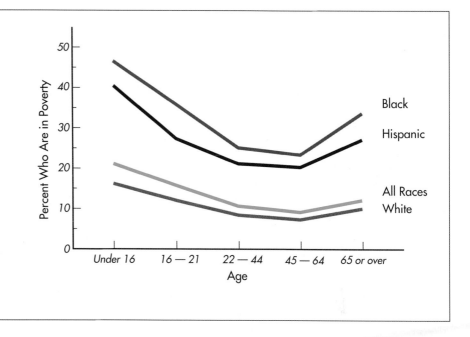

**Figure 6
Age, Race, Hispanic Origin, and Poverty**
The young and old constitute most of the poverty group: 22.8 percent of the children under age six live in poverty, as do 19.4 percent of the children between ages six and seventeen. And 12.2 percent of people sixty-five or older also live in poverty. The poverty rate among whites is 10.5 percent; among blacks, 33.1 percent, and among Hispanics, 28.2 percent. Source: U.S. Bureau of the Census, *Current Population Reports* (Washington, D.C.: U.S. Government Printing Office, 1988, 1991).

Poverty does not affect races, sexes , or different age groups equally.

Studies indicate that approximately 25 percent of all Americans fall below the poverty line at some time in their lives. Many of these spells of poverty are relatively short; nearly 45 percent last less than a year. However, more than 50 percent of those in poverty at a particular time remain in poverty for at least ten years.[5]

One major determinant of an individual's income is age. A young person or a senior citizen has a much greater chance of suffering a low income than a person who is between thirty and sixty years old. Figure 6 shows the percentage of the population below the poverty level by race and age in 1991. The highest incidence of poverty by age occurs among those under sixteen years. The second highest occurs among those between sixteen and twenty-one. The third highest occurs among those sixty-five years and older.

Poverty does not affect all racial and all age groups equally. As Figure 7 shows, the percentages of the population of different groups that fall below the poverty level each year are not equal. Blacks and Hispanics carry a much heavier burden of poverty relative to the size of their populations than do whites. A growing economy helps all groups but helps whites more than it helps the others. A recession harms all groups but harms whites less than it harms other groups. It appears from these data that blacks and Hispanics have less opportunity to break out of poverty than do whites.

Poverty does not affect males and females equally either. Approximately 35 percent of all families headed by a female have poverty-level incomes.

---

[5]Mary Jo Bane and David T. Ellwood, "Slipping into and out of Poverty," *Journal of Human Resources* 21, no. 1 (Winter 1986), pp. 1–23.

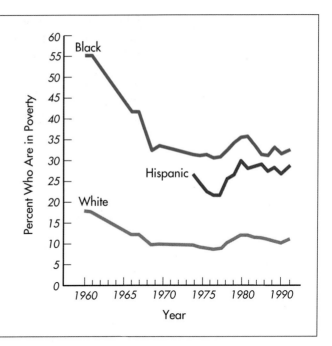

Figure 7
The Incidence of Poverty by Race and Hispanic Origin
The incidence of poverty is higher for blacks and Hispanics than it is for whites. Good times help whites more than they help other races, and bad times harm whites less than they harm other races. Sources: U.S. Bureau of the Census, *Current Population Reports* (Washington, D.C.: U.S. Government Printing Office, 1988, 1991); U.S. Department of Commerce, *Statistical Abstract of the United States, 1991.*

Only 8 percent of all families headed by a male have incomes so low. More than 55 percent of households with a female head and children are living in poverty.

2.b. Causes of Poverty

What are the determinants of income?

The primary characteristic of those who fall below the poverty line is the lack of a job.

The less education a person has, the greater his or her chance of experiencing poverty.

The primary characteristic of those who fall below the poverty line is the lack of a job. In 1991, almost half of all such households were headed by people sixty-five years of age and over. Another 12 percent were headed by disabled people. Another 7 percent of such households were headed by women with children under six. Nonworking students constituted 5 percent of the poverty group. Thus, those not working accounted for nearly three-fourths of the poverty group.

People who fall below the poverty line may have jobs but work less than full time, or their jobs may pay so little that their income does not exceed the poverty cutoff. For instance, a job paying $4.65 per hour for 40 hours a week and 50 weeks a year yields an income of $9,300, fully $2,000 below the poverty level.

Place of residence also affects a person's ability to earn income. A little over half of the poor live in big cities, where they tend to be concentrated downtown. The remainder live in rural areas.

The less education an individual has, the lower the income that individual earns. The less education an individual has, the greater the chance that individual will experience poverty. A significant percentage of those in poverty have less than eight years of education. Fully 25 percent of the people with less than eight years of education fall below the poverty level of income. Only 4 percent of those with one year or more of college fall below the poverty cutoff. Lack of education prevents people from securing well-paying jobs. Without the human capital obtained from education or training programs, finding a job that is stable and will not disappear during a recession is very difficult. Even someone who has the desire to work but has no exceptional abilities and has not acquired the skills necessary for a well-paying job is unlikely to escape poverty completely. Minorities and women, the young, the disabled, and the old have disproportionately less education than the rest of the population and as a result have a higher likelihood of falling into poverty.

RECAP

1. Many people experience poverty only temporarily. Nearly 45 percent of the spells of poverty last less than a year. However, nearly 50 percent of those in poverty remain there for at least ten years.
2. The highest incidences of poverty occur among those who are under twenty-one or over sixty-five.
3. The incidence of poverty is much higher among blacks and Hispanics than it is among whites.
4. A poor person may be poor because of age, lack of a job, lack of education, or place of residence.

3. GOVERNMENT ANTIPOVERTY POLICIES

How does the government try to reduce poverty?

Why are economists and others concerned with income inequality and poverty? One reason might be normative. People might have compassion for those who have less than they do, or people might not like to see the squalid living conditions endured by some in poverty. In other words, the existence of poverty may mean lower levels of utility for members of society not in poverty. If increases in poverty mean decreases in utility, then people will want less poverty. They will be willing and able to purchase less poverty by allocating portions of their income or their time to alleviating the problem.

Another reason for concern about income inequality and poverty might be positive, or not dependent on value judgments. Perhaps the inequality is a result of inefficiency, and a correction of the situation that creates the inefficiency will improve the functioning of the economy. For instance, if inequality is partly the result of a market failure (see the next chapter for a full discussion of externalities and market failures), then the economic system will function more efficiently after the market failure is corrected. If education provides benefits for society that are not taken into account in individual decisions to acquire education, for example, then too few people acquire education. People who would have acquired education if the positive benefits for society had been subsidized, but did not, are wasted resources. These people would have earned more income; fewer would have fallen into poverty; and the distribution of income might have been more equal. In this sense, the number of people in poverty and the existence of income inequality provide indications that allocative efficiency has failed to occur.

The government is often called on to resolve market failures. If income inequality and poverty are the result of such failures, then the government plays a role in resolving the failures and thereby decreasing poverty and reducing income inequality. If poverty is distasteful to society, then citizens, by paying taxes and through their votes, may ask the government to reduce poverty. Whatever the rationale, positive or normative, the fact is that the government is involved in antipoverty programs and in the attempt to reduce income inequality. Having accepted this fact, several questions arise. For instance, is the government carrying out its antipoverty programs efficiently? What are the ramifications of the government programs? Have the programs reduced poverty?

Once levels of poverty and degrees of inequality are identified, the first question to be answered is whether to reallocate resources to reduce them. If resources are to be reallocated, the next question is how to reallocate them. Clearly, an important way to decrease poverty is by increasing the rate of growth of national income and avoiding recessions. The incidence of poverty declines during periods of economic growth and rises during recessionary periods. Government policies designed to stimulate economic growth over the short and long terms may be important weapons against poverty. Whether these policies are effective in reducing poverty, and the policies themselves, are the subject matter of macroeconomics. Another way to approach the poverty problem is through tax and transfer programs.

3.a. Tax Policy

One approach to reducing poverty is to provide people with enough income to bring them above the poverty level. Funds used to supplement the incomes of the poor must come from somewhere. Many societies adopt a Robin Hood approach, taxing the rich to give to the poor. Income taxes can influence income distribution through their impact on after-tax income. Taxes may be progressive, proportional, or regressive.

progressive income tax:
a tax whose rate increases as income increases

A **progressive income tax** is a tax that rises as income rises—the marginal tax rate increases as income increases. If someone with an annual income of $20,000 pays $5,000 in taxes while someone else with an annual income of $40,000 pays $12,000 in taxes, the tax rate is progressive. The first person is paying a 25 percent rate, and the second is paying a 30 percent rate.

proportional tax:
a tax whose rate does not change as the tax base changes

A **proportional tax** is a tax whose rate does not change as the tax base changes. The rate of a proportional income tax remains the same at every level of income. If the tax rate is 20 percent, then individuals who earn $10,000 or $100,000 pay 20 percent.

regressive tax:
a tax whose rate decreases as the tax base changes

A **regressive tax** is a tax whose rate decreases as the tax base changes. The social security tax is regressive; a specified rate is paid on income up to a specified level. On income beyond that level, no social security taxes are paid. In 1993, the cutoff level of income was nearly $58,000 and the tax rate was 7.65 percent. A person earning $300,000 paid no more social security taxes than someone earning $58,000.

A progressive tax rate tends to reduce income inequality; a proportional tax does not affect income distribution; and a regressive tax increases inequality. The progressive tax takes larger percentages of income from high-income members of society than it takes from low-income members. This tends to equalize after-tax incomes. In the United States, the federal income tax is progressive. The tax rate rises from zero to 36 percent as income rises (39 percent for incomes above $1 million).

3.b. Transfers

The main transfer programs are social insurance, cash welfare or public assistance, in-kind transfers, and employment programs. The programs, the numbers receiving transfers, and the dollars received are listed in Table 2.

Social security—officially known as Old Age, Survivors, and Disability Insurance (OASDI) and listed as FICA on your paycheck stubs—is the largest social insurance program. It helps a family replace income that is lost when a worker retires in old age, becomes severely disabled, or dies. Coverage is nearly universal, so the total amount of money involved is immense—over $180 billion annually. Two-thirds of the aged rely on social security for more than half of their income.

Unemployment insurance provides temporary benefits to regularly employed people who become temporarily unemployed. Funded by a national tax on payrolls levied on firms with eight or more workers, the system is run by state governments. Benefits normally amount to about 50 percent of a worker's usual wage.

TABLE 2
Transfer Programs

Program	Average Number of Monthly Recipients (in millions)	Dollars per Month per Recipient
Social insurance		
Social security	37.1	$421
Unemployment insurance	2.9	466
Medicare	17.9	218
Cash welfare		
Aid to Families with Dependent Children	10.9	119
Supplemental Security Income	3.8	202
In-kind transfers		
Medicaid	21.9	143
Food stamps	22.4	50
School lunch program	12.1	18
Energy assistance	8.5	20
Employment programs		
Jobs and training	2.5	137
Head Start	0.4	225

Sources: *Social Security Bulletin*, various issues; U.S. Bureau of the Census, *Statistical Abstract of the United States, 1991* (Washington, D.C.: U.S. Government Printing Office).

Aid to Families with Dependent Children (AFDC) is the largest cash welfare program. The average AFDC family is headed by a mother with two small children and receives $300 per month. Recipients of AFDC must not have savings of more than $1,000 and must not earn more than about $8,000.

Supplemental Security Income (SSI) ranks second among cash welfare programs. Fully 65 percent of the SSI population is blind or otherwise disabled. The rest are over age sixty-five. Unlike social security recipients, who are *entitled* to receive benefits because they are a certain age or otherwise qualify, recipients of SSI must meet certain disability requirements or be of a certain age and must have incomes below about $4,500 per year.

About 60 percent of all poor households receive in-kind transfers. The largest of these programs is Medicaid (for a discussion of Medicaid and the medical-care industry, see the chapter The Economics of Aging and Health Care). Medicaid provides federal funds to states to help them cover the costs of long-term medical and nursing home care. Second in magnitude is the food stamp program, which gives households coupons that are redeemable at grocery stores. The amounts vary with income and household size. Other programs include jobs and training directed toward disadvantaged workers and the Head Start program, an education program available to poor children. Total government outlays for social service (welfare) programs run more than $700 billion annually.

3.c. The Effectiveness of Welfare Programs

In 1964, President Lyndon Johnson declared "unconditional war on poverty." In 1967, total transfers were about $10 billion. After nearly a quarter-century of increasing outlays to reduce poverty, is the war being won? Unfortunately, there is no easy or straightforward answer to that question. In fact, there is disagreement about whether antipoverty programs have reduced or increased poverty. Some people maintain that without the programs, income inequality and poverty would have been much more severe. Others argue that welfare has been a drag on the economy and may have made poverty and inequality worse than they otherwise would have been.

It is impossible to compare what did happen with what would have happened in the absence of the government's programs. All economists can do is look at what actually occurred. The distribution of money income among families in 1929 and 1991 is shown in Figure 8. The Lorenz curve has shifted in toward the line of income equality since 1929. In 1929, the lowest 20 percent of the population had 4 percent of the income and the top 5 percent had 30 percent of the income. In 1991, the lowest 20 percent had about 5 percent and the top 5 percent had about 16 percent.

Gini ratio:
a measure of the dispersion of income ranging between 0 and 1; 0 means all families have the same income; 1 means one family has all of the income.

Another measure of income distribution is provided by a **Gini ratio**. The Gini ratio is a measure of the dispersion of income that ranges between 0 and 1. The Gini ratio measures the deviation between the Lorenz curve and the line of perfect equality; it is a measure of the area between the Lorenz curve and the line of perfect equality divided by the total area if one family had all of the income. A lower Gini value indicates less dispersion in the income distribution: a Gini of 0 would occur if every family had the exact same amount of income; a Gini of 1 would occur if all income accrued to only one family. Figure 9 shows that from 1947 to 1968 the dispersion of income fell gradually but has risen slowly since.

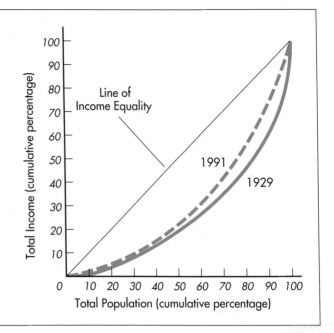

Figure 8
Income Distribution over Time
Income distribution in the United States has become more equal since 1929. This is shown by the movement of the Lorenz curve in toward the line of income equality. Sources: World Bank, *World Development Report, 1992* (New York: Oxford University Press), Table 30; U.S. Bureau of the Census, *Current Population Reports* (Washington, D.C.: U.S. Government Printing Office, 1988, 1992).

Figure 10 shows the annual expenditures on poverty programs along with the incidence of poverty from 1960 to 1990. The incidence-of-poverty curve is taken from Figure 5. During the 1960s, as transfers and spending increased, the incidence of poverty fell. Since the early 1970s, transfers and spending have increased much more rapidly than in the previous decade, but the incidence of poverty has changed little, and in fact, it rose during the recessions of the early 1980s and the early 1990s.

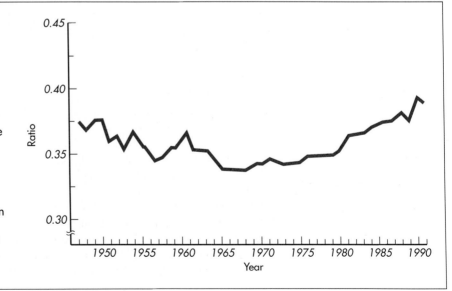

Figure 9
The Gini Ratio
The Gini ratio is a measure of the dispersion of income that ranges between 0 and 1. A lower value indicates less dispersion in the income distribution: a Gini of 0 would occur if every family had the exact same amount of income, while a Gini of 1 would occur if all income accrued to only one family. Figure 9 shows that from 1947 to 1968 the dispersion of income fell gradually. Since then the dispersion has risen slowly. Source: *Economic Report of the President, 1992*, p. 123.

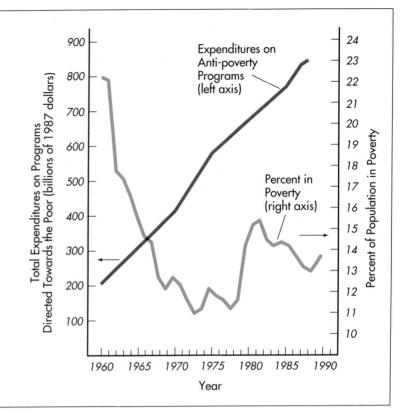

Figure 10
Spending and Poverty, 1960–1990
Curves representing total government spending in real (1987) billions of dollars on poverty programs since 1960 and the incidence of poverty since 1960 are shown. Total expenditures on antipoverty programs in equal purchasing power terms (real terms) are measured on the left vertical axis, and the percent of population in poverty is shown on the right vertical axis. During the 1960s, the incidence of poverty decreased as spending increased. Since then, spending has continued to increase, but the incidence of poverty has not declined.
Source: Department of Commerce, *Statistical Abstract of the United States, 1992.*

Those who argue that welfare programs are a drag on the economy and may make poverty and income inequality worse typically focus on the disincentives created by the transfers.

3.c.1. Disincentives Created by the Welfare System Incentives for both the rich and the poor to work hard and increase their productivity may be reduced by programs that take from the rich and give to the poor. Those paying taxes may ask themselves, "Why should I work an extra hour every day if all the extra income does is pay additional taxes?" Someone who gets to keep only 60 cents out of the next dollar earned has less incentive to earn that dollar than if he or she got to keep it all.

Those who receive benefits may lose the incentive to change their status. Why should someone take a job paying $6,000 per year when he or she can remain unemployed and receive $8,000? Someone out of work might wonder, "Why should I spend eight hours a day in miserable working conditions when I can relax every day and bring home nearly the same amount of income?" If incentives to work are weak, then the total income created in the economy is less than it otherwise would be. Less income and lower economic growth mean more people in poverty.

3.c.2. Welfare Dependency Some have argued that the welfare system causes welfare dependency—that children who grow up on welfare are likely to become welfare recipients as adults and to have children who eventually become dependent on welfare. Evidence that such a situation occurs is not strong, but the incentives for it to occur do exist. Society tries to provide families with decent living standards but does not want transfers to go to those who do not need them. As a result, transfer programs are designed to provide the greatest benefits to the people with the lowest incomes. As incomes rise, benefits decrease.

Transfer programs are designed much like a progressive income tax. The higher the person's income, the fewer benefits he or she gets. In 1990, a family of four with no earned income could receive about $260 worth of food stamps per month. A family of four with $100 of income per month could receive only $230 worth of food stamps per month. For earning $100, the second family received food stamps worth $30 less than the stamps received by the nonworking family. This is a 30 percent marginal penalty on working. A family of four with a monthly income of $300 could receive $210 of benefits per month; a family of four with $400 could receive only $130 worth of benefits per month. The additional $100 of income, from $300 to $400 per month, meant a reduction in benefits of $80 per month. This is an 80 percent marginal penalty on working. Eventually, as earned income rises, benefits are reduced dollar for dollar—there is a 100 percent marginal penalty on working.

3.d. Welfare Reform

workfare:
a plan that requires welfare recipients to accept public service jobs or participate in job training

Unhappiness with the results of transfer programs has led to various attempts at welfare reform. Welfare reform has taken two tacks: tying benefits to work and establishing parents' responsibility for children.

Workfare is the name given to plans that require welfare recipients to accept public service jobs or participate in job training. To receive benefits, a person must accept a job provided by the state. To receive AFDC, the head of the household must agree to search for work or obtain training or education. Many states have introduced a work-for-pay component to their welfare programs. In 1988, Congress passed the Family Support Act. This legislation provides federal funding and considerable flexibility to states in designing programs that will encourage work and reduce welfare participation. Under the new legislation, states can make participation in a training or employment program mandatory and can impose penalties on welfare recipients who refuse to accept a job that is offered to them.

The second approach to welfare reform focuses on children and child support. The incidence of poverty among families with children and a female head of household has always been high. More than half of these families are poor, a condition that has changed little since 1930. However, sixty years ago there were fewer such families. Today, as a result of increased divorce rates and more out-of-wedlock childbearing, more than one in five children live in a female-headed family, though in nine out of ten cases these children have a living father. The proportion of all children under age eighteen who are dependent on AFDC rose from around 3 percent in 1960 to 11 percent in 1985. These developments led to an interest in establishing parental financial responsibility for children.

This objective has been approached in three ways: (1) by discouraging teenage pregnancy, (2) by requiring absent parents to contribute to the support of their children, and (3) by requiring welfare mothers to work. The

The top 20 percent of household income earners in the United States earn 42 percent of total household income while the bottom 20 percent earn just 4.7 percent. The government provides assistance to the lowest rungs of income recipients though food stamps, aid to families with dependent children, Medicare, Medicaid, and public housing. In urban areas, public housing known as the projects are multi-story buildings housing hundreds of families. In rural areas, the government-provided housing often takes the form of wide trailers located on the outskirts of small towns.

1975 Child Support Enforcement Program required each state to develop a system to establish paternity, locate absent fathers, and enforce child-support obligations. The 1988 Family Support Act increased the responsibility of absent fathers for their children and provided federal funding for enforcement of child-support payments by absentee fathers.

3.e. Equity and Efficiency

Efficiency requires that goods and services go to those willing and able to pay the price. The allocation of goods and services on the basis of equity would provide goods to those who meet the definition of *equity*. For instance, if *equity* means "equality," then all persons would receive the same goods and services whether or not they had the ability to pay. If *equity* means "goods and services go to those with the greatest need," then some definition of *need* must be created. *Equity* requires a definition.

There are two general definitions of *equity*: the means test and the ends test. The *ends test* examines the existing situation, the results of whatever has gone on in the past. For instance, the distribution of income is more equal now than it was fifty years ago. This is an end result of whatever occurred during the past fifty years. The *means test* considers the means to achieve the end. If the opportunity to earn income were equally distributed, then according to the means definition, equity would occur even if the existing distribution of income were unequal.

Policymakers who rely on the ends test tend to support policies directed toward changing the existing distribution of income, such as providing assistance to the poor by taking from the rich. A problem with the ends test is that it may be antithetical to efficiency. Policies intended to create a more equal distribution of income can reduce incentives to earn income and thereby reduce the efficiency with which the economy functions.

Policymakers who advocate a means test of equity look not at whether income is distributed equally but instead at whether the opportunity to earn income is distributed equally. To them, *equity* means "equal opportunities to earn, to accumulate wealth, to obtain human capital, and to be an entrepreneur." There need be no tradeoff between efficiency and equity if the means definition is used. Efficiency is achieved when entry and exit are free and there are no market failures. Once barriers are erected, efficiency is decreased. Thus, policies that tear down the barriers and resolve the market failures increase the efficiency of the market.

3.f. The Negative Income Tax and Family Allowance Plans

negative income tax (NIT):
a tax system that transfers increasing amounts of income to households earning incomes below some specified level as their income declines

The solution to the welfare system problems most often proposed by economists is the **negative income tax (NIT)**—a tax system that transfers increasing amounts of income to households earning incomes below some specified level. The lower the income, the more that is transferred. As income rises above the specified level, a tax is applied. Economists like the NIT because, at least in theory, it attacks the distribution of income and reduces poverty without reducing efficiency.

Suppose policymakers determine that a family of four is to be guaranteed an income of $10,000. If the family earns nothing, then it will get a transfer of $10,000. If the family earns some income, it will receive $10,000 less a tax on the earned income. If the tax rate is 50 percent, then for each dollar earned, $.50 will be taken out of the $10,000 transfer.

With a 50 percent tax rate, there would always be some incentive to work under the NIT system because each additional dollar of earnings would bring the recipient of the transfer $.50 in additional income. At some income level, the tax taken would be equal to the transfer of $10,000. This level of income is referred to as the *break-even income level*. The break-even income level in the case of a $10,000 guaranteed income and a 50 percent tax rate is $20,000. Once a family of four earns more than $20,000, its taxes exceed the transfer of $10,000.

The break-even level of income is determined by the income floor and the tax rate:

$$\text{Break-even income} = \frac{\text{income floor}}{\text{negative income tax rate}}$$

If the guaranteed income floor is $13,000 and the tax rate is 50 percent, then the break-even income would be $26,000. If the guaranteed income floor is

$13,000 but the tax rate is 33 percent, then the break-even income would be $39,000.

In order for the negative income tax to eradicate poverty, the guaranteed level of income has to be equal to the poverty level, $13,950 in 1992. But if the tax rate is less than 100 percent, the break-even income level will be above the poverty level and families who are not officially considered "poor" will also receive benefits. At a guaranteed income level of $13,950 and a 33 percent tax rate, the break-even income level is $42,272. All families of four earning less than $42,272 would receive some income benefits.

For people now covered by welfare programs, the negative income tax would increase the incentive to work, and that is what proponents of the negative income tax like. However, for people who are too well off to receive welfare but would become eligible for NIT payments, the negative income tax might create work disincentives. It provides these families with more income, and they may choose to buy more leisure.

The possibility of disincentive effects worried both social reformers and legislators, so in the late 1960s the government carried out a number of experiments to estimate the effect of the negative income tax on the supply of labor. Families from a number of American cities were offered negative-income-tax payments in return for allowing social scientists to monitor their behavior. A matched set of families, who were not given NIT payments, were also observed. The idea was to compare the behavior of the families receiving NIT payments with that of the families who did not receive them. The experiments lasted about a decade and showed pretty clearly that the net effects of the negative income tax on labor supply were quite small.

Even though disincentive effects did not seem to occur to any great extent, the negative income tax has not gained political acceptability. One reason is the high break-even income level. Politicians are not very supportive of programs that may provide income transfers to a family earning significantly more than the poverty income level. Another reason is the transfer of dollars rather than in-kind benefits (food and medical care). Policymakers do not look favorably on the idea of giving a family cash that the family can use as it pleases.

RECAP

1. Tax policies can affect the distribution of income. A progressive income tax has a rate that increases as income increases. Thus, a progressive tax reduces income inequality. A proportional tax has a rate that is the same no matter the income level. A regressive tax has a rate that declines as income increases.

2. The federal income tax in the United States is slightly progressive, with rates rising from zero to 36 percent as income increases.

3. Spending programs used by the government to fight poverty include social insurance, cash welfare, in-kind transfers, and employment programs.

4. Incomes in the United States have become more equally distributed since 1929.

5. There have been two approaches to welfare reform: workfare and establishing parents' financial responsibility.

6. *Equity* can be defined as an end or as the means to an end. Defined as an end, *equity* means "equal distribution of income." Defined as the means to an end, *equity* means "equal opportunities to earn income."

7. Economists often propose the negative income tax as a way to resolve the welfare issue. It has not gained political acceptability, however.

SUMMARY

▲▼ *Are incomes distributed equally in the United States?*

1. The Lorenz curve illustrates the degree of income inequality. §1.a

2. If the Lorenz curve corresponds with the line of income equality, then incomes are distributed equally. If the Lorenz curve bows down below the line of income equality, then income is distributed in such a way that more people earn low incomes than earn high incomes. §1.a

3. As a rule, incomes are distributed more unequally in less developed countries than in developed countries. §1.b

▲▼ *How is poverty measured, and does poverty exist in the United States?*

4. Poverty is a measure of how well basic human needs are being met. Poverty is both a relative and an absolute concept. §1.c

5. Income consists of resource earnings and transfers. Transfers may be in cash or in kind. The distribution of income in the United States is more unequal when only market earnings are considered than it is when transfers as well as market earnings are considered. §1.d

6. The incidence of poverty decreases as the economy grows and increases as the economy falls into recession. §1.e

▲▼ *Who are the poor?*

7. Many people fall below the poverty line for a short time only. However, a significant core of people remain in poverty for at least ten years. §2.a

8. The poor are primarily those without jobs (the youngest and oldest members of society), those residing in the centers of large cities and in rural areas, and those without education. §2.b

▲▼ *What are the determinants of income?*

9. Age, a lack of education, and a lack of a full-time or well-paying job are the primary determinants of income. §2.b

▲▼ *How does the government try to reduce poverty?*

10. Tax policies can be used to alter income distribution. A progressive tax takes a higher rate from higher-income groups than from lower-income groups, thus reducing income inequality. §3.a

11. Transfer programs are used to fight poverty. The main transfer programs are social insurance, cash welfare or public assistance, in-kind transfers, and employment programs. §3.b

12. Welfare systems may reduce incentives to work and thereby harm the economy and cause more poverty. §3.c.1

13. Two approaches to welfare reform are tying benefits to work (workfare) and establishing parental financial responsibility. §3.d

14. *Equity* can be defined as an end or as the means to an end. *Equity* defined as an end is judged on the basis of actual income distributions. *Equity* defined as the means to an end is judged on the basis of equal opportunities to earn income, not on the existing income distribution. §3.e

15. The negative income tax is often proposed as a solution to the disincentives created by welfare. The negative income tax would provide income to the lowest-income families. The lower the income, the greater the benefit received by the family. As family income rose, the amount of income transferred to the family would decrease until it reached some break-even level of income. §3.f

KEY TERMS

Lorenz curve §1.a
cash transfers §1.d
in-kind transfers §1.d
progressive income tax §3.a
proportional tax §3.a

regressive tax §3.a
Gini ratio §3.c
workfare §3.d
negative income tax (NIT) §3.f

EXERCISES

1. What is a Lorenz curve? What would the curve look like if income were equally distributed? Could the curve ever bow upward above the line of income equality?

2. Why does the health of the economy affect the number of people living in poverty?

3. What would it mean if the poverty income level of the United States were applied to Mexico?

4. What is the difference between a means and an ends definition of *equity*? What policies in force today would not be used under the means test of equality?

5. What positive arguments can be made for reducing income inequality? What normative arguments are made for reducing income inequality?

6. What does it mean to say that poverty is a luxury good?

7. Are people who are poor today in the United States likely to be poor for the rest of their lives? Under what conditions is generational poverty likely to exist?

8. Use the following information to plot a Lorenz curve.

Percent of Population	Percent of Income
20	5
40	15
60	35
80	65
100	100

9. If the incidence of poverty decreases during periods when the economy is growing and increases during periods when the economy is in recession, what government policies might be used to reduce poverty most effectively?

10. If the arguments for reducing income inequality and poverty are normative, why rely on the government to reduce the inequality? Why doesn't the private market resolve the problem?

11. How could transfer programs (welfare programs) actually increase the number of people in poverty?

12. What is the difference between in-kind and cash transfers? Which might increase the utility of the recipients the most? Why is there political resistance to the negative income tax?

13. Is it possible to eradicate poverty? The government's definition of poverty is a family of four with reported income less than $13,950. According to a recent study by the Heritage Foundation, this figure does not include the housing that 40 percent of those in poverty own or the cars that 62 percent own. Nor does it consider how the poorest 20 percent of households manage to consume twice as much as they earn. Is poverty a relative concept or an absolute concept?

14. Consider the following three solutions offered to get rid of homelessness and discuss whether any would solve the problem. First, provide permanent housing for all who are homeless. Second, provide free hospital care for the one-third of homeless who are mentally ill. Third, provide subsidies for the homeless to purchase homes.

15. What is the relationship between the Gini coefficient and the Lorenz curve? Illustrate your answer using question 8.

Recession's Human Toll

WASHINGTON—The stress and strain of the 1989–90 recession took a human toll in terms of health and behavior, according to a new Johns Hopkins University study.

The tally: 35,000 extra fatal heart attacks and strokes, and an additional 1,500 homicides and 2,300 suicides.

The study, by Harvey Bren-ner, professor of health policy and management at the School of Hygiene and Public Health, sought to measure the effect that economic hard times may have on ill health and crime.

The triggers for health deterioration and increased crime were loss of normal income growth, increased unemployment and an accelerated rate of business failures, the study says. All can produce family stress, job anxiety, and possibly altered social behavior and status.

"It is now evident that severe anxiety and loss, as well as damage to social relations, are significant risks to disorders of the immune, cardiovascular and central nervous systems," said Brenner, in a paper presented at the Harvard School of Public Health on Friday.

"These disorders are significant sources of ill health, including infections, heart disease, hypertension, stroke, kidney disease, diabetes, mental disorders and uncontrolled violence."

A recession can encourage people to resort to such dangerous "coping mechanisms" as alcohol, drugs, tobacco and diminished dietary control, the study says. Hard times can produce alienation from society, which "may also involve a sense of injustice over life's misfortunes," leading to crime to recoup income or status, or to violence as an expression of rage, according to the study.

Since World War II, normal annual income growth has been about 3 percent. In the 1989–90 recession, it was zero. The unemployment rate increased by 1.3 percentage points during the recession, to 6.8 percent, lower than it is today but sufficient to contribute to the health and behavioral problems, according to the study. Business failures increased to 75 per 1,000 businesses during the recession from 65 per 1,000 businesses before it.

The result, according to Brenner, who worked out a series of equations relating economic indexes to medical and social conditions: a 3.6 percent increase in deaths due to heart disease and strokes; a 4.2 percent increase in homicides; and a 3.9 percent increase in suicides.

He estimated that in each year of the two-year recession, an extra 17,800 people died from heart disease and strokes, 760 were slain, and 1,170 committed suicide.

"Economic-policy decisions, therefore, can be assumed to have a profound effect on many aspects of societal health and well-being," said Brenner, adding, "Action is obviously required to remedy the short- and long-term problems of the United States' economy—especially low investment, wage stagnation, continuing and relatively high unemployment rates, and poverty."

Brenner's report was issued by the Economic Policy Institute, with a corroborating study by two economists at the University of Utah, who came to similar findings using different methodology after studying recession-related health and behavioral problems in 30 major metropolitan areas with a combined population of 80 million.

The release of such recession-related analyses less than three weeks from Election Day by a research group that actively is supporting the Democratic ticket of Bill Clinton and Al Gore clearly had political overtones. The institute's director, Jeff Faux, is an informal economic adviser to Clinton, and this month, he organized an endorsement by 556 economists, including nine Nobel laureates.

Source: Gilbert A. Lewthwaite, "Recession's Human Toll," Arizona Republic, Oct. 20, 1992, p. A1. Reprinted with permission of the Baltimore Sun.

Arizona Republic/October 20, 1992

Commentary

Public health officials tell us that recessions and unemployment lead to stress, heart disease, murders, suicides, and crime. Psychologists tell us that happiness is not related to wealth but that the lack of wealth, the lack of a job, and relative poverty—having little among those who have plenty—create unhappiness. And the columnist indicates that a study pointing out these connections is politically motivated. What do these things have to do with economics? For one thing, they indicate what some of the costs of poverty, unemployment, and recessions are. For another thing, they tell us why people might be willing to give up some of their own income to help others avoid poverty and unemployment, and why they might vote for a president on the basis of commitments the candidate might make to avoid poverty, unemployment, business failure, and recession.

These factors can be represented in a simple demand and supply diagram. Let's group job loss, business failure, and poverty into one "good" we will call unemployment. The costs of job loss, business failure, and recession—unemployment—include not only the lost income but the increased stress and ill health, the additional crime, drug use, alcohol abuse, and the child abuse, additional divorces, and family disruptions that may result. The benefits of job loss, business failure, and recession—unemployment—include the increased flow of resources from low-value to higher-valued uses, the increased efficiency and productivity that result, and perhaps the increased incentives to innovate and succeed.

In the diagram, we measure the costs and benefits along the vertical axis and the percentage of the population unemployed along the horizontal axis. The demand curve is downward-sloping, illustrating the idea that as the costs of unemployment fall, the quantity of unemployment people are willing and able to abide by rises. Conversely, as the benefits of unemployment (the potential of rising productivity, rising innovation, new products, etc.) rise, the quan-

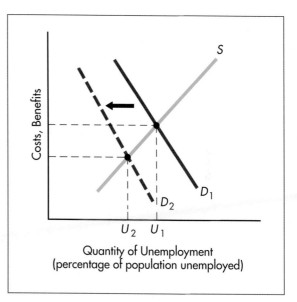

tity supplied rises: Firms are more willing to cut employees; people are more willing to see others be unemployed. The intersection between demand and supply determines the optimal unemployment rate, U_1.

Now suppose that the public's attitude toward poverty and unemployment changes because people learn that the costs of unemployment are higher than they previously thought. Then, the demand for unemployment shifts in, reflecting the idea that people are less tolerant of the conditions and effects of poverty, job loss, and business failure. They are willing to purchase more antipoverty programs and less of other goods and services. As a result, the optimal unemployment rate declines, to U_2.

The last paragraph of the newspaper article tells us that being more aware of the personal burdens that job loss and business failure inflict may induce people to purchase less unemployment—to demand more programs to combat job loss and business failure—and to vote for one candidate instead of another in a presidential election.

537

21

Market Failure and Environmental Policy

FUNDAMENTAL
QUESTIONS

1. What is a market failure?
2. Why is an externality considered to be a source of market failure?
3. What is a public good?
4. How can market failures be resolved?
5. How do global environmental problems differ from domestic environmental problems?

How much are Americans willing to pay to make the Blue Ridge Mountains look bluer, to save the brook trout from acid rain, to make living next door to a chemical plant no riskier than smoking a few cigarettes a year, or to ensure that the ozone layer isn't destroyed? To achieve these goals might be expensive. Utility consumers in the Midwest might stagger under double-digit increases in the cost of electricity for several years; thousands of coal-mining jobs in Appalachia could be lost; the cost of a new car could rise by as much as $600 because of new emission standards; and productivity and income growth could slow appreciably. But fears of air-quality deterioration, acid rain, overflowing landfills, and global warming have spurred the public's call for government action.

Why does the government play such an important role in environmental issues? As discussed in Chapter 5, "Households, Businesses, Government, and the International Sector," and examined in more detail in the next chapter, "The Government and Public Choice," the rationale for government intervention is either to protect the public interest or to capture benefits for special interest groups. In the environmental arena, the public interest rationale for government intervention stems from the failure of market-based economies to automatically provide the level of environmental quality that consumers desire. In this chapter we discuss the market failure problem and examine solutions to it.

I. MARKETS AND EFFICIENCY

You have seen how the market system works. Profit-seeking entrepreneurs undertake those activities in which the profit potential is highest, ensuring that resources flow to their most highly valued uses. In addition, you have seen that entrepreneurs or firms provide what consumers want by using resources efficiently, and consumers get what they want at the lowest possible prices. Markets, demand and supply, and the resulting equilibrium prices allocate goods and services and resources so that no one could be made better off without making someone else worse off. Economists refer to this as economic efficiency.

I.a. Perfect Competition

You have also learned that if entrepreneurs are free to enter and exit alternative activities in their quest for profit, and if no one producer can affect the

market price, then consumers get what they want at a price that equals the
marginal cost of production, and resources are paid their marginal revenue
products—including entrepreneurs, who earn a normal profit. Thus, the result
of perfect competition is economic efficiency.

Figure 1 shows a perfectly competitive market; the equilibrium price and
quantity are the economically efficient price and quantity. A different price
would mean that consumers are not getting what they want at the lowest possible price or that resources are not being used efficiently. But there is no
reason for the price and quantity to be different from that determined in
the perfectly competitive market, because a higher price results in a surplus and a movement back to equilibrium, and a lower price leads to a shortage and a movement back to equilibrium. In short, the market works.

I.b. Imperfect Competition

The perfectly competitive market "works" as long as the conditions of perfect
competition are met. A firm other than a perfectly competitive firm can set a
price that is not equal to marginal cost. And if consumers and producers do
not know everything about the market, if information is not perfect, price or
quantity can be "too high" or "too low." But how much do these real-world
situations cause us to diverge from the economically efficient prices and
quantities? The monopolistic competitor produces differentiated goods
because that is what consumers want; the oligopolist or monopolist may earn
above-normal profit and the monopsonist may pay resources less than their
marginal revenue products as long as entry is restricted. If entry is not
restricted or if the potential for entry by profit-seeking entrepreneurs exists
whenever above-normal profits are earned (what we earlier referred to as
contestable markets), these situations correspond closely to the results of perfect competition. Although we might not achieve the results of our textbook
description of perfect competition, we can argue that the markets in the real
world tend to move toward economic efficiency. The markets tend to work
even if perfect competition does not hold.

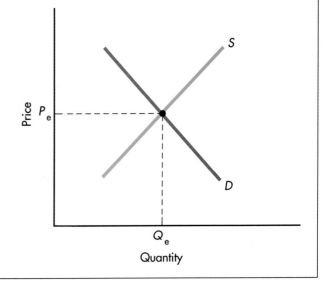

Figure 1
The Efficiency of the Market System
In a perfectly competitive market, equilibrium price and
quantity are the efficient price and quantity. A different
price would mean that consumers are not getting what
they want at the lowest possible price or that resources
are not being used efficiently. But there is no reason for
the price and quantity to be different from that determined in the perfectly competitive market, because a
higher price results in a surplus and a movement back
to equilibrium, and a lower price leads to a shortage
and a movement back to equilibrium. In short, the
market works.

I.c. Market Failure

What is a market failure?

market failure:
the failure of the market system to achieve economic efficiency

However, even if the conditions of perfect competition hold, there are situations where the market does not work, where markets *fail*. If consumers do not have to pay a price that covers the full cost of producing a product or if producers do not have to pay all their costs of production, then "too much" or "too little" might be produced. When this occurs, economists refer to a **market failure**. A market failure occurs when the unrestrained operations of a market generate an output level that society believes is undesirable, an output level that is different from the economically efficient level.

2. EXTERNALITIES AND PUBLIC GOODS: MARKET FAILURES

Why is an externality considered to be a source of market failure?

Market failures occur when consumers or producers do not have to bear the full costs of transactions they undertake.

In the chapter "Capital, Land, and Entrepreneurial Ability," we discussed the market for natural resources, and you saw how the market functions to ensure that resources are used at a rate that maximizes their value. If the market for natural resources allocates resources to their most highly valued use today and in the future, why do we hear so much about the depletion of the ozone, the destruction of the rain forest, the pollution of the oceans and rivers, and the depletion of wildlife? If the market for labor ensures that people acquire skills and education when doing so is valuable, then why are dropout rates so high? Part of the answer may stem from market failures.

Problems may arise in market economies when private individuals and businesses lack incentives to take full account of the consequences of their actions. When consumers or producers do not have to bear the full costs of transactions they undertake, a market failure is said to have occurred. These market failures can be traced to two sources: externalities and public goods.

2.a. The Definition of Externalities

private costs:
costs borne by the individual involved in the transaction that created the costs

A business firm knows how much it costs to employ workers, and it knows the costs of purchasing materials or constructing buildings. An individual who buys a new car or pays for a pizza knows exactly what the cost will be. Such costs are **private costs**: They are costs borne solely by the individuals involved in the transaction that created the costs. Many environmental problems arise, however, because the costs of an individual's actions are *not* borne directly by that individual. When a firm pollutes the air or water, or when a tourist leaves trash in a park, the costs of these actions are not easily determined and are not borne by the individual or firm creating them. This situation represents a market failure because the price of the good and the equilibrium quantity produced and consumed do not reflect the full costs of producing or consuming the good. In this sense, "too much" or "too little" is produced.

Consider an oil tanker that runs aground and dumps crude oil into a pristine ocean area teeming with wildlife, or a public beach where people litter. A cost is involved in these actions: the crude oil may kill wildlife and ruin fishing industries, and the trash may discourage families from using the beach. But in neither of these cases is the cost of the action borne by the individuals who took the action. Instead, the cost is borne by those who were not participants in the activity. The fishermen, the fish, and other wildlife did not spill the oil, yet they have to bear the cost. The beachgoers who encounter trash and broken bottles were not the litterers, yet they must bear the cost.

externality:
a cost or benefit of an activity that is borne by parties not directly involved in the activity; an external cost or benefit

social costs:
the sum of private costs and externalities

When social and private costs are not the same, then either too much or too little production occurs.

The cost is external to the activity and is thus called an **externality**, specifically a *negative externality*. When externalities are added to private costs, the result is **social costs**:

Social costs = private costs + externalities

When private costs differ from social costs, individual decision-makers are ignoring externalities. The full opportunity cost of using a scarce resource, for example, is borne not by the producer or the consumer but by society. The difference between the private cost and the full opportunity, or social, cost is the externality.

A *positive externality* may result from an activity in which benefits are received by consumers or firms not involved directly in the activity. For instance, a literate populace may provide benefits to society as a whole that exceed the benefits received by those individuals who acquire an education. In this case, the private costs of acquiring an education exceed the social costs by the amount of the externality.

When there is a divergence between social costs and private costs, the result is either too much or too little production and consumption. In either case, resources are not being used in their highest-valued activity, and there is a market failure. For instance, those who pollute do not bear the entire costs of the pollution, and therefore pollute more than they otherwise would. Although chlorofluorocarbons (CFCs) from air conditioners and aerosol sprays damage the ozone layer, the people producing aerosol cans and those buying aerosol sprays do not pay for the damage to the ozone layer. As a result, more aerosols are produced and consumed than would be the case if the external costs (externalities) were part of the cost of production or consumption.

In contrast to negative externalities such as with CFCs, private costs exceed social costs when external benefits are created. From society's viewpoint, too little education would take place if individuals bore all the costs of education. Similarly, vaccinations from communicable diseases provide positive externalities. If individuals bear all the costs of obtaining vaccinations, too few are vaccinated.

2.b. Private Property Rights and Externalities

private property right:
the right to claim ownership of an item

The absence of a well-defined private property right may result in a market failure.

marginal benefits (MB):
the additional benefits of producing or consuming one more unit of a good or service

Market failures may result because of the absence of well-defined **private property rights**. A private property right is the right to claim ownership of an item; it is well-defined if there is a clear owner and if the right is recognized and enforced by society. Suppose you sit next to a person who gets very nervous during exams and as a result coughs, drops pencils, papers, and calculators, and spreads out over the desk, encroaching on your space. The nervous person, Bob, is imposing an externality on you. The problem is that neither you nor Bob owns the space or the noise level. If you did, you could restrict Bob's noise activity or you could charge him for it. If Bob owned it, you could pay him not to make noise. In either case, the externality would no longer be external, it would be part of the private costs.

Figure 2 shows Bob's demand (the marginal revenue product) for the distractions and noise he causes, what we will call his **marginal-benefits (MB)** curve. The marginal-benefits curve measures the additional benefits of consuming one more quantity of something. The first few coughs and the first few dropped pencils provide Bob large benefits. They help him take the

Figure 2
Externalities

The marginal costs borne by the noisy student, Bob, are shown by the rising curve MC. The costs Bob imposes on others exceed his private costs. As a result, the marginal-social-cost curve, MSC, lies above Bob's marginal-cost curve. Bob's marginal benefits from creating distractions are indicated by the downward-sloping curve, MB. The amount of noise and distraction that Bob creates is given by the point where the MC curve and the MB curve intersect, Q_B. According to society, too much noise and other distractions occur. Society would choose the quantity Q_S, where marginal social costs and marginal benefits are equal. The solution to the externalities problem is to equate private costs and social costs.

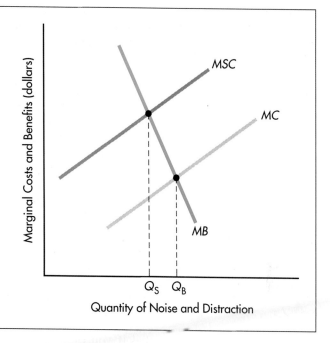

marginal social costs:
the additional private and external or social costs of producing or consuming one more unit of a good or service

exam. But as coughing continues and the dropping of materials increases, Bob gets fewer benefits with each additional cough. The marginal cost (MC) to Bob of his noise and distractions rises as more noise and distractions occur because he has to devote increasing amounts of time to making noise and dropping materials, and this distracts from his taking the examination. The marginal cost Bob faces does not measure the full costs of his actions. The *full costs*, the costs imposed on you and everyone else, are the **marginal social costs**, shown as the upward-sloping curve MSC, which lies above the MC curve.

Bob chooses the amount of distraction indicated by the intersection of his MC and MB curves, quantity Q_B. This is an amount greater than is desired by society (you and other students). The amount of activity you would desire is indicated by the intersection of the MSC curve and Bob's MB curve, quantity Q_S. Thus, "too much" noise is provided because the MC curve does not take into account all costs. The market has failed to generate the "right" amount of noise. The reason stems from the fact that no one owns the noise level; that is, no one has a private property right to the noise level.

The lack of private property ownership or rights is a common one in the natural resources area. No one has a private property right to the ocean or air. No one owns the fish in the sea; no one owns the elephants that roam the African plains; and during the past one hundred years no one owned the American buffalo or bald eagle. Because no one owns these natural resources, a "too rapid" rate of use or harvest occurs.

The waters off New England once were among the world's most fertile fishing grounds. Now, fish are severely depleted in the area known as Georges Bank. Overfishing resulting from a lack of private property rights was fueled by the nation's increasing appetite for fish and by technological changes in fishing. A single fishing vessel using radar, sonar, spotter planes, sea-surface observations from satellites, advanced catching gear, onboard processing, and refrigeration can do the job of a hundred older boats and in less time. For some species, the entire fishing season lasts only a few hours. The Economic Insight "The Problems of Common Ownership" discusses some of the results of private and common ownership of resources.

The resource markets would solve the problem of harvesting now or in the future if someone owned the oceans or the fish. As we discussed in the chapter on capital, land, and entrepreneurial ability, the prices would adjust until the present values of harvesting and not harvesting would be the same. Without private ownership, however, no one has the incentive to sell the resources at the profit-maximizing rate. A fishing crew has no incentive to harvest the "right" amount of fish, since leaving fish until the future simply leaves them for other fishing crews today. If someone owned the fish, that resource owner would sell the fish only up to the point that the present value of fish caught in the future would equal the present value of the revenue obtained from the fish caught today.

2.c. Public Goods

What is a public good?

principle of mutual exclusivity:
the owner of private property is entitled to enjoy the consumption of private property privately

public good:
a good for which the principle of mutual exclusivity does not hold

free rider:
a consumer or producer who enjoys the benefits of a good without paying for it

According to the **principle of mutual exclusivity**, the owner of private property is entitled to enjoy the consumption of private property privately. The principle of mutual exclusivity is a well-defined private property right. It says that if you own a good, I cannot use it; and if I own a good, you cannot use it. When I purchase a pizza, it is mine to consume as I wish. You have absolutely no right to the pizza unless I provide that right. However, a good or service may also be a **public good**, a good for which the principle of mutual exclusivity does not apply. If you use a public good, I may also. Moreover, a public good is a good or service whose use by one consumer does not diminish the quantity available for other consumers.

The airwaves illustrate the characteristics of a public good quite well. A television station broadcasts on a certain frequency, and anyone can pick up that station. It doesn't matter whether one person or 1 million people tune in to the station, the signal is the same and additional users do not deprive others of any of the public good. If your neighbor tunes in to the channel you are watching, you don't receive a weaker signal.

When goods are public, people have an incentive to be **free riders**—consumers or producers who enjoy a good without paying for it. As an example, suppose that national defense was not provided by the government and paid for with tax money. Suppose that you would not be protected by the armed forces unless you paid a fee. A problem would arise because national defense is a public good; you would be protected whether or not you paid for it as long as others paid. Of course, since each person has an incentive not to pay for it, few voluntarily do and the quantity of the good produced is too small from society's viewpoint. Similarly, clean air and the ozone layer may be public goods. Each person has an incentive to use the good without paying for it, and many people can consume the good simultaneously. As a result, not enough people pay to improve the air quality or to protect the ozone layer, and the resulting environmental quality is lower than society would like.

2.c.1. The Demand for Public Goods A private good comes in units that can be purchased by individuals, and once the good is purchased, the individual owns it and can decide how to consume it. The market demand curve is the *horizontal* summation of the individual demand curves. A public good, in contrast, is not divisible into units that can be purchased and owned by the

The Problems of Common Ownership

Lured by the opportunity to earn a year's wages with one squeeze of the trigger, poachers have slaughtered elephants by the tens of thousands. A decade ago, Africa's elephant population was more than a million; it has now fallen to less than half of that. Environmentalists in the United States trying to save the flora and fauna of the ancient forests in the Pacific Northwest are battling local loggers, who see the trees as a means to feed their families. Thousands of acres of Amazon forest are burned each year to provide land for Brazil's ranchers and subsistence farmers, eliminating hundreds of species of plants and animals. The swordfish is being fished to extinction. These and other similar problems result from common ownership. When no one owns the land or the wildlife, no one has an incentive to harvest quantities that ensure reproduction and renewal.

Policies regarding forests illustrate the problem of common ownership. The government of Ontario, Canada, fights with small, private owners of forest lands over how to manage the trees. The Ontario government wants to cut the trees down and sell them, but private owners refuse to clear-cut their private forests (the process of cutting down all the trees in an area). Stories about deforestation and the degradation of Ontario's forest lands make the papers every day in Ontario, but the private sector, which owns less than 10 percent of the timber, is not to blame.

The deforestation is occurring on the government's land.

Sweden has more standing forest today than at any time in its past. Unlike Canada, most of the forest land in Sweden is privately owned. Neighboring Finland also has a huge forest industry and more forest than ever before. It too has mostly privately owned forest lands. In the less developed countries as well, common ownership encourages deforestation. In Brazil's Amazon basin, the government has subsidized the tearing down and burning of a forested area bigger than France. Deforestation has occurred in other regions of Latin America, several Asian nations, and much of Africa. In each case where there is common ownership, there is a problem with the rate of harvest. The difference is that private owners do not cut at a loss and do not cut to maintain employment levels or for other political reasons. They cut at a rate that yields them the greatest return—a rate of return that matches the rates of return earned on alternative assets.

The problems of the African elephant, the swordfish, and other species of plants and animals that are being depleted are no different from the problem of the forests. Proposed solutions typically call for bans on the killing of the species. For example, Kenya, Tanzania, and several other African nations, with the support of most of the developed nations, are banning the trade of ivory in order to protect African

elephants. The elephants' problem may stem partly from the demand for ivory, but it also stems from common ownership of the elephant and the low incomes of the African peoples. To a small farmer in Kenya whose crops are threatened by an elephant, the killing of the elephant means the survival of his family. If the farmer owned the elephants, had enough land to harvest food for them, and could then sell them, the plight of the elephant would change. Once in a while, someone proposes and implements a private ownership system. In South Africa, Zimbabwe, and Botswana, the government gives elephants to certain tribes to be harvested for ivory and for tourism. In those countries, elephants have not declined, and the living standards of the poorest tribes have improved. A ban on ivory in these countries would destroy the industry and lead to the destruction of the animals.

Sources: Gordon L. Brady and Michael L. Marlow, "The Political Economy of Endangered Species Management: The Case of Elephants," *Journal of Public Finance and Public Choice* I (1991), pp. 29–39; "Saving the Elephant," *The Economist*, July 1, 1989, pp. 15–17; "Fishing," *The Economist*, Nov. 4, 1989, p. 36; William F. Allman, "Can They Be Saved?" *U.S. News & World Report*, Oct. 2, 1989, pp. 52–61; David Brooks, "Saving the Earth from Its Friends," *National Review*, June 30, 1989, pp. 28–33.

buyers. Once the good is produced, the producer is unable to exclude non-payers from consuming the good. Since they can enjoy the good without paying for it, many individuals will not pay for it. The demand curve for the public good may not exist.

TABLE 1
The Demand for a Public Good

Quantity	Willingness to Pay		Total Willingness to Pay
	Jesse	Rafael	
1	$5	$3	$8
2	4	2	6
3	3	1	4
4	2	0	2

Suppose there are two people in society, Jesse and Rafael, whose demands for a public good are shown in Table 1. The demands show how much each would be *willing* and *able* to pay for the various quantities of the public good. Once the good is produced, however, neither Jesse nor Rafael has any incentive to pay for it. Jesse would be willing and able to pay $5 for one unit of the good, and Rafael would be willing and able to pay $3 for the one unit. But neither has an incentive to actually pay anything. The last column in Table 1 shows the total amount society (Jesse and Rafael) would be willing and able to pay for various quantities of the public good. In contrast to the private good, where the market demand is the horizontal summation of the individual demands, the market demand for the public good is the *vertical* summation of the individual demand curves. The market demand for the public good shows how much society would be willing and able to pay for various quantities of a public good. Again, the problem is that the existence of this market demand curve does not mean that people will actually pay for the good; once produced, no one has an incentive to pay for it. There is, therefore, a market failure.

The market demand curve for a public good is derived by summing vertically all individual demand curves.

RECAP

1. Externalities occur when all of the costs of production or consumption are not borne by the private individuals involved in a transaction.

2. Externalities are market failures because the market does not determine the level of a good that society desires. A market failure occurs when social costs and benefits are not equal.

3. A market failure may result when private property rights are not well defined.

4. A public good is a good for which the principle of mutual exclusivity does not hold and thus free riding exists.

5. Free riding occurs when people can enjoy an activity without having to bear any costs for the activity.

6. Market failures may occur in the case of a public good. The demand for the public good may not exist because no one has an incentive to pay for the public good once it is produced.

3. PUBLIC POLICIES

How can market failures be resolved?

3.a. Externalities

The government is called on to resolve market failures. It may levy taxes or subsidies, produce public goods, or assign private property rights.

emission standard:
a maximum allowable level of pollution from a specific source

How is a market failure to be resolved? If we call on the government to solve the problem, do we have the government impose regulations, as it does in the case of natural monopolies, or should it impose taxes and subsidies? In this section, we look at some of the approaches the government takes in the case of market failures.

Let's begin with the externality problem. Since the problem is that the MSC is not equal to the MC, the solution requires that the two be made equal. How can the creators of the externality be required to take the externality into account, to *internalize* the externality? Externalities can be internalized through the imposition of regulations or taxes, the use of subsidies, or the assignment of private property rights.

3.a.1. Regulation   Let's consider your noisy classmate Bob again. Suppose your professor owns the property right to the noise level in your class. The professor can regulate the noise, specifying that Bob can cough only *x* times per hour. But to ensure that the entire class is made better off, how much noise should the professor allow—5, 10, or 50 coughs per hour? The optimal amount for all of the class would be to restrict Bob's noise to the level where MSC = MB.

Environmental regulation is analogous to the regulation of Bob's noise-making. One form of environmental regulation is an **emission standard** that specifies the maximum level of pollution allowed from a specific source. Each automaker, for instance, must create a line of cars that meets fixed emission standards. Emission standards are also applied to steel factories, electric-power plants, and many other industries.

The Botswana, Zimbabwe, and South African governments allow individuals to own elephants. These elephant "farmers" ensure that the elephants breed and reproduce so that they can be sold for their tusks, for hunting in special hunting parks, or to zoos in developed nations. This privatization has led to a revival of the elephant population in these nations. Most other nations have created national parks in which hunting is forbidden, and the results have not stemmed the tide of extinction of the species. These orphaned elephants are being cared for at a wildlife preserve in Kenya.

The government defines an emission level and requires firms to meet the standards. Economists argue that the level should be determined by demand and supply—that is, by equating marginal benefits and marginal social costs. Figure 3 shows the market for pollution. (Alternatively, we could show the market for clean air, since the two, clean air and polluted air, add up to 100 percent). The marginal costs and benefits of pollution are measured on the vertical axis. The horizontal axis measures the quantity of pollution, from perfectly clean air (0 on the graph) to perfectly filthy air (100 on the graph). Moving away from the origin along the horizontal axis, the percentage of polluted air rises (the particles of dirty air increase). When the air is perfectly clean (0 on the graph), the marginal benefit of a particle of pollutants emitted in the air is quite high. As the air becomes dirtier and dirtier, the marginal benefit of a few more polluted particles of air falls, as seen by the downward slope of the marginal-benefit curve, *MB*.

The marginal cost of dirty air (*MC*) rises at an accelerating rate because of diminishing marginal returns. The first 10 percent increase in pollutants occurs easily and is accomplished by not using the very expensive pollution abatement devices installed on automobiles and smokestacks. As the air gets dirtier and dirtier, the benefits a firm or individual might get from some additional pollution are quite small. The difference between the marginal cost and the marginal social cost (*MSC*) is that the marginal cost refers to the individual's private costs while the marginal social cost refers to society's marginal costs. When I drive my automobile, the costs of the pollution I create are borne by me in the sense that I have to purchase oxygenated fuels and maintain the quality of my car, but costs are also borne by others. Everyone has to breathe the polluted air I create.

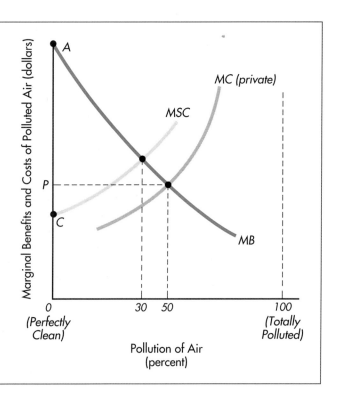

Figure 3
The Optimal Amount of Pollution
The horizontal axis measures the quantity of pollution, from perfectly clean air (0 on the graph) to perfectly filthy air (100 on the graph). Moving away from the origin along the horizontal axis, the percentage of polluted air rises (the particles of dirty air increase). When the air is perfectly clean (0 on the graph), the marginal benefit of a particle of pollutants emitted in the air is quite high. As the air becomes dirtier and dirtier, the marginal benefit of a few more polluted particles of air falls, as seen by the downward slope of the marginal-benefit curve, *MB*. The optimal amount of pollution is determined by the intersection of the *MSC* and *MB* curves: 30 percent dirty air. This is a greater amount of clean air (less pollution) than is determined in the market, where private marginal costs, *MC (private)*, are equal to marginal benefits (*MB*), or 50 percent dirty air. If a standard greater than 70 percent clean air is set by the government, the demand exceeds the marginal social costs. If a 100 percent clean air standard is set, the marginal benefits exceed the marginal social costs by the distance *AC*.

The optimal amount of pollution for society is indicated by the intersection of the marginal-social-cost and marginal-benefit curves. This amount—30 percent in this example—is optimal because marginal social costs and marginal benefits are equalized, not because pollution is eliminated (it isn't). At 100 percent cleanliness, the demand for pollution (the marginal benefits) would greatly exceed the marginal costs, by the distance *AC*.

In reality, the emission level is seldom set at the optimal level. Moreover, the regulations may cause other problems. One hallmark of the standards approach is uniformity: standards apply to all firms and all areas. However, standards appropriate for small firms may be inappropriate for large firms, or standards appropriate for one area might be inappropriate for another. An emission standard for automobiles that is appropriate for Los Angeles would not necessarily be appropriate for Salem, Idaho. An emission standard applied to fishing might restrict the quantity of fish caught per shift. This might be appropriate in the mountain streams of Vermont, but not in Chesapeake Bay.

The regulatory approach also fails to account for private responses that tend to neutralize its impact. For example, a common regulatory practice is to impose standards for new products that are tougher than standards for existing products. This practice induces producers to remain with older products even though they may be environmentally damaging. As a result, the regulation may raise pollution levels higher than they would have been without regulation. Such is the case with the 1990 Clean Air Act. Standards for planned coal plants are tougher than for existing plants. The effect is that firms continue to use old plants even when more efficient or environmentally less damaging plants would be feasible.

Uniform standards can also be problematic if they aid large or existing firms in their attempts to keep smaller or new firms from competing. For instance, the Resource Conservation and Recovery Act, which covers the disposal of more than 450 substances, has 17,000 rulings related to it. These rulings mean that it can cost as much as $1 million and take as long as four years to get approval to operate a business.[1] This is a fixed cost that makes it more difficult for new firms to enter the industry and begin competing with existing firms.

3.a.2. Taxes or Subsidies An alternative to the problems caused by regulatory standards is to levy taxes or provide subsidies to resolve the market failure. Society might want to tax actions that cause a negative externality and subsidize actions that cause a positive externality, by the amount of the externality. In this way, social costs and private costs would be the same. A tax could be placed on automobiles or smokestacks or on products that create litter or damage the ozone layer. The tax would increase the price to the full cost—internal plus external costs—and consumers and producers would have to take the full cost into account in their decision-making.

For instance, instead of mandating that automobile manufacturers install expensive pollution-control equipment on all new cars (the costs of which would be paid by every car buyer nationwide), the government could impose a tax on drivers whose cars exceed federally set emission limits. That way the

---

[1]David Brooks, "Saving the Earth from Its Friends," *National Review*, April 1, 1990, pp. 28–31.

individual could decide whether or not to drive an old junker that produces a lot of pollution. With the government mandate, new cars become relatively more expensive than the "junkers" and so people drive junkers longer than they otherwise would have.

Disposable diapers are a huge contributor to the solid-waste problem in the United States. They account for 2 percent of the nation's municipal solid waste. In 1990, nearly 20 billion paper and plastic diapers were dumped in landfills in the United States—3.6 million tons of waste that researchers believe will take five hundred years to decompose. A tax could be imposed on single-use diapers to pay the costs of their disposal. In this way people could choose whether to use the diapers or not. Under regulation, the diapers would most likely be banned.

A common use of taxes on externalities is the effluent charge—a charge on waste produced or emissions generated. With a tax on emissions, polluters can choose to install pollution-abatement equipment, change production techniques so as to reduce pollution-causing activities, or pay the tax and continue to pollute.

Figure 4 illustrates the demand for and supply of pollution. The amount of pollution that occurs in the absence of a tax is Q_1, at the intersection of S_1 and D_1. An emissions charge levied on waste tends to make pollution more expensive by the amount of the tax. In other words, producers can decide to pollute the same amount and pay the tax or pollute less and pay less tax. The supply curve shifts up to S_2, and the new amount of pollution is Q_2.

Although the effluent tax enables individuals to decide whether to pollute and thus relies on self-interest to reduce pollution, the tax can be difficult to administer. A problem with effluent charges is discovering where the supply and demand curves are located and determining what charge is necessary to cover the externality.

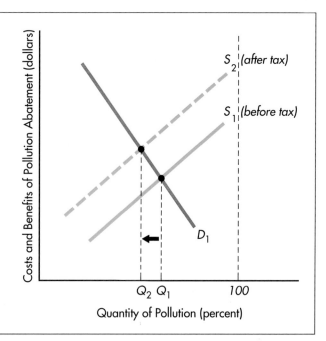

Figure 4
The Effect of an Effluent Charge
The figure illustrates the demand for and supply of pollution. The amount of pollution that occurs in the absence of a tax is Q_1, at the intersection of S_1 and D_1. An emissions charge levied on waste tends to make pollution more expensive by the amount of the tax. In other words, producers can decide to pollute the same amount and pay the tax or pollute less and pay less tax. The supply curve shifts up to S_2, and the new amount of pollution is Q_2.

3.a.3. The Coase Theorem

In cases where the market failure results from a lack of private property rights, it can be corrected by the assignment of private property rights rather than by having the government regulate or impose taxes and subsidies. To solve the problem of your classmate Bob imposing an externality on you by being too noisy and distracting, your professor could assign either you or Bob the ownership of the sound level and then allow the two of you to work out the noise pollution problem. If the professor told you that Bob owns the property rights, then you would have to decide how much of his noise and activity you could stand. You would then offer to pay Bob some amount to refrain from any more noise and activity. You would be willing to pay him enough so that your marginal cost just equals the marginal benefits you get from less noise and fewer distractions. Bob would accept a payment that just offsets his marginal cost of not making noise and creating distractions. If the *MSC* curve of Figure 5 represents your marginal-cost curve, and the *MC* curve represents Bob's marginal costs, then you would be willing to pay Bob any amount up to the difference between the *MC* and *MSC* curves because that would induce him to reduce his activity to the level you find best. Bob would be willing to accept any amount equal to or greater than the difference between the *MC* and *MSC* curves to reduce his activity to Q_S.

Conversely, if your professor assigned you the property right, Bob would have to buy some noise and activity level from you. Bob would be willing to pay up to the difference between the *MC* and *MSC* curves, and you would accept anything equal to or greater than that difference.

Notice that no matter to whom the property rights are assigned, the quantity of noise produced is the same. You and Bob come to an agreement in which the marginal cost to you equals the marginal benefit to Bob and vice versa. The only difference is that one of you provides payments to the other. When bargaining is costless and property rights can be assigned without dif-

---

Figure 5
The Assignment of Property Rights
If the *MSC* curve of Figure 5 represents your marginal-cost curve, then you would be willing to pay Bob any amount up to the difference between the *MC* and *MSC* curves because that would induce him to reduce his activity to a level you find acceptable. Bob would be willing to accept any amount equal to or greater than the difference between the *MC* and *MSC* curves to reduce his activity to Q_S.

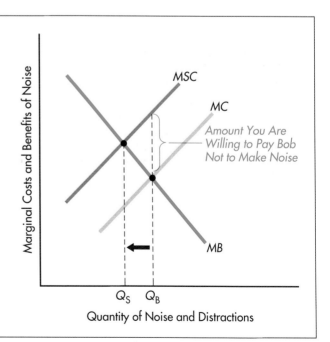

Coase Theorem:
when bargaining is costless and property rights can be assigned without difficulty, the amount of an externality-generating activity will not depend on who is assigned the property rights

ficulty, the amount of the externality-creating activity will be the same no matter who has the property right. This is known as the **Coase Theorem**, named after Ronald Coase, the University of Chicago economist and 1991 Nobel Prize winner who discovered the principle.

In some cases where private property rights do not exist, it is not possible for the government to assign private property rights or to enforce them once assigned, and the Coase Theorem does not hold. For instance, society cannot easily assign individual homeowners private rights to air and expect motorists to buy pollution rights from them. It would be virtually impossible for each motorist to speak with each homeowner. In this case the transaction costs are too high. It is possible, in cases where the transaction costs are too high for the Coase Theorem to work, that a market can be created for the property rights and that the market for property rights will reduce the externality problem. The Economic Insight "The Coase Theorem and Government Interventions" explores the theorem further.

3.a.4. A Market for the Property Rights For the 2,700 Southern California plants that account for 85 percent of the region's hydrocarbons and 95 percent of the nitrogen oxides that do not come from automobiles, a new approach is being used to clean up the air. Under the old approach, the amount of pollution allowed from each generator, boiler, baking oven, or other piece of equipment was specified by the smog-control agency. The new approach is to allow a company to choose the least expensive mix of new controls as long as total pollution does not exceed some assigned level. Each business gets a certificate indicating the amount of pollution it is permitted each year; each is given a property right to that amount of pollution. These permits can then be bought and sold in a market, what is referred to as a "smog" market. A firm easily meeting its standards could sell its excess to a firm having some difficulty meeting its standards. For example, Mobil Corporation purchased the permission to spew out an additional 900 pounds of noxious gas vapors each day, for about $3 million, from the city of South Gate, California. South Gate had acquired the credits from General Motors, which closed a plant there and sold the city the property and the pollution permits that went with the property.[2]

emissions offset policy:
an environmental policy wherein pollution permits are issued and a market in the permits then develops

In many regions of the country the Environmental Protection Agency uses an **emissions offset policy**. The EPA owns the air and sells permits to "use" the air. Companies with permits must not produce more pollution than their permits allow. But if they produce less pollution than their permits allow, they can "bank" the difference and use it later, or they can sell it to other polluters. This, like the approach in Southern California, creates a market for the right to pollute.

The amount of pollution wanted by the Environmental Protection Agency is indicated by the vertical supply curve of pollution rights in Figure 6. The demand for permits to pollute is shown by the downward-sloping curve, *MB*. With a price (*P*) for pollution rights determined, firms *internalize* the exter-

---

[2]"A Promising New Weapon in the Battle to Clean Up the Air," *Los Angeles Times*, Feb. 16, 1992, p. M4; Jeffrey Taylor, "Smog Swapping," *Wall Street Journal*, April 14, 1992, p. 1; *Economic Report of the President, 1992*, p. 184.

Figure 6
The Value of Pollution Permits
The value of pollution permits depends on the demand for and supply of such permits. The vertical supply curve shows the amount of pollution allowed by EPA standards. The marginal benefits of polluting are shown by the downward-sloping curve, *MB*. With a price for pollution rights determined, firms internalize the externality of polluting by using the price of the pollution rights to define the quantity of pollution they will undertake.

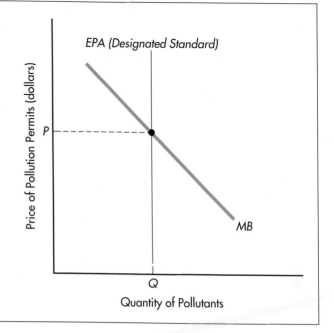

How do global environmental problems differ from domestic environmental problems?

nality of polluting by using the price of the pollution rights to define the quantity (*Q*) of pollution they will undertake.

3.a.5. Global Problems Global environmental issues arise because of externalities and public goods, and the global problems are complicated by the fact that the individuals involved live in many nations. Sulfur dioxide and nitrogen dioxide emitted by factories in the United States are blown to Canada, where they mix with moisture and fall as acid rain. Manufacturing plants located along the Mexican side of the U.S.-Mexico border emit pollutants that flow across the border into the United States. Because one nation cannot impose its wishes on another, developing and enforcing international policies to resolve market failures is difficult.

The ozone layer poses another international challenge. Many scientists claim that the stratospheric ozone layer has been damaged by several chemical compounds, most notably chlorofluorocarbons and bromofluorocarbons (halons). The appearance of a major hole in the ozone layer over Antarctica, where no emissions originate, indicates the global nature of the externality. The problem is that no one government can claim ownership of the ozone. The standard approach has been to develop a nonbinding policy to which several countries will agree. In 1985, a convention of nations established a framework for international scientific and technical cooperation. In 1987, the Montreal Protocol committed signatories to freeze production levels of chlorofluorocarbons by 1989 and then cut their production in half by 1998. In 1989 in Paris, the world's seven biggest industrial economies agreed to begin major assaults on many environmental problems. The group set a goal of a total ban on chlorofluorocarbon emissions by the year 2000.

The 1985, 1987, and 1989 meetings seemed to imply that the industrialized nations of the West were in agreement about environmental policy. On

The Coase Theorem and Government Interventions

Policies to minimize negative externalities must be carefully considered. The policy implemented might not be the best means to reduce the externalities. Often this is the case with what initially seems to be the simplest solution to a problem—banning the activity that creates the noxious negative externality. Consider, for instance, the regulatory approach to the pollution problems in Mexico City. A ban on driving each car a specific day of the week failed to reduce the pollution problem. Many drivers bought a second car to circumvent the regulation, and the added cars pushed up their costs. Moreover, with more cars in the city, many of them older, the regulation actually ended up increasing pollution rather than reducing it.*

Consider also recent attempts to deal with the negative externalities smokers impose on nonsmokers. Reports on the established link between secondhand smoke and cancer have stimulated demands for outright bans on smoking in public places. In Italy, France, and an increasing number of cities in the United States, these bans are in fact being imposed. The basis for the bans is the externalities that smokers impose on nonsmokers.

The question that arises is whether the ban is the best solution to the externality problem. The Coase Theorem suggests that a private market solution would be the economically efficient one. A private market solution would come about because profit-maximizing owners have an incentive to please their customers by catering to their smoking/nonsmoking desires. Whether a business caters solely to smokers or to nonsmokers, or attempts to satisfy both by providing smokers with the right to smoke while at the same time providing nonsmokers with cleaner air through air filtration systems and nonsmoking sections, depends on the extent to which customers want smoking environments and on the marginal costs of one option relative to another. The important point is that when businesses own the airspace, they will manage that scarce resource so as to promote its long-term value.

The secondhand smoke issue involves people in close proximity to each other interacting over airspace. To the extent that smokers and nonsmokers share the airspace, they must come to some agreement about the allocation of the resource. It is unlikely that these customers will want to bargain with each other over the right to smoke or to have smoke-free air every time they enter a public building, but they can demand that the owner of the restaurant or building accommodate their diverse preferences in mutually advantageous ways. Businesses cater to either smokers or nonsmokers (or some combination) based on which of these two groups values the airspace more.

Regulations that prohibit smoking shift ownership of the airspace within those bars and restaurants. Before a ban, smokers and nonsmokers have equal access to negotiate with business owners over the use of the airspace, and therefore the private market internalizes the negative externalities. Smoking bans, however, eliminate the negotiation process and do not allow the Coase Theorem to work.

*The World Bank, "Development Brief," December 1992, number 5.

November 7, 1989, however, the United States and Japan refused to sign a draft resolution at an international conference on global climate change held in the Netherlands. The resolution called for stabilization of carbon dioxide emissions and the emissions of other greenhouse gases by the year 2000. The United States and Japan made the conference drop all reference to a specific year and to a specific target for carbon dioxide. The reason the United States gave for refusing to sign the draft was that it was unfair to less developed nations. For more than one hundred years, the developed nations have benefited from the use of fossil fuels, which emit carbon dioxide when they are burned. Now, those developed nations, concerned about the environmental impact of carbon dioxide emissions, want to limit the use of fossil fuels by less developed nations. Such a limitation would deprive people in poor countries of the advantages offered by the use of coal and oil in production—advantages enjoyed for years by people in developed countries.

The fairness issue is at the heart of the debate about global warming. The unequal distribution of income among nations (see the chapter on income distribution, poverty, and government policy) creates a sticking point for policies intended to resolve global environmental problems. Environmental quality can be thought of as a normal good or even as a luxury good. The richest nations can better afford the sacrifices needed to improve environmental conditions than the poorest nations. Similarly, within one nation, the richest members of society can better afford environmental improvements than the poorest members. Yet the poor often pay significant costs for improvements to the environment. They usually reside near airports, chemical plants, and other undesirable locations because land values in such places have been driven down. When these areas are improved environmentally and noise is reduced, the value of the land rises and the poor are driven out. The marginal increase in the price of cars due to emission controls or mandatory safety equipment adversely affects the poor more than the wealthy in the sense that the auto purchase is a greater share of their income.

3.b. Government Regulation of Public Goods

Public goods, as you learned earlier, are those goods or services for which the producer is unable to exclude nonpayers so that a free rider problem emerges. Because users have no incentive to pay for the public good, the demand curve for the good will lie far below the demand that would exist if users had to purchase the good. As a result, "too little" of the public good is

This mighty saguaro (sa-war-o) cactus, native only to Arizona, is 150 to 200 years old. Many of the cacti, along with a great deal of the Southwestern desert, have disappeared under the bulldozer, pavement, and building as the population of the Southwest has risen. To preserve the desert, private organizations and the city of Phoenix, using private funds, have purchased portions of the desert to set aside as preserves. Around Phoenix, the North and South Mountain preserves ensure that the saguaro cactus remains for residents and visitors alike to enjoy. Outside of Tucson, the Saguaro National Monument sets aside desert land as a federally owned park.

produced. Since too little is produced, too few resources flow to the production of the public good. How is the public good problem solved?

There have been attempts by private entrepreneurs to convert public goods into private goods. Large stadiums built around baseball or football fields restrict the viewing of the games outside of the stadiums; you have to purchase a ticket to see the contest. The Rural Metro Company of Scottsdale, Arizona, provided private subscription fire protection to residents of Scottsdale and surrounding communities. The company would put out fires at no cost to subscribers but would put out fires for nonsubscribers for a price that equaled Rural Metro's average total cost. In general, however, the solution for the free rider problems of public goods is to have the government produce the good. National defense, wildlife reserves in Kenya, wilderness areas in the United States, and the park systems in every country would probably not exist if a government did not provide them. Radio and television airwaves, and perhaps police and fire protection, are public goods as well and might not exist unless provided by the government.

How much of a public good should the government provide? The optimal amount is the amount where the market demand curve and the marginal-cost curve (supply curve) of producing the good intersect. If we could measure how much society would actually be willing and able to pay for a public good, we could determine the optimal quantity to produce very readily. For example, we know the marginal cost of producing a missile—all we have to do is equate it to the market demand for the missile to determine the number of missiles to produce. The problem is that we cannot easily determine the market demand. Surveys do not help because people have an incentive not to tell the truth—by indicating they would pay a lot when in reality they know they get it for free, or by indicating they would pay nothing because they know their taxes will be set according to what they say. The only way that the public can register its demand for public goods is through the ballot box. But, as we will discuss in the next chapter, the ballot box does not measure the intensity of consumer preferences, and it too can fail to produce the optimal quantity of the public good.

RECAP

1. The solution to an externality is to ensure that those creating an externality internalize it.

2. Externalities may be internalized through the imposition of regulations or taxes, the use of subsidies, or the assignment of private property rights.

3. The Coase Theorem illustrates the way private individuals can resolve externalities if property rights are assigned. Who has the property right does not matter; what matters is the assigning of the property right.

4. Global environmental issues are particularly difficult to solve because no one government can claim ownership of the property.

5. If a public good cannot be converted to a private good, the solution to providing the right amount of the public good is to have the government provide it.

SUMMARY

▲▼ What is a market failure?

1. A market failure occurs when the market fails to produce the right amount of output and to allocate the right amount of resources to alternative uses. The right amount refers to the amount that would occur in a world of perfect competition—the economically efficient amount. §§1.a, 1.c

▲▼ Why is an externality considered to be a source of market failure?

2. When an externality occurs, private costs and benefits differ from social costs. Either too much or too little is consumed or produced relative to the quantities that would occur if all costs and benefits were included. §2.a

3. An externality may result from the lack of private property rights. §2.b

▲▼ What is a public good?

4. A public good is a good for which the principle of mutual exclusivity does not hold. §2.c

▲▼ How can market failures be resolved?

5. Possible solutions to externalities include regulations, taxes, subsidies, and the assignment of private property rights. §§3.a, 3.a.1, 3.a.2, 3.a.3

6. The most common solution to public goods is for the government to supply the good. §3.b

▲▼ How do global environmental problems differ from domestic environmental problems?

7. Global environmental problems are more difficult to resolve than domestic ones because of the lack of property rights. When no one government owns the resource being damaged by an externality, then the externality cannot be resolved by any one government. §3.a.5

KEY TERMS

market failure §1.c
private costs §2.a
externality §2.a
social costs §2.a
private property right §2.b
marginal benefits (MB) §2.b
marginal social costs §2.b

principle of mutual exclusivity §2.c
public good §2.c
free rider §2.c
emission standard §3.a.1
Coase Theorem §3.a.3
emissions offset policy §3.a.4

EXERCISES

1. The three demand schedules listed below constitute the total demand for a particular good.
   a. Determine the market demand schedule for the good if it is a private good.

   b. Determine the market demand schedule for the good if it is a public good.

Bob		Sally		Rafael	
P	Q_d	P	Q_d	P	Q_d
$6	0	$6	0	$6	1
5	1	5	0	5	2
4	2	4	1	4	3
3	3	3	2	3	4
2	4	2	3	2	5
1	5	1	4	1	6

2. Using the public good described in question 1 and the following supply schedule, determine the optimal quantity of the good. Explain how you determined this quantity.

P	Q_s
$10	15
9	11
7	9
6	8
4	7
2	4
1	3

3. Use the following information to answer the questions listed below.

   a. What is the external cost per unit of output?

   b. What level of output will be produced?

   c. What level of output should be produced to achieve economic efficiency?

   d. What is the value to society of correcting the externality?

Quantity	MC	MSC	MB
1	$ 2	$ 4	$12
2	4	6	10
3	6	8	8
4	8	10	6
5	10	12	4

4. What level of tax would be appropriate to internalize the externality in question 3?

5. If, in question 3, the MC and MSC columns were reversed, you would have an example of what? Would too much or too little of the good be produced? How would the market failure be resolved, by tax or by subsidy?

6. What is meant by the term *overfishing*? What is the fundamental problem associated with overfishing of the oceans? What might lead to *underfishing*?

7. Explain why the optimal amount of pollution is not a zero amount. Use the same explanation to discuss the amount of health and safety that the government should require in the workplace.

8. Suppose the following table describes the marginal costs and marginal benefits of waste (garbage) reduction. What is the optimal amount of garbage? What is the situation if no garbage is allowed to be produced?

Percentage of Waste Eliminated	Marginal Costs (millions of dollars)	Marginal Benefits (millions of dollars)
10%	$ 10	$1,000
20	15	500
30	25	100
40	40	50
50	70	20
60	110	5
70	200	3
80	500	2
90	900	1
100	2,000	0

9. Elephants eat 300 pounds of food per day. They flourished in Africa when they could roam over huge areas of land, eating the vegetation in one area and then moving on so that the vegetation could renew itself. Now, the area over which elephants can roam is declining. Without some action, the elephants will become extinct. What actions might save the elephants? What are the costs and benefits of such actions?

10. What could explain why the value of pollution permits in one area of the country is rising 20 percent per year while in another it is unchanged from year to year? What would you expect to occur as a result of this differential?

11. Smokers impose negative externalities on non-smokers. Suppose the airspace in a restaurant is a resource owned by the restaurant owner.

    a. How would the owner respond to the negative externalities of smokers?

    b. Suppose that the smokers owned the airspace. How would that change matters?

    c. How about if the nonsmokers owned the airspace?

d. Finally, consider what would occur if the government passed a law banning all smoking. How would the outcome compare with the outcomes described above?

12. Discuss the argument that education should be subsidized because it creates a positive externality.

13. If the best solution to solving the positive externality problem of education is to provide a subsidy, explain why education systems in all countries are nationalized, that is, are government entities.

Sold: $21 Million of Air Pollution

CHICAGO, March 29—The Environmental Protection Agency's first auction of rights to pollute the air attracted more participants than had been expected and reaped $21 million, according to a participant in the sale who declined to be named.

The results, which are to be announced at a news conference here Tuesday, were less pleasing for utilities that tried to piggyback on the auction to sell pollution allowances that the Federal agency had previously granted them. The utilities set such high minimum prices that almost none of their allowances were sold, the participant said.

At stake were more than 275,000 pollution allowances, each permitting a utility to emit a ton of sulfur dioxide, the chemical that causes acid rain. Under the 1990 Clean Air Act, the E.P.A. set strict "spot" emissions limits to take effect in 1995, covering 110 of the nation's largest, dirtiest power plants. . . .

The act allows utilities that can reduce emissions below the permitted levels to sell the allowances they do not need to others that are having trouble meeting the limits. In theory, market forces will encourage utilities that can cut pollution the most for the least investment in scrubbers or fuel changes to lead the way. That would allow the nation to shave billions of dollars off the cost of meeting pollution-reduction goals.

The E.P.A. is said to have received 106 bids for the 50,000 spot allowances it offered, 36 of which were successful at prices ranging from $131 an allowance to $450. Utilities offered 95,010 spot allowances, only 10 of which were sold, the sources said.

The E.P.A. received 65 bids for the 100,000 advance allowances it offered and sold them to 30 bidders at prices of $122 to $310. None of the 30,500 advance allowances offered by the utilities were sold.

The annual auction is intended to help utilities figure out the value of the allowances, encourage trading, and spur investment by utilities that want to build up reserves of allowances for future trading. Experts said that the level of interest had been unexpectedly high.

"It looked like a lot of utilities would stay out because they didn't have a pressing need to get in," said Michael Gildea, a regulatory analyst for the Edison Electric Institute, the Washington-based trade organization for the nation's largest investor-owned utilities. "But it seems that people were hunting for bargains and just testing the water."

Complete results will be announced by E.P.A. officials and the Chicago Board of Trade, which was selected to run the annual auctions for three years. The Board of Trade expects eventually to create a pollution allowance futures contract that will allow utilities to shift the risk of price changes in allowances to investors, just as farmers use futures markets to shift the risks of changes in crop prices.

"This auction will be remembered as a classic case of the exchange's role in price discovery," said Richard Sandor, a director of the Board of Trade and early proponent of pollution rights trading on established exchanges. "Up until now, you have only had a handful of small trades with wide ranges in prices."

The lowest winning bids were well under Mr. Sandor's predictions last week. Private transactions in recent months have reportedly taken place at prices up to $400 per allowance. . . .

In general, falling prices would indicate that utilities have been investing more heavily in compliance than projected and expect to have more allowances than they need in 1995. But lower prices might also cause utilities that are planning such investments to reconsider, because it might prove cheaper to buy enough allowances to continue polluting at current levels—or even higher.

Indeed, one utility that bid in the auction, the Illinois Power Company, has already stopped construction on a $350 million scrubber and begun in private deals to stockpile permits that it will use between 1995 and 2000. "The state requires us to meet emissions standards in the least costly way, said John Dewey, a spokesman for the Decatur, Ill., utility. "Using the permits will save us at least $250 million over the next 20 years and save Illinois coal-mining jobs as well." . . .

Source: Barnaby J. Feder, "Sold: $21 Million of Air Pollution," *New York Times,* March 30, 1993, *p. 1.* Copyright © 1993 by The New York Times Company. Reprinted with permission.

Commentary

Externalities—costs and benefits borne by those not directly involved—are often a consequence of the lack of private property rights for a natural resource. Unless property rights have been assigned so that the parties who own the rights to the property are clearly stated, the private market will not allocate natural resources in a way that maximizes society's benefits. Often in such cases the role of government is to assign private property rights. This has occurred with land, forests, and some species of animals and plants.

Not all natural resources lend themselves to ordinary boundaries and fences, however. For instance, it is difficult to assign ownership of the atmosphere. To address this problem, the government has created a special kind of property right—the right to *use* the resource—and it allows holders of the right to sell it like any other property. Here is how the system works: Yearly caps (ceilings) on sulfur dioxide emissions from electric utilities are set by law. Over time, the caps will be lowered, so that by the year 2000 these emissions will be about one-half of their 1990 levels. The utilities are given permits each year for the amount of the sulfur dioxide that may legally be released. Since the cost of limiting emissions may be much higher at some facilities than at others, it would be very inefficient to force each plant to reduce emissions by the same amount. So, the law allows the permits to be bought and sold. Utilities that would find it expensive to reduce emissions may be willing to pay a high price for the permits. Plants that can reduce emissions relatively inexpensively may be willing to sell their permits. In this way, the market for permits allocates the permits so that those plants able to reduce pollution inexpensively will reduce pollution the most.

To illustrate how the market for permits works, let's assume the government issues 300,000 permits, each permit allowing one ton of sulfur dioxide to be emitted. The owners of those permits are the utilities. But the utilities do not know what the permits are worth. They can calculate their own value and offer to sell permits if someone will pay a higher price, but they really do not even know who might want to purchase a permit.

To establish a price for the permits, an auction is held where buyers and sellers offer to buy or sell a permit for a certain price. The resulting equilibrium price is the price established by the intersection of the demand and supply curves. The suppliers of permits are the holders of the permits. They decide what price and quantity to offer for sale. The higher the price, the greater the quantity supplied. The market demand for the permits is the sum of the individual demands. A utility will compare the marginal cost of the permit to the marginal cost of pollution-abatement expenditures and decide whether to purchase permits or to offer permits for sale. The utilities are not the only ones who enter the market for pollution permits. Environmental groups that want to reduce the quantity of pollution in the atmosphere may also bid for permits; owning one permit means that firms cannot emit one ton of sulfur dioxide.

Once a price is established, the electric utilities have information with which to decide whether to purchase pollution-abatement equipment or additional permits in the future. If the marginal cost of pollution-abatement equipment exceeds the equilibrium price of the permits, the utilities are better off purchasing additional permits. However, if the price of the permits rises, some utilities that are not currently buying pollution-abatement equipment will find that they are better off devoting expenditures to abatement.

As the supply of permits is reduced by the government and the price of the permits rises, more and more utilities will be willing to sell their permit and purchase pollution-abatement equipment: The supply curve will shift up.

22

Government and Public Choice

FUNDAMENTAL QUESTIONS

1. What is collective decision-making?
2. Individuals maximize utility. What does the government maximize?
3. What is rent seeking?

M any policies and practices are the result of collective rather than individual decisions. Collective decisions are made by groups of people: the members of a union decide whether to accept a contract offered by management; voters decide whether to support a bond issue providing more funds for education; a board of directors of a corporation decides whether the firm should enter new markets; Congress decides whether to support President Clinton's plans on health care.

Collective decision-making differs from the private decision-making discussed so far. In private decision-making, individuals make the decisions that maximize their utility given the information they have at the time. In a private market, individual decisions are expressed in terms of a willingness and ability to purchase or produce a good or service. Collective decisions are not as straightforward. Individual decisions to maximize utility are expressed as votes. The votes are then combined to reach a collective decision.

PREVIEW

This chapter focuses on the government, or what we call the public sector. As you have seen in previous chapters, the government intervenes in the private market frequently. We will now examine the process which drives the government to take action. We first look at collective decision-making, because it is this mechanism, specifically voting, through which we choose our government officials and make our preferences for government action known.

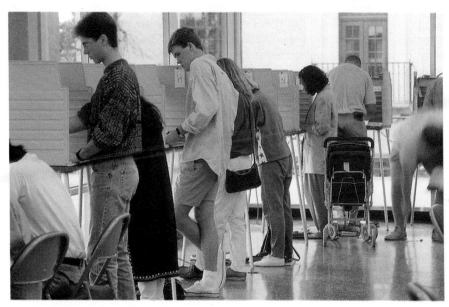

The study of the public sector and collective decision-making is the study of public choice. **Public choice theory** uses economics to analyze the actions and inner workings of the public sector.

public choice theory:
the use of economics to analyze the actions and inner workings of the public sector

In Chapter 5 we defined public choice as the study of how government actions result from the self-interested behavior of voters and politicians. In this chapter we broaden the definition somewhat to include the role collective decision-making plays in determining the activities of the public sector. As we examine how the government functions, it will become clear that the outcomes of collective decision-making differ from those of individual choice as expressed in the private marketplace. We will also see, as a result, how the government's behavior deviates from the workings of the private marketplace. By the end of this chapter we will have built an explanation for why and how this deviation comes about.

I. COLLECTIVE DECISION-MAKING

If we analyze government in economic terms, we have one large market, where the public's demand for particular actions in the form of votes meets

What is collective decision-making?

the supply of legislation enacted by politicians. Where is equilibrium? Are the decisions made and actions carried out optimal? As we will see in this section, the process through which the public's votes get translated into government policy is different from the way in which equilibrium is reached in a private market, resulting in different outcomes from collective decision-making than we would expect from the private market at work.

1.a. Differences Between Collective Decision-Making and the Private Marketplace

Unlike individual decision-making in the private marketplace, collective decisions are made by voting, not by consuming or producing goods and services. In collective decision-making, votes replace dollars, bundles of issues or goods are considered rather than one good at a time, and consumers are rationally ignorant.

Dollars versus votes   Collective decisions are made on the basis of one vote per person, whereas in the private marketplace, there is one vote per dollar. If you decide to spend a lot of money on a particular good or service, you are expressing the intensity with which you desire that good or service. You vote once in an election no matter what your income is and no matter how intensely you feel about an issue. You cannot express how much you want something with your vote since your vote counts no more than a vote by someone who cares little about the issue being decided.

Full-line supply   Voters do not purchase one good at a time as consumers do in the marketplace; instead, they must choose a *full-line supply* of products when they cast their votes. A **full-line supply** is the entire bundle of policies offered by a candidate for office or comprised in an issue. Voters cast a vote for a candidate knowing that the candidate will take stands on many issues. An individual who agrees with a candidate's environmental policies but not with the candidate's support for income redistribution does not vote yes for the environmental policy and no for the income-distribution policy. The voter casts a yes or no vote for the candidate's entire bundle of policies. Similarly, a voter may support a bond issue even though a portion of the funds to be raised with the sale of the bonds is to be used for a baseball field, something the voter does not want, because the remainder of the funds are to be used for community hiking paths, something the voter wants.

full-line supply:
the entire bundle of policies offered by a candidate

Rational ignorance   As we discussed in the chapter on the economics of information, individuals will compare the marginal costs and marginal benefits of devoting time and income to gathering more information. In the private market, individuals have a greater incentive to gather information than they do in a collective decision-making process because they have to bear the full costs of any mistakes they make in purchasing a good or service. With collective decisions, the entire collectivity bears the costs of any mistakes; one well-informed individual bears the same costs as one ill-informed individual. As a result, no individual has an incentive to become really well informed about each issue.

Knowing all sides of an issue, determining the ramifications of a piece of legislation, knowing all the candidates' stands on issues, and in general, having perfect information prior to voting would take an inordinate amount of time and money. Because information gathering is costly and because individuals have little incentive to become well informed, we say that voters are

rationally ignorant voters:
voters who do not have perfect
information because it is too
costly to acquire

rationally ignorant—they choose to make decisions on the basis of limited information. Many voters, in fact, go to the polls without having any knowledge of the issues being voted on.

For all of these reasons, you can see that voting is a much less exact expression of individual preference than the process of purchasing a good or service. In the next section, we look at some of the problems that can result from collective decision-making that do not occur in a private market.

I.b. Problems That Can Arise in Collective Decision-Making

In examining group decision-making we must first acknowledge the set of voting rules used. Under a democratic system the majority is usually favored. The issue or candidate receiving one vote more than one-half of the votes cast wins. There are instances, though, where a clear majority may not emerge and thus where collective decision-making provides no solution.

I.b.1. Voting Cycles

Consider, as an example, a decision of what type of budget to offer to the citizens of the Kyrene School District. The three members of the school board must decide whether to offer a low-budget program, a moderate-budget program, or a high-budget program. Suppose that school board member Melissa High prefers that new schools be built, class sizes be kept small, computers be provided, sports and music be available, and the maintenance of the schools be upgraded. Moreover, if the district does not want to have a high-budget program, Melissa believes most people will enroll their children in private schools. Thus, if she can't have the high-budget program, Melissa would prefer the low budget to the middle budget for the school district. John Middle is not comfortable with the size of tax payments necessary to support the high-quality package Melissa desires. He supports a more moderate budget, but he believes families would be willing to sacrifice to have the high budget if necessary. His least-preferred option is the low budget. Sharon Low prefers a low budget but would go along with a moderate budget if necessary. She is totally opposed to the high-budget program. The three board members must decide which of the programs to offer to the school district.

The choices of the three board members are illustrated in Figure 1. Along the vertical axis are the preferences of each board member ranked from least preferred to most preferred. Along the horizontal axis are the three proposals, low budget, moderate budget, and high budget. Melissa most prefers the high budget and least prefers the moderate budget; her preferences are indicated along the line labeled "Melissa." John most prefers the moderate budget and least prefers the low budget; his preferences are indicated by the line labeled "John." Sharon most prefers the low budget and least the high budget; her preferences are indicated by the line labeled "Sharon."

The board decides to vote on each budget program compared to the other; high budget versus middle budget, then high budget versus low budget, and then middle budget versus low budget. If the board members are asked to choose between the low budget and the moderate budget, the low budget gets the most votes. If they are asked to choose between the low budget and the high budget, the high budget gets the most votes. If they are asked to choose between the moderate budget and the high budget, the moderate budget gets the most votes. There is no clear decision: each alternative wins an election and each loses an election when paired against the other alternatives. A series

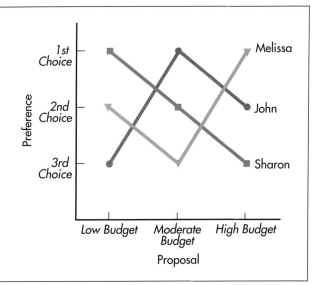

Figure 1
Voting Cycles
The preferences of three groups of voters are measured along the vertical axis; the issues among which the voters must choose are measured on the horizontal axis. Because each issue is the first choice of one group, the second choice of another group, and the third choice of the third group, there is no clear majority supporting any one issue.

voting cycle:
the situation where a collective decision process does not reach a conclusion

logrolling:
trading votes or support on one issue in return for votes or support on another issue

of votes or runoffs to determine the winner would result in an endless cycle. This result of the collective decision-making process is referred to as a **voting cycle**.

Voting cycles are a possible outcome in any election. They are a *failure of collective decision-making*. As a result of the failure, either no decision will be reached or another voting rule or procedure must be used. Often, a two-thirds voting rule is required instead of a simple majority in order to reduce the chance of a voting cycle. In the case we have outlined, a two-thirds voting rule is no different than the majority voting rule, and a change in the rule would not alter the outcome. Unanimity does not work either since there is no compromise position all could agree on. The ultimate outcome in the school board case will depend on whether any one of the three board members can dominate or influence the other members and convince one or both to alter their preferences.

I.b.2. Logrolling   The frustration voters may feel when the collective decision-making process fails may induce them to trade votes. John Middle may agree to support Melissa High's preference on the school budget issue if Melissa will agree to support his preference on some other issue. In this case, the voting cycle will be resolved and the high-budget program will be selected. John traded his vote on the budget issue to Melissa in return for a similar trade from Melissa on some other issue in the future. Vote trading is called **logrolling**.

Vote trading, or logrolling, is common in collective decision-making. It occurs regularly in the U.S. Congress. Suppose voters in Massachusetts want the government to build a large ship in their harbor and voters in Kansas want the government to purchase large quantities of wheat. The senator from Kansas has no reason to support the shipbuilding program in Massachusetts, and the senator from Massachusetts has no incentive to support the wheat-purchase plan. However, if the two senators agree to support each other's program, both can gain. Thus the senator from Kansas will promise to support a bill subsidizing the construction of a ship in Boston Harbor in return for the support of the senator from Massachusetts for an increase in the price of wheat. In this way, each senator is able to get something he or she desires. Notice, however, that the outcomes may not be something desired by a majority of voters. As in the school board case, an outcome was determined through vote trading, but no clear majority prevailed.

1.c. The Importance of Brand Names

In private markets brand names provide information about the quality or reliability of products, as you saw in the chapter on the economics of information. In collective decision-making, where voters are rationally ignorant, brand names may play even more important roles. For instance, although their policies may seem to differ only slightly from one another, Republicans generally support smaller government, lower taxes, fewer benefits for lower-income citizens, and lower inflation, while Democrats are more likely to favor more government, tax increases, more support for the disadvantaged, and lower unemployment. A voter expects that a vote for a Republican will be a vote in support of a certain type of policy, whereas a vote for a Democrat will be a vote in support of a different type of policy. Political party identification thus provides at least general information to voters.

Incumbency also provides brand-name information; incumbents are better known than newcomers simply because the incumbents have a track record from having been in office. Just as consumers tend to purchase products with brand names, voters tend to support incumbent candidates: over 90 percent of incumbents in the U.S. Congress running for reelection win.

Voters' reliance on the brand names of "Republican" and "Democrat" has made it difficult for members of any other party to be successfully elected to office. Independents seldom enter campaigns for office at the federal or state level and, when they do, seldom win. The fixed costs of the brand name are extremely high: Ross Perot had to outspend George Bush and Bill Clinton in order to run a respectable third place in the 1992 presidential election.

RECAP

1. Collective decisions are reached by a group. The group may be a club or organization, a board of directors, or the citizens of a state or nation.

2. Collective decision-making differs from private decision-making. Collective decisions are made on the basis of one person–one vote; thus, intensity of preference cannot be registered. A full-line supply of issues is voted on rather than a single issue, and, since gathering information about issues is too costly, most voters choose rational ignorance.

3. Collective decision-making may not reach a conclusion or decision; a voting cycle may occur.

4. Logrolling is the trading of votes: One voter agrees to support the preference of another voter on one issue in return for the support of the second voter on an issue preferred by the first voter.

5. Due to rational ignorance, brand names—in this case, identification with a specific political party—may provide the information voters rely on.

2. GOVERNMENT ACTIVITIES AS DETERMINED BY COLLECTIVE DECISION-MAKING

Individuals maximize utility. What does the government maximize?

Although collective decision-making occurs in the private sector—boards of directors, unions, private clubs, and organizations all make collective or group decisions—its most important manifestation is in government: the public's choice with respect to levels of national defense, macroeconomic policy, government intervention in private markets, and other activities is expressed through this process.

2.a. Representative Democracy

In direct democracy, each action is voted on by all of the citizens. In representative democracy, citizens select individuals to represent them, to vote on issues and carry out the day-to-day activities of government. Representative democracy is more common than direct democracy because the transaction costs of direct democracy are too high. Just imagine how difficult it would be to have all of the nearly 200 million eligible voters in the United States vote on every issue confronting the country.

The participants in representative democracy are the voters and the politicians who attempt to become their representatives. Voters are like consumers, demanding the benefits that government can provide, and the representatives are the suppliers, providing the legislation that consumers want. The behavior of voters and representatives thus influences the outcome of the collective decision-making process in representative democracy.

2.b. Representatives Behave in Their Self-Interest

Self-interest characterizes all individuals.

Self-interest characterizes the behavior of every individual. Government representatives are no exception: they act to maximize their own utility. The central objective of any politician is to get elected and then maintain enough support to remain in office. Thus, each candidate running for office and each elected official must behave as his or her constituents want in order to win the election. Yet, each may have personal goals and objectives that do not correspond to what the constituents want. To the extent that the voters cannot monitor the actions of the elected officials, the officials can pursue their own objectives even at the expense of the voters.

Because voters cannot vote directly on every piece of legislation but must instead elect representatives to vote for them, the possibility exists that politicians will allow their own personal interests to enter into their voting decisions.

A great deal of evidence exists to suggest that self-interest characterizes the behavior of elected officials. Consider the difference between senators who are subject to election only once every six years and the members of the House of Representatives, who must compete every other year. Citizens can more easily monitor the behavior of the representatives, while senators have a longer period of time during which entry is barred. We would thus expect senators to act more like monopolists than would representatives. We would expect senators to pursue their own interests rather than their constituents' interests more often than the representatives do. And indeed this is the case. Senators vote their own interests rather than the interests of their constituents much more often than do the representatives.

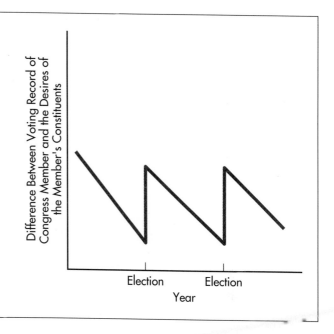

Figure 2
Senatorial Voting Record
Senators face election every six years. As a result, once elected they can vote their own interests for a few years. As an election nears, however, they begin to vote more along the lines desired by their constituents. The jagged curve represents the difference between the voting record of a senator and the voting record desired by the senator's constituents. The difference decreases as an election nears and rises by the greatest amount immediately after an election.

Senators vote their own interests during the first two or three years immediately following an election and then vote as their constituents want in the year or two prior to an election, because the voters forget the earlier actions and focus on the more recent ones when going to the polls. Senators thus have a cyclical voting record relative to the desires of their constituents, as shown in Figure 2. They vote a more conservative line as an election nears if they are from a conservative state, and they vote a more liberal line as an election nears if they are from a liberal state. Once the election is over, they once again vote as their own self-interest dictates. This pattern does not show up in the voting behavior of members of the House of Representatives.

All politicians behave in their own self-interest, and all must appeal to a majority of their constituents at the time of election. Thus policies and programs are offered and implemented in order to ensure election or reelection. A dramatic illustration of this was described by Gore Vidal in his historical novel *Lincoln*. Vidal noted that President Lincoln used troop deployment to ensure his reelection in 1864. Units from states in which his election was in question were moved to the rear or out of the fighting in the hope that they and their friends and families would support Lincoln or at least would not have reason not to support him. Troops from states in which his reelection was virtually either a certainty or an impossibility saw front-line action.[1]

2.c. Public Choice Theory at Work

What results can we expect a system of representative democracy, with its rationally self-interested participants, to yield? In the next sections, we look

---

[1]Gore Vidal, *Lincoln* (New York: Ballantine Books, 1984). Robert Tollison examined Vidal's thesis and found evidence to support it. See Robert Tollison, "Dead Men Don't Vote," Public Choice Center, George Mason University, 1989.

at four outcomes of our own representative democracy: growth of government; public production of public goods; taxation and spending legislation; and the median voter theorem.

2.c.1. Agencies and the Growth of Government Government consists not just of the representatives directly elected by the public but also the bureaucrats appointed by the elected representatives to run the government. This includes the agencies like the Food and Drug Administration, the Federal Communications Commission, the Departments of Labor, State, Health and Human Resources, Treasury, and many others. Although these individuals may be appointed by the president or members of Congress, they have their own objectives.

Agencies of government may grow because of the self-interested behavior of employees of government.

How does self-interest show up in the bureaucracy? It could mean that a director will attempt to gain visibility and access to power in order to maximize personal income. Books can be written and speeches given after one leaves government service. Not only is the potential of personal wealth enticing, but power and influence alone provide utility. To be the director of a large and powerful agency is better than to be the director of a small, unknown agency. For this reason, it is not at all unusual for an agency to increase its sphere of influence and for the number of employees in an agency to rise over time. In fact, nearly every agency in government has grown, and at a very fast pace, as discussed in the Economic Insight "The Growth of Government." As you learned in Chapter 5, the number of government employees has risen significantly since 1930, and they now constitute about 20 percent of the labor force, at least partly due to the individual self-interest of those involved in the bureaucracy of government.

2.c.2. Private versus Public Production of Public Goods Although society believes that government should provide public goods, it does not say the government should produce the goods itself. Why doesn't the government have private firms produce the public goods, such as fire protection and police protection, under contract to the government? In this way, the government could rely on the efficiency of the private market to produce high-quality goods at the lowest prices. For instance, the national park service, national postal service, local police and fire protection services, and refuse collection and water supply services could all be run by private firms for the government rather than run and staffed by government employees. Private firms could provide these services for the government at a lower cost in most instances.

One reason that private firms aren't used is that the representatives of government have more control of the public goods if the government produces them than if private firms produce them. If services were provided by the private sector, politicians would have much more difficulty influencing the behavior of the agencies. Not only can politicians influence the behavior of government agencies and bureaus, but they can provide employment in an agency for constituents. It would be more difficult to place an important constituent in a position in a private firm than in a government agency.

Another reason that such a combination of government and private enterprise is problematic is that the private sector may not be able to perform as the public wants. Perhaps a private firm would not produce the quality of goods the public desires. (However, it would be difficult to know how the public felt about the quality of the goods, since the public couldn't switch to another brand; only one would be provided.) Thus, the performance of the

A market-failure problem common to nations is that of lands or natural resources commonly or publicly owned. Nations have the option of having private firms rather than government employees manage the public property. Here, a park ranger in Puerto Rico directs attention to the public land; the ranger is an employee of the government rather than an employee of a private firm that contracts with the government to manage the public lands.

private firm would have to be controlled or monitored by some government agency, and it is possible the costs of such monitoring would exceed the efficiencies gained from the private production of the good. While such a system might appear to offer a solution to the problem of government inefficiencies, it creates other problems which outweigh the efficiencies.

2.c.3. Taxes versus Spending Representatives want to offer a package of policies that voters believe will improve their well-being. If a representative can ensure that benefits flow to many constituents, the representative can gain more support. Government expenditures create income and provide benefits to constituents. Taxes, in contrast, reduce income and take away benefits from constituents. Thus, politicians favor increasing government spending a lot more than they favor increasing taxes.

The problem for the representatives is that an increase in benefits usually means an increase in costs. An increase in government expenditures must be paid for either through raising taxes or through borrowing. How can a representative increase benefits and support without increasing costs and losing support? One way is to provide benefits to constituents but have everyone, constituents and nonconstituents, pay taxes. In this way, the benefits the constituents receive are substantially more than the costs they pay.

Of course, all representatives are attempting to do the same thing since none want taxes imposed on their constituents. As a result, it is much easier to implement expenditure increases than tax increases. An alternative is to provide benefits to the constituents today but not pay for the benefits until sometime in the future, thereby imposing the costs on future generations. There is a natural bias, then, toward increased government expenditures paid for by borrowing or debt, since debt does not have to be paid until some point in the future.

2.c.4. The Median Voter Theorem Programs aiming to improve the lot of everyone are prominent features in every representative's policies. The problem for the representative is that there is usually a diversity of opinion on

The Growth of Government

Most federal agencies have grown significantly since the 1970s. Even in the Reagan and Bush administrations, which were purportedly antigovernment, the growth was substantial. The Justice Department increased its staff by 30.4 percent between 1982 and 1988, the Treasury by 23 percent, the Environmental Protection Agency by 11.5 percent, the State Department by 11 percent, and the Department of Defense by about 7 percent. Growth has been pervasive, occurring in virtually every government agency and department.

The desire for growth has implications for the economy. How is it to be paid for? The growth of most agencies is supported by an increase in general government expenditures. The growth of the Federal Reserve System (Fed), however, is covered not by general government revenues but by the Fed's own revenues. The Federal Reserve obtains its funding in a roundabout way from the Treasury: the Fed pays direct expenses and transfers the remainder to the Treasury. The greater the Fed's revenue, the more expenses it is allowed to generate and still be able to transfer profit to the Treasury. How does the Federal Reserve earn revenue? It increases sales of the goods and services it provides—and the primary good it provides is money. In other words, the Federal Reserve increases its revenue by increasing the quantity of money it creates.

William Shughart and Robert Tollison speculate that the growth of the Federal Reserve has been accompanied by a money-supply growth that has exceeded the rate of growth necessary for a stable, noninflationary economy, and this may explain why inflation has been a problem in the United States for the past four decades. A monetary policy that expands the supply of money and thereby causes inflation may have resulted from the desires of Fed officials to increase their power, prestige, and income by increasing the size of the Federal Reserve rather than through safeguarding the public interest.

According to Professor Eugenia Toma, the Supreme Court too can be shown to be influenced by the objective of increased growth. The Supreme Court receives its funds from Congress. Toma has shown that the opinions of the Court change in response to the budgetary largesse of Congress.

Sources: William Shughart and Robert Tollison, "Preliminary Evidence on the Federal Reserve Use of Inputs," *American Economic Review* 73, no. 3 (June 1983), pp. 291–304; Eugenia Toma, "Congressional Influence and the Supreme Court: The Budget as a Signalling Device," *Journal of Legal Studies*, Jan. 1991, pp. 131–146.

each issue. Some voters favor a large national defense budget; others urge disarmament. Some want a great deal of income redistribution; others urge tax cuts for everyone. Some want large-scale government intervention to protect the environment; others want little government intervention. Faced with this diversity of opinion, it is almost impossible to please everyone. Nevertheless, to attain office, a party must put together a package that attracts a majority of the votes. The search for a majority often results in each candidate offering policies that are very similar to the policies of the other candidates and very similar to the preferences of the median voter.

Suppose all voters are aligned along the continuum of attitudes toward environmental protection shown in Figure 3. The horizontal axis measures the number of voters, and the vertical axis measures the level of government spending on environmental issues supported by each voter. Voter D, labeled *median*, is exactly in the middle: half of the voters support more spending and half support less spending than voter D. Given this range of attitudes, which position will the party stake out?

The greatest support can be gained by selecting a level of spending that corresponds with the level supported by the median voter. The median posi-

Figure 3
The Median Voter Theorem
Voters are aligned in the order of the amount of government spending on environmental issues they desire. The median voter is the voter whose interests put him or her exactly in the middle of all voters: half want more spending and half want less spending than the median voter. A candidate gains maximum political support by staking out positions that are identical to the positions favored by the median voter.

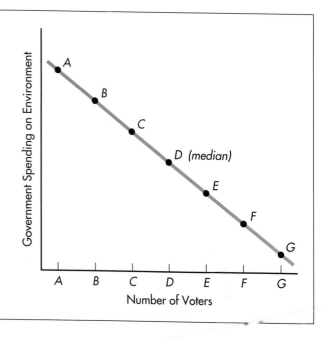

tion differs from the level of spending supported by each other voter by less than any other position. Suppose the party goes along with voter C. Candidates would pick up more support from voters A and B. Voters D, E, F, and G, however, would decrease their support. The difference between the levels of spending that they favor and the party's chosen position would be larger than it was when the candidate chose to support the median position. Similarly, choosing a position at E would decrease the difference between the spending that F supports and the party's position, but it would increase the differences between the spending levels supported by A, B, and C and by the candidate relative to the median position. By staking out a position that is the median voter position, the party or candidate maximizes support.

The first party stakes out *D*, the median position. Where should the second party stake out its position? If it chooses point *E*, it will attract all voters to the right of *E* and half of the voters between the median position and *E*; but the first party will obtain the support of all voters between *A* and the median as well as half of those between the median and *E* and will win the election. The closer the second party moves to the median voter, the larger the number of votes the second party will receive. Therefore, it too will stake out a position identical to the median voter position. This decision is explained by the **median voter theorem**: parties or candidates select positions on issues that reflect the median voter's position.

The median voter theorem is the result of competition among candidates seeking to maximize votes. The identical result is obtained when profit-maximizing firms look at locations or introduce new products, as discussed in the chapter on monopolistic competition and oligopoly. The median position is the profit-maximizing position—or, in the case of votes, the vote-maximizing position.

Logrolling in collective decision-making can invalidate the median voter theorem and result in voter frustration. Suppose, for example, that voters are deciding on a health-care system. Senior citizens prefer increased spending

median voter theorem:
parties or candidates select positions on issues that reflect the median voter's positions on those issues

on health care and want the most lavish system available for preserving lives. The middle-aged citizens prefer a more moderate system, one that will help them provide for their children's health. Younger citizens prefer no system. The middle-aged citizens are the median voters in this case. But suppose the younger citizens agree to support the lavish health-care system if the seniors will support a system of free education for all college students. In this case, logrolling has led to a decision not favored by the median voter.

RECAP

1. The economic principle of self-interest accounts for the actions of the government.

2. Political outcomes are the result of participants maximizing their self-interest. Political candidates want to be elected to office. Bureaucrats want to acquire income, power, and prestige.

3. According to the median voter theorem, politicians tend to stake out policies and programs that are supported by the median voter.

4. The median voter theorem may not hold because of logrolling in the collective decision-making process.

3. RENT SEEKING

What is rent seeking?

In Chapter 5 we discussed how people attempt to acquire benefits or wealth through government actions rather than through creating goods and services. We referred to this as *rent-seeking activity*. Having discussed collective decision-making in this chapter, we can now see how representative democracy allows rent seeking to occur: people cannot express their intensity of preferences with a single vote; people must find ways to influence others; and representatives pursue their own self-interest as long as constituents cannot closely monitor their actions. These three elements combine to create the conditions for rent seeking.

Representative democracy provides an incentive to citizens to increase their wealth through government regulations, transfers, or direct expenditures without increasing the supply or ownership of resources. If special interest groups want to increase their wealth, are well organized, and are politically powerful, politicians will grant benefits that enable these groups to increase their wealth. Such benefits are called rents because, like economic rents, they represent a payment that is larger than necessary for the resource to be supplied. Activities undertaken to obtain special favors (rents) from government are called **rent seeking**; these activities produce zero output but use up resources.

rent seeking:
activities directed toward securing income without increasing the production of output

3.a. Profit Seeking versus Rent Seeking

Rent seeking may increase the efficiency of government.

Throughout the book we have pointed out how profit-seeking resource owners enter industries in which economic profits are positive and exit industries in which economic profits are negative. Profit seeking is an important aspect of competition—it ensures that resources are allocated to their highest-valued uses. Rent seeking, in contrast, simply transfers wealth from one group to another. It does not create wealth or produce goods and services. As a result, it does not ensure that resources flow to their most highly valued use.

3.a.1. An Application of Rent Seeking

In the mid-1930s the Agricultural Marketing Agreement was implemented to stop U.S. farmers from ruining each other with too much competition. Since then a number of government policies have been implemented to benefit farmers. Let's see how rent seeking might explain some of these programs.

Assume the market for wheat is shown in Figure 4. The demand for and supply of wheat determine a price of $.80 per bushel and a quantity of 80 million bushels. This represents a long-run equilibrium in a competitive market so that wheat farmers are earning a normal rate of return. Farmers, however, are able to convince Congress that $.80 is too low a price, and Congress passes legislation that sets a minimum price for wheat of $1 per bushel. Farmers clearly have an incentive to increase production at this higher price. As shown in the figure, the quantity supplied at $1 per bushel is 100 million bushels, but the quantity demanded at this price is only 60 million bushels. A surplus of 40 million bushels is created by the government's program.

With a surplus, the price should fall. However, the government has mandated that the price cannot fall. To keep the higher price in force, the government must buy all of the surplus or must restrict the supply without affecting domestic farmers. By placing quotas on the importing of foreign agriculture, the total supply of agricultural products in the United States declines. Thus, consumers are paying a direct subsidy to the farmer (the difference between $.80 per bushel and $1 per bushel), and the government is paying a subsidy to the farmer by purchasing the wheat at $1 per bushel for all wheat not sold to the consumer or by restricting foreign agricultural products.

Each U.S. farmer receives an extra $.20 per bushel over what would have prevailed in the market without government intervention. In addition, the

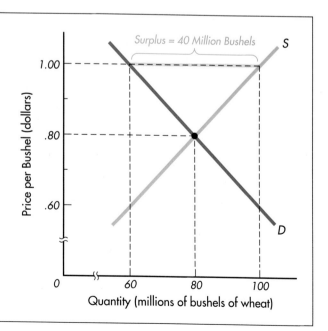

Figure 4
Rent Seeking
The demand for and supply of wheat determine a price of $.80 per bushel and a quantity of 80 million bushels. Farmers, however, are able to convince Congress that $.80 is too low a price, and Congress passes legislation that sets a minimum price for wheat of $1 per bushel. Farmers clearly have an incentive to increase their production at this higher price, to 100 million bushels. To keep the higher price in force, the government must buy all of the surplus. Thus, consumers are paying $1 per bushel instead of $.80 per bushel and the government is paying a direct subsidy to the farmer of $1 per bushel for all wheat not sold to the consumer.

Rent seeking may benefit few at the expense of many. A government subsidy may benefit those receiving the subsidy, but cost the general public in the form of higher prices and large surpluses. Here we see that a price floor leads to surpluses. The question is how to dispose of the surplus. In many nations the government purchases the surplus. In Sicily, however, the least-cost solution may have been simply to dump this surplus of blood oranges.

total U.S. farming industry expands. As it expands, the marginal costs of production may rise (if the industry is an increasing-cost industry). As land prices rise, as capital equipment costs rise, as the cost of fertilizer and pesticides rise, the farmer's total operating costs rise. Over the long run, because of the relatively free entry into the wheat-producing business, the farmer ends up earning just a normal rate of return at the higher, subsidized price.

The rent-seeking activity by the farmers has led to deadweight losses—higher costs to consumers and no more profits to farmers. Yet the subsidies persist and increase. In 1990, direct subsidies to agriculture from the federal government exceeded $30 billion. Why does rent seeking occur? It occurs because the first group to receive the rewards of rent seeking earns economic rents. Much as the entrepreneur who introduces a new, unique product earns monopoly profit in the short run, special interests who are first to receive a benefit earn economic rents. Since rents are available from special legislation, there is a demand for this legislation. Legislators supply the legislation in return for political support.

When President Clinton was considering how to reduce the government deficit, one proposal was to reduce the expenditures on social security. As discussed in the chapter on aging and health care, retirees in the United States receive their entire contributions to the social security system in fewer than six years following retirement. Since the average lifespan following retirement far exceeds six years, the retirees receive huge transfers. Thus, reductions in social security benefits appeared to be a fair and reasonable proposal. But the retirees are a very powerful interest group. The American Association of Retired Persons (AARP) placed tremendous pressure on the representatives not to support a reduction in social security benefits. Their rent seeking was successful: no new legislation reducing benefits to retirees was introduced. Another example of rent seeking is discussed in the Economic Insight "The Sherman Act: Special Interest Legislation?"

ECONOMIC INSIGHT

The Sherman Act: Special Interest Legislation?

The legislative basis for the federal government's intervention in the U.S. economy to solve the problems of monopoly was established with the Sherman Act of 1890. Though the Sherman Act is commonly considered public interest legislation that was designed to promote competition and efficiency in markets, Professor Gary Libecap has examined the history of the legislation and believes that the act came about primarily as the result of rent seeking by specific interest groups.

Libecap found it curious that the Sherman Act and the Meat Inspection Acts of 1887 and 1891 were introduced and considered by the same congressional committees and had the same supporters. An inquiry into the events surrounding the Meat Inspection Acts showed that major changes in the cattle industry occurred in the 1880s with the introduction of refrigeration. Refrigeration, which made possible the centralized slaughter of cattle and the shipment and cold storage of carcasses for year-round consumption, fundamentally changed the cattle and meat industries. It led to the dressed beef trade, in which cattle were slaughtered in Chicago and shipped in refrigerated railroad cars to East Coast and export markets more cheaply than before. The new technology led to the rise of the large Chicago meat

packers. Beef imported from Chicago competed with beef slaughtered locally, near the point of consumption. Eventually local slaughterhouses were forced either to become retailers for the large houses or to exit the industry. By 1884, four slaughterhouses controlled close to 90 percent of the market.

The new technology increased the demand for cattle as people in the East could more easily acquire fresh beef in their local markets. The heightened demand led first to price increases and then to a precipitous decline in the price of cattle, as more cattle were raised in anticipation of greater profits.

The stage was set for rent seeking. Small slaughterhouses were upset at the concentration of slaughtering into four major houses and at being forced out of the business. The cattle growers were upset with falling prices and wanted higher and more stable prices. And the emergence of Chicago as the beef slaughter capital meant a loss of business in other midwestern states. These special interests merged into a powerful political group ready to take action to protect themselves from the slaughterhouses and the advent of refrigeration. Libecap theorizes that in order for the group to be successful it needed a cause that would win the support of the gen-

eral public, and so it chose disease. At the time, claims that the large slaughterhouses in Chicago used diseased meats occurred in papers throughout the cattle-producing areas of the country. Upton Sinclair's *The Jungle* popularized these claims. And so Libecap believes that the Meat Inspection Acts were the result of rent seeking by special interests. But the Meat Inspection Acts merely justified the government's regulation of the cattle industry. They did not reduce the monopsony power that the big slaughterhouses were alleged to have. Libecap reasons that additional legislation was needed to attack the monopsonistic slaughterhouses, legislation that would enable the government to control the size of a market that firms could have command over. It was these circumstances that Libecap believes caused the Sherman Antitrust Act to be passed. Rent seeking by various members of the cattle industry may have been the driving force behind one of the most important pieces of antitrust legislation in U.S. history.

Source: Gary D. Libecap, "Origins of Meat Inspection and Antitrust," *Economic Inquiry*, April 1992, pp. 242–262.

3.b. The Costs and Benefits of Rent Seeking

Because profits can be made by a firm or industry that succeeds in acquiring a privilege, firms compete with each other to acquire these privileges. Some of the rents that are created are competed away with resources that could otherwise have been put to productive uses. An industry receiving protection from foreign competition worth $20 million per year is willing to spend up to

$20 million a year on lobbyists, campaign committees, and other rent-seeking activities to maintain the special privilege.

The value of rent-seeking activity occurring each year is substantial, ranging upward from about 5 percent of a nation's total output. The amount of rent seeking that occurs depends on the extent to which a government doles out special privileges. The more involved government is in the economy, the greater the extent of rent seeking. The World Bank estimates that rent-seeking activities account for nearly one-fourth of the national income of many developing countries, countries in which the government plays a major role.

Although rent seeking is not considered a productive activity, many economists argue that it may offer some social benefits. Figure 5 shows a firm that has received a government privilege; the firm is earning rents (monopoly profits) of *ABCE*. If the firm were assured of maintaining the privilege—if its costs could rise and it would still earn a profit—it might become lazy and sloppy. However, other firms, seeing the benefits of the privilege, want to have that special benefit themselves. They lobby politicians and make donations to political campaigns in order to get politicians to bestow the privilege on them. The firm portrayed in Figure 5 is thus willing to devote some resources to safeguarding its rents. It cannot become lazy and sloppy because if it does it will not have the economic rents to offset its increased costs. The competition for special privileges and the resulting rents tends to dissipate those rents. The most effective rent seekers receive the benefits, but competition for rents forces the firm to be as efficient as a firm without the special privilege.

3.c. Should Government Intervene?

Barriers to entry, above-normal profit, imperfect information, and market failures in the private sector suggest that the government should intervene. If the government were a single entity whose sole purpose was to act in the

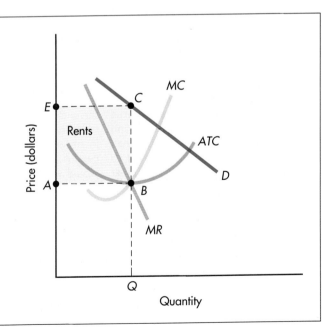

Figure 5
Economic Rents
A firm receives a special privilege from government that enables it to earn rents or monopoly profits of *ABCE*. The firm is willing to devote an amount up to *ABCE* to ensure that it retains those rents. As a result of the competition for the special privilege, the rents are dissipated, used in rent seeking to maintain the rents.

public interest, there would be little question regarding its intervention. But when the government is understood to be composed of individuals with differing objectives, each a self-interested rational being, then its activities may be the result of rent seeking or the self-interest of bureaucrats or elected officials. In such a case, government actions may *not* be in the best interest of the public. In this chapter we have seen that barriers to entry, imperfect information, and failures occur in the public sector as they do in the private sector. We have seen that collective decision-making may not come to a conclusion. Yet we have provided no definitive answer as to the optimal role of the public sector in an economy. Instead, our discussion has been directed toward creating a healthy skepticism: solving private market problems through the public sector may not always make society better off.

RECAP

1. Rent seeking refers to activities that attempt to secure income without an increase in resource supplies.
2. Rent seeking in a representative democracy may serve to create efficiency within government.

SUMMARY

▲▼ *What is collective decision-making?*

1. Collective decision-making is the process of reaching a group decision. §Preview

2. Collective decisions differ from private market decisions in that there is one vote per person, a full-line supply of goods is "purchased" (voted on) at one time, and voters are rationally ignorant. §1.a

3. Voting cycles are failures of the collective decision-making process. §1.b.1

4. Logrolling is the process of vote trading. §1.b.2

5. Brand-name recognition (political party identification) plays a key role in collective decision-making. §1.c

▲▼ *Individuals maximize utility. What does the government maximize?*

6. Self-interest characterizes the behavior of individuals involved in collective decision-making. Politicians, representatives, bureaucrats, and citizens behave so as to maximize their own self-interest. §2.b

7. Government grows partly through the growth of agencies and bureaus. §2.c.1

8. There is a bias toward expenditures and away from taxes, and toward expenditures financed by debt, because representatives attempt to maximize their support. §2.c.3

9. According to the median voter theorem, the competition among candidates for votes induces the candidates to stake out similar positions on issues. §2.c.4

10. Logrolling can invalidate the median voter theorem. §2.c.4

▲▼ *What is rent seeking?*

11. Rent-seeking activities are directed toward securing income without increasing the production of output. §3

12. Competition for rents may decrease the amount of inefficiency that results from special legislation. §3.b.

KEY TERMS

public choice theory §Preview
full-line supply §1.a
rationally ignorant voters §1.a
voting cycle §1.b.1

logrolling §1.b.2
median voter theorem §2.c.4
rent seeking §3

EXERCISES

1. Individuals act to maximize their utility. What does the government maximize?

2. Explain why it is easier for the government to spend than to tax. What would occur if the law required the government to spend only what it collected in taxes?

3. Why do political parties exist? What purpose do they serve for voters? What purpose do they serve for candidates?

4. In the Civil War, the Union Army was organized into state regiments. A soldier from Pennsylvania fought with the Pennsylvania regiment, a soldier from New York fought with the New York regiment, and so on. In the Vietnam War, there were state quotas for draftees, but draftees were assigned to regiments regardless of the state in which they were drafted. Explain how President Lincoln in the Civil War and Presidents Johnson and Nixon in the Vietnam War might have used the armies to enhance their chances for reelection.

5. What is the optimal amount of rent seeking? What could cause this amount to be reduced or increased?

6. Why is voter turnout in the United States usually less than 50 percent of the total eligible voters, while in the former Soviet Union it was 100 percent?

7. U.S. automobile producers are asking Congress to place limits, or quotas, on the number of foreign-made cars and trucks that can be sold in the United States. What would be the outcome of such a policy, if implemented, for consumers and producers? Why would legislators support such a policy?

8. In most national campaigns, the Republican and Democratic platforms are not much different. Other parties, such as the Libertarian party, the Science party, and Up With America, stake out more extreme policies. Why?

9. The U.S. government is in debt to the tune of nearly $4 trillion and the debt keeps growing. Why, when nearly everyone calls the debt bad for the economy and bad for society, does it continue to grow?

10. Evaluate the following statement: "To demonstrate that there are market failures in the private sector is not sufficient to justify government intervention in the private sector."

11. Use the following table to determine whether a voting cycle may occur using majority rule. Can you think of any other voting rule that would reduce the chance of a voting cycle?

Public Good	Sally	Jesse	Rafael
Park	2nd choice	1st choice	3rd choice
School	3rd choice	2nd choice	1st choice
Bike Path	1st choice	3rd choice	2nd choice

12. Explain what term limits might mean for the political market. (A term limit would allow a senator to serve only two terms of six years and a representative to serve four terms of two years.)

13. Discuss the following three ways to finance political campaigns.

    a. Anyone, any firm, or any entity can contribute as much to a politician's campaign as desired.

    b. No donation of more $50 can be made.

    c. Campaign expenditures are limited to $100,000 for House of Representative campaigns and $300,000 for Senate campaigns.

14. President Clinton forbade his appointees to lobby for a private firm or group for several years following their departure from government service. Explain how this policy might actually reduce the efficiency of government.

15. "Here they go again." This is the statement with which Ronald Reagan defeated Jimmy Carter and which he later used to lament the policies of President Clinton. The statement refers to the tendency of Democrats to increase government involvement in the private sector. Reagan, on the other hand, argues that the government that governs least governs best. How do such apparently opposite views match with the median voter theorem?

Economically Speaking

Feinstein: Base Losses Would Be Devastating

WASHINGTON—Defense Secretary Les Aspin promised the "mother of all base-closing lists" Sunday but said he will try to be "fair to the various regions of the country."

Aspin declined to say how many military installations he will seek to shut down. He confirmed the armed services have presented their proposals to him to close about 30 bases across the country and said he will make his own recommendations on Friday.

"We have the suggestions from the services. We need to integrate them and balance them and make sure we are fair to the various regions of the country as we do this," he said on ABC's "This Week with David Brinkley."

That heartened some California lawmakers who believe the state would be especially hard-hit by the armed services' recommendations. The Air Force, Navy and Army have called for closing Sacramento's McClellan Air Force Base and eight other California installations.

California Sen. Dianne Feinstein said shutting down the nine California bases the armed services targeted would be a "devastating hit" in a state already buffeted by rising unemployment and a sagging economy.

"Our unemployment rate is already at 9.8 percent," the Democrat said. "That is 17 percent of all the unemployment in the country. That is the total of unemployment in 13 states. I, for one, am extraordinarily concerned about what this round of base closures would do."

If Aspin follows through on his promise to be fair to other regions of the country, she said, he won't close any bases in the state.

"California has already accepted 60 percent of the personnel reductions (from base closures) since 1988," she said. "I see no rush to proceed with this round of base closures with the current condition of California's economy."

The senator is urging President Clinton to impose a moratorium on shutting down military installations in California and other states with unemployment rates of 9.5 percent or more.

Feinstein also said she will join Sens. Barbara Boxer, D-Calif., and Ernest Hollings, D-S.C., in introducing a resolution Wednesday calling for the cumulative economic impact of base closures to play a larger role in deciding which installations to shut down.

Boxer was unavailable for comment, but she has complained before that economic impact is not being given enough consideration. Under current regulations, it is No. 7 out of eight criteria used in deciding closures.

"If we are concerned about economic stimulus, we can do more by delaying this round of base closures and continuing these jobs," she said.

Aspin, however, pointed out that Clinton has pledged to cut another $122 billion from defense spending, and he contended base closings are needed to achieve those savings.

"If we are going to cut the defense budget, we are going to have to cut overhead," the secretary said. "And a large part of the overhead is the bases."

Feinstein contended more foreign bases could be shut down and said closing domestic bases is "unnecessary when America is in the midst of a very shaky recovery."

The senator said the proposed closures of just two of the California bases—McClellan and Mare Island Naval Shipyard in Vallejo—could mean a loss of 60,000 jobs from the bases and businesses reliant on the installations for their livelihoods.

McClellan employs 16,000 and has a $548 million payroll. Mare Island employs 11,000 and has a $227 million payroll. Feinstein pointed out the impact will reach far behind the gates of these two installations if they are shut down. . . .

Gov. Pete Wilson said that the state ultimately could lose 100,000 more jobs if the nine California bases the armed services targeted were to shut down. . . .

Source: Copyright, *The Sacramento Bee*, 1993.

Commentary

National defense is a public good; unless the government provides it, too little will be produced. How can we identify the demand for a public good? We could undertake a survey asking each citizen how much he or she would be willing to pay for alternative quantities of the public good. We could then sum the demands to get the market demand. The government could then ensure that a quantity was produced such that the marginal cost of producing it and the amount consumers were willing to pay were equal. Then society would get the quantity of the public good it wanted.

Since such a survey is not feasible, the demand for the public good is usually expressed through the ballot box. Voters choose a president and members of the House and Senate to represent their desires. If, on the whole, they want less national defense, they vote for candidates who promise to supply that, as Clinton did in the 1992 presidential election.

Since the public chose to pay for less national defense, it would seem logical that the public sector would supply less of the good. In other words, the demand curve for the public good has shifted down so the quantity supplied should decline. However, the democratic process does not work quite that smoothly. As the Clinton administration began the process of reducing government expenditures on national defense, the voters began saying, "Yes, reduce expenditures, but not in my back yard."

California Senators Feinstein and Boxer were elected to help shift government expenditures from national defense to domestic issues. However, once California appeared to become a target of base closings, the potential impacts of job and spending reductions in a state already reeling under recession were greater than the California residents wanted. Senators Feinstein and Boxer began backpedaling, calling on President Clinton to close bases in states other than California.

This issue provides insights into why it is so difficult for the public sector to reduce expenditures and why there is a tendency for the public sector to grow. Representatives want to be reelected. To win elections, they need to provide the services their constituents want. Increased government expenditures and transfers provide benefits to constituents, while reduced expenditures and transfers impose costs. Thus, all representatives want to increase the benefits their constituents receive.

When the government increases expenditures, say by opening new military bases around the country, the communities in which the bases are located benefit considerably. Incomes rise and jobs are created. To pay for the bases, taxes are imposed on all citizens of the nation. As a result, the benefits accrue to a small group while the costs are borne by many. Because the benefits are larger than the costs to those citizens realizing the benefits, the support for their representative rises. At the same time, the costs imposed on all other citizens are not significant enough to cause them to reduce support for all other representatives. The other representatives thus have little incentive to vote against the project. Moreover, if they have participated in logrolling, they support the project knowing that their constituents will receive benefits in the future.

To ensure that benefits can be bestowed on constituents and that the citizens bearing the additional costs do not object to the additional expenditures, taxes are not designated as going to pay for a particular project. Citizens are not asked to identify how much they would be willing to pay for various quantities of a public good but instead are allowed to purchase the good without paying its full cost. Congress has ensured that new government programs are not paid for with a specific tax or financing mechanism. To do so would make it much more difficult for the logrolling process to occur.

Suppose each new dollar of spending had to be accompanied by a new dollar of taxes. In other words, if a new swimming pool was to be built for the senators in Washington D.C., the money to pay for the pool would be designated on a ballot. Voters could choose to support the pool or not. If a scientific project in Texas was to cost three billion dollars, then a tax increase of three billion dollars would have to be imposed. If a base was to benefit the citizens of California, then those citizens should provide the taxes to pay for the base. Would voters support the expenditure? Would they get the quantity of the public good they are willing and able to pay for?

VI

Issues in International Trade and Finance

23

World Trade Equilibrium

FUNDAMENTAL
QUESTIONS

1. What are the prevailing patterns of trade between countries? What goods are traded?
2. What determines the goods a nation will export?
3. How are the equilibrium price and the quantity of goods traded determined?
4. What are the sources of comparative advantage?

T he United States's once-dominant position as an exporter of color television sets has since been claimed by nations like Japan and Taiwan. What caused this change? Is it because Japan specializes in the export of high-tech equipment? If countries tend to specialize in the export of particular kinds of goods, why does the United States import Heineken beer at the same time it exports Budweiser? This chapter will examine the volume of world trade and the nature of trade linkages between countries. As you saw in Chapter 2, trade occurs because of specialization in production. No single individual or country can produce everything better than others can. The result is specialization of production based on comparative advantage. Remember that comparative advantage is in turn based on relative opportunity costs: a country will specialize in the production of those goods for which its opportunity costs of production are lower than costs in other countries. Nations then trade what they produce in excess of their own consumption to acquire other things they want to consume. In this chapter, we will go a step further to discuss the sources of comparative advantage. We will look at why one country has a comparative advantage in, say, automobile production while another country has a comparative advantage in wheat production.

PREVIEW

The world equilibrium price and quantity traded are derived from individual countries' demand and supply curves. This relationship between the world trade equilibrium and individual country markets will be utilized in Chapter 38 to discuss the ways that countries can interfere with free international trade to achieve their own economic or political goals.

I. AN OVERVIEW OF WORLD TRADE

What are the prevailing patterns of trade between countries? What goods are traded?

Trade occurs because it makes people better off. International trade occurs because it makes people better off than they would be if they could consume only domestically produced products. This section will consider the direction of international trade, who trades with whom, and what sorts of goods are traded.

1.a. The Direction of Trade

Table 1 shows patterns of trade between two large groups of countries: the industrial countries and the developing countries. The industrial countries include all of Western Europe, Japan, Australia, New Zealand, Canada, and the United States. The developing countries are, essentially, the rest of the

TABLE I
The Direction of Trade
(in billions of dollars and percentages of world trade, 1991)

| | Destination: | |
	Industrial Countries	Developing Countries
Origin:		
Industrial Countries	$1,913	$632
	54.2%	17.9%
Developing Countries	$ 622	$323
	17.6%	9.2%

Source: International Monetary Fund, *Direction of Trade Statistics Yearbook*, 1991.

world. The table shows the dollar values and percentages of total trade between these groups of countries. The vertical column at the left lists the origin of exports, and the horizontal row at the top lists the destination of imports.

Trade between industrial countries accounts for the majority of international trade.

As Table 1 shows, trade between industrial countries accounts for the bulk of international trade. Trade between industrial countries is a little less than $2 trillion in value and amounts to 54.2 percent of world trade. Exports from industrial countries to developing countries represent 17.9 percent of total world trade. Exports from developing countries to industrial countries account for 17.6 percent of total trade, while exports from the developing countries to other developing countries currently represent only 9.2 percent of international trade.

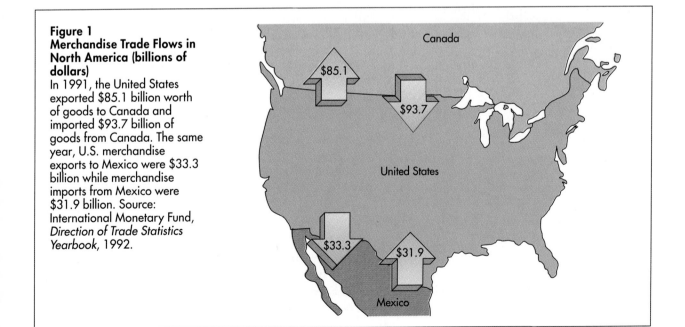

Figure 1
Merchandise Trade Flows in North America (billions of dollars)
In 1991, the United States exported $85.1 billion worth of goods to Canada and imported $93.7 billion of goods from Canada. The same year, U.S. merchandise exports to Mexico were $33.3 billion while merchandise imports from Mexico were $31.9 billion. Source: International Monetary Fund, *Direction of Trade Statistics Yearbook*, 1992.

Table 2 lists the major trading partners of selected countries and the percentage of total exports and imports accounted for by each country's top ten trading partners. For instance, 20.2 percent of U.S. exports went to Canada, and 18.7 percent of U.S. imports came from Japan. From a glance at the other countries listed in Table 2, it is clear that the United States is a major trading partner for many nations. This is true because of the size of the U.S. economy and the nation's relatively high level of income. It is also apparent that Canada and Mexico are very dependent on trade with the United States: about three-fourths of Canadian exports and more than 60 percent of imports, and almost three-fourths of Mexican exports and over 70 percent of imports, involve the United States. The dollar value of trade among the three North American nations is shown in Figure 1.

1.b. What Goods Are Traded

Because countries differ in their comparative advantages, they will tend to export different goods. Countries also have different tastes and technological needs, and thus tend to differ in what they will import. Some goods are more widely traded than others, as Table 3 shows. Crude petroleum is the most

TABLE 2
Major Trading Partners of Selected Countries

United States					Canada			
Exports		**Imports**			**Exports**		**Imports**	
Canada	20.2%	Japan	18.7%		U.S.	75.2%	U.S.	61.7%
Japan	11.4	Canada	18.4		Japan	4.9	Japan	7.3
U.K.	5.2	Mexico	6.3		U.K.	2.0	U.K.	3.0
Germany	5.0	Germany	5.3		Germany	1.6	Germany	2.6
Mexico	3.9	U.K.	3.7		Korea	1.3	France	1.9

Germany					Mexico			
Exports		**Imports**			**Exports**		**Imports**	
France	13.1%	France	12.2%		U.S.	74.5%	U.S.	70.8%
Italy	9.2	Netherlands	9.7		Canada	5.5	Japan	6.0
Netherlands	8.4	Italy	9.3		Japan	4.1	Germany	5.3
U.K.	7.6	Belgium	7.1		Spain	3.1	France	2.3
U.S.	6.3	U.K.	6.6		Germany	1.5	Italy	1.4
		U.S.	6.6					

Japan					United Kingdom			
Exports		**Imports**			**Exports**		**Imports**	
U.S.	29.3%	U.S.	22.6%		Germany	14.0%	Germany	14.9%
Germany	6.6	China	6.0		France	11.0	U.S.	11.6
Korea	6.4	Australia	5.5		U.S.	10.9	France	9.3
Hong Kong	5.2	Indonesia	5.4		Netherlands	7.9	Netherlands	8.4
Singapore	3.9	Korea	5.1		Italy	5.8	Japan	5.7

Source: Data for all countries from International Monetary Fund, *Direction of Trade Statistics Yearbook*, 1991.

TABLE 3
The Top Ten Exported Products
(in millions of dollars and percentages of world exports)

Product Category	Value	Percentage of World Trade
Crude petroleum	$145,594	5.58%
Motor vehicles	131,394	5.01
Petroleum products	66,597	2.55
Motor vehicle parts	65,847	2.51
Data processing equipment	49,944	1.90
Special transactions	42,823	1.62
Transistors, valves, etc.	42,170	1.60
Telecom equipment, parts	42,130	1.60
Aircraft	38,406	1.46
Paper and paperboard	37,600	1.43

Source: Data from United Nations Conference on Trade and Development: *Handbook of International Trade and Development Statistics, 1990*, (TD/STAT.18), p. 182: United Nations publication Sales No. E/F.91.II.D.1.

The volume of trade in crude petroleum exceeds that of any other good.

heavily traded good in the world, accounting for 5.58 percent of the total volume of world trade. Crude petroleum is followed by motor vehicles, petroleum products, motor vehicle parts, and automatic data processing equipment. The top ten exported products, however, represent only 25 percent of world trade. The remaining 75 percent is distributed among a great variety of products. The importance of petroleum and motor vehicles in international trade should not obscure the fact that international trade involves all sorts of products from all over the world.

RECAP

1. Trade between industrial countries accounts for the bulk of international trade.
2. The most important trading partners of the United States are Canada (for U.S. exports) and Japan (for U.S. imports).
3. Crude petroleum is the most heavily traded good in the world, in terms of value of exports.
4. World trade is distributed across a great variety of products.

2. AN EXAMPLE OF INTERNATIONAL TRADE EQUILIBRIUM

The international economy is very complex. Each country has a unique pattern of trade, in terms both of trading partners and of goods traded. Some countries trade a great deal and others trade very little. We already know that countries specialize and trade according to comparative advantage, but what are the fundamental determinants of international trade that explain the pattern of comparative advantage?

Comparative advantage is based on what a country can do relatively better than other countries. Italy is one of the few European countries that exports a significant amount of wine. Due to favorable growing conditions (a natural resource), these countries have a comparative advantage in wine production. These Tuscan grapes will be used to make Chianti.

The answer to this question will in turn provide a better understanding of some basic questions about how international trade functions: What goods will be traded? How much will be traded? What prices will prevail for traded goods?

2.a. Comparative Advantage

What determines the goods a nation will export?

absolute advantage:
an advantage derived from one country having a lower absolute input cost of producing a particular good than another country

Comparative advantage is found by comparing the relative costs of production in each country. We measure the cost of producing a particular good in two countries in terms of opportunity costs—what other goods must be given up in order to produce more of the good in question.

Table 4 presents a hypothetical example of two countries, the United States and India, that both produce two goods, wheat and cloth. The table lists the hours of labor required to produce 1 unit of each good. This example assumes that labor productivity differences alone determine comparative advantage. In the United States, 1 unit of wheat requires 3 hours of labor, and 1 unit of cloth requires 6 hours of labor. In India, 1 unit of wheat requires 6 hours of labor, and 1 unit of cloth requires 8 hours of labor.

The United States has an **absolute advantage**—a lower resource cost—in producing both wheat and cloth. Absolute advantage is determined by comparing the absolute cost in different countries of producing each good. Since

TABLE 4
An Example of Comparative Advantage

Labor Hours Required to Produce 1 Unit Each of Two Goods		
	U.S.	**India**
1 unit of wheat	3	6
1 unit of cloth	6	8

it requires fewer hours of labor to produce either good in the United States than in India, the United States is the more efficient producer of both goods in terms of the domestic labor hours required.

It might seem that since the United States is the more efficient producer of both goods, there would be no need for trade with India. But absolute advantage is not the critical consideration. What matters in determining the benefits of international trade is comparative advantage, as originally discussed in Chapter 2. To find the **comparative advantage**—the lower opportunity cost—we must compare the opportunity cost of producing each good in each country.

comparative advantage:
an advantage derived from comparing the opportunity costs of production in two countries

The opportunity cost of producing wheat is what must be given up in cloth using the same resources, or number of labor hours. Look again at Table 4 to see the labor hours required for the production of wheat and cloth in the two countries. If the 3 labor hours it takes to produce wheat in the United States are devoted to cloth production, only 1/2 unit of cloth will result, since 6 labor hours are required to produce a full unit of cloth. The opportunity cost of producing wheat equals 3/6, or 1/2 unit of cloth:

$$\frac{\text{No. of labor hours to produce 1 unit of wheat}}{\text{No. of labor hours to produce 1 unit of cloth}} = \begin{array}{l}\text{Opportunity cost of} \\ \text{producing 1 unit of wheat} \\ \text{(in terms of cloth given up)}\end{array}$$

$$3/6 = 1/2$$

Applying the same thinking to India, we find that devoting 6 hours of wheat production to the production of cloth yields 6/8, or 3/4 unit of cloth. The opportunity cost of producing 1 unit of wheat in India is 3/4 unit of cloth.

A comparison of the domestic opportunity costs in each country will reveal which one has the comparative advantage in producing each good. The U.S. opportunity cost of producing 1 unit of wheat is 1/2 unit of cloth; the Indian opportunity cost is 3/4 unit of cloth. Because the United States has a lower domestic opportunity cost, it has the comparative advantage in wheat production and will export wheat. Since wheat production costs are lower in the United States, India is better off trading for wheat rather than trying to produce it domestically.

The comparative advantage in cloth is found the same way. A unit of cloth requires 6 hours of labor in the United States. Since a unit of wheat requires 3 hours of labor, producing 1 more unit of cloth costs 2 units of wheat:

$$\frac{\text{No. of labor hours to produce 1 unit of cloth}}{\text{No. of labor hours to produce 1 unit of wheat}} = \begin{array}{l}\text{Opportunity cost of} \\ \text{producing 1 unit of cloth} \\ \text{(in terms of wheat given up)}\end{array}$$

$$6/3 = 2$$

In India, 1 unit of cloth requires 8 hours of labor. Since 1 unit of wheat requires 6 hours of labor, shifting 8 hours of labor from wheat production to cloth production means an opportunity cost of 8/6, or 1 1/3 units of wheat for 1 unit of cloth. Comparing the U.S. opportunity cost of 2 units of wheat with the Indian opportunity cost of 1 1/3 units, we see that India has the comparative advantage in cloth production and will therefore export cloth. In this case, the United States is better off trading for cloth than producing it since India's costs of production are lower.

In international trade, as in other areas of economic decision-making, it is opportunity cost that matters—and opportunity costs are reflected in comparative advantage. Absolute advantage is irrelevant, because knowing the absolute number of labor hours required to produce a good does not tell us if we can benefit from trade. We benefit from trade if we are able to obtain a good from a foreign country by giving up less than we would have to give up to obtain the good at home. Because only opportunity cost can allow us to make such comparisons, international trade proceeds on the basis of comparative advantage.

Countries export goods in which they have a comparative advantage.

2.b. Terms of Trade

Based on comparative advantage, India will specialize in cloth production and the United States will specialize in wheat production. The two countries will then trade with each other to satisfy the domestic demand for both goods. International trade permits greater consumption than would be possible from domestic production alone. Since countries trade when they can obtain a good more cheaply from a foreign producer than they can at home, international trade allows all traders to consume more. This is evident when we examine the terms of trade.

terms of trade:
the amount of an export good that must be given up to obtain one unit of an imported good

The **terms of trade** are the amount of an export good that must be given up to obtain one unit of an imported good. As you saw earlier, comparative advantage dictates that the United States will specialize in wheat production and export wheat to India in exchange for Indian cloth. But the amount of wheat that the United States will exchange for a unit of cloth is limited by the domestic tradeoffs. If a unit of cloth can be obtained domestically for 2 units of wheat, the United States will be willing to trade with India only if the terms of trade are less than 2 units of wheat for a unit of cloth.

India in turn will be willing to trade its cloth for U.S. wheat only if it can receive a better price than its domestic opportunity costs. Since a unit of cloth in India costs 1 1/3 units of wheat, India will gain from trade if it can obtain more than 1 1/3 units of wheat for its cloth.

The limits of the terms of trade are determined by the opportunity costs in each country:

1 unit of cloth for more than 1 1/3 but less than 2 units of wheat

Within this range, the actual terms of trade will be decided by the bargaining power of the two countries. The closer the United States can come to giving up only 1 1/3 units of wheat for cloth, the better the terms of trade for the United States. The closer India can come to receiving 2 units of wheat for its cloth, the better the terms of trade for India.

Though each country would like to push the other as close to the limits of the terms of trade as possible, any terms within the limits set by domestic opportunity costs will be mutually beneficial. Both countries benefit because they are able to consume goods at a cost less than their domestic opportunity costs. To illustrate the *gains from trade*, let us assume that the actual terms of trade are 1 unit of cloth for 1 1/2 units of wheat.

Suppose the United States has 60 hours of labor, half of which goes to wheat production and the other half to cloth production. Since a unit of wheat requires 3 labor hours, 10 units of wheat are produced. Cloth requires 6 labor hours, so 5 units of cloth are produced. Without international trade, the United States can produce and consume 10 units of wheat and 5 units of cloth. If the United States, with its comparative advantage in wheat produc-

The Dutch Disease

The terms of trade are the amount of an export that must be given up for a certain quantity of an import. The price of an import will be equal to its price in the foreign country of origin multiplied by the exchange rate (the domestic-currency price of foreign currency). As the exchange rate changes, the terms of trade will change. This can have important consequences for international trade.

A problem can arise when one export industry in an economy is booming relative to others. In the 1970s, for instance, the Netherlands experienced a boom in its natural gas industry. The dramatic energy price increases of the 1970s resulted in large Dutch exports of natural gas. Increased demand for exports from the Netherlands caused the Dutch currency to appreciate, making Dutch goods more expensive for foreign buyers. This situation caused the terms of trade to worsen for the Netherlands. Although the natural gas sector boomed, Dutch manufacturing was finding it difficult to compete in the world market.

The phenomenon of a boom in one industry causing declines in the rest of the economy is popularly called the Dutch Disease. It is usually associated with dramatic increases in the demand for a primary commodity and can afflict any nation experiencing such a boom. For instance, a rapid rise in the demand for coffee could lead to a Dutch Disease problem for Colombia, where a coffee boom would be accompanied by decline in other sectors of the economy.

tion, chooses to produce only wheat, it can use all 60 labor hours to produce 20 units. If the terms of trade are 1 1/2 units of wheat per unit of cloth, the United States can keep 10 units of wheat and trade the other 10 for 6 2/3 units of cloth (10 divided by 1 1/2). By trading U.S. wheat for Indian cloth, the United States is able to consume more than it could without trade. With no trade, and half its labor hours devoted to each good, the United States could consume 10 units of wheat and 5 units of cloth. After trade, the United States consumes 10 units of wheat and 6 2/3 units of cloth. By devoting all its labor hours to wheat production and trading wheat for cloth, the United States gains 1 2/3 units of cloth. This is the gain from trade—an increase in consumption, as summarized in Table 5.

The gain from trade is increased consumption.

TABLE 5
Hypothetical Example of U.S. Gains from Specialization and Trade

Without International Trade
30 labor hours in wheat production: produce and consume 10 wheat
30 labor hours in cloth production: produce and consume 5 cloth

With Specialization and Trade
60 labor hours in wheat production: produce 20 wheat and consume 10; trade 10 wheat for 6 2/3 cloth

Before trade: consume 10 wheat and 5 cloth

After trade: consume 10 wheat and 6 2/3 cloth
Gain 1 2/3 cloth by specialization and trade

2.c. Export Supply and Import Demand

The preceding example suggests that countries all benefit from specialization and trade. Realistically, however, countries do not completely specialize. Typically, domestic industries satisfy part of the domestic demand for goods that are also imported. To understand how the quantity of goods traded is determined, we must construct demand and supply curves for each country, and use them to create export supply and import demand curves.

The proportion of domestic demand for a good that is satisfied by domestic production and the proportion that will be satisfied by imports are determined by the domestic supply and demand curves and the international equilibrium price of a good. The international equilibrium price and quantity may be determined once we know the export supply and import demand curves for each country. These curves are derived from the domestic supply and demand in each country. Figure 2 illustrates the derivation of the export supply and import demand curves.

Figure 2(a) shows the domestic supply and demand curves for the U.S. wheat market. The domestic equilibrium price is $6 and the domestic equilibrium quantity is 200 million bushels. (The domestic "no-trade" equilibrium price is the price that exists prior to international trade.) A price above $6 will yield a U.S. wheat surplus. For instance, at a price of $9, the U.S. surplus will be 200 million bushels. A price below equilibrium will produce a wheat shortage: at a price of $3, the shortage will be 200 million bushels. The key point here is that the world price of a good may be quite different than the domestic "no-trade" equilibrium price. And once international trade occurs, the world price will prevail in the domestic economy.

If the world price of wheat is different than a country's domestic "no-trade" equilibrium price, the country will become an exporter or importer. For instance, if the world price is above the domestic "no-trade" equilibrium price, the domestic surplus can be exported to the rest of the world. Figure 2(b) shows the U.S. **export supply curve**. This curve illustrates the U.S. domestic surplus of wheat for prices above the domestic "no-trade" equilibrium price of $6. At a world price of $9, the United States would supply 200 million bushels of wheat to the rest of the world. The export supply is equal to the domestic surplus. The higher the world price above the domestic "no-trade" equilibrium, the greater the quantity of wheat exported by the United States.

If the world price of wheat is below the domestic "no-trade" equilibrium price, the United States will import wheat. The **import demand curve** is the amount of the U.S. shortage at various prices below the "no-trade" equilibrium. In Figure 2(b), the import demand curve is a downward-sloping line, indicating that the lower the price below the domestic "no-trade" equilibrium of $6, the greater the quantity of wheat imported by the United States. At a price of $3, the United States will import 200 million bushels.

The domestic supply and demand curves and the export supply and import demand curves for India appear as parts (c) and (d) of Figure 2. The domestic "no-trade" equilibrium price in India is $12. At this price, India would neither import nor export any wheat because the domestic demand would be satisfied by domestic supply. The export supply curve for India is shown in Figure 2(d) as an upward-sloping line that measures the amount of the domestic surplus as the price level rises above the domestic "no-trade" equilibrium price of $12. According to Figure 2(c), if the world price of wheat is

export supply curve:
a curve showing the relationship between the world price of a good and the amount that a country will export

import demand curve:
a curve showing the relationship between the world price of a good and the amount that a country will import

Figure 2
The Import Demand and Export Supply Curves

Figures 2(a) and 2(c) show the domestic demand and supply curves for wheat in the United States and India, respectively. The domestic "no-trade" equilibrium price is $6 in the United States and $12 in India. Any price above the domestic "no-trade" equilibrium prices will create domestic surpluses, which are reflected in the export supply curves in Figures 2(b) and (d). Any price below the domestic "no-trade" equilibrium prices will create domestic shortages, which are reflected in the import demand curves in Figures 2(b) and (d).

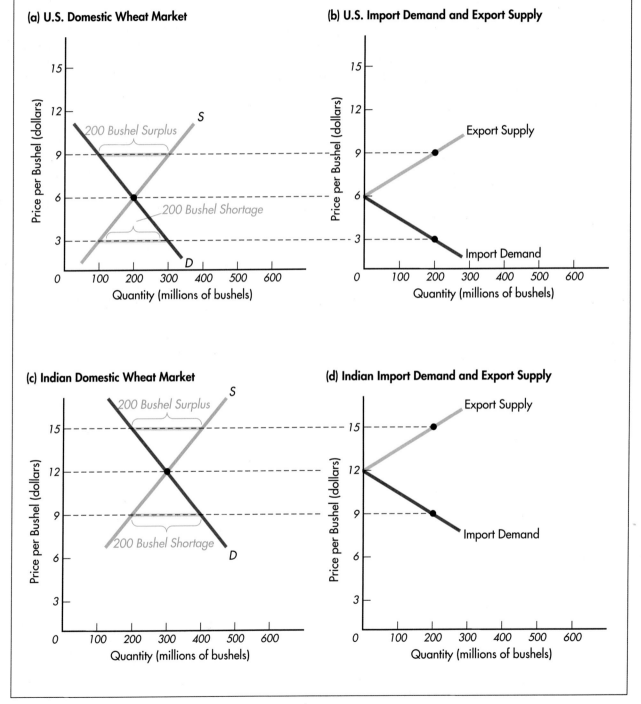

(a) U.S. Domestic Wheat Market

(b) U.S. Import Demand and Export Supply

(c) Indian Domestic Wheat Market

(d) Indian Import Demand and Export Supply

$15, the domestic surplus in India is equal to 200 million bushels. The corresponding point on the export supply curve indicates that, at a price of $15, 200 million bushels will be exported. The import demand curve for India reflects the domestic shortage at a price below the domestic "no-trade" equilibrium price. At $9, the domestic shortage is equal to 200 million bushels: the import demand curve indicates that, at $9, 200 million bushels will be imported.

2.d. The World Equilibrium Price and Quantity Traded

How are the equilibrium price and the quantity of goods traded determined?

International equilibrium occurs at the point where the quantity of imports demanded by one country is equal to the quantity of exports supplied by the other country.

The international equilibrium price of wheat and the quantity of wheat traded are found by combining the import demand and export supply curves for the United States and India, as in Figure 3. International equilibrium occurs if the quantity of imports demanded by one country is equal to the quantity of exports supplied by the other country. In Figure 3, this equilibrium occurs at the point labeled *e*. At this point, the import demand curve for India indicates that India wants to import 200 million bushels at a price of $9. The export supply curve for the United States indicates that the United States wants to export 200 million bushels at a price of $9. Only at $9 will the quantity of wheat demanded by the importing nation equal the quantity of wheat supplied by the exporting nation. So the equilibrium world price of wheat is $9 and the equilibrium quantity of wheat traded is 200 million bushels.

RECAP

1. Comparative advantage is based on the relative opportunity costs of producing goods in different countries.

2. A country has an absolute advantage when it can produce a good for a lower input cost than can other nations.

Figure 3
International Equilibrium Price and Quantity
The international equilibrium price is the price at which the export supply curve of the United States intersects with the import demand curve of India. At the equilibrium price of $9, the United States will export 200 million bushels to India.

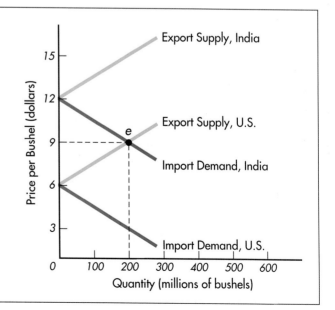

3. A country has a comparative advantage when the opportunity cost of producing a good, in terms of forgone output of other goods, is lower than that of other nations.

4. The terms of trade are the amount of an export good that must be given up to obtain one unit of an import good.

5. The limits of the terms of trade are determined by the domestic opportunity costs of production in each country.

6. The export supply and import demand curves measure the domestic surplus and shortage, respectively, at different world prices.

7. International equilibrium occurs at the point where one country's import demand curve intersects with the export supply curve of another country.

3. SOURCES OF COMPARATIVE ADVANTAGE

We know that countries specialize and trade in accordance with comparative advantage, but what gives a country a comparative advantage? Economists have suggested several theories of the source of comparative advantage. Let us review these theories.

What are the sources of comparative advantage?

3.a. Productivity Differences

The example of comparative advantage earlier in this chapter showed the United States to have a comparative advantage in wheat production and India to have a comparative advantage in cloth production. Comparative advantage was determined by differences in the labor hours required to produce each good. In this example, differences in the *productivity* of labor accounted for comparative advantage.

Comparative advantage due to productivity differences between countries is often called the Ricardian model of comparative advantage.

For over two hundred years, economists have argued that productivity differences account for comparative advantage. In fact, this theory of comparative advantage is often called the *Ricardian model*, after David Ricardo, a nineteenth-century English economist who explained and analyzed the idea of productivity-based comparative advantage. Variation in the productivity of labor can explain many observed trade patterns in the world.

Although we know that labor productivity differs across countries—and that this can help explain why countries produce the goods they do—there are factors other than labor productivity that determine comparative advantage. Furthermore, even if labor productivity were all that mattered, we would still want to know why some countries have more productive workers than others. The standard interpretation of the Ricardian model is that technological differences between countries account for differences in labor productivity. The countries with the most advanced technology would have a comparative advantage with regard to those goods that can be produced most efficiently with modern technology.

3.b. Factor Abundance

Goods differ in terms of the resources, or factors of production, required for their production. Countries differ in terms of the abundance of different factors of production: land, labor, capital, and entrepreneurial ability. It seems self-evident that countries would have an advantage in producing those goods that use relatively large amounts of their most abundant factor of production. Certainly countries with a relatively large amount of farmland would have a comparative advantage in agriculture, and countries with a relatively large amount of capital would tend to specialize in the production of manufactured goods.

The idea that comparative advantage is based on the relative abundance of factors of production is sometimes called the *Heckscher-Ohlin model*, after the two Swedish economists, Eli Heckscher and Bertil Ohlin, who developed the original argument. The original model assumed that countries possess only two factors of production: labor and capital. Thus, researchers have examined the labor and capital requirements of various industries to see whether labor-abundant countries export goods whose production is relatively labor-intensive, and capital-abundant countries export goods that are relatively capital-intensive. In many cases, factor abundance has served well as an explanation of observed trade patterns. However, there remain cases in which comparative advantage seems to run counter to the predictions of the factor-abundance theory. In response, economists have suggested other explanations for comparative advantage.

Comparative advantage based on differences in the abundance of factors of production across countries is described in the Heckscher-Ohlin model.

3.c. Other Theories of Comparative Advantage

New theories of comparative advantage have typically come about in an effort to explain the trade pattern in some narrow category of products. They are not intended to serve as general explanations of comparative advantage, as do factor abundance and productivity. These supplementary theories emphasize human skills, product cycles, and preferences.

Human skills   This approach emphasizes differences across countries in the availability of skilled and unskilled labor. The basic idea is that countries with a relatively abundant stock of highly skilled labor will have a comparative advantage in producing goods that require relatively large amounts of skilled labor. This theory is similar to the factor-abundance theory, except that here the analysis rests on two segments (skilled and unskilled) of the labor factor.

The human-skills argument is consistent with the observation that most U.S. exports are produced in high-wage (skilled-labor) industries, and most U.S. imports are products produced in relatively low-wage industries. Since the United States has a well-educated labor force, relative to many other countries, we would expect the United States to have a comparative advantage in industries requiring a large amount of skilled labor. Developing countries would be expected to have a comparative advantage in industries requiring a relatively large amount of unskilled labor.

Product life cycles   This theory explains how comparative advantage in a specific good can shift over time from one country to another. This occurs because goods experience a *product life cycle*. At the outset, development and testing are required to conceptualize and design the product. For this reason, the early production will be undertaken by an innovative firm. Over time, however, a successful product tends to become standardized, in the sense that many manufacturers can produce it. The mature product may be produced by firms that do little or no research and development, specializing instead in copying successful products invented and developed by others.

Manufactured goods have life cycles. At first they are produced by the firm that invented them. Later, they may be produced by firms in other countries that copy the technology of the innovator.

The product-life-cycle theory is related to international comparative advantage in that a new product will be first produced and exported by the nation in which it was invented. As the product is exported elsewhere and foreign firms become familiar with it, the technology is copied in other countries by foreign firms seeking to produce a competing version. As the product matures, comparative advantage shifts away from the country of origin if other countries have lower manufacturing costs using the now-standardized technology.

The history of color television production shows how comparative advantage can shift over the product life cycle. Color television was invented in the United States, and U.S. firms initially produced and exported color TVs. Over time, as the technology of color television manufacturing became well known, countries like Japan and Taiwan came to dominate the business. Firms in these countries had a comparative advantage over U.S. firms in the manufacture of color televisions. Once the technology is widely available, countries with cheaper assembly lines, due to lower wages, can compete effectively against the higher-wage nation that developed the technology.

Preferences The theories of comparative advantage we have looked at so far have all been based on supply factors. It may be, though, that the demand side of the market can explain some of the patterns observed in international trade. Seldom are different producers' goods exactly identical. Consumers may prefer the goods of one firm to those of another firm. Domestic firms usually produce goods to satisfy domestic consumers. But since different consumers have different preferences, some consumers will prefer goods produced by foreign firms. International trade allows consumers to expand their consumption opportunities.

Consumers who live in countries with similar levels of development can be expected to have similar consumption patterns. The consumption patterns of consumers in countries at much different levels of development are much less similar. This would suggest that firms in industrial countries will find a larger market for their goods in other industrial countries than in developing countries.

As you saw earlier in this chapter, industrial countries tend to trade with other industrial countries. This pattern runs counter to the factor-abundance theory of comparative advantage, which would suggest that countries with the most dissimilar endowments of resources would find trade most beneficial. Yet rich countries, with large supplies of capital and skilled labor forces, trade more actively with other rich countries than they do with poor countries. Firms in industrial countries tend to produce goods that relatively wealthy consumers will buy. The key point here is that we do not live in a world based on simple comparative advantage, in which all cloth is identical, regardless of the producer. We inhabit a world of differentiated products, and consumers want choices between different brands or styles of a seemingly similar good.

intraindustry trade:
simultaneous import and export of goods in the same industry by a particular country

Another feature of international trade that may be explained by consumer preference is **intraindustry trade**, a circumstance in which a country both exports and imports goods in the same industry. The fact that the United States exports Budweiser beer and imports Heineken beer is not surprising when preferences are taken into account. Supply-side theories of comparative advantage rarely provide an explanation of intraindustry trade, since they

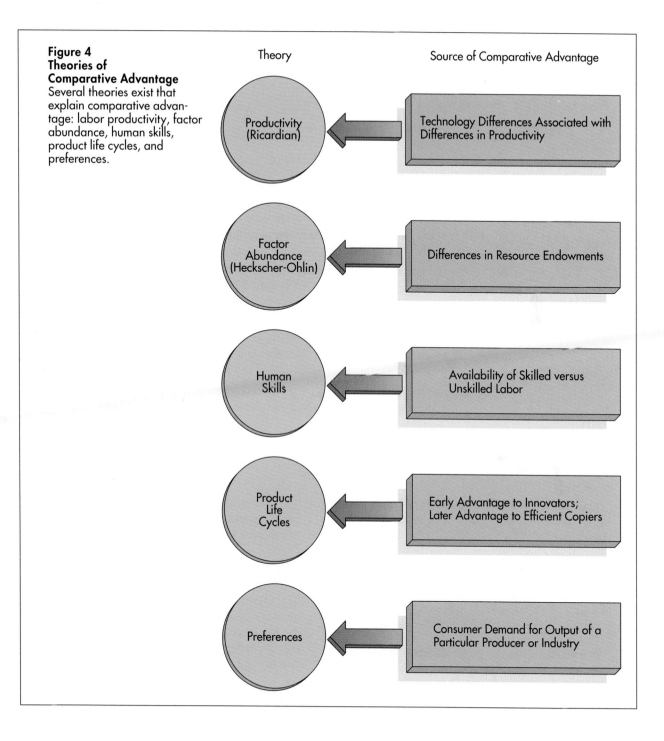

**Figure 4
Theories of
Comparative Advantage**
Several theories exist that
explain comparative advantage: labor productivity, factor
abundance, human skills,
product life cycles, and
preferences.

Theory

Source of Comparative Advantage

Productivity (Ricardian) — Technology Differences Associated with Differences in Productivity

Factor Abundance (Heckscher-Ohlin) — Differences in Resource Endowments

Human Skills — Availability of Skilled versus Unskilled Labor

Product Life Cycles — Early Advantage to Innovators; Later Advantage to Efficient Copiers

Preferences — Consumer Demand for Output of a Particular Producer or Industry

would expect each country to export only those goods produced in industries in which a comparative advantage exists. Yet the real world is characterized by a great deal of intraindustry trade.

We have discussed several potential sources of comparative advantage: labor productivity, factor abundance, human skills, product cycles, and preferences. Each of these theories, summarized in Figure 4, has proven useful in understanding certain trade patterns. Each has also been shown to have limitations as a general theory applicable to all cases. Once again we are reminded that the world is a very complicated place. Theories are simpler than reality. Nevertheless, they help us to understand how comparative advantage arises.

RECAP

1. Comparative advantage can arise because of differences in labor productivity.

2. Countries differ in their resource endowments, and a given country may enjoy a comparative advantage in products that intensively use its most abundant factor of production.

3. Industrial countries may have a comparative advantage in products requiring a large amount of skilled labor. Developing countries may have a comparative advantage in products requiring a large amount of unskilled labor.

4. Comparative advantage in a new good initially resides in the country that invented the good. Over time, other nations learn the technology and may gain a comparative advantage in producing the good.

5. In some industries, consumer preferences for differentiated goods may explain international trade flows, including intraindustry trade.

SUMMARY

▲▼ *What are the prevailing patterns of trade between countries? What goods are traded?*

1. International trade flows largely between industrial countries. §1.a

2. International trade involves many diverse products, but crude petroleum accounts for more than 5 percent of its total value. §1.b

▲▼ *What determines the goods a nation will export?*

3. Comparative advantage is based on the opportunity costs of production. §2.a

4. Domestic opportunity costs determine the limits of the terms of trade between two countries—that is, the amount of exports that must be given up to obtain imports. §2.b

5. The export supply curve shows the domestic surplus and amount of exports available at alternative world prices. §2.c

6. The import demand curve shows the domestic shortage and amount of imports demanded at alternative world prices. §2.c

▲▼ *How are the equilibrium price and the quantity of goods traded determined?*

7. The international equilibrium price and quantity of a good traded are determined by the intersection of the export supply of one country with the import demand of another country. §2.d

▲▼ *What are the sources of comparative advantage?*

8. The productivity-differences and factor-abundance theories of comparative advantage are general theories that seek to explain patterns of international trade flow. §§3.a, 3.b

9. Other theories of comparative advantage aimed at explaining trade in particular kinds of goods focus on human skills, product life cycles, and consumer preferences. §3.c

KEY TERMS

absolute advantage §2.a
comparative advantage §2.a
terms of trade §2.b

export supply curve §2.c
import demand curve §2.c
intraindustry trade §3.c

EXERCISES

1. Why must voluntary trade between two countries be mutually beneficial?

   Use the following table to answer questions 2–6.

Labor Hours Required to Produce 1 Unit of Each Good

	Canada	Japan
Beef	2	4
Computers	6	5

2. Which country has the absolute advantage in beef production?

3. Which country has the absolute advantage in computer production?

4. Which country has the comparative advantage in beef production?

5. Which country has the comparative advantage in computer production?

6. What are the limits of the terms of trade? Specifically, when is Canada willing to trade with Japan, and when is Japan willing to trade with Canada?

7. Use the following supply and demand schedule for two countries to determine the international equilibrium price of shoes. How many shoes will be traded?

Demand and Supply of Shoes (1,000s)

	Mexico		Chile	
Price	Qty. Demanded	Qty. Supplied	Qty. Demanded	Qty. Supplied
$10	40	0	50	0
20	35	20	40	10
30	30	40	30	20
40	25	60	20	30
50	20	80	10	40

8. How would each of the following theories of comparative advantage explain the fact that the United States exports computers?

   a. Productivity differences

   b. Factor abundance

   c. Human skills

   d. Product life cycle

   e. Preferences

9. Which of the theories of comparative advantage could explain why the United States exports computers to Japan at the same time that it imports computers from Japan? Explain.

10. Developing countries have complained that the terms of trade they face are unfavorable. If they voluntarily engage in international trade, what do you suppose they mean by "unfavorable terms of trade"?

11. If two countries reach equilibrium in their domestic markets at the same price, what can be said about their export supply and import demand curves and about the international trade equilibrium?

Should We Attempt to Eliminate the U.S.-Japan Trade Deficit?

Business leaders and politicians have argued recently that the U.S.-Japan merchandise trade deficit, currently estimated to be $42.5 billion for 1991, is "abnormally" high. Many contend that a large bilateral trade deficit like this indicates unfair trade practices in the country with the surplus. In response to this, a current legislative proposal requires that the U.S.-Japan trade deficit be eliminated in five years—if necessary, by restricting imports of motor vehicles. This proposal raises two important questions: First, is a bilateral trade deficit undesirable, and second, should action be taken to eliminate this imbalance in five years?

On the first issue, there is no economic reason for trade to be balanced between any pair of countries in a world with many trading partners; in fact, the opposite should be expected. Why? Because different endowments of national resources and different skills and technologies encourage nations to specialize in the production of things they pro-

duce efficiently and import those that are costly to produce domestically. Indeed, most studies show that the U.S.-Japan trade deficit can be attributed to this "comparative advantage." In fact, the composition of imports and exports is quite different in the two countries. Approximately 80 percent of U.S. exports—but 50 percent of Japanese imports—are manufactured products. The other 50 percent of Japanese imports consists of food, tobacco, beverages, crude materials and mineral fuels, which constitute only 20 percent of U.S. exports. Japanese exports are almost entirely in manufactured products and these products make up approximately 80 percent of U.S. imports. In general, Japan tends to run a surplus with countries that import primarily manufactured products, and a deficit against countries that export primarily food and raw materials. Thus, even if both the United States and Japan had balanced trade overall, one would not expect trade between these two countries to balance.

Meanwhile, except for a slight increase in 1991, the bilateral deficit has been shrinking since it peaked at $57 billion in 1987. Over the same period, U.S. exports to Japan have grown, on average, over seven times as fast as Japanese exports to the United States (15.8 percent vs. 2 percent). If these relative growth rates continue, the U.S.-Japan merchandise trade deficit will be eliminated within five years without any government intervention. Even with somewhat slower growth rates of U.S. exports to Japan, the deficit should be reduced substantially over the next five years. Thus, a variety of market forces—increased U.S. productivity and exchange rate adjustments, among others—appear to be reducing the U.S.-Japan trade deficit on their own.

Source: Alison Butler, "Should We Attempt to Eliminate the U.S.-Japan Trade Deficit?" *International Economic Conditions*, Federal Reserve Bank of St. Louis, February 1992.

Commentary

There is no lack of stories in the American media on the threat of Japanese economic domination. The main piece of evidence used in arguing that the United States will soon become an economic vassal state of Japan is the large trade imbalance between the two countries.

However, the bilateral trade accounts provide little, if any, information on relative economic strengths. Indeed, it is easy to think of an example in which a country has a persistent trade deficit with one of its trading partners but has its overall trade account in balance. Suppose there are three countries that trade among themselves, which we will call countries A, B, and C. The people of each country produce only one type of good and consume only one other type of good. The people of country A produce apples and consume bananas, the people of country B produce bananas and consume cucumbers, and the people of country C produce cucumbers and consume apples. Even when the trade account of each country is balanced, each has a deficit with one of its trading partners and a surplus with the other. Furthermore, a larger trade deficit between countries A and B (with each country retaining balanced trade) implies that the people of country A are better off since they are consuming more. If the government of country A tried to impose a law forcing bilateral trade balance with country B, citizens of country A could not consume as many bananas as before and would be forced to attempt to sell apples to the uninterested citizens of country B.

This simple example demonstrates that the U.S. trade deficit with Japan should not in itself be a cause for concern, especially if the overall trade surplus is shrinking. The United States could have a persistent trade deficit with Japan and yet maintain an overall balanced trade account. In fact, any country would be expected to have a trade deficit with some countries and a trade surplus with others. This reflects comparative advantage. Trade between

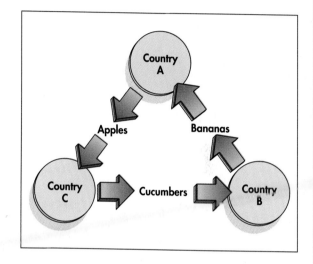

countries makes both the exporting and the importing countries better off.

This is not to say that concern about the *overall* trade deficit is not well founded. An overall trade deficit indicates that a country is consuming more than it is producing. Just as an individual can do this through borrowing (as you may very well be borrowing to finance your college education), a country can run a trade deficit by borrowing from the rest of the world. Borrowing may not be a problem if the loans are used to finance investment that will enable the country to become more productive (just as you may be willing to take out college loans since you expect higher future income because of your college degree). If, on the other hand, the loans only finance consumption, the future repayment of the debt will not be possible because any potential future income will have been consumed in the present.

At any particular time, a country may want to run a trade deficit or a trade surplus, depending on the circumstances it faces. But regardless of the overall trade account of a country, we should expect bilateral trade imbalances among trading partners.

24

Commercial Policy

FUNDAMENTAL
 QUESTIONS

1. Why do countries restrict international trade?
2. How do countries restrict the entry of foreign goods and promote the export of domestic goods?
3. What sorts of agreements do countries enter into to reduce barriers to international trade?

T he Japanese government once announced that foreign-made skis would not be allowed into Japan because they were unsafe. Japanese ski manufacturers were active supporters of the ban. The U.S. government once imposed a tax of almost 50 percent on imports of motorcycles with engines larger than 700cc. The only U.S.-owned motorcycle manufacturer, Harley-Davidson, produced no motorcycles with engines smaller than 1,000cc and so did not care about the small-engine market. In the mid-1980s, Britain began replacing the distinctive red steel telephone booths that were used all through the country with new booths. Many U.S. residents were interested in buying an old British phone booth to use as a decorative novelty, so the phone booths were exported to the United States. However, when the phone booths arrived, the U.S. Customs Service impounded them because there was a limit on the amount of iron and steel products that could be exported from Britain to the United States. The phone booths would be allowed to enter the country only if British exports of some other

PREVIEW

iron and steel products were reduced. The British exporters protested the classification of the phone booths as iron and steel products and argued that they should be considered antiques (which have no import restrictions). The phone booths were not reclassified, so as a result, few have entered the United States, and prices of old British phone booths have been in the thousands of dollars. There are many examples of government policy influencing the prices and quantities of goods traded internationally.

International trade is rarely determined solely by comparative advantage and the free market forces of supply and demand. Governments often find that political pressures favor policies that at least partially offset the prevailing comparative advantages. Government policy aimed at influencing international trade flows is called **commercial policy**. This chapter first examines the arguments in support of commercial policy and then discusses the various tools of commercial policy employed by governments.

commercial policy:
government policy that influences international trade flows

I. ARGUMENTS FOR PROTECTION

Why do countries restrict international trade?

Governments restrict foreign trade to protect domestic producers from foreign competition. In some cases the protection may be justified; in most cases it harms consumers. Of the arguments used to promote such protection, only a few are valid. We will look first at arguments widely considered to have little or no merit, and then at those that may sometimes be valid.

International trade on the basis of comparative advantage maximizes world output and allows consumers access to better-quality products at lower prices than would be available in the domestic market alone. If trade is restricted, consumers pay higher prices for lower-quality goods, and world output declines. Protection from foreign competition imposes costs on the domestic economy, as well as on foreign producers. When production does not proceed on the basis of comparative advantage, resources are not expended on their most efficient uses. Whenever government restrictions alter the pattern of trade, we should expect someone to benefit and someone else to suffer. Generally speaking, protection from foreign competition benefits domestic producers at the expense of domestic consumers.

Protection from foreign competition generally benefits domestic producers at the expense of domestic consumers.

I.a. Creation of Domestic Jobs

If foreign goods are kept out of the domestic economy, it is often argued, jobs will be created at home. This argument holds that domestic firms will produce the goods that otherwise would have been produced abroad, thus employing domestic workers instead of foreign workers. The weakness of this argument is that only the protected industry would benefit in terms of employment. Since domestic consumers will pay higher prices to buy the output of the protected industry, they will have less to spend on other goods and services, which could cause employment in other industries to drop. If other countries retaliate by restricting entry of U.S. exports, the output of U.S. firms that produce for export will fall as well. Typically, restrictions to "save domestic jobs" simply redistribute jobs by creating employment in the protected industry and reducing employment elsewhere.

Table 1 shows estimates of consumer costs and producer gains associated with protection in certain U.S. industries. The first column lists the total cost to U.S. consumers, in terms of higher prices paid, for each industry. For instance, the consumer cost of protecting U.S. book manufacturing is $500 million. The second column lists the cost to consumers of saving one job in each industry (found by dividing the total consumer cost by the number of jobs saved by protection). In book manufacturing, each job saved costs U.S. consumers $100,000. The gain to U.S. producers appears in the third column. Government protection of book manufacturers allowed them to gain $305 million. This gain is less than the costs to consumers of $500 million.

Saving domestic jobs from foreign competition may cost domestic consumers more than it benefits the protected industries.

Table 1 demonstrates the very high cost per job saved by protection. If the costs to consumers are greater than the benefits to protected industries, you may wonder why government provides any protection aimed at saving jobs. The answer, in a word, is politics. Protection of book manufacturing means that all consumers pay a higher price for books. But the individual consumer does not know how much of the book's price is due to protection, and consumers rarely lobby their political representatives to eliminate protection and reduce prices. Meanwhile, there is a great deal of pressure for protection. Employers and workers in the industry know the benefits of protection: higher prices for their output, higher profits for owners, and higher wages for workers. As a result, there will be active lobbying for protection against foreign competition.

I.b. Creation of a "Level Playing Field"

Special interest groups sometimes claim that other nations that export successfully to the home market have unfair advantages over domestic produc-

TABLE 1

Benefits and Costs of Protection from Foreign Competition: Some U.S. Case Histories

Case	Consumer Losses		Producer Gains
	Totals (million dollars)	Per job saved[1] (dollars)	Totals (million dollars)
Manufacturing			
Book manufacturing	$ 500	$ 100,000	$ 305
Benzenoid chemicals	2,650	over 1 million	2,250
Glassware	200	200,000	130
Rubber footwear	230	30,000	90
Ceramic articles	95	47,500	25
Ceramic tiles	116	135,000	62
Orange juice	525	240,000	390
Canned tuna	91	76,000	74
Textiles and apparel: Phase I	9,400	22,000	8,700
Textiles and apparel: Phase II	20,000	37,000	18,000
Textiles and apparel: Phase III	27,000	42,000	22,000
Carbon steel: Phase I	1,970	240,000	1,330
Carbon steel: Phase II	4,350	620,000	2,770
Carbon steel: Phase III	6,800	750,000	3,800
Ball bearings	45	90,000	21
Specialty steel	520	1,000,000	420
Nonrubber footwear	700	55,000	250
Color televisions	420	420,000	190
CB radios	55	93,000	14
Bolts, nuts, large screws	110	550,000	60
Prepared mushrooms	35	117,000	13
Automobiles	5,800	105,000	2,600
Motorcycles	104	150,000	67
Services			
Maritime industries	3,000	270,000	2,000
Agriculture and fisheries			
Sugar	930	60,000 (690/acre)	550
Dairy products	5,500	220,000 (1,800/cow)	5,000
Peanuts	170	1,000/acre	170
Meat	1,800	160,000 (225/head)	1,600
Fish	560	21,000	200
Mining			
Petroleum	6,900	160,000	4,800
Lead and zinc	67	30,000	46

[1]Unless otherwise specified, figures are per worker.

Sources: Data from Cletus C. Coughlin, et al., "Protectionist Trade Policies: A Survey of Theory, Evidence, and Rationale," *Federal Reserve Bank of St. Louis Review,* January/February 1988, p. 18; based on data reported in Gary Clyde Hufbauer, et al., *Trade Protection in the United States: 31 Case Studies,* Institute for International Economics, Washington, D.C., 1986.

ers. Fairness, however, is often in the eye of the beholder. People who call for creating a "level playing field" believe that the domestic government should take steps to offset the perceived advantage of the foreign firm. They often claim that foreign firms have an unfair advantage because foreign workers are willing to work for very low wages. "Fair trade, not free trade" is the cry that this claim generates. But advocates of fair trade are really claiming that production in accordance with comparative advantage is unfair. This is clearly wrong. A country with relatively low wages is typically a country with an abundance of low-skilled labor. Such a country will have a comparative advantage in products that use low-skilled labor most intensively. To create a "level playing field" by imposing restrictions that eliminate the comparative advantage of foreign firms will make domestic consumers worse off and undermine the basis for specialization and economic efficiency.

Calls for "fair trade" are typically aimed at imposing restrictions to match those imposed by other nations.

Some calls for "fair trade" are based on the notion of reciprocity. If a country imposes import restrictions on goods from a country that does not have similar restrictions, reciprocal tariffs and quotas may be called for in the latter country in order to stimulate a reduction of trade restrictions in the former country. For instance, it has been claimed that U.S. construction firms are discriminated against in Japan, because no U.S. firm has had a major construction project in Japan since the 1960s. Yet Japanese construction firms do billions of dollars' worth of business in the United States each year. Advocates of fair trade could argue that U.S. restrictions should be imposed on Japanese construction firms. Reciprocity is generally a more valid reason for restrictions on free trade than protection of domestic jobs.

Calls for fairness based on reciprocity are becoming more common. One danger is that calls for fair trade may be invoked in cases where, in fact, foreign restrictions on U.S. imports do not exist. For instance, suppose the U.S. auto industry wanted to restrict the entry of imported autos to help stimulate sales of domestically produced cars. One strategy might be to point out that U.S. auto sales abroad had fallen and to claim that this was due to unfair treatment of U.S. auto exports in other countries. Of course, there are many other possible reasons why foreign sales of U.S. autos might have fallen. But blaming foreign trade restrictions might win political support for restricting imports of foreign cars into the United States.

1.c. Government Revenue Creation

Developing countries often justify tariffs as an important source of government revenue.

Tariffs on trade generate government revenue. Industrial countries, which find income taxes easy to collect, rarely justify tariffs on the basis of the revenue they generate for government spending. But many developing countries find income taxes difficult to levy and collect, while tariffs are easy to collect. Customs agents can be positioned at ports of entry to examine all goods that enter and leave the country. The observability of trade flows makes tariffs a popular tax in developing countries, whose revenue requirements may provide a valid justification for their existence. Table 2 shows that tariffs account for a relatively large fraction of government revenue in many developing countries, and only a small fraction in industrial countries.

1.d. National Defense

It has long been argued that industries crucial to the national defense, like shipbuilding, should be protected from foreign competition. Even though the

TABLE 2
Tariffs as a Percentage of Total Government Revenue

Country	Tariffs as Percentage of Government Revenue
United Kingdom	0.1%
Japan	1.3
United States	1.6
Costa Rica	23.0
Bangladesh	27.3
Ghana	35.2
Dominican Republic	41.1
Zaire	47.3

Source: Data are from World Bank, *World Development Report*, 1992.

Industries that are truly critical to the national defense should be protected from foreign competition if that is the only way to ensure their existence.

United States does not have a comparative advantage in shipbuilding, a domestic shipbuilding industry is necessary since foreign-made ships may not be available during war. This is a valid argument as long as the protected industry is genuinely critical to the national defense. In some industries, like copper or other basic metals, it might make more sense to import the crucial products during peacetime and store them for use in the event of war; these products do not require domestic production to be useful. Care must be taken to ensure that the national-defense argument is not used to protect industries other than those truly crucial to the nation's defense.

1.e. Infant Industries

Countries sometimes justify protecting new industries that need time to become competitive with the rest of the world.

If a nation sees an opportunity to develop a new industry to compete with established foreign firms, it may want to ensure that industry adequate time to develop. The new industry will need time to establish itself and to become efficient enough that its costs are no higher than those of its foreign rivals. An alternative to protecting young and/or critical domestic industry with tariffs and quotas is to subsidize them. Subsidies allow such firms to charge lower prices and to compete with more efficient foreign producers, while permitting consumers to pay the world price rather than the higher prices associated with tariffs or quotas on foreign goods.

Protecting an infant industry from foreign competition may make sense, but only until the industry matures. Once the industry achieves sufficient size, protection should be withdrawn, and the industry should be made to compete with its foreign counterparts. Unfortunately, such protection is rarely withdrawn, because the larger and more successful the industry becomes, the more political power it wields. In fact, if an infant industry truly has a good chance to become competitive and produce profitably once it is well established, it is not at all clear that government should even offer protection to reduce short-run losses. New firms typically incur losses, but they are only temporary if the firm is successful.

I.f. Strategic Trade Policy

increasing-returns-to-scale industry:
an industry in which the costs of producing a unit of output fall as more output is produced

Government can use trade policy as a strategy to stimulate production by a domestic industry capable of achieving increasing returns to scale.

There is a new view of international trade that regards as misleading the simple formula of comparative advantage presented in the previous chapter. According to this new outlook, which advocates what it calls strategic trade policy, international trade largely involves firms that pursue economies of scale—that is, firms that achieve lower costs per unit of production the more they produce. In contrast to the constant opportunity costs illustrated in the example of wheat and cloth in Chapter 37, opportunity costs in some industries may fall with the level of output. Such **increasing-returns-to-scale industries** will tend to concentrate production in the hands of a few very large firms, rather than many competitive firms. Proponents of strategic trade policy contend that government can use tariffs or subsidies to allow domestic firms with decreasing costs an advantage over their foreign rivals.

A monopoly exists when there is only one producer in an industry, and no close substitutes for the product exist. If the average costs of production decline with increases in output, then the larger a firm is, the lower its per unit costs will be. One large producer will be more efficient than many small ones. A simple example of a natural-monopoly industry will indicate how strategic trade policy can make a country better off. Suppose that the production of buses is an industry characterized by increasing returns to scale and that there are only two firms capable of producing buses: Mercedes-Benz in Germany and General Motors in the United States. If both firms produce buses, their costs will be so high that both will experience losses. If only one of the two produces buses, however, it will be able to sell buses at home and abroad, creating a level of output that allows the firm to earn a profit.

Assume further that a monopoly producer will earn $100 million and that if both firms produce, they will each lose $5 million. Obviously, a firm that doesn't produce earns nothing. Which firm will produce? Because of the decreasing-cost nature of the industry, the firm that is the first to produce will realize lower costs and be able to preclude the other firm from entering the market. But strategic trade policy can alter the market in favor of the domestic firm.

Suppose Mercedes-Benz is the world's only producer of buses. General Motors does not produce them. The U.S. government could offer General Motors an $8 million subsidy to produce buses. General Motors would then enter the bus market, since the $8 million subsidy would more than offset the $5 million loss it would suffer by entering the market. Mercedes-Benz would sustain losses of $5 million once General Motors entered. Ultimately, Mercedes-Benz would stop producing buses to avoid the loss, and General Motors would have the entire market and earn $100 million plus the subsidy.

Strategic trade policy is aimed at offsetting the increasing-returns-to-scale advantage enjoyed by foreign producers and at stimulating production in domestic industries capable of realizing decreasing costs. One practical problem for government is the need to understand the technology of different industries and to forecast accurately the subsidy needed to induce domestic firms to produce new products. A second problem is the likelihood of retaliation by the foreign government. If the U.S. government subsidizes General Motors in its attack on the bus market, the German government is likely to subsidize Mercedes-Benz rather than lose the entire bus market to a U.S. producer. As a result, taxpayers in both nations will be subsidizing two firms, each producing too few buses to earn a profit.

RECAP

1. Government restrictions on foreign trade are usually aimed at protecting domestic producers from foreign competition.

2. Import restrictions may save domestic jobs, but the costs to consumers may be greater than the benefits to those who retain their jobs.

3. Advocates of "fair trade," or the creation of a "level playing field," call for import restrictions as a means of lowering foreign restrictions on markets for domestic exports.

4. Tariffs are an important source of revenue in many developing countries.

5. The national-defense argument in favor of trade restrictions is that protection from foreign competition is necessary to ensure that certain key defense-related industries continue to produce.

6. The infant-industries argument in favor of trade restriction is to allow a new industry a period of time in which to become competitive with its foreign counterparts.

7. Strategic trade policy is intended to provide domestic increasing-returns-to-scale industries an advantage over their foreign competitors.

2. TOOLS OF POLICY

How do countries restrict the entry of foreign goods and promote the export of domestic goods?

Commercial policy makes use of several tools, including tariffs, quotas, subsidies, and nontariff barriers like health and safety regulations that restrict the entry of foreign products. Since 1945, barriers to trade have been reduced. Much of the progress toward free trade may be linked to the *General Agreement on Tariffs and Trade*, or *GATT*, that began in 1947. The Economic Insight "The GATT" describes how this document and the continuing negotiations under its auspices have worked to eliminate quotas on manufactured goods and to lower tariffs.

2.a. Tariffs

tariffs:
taxes on imports or exports

A **tariff** is a tax on imports or exports. Every country imposes tariffs on at least some imports. Some countries also impose tariffs on selected exports as a means of raising government revenue. Brazil, for instance, taxes coffee exports. The United States does not employ export tariffs, which are forbidden by the U.S. Constitution.

Tariffs are frequently imposed in order to protect domestic producers from foreign competition (see the Economic Insight "Smoot-Hawley Tariff"). The effect of a tariff is illustrated in Figure 1, which shows the domestic market for oranges. Without international trade, the domestic equilibrium price, P_d, and quantity demanded, Q_d, are determined by the intersection of the domestic demand and supply curves. If the world price of oranges, P_w, is lower than the domestic equilibrium price, this country will import oranges. The quantity imported will be the difference between the quantity Q_1 produced domestically at a price of P_w and the quantity Q_2 demanded domestically at the world price of oranges.

When the world price of the traded good is lower than the domestic equilibrium price without international trade, free trade causes domestic produc-

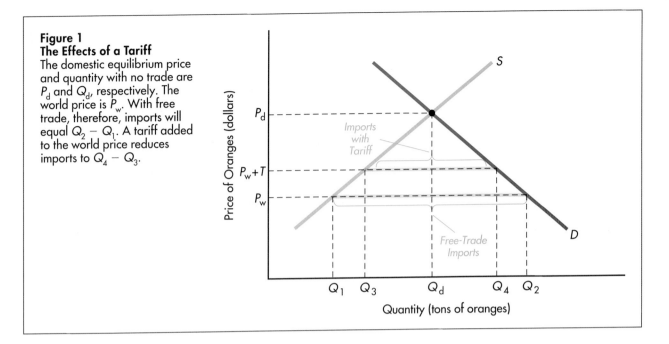

Figure 1
The Effects of a Tariff
The domestic equilibrium price and quantity with no trade are P_d and Q_d, respectively. The world price is P_w. With free trade, therefore, imports will equal $Q_2 - Q_1$. A tariff added to the world price reduces imports to $Q_4 - Q_3$.

tion to fall and domestic consumption to rise. The domestic shortage at the world price is met by imports. Domestic consumers are better off, since they can buy more at a lower price. But domestic producers are worse off, since they now sell fewer oranges and receive a lower price.

Suppose a tariff of T (the dollar value of the tariff) is imposed on orange imports. The price paid by consumers is now $P_w + T$, rather than P_w. At this higher price, domestic producers will produce Q_3 and domestic consumers will purchase Q_4. The tariff has the effect of increasing domestic production and reducing domestic consumption, relative to the free trade equilibrium. Imports fall accordingly, from $Q_2 - Q_1$ to $Q_4 - Q_3$.

Domestic producers are better off, since the tariff has increased their sales of oranges and raised the price they receive. Domestic consumers pay higher prices for fewer oranges than they would with free trade, but they are still better off than they would be without trade. If the tariff had raised the price paid by consumers to P_d, there would be no trade, and the domestic equilibrium quantity, Q_d, would prevail.

The government earns revenue from imports of oranges. If each ton of oranges generates tariff revenue of T, the total tariff revenue to the government is found by multiplying the tariff by the quantity of oranges imported. In Figure 1, this amount is $T \times (Q_4 - Q_3)$. As the tariff changes, so does the quantity of imports and the government revenue.

2.b. Quotas

quantity quota:
a limit on the amount of a good that may be imported

Quotas are limits on the quantity or value of goods imported and exported. A **quantity quota** restricts the physical amount of a good. For instance, in 1987 the United States allowed only 1 million tons of sugar to be imported. Even though the United States is not a competitive sugar producer compared to other nations like the Dominican Republic or Cuba, the quota allowed approximately 6.5 million tons of sugar to be produced by U.S. firms. A

The GATT

The General Agreement on Tariffs and Trade, or GATT, is both a document that establishes rules for international trade and an international organization that manages negotiations among nations to lower trade barriers. The basic principles reflected in the GATT document are these:

1. Quotas should be eliminated and other barriers to international trade should be reduced.

2. Barriers to trade should apply equally to all countries, rather than selectively to some.

3. Once tariffs have been lowered, they cannot be increased without compensating trading partners.

4. Disagreements should be settled in consultation, according to the GATT rules.

The Secretariat of the GATT oversees the international trading system and provides a forum for periodic meetings of nations to negotiate reduced trade barriers. Currently, 124 countries agree to abide by the GATT rules. These 124 countries account for the great bulk of world trade.

value quota:
a limit on the monetary value of a good that may be imported

value quota restricts the monetary value of a good that may be traded. Instead of a physical quota on sugar, the United States could have limited the dollar value of sugar imports.

Quotas are used to protect domestic producers from foreign competition. By restricting the amount of a good that may be imported, they increase its price and allow domestic producers to sell more at a higher price than they would with free trade. Figure 2 illustrates the effect of a quota on the domestic orange market. The domestic equilibrium supply and demand curves determine the equilibrium price and quantity without trade to be P_d and 250

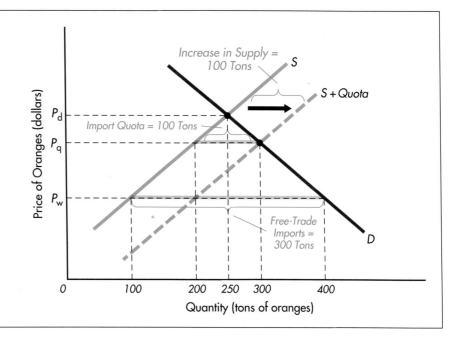

Figure 2
The Effects of a Quota
The domestic equilibrium price with no international trade is P_d. At this price, 250 tons of oranges would be produced and consumed at home. With free trade, the price is P_w and 300 tons will be imported. An import quota of 100 tons will cause the price to be P_q, where the domestic shortage equals the 100 tons allowed by the quota.

tons, respectively. The world price of oranges is P_w. Since P_w lies below P_d, this country will import oranges. The quantity of imports is equal to the amount of the domestic shortage at P_w. The quantity demanded at P_w is 400 tons, and the quantity supplied domestically is 100 tons, so imports will equal 300 tons of oranges. With free trade, domestic producers sell 100 tons at a price of P_w.

But suppose domestic orange growers convince the government to restrict orange imports. The government then imposes a quota of 100 tons on imported oranges. The effect of the quota on consumers is to shift the supply curve to the right by the amount of the quota, 100 tons. Since the quota is less than the quantity of imports with free trade, the quantity of imports will equal the quota. The domestic equilibrium price with the quota occurs at the point where the domestic shortage equals the quota. At price P_q, the domestic quantity demanded (300 tons) is 100 tons more than the domestic quantity supplied (200 tons).

Quotas benefit domestic producers in the same way that tariffs do. Domestic producers receive a higher price (P_q instead of P_w) for a greater quantity (200 instead of 100) than they do under free trade. The effect on domestic consumers is also similar to that of a tariff: They pay a higher price for a smaller quantity than they would with free trade. A tariff generates government tax revenue; quotas do not (unless the government auctioned off the right to import under the quota). Furthermore, a tariff only raises the price of the product in the domestic market. Foreign producers receive the world price, P_w. With a quota, both domestic and foreign producers receive the higher price, P_q, for the goods sold in the domestic market. So foreign producers are hurt by the reduction in the quantity of imports permitted, but they do receive a higher price for the amount they sell.

Voluntary export restraints are a substitute for quotas. They limit the amount exporters ship to an importing country.

In some cases, countries negotiate *voluntary export restraints* rather than imposing quotas. A voluntary export restraint limits the quantity of goods shipped from the exporting country to an importing country, so such restraints have the same practical effect as a quota. For instance, in the 1980s the United States negotiated voluntary export restraints on Japanese auto exports to the United States, limiting such exports to 1.62 million autos in 1981 (U.S. firms produced 1.3 million small cars and 2.6 million large cars that year). The agreement lasted until 1985, with the quantity of exports rising over time.

2.c. Other Barriers to Trade

Tariffs and quotas are not the only barriers to the free flow of goods across international borders. There are three additional sources of restrictions on free trade: subsidies, government procurement, and health and safety standards. Though often enacted for reasons other than protection from foreign competition, a careful analysis reveals their import-reducing effect.

Before discussing these three types of barriers, let us note the cultural or institutional barriers to trade that also exist in many countries. Such barriers may exist independently of any conscious government policy. For instance, Japan has frequently been criticized by U.S. officials for informal business practices that discriminate against foreigners. Under the Japanese distribution system, goods typically pass through several layers of middlemen before appearing in a retail store. A foreign firm faces the difficult task of gaining

Smoot-Hawley Tariff

Many economists believe that the Great Depression of the 1930s was at least partly due to the Smoot-Hawley Tariff Act, signed into law by President Herbert Hoover in 1930. Hoover had promised that, if elected, he would raise tariffs on agricultural products to raise U.S. farm income. Congress began work on the tariff increases in 1928. Congressman Willis Hawley and Senator Reed Smoot conducted the hearings.

In testimony before Congress, manufacturers and other special interest groups also sought protection from foreign competition. The resulting bill increased tariffs on over twelve thousand products. Tariffs reached their highest levels ever, about 60 percent of average import values. Only twice before in

U.S. history had tariffs approached the levels of the Smoot-Hawley era.

Before President Hoover signed the bill, thirty-eight foreign governments made formal protests, warning that they would retaliate with high tariffs on U.S. products. A petition signed by 1,028 economists warned of the harmful effects of the bill. Nevertheless, Hoover signed the bill into law.

World trade collapsed as other countries raised their tariffs in response. Between 1930 and 1931, U.S. imports fell 29 percent, but U.S. exports fell 33 percent. By 1933, world trade was about one-third of the 1929 level. As the level of trade fell, so did income and prices. In 1934, in an effort to correct the mistakes of Smoot-

Hawley, Congress passed the Reciprocal Trade Agreements Act, which allowed the president to lower U.S. tariffs in return for reductions in foreign tariffs on U.S. goods. This act ushered in the modern era of relatively low tariffs. In the United States today, tariffs are about 5 percent of the average value of imports.

Many economists believe the collapse of world trade and the Depression to be linked by a decrease in real income caused by abandoning production based on comparative advantage. Few economists argue that the Great Depression was caused solely by the Smoot-Hawley tariff, but the experience serves as a lesson to those who support higher tariffs to protect domestic producers.

entry to this system to supply goods to the retailer. Furthermore, a foreigner cannot easily open a retail store. Japanese law requires a new retail firm to receive permission from other retailers in the area in order to open a business. A firm that lacks contacts and knowledge of the system cannot penetrate the Japanese market.

In the fall of 1989, the U.S. toy firm Toys "R" Us announced its intent to open several large discount toy stores in Japan. However, local toy stores in each area objected to having a Toys "R" Us store nearby. The U.S. government has argued that the laws favoring existing firms are an important factor in keeping Japan closed to foreign firms that would like to enter the Japanese market. Eventually, Toys "R" Us opened stores in Japan.

subsidies:
payments made by government to domestic firms to encourage exports

2.c.1. Subsidies **Subsidies** are payments by a government to an exporter. Subsidies are paid to stimulate exports by allowing the exporter to charge a lower price. The amount of a subsidy is determined by the international price of a product relative to the domestic price in the absence of trade. Domestic consumers are harmed by subsidies in that their taxes finance the subsidies. Also, since the subsidy diverts resources from the domestic market toward export production, the increase in the supply of export goods could be associated with a decrease in the supply of domestic goods, causing domestic prices to rise.

Subsidies may take forms other than direct cash payments. These include tax reductions, low-interest loans, low-cost insurance, government-sponsored research funding, and other devices. The U.S. government subsidizes export activity through the U.S. Export-Import Bank, which provides loans and insurance to help U.S. exporters sell their goods to foreign buyers. Subsidies are more commonplace in Europe than in Japan or the United States.

2.c.2. Government Procurement

Governments are often required by law to buy only from local producers. In the United States, a "buy American" act passed in 1933 requires U.S. government agencies to buy U.S. goods and services unless the domestic price is more than 12 percent above the foreign price. This kind of policy allows domestic firms to charge the government a higher price for their products than they charge consumers; the taxpayers bear the burden. The United States is by no means alone in requiring the federal government to purchase domestic goods. Many other nations also use such policies to create larger markets for domestic goods.

2.c.3. Health and Safety Standards

Government serves as a guardian of the public health and welfare by requiring that products offered to the public be safe and fulfill the use for which they are intended. Government standards for products sold in the domestic marketplace can have the effect (intentional or not) of protecting domestic producers from foreign competition. These effects should be considered in evaluating the full impact of such standards.

As mentioned in the Preview, the government of Japan once threatened to prohibit foreign-made snow skis from entering the country for reasons of safety. Only Japanese-made skis were determined to be suitable for Japanese snow. Several Western European nations announced that U.S. beef would not be allowed into Europe because hormones approved by the U.S. government are fed to U.S. beef cattle. In the late 1960s, France required tractors sold there to have a maximum speed of 17 miles per hour; in Germany, the permissible speed was 13 mph, and in the Netherlands it was 10 mph. Tractors produced in one country had to be modified to meet the requirements of the other countries. Such modifications raise the price of goods and discourage international trade.

Product standards may not eliminate foreign competition, but standards different from those of the rest of the world do provide an element of protection to domestic firms.

RECAP

1. A tariff is a tax on imports or exports. Tariffs protect domestic firms by raising the prices of foreign goods.

2. Quotas are government-imposed limits on the quantity or value of an imported good. Quotas protect domestic firms by restricting the entry of foreign products to a level less than the quantity demanded.

3. Subsidies are payments by the government to domestic producers. Subsidies lower the price of domestic goods.

4. Governments are often required by law to buy only domestic products.

What sorts of agreements do countries enter into to reduce barriers to international trade?

In an effort to stimulate international trade, groups of countries sometimes enter into agreements to abolish most barriers to trade among themselves. Such arrangements between countries are known as preferential trading agreements. The European Economic Community and the North American Free Trade Agreement (NAFTA) are examples of preferential trading agreements.

3.a. Free Trade Areas and Customs Unions

free trade area:
an organization of nations whose members have no trade barriers among themselves but are free to fashion their own trade policies toward nonmembers

customs union:
an organization of nations whose members have no trade barriers among themselves but impose common trade barriers on nonmembers

Two common forms of preferential trade agreements are **free trade areas** (FTAs) and **customs unions** (CUs). These two approaches differ with regard to treatment of countries outside the agreement. In an FTA, member countries eliminate trade barriers among themselves, but each member country chooses its own trade policies toward nonmember countries. Members of a CU agree to eliminate trade barriers among themselves and to maintain common trade barriers against nonmembers.

The best-known CU is the European Economic Community (EEC), created in 1957 by France, West Germany, Italy, Belgium, the Netherlands, and Luxembourg. The United Kingdom, Ireland, and Denmark joined in 1973, followed by Greece in 1981 and Spain and Portugal in 1986. The EEC agreement has eliminated most tariffs within the CU, but full-fledged free trade within the union has been slow in coming, due to the presence of nontariff barriers. Besides free trade in goods, European financial markets and institutions will eventually be able to operate across national boundaries. For instance, a bank in any EEC country will be permitted to operate in any or all other EEC countries.

In 1989, the United States and Canada negotiated a free trade area. The United States, Canada, and Mexico negotiated a free trade area in 1992. Once it is signed, tariffs are to be lowered on eight thousand different items,

The North American Free Trade Agreement will stimulate trade between Mexico, Canada, and the United States. In coming years, there will be more and more container ships from Mexico unloading their cargo at U.S. docks. This ship, Mexicana, tied up in Long Beach, California, is a sign of the times ahead for U.S. ports. Similarly, freight from Canada and the United States will increase in volume at Mexican ports as trade barriers between the three nations fall.

and each nation's financial market will be opened to competition from the other two nations. The North American Free Trade Agreement (NAFTA) will not eliminate all barriers to trade among the three nations but does represent a significant step in that direction.

3.b. Trade Creation and Diversion

Free trade agreements provide for free trade among a group of countries, not worldwide. As a result, a customs union or free trade area may make a nation better off or worse off compared to the free trade equilibrium.

Figure 3 illustrates the effect of a free trade area. With no international trade, the U.S. supply and demand curves for oranges would result in an equilibrium price of $500 per ton and an equilibrium quantity of 425 tons. Suppose there are two other orange-producing countries, Israel and Brazil. Israel, the low-cost producer of oranges, is willing to sell all the oranges the United States can buy for $150 per ton, as represented by the horizontal supply curve S_I. Brazil will supply oranges for a price of $200 per ton, as represented by the horizontal supply curve S_B.

With free trade, the United States would import oranges from Israel. The quantity demanded at $150 is 750 tons, and the domestic quantity supplied at this price is 100 tons. The shortage of 650 tons is met by imports from Israel.

Now suppose a 100 percent tariff is imposed on orange imports. The price domestic consumers pay for foreign oranges is twice as high as before. For oranges from Israel the new price is $300, twice the old price of $150. The new supply curve for Israel is represented as $S_I + Tariff$. Oranges from Brazil now sell for $400, twice the old price of $200; the new supply curve for Brazil is shown as $S_B + Tariff$. After the 100 percent tariff is imposed, oranges are still imported from Israel. But at the new price of $300, the domestic quantity demanded is 600 tons and the domestic quantity supplied

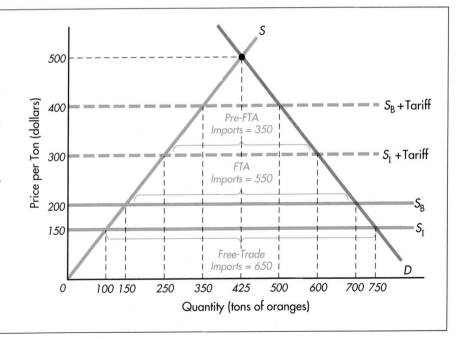

Figure 3
Trade Creation and Trade Diversion with a Free Trade Area
With no trade, the domestic equilibrium price is $500 and the equilibrium quantity is 425 tons. With free trade, the price is $150, and 650 tons would be imported, as indicated by the supply curve for Israel, S_I. A 100 percent tariff on imports would result in imports of 350 tons from Israel, according to the supply curve $S_I + Tariff$. A free trade agreement that eliminates tariffs on Brazilian oranges only would result in a new equilibrium price of $200 and imports of 550 tons from Brazil, according to supply curve S_B.

is 250 tons. Thus only 350 tons will be imported. The tariff reduces the volume of trade relative to the free trade equilibrium, at which 650 tons were imported.

Now suppose that the United States negotiates a free trade agreement with Brazil, eliminating tariffs on imports from Brazil. Israel is not a member of the free trade agreement, so imports from Israel are still covered by the 100 percent tariff. The relevant supply curve for Brazil is now S_B, so oranges may be imported from Brazil for $200, a lower price than Israel's price including the tariff. At a price of $200, the domestic quantity demanded is 700 tons and the domestic quantity supplied is 150 tons; 550 tons will be imported.

The effects of the free trade agreement are twofold. First, trade was diverted away from the lowest-cost producer, Israel, to the FTA partner, Brazil. This **trade diversion** effect of an FTA reduces worldwide economic efficiency, since production is diverted from the country with the comparative advantage. Oranges are not being produced as efficiently as possible. The other effect of the FTA is that the quantity of imports increases relative to the effect of a tariff applicable to all imports. Imports rise from 350 tons (the quantity imported from Israel with the tariff) to 550 tons. The FTA thus has a **trade creation** effect, resulting from the lower price available after the tariff reduction. Trade creation is a beneficial aspect of the FTA: the expansion of international trade allows this country to realize greater benefits from trade than would be possible without trade.

Countries form preferential trade agreements because they believe FTAs will make each member country better off. The member countries view the trade-creation effects of such agreements as benefiting their exporters by increasing exports to member countries and as benefiting consumers by making a wider variety of goods available at a lower price. From the point of view of the world as a whole, preferential trade agreements are more desirable the more they stimulate trade creation to allow the benefits of trade to be realized and the less they emphasize trade diversion, so that production occurs on the basis of comparative advantage. This principle suggests that the most successful FTAs or CUs are those that increase trade volume but do not change the patterns of trade in terms of who specializes and exports each good. In the case of Figure 3, a more successful FTA would reduce tariffs on Israeli as well as Brazilian oranges, so that oranges would be imported from the lowest-cost producer, Israel.

trade diversion:
an effect of a preferential trade agreement, reducing economic efficiency by shifting production to a higher-cost producer

trade creation:
an effect of a preferential trade agreement, allowing a country to obtain goods at a lower cost than is available at home

RECAP

1. Countries form preferential trade agreements in order to stimulate trade among themselves.

2. The most common forms of preferential trade agreement are free trade areas (FTAs) and customs unions (CUs).

3. Preferential trade agreements have a harmful trade-diversion effect when they cause production to shift from the nation with a comparative advantage to a higher-cost producer.

4. Preferential trade agreements have a beneficial trade-creation effect when they reduce prices for traded goods and stimulate the volume of international trade.

SUMMARY

1. Commercial policy is government policy that influences the direction and volume of international trade. §Preview

2. Protecting domestic producers from foreign competition usually imposes costs on domestic consumers. §1

3. Rationales for commercial policy include saving domestic jobs, creating a fair-trade relationship with other countries, raising tariff revenue, ensuring a domestic supply of key defense goods, allowing new industries a chance to become internationally competitive, and giving domestic industries with increasing returns to scale an advantage over foreign competitors. §§1.a–1.f

4. Tariffs protect domestic industry by increasing the price of foreign goods. §2.a

5. Quotas protect domestic industry by limiting the quantity of foreign goods allowed into the country. §2.b

6. Subsidies allow relatively inefficient domestic producers to compete with foreign firms. §2.c.1

7. Government procurement practices and health and safety regulations can protect domestic industry from foreign competition. §§2.c.2, 2.c.3

8. Customs unions and free trade areas are two types of preferential trade agreements that reduce trade restrictions among member countries. §3.a

9. Preferential trade agreements have harmful trade-diversion effects and beneficial trade-creation effects. §3.b

KEY TERMS

commercial policy §Preview

increasing-returns-to-scale industry §1.f

tariff §2.a

quantity quota §2.b

value quota §2.b

subsidy §2.c.1

free trade area §3.a

customs union §3.a

trade diversion §3.b

trade creation §3.b

EXERCISES

1. What are the potential benefits and costs of a commercial policy designed to pursue each of the following goals?

   a. Save domestic jobs

   b. Create a level playing field

   c. Increase government revenue

   d. Provide a strong national defense

   e. Protect an infant industry

   f. Stimulate exports of an industry with increasing returns to scale

2. For each of the goals listed in question 1, discuss what the appropriate commercial policy is likely to be (in terms of tariffs, quotas, subsidies, etc.).

3. Tariffs and quotas both raise the price of foreign goods to domestic consumers. What is the difference between the effects of a tariff and the effects of a quota on the following?

a. The domestic government

b. Foreign producers

c. Domestic producers

4. Would trade-diversion and trade-creation effects occur if the whole world became a free trade area? Explain.

5. What is the difference between a customs union and a free trade area?

6. Draw a graph of the U.S. automobile market in which the domestic equilibrium price without trade is P_d and the equilibrium quantity is Q_d. Use this graph to illustrate and explain the effects of a tariff if the United States were an auto importer with free trade. Then use the graph to illustrate and explain the effects of a quota.

7. If commercial policy can benefit U.S. industry, why would any U.S. resident oppose such policies?

8. Suppose you were asked to assess U.S. commercial policy to determine whether the benefits of protection for U.S. industries are worth the costs. Does Table 1 provide all the information you need? If not, what else would you want to know?

9. How would the effects of international trade on the domestic orange market change if the world price of oranges were above the domestic equilibrium price? Draw a graph to help explain your answer.

10. Suppose the world price of kiwi fruit is $20 per case and the U.S. equilibrium price with no international trade is $35 per case. If the U.S. government had previously banned the import of kiwi fruit but then imposed a tariff of $5 per case and allowed kiwi imports, what would happen to the equilibrium price and quantity of kiwi fruit consumed in the United States?

Imports and Competition in Domestic Markets

Foremost among the asserted benefits of reducing trade barriers is competition: firms that operate in an economy with relatively weak domestic competition are supposed to be forced by the onslaught of foreign goods to improve their quality and service and to keep costs and prices down. The benefits of trade liberalization are assumed to be particularly great in developing countries, where a relatively few firms may control a given industry. But while the theoretical benefits of freer trade are well understood, do businesses actually respond in that way? After studying the effects of trade liberalization in Turkey, NBER researcher James Levinsohn concludes that the answer is "yes."

Until 1984, the Turkish economy was highly protected against imports, with tariffs averaging 49 percent and an array of nontariff barriers including quotas, import licenses, and foreign exchange regulations. In 1984, however, tariffs were reduced to an average of 20 percent and restrictions on many types of imports were eliminated. . . . Levinsohn investigated the impact of this sweeping liberalization by using detailed data on individual firms from the Turkish manufacturing census. . . .

Prior to the change in trade policy, Levinsohn finds, firms in six of the eleven industries studied were pricing at marginal cost, indicating a high level of competition. In three industries, companies were pricing above marginal cost, indicating the existence of imperfect competition, while in two industries, including the largely government-owned steel industry, firms were losing money on each unit of output. The 1984 trade liberalization reduced the level of protection enjoyed by nine of the eleven industries. In the three high-margin industries, miscellaneous chemicals, pottery, and electrical machinery, price markups declined as import competition increased. For two of the previously competitive industries, transport equipment and scientific equipment, the trade reform resulted in higher levels of import protection, and price markups in those industries increased. Of the six previously competitive industries that had their protection reduced by the trade reform, three had lower markups and one was unchanged; one of the two industries in that category with higher markups was the steel industry.

Levinsohn warns that the price markups reported by companies to census officials may not be completely accurate. Firms with high profits may be inclined to understate their revenues or overstate costs in case tax officials learn of their reports, while firms with losses may exit the industry and not report. Nonetheless, Levinsohn writes, the Turkish data indicate that imports increase competition and restrict the ability of domestic firms to exercise market power.

Source: Reprinted by permission of the National Bureau of Economic Research.

Commentary

onsider the following hypothetical situation: The legislature of the state of Maine considers a tax to support the pineapple farmers of the state. Of course, Maine's climate is not conducive to growing pineapples, but it is possible, at great cost, to grow a few pineapples in greenhouses. The tax on pineapples brought into the state raises the price of Hawaiian pineapples by enough to make pineapples grown in Maine competitive. Thus Maine's pineapple industry is saved from competitors whose price reflects their unfair climatic advantage, though the consumers of the state must pay exorbitant prices for their pineapples.

This scenario, with its absurd distortion of the workings of the market, differs in degree but not in kind from the description of the effects of import competition in the accompanying article. The protectionist measure of imposing quotas or tariffs on imports saves jobs in the domestic import-competing industries, but at a great cost to consumers. It is estimated that the cost of protecting the U.S. domestic textile industry is $238 per family in the United States.

The effect of reducing domestic competition with quotas can be understood using supply and demand analysis. Let's analyze the case of quotas on textile imports into the United States. In the diagram, S_1 is the domestic supply of textiles, S_2 is the sum of the domestic supply and the foreign supply allowed in by the quotas, and D is the demand for textiles. Under the quota system, the price of textiles in the United States is represented by P_q and the quantity of textiles consumed is Q_q. If the quotas were removed, the price of textiles in the United States would equal the world price of P_w, and this lower price would be associated with an increase in the consumption of textiles to Q_w. The quota represents a cost to society in terms of a loss of consumer welfare as well as a loss from the inefficient use of resources in an industry in which this country has no comparative advantage, just as Maine has no comparative advantage in the production of pineapples.

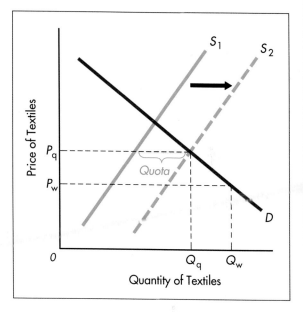

Given the costs to society of these quotas, why is there such strong support for them in Congress? An important political aspect of protectionist policies is that their benefits are concentrated among a relatively small number of people while their costs are diffuse and spread across all consumers. Each individual import-competing producer faces very large losses from free trade while the cost to each consumer of a protectionist policy is less dramatic. It is also easier to organize a relatively small number of manufacturers than to mobilize a vast population of consumers. These factors explain the strong lobby for the protection of industries like textiles and the absence of a legislative lobby that operates specifically in the interest of textile consumers.

It is possible to patch together a case for the protection of the textile or any other industry, just as it is possible to concoct an argument for the protection of the hypothetical Maine pineapple industry. But these arguments should be seen for what they are: an attempt by an industry to increase its profits at the expense of the general public.

25

Exchange-Rate Systems and Practices

FUNDAMENTAL QUESTIONS

1. How does a commodity standard fix exchange rates between countries?
2. What kinds of exchange-rate arrangements exist today?
3. How is equilibrium determined in the foreign exchange market?
4. How do fixed and floating exchange rates differ in their adjustment to shifts in supply and demand for currencies?
5. What are the advantages and disadvantages of fixed and floating exchange rates?
6. What determines the kind of exchange-rate system a country adopts?

xchange-rate policy is an important element of macroeconomic policy. An exchange rate is the link between two nations' monies. The value of a U.S. dollar in terms of Japanese yen or German marks determines how many dollars a U.S. resident will need to buy goods priced in yen or marks. Thus changes in the exchange rate can have far-reaching implications. Exchange rates may be determined in free markets, or through government intervention in the foreign exchange market, or even by law.

At the beginning of 1992, one U.S. dollar was worth 1.61 German marks. By late August of that year, the dollar was worth 1.41 marks. Why did the dollar fall in value relative to the mark? What are the effects of such changes? Should governments permit exchange rates to change? What can governments do to discourage changing exchange rates? These are all important questions, which this chapter will help to answer.

PREVIEW

This chapter begins with a review of the history of exchange-rate systems. Then follows an overview of exchange-rate practices in the world today and an analysis of the benefits and costs of alternative exchange-rate arrangements. Along the way, we will introduce terminology and institutions that play a major role in the evolution of exchange rates.

I. PAST AND CURRENT EXCHANGE-RATE ARRANGEMENTS

I.a. The Gold Standard

How does a commodity standard fix exchange rates between countries?

gold standard:
a system whereby national currencies are fixed in terms of their value in gold, thus creating fixed exchange rates between currencies

In ancient times, government-produced monies were made of precious metals like gold. Later, when governments began to issue paper money, it was usually convertible into a fixed amount of gold. Ensuring the convertibility of paper money into gold was a way to maintain confidence in the currency's value, at home and abroad. If a unit of currency was worth a fixed amount of gold, its value could be stated in terms of its gold value. The countries that maintained a constant gold value for their currencies were said to be on a **gold standard**.

Some countries had backed their currencies with gold long before 1880; however, the practice became widespread around 1880 so that economists typically date the beginning of the gold standard around this period. From roughly 1880 to 1914, currencies had fixed values in terms of gold. For instance, the U.S. dollar's value was fixed at $20.67 per ounce of gold. Any other currency that was fixed in terms of gold also had a fixed exchange rate against the dollar. A simple example will illustrate how this works.

Suppose the price of an ounce of gold is $20 in the United States and £4 in the United Kingdom. The pound is worth five times the value of a dollar, since it takes five times as many dollars as pounds to buy one ounce of gold. Because one pound buys five times as much gold as one dollar, the exchange rate is £1 = $5. Since currency values are linked by gold values, as the supply of gold fluctuates, there will be pressure to alter prices of goods and services. The gold standard fixes only the current price of gold. As the stock of gold increases, everything else held constant, the gold and currency prices of goods and services will tend to rise (as would occur when the money supply increases).

A commodity money standard exists when exchange rates are fixed based on the values of different currencies in terms of some commodity.

A gold standard is only one possible *commodity money standard*. Any other highly valued commodity (silver, for instance) could serve as a standard linking monies in a fixed exchange-rate system.

The gold standard ended with the outbreak of World War I. War financing was partially funded by increases in the money supplies of the hostile nations. A gold standard would not permit such a rapid increase in the money supply unless the stock of gold increased dramatically, which it did not. As money supplies grew faster than gold supplies, the link between money and gold had to be broken. During the war years and the Great Depression of the 1930s, and on through World War II, there was no organized system for setting exchange rates. Foreign trade and investment shrunk as a result of the war, obviating the need for a well-functioning method of determining exchange rates.

1.b. The Bretton Woods System

At the end of World War II, there was widespread political support for an exchange-rate system linking all monies in much the same way as the gold standard had. It was believed that a system of fixed exchange rates would promote the growth of world trade. In 1944, delegates from forty-four nations met in Bretton Woods, New Hampshire, to discuss the creation of such a system. The agreement reached at this conference has had a profound impact on the world.

The Bretton Woods agreement established a system of fixed exchange rates.

The exchange-rate arrangement that emerged from the Bretton Woods conference is often called a **gold exchange standard**. Each country was to fix the value of its currency in terms of gold, just as it had under the gold standard. The U.S.-dollar price of gold, for instance, was $35 an ounce. However, there were fundamental differences between this system and the old gold standard. The U.S. dollar, rather than gold, served as the focal point of the system. Instead of buying and selling gold, countries bought and sold U.S. dollars to maintain a fixed exchange rate with the dollar. Since the United States was the major victor nation, its currency was the dominant world currency. The United States had the productive capacity to supply much-needed goods to the rest of the world, and these goods were priced in dollars.

gold exchange standard:
an exchange-rate system in which each nation fixes the value of its currency in terms of gold but buys and sells the U.S. dollar rather than gold to maintain fixed exchange rates

reserve currency:
a currency that is used to settle international debts and is held by governments to use in foreign exchange market interventions

The U.S. dollar was the **reserve currency** of the system. International debts were settled with dollars, and international trade contracts were often denominated in dollars. In effect, the world was on a dollar standard following World War II.

1.c. The International Monetary Fund and the World Bank

International Monetary Fund (IMF):
an international organization that supervises exchange-rate arrangements and lends money to member countries experiencing problems meeting their external financial obligations

Two new organizations also emerged from the Bretton Woods conference: the International Monetary Fund and the World Bank. The **International Monetary Fund**, or **IMF**, was created to supervise the exchange-rate practices of member countries and to encourage the free convertibility of any national money into the monies of other countries. The IMF also lends money to countries that are experiencing problems meeting their international payment obligations. The funds available to the IMF come from the annual membership fees (called *quotas*) of the 151 member countries of the IMF. The U.S. quota, for instance, is almost $23 billion. (The term *quota* has a different meaning in this context than it does in international trade.)

World Bank:
an international organization that makes loans and provides technical expertise to developing countries

The **World Bank** was created to help finance economic development in poor countries. It provides loans to developing countries at more favorable terms than are available from commercial lenders and also offers technical expertise. The World Bank obtains the funds it lends by selling bonds. It is one of the world's major borrowers. See the Economic Insight "The IMF and the World Bank" for an explanation of how these institutions work.

1.d. The Transition Years

foreign exchange market intervention:
buying or selling of currencies by a government or central bank to achieve a specified exchange rate

The Bretton Woods system of fixed exchange rates required countries to actively buy and sell dollars to maintain fixed exchange rates when the *free market equilibrium* in the foreign exchange market differed from the fixed rate. The free market equilibrium exchange rate is the rate that would be established in the absence of government intervention. Governmental buying and selling of currencies to achieve a target exchange rate is called **foreign exchange market intervention**. The effectiveness of such intervention was limited to situations in which free market pressure to deviate from the fixed exchange rate was temporary. For instance, suppose a country has a bad harvest and earns less foreign exchange than usual. This may only be a temporary situation if the next harvest is plentiful and the country resumes its typical export sales. During the period of reduced exports, it will be necessary for the government of this country to intervene to avoid a depreciation of its domestic currency. In the 1960s, however, there were several episodes of permanent rather than temporary changes that called for changes in exchange rates rather than government foreign exchange market intervention. The problems that arise in response to permanent pressures to change the exchange rate will be discussed further in Section 2, when we analyze the benefits and costs of alternative exchange-rate systems.

devaluation:
a deliberate decrease in the official value of a currency

The Bretton Woods system officially dissolved in 1971, at a meeting of the finance ministers of the leading world powers at the Smithsonian Institution in Washington, D.C. The Smithsonian agreement changed the exchange rates set during the Bretton Woods era. One result was a **devaluation** of the U.S. dollar. (A currency is said to be devalued when its value is officially lowered.) The official dollar value of gold dropped from $35 an ounce to $38 an ounce.

equilibrium exchange rates:
the exchange rates that are established in the absence of government foreign exchange market intervention

Under the Smithsonian agreement, countries were to maintain fixed exchange rates at newly defined values. It soon became clear, however, that the new exchange rates were not **equilibrium exchange rates** that could be maintained without government intervention, and that government intervention could not maintain the disequilibrium fixed exchange rates forever. The

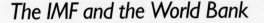
The IMF and the World Bank

The International Monetary Fund (IMF) and the World Bank were both created at the Bretton Woods conference in 1944. The IMF oversees the international monetary system, promoting stable exchange rates and macroeconomic policies. The World Bank promotes the economic development of the poor nations. Both organizations are owned and directed by their 151 member countries.

The IMF provides loans to nations having trouble repaying their foreign debts. Before the IMF lends any money, however, the borrower must agree to certain conditions. IMF *conditionality* usually requires that the country meet targets for key macroeconomic variables like money-supply growth, inflation, tax collections, and subsidies. The conditions attached to IMF loans are aimed at promoting stable economic growth.

The World Bank assists developing countries by providing long-term financing for development projects and programs. The Bank also provides expertise in many areas in which poor nations lack expert knowledge: agriculture, medicine, construction, and education, as well as economics. The IMF primarily employs economists to carry out its mission.

The diversity of World Bank activities results in the employment of about 6,500 people. The IMF has a staff of approximately 1,700. Both organizations post employees around the world, but most work at the headquarters in Washington, D.C.

World Bank funds are largely acquired by borrowing on the international bond market. The IMF receives its funding from member-country subscription fees, called *quotas*. A member's quota determines its voting power in setting IMF policies. The United States, whose quota accounts for the largest fraction of the total, has the most votes.

U.S. dollar was devalued again in February 1973, when the dollar price of gold was raised to $42.22. This new exchange rate was still not an equilibrium rate, and in March 1973 the major industrial countries abandoned fixed exchange rates.

1.e. Floating Exchange Rates

What kinds of exchange-rate arrangements exist today?

In March 1973, the major industrial countries abandoned fixed exchange rates for floating rates.

managed floating exchange rates:
the system whereby central banks intervene in the floating foreign exchange market to influence exchange rates; also referred to as *dirty float*

When fixed exchange rates were abandoned by the major industrial countries in March 1973, the world did not move to freely floating exchange rates determined by the forces of free market supply and demand alone. Under the system in existence since that time, the major industrial countries intervene to keep their currencies within acceptable ranges, while many smaller countries maintain fixed exchange rates.

The world today consists of some countries with fixed exchange rates, whose governments keep the exchange rates between two or more currencies constant over time; other countries with floating exchange rates, which shift on a daily basis according to the forces of supply and demand; and still others whose exchange-rate systems lie somewhere in between. Table 1, which lists the exchange-rate arrangements of over 150 countries, illustrates the diversity of exchange-rate arrangements currently in effect. We will focus here on the differences between fixed and floating exchange rates. All of the other exchange-rate arrangements listed in Table 1 are special versions of these two general exchange-rate systems.

As Table 1 shows, the major industrial countries maintain **managed floating exchange rates**, also called a *dirty float*. Although Table 1 lists countries like Japan and the United States as "independently floating," in fact their

TABLE I
Exchange-Rate Arrangements

		Currency Pegged to		
U.S. Dollar	**French Franc**	**Other Currency**	**SDR**	**Other Composite**[1]
Angola	Benin	Bhutan (Indian rupee)	Iran, I. R. of	Algeria
Antigua and Barbuda	Burkina Faso	Estonia (deutsche mark)	Libya	Austria
Argentina	Cameroon	Latvia (Russian ruble)	Myanmar	Bangladesh
Bahamas, The	C. African Rep.	Lesotho (South African rand)	Rwanda	Botswana
Barbados	Chad	Swaziland (South African rand)	Seychelles	Burundi
Belize	Comoros			Cape Verde
Djibouti	Congo			Cyprus
Dominica	Côte d'Ivoire			Czechoslovakia
Ethiopia	Equatorial Guinea			Fiji
Grenada	Gabon			Finland
Iraq	Mali			Hungary
Liberia	Niger			Iceland
Mongolia	Senegal			Jordan
Nicaragua	Togo			Kenya
Oman				Kuwait
Panama				Malawi
St. Kitts and Nevis				Malaysia
St. Lucia				Malta
St. Vincent and the Grenadines				Mauritania
Suriname				Mauritius
Syrian Arab Rep.				Morocco
Trinidad and Tobago				Nepal
Yemen, P.D. Rep.				Norway
				Papua New Guinea
				Solomon Islands
				Sweden
				Tanzania
				Thailand
				Tonga
				Vanuatu
				Western Samoa
				Zimbabwe

[1]Comprises currencies that are pegged to various "baskets" of currencies of the members' own choice, as distinct from the SDR basket.

(continued)

TABLE I
Exchange-Rate Arrangements (cont.)

Flexibility Limited in Terms of a Single Currency or Group of Currencies			More Flexible	
Single Currency[2]	Cooperative Arrangements[3]	Adjusted According to a Set of Indicators[4]	Other Managed Floating	Independently Floating
Bahrain	Belgium	Chile	China, P.R.	Afghanistan
Qatar	Denmark	Colombia	Ecuador	Albania
Saudi	France	Madagascar	Egypt	Australia
Arabia	Germany	Zambia	Greece	Bolivia
United	Ireland		Guinea	Brazil
Arab	Italy		Guinea-	Bulgaria
Emirates	Luxembourg		Bissau	Canada
	Netherlands		India	Costa Rica
	Portugal		Indonesia	Dominican
	Spain		Israel	Rep.
	United		Korea	El Salvador
	Kingdom		Lao P.D.	Gambia
			Rep.	Ghana
			Maldives	Guatemala
			Mexico	Guyana
			Pakistan	Haiti
			Poland	Honduras
			Singapore	Jamaica
			Somalia	Japan
			Sri Lanka	Kiribati
			Tunisia	Lebanon
			Turkey	Marshall
			Uruguay	Islands
			Vietnam	Mozambique
				Namibia
				New Zealand
				Nigeria
				Paraguay
				Peru
				Philippines
				Romania
				Sierra Leone
				South Africa
				Sudan
				Uganda
				United States
				Venezuela
				Zaire

[2]Exchange rates of all currencies have shown limited flexibility in terms of the U.S. dollar.

[3]Refers to the cooperative arrangement maintained under the European Monetary System.

[4]Includes exchange arrangements under which the exchange rate is adjusted at relatively frequent intervals, on the basis of indicators determined by the respective member countries.

Source: International Monetary Fund, *International Financial Statistics*, Washington, D.C., October 1992. Used by permission.

central banks, such as the Federal Reserve in the United States and the Bank of Japan in Japan, intervene from time to time in the foreign exchange market. Since exchange-rate variations can alter the prices of goods traded internationally, governments often attempt to push exchange rates to values consistent with some target value of international trade or investment. For example, in late summer 1989, the U.S. Treasury and the Federal Reserve were concerned that a rise in the value of the dollar would hurt the competitiveness of U.S. goods. As a result, the Fed sold $1,452 million in exchange for German marks and $1,699 million in exchange for Japanese yen. This intervention in the foreign exchange market caused the dollar to fall lower in value than private-market pressures would have done.

Some countries, like Angola and Benin, maintain a fixed value (or peg) relative to a single currency, such as the dollar or French franc. Fixed exchange rates are often called *pegged* exchange rates. Other countries, like Algeria and Austria, peg to a composite of currencies by setting the value of their currency at the average value of several foreign currencies.

Some currencies are pegged to the *SDR*, as you learned in the chapter on money and banking. The SDR, which stands for **special drawing right**, is an artificial unit of account. Its value is determined by combining the values of the U.S. dollar, German mark, Japanese yen, French franc, and British pound. A country that pegs to the SDR determines its currency's value in terms of an average of the five currencies that make up the SDR.

The column entitled "Cooperative Arrangements" in Table 1 lists the countries that belong to the **European Monetary System**, or **EMS**. These countries maintain fixed exchange rates against each other but allow their currencies to float jointly against the rest of the world. In other words, the values of currencies in the EMS all shift together relative to currencies outside the EMS.

Table 2 lists the end-of-year exchange rates for several currencies versus the U.S. dollar from the 1950s to 1992. For most of the currencies, there was

Fixed (pegged) exchange rates are held constant over time.

special drawing right:
an artificial unit of account created by averaging the values of the U.S. dollar, German mark, Japanese yen, French franc, and British pound

European Monetary System (EMS):
an organization composed of Western European nations that maintain fixed exchange rates among themselves and floating exchange rates with the rest of the world

TABLE 2
Exchange Rates of Selected Countries (currency units per U.S. dollar)

Year	Canadian Dollar	Japanese Yen	French Franc	German Mark	Italian Lira	British Pound
1950	1.06	361	3.50	4.20	625	.36
1955	1.00	361	3.50	4.22	625	.36
1960	1.00	358	4.90	4.17	621	.36
1965	1.08	361	4.90	4.01	625	.36
1970	1.01	358	5.52	3.65	623	.42
1975	1.02	305	4.49	2.62	684	.50
1980	1.19	203	4.52	1.96	931	.42
1985	1.40	201	7.56	2.46	1,679	.69
1990	1.16	134	5.13	1.49	1,130	.52
1992	1.27	124	5.51	1.61	1,471	.66

Source: End-of-year exchange rates from International Monetary Fund, *International Financial Statistics*, Washington, D.C.

little movement in the 1950s and 1960s, the era of the Bretton Woods agreement. In the early 1970s, exchange rates began to fluctuate. More recently, there has been considerable change in the foreign exchange value of a dollar, as Table 2 illustrates.

RECAP

1. Under a gold standard, each currency has a fixed value in terms of gold. This arrangement provides for fixed exchange rates between countries.

2. At the end of World War II, the Bretton Woods agreement established a new system of fixed exchange rates. Two new organizations—the International Monetary Fund (IMF) and the World Bank—also emerged from the Bretton Woods conference.

3. Fixed exchange rates are maintained by government intervention in the foreign exchange market; governments or central banks buy and sell currencies to keep the equilibrium exchange rate steady.

4. The governments of the major industrial countries adopted floating exchange rates in 1973. In fact, the prevailing system is characterized by "managed floating"—that is, by occasional government intervention rather than a pure free-market-determined exchange-rate system.

5. Some countries choose independently floating exchange rates; others peg their currencies to a single currency or a composite.

6. The European Monetary System maintains fixed exchange rates among several Western European currencies, which then float jointly against the rest of the world.

2. FIXED OR FLOATING EXCHANGE RATES

Is the United States better off today, with floating exchange rates, than it was with the fixed exchange rates of the post–World War II period? This question is difficult to answer, since much else has changed along with the exchange-rate system.

The choice of an exchange-rate system has multiple implications for the performance of a nation's economy and, therefore, for the conduct of macroeconomic policy. As is true of many policy issues in economics, economists often disagree about the merits of fixed versus flexible exchange rates. Let us look at the characteristics of the different exchange-rate systems.

2.a. Equilibrium in the Foreign Exchange Market

How is equilibrium determined in the foreign exchange market?

An exchange rate is the price of one money in terms of another. Equilibrium is determined by the supply of and demand for the two currencies in the foreign exchange market. Figure 1 contains two supply and demand diagrams for the U.S. dollar–French franc foreign exchange market. The downward-sloping demand curve indicates that the higher the dollar price of French francs, the fewer francs will be demanded. The upward-sloping supply curve indicates that the higher the dollar price of French francs, the more francs will be supplied.

Equilibrium in the foreign exchange market occurs at the point where the foreign exchange demand and supply curves intersect.

In Figure 1(a), the initial equilibrium occurs at the point where the demand curve D_1 intersects the supply curve. At this point, the equilibrium exchange rate is $.15 (1 franc costs $.15) and the quantity of francs bought and sold is Q_1.

Suppose U.S. residents increase their demand for French wine. Because francs are needed to pay for the wine, the greater U.S. demand for French wine generates a greater demand for francs by U.S. citizens, who hold dollars. The demand curve in Figure 1(a) thus shifts from D_1 to D_2. This increased demand for francs causes the franc to appreciate relative to the dollar. The new exchange rate is $.18, and a greater quantity of francs, Q_2, is bought and sold.

If the U.S. demand for French wine falls, the demand for francs also falls, as illustrated by the shift from D_1 to D_3 in Figure 1(a). The decreased demand for francs causes the franc to depreciate relative to the dollar, so that the exchange rate falls to $.12.

So far, we have considered how shifts in the U.S. demand for French goods affect the dollar-franc exchange rate. We can also use the same supply and demand diagram to analyze how changes in the French demand for U.S.

Figure 1
The Supply of and Demand for Foreign Exchange
This figure represents the foreign exchange market for francs traded for dollars. The demand curve for francs is based on the U.S. demand for French products, and the supply curve of francs is based on the French demand for U.S. products: an increase in demand for French wine causes demand for francs to increase from D_1 to D_2. This shift causes an increase from Q_1 to Q_2 in the equilibrium quantity of francs traded and causes the franc to appreciate to $.18 from the initial equilibrium exchange rate of $.15. A decrease in demand for

French wine causes the demand for francs to fall from D_1 to D_3. This shift leads to a fall in the equilibrium quantity traded to Q_3 and a depreciation of the franc to $.12. If the French demand for U.S. tractors falls, fewer francs are supplied for exchange for dollars, as illustrated by the fall in supply from S_1 to S_3. This shift causes the franc to appreciate to $.18 and the equilibrium quantity of francs traded to fall to Q_3. If the French demand for U.S. tractors rises, then more francs are supplied for dollars and the supply curve increases from S_1 to S_2. This causes the franc to depreciate and the equilibrium quantity of francs traded to rise to Q_2.

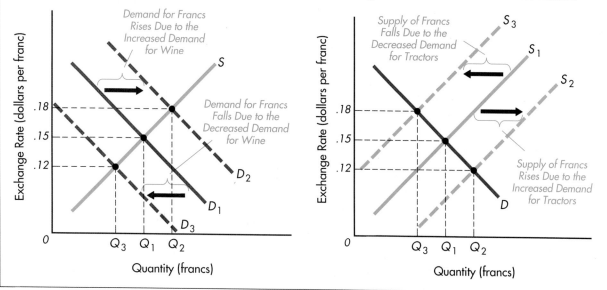

(a) A Change in the U.S. Demand for French Wine

(b) A Change in the French Demand for U.S. Tractors

goods affect the equilibrium exchange rate. The supply of francs to the foreign exchange market originates with French residents who buy goods from the rest of the world. If a French importer buys a tractor from a U.S. firm, the importer must exchange francs for dollars to pay for the tractor. As French residents' demand for foreign goods and services rises and falls, the supply of francs to the foreign exchange market changes.

Suppose the French demand for U.S. tractors increases. This brings about a shift of the supply curve: as francs are exchanged for dollars to buy the U.S. tractors, the supply of francs increases. In Figure 1(b), the supply of francs curve shifts from S_1 to S_2. The greater supply of francs causes the franc to depreciate relative to the dollar, and the exchange rate falls from $.15 to $.12. If the French demand for U.S. tractors decreases, the supply of francs decreases from S_1 to S_3, and the franc appreciates to $.18.

Foreign exchange supply and demand curves are affected by changes in tastes and technology and by changing government policy. As demand and supply change, the equilibrium exchange rate changes. In fact, continuous shifts in supply and demand cause the exchange rate to change as often as every day, based on free market forces. Now let us consider how fixed exchange rates differ from floating exchange rates.

2.b. Adjustment Mechanisms Under Fixed and Flexible Exchange Rates

How do fixed and floating exchange rates differ in their adjustment to shifts in supply and demand for currencies?

Figure 2 shows the dollar-franc foreign exchange market. The exchange rate is the number of dollars required to buy one franc; the quantity is the quantity of francs bought and sold. Suppose that, initially, the equilibrium is at point A, with quantity Q_1 francs traded at $.15 per franc.

Suppose French wine becomes more popular in the United States, and the demand for francs increases from D_1 to D_2. With flexible exchange rates (as in Figure 1), a new equilibrium is established at point B. The exchange rate rises to $.18 per franc, and the quantity of francs bought and sold is Q_2. The

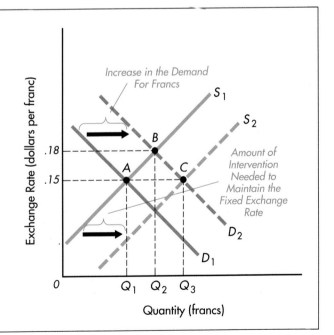

Figure 2
Foreign Exchange Market Equilibrium
Under Fixed and Flexible Exchange Rates
Initially, equilibrium is at point A; the exchange rate is $.15 and Q_1 francs are traded. An increase in demand for French wine causes the demand for francs to increase from D_1 to D_2. With flexible exchange rates, the franc appreciates in value to $.18 and Q_2 francs are traded; equilibrium is at point B. If the government is committed to maintaining a fixed exchange rate of $.15, the supply of francs must be increased to S_2 so that a new equilibrium can occur at point C. The government must intervene in the foreign exchange market and sell francs to shift the supply curve to S_2.

The Plaza Agreement

In September 1985, representatives of the United States, Germany, Japan, the United Kingdom, and France (the so-called *Group of 5*, or *G5* countries) met at the Plaza Hotel in New York City to plan coordinated foreign-exchange-market interventions aimed at bringing about a depreciation of the dollar. Although the meeting was secret, the participants announced their plan immediately after they adjourned. The dollar had appreciated throughout the early 1980s, and it was widely believed that this appreciation was causing U.S. exports to drop; U.S. goods were becoming too expensive for foreign buyers. The dollar had begun to depreciate in early 1985, and this turn of events was welcomed as a means of stimulating U.S. exports. By late summer, however, the dollar began again to appreciate. The G5 leaders considered further dollar appreciation undesirable (the U.S. Congress was threatening to impose restrictions on imports in order to reduce the U.S. international trade deficit), so they agreed to sell dollars simultaneously. The resulting sudden increase in supply was intended to drive down the value of the dollar.

The intervention succeeded in pushing down the value of the dollar against other currencies, just as the G5 officials desired. It is important to realize that governments intervene in foreign exchange markets not only to maintain fixed exchange rates but also to manage floating exchange rates. The Plaza Agreement was a notable attempt at *coordinated intervention* involving several countries—notable both for the effect on exchange rates and for the public nature of the agreement. Central banks rarely hold press conferences to discuss their plans. The public announcement was considered a major shift in the foreign exchange policy of the previously noninterventionist Reagan administration, signaling a new desire for international coordination of policy among the G5.

appreciate:
when the value of a currency increases under floating exchange rates—that is, exchange rates determined by supply and demand

depreciate:
when the value of a currency decreases under floating exchange rates

An increase in demand for a currency will cause an appreciation of its exchange rate, unless governments intervene in the foreign exchange market to increase the supply of that currency.

fundamental disequilibrium:
a permanent shift in the foreign-exchange-market supply and demand curves, such that the fixed exchange rate is no longer an equilibrium rate

increased demand for francs has caused the franc to **appreciate** (rise in value against the dollar) and the dollar to **depreciate** (fall in value against the franc). This is an example of a freely floating exchange rate, determined by the free market forces of supply and demand.

Now suppose the Federal Reserve is committed to maintaining a fixed exchange rate of $.15 per franc. The increase in demand for francs causes a shortage of francs at the exchange rate of $.15. According to the new demand curve, D_2, the quantity of francs demanded at $.15 is Q_3. The quantity supplied is found on the original supply curve S_1, at Q_1. The only way to maintain the exchange rate of $.15 is for the Federal Reserve to supply francs to meet the shortage of $Q_3 - Q_1$. In other words, the Fed must sell $Q_3 - Q_1$ francs to shift the supply curve to S_2 and thus maintain the fixed exchange rate.

If the increased demand for francs is temporary, the Fed can continue to supply francs for the short time necessary. However, if the increased demand for francs is permanent, the Fed's intervention will eventually end when it runs out of francs. This situation—a permanent change in supply or demand—is referred to as a **fundamental disequilibrium**. The fixed exchange rate is no longer an equilibrium rate. Under the Bretton Woods agreement, a country was supposed to devalue its currency in such cases.

Suppose that the shift to D_2 in Figure 2 is permanent. In this case, the dollar should be devalued. A devaluation to $.18 per franc would restore equilibrium in the foreign exchange market without requiring further intervention by the government. Sometimes, however, governments try to maintain the old exchange rate ($.15 per franc, in this case) even though most people

speculators:
people who seek to profit from
an expected shift in an exchange rate by selling the currency expected to depreciate
and buying the currency
expected to appreciate, then
exchanging the appreciated currency for the depreciated currency after the exchange rate
adjustment

believe the shift in demand to be permanent. When this happens, **speculators** buy the currency that is in greater demand (francs, in our example) in
anticipation of the eventual devaluation of the other currency (dollars, in
Figure 2). A speculator who purchases francs for $.15 prior to the devalua-
tion and sells them for $.18 after the devaluation earns $.03 per franc purchased—a 20 percent profit.

Speculation puts greater devaluation pressure on the dollar: the speculators
sell dollars and buy francs, causing the demand for francs to increase even
further. Such speculative activity contributed to the breakdown of the Bretton
Woods system of fixed exchange rates. Several countries intervened to support exchange rates that were far out of line with free market forces. The
longer a devaluation was put off, the more obvious it became that devaluation
was forthcoming and the more speculators entered the market. In 1971 and
1973, speculators sold dollars for yen and German marks. They were betting
that the dollar would be devalued; both times they were correct. The speculative activity of the early 1970s drew attention to the folly of efforts to maintain fixed exchange rates in the face of a change in the fundamental
equilibrium exchange rate.

2.c. Constraints on Economic Policy

What are the advantages and
disadvantages of fixed and
floating exchange rates?

Fixed exchange rates can be maintained over time only between countries
with similar economic policies and similar underlying economic conditions.
As prices rise within a country, the domestic value of a unit of its currency
falls, since the currency buys fewer goods and services. In the foreign
exchange market too, the value of a unit of domestic currency falls, since it
buys relatively fewer goods and services than the foreign currency does. A
fixed exchange rate thus requires that the purchasing power of the two currencies change at roughly the same rate over time. Only if two nations have
approximately the same inflation experience will they be able to maintain a
fixed exchange rate. This condition was a frequent source of problems in the
Bretton Woods era of fixed exchange rates. In the late 1960s, for instance, the
U.S. government was following a more expansionary macroeconomic policy
than was Germany. U.S. government expenditures on the war in Vietnam and
domestic antipoverty initiatives led to inflationary pressures that were not
matched in Germany. Between 1965 and 1970, price levels rose by 23.2 percent in the United States but only 12.8 percent in Germany. Since the purchasing power of a dollar was falling faster than that of the mark, the fixed
exchange rate could not be maintained. The dollar had to be devalued.

One of the advantages of floating exchange rates is that countries are free
to pursue their own macroeconomic policies without worrying about maintaining an exchange-rate commitment. If U.S. policy produces a higher inflation rate than Japanese policy, the dollar will automatically depreciate in
value against the yen. The United States can choose the macroeconomic policy it wants, independent of other nations, and let the exchange rate adjust if
its inflation rate differs markedly from that of other nations. If the dollar
were fixed in value relative to the yen, the two nations couldn't follow independent policies and expect to maintain the exchange rate.

It became obvious in the late 1960s that many governments considered
other issues more important than maintenance of a fixed exchange rate. A
nation that puts a high priority on reducing unemployment will typically

stimulate the economy to try to increase income and create jobs. This initiative may cause the domestic inflation rate to rise and the domestic currency to depreciate relative to other currencies. If one goal or the other—lower unemployment or a fixed exchange rate—must be given up, it is likely that the exchange-rate goal will be sacrificed.

Floating exchange rates allow countries to formulate domestic economic policy solely in response to domestic issues; attention need not be paid to the exchange rate of the rest of the world. For residents of some countries, this freedom may be more of a problem than a benefit. The freedom to choose a rate of inflation and let the exchange rate adjust itself can have undesirable consequences in countries whose politicians, for whatever reason, follow highly inflationary policies. In these countries a fixed-exchange-rate system would impose discipline, since maintenance of the exchange rate would not permit policies that diverged sharply from those of its trading partner.

Floating exchange rates allow countries to formulate their macroeconomic policies independently of other nations. Fixed exchange rates require the economic policies of countries linked by the exchange rate to be similar.

RECAP

1. Under a fixed-exchange-rate system, governments must intervene in the foreign exchange market to maintain the exchange rate. A fundamental disequilibrium requires a currency devaluation.

2. Fixed exchange rates can be maintained only between countries with similar macroeconomic policies and similar underlying economic conditions.

3. Fixed exchange rates serve as a constraint on inflationary government policies.

3. THE CHOICE OF AN EXCHANGE-RATE SYSTEM

What determines the kind of exchange-rate system a country adopts?

Different countries choose different exchange-rate arrangements. Why does the United States choose floating exchange rates while Guatemala adopts a fixed exchange rate? Let us compare the characteristics of countries that choose to float with those of countries that choose to fix their exchange rates.

3.a. Country Characteristics

The choice of an exchange-rate system is an important element of the macroeconomic policy of any country. The choice seems to be related to country size, openness, inflation, and diversification of trade.

3.a.1. Size Large countries (measured by economic output or GDP) tend to be both independent and relatively unwilling to forgo domestic policy goals in order to maintain a fixed exchange rate. Because large countries have large domestic markets, international issues are less crucial to everyday business than they are in a small country.

3.a.2. Openness Closely related to size is the relative openness of the economy. By openness, we mean the degree to which the country depends on international trade. Because every country is involved in international trade, openness is very much a matter of degree. An **open economy**, according to economists, is one in which a relatively large fraction of the GDP is devoted

open economy:
an economy in which a relatively large fraction of the GDP is devoted to internationally tradable goods

to internationally tradable goods. In a closed economy, a relatively small fraction of the GDP is devoted to internationally tradable goods. The more open an economy, the greater the impact of variations in the exchange rate on the domestic economy. The more open the economy, therefore, the greater the tendency to establish fixed exchange rates.

3.a.3. Inflation Countries whose policies produce inflation rates much higher or lower than those of other countries tend to choose floating exchange rates. A fixed exchange rate cannot be maintained when a country experiences inflation much different from that of the rest of the world.

3.a.4. Trade Diversification Countries that trade largely with a single foreign country tend to peg their currencies' value to that of the trading partner. For instance, South Africa accounts for the dominant share of the total trade of Swaziland. By pegging its currency, the lilangeni, to the South African rand, Swaziland enjoys more stable lilangeni prices of goods than it would with floating exchange rates. Trade with South Africa is such a dominant feature of the Swaziland economy that a fluctuating lilangeni price of the rand would be reflected in a fluctuating price level in Swaziland. If the lilangeni depreciated against the rand, the lilangeni prices of imports from South Africa would rise: this would bring about a rise in the Swaziland price level. Exchange-rate depreciation tends to affect the domestic price level in all countries, but the effect is magnified if a single foreign country accounts for much of a nation's trade. Countries with diversified trading patterns find fixed exchange rates less desirable, because price stability would prevail only in trade with a single country. With all other trading partners, prices would still fluctuate.

Table 3 summarizes the national characteristics associated with alternative exchange-rate systems. Many countries do not fit into the neat categorization of Table 3, but it is nonetheless useful for understanding the great majority of countries' choices.

3.b. Multiple Exchange Rates

multiple exchange rates:
a system whereby a government fixes different exchange rates for different types of transactions

Most countries conduct all their foreign exchange transactions at a single exchange rate. For instance, if the dollar-pound exchange rate is $1.80, residents of the United States can purchase British pounds at $1.80, no matter what use they make of the pounds. In 1992, however, the twenty-eight countries listed in Table 4 had **multiple exchange rates**—different exchange rates for different types of transactions. A typical arrangement is a dual exchange-

TABLE 3
Characteristics of Countries with Fixed and Floating Exchange Rates

Fixed-Rate Countries	*Floating-Rate Countries*
Small size	Large size
Open economy	Closed economy
Harmonious inflation rate	Divergent inflation rate
Concentrated trade	Diversified trade

TABLE 4

Countries with Multiple Exchange Rates (as of March 31, 1992)

Afghanistan	India	Nigeria
Albania	Iran	Peru
The Bahamas	Iraq	Poland
Brazil	Kenya	Somalia
Chile	Lesotho	South Africa
China	Mongolia	Syrian Arab Republic
Colombia	Mozambique	Uganda
Ecuador	Namibia	Zambia
El Salvador	Nepal	
Ghana	Nicaragua	

Source: International Monetary Fund, *IMF Survey*, Washington, D.C., June 8, 1992, p. 185.

rate system, consisting of a free-market-determined floating exchange rate for financial transactions and a fixed exchange rate that overvalues the domestic currency for transactions in goods and services. Some countries adopt even more elaborate arrangements, with special exchange rates for a variety of different transactions. For example, at the end of 1985, Venezuela had a four-tier system. The central bank traded dollars for bolivars (Bs) at the following rates: sell dollars for Bs4.30 for interest payments on foreign debt; sell dollars for Bs6.00 for national petroleum and iron-ore companies; and sell dollars for Bs7.50 for other government agencies. All other transactions took place at the free market floating exchange rate of Bs14.40.

Countries with multiple exchange rates use them as an alternative to taxes and subsidies. Activities that the policymakers want to encourage are subsidized by allowing participants in them to buy foreign exchange at an artificially low price or sell foreign exchange at an artificially high price. Participants in activities that policymakers want to discourage are forced to pay an artificially high price to buy foreign exchange and an artificially low price to sell foreign exchange. For instance, firms that manufacture goods for export, but import some of the resources used in production, may be permitted to buy foreign exchange at an artificially low price. This allows them to pay a lower domestic-currency price for their imported resources and consequently to charge a lower price for their output, which increases exports. In Venezuela, as you just saw, petroleum companies could buy dollars from the Central Bank for Bs6.00 even though the free-market rate was Bs14.40. In order to encourage greater production and export of Venezuelan petroleum, the Central Bank subsidized the dollars the petroleum companies needed for imports.

In an effort to discourage imports, developing countries often charge an artificially high price for foreign exchange that will be used to import consumer goods. Such multiple-exchange-rate systems have the same effects as direct government subsidies to exporting manufacturers and taxes on the importation of consumer goods: exports are stimulated and consumer-goods imports are reduced.

The IMF has tried to discourage multiple exchange rates, because they cause the domestic prices of internationally traded goods to differ from the international prices. The result is inefficient resource utilization in consumption and production, since domestic residents respond to the contrived relative prices rather than the true prices set on world markets. Monitoring and administering compliance with multiple exchange rates create additional costs, and people devote resources to avoiding the unfavorable aspects of multiple exchange rates (for example, by getting their transactions classified to the most favorable exchange rate).

3.c. Overvalued Exchange Rates

Developing countries often establish an official exchange rate—the exchange rate set by law—that differs from the equilibrium exchange rate. Figure 3 illustrates an overvalued exchange rate. Assume that a developing country whose currency is called the peso fixes an official peso-dollar exchange rate of 150 pesos per dollar, while the free market equilibrium exchange rate is 200 pesos per dollar. Since the official rate is less than the equilibrium rate, a dollar shortage results. Q_2 dollars are demanded at 150 pesos per dollar, but only Q_1 are supplied.

When the official peso-dollar rate is less than the free market rate, the peso is overvalued. To support the official rate, the country must impose tariffs or other restrictions on trade to reduce the demand for dollars. Overvaluing the domestic currency subsidizes favored activities or groups: if everyone had access to the official rate, there would be a dollar shortage. In addition to imposing quotas or tariffs on international trade in goods or financial assets, the country can use multiple exchange rates to ensure that only favored

Overvalued exchange rates are used to subsidize favored transactions.

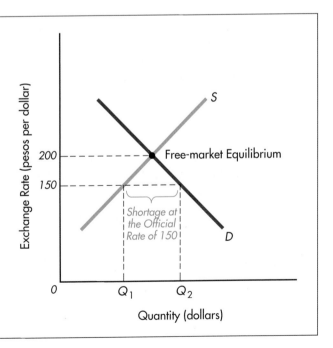

Figure 3
Overvalued Exchange Rate
The official exchange rate is 150 pesos per dollar, while the free market equilibrium exchange rate is 200 pesos per dollar. Since the official peso price of a dollar is below the equilibrium, the peso is said to be overvalued.

groups buy dollars at the official rate. In fact, a typical feature of multiple-exchange-rate regimes is the availability of an overvalued domestic-currency rate for favored transactions. Other residents are forced into the free market, where in this case they pay 200 pesos for their dollars.

RECAP

1. Countries with fixed exchange rates tend to be small, open economies with inflation rates similar to those of their trading partners. Their currencies are typically pegged to that of their main trading partner.

2. Some countries adopt multiple exchange rates for different kinds of transactions.

3. Multiple exchange rates resemble a system of subsidies for favored activities and taxes for activities that are discouraged.

4. An exchange rate is overvalued when the official domestic-currency price of foreign currency is lower than the equilibrium price.

SUMMARY

▲▼ *How does a commodity standard fix exchange rates between countries?*

1. Between 1880 and 1914, a gold standard provided for fixed exchange rates among countries. §1.a

2. The gold standard ended with World War I, and no established international monetary system replaced it until after World War II, when the Bretton Woods agreement created a fixed-exchange-rate system. §1.b

▲▼ *What kinds of exchange-rate arrangements exist today?*

3. Today some countries have fixed exchange rates, others have floating exchange rates, and still others have managed floats or other types of systems. §1.e

▲▼ *How is equilibrium determined in the foreign exchange market?*

4. Foreign-exchange-market equilibrium is determined by the intersection of the demand and supply curves for foreign exchange. §2.a

▲▼ *How do fixed and floating exchange rates differ in their adjustment to shifts in supply and demand for currencies?*

5. Under fixed exchange rates, central banks must intervene in the foreign exchange market to keep the exchange rate from shifting. §2.b

▲▼ *What are the advantages and disadvantages of fixed and floating exchange rates?*

6. Floating exchange rates permit countries to pursue independent economic policies. A fixed exchange rate requires a country to adopt policies similar to those of the country whose currency it pegs to. A fixed exchange rate may serve to prevent a country from pursuing inflationary policies. §2.c

▲▼ *What determines the kind of exchange-rate system a country adopts?*

7. The choice of an exchange-rate system is related to the size and openness of a country, its inflation experience, and the diversification of its international trade. §3.a

8. Multiple exchange rates are used to subsidize favored activities and raise costs for other activities. §3.b

KEY TERMS

gold standard §1.a

gold exchange standard §1.b

reserve currency §1.b

International Monetary Fund (IMF) §1.c

World Bank §1.c

foreign exchange market intervention §1.d

devaluation §1.d

equilibrium exchange rates §1.d

managed floating exchange rates §1.e

special drawing right §1.e

European Monetary System (EMS) §1.e

appreciate §2.b

depreciate §2.b

fundamental disequilibrium §2.b

speculators §2.b

open economy §3.a.2

multiple exchange rates §3.b

EXERCISES

1. Under a gold standard, if the price of an ounce of gold is 400 U.S. dollars and 500 Canadian dollars, what is the exchange rate between U.S. and Canadian dollars?

2. What were the three major results of the Bretton Woods conference?

3. What is the difference between the IMF and the World Bank?

4. How can Mexico fix the value of the peso relative to the dollar when the demand for and supply of dollars and pesos changes continuously? Illustrate your explanation with a graph.

5. Draw a foreign-exchange-market supply and demand diagram to show how the mark-dollar exchange rate is determined. Set the initial equilibrium at a rate of 2.5 marks per dollar.

6. Using the diagram in question 5, illustrate the effect of a change in tastes prompting German residents to buy more goods from the United States. If the exchange rate is floating, what will happen to the foreign-exchange-market equilibrium?

7. Using the diagram in question 5, illustrate the effect of the change in German tastes if exchange rates are fixed. What will happen to the foreign-exchange-market equilibrium?

8. When and why should exchange rates change under a fixed exchange-rate system?

9. Other things being equal, what kind of exchange-rate system would you expect each of the following countries to adopt?

   a. A small country that conducts all of its trade with the United States

   b. A country that has no international trade

   c. A country whose policies have led to a 300 percent annual rate of inflation

   d. A country that wants to offer exporters cheap access to the imported inputs they need but to discourage other domestic residents from importing goods

   e. A large country like the United States or Japan

10. Illustrate and explain the meaning and likely effects of an overvalued exchange rate.

11. The countries listed as pegging to the French franc in Table 1 have a characteristic in common that helps to explain why they maintain fixed exchange rates with the franc. Explain what that characteristic is.

12. Suppose you just returned home from a vacation in Mazatlán, Mexico, where you exchanged U.S. dollars for Mexican pesos. How did your trip to Mexico affect the supply and demand for dollars and the exchange rate (assume that all other things are equal)?

13. What does it mean to say that a currency appreciates or depreciates in value? Give an example of each and briefly mention what might cause such a change.

14. If you were an economic policy czar with total power to choose your country's economic pol-icy, would you want a fixed or floating exchange rate for your currency? Why?

15. How does a currency speculator profit from exchange-rate changes? Give an example of a profitable speculation.

A Single Currency for the European Community

The meeting of European heads of state and government in the Dutch city of Maastricht in December 1991 not only reaffirmed the commitment of the European Community (EC) to the creation of a single market but also resulted in agreement on the creation of an economic and monetary union (EMU). More specifically, the Maastricht agreement provides a framework for the transition to a common monetary policy and to a single EC currency managed by an independent European central bank.

... The creation of an economic and monetary union is a complex task, both technically and politically, that requires a high degree of convergence of economic policies and performance. At the same time, it would significantly reduce the economic sovereignty of the participating states. Indeed, the often different economic and monetary policy traditions of the EC member states have given rise to conflicts that were resolved only after protracted negotiations. Agreement hinged on a number of fundamental issues: the timing of the union, the conditions for participation, and the independence of monetary policy from government influence. More generally, there was the question regarding to what extent countries would be willing to cede national sovereignty to EC institutions. These issues, among others, also dominate the current debate over ratification of the treaty.

Under the Maastricht agreement, EMU would be reached in three stages. During the first two stages, member governments would endeavor to achieve greater convergence of their economies as measured by four criteria: inflation, interest rates, exchange rate stability, and the sustainability of the fiscal position. In the third stage, which could begin as early as 1997 but no later than 1999, member states that meet the economic criteria would irrevocably fix their exchange rates and issue a single currency.

... From the beginning, there was widespread agreement that a stable monetary union would require close coordination of national fiscal policies, as well as some kind of restriction on public sector deficits and debt. ... To enforce fiscal discipline, the treaty provides for sanctions....

... Participation in the EMU described above will require profound changes in the economic policies and institutions of many EC member states. For some countries, these changes will mean nothing less than a shift in the framework governing economic policy. Not only must there be further convergence of inflation and interest rates in order to engender greater exchange rate stability, but fiscal deficits and debt also must be brought under control. Moreover, the instruments of monetary policy, financial market laws, and economic statistics will need to be harmonized.

... The agreement of Maastricht on economic and monetary union of the EC provides a solid legal basis for a single currency and a common monetary policy. However, the treaty by itself will not guarantee monetary and price stability. Since the economic criteria, especially the fiscal criteria, allow considerable discretion, the fear is that countries that are not ready to adopt the single currency on purely economic grounds may nonetheless be permitted to do so for political reasons. In the past, not all EC member states have shown a strong commitment to stability-oriented macroeconomic policies. In particular, budget deficits and public debt of some countries are far higher than would be consistent with medium-term financial stability....

Source: Karl Habermeier and Horst Ungerer, "A Single Currency for the European Community," *Finance and Development*, Sept. 1992. Reprinted by permission.

Commentary

A fixed exchange-rate system represents an agreement among countries to convert their individual currencies from one to another at a given rate. The adoption of one money for Europe would be the strongest possible commitment to fixed exchange rates among the EC countries. If every nation used the same currency, then all would be linked to the same inflation rate and there would be no fluctuation of the value of the currency across the EC nations using the currency—just as each state in the United States uses the same money, the U.S. dollar. The adoption of a single currency requires that economic policies be similar across EC countries. This means that individual countries must subjugate their monetary policies to the goals of the European monetary and fiscal authority. If each nation insists on exercising its own monetary and fiscal policy and chooses different interest and inflation rates, there can never be one money.

For most of the 1980s eight European countries participated in the fixed exchange-rate system of the EC. This means that there were only seven independent exchange rates within the system and that one country could have played the role of "leader" in terms of monetary policy. In fact, much evidence points to the fact that Germany served as the leader of the EC, and other member nations followed its monetary policy. Germany's monetary policy in the 1980s was geared toward keeping inflation low. From the beginning of the EC in 1979 until 1987, the inflation rate in Germany averaged 3.2 percent. The inflation rates of other countries in the EC, which were generally higher than the inflation rate in Germany in 1979, have all decreased toward the German rate during the 1980s.

This convergence in inflation rates is necessary for the smooth operation of the EMS. Persistent inflation differentials across the members of a fixed exchange-rate system affect the competitiveness of each member's exports in the world market. Though a fixed exchange-rate system maintains stable *nominal exchange rates* (the rate observed in the foreign exchange market), the competitiveness of a currency is represented by the *real exchange rate*. The real exchange rate is the nominal exchange rate adjusted for the price level at home compared to the price level abroad. It is calculated as follows:

$$\text{real exchange rate} = \frac{(\text{nominal exchange rate} \times \text{foreign price level})}{\text{domestic price level}}$$

The disruptive changes in competitiveness caused by persistent inflation differentials require a realignment of a fixed exchange-rate system that adjusts nominal exchange rates to keep real exchange rates from drifting too far from their correct value. For instance, if the U.S. price level starts to rise faster than foreign prices, U.S. goods will be priced out of the world market unless the dollar depreciates on the foreign exchange market. According to the equation just presented, if the United States is the domestic country and its price level rises, the real exchange rate falls and U.S. goods are, therefore, relatively more expensive unless the nominal exchange rate rises to offset the higher domestic price level. The need for similar inflation rates within a fixed exchange-rate system indicates that a country could successfully join the fixed exchange-rate system or a region with one money only when its inflation rate fell to a level closer to that of other European countries.

Plans have been put forward for the evolution of the EC toward greater exchange-rate convergence, culminating in a single European currency. This plan would force individual countries to abandon completely any control over monetary policy. Proponents of the plan argue that one currency in Europe would facilitate international trade and investment by eliminating exchange-rate fluctuations and the associated uncertainty they add. Opponents of the plan think that the cost of giving up national control over monetary policy is too high relative to the benefits of a single currency. This issue is far from settled, and we can expect to continue to read about the debate over European integration well into the 1990s.

26

The Transition from Socialism to Capitalism

FUNDAMENTAL QUESTIONS

1. What is socialism, and why did it fail?
2. What microeconomic issues are involved in the transition to capitalism?
3. What macroeconomic issues are involved in the transition to capitalism?

"It is becoming more and more clear to all East Europeans, and the Czechs and Slovaks in particular, that the only practical and realistic way to improve their living standards is the total abolition of institutions of central planning, the dismantling of price and wage, exchange rate and foreign trade controls, and the radical transformation of property rights"—Vaclav Klaus, minister of finance for Czechoslovakia at a 1990 conference held by the Federal Reserve Bank of Kansas City.

As the world left the 1980s behind for the 1990s, the economies of the former Soviet Union and its Eastern European satellites were leaving socialism behind and embracing capitalism as the road to future prosperity. In this chapter, we review the basic institution of socialism and provide an analysis of what went wrong. In a nutshell, the problems were largely related to low productivity and lack of consumption goods—or, as Soviet workers were fond of saying, "We pretend to work and the state pretends to pay us." Next we turn to a discussion of the current problem facing all of the formerly

socialist countries: How does a country move from socialism, with widespread government ownership of productive resources and massive government intervention in economic decision-making, to capitalism and its emphasis on private property and private decision-making? The answers are not yet clear, and there is much learning going on as each nation attempts to implement its variant of transition. As a result, we can only suggest certain fundamentals required for a successful transition and then examine the experiences of several countries that are in the process of implementing change to see what lessons may be gained from their experience.

What is socialism and why did it fail?

I. SOCIALISM

capitalism:
an economic system characterized by private ownership of most resources and the use of markets to allocate goods and services

socialism:
an economic system characterized by government ownership of most resources and centralized decision-making

Socialism and capitalism are types of economic systems. **Capitalism** is characterized by private ownership of most resources and the use of markets to allocate goods and services, while **socialism** is characterized by government ownership of most resources and centralized decision-making or planning to allocate resources. As a specific example of a centrally planned socialist state, let's consider the characteristics of the Soviet Union prior to the era of *perestroika* (the recent reform movement). Of course, today, the Soviet Union has fragmented into independent nations (Russia and the CIS states) and the face of Eastern Europe has been changed, as illustrated by the map in Figure 1.

Figure 1
Republics of the Former U.S.S.R.

Source: *Finance and Development*, September 1992, pp. 24–25. Reprinted with permission.

I.a. Socialism in the Soviet Union

The Soviet Union was characterized by state ownership of all natural resources and almost all of the capital stock. In the late 1980s, state-run enterprises produced more than 88 percent of agricultural output and 98 percent of retail trade, and owned 75 percent of the urban housing space.

The government operation of a large economy spread over a vast geographical space required a huge bureaucracy of government planners and ministries. At the top were the highest authorities of the Communist party. The top party officials held the political power that moved the system and made broad policy decisions. Below the top level, planners were responsible for making party directives operational. Below the planners were agencies (ministries) responsible for specific functions of the economy like construction or agricultural equipment. Each of the agencies supervised a network of lesser agencies and departments under its direction, with the level of responsibility narrowing the further one went down the hierarchy by industrial branch and by region. At the base of the hierarchy were the enterprises and farms that actually carried out the productive activity. In the late 1980s, there were about 47,000 construction enterprises, 46,000 industrial enterprises, and almost 1 million wholesale and retail trade organizations.

The general direction of the economy was defined in five-year plans. More detailed operational plans were specified on an annual basis. The planning process began with goals set by the highest authorities. Government planners would use these goals to determine production priorities and set production targets. As the plans reached the production units through the ministries, enterprises responded with requests for resources needed to achieve the plan. Thus, there was a "give and take" as information flowed down the hierarchy and then back up. The higher authorities sought to maximize the productivity of the producing units by having them increase output with little or no increase in resources, while the producing units sought to lower their goals or quotas of output ordered from above in order to receive more easily attainable tasks. Achievement of tasks meant rewards for managers and workers.

Prices and wages were set by the state authorities and were based on political priorities rather than economic costs or scarcity. Furthermore, prices and wages tended to remain fixed for long periods regardless of actual market supply and demand conditions. Since the state administrators controlled prices of millions of goods and services, there was no practical way to adjust these continuously as supply and demand pressures varied.

1.b. Shortcomings of Socialism

Why did the leaders of the socialist economies of Eastern Europe decide to abandon government ownership and control for private property and individual market-type decision-making? The basic problem with central planning of an economy is that the authorities doing the planning do not possess information regarding the true opportunity costs of their decisions. Since everybody else in the system simply follows the planners' directives, only the top planners have an incentive to consider opportunity costs to maximize efficiency. But there is no possible way that they could monitor all of the relevant costs, even if such information were available.

The biggest disadvantages of socialism were the inability to take opportunity costs into account and the lack of incentives to increase efficiency and produce in sufficient quantity the goods and services desired by consumers.

An additional problem is that those actually carrying out the production have no incentive to use innovative production methods that increase efficiency. The incentives relate to carrying out the plan rather than taking risks in employing new technology. As the Eastern European economies became more developed and complex, the drawbacks to central planning became increasingly obvious. Waste and inefficiency grew, and the achievement of planners' goals were more often than not frustrated. The incentives to produce simply did not create the goods and services that consumers wanted in sufficient quantity and quality. Table 1 provides some comparative information on the demographics and economies of the (formerly) socialist economies of Eastern Europe and of the United States. The data on per capita GDP, cars, and telephones indicate the extent to which the selected Eastern European economies listed lagged behind the United States in terms of production and availability of consumer goods.

The lack of attention to technological advance resulted in a capital stock that became obsolete and uncompetitive internationally. Furthermore, the reliance on old production technologies with steadily growing populations resulted in environmental decay of massive proportions.

TABLE I
Comparative Data on Eastern Europe, the Former U.S.S.R., and the United States

Country	Population (millions)	Population Density (population per square kilometer)	Infant Mortality (per 1,000 births)	Per Capita GDP as Percent of U.S. Per Capita GDP	Cars per 1,000 Persons	Telephones per 1,000 Persons
Bulgaria	8.9	81	12	26%	127	248
Czechoslovakia	15.7	125	11	35	186	246
East Germany	16.3	154	7	43	214	233
Hungary	10.6	114	15	30	156	152
Poland	37.8	124	13	25	112	122
Romania	23.3	101	19	19	na	111
U.S.S.R.	290.9	13	24	31	46	124
United States	250.4	27	10	100	565	789

Source: Selected data taken from tables in Peter Murrell, "Symposium on Economic Transition in the Soviet Union and Eastern Europe," *Journal of Economic Perspectives*, Fall 1991, pp. 5–6.

An understanding of why socialism has failed is necessary to effectively bring about efficient reforms. Moreover, as the transition from plan to market takes place, reformers must deal with the legacies of the past. The rest of the chapter is devoted to the process of turning a centrally planned economy into a market-oriented system.

RECAP

1. Capitalism is characterized by private ownership of most resources and the use of markets to allocate goods and services.
2. Socialism is characterized by government ownership of most resources and centralized decision-making.
3. Socialist economies are centrally planned: the enterprises carrying out actual production are following orders from higher authorities.
4. The two main shortcomings of socialism were the inability of the planners to take opportunity costs into account and the lack of adequate incentives to increase efficiency and produce the goods and services that consumers wanted.

2. MICROECONOMIC ISSUES

The transformation of a socialist economy into a capitalist economy requires the creation of markets. Resources that were formerly owned and allocated

What microeconomic issues are involved in the transition to capitalism?

privatize:
to convert state-owned enterprises to private ownership

by government must be **privatized**, or converted from state ownership to private ownership. The state still has a role, since private property rights must be developed, recognized, and protected by government. Privately owned resources will then be allocated by the market system through prices set by supply and demand in a competitive environment with incomes that are based on productivity. Although it is easy to state where an economy should be in terms of free markets rather than central planning, getting there is easier said than done. The issue of privatization is the most obvious case.

2.a. Privatization

Socialist economies are characterized by many state-owned enterprises (SOEs). These enterprises are frequently large, technologically outdated, and unprofitable. The move to a market economy requires that these enterprises be privatized. How should SOEs be sold or otherwise converted to private ownership?

One alternative is to issue shares of ownership (like shares of stock) to existing workers and managers in an enterprise. This method has the advantage of simplicity—the new private owners are easy to identify, and ownership is easy to transfer. The disadvantage is that some SOEs may be uncompetitive in a capitalist environment so that ownership of such a firm is worthless, while other SOEs may be able to compete effectively so that ownership may have considerable value. This privatization system would reward and penalize the working population based on where they were previously assigned to work by the state rather than on the basis of individual investment and risk-taking. Moreover, a simple change of ownership may not change the manner in which the firm operates.

Another alternative is to issue shares of ownership randomly to the public in a kind of lottery. You may have an equal chance of becoming one of the owners of a steel mill, a shoe factory, or a farm. In a truly random assignment of ownership, everyone has an equal chance of receiving a profitable share. This scheme does away with the unfortunate circumstance associated with those who have the misfortune to be employed by the state in an unproductive job when shares are issued only to existing employees of each firm. A problem with this scheme is that those interested in, or knowledgeable about, a particular firm or industry would have no better chance to be involved in that industry than would those who had no interest.

Yet another alternative is to auction ownership of SOEs to the highest bidder. In addition to raising revenue for the state, this method is quite straightforward to carry out. A common argument against this method is that those with enough wealth to make winning bids are likely to be former Communist party leaders or individuals who traded on black markets under the socialist regime. Such people are not favorably viewed by the masses, and as a result, auctions are controversial.

The privatization method chosen by Czechoslovakia (before its split into two nations) was a coupon giveaway to millions of citizens, who then used the coupons to buy stock in SOEs. The goal of this kind of plan was to create a broad-based democratic capitalism with millions of citizens holding ownership positions in productive firms. An advantage of this plan is that the government does not have to find buyers willing to exchange real money for

Just as in Florida, California, and many other U.S. states, residents in Moscow can play the "Lotto Million" in hopes of becoming a millionaire. Aside from such lucky windfalls, we should expect to see a class of successful entrepreneurs emerge from the chaos of the transition from socialism. The first wave of successful enterprises should provide useful models for the next generation of risk takers by efficiently providing the goods and services people want and rewarding the owners with profits not legally obtainable to private citizens under socialism.

SOEs. Since many SOEs have a questionable initial money value, by granting ownership to a wide group of citizens, the state pushes the burden of managing relatively unproductive firms to the general public.

At this time, the experience with privatization is still in an experimental stage. In Hungary and Poland, it became politically difficult for worker-managed firms to be sold to any willing buyer, since the employees felt that they had legitimate claims on the control of the firm. As a result, the privatization plan in those countries is proceeding relatively slowly. In countries where privatization schemes have been pushed forward rapidly, the ultimate goal is for shares of firms to trade openly on stock markets.

There is no universal approach to converting SOEs into privately owned firms. Each nation has taken the approach that best seems to fit its particular political and economic system. In all cases, it has been relatively easy to privatize small, profitable firms but much more difficult to privatize large, unprofitable firms. For an example of the Romanian approach, see the Economic Insight "Privatization in Romania."

2.b. Price Reform

Under socialism, prices of goods and services are established by the state. These prices need not reflect economic costs or scarcity. But in a market-oriented economy, prices serve an important signaling role. If consumers want more of a good or service, its price rises, and that induces producers to offer more for sale. If consumer tastes change so that demand for a good or service falls, then the price should fall to induce producers to offer less for sale. If there is an excess supply of a good, its price falls, and that induces consumers to buy more. If there is an excess demand for a good, the price rises

Privatization in Romania

The Romanian authorities regard the privatization of state-owned assets as essential for building a market-based economy, strengthening the financial discipline of enterprises, and improving their productivity and efficiency. To this end, they have embarked on a massive privatization program that involves selling or leasing to the private sector state-owned equipment and structures, enterprises, and housing, as well as land held by agricultural cooperatives. Some 6,000 state enterprises have been commercialized since September 1990. The remaining such enterprises (about 320), which operate in sectors considered strategic, will be commercialized later, except for natural monopolies, such as utilities.

In August 1991, the Parliament enacted a sweeping privatization law for the commercial enterprises. Under this law, 30 percent of the share capital of each enterprise will be transferred to five Private Ownership Funds (POFs) and 70 percent to a State Ownership Fund (SOF). Starting in June 1992, the certificates of ownership of the POFs were distributed in bearer form, free of charge, to about 16.5 million Romanian citizens. These certificates can be traded in the stock market (which is being established), exchanged for shares in the commercial enterprises, or transformed into shares of mutual funds that will replace the POFs after five years. The SOF is obliged to sell enterprises so that its holding of share capital is reduced by at least 10 percent a year.

The privatization law also allows commercial units that can be organized and operated independently (such as shops, restaurants, and hotels) to sell up to 75 percent of the total value of their assets. Sales of about 4,400 commercial units began in February 1992.

As of February 1992, more than 250,000 authorizations for general private-sector activity had been issued. Of these, almost 100,000 were for private commercial enterprises, and the rest were for private individuals or family partnerships. Of the commercial enterprises, almost 10,000 were joint ventures with foreign capital. It is estimated that about 20 percent of GDP is now generated by the private sector.

The government's privatization strategy also involves selling state-owned housing to the population. Out of more than 2 million houses built by state companies, more than half have been sold to their tenants. In addition, the authorities adopted a land reform program under which about 80 percent of all agricultural land was transferred to the private sector by the end of 1992.

A market system requires that prices be free to fluctuate to reflect supply and demand fluctuations.

to induce consumers to buy less. A major problem with socialism is that prices are not free to serve this role of a signal to producers and consumers. Therefore, an important step in the transition from socialism to capitalism is the freeing of prices so that they may seek their free market levels.

Considering that there are around 25 million goods and services to be priced in the Soviet Union, it is impossible for government officials to know and then plan a shift from the state-regulated price to the appropriate free market price for each item. However, there is a way to allow the correct prices to be set very quickly. There are prices existing for every good in the rest of the world. By opening the economy to competition from foreign countries, foreign trade will force the domestic prices to be comparable to foreign prices. Of course, the presence of tariffs or quotas on foreign goods will distort the price comparisons, but the lower the restrictions on trade, the more domestic prices will conform to prices in the rest of the world. For goods that are not traded internationally or for many services, foreign trade will not set a domestic price. In this case, the market may be allowed to adjust the price over time to the internal domestic pressures of supply and demand.

The normal response to a freeing of prices from state control is an increase in the availability of goods and services, although initially output may fall. However, the beneficial aspects of price reform require privatization of the economy. Price changes bring about profits and losses that induce profit-seeking producers to provide what buyers want. If production is still controlled by state-owned enterprises that have no profit incentive, then price reform will not have the desired effect of increasing output and efficiency.

It is important to realize that price reform has an initial shock effect on the economy. Prices under socialism are typically well below the true opportunity cost for most items considered to be necessities. Speaking of price reform in Bulgaria, the Bulgarian National Bank's chief economist said, "One no longer has to get up at four or five A.M. to line up for bread and milk. Items that in the past might not even be available when one finally reached the counter now are available, but at ten times higher prices." This is a source of political conflict in taking an economy on the transition path from socialism to capitalism. People have to learn the new rules of the game, and the lessons are often quite harsh to those who have lived under decades of socialism.

2.c. Social Safety Net

Moving from socialism to capitalism will harm many people during the transition period as enterprises are closed and unemployment increases at the same time that prices of many goods and services rise. As a result, it is critical to have a program in place to provide a minimal standard of living for all citizens in order to avoid massive political unrest. Under socialism, the state provided for health care and took care of the disabled, aged, and unemployed. Moreover, many goods such as housing were heavily subsidized. It is politically necessary that such government activity continue, although as more and more of the economy is privatized, government programs will have to be financed by explicit taxation of workers and firms. In other cases, user charges will be introduced, a phenomenon much less common under socialism.

The abandonment of socialism was due to populist sentiment in Eastern Europe. The populations of these nations were tired of stagnant or declining standards of living and were ready for change. However, market-oriented economies operate in a democratic framework, and political unrest due to dissatisfaction with the operation of the economy can much more easily be demonstrated in a democratic setting than under the authoritarian rule of the centrally planned economy. A social safety net must be generous enough to buy time for the transition to capitalism to yield benefits for the majority of citizens. Otherwise, the movement toward capitalism may never survive the transition period.

RECAP

1. The transition from socialism to capitalism requires that state-owned enterprises be privatized.

2. A market system requires that prices fluctuate freely to allow producers and consumers to make efficient production and consumption decisions.

3. Since the transition from socialism will create unemployment and lower incomes for many, the government must provide a social safety net.

3. MACROECONOMIC ISSUES

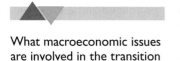

What macroeconomic issues are involved in the transition to capitalism?

Good macroeconomic policy is aimed at providing steady income growth with low inflation. This is true whether we are talking about the United States, Japan, or Russia. Good macroeconomic policy, then, requires limited use of government budget deficits and tight control over monetary and credit growth. Although these features of good macroeconomic policy are universal, there are some macro issues that are unique to the transition from socialism to capitalism.

3.a. Monetary Policy

monetary overhang:
money accumulated by households because there was nothing available that they wanted to buy

3.a.1. Monetary Overhang In many socialist countries, there is believed to be a substantial **monetary overhang**, which is the term used to describe the money that households have accumulated because there was nothing they could buy with it. With limited access to consumer goods, and subsidized housing, food, and health care, the typical household had savings in the form of money building up over time that they would not have had if they had access to more consumer goods. In early 1991, the monetary overhang in the (former) Soviet Union was estimated to be half of household savings deposits.

The transition from central planning to a market-based economy is creating opportunities for hard-working, enterprising individuals to earn a standard of living previously available only to high-ranking members of the socialist elite. This family in Hungary is a visible result of the opportunities available to the new business leaders in Eastern Europe. At the same time, there are large masses who have been disenfranchised by the termination of their jobs or income security that existed under socialism. A major problem during the early transition from socialism is providing a social safety net to protect the disenfranchised.

The potential problem with a large monetary overhang is that inflation could result if goods become available to induce spending of the saved funds. How can the monetary overhang be eliminated? One way is for the state to decontrol prices suddenly and have prices rise sharply, thereby decreasing the purchasing power of the money held by households. The state basically imposes its own inflation tax on the purchasing power of the monetary overhang early in the transition period rather than let the households create their own inflation later in the transition period. This was the approach taken in Poland and Yugoslavia in 1989 and the Soviet Union in 1991. Of course, it is critical that the one-time inflation not turn into a prolonged inflation if the economy is to enjoy long-term prosperity.

An alternative way of reducing the monetary overhang is to privatize—sell state-owned property (like houses or land) to private households. Another alternative is to allow greater access to Western consumer goods so that households spend their excess money balances on such goods. Yet another alternative is to allow interest rates to rise on household savings accounts so that households willingly hold on to their accumulated money.

Beyond the issue of monetary overhang, monetary policy will be primarily aimed at controlling inflation during the transition to capitalism. By maintaining a steady and low rate of inflation, a nation will also realize stable exchange rates, which will contribute to its speedy integration into trade with the rest of the world.

During the transition from social-ism, monetary policy should be aimed at achieving a low and stable inflation rate.

3.a.2. Currency Convertibility

Closely related to the issue of foreign trade and exchange rates is **currency convertibility**. The currency of the country must be freely convertible into other currencies if domestic prices are to be linked to (and disciplined by) foreign markets. One cannot compare the cost of a tractor in Romania with a tractor in Germany if the currency of Romania cannot be freely traded for the currency of Germany at a market-determined exchange rate.

currency convertibility: the ease with which the domestic currency can be converted into foreign currency so foreign exchange rates can properly reflect the domestic currency value of foreign prices

Socialist countries traditionally did not permit free exchange of their currencies for other currencies. Government controls on foreign exchange trading allowed the government to fix an official exchange-rate value of the domestic currency that was often far from the true market value. As a result, international prices were unable to serve their purpose of increasing production of the goods a country could produce relatively cheaply and increasing imports of those goods that could be produced more cheaply in the rest of the world. For instance, if the true value of a Soviet ruble relative to the U.S. dollar was 30 rubles per dollar, yet the official exchange rate set by the Soviet Union was 3 rubles per dollar, then the ruble was officially overvalued. Suppose a computer monitor produced in the United States sold for $200. At the official exchange rate, the monitor was worth 600 rubles ($200 at 3 rubles per dollar). At the true market value of the currencies, the monitor was worth 6,000 rubles ($200 at 30 rubles per dollar). Since Soviet citizens were unable to buy foreign goods (all foreign trade was in the hands of the state), the official exchange rate was largely irrelevant. However, the absence of free trading in a ruble that was convertible into dollars meant that there was no way to identify which goods the Soviet Union could produce more cheaply than other nations. The absence of such relative cost information made specialization according to comparative advantage a difficult task. If a country cannot determine which goods it can produce more cheaply than others, it will not know which goods it should specialize in.

Under socialism, with central planning of production, the absence of relative price information was not as critical a problem as it is with capitalism. When private decision-makers must decide which goods to produce, they must rely on relative prices to guide them. In international trade, this requires a currency that is convertible into other currencies at market-determined exchange rates.

3.a.3. Money and Credit

In industrial countries with well-developed financial markets, monetary policy is often aimed at changing interest rates in order to change aggregate demand. For instance, when the monetary authorities are concerned that inflation is a problem, money growth is slowed and interest rates tend to rise. The higher interest rates reduce investment and consumption spending and lower (or at least slow the growth of) aggregate demand, or total spending in the economy. In a socialist system just beginning the transformation toward capitalism, financial markets are generally undeveloped, since the state under socialism regulated interest rates and limited the saving and borrowing opportunities for citizens. Changes in the money supply may have little or no effect on interest rates. Therefore, the role of monetary policy in terms of money growth rates should be to maintain a low and steady rate of inflation. Any other effects of money growth on the economy are likely to be of secondary importance until further development of the economy occurs.

Under socialism, credit was often extended to enterprises on the basis of political connections or central planner preferences. A market economy requires that credit occur on the basis of productive potential. Firms that offer good prospects of earning a sufficient profit to repay debts should receive greater credit access than firms that have little hope of competing profitably. The move toward a market economy must include the development of financial institutions like banks that are able to efficiently evaluate creditworthiness and allocate credit accordingly.

3.b. Fiscal Policy

Reform of fiscal policy involves reducing government subsidies and reforming tax policy to avoid large budget deficits. Socialist countries have been characterized by subsidies to enterprises that produced a value of output less than the costs of production. Under a market system, firms that cannot operate at a profit should not be allowed to exist forever by continued subsidies from the government. It is for this reason that, as noted earlier, a safety net is necessary since lower subsidies lead to transitional unemployment.

A socialist government does not rely on explicit or direct taxes on the public since the state controls prices, wages, and production. By paying workers less than the value of their output, the state can extract the revenue needed to operate the government. However, once private ownership and free markets have replaced central planning, the activities of government must be financed by explicit taxes. Reforming countries are implementing income, value-added, and profit taxes to produce revenue for the remaining functions of government. Again, the goal should be to match government revenue and expenditures as closely as possible to avoid a large budget deficit.

The Debate on Phasing

Should price reform come before or after enterprise reform?

Before: Enterprise reform and privatization will not succeed if the market cannot judge efficiency and value because prices do not reflect true costs. Budgets cannot be "hardened" before introducing market prices.

After: Freeing prices in the presence of monopolies will lead to excessive prices and profits, undercutting the political consensus for reform. Domestic competition policy should be in place before price liberalization.

Should large-scale privatization be "quick and dirty" or slower and more careful?

Quick: Rapid privatization is of utmost importance. It raises effi-

ciency, speeds restructuring, establishes a constituency for further reforms, and weakens the traditional power centers opposing reform.

Slow: Sales revenues are needed by the government, and preserving fairness in the process is vital for public support. Restructuring should thus precede privatization, and firms should not be given away hastily.

Should trade liberalization come early and fast or later and slowly?

Early: It supports price reform by importing the world price structure and heightens competitive forces.

Later: It shocks the economy in the right direction but with exces-

sive costs and is risky until the economy is stabilized.

Must full-scale financial-sector reform go hand in hand with enterprise reform, or can it come earlier?

Hand in hand: Competitive financial markets require enforceable loan contracts and timely repayment of debt obligations, and enterprise reform and bank portfolio restructuring are best accomplished simultaneously. Cleaning up loan portfolios is futile without enterprise reform.

Earlier: Only independent financial institutions and liberalized financial markets can play the critical role of allocating capital as enterprises are restructured.

RECAP

1. Since households could not buy all of the consumer goods they wanted, socialist economies often had a monetary overhang of excess money holdings.

2. The convertibility of the domestic currency into foreign currencies is necessary to link the domestic country with prices in the rest of the world.

3. The transition economy will aim monetary policy at the creation of a low and stable rate of inflation.

4. Credit must be available to firms on the basis of potential profitability rather than political relationships in order to increase productivity.

5. Fiscal policy should be reformed to reduce subsidies from government to firms and also to collect explicit taxes.

4. THE SEQUENCING OF REFORMS

Considering all of the reforms necessary in the transition from socialism to capitalism, how should a country proceed? Are some measures needed before others can be undertaken? How rapidly should the changes be introduced? There are no certain answers to these questions, and there is an ongoing debate regarding the proper order of the reforms (see the Economic Insight "The Debate on Phasing").

Some economists argue that all reforms should be undertaken simultaneously (or as nearly so as possible). Most tend to agree that macroeconomic stabilization is necessary for any serious conversion of the economy to a market system. Inflation must be stabilized at a reasonably low and steady rate, and the fiscal deficit must be brought to a level low enough to support a noninflationary monetary policy (so that the monetary authorities are not creating money to fund the budget deficit). Included in the macroeconomic stabilization is the development of a convertible currency.

Following the macroeconomic reform, micro reforms like privatization may proceed, along with the opening of the economy to foreign trade and competition. Then the foreign prices will guide the deregulation of industry in setting appropriate prices for domestic products. It is generally thought that the micro reforms are intertwined and support one another. In this case, they should be carried out simultaneously. Otherwise, each element will tend to be less effective than it otherwise would be. For instance, privately owned firms need deregulated prices and wages to respond to changing relative prices and produce what consumers want.

RECAP

1. Macroeconomic reform must provide a stable, low-inflation environment for microeconomic reform to succeed.

2. Since microeconomic reforms tend to reinforce one another, they should generally be carried out simultaneously.

SUMMARY

▲▼ What is socialism, and why did it fail?

1. Capitalism is characterized by private ownership of most resources and the use of markets to allocate goods and services. §1

2. Socialism is characterized by government ownership of most resources and centralized decision-making. §1

3. Socialism failed because of the planners' inability to consider opportunity costs and because of a lack of incentive to increase efficiency and produce the goods and services consumers wanted. §1.b

▲▼ What microeconomic issues are involved in the transition to capitalism?

4. The move toward capitalism requires that state-owned enterprises be privatized. §2.a

5. Prices and incomes must be freed from state control if markets are to work efficiently. §2.b

6. Since many workers may be unemployed and incomes may fall during the transition, there must be a social safety net provided by the government. §2.c

7. There may be a substantial monetary overhang as a result of limited opportunities to exchange money for goods under socialism. §3.a.1

8. Exchange rates can link economies together, but the currency must be freely convertible into other currencies if exchange rates are to indicate accurate price information. §3.a.2

9. Monetary policy should be aimed at providing a low and steady rate of inflation. §§3.a.1, 3.a.3

10. Credit must be allocated on the basis of productivity and profitability rather than political connections. §3.a.3

11. Fiscal policy must avoid large deficits and must raise explicit taxes. §3.b

12. Macroeconomic stabilization is generally necessary before microeconomic reforms are implemented. §4

KEY TERMS

capitalism §1
socialism §1
privatize §2

monetary overhang §3.a.1
currency convertibility §3.a.2

EXERCISES

1. Explain the difference between capitalism and socialism and use the key elements of your definitions to explain why socialism failed in the Soviet Union and Eastern Europe.

2. Why would socialism not be as likely as capitalism to take opportunity costs into account in economic decision-making?

3. Discuss the alternative ways in which state-owned enterprises can be privatized.

4. One problem associated with the transition from socialism to capitalism is deregulating prices of goods and services. How can government officials find the appropriate prices to use when ending the government regulation of prices?

5. What is monetary overhang, and how can government eliminate it?

6. Suppose the official exchange rate is set by the government at 10 rubles per dollar. If the government does not allow its citizens to freely trade rubles for dollars, what is the use of such an exchange rate? How would currency convertibility change things?

7. What is the proper role of monetary policy during the transition from socialism to capitalism?

8. Is there any particular order in which the reforms needed in the transition from socialism to capitalism should occur? If so, discuss why.

9. The socialist economies of Eastern Europe had outdated production methods following years of technological stagnation. Why didn't these economies invest in new technology like the industrial countries of Western Europe?

10. The social safety net necessary for easing the transition from socialism will require the government to continue many of its health and public welfare policies to protect the unemployed from creating social and political unrest

that threatens the transition. In what sense does the social safety net program also hinder the movement toward a market-based economy?

11. What is the proper role of fiscal policy during the transition from socialism to capitalism?

12. Imagine the United States changing from a market-oriented economy to a socialist economy. If you are appointed chief of economic planning for the nation, how would you go about planning the right amount and kind of output for each firm, the proper prices for goods, and the appropriate incomes for workers? Write a brief essay addressing each of these planning issues and include a discussion of the problems central planners face that are solved by the use of free markets.

Tough Times in Tiny German Village of Amerika

Cheer up, America. In Amerika, things are really tough.

In this tiny village in the former East Germany, every worker is unemployed and every family is afraid of losing its home. With the closing of the Spinnerei Amerika textile mill, the community's economic lifeline since 1849, the Amerikan way of life is in danger.

"This is a difficult time for Amerika," says Hans Friedrich, a third-generation Amerikan and Amerika's leading—probably only —historian.

Although technically a district of the neighboring village of Arnsdorf, Amerika has its own identity. Road signs point it out, and if you mail a letter to "Amerika, Germany," residents say it will get here.

Amerika's 120 residents have apartment houses, a train station, a health clinic and a long, asphalt path that lets them stroll to the edge of the swift, wide Zwickauer Mulde River.

Sitting on 200 acres just north of the Czechoslovak border, Amerika is one of the prettiest places in the former East Germany. It is surrounded by a majestic panorama of pine-covered hills, spacious skies and—after planting season—a fruited plain, complete with amber waves of grain.

According to Friedrich, the village got its name nearly a century and a half ago when new mill employees, trudging through dense forest and crossing a wide river, kept asking, "What are we doing, discovering America?"

The Germanized name stuck and was officially adopted by owner Bernhard Schmidt. The mill thrived, employing 1,300 people by 1932.

The communists didn't tamper with the name, although they did change the nearest big town, Chemnitz, to Karl Marx City. For four decades, Amerika was in Karl Marx County.

But the arrival of German unification, the free market and a flood of cheap, imported sweaters, trousers and shirts have mercilessly hammered the East German textile industry.

On Jan. 1, Spinnerei Amerika was shut down and transferred to the state holding company, idling 260 people—including everyone in Amerika.

Arnsdorf Mayor Gerald Merkel says there are at least three prospective buyers who want to revive the mill, and one who wants to sell off the equipment. He expects a decision next month.

He said it is unclear what will happen to the residents who live on the grounds, although he said he personally doubts anybody would be evicted.

"My own hope is to convert the community into a tourist attraction," he said. "The name is the most important thing."

The average Amerikan is fairly old. Most began drawing pension rather than jobless benefits after they were laid off.

Then there are people like Karl Heinz Kunze, the single father of a handicapped child who worked at the plant for 21 years.

"I'm 40," he said. "If I was 15 years younger I could start over. If I was 15 years older I could get my pension."

Friedrich, the self-appointed historian, worked in the mill's laboratory for 45 years. He shares a two-room apartment with his widowed, 80-year-old mother. His father and grandfather also toiled in Amerika.

In 1984, he began chronicling the history of Amerika and has compiled a thick binder of photos and papers dating to the 19th century. Included are postcards that say "Greetings from Amerika."

"It's important for people to know that Amerika exists," he said.

Residents only hope that remains the case.

"I worked on the looms for 40 years," says Thea Stoeber, 56. "This sweater I'm wearing was made there. I hope if somebody buys the plant we can keep our homes."

Source: Copyright © 1992. Reprinted with permission of Associated Press.

The Associated Press/March 21, 1992

Commentary

One of the primary reasons that Eastern European nations abandoned socialism was a desire to achieve living standards comparable to those enjoyed by the industrial nations of Western Europe. However, in the early stages of the transition from socialism to capitalism, output fell substantially in the Eastern European nations as inefficient firms like the textile mill in Amerika were forced to close. This short-run effect of the transition makes for a difficult political climate to carry out further reforms. The transition process involves more pain than many reformers initially expected. Why has the decline in output occurred, and what should be expected in the future?

The article emphasizes the role of competitive market pressures in forcing the old, inefficient firms that existed under socialism to either reform or close. The Eastern European countries face many other economic shocks during the early stages of the transition process—for instance, major relative price shocks of important goods, like oil, which were provided at artificially low prices under socialism but have now been freed to rise substantially. We would expect such a price shock to have a negative effect on output in the short run as producers and consumers adjust to the new relative prices. Furthermore, these countries face restrictions on the availability of credit from willing lenders, yet such credit would allow the government to ease the transition by providing a more generous social safety net and financing an imbalance in the current account of the balance of payments. Without the more generous availability of funds from foreign creditors, the countries have to substantially reduce domestic consumption to finance imports of goods at now-higher prices.

The international trade effects of the reforms were worsened by the collapse of the CMEA (Council for Mutual Economic Assistance) agreement that tied the socialist countries of Eastern Europe and the U.S.S.R. together to stimulate trade among the group. Over time, each nation will develop new trade relationships with the rest of the world, and trade within the Eastern bloc will become less important. But the short-run costs of moving away from the old relationships include a decrease in the volume of international trade and a consequent drop in output.

If the reforms are allowed sufficient time to work, then producers, consumers, and governments will adjust to the new relative prices and competitive incentives, and the goal of convergence toward the incomes of the West will be achieved. The danger is that the political costs of falling output and the short-run appearance of the failure of reforms to increase living standards will lead to a resurgence of popularity for the old socialist ways and a return to central planning and the inefficiencies of the past.

Glossary

adverse selection   a process by which low-quality consumers or producers drive the higher-quality consumers or producers out of the market

age-earnings profile   the relationship between a worker's earnings and age

age-productivity profile   the relationship between a worker's productivity and age

antitrust policy   government policies and programs designed to control the growth of monopoly and enhance competition

arc elasticity   the price elasticity of demand measured over a price range using the midpoint or average as the base

association as causation   the mistaken assumption that because two events seem to occur together, one causes the other

assumptions   statements that are taken for granted without justification

asymmetric information   when participants to an economic transaction have different information about the transaction

average fixed costs (AFC)   total fixed costs divided by the quantity produced

average physical product (APP)   output per unit of resource

average total cost (ATC)   total costs divided by the total quantity of the good that is produced

average variable cost (AVC)   total variable costs divided by the quantity produced

backward-bending labor supply curve   a labor supply curve indicating that a person is willing and able to work more hours as the wage rate increases until, at some sufficiently high wage rate, the person chooses to work fewer hours

barrier to entry   anything that impedes the ability of firms to begin a new business in an industry in which existing firms are earning positive economic profits

barter   the direct exchange of goods and services without the use of money

bilateral monopoly   a market in which a monopsonistic buyer of resources faces a monopoly seller of resources

break-even price   the price that is just equal to the minimum value of the average total cost

budget line   a line showing all the combinations of goods that can be purchased with a given level of income

budget deficit   the shortage that results when government spending is greater than revenue

budget surplus   the excess that results when government spending is less than revenue

business cycle   the recurrent pattern of rising real GDP followed by falling real GDP

business firm   a business organization controlled by a single management

capital   products such as machinery and equipment that are used in production

capitalized value   the present value of an expected future income stream

capture theory of government   government actions benefit some special-interest group that has captured control of regulations, legislation, or governing authority

cartel   an organization of independent firms whose purpose is to control and limit production and maintain or increase prices and profits

cash transfers   money allocated away from one group in society to another

centrally planned system   an economic system in which the government determines what goods and services are produced and the prices at which they are sold

ceteris paribus   other things being equal, or everything else held constant

circular flow diagram   a model showing the flow of output and income from one sector of the economy to another

closed shop   a workplace in which union membership is a condition of employment

Coase Theorem   when bargaining is costless and property rights can be assigned without difficulty, the amount of an externality-generating activity will not depend on who is assigned the property rights

collective bargaining   the process by which union and management negotiate labor contracts

comparable worth   the idea that pay ought to be determined by job characteristics rather than by supply and demand and that jobs with comparable requirements should receive comparable wages

comparative advantage   the ability to produce a good or service at a lower opportunity cost than someone else

compensating wage differentials   wage differences that make up for the higher risk or poorer working conditions of one job over another

complementary goods   goods that are used together (as the price of one rises, the demand for the other falls)

concentration   the degree to which a few firms control the output and pricing decisions in a market

constant-cost industry   an industry that can expand or contract without affecting the prices of the resources it purchases

constant returns to scale   unit costs that remain constant as the quantity of production is increased and all resources are variable

consumer equilibrium the point at which the marginal utilities per dollar of expenditure on the last unit of each good purchased are equal

consumer sovereignty the supreme authority of consumers to determine, by means of their purchases, what is produced

consumer surplus the difference between what the consumer is willing to pay for a unit of a good and the price that the consumer actually has to pay

consumption household spending

consumption function the relationship between disposable income and consumption

contestable market a market where the potential of entry is high

contracting out hiring a private firm to provide a product or service for a government entity

corporation a legal entity owned by shareholders whose liability for the firm's losses is limited to the value of the stock they own

cost-plus pricing a pricing policy whereby a firm computes its average cost of producing a product and then sets the price at some percentage above this cost

cross-price elasticity of demand the percentage change in the demand for one good divided by the percentage change in the price of a related good, ceteris paribus

crowding forcing a group into certain kinds of occupations

deadweight loss the reduction of consumer surplus without a corresponding increase in monopoly profit when a perfectly competitive firm is monopolized

decreasing-cost industry an industry in which the costs of producing a unit of output fall as more output is produced

demand the quantities of a well-defined commodity that consumers are willing and able to buy at each possible price during a given period of time, ceteris paribus

demand curve a graph of a demand schedule that measures price on the vertical axis and quantity demanded on the horizontal axis

demand schedule a list or table of the prices and the corresponding quantities demanded of a particular good or service

dependent variable the variable whose value depends on the value of the independent variable

derived demand demand stemming from what a good or service can produce, not demand for the good or service itself

determinants of demand factors other than the price of the good that influence demand—income, tastes, prices of related goods and services, expectations, and number of buyers

determinants of supply factors other than the price of the good that influence supply—prices of resources, technology and productivity, expectations of producers, number of producers, and the prices of related goods and services

differentiated products products that consumers perceive to be different from one another

diminishing marginal utility the principle that the more of a good that one obtains in a specific period of time, the less is the additional utility by each additional unit of that good

direct or positive relationship the relationship that exists when the values of related variables move in the same direction

discrimination prejudice that occurs when factors unrelated to marginal productivity affect the wages or jobs that are obtained

diseconomies of scale the increase of unit costs as the quantity of production increases and all resources are variable

disequilibrium a point at which quantity demanded and quantity supplied are not equal at a particular price

disparate impact an impact that differs according to race, sex, color, religion, or national origin, regardless of the motivation

disparate treatment treatment of individuals differently because of their race, sex, color, religion, or national origin

disutility dissatisfaction

dominant strategy a strategy that produces better results no matter what strategy the opposing firm follows

double coincidence of wants the situation that exists when A has what B wants and B has what A wants

dumping selling goods at a lower price in foreign markets than at home

economic costs total costs including explicit costs and the full opportunity costs of the resources that the producer does not buy or hire but already owns

economic efficiency a situation where no one in society can be made better off without making someone else worse off

economic bad any item for which we would pay to have less of

economic good any good that is scarce

economic profit total revenue less total costs including opportunity costs

economic regulation the prescription of price and output for a specific industry

economic rent the portion of earnings above transfer earnings

economies of scale the decrease of unit costs as the quantity of production increases and all resources are variable

efficiency wages wages that are higher than equilibrium wages in order to elicit a certain type of behavior

emission standard a maximum allowable level of pollution from a specific source

emissions offset policy an environmental policy wherein pollution permits are issued and a market in the permits then develops; an increase in pollutants by one source is acceptable if met by a decrease by another source

entrepreneur someone who recognizes an opportunity for earning economic profit and is able to collect and organize the resources and undertake the risk necessary to obtain this profit

entrepreneurial ability the ability to recognize a profitable opportunity and the willingness and ability to organize land, labor, and capital and assume the risk associated with the opportunity

equilibrium the point at which quantity demanded and quantity supplied are equal at a particular price

equimarginal principle to maximize utility, consumers must allocate their scarce incomes among goods so as to equate the marginal utilities per dollar of expenditure on the last unit of each good purchased

exchange rate   the price of one country's money in terms of another country's money

exports   products that a country sells to other countries

externalities   costs or benefits of a transaction that are borne by someone not directly involved in the transaction

facilitating practices   actions on the part of firms that lead to cooperation or collusion where such cooperation has not formally been agreed to

fair rate of return   a price that allows a monopoly firm to earn a normal profit

fallacy of composition   the mistaken assumption that what applies in the case of one applies to the case of many

featherbedding   using an inefficient combination of resources in order to preserve union jobs

Federal Reserve   the central bank of the United States

financial intermediaries   institutions that accept deposits from savers and make loans to borrowers

fiscal policy   policy directed toward government spending and taxation

free good   a good for which there is no scarcity

free ride   the enjoyment of the benefits of a good by a producer or consumer without having to pay for it

free rider   a consumer or producer who enjoys the benefits of a good without paying for it

full-line supply   the bundle of policies offered by a candidate

future value   the equivalent value in the future of some amount received today

game theory   a description of oligopolistic behavior as a series of strategic moves and countermoves

Gini ratio   a measure of the dispersion of income ranging between 0 and 1; 0 means all families have same income; 1 means 1 family has all income

health maintenance organization (HMO)   an organization that provides comprehensive medical care to a voluntarily enrolled consumer population in return for a fixed, prepaid amount of money

Herfindahl index   a measure of concentration calculated as the sum of the squares of the market share of each firm in an industry

household   one or more persons who occupy a unit of housing

human capital   skills, training, and personal health acquired through education and on-the-job training

imports   products that a country buys from other countries

in-kind transfers   the allocation of goods and services from one group in society to another

income effect   the change in quantity demanded that occurs when the purchasing power of income is altered as a result of a price change

income elasticity of demand   the percentage change in the demand for a good divided by the percentage change in income, ceteris paribus

increasing-cost industry   an industry in which the costs of resources rise when the industry expands

increasing marginal opportunity cost   a rising amount of one good or service that must be given up to obtain one additional unit of any good or service, no matter how many units are being produced

independent variable   the variable whose value does not depend on the value of other variables.

indifference curve   a curve showing all combinations of two goods that the consumer is indifferent among

indifference map   a complete set of indifference curves

indifferent   lacking any preference

industrial policy   government direction and involvement in defining an economy's industrial structure

inferior goods   goods for which the income elasticity of demand is negative

inverse or negative relationship   the relationship that exists when the values of related variables move in opposite directions.

labor   the physical and intellectual services of people, including the training, education, and abilities of the individuals in a society

labor force participation   entering the work force

lagging indicator   a variable that changes after real output changes

land   all natural resources, such as minerals, timber, and water, as well as the land itself

law of diminishing marginal returns   when successive equal amounts of a variable resource are combined with a fixed amount of another resource, marginal increases in output that can be attributed to each additional unit of the variable resource will eventually decline

law of supply   as the price of a good or service that producers are willing and able to offer for sale during a particular period of time rises (falls), the quantity of that good or service supplied rises (falls), ceteris paribus

local monopoly   a monopoly that exists in a limited geographic area

logrolling   trading votes or support on one issue in return for votes or support on another issue

long run   a period of time just long enough that the quantities of all resources can be varied

long-run average total cost curve (LRAC)   the lowest-cost combination of resources with which each level of output is produced when all resources are variable

Lorenz curve   a curve measuring the degree of inequality of income distribution within a society

managed competition   government intervention in the health care market to guide competition so that costs are reduced

mandatory retirement   a policy that required workers to retire at a certain age

marginal   extra, additional

marginal benefit   additional benefit

marginal cost (MC)   the additional costs of producing one more unit of output

marginal factor cost (MFC)   the additional cost of an additional unit of a resource

marginal opportunity cost   the amount of one good or service that must be given up to obtain one additional unit of another good or service

marginal physical product (MPP)   the additional quantity that is produced when one additional unit of a resource is used in combination with the same quantities of all other resources

marginal revenue the additional revenue obtained by selling an additional unit of output

marginal revenue product (MRP) the value of the additional output that an extra unit of a resource can produce, MPP × MR

marginal social cost the additional social cost that results from a 1-unit increase in production

marginal utility the extra utility derived from consuming one more unit of a good or service

market a place or service that enables buyers and sellers to exchange goods and services

market failure the failure of the market system to achieve economic and technical efficiency

market imperfection a lack of efficiency that results from imperfect information in the market place

median voter theorem candidates or parties select positions on issues that reflect the median voter's positions on those issues

Medicaid a joint federal-state program providing long-term health care for the elderly and disabled

Medicare a federal program providing health care for the elderly and disabled

microeconomics the study of economics at the level of the individual

minimum efficient scale (MES) the minimum point of the long-run average cost curve; the output level at which the cost per unit of output is the lowest

monetary policy policy directed toward control of the money supply

monopoly a market structure in which there is a single supplier of a product

monopoly firm (monopolist) a single supplier of a product for which there are no close substitutes

monopoly power market power, the ability to set prices

monopsonist a firm that is the only buyer of a resource

moral hazard the chance that people will alter their behavior in unanticipated ways after an agreement or contract has been defined

most-favored customer any customer to whom a producer guarantees the lowest price for a certain period of time

multinational business a firm that owns and operates producing units in foreign countries

natural monopoly a monopoly that emerges because of economies of scale

negative income tax (NIT) a tax system that transfers increasing amounts of income to households earning incomes below some specified level as their income declines

net exports exports minus imports

nonrenewable (exhaustible) natural resources resources that can not be replaced or renewed

normal goods goods for which the income elasticity of demand is positive

normative analysis analysis of what ought to be

occupational segregation the separation of jobs by sex

opportunity cost the highest-valued alternative that must be forgone when a choice is made

opportunity cost of capital the forgone return on an entrepreneur's funds used in business

partnership a business with two or more owners who share the firm's profits and losses

per se rule actions that could be anticompetitive are intrinsically illegal

perfectly elastic demand curve a horizontal demand curve indicating that consumers can and will purchase all they want at one price

perfectly inelastic demand curve a vertical demand curve indicating that there is no change in the quantity demanded as the price changes

personnel practices a firm's policies toward its employees

positive analysis analysis of what is

positive economic profit (above normal profit) total revenue equals the sum of direct and opportunity costs

potential competition entry or rivalry capable of forcing existing producers to behave as if the competition actually existed

predatory dumping dumping to drive competitors out of business

preferred provider organization (PPO) group of physicians who contract to provide services at a price discount

present value the equivalent value today of some amount to be received in the future

price ceiling a situation where the price is not allowed to rise above a certain level

price discrimination charging different customers different prices for the same product; charging different prices for different quantities of the same product

price elasticity of demand the percentage change in the quantity demanded of a product divided by the percentage change in the price of that product

price elasticity of supply the percentage change in quantity supplied divided by the percentage change in price ceteris paribus

price floor a situation where the price is not allowed to decrease below a certain level

price maker a firm that sets the price of the product it sells

price taker a firm that is unable to set a price that differs from the market price without losing profit

principle of mutual exclusivity the owner of private property is entitled to enjoy the consumption of the property privately

private costs costs borne by the individual in the transaction that created the costs

private property right the limitation of ownership to an individual

privatization transferring a publicly owned enterprise to private ownership

producer surplus the difference between the price firms would have been willing to accept for their products and the price they actually receive

production possibilities curve (PPC) a graphical representation showing the maximum quantity of goods and services that can be produced using limited resources to the fullest extent possible

productivity the quantity of output produced per unit of resource

progressive tax a tax whose rate rises as income rises

proportional tax   a tax whose rate does not change as the tax base changes

prospective payment system (PPS)   the use of a preas- signed reimbursement rate by Medicare to reimburse hos- pitals and physicians

public choice   the use of economics to analyze the actions and inner workings of the public sector

public choice theory of government   government actions result from the effort of politicians and government work- ers to maximize their own interests

public goods   goods whose consumption cannot be limited only to the person who purchased the good

public interest theory   government actions improve the well-being of the general public

quantity demanded   the amount of a product that people are willing and able to purchase at a specific price

quantity supplied   the amount sellers are willing and able to offer at a given price, during a given period of time, everything else held constant

rational self-interest   the term economists use to describe how people make choices

rationally ignorant voters   voters who do not have perfect information because it is too costly to acquire

regressive tax   a tax whose rate decreases as the tax base changes

regulated monopoly   a monopoly firm whose behavior is monitored and prescribed by a government entity

relative price   the price of one good expressed in terms of another good

rent seeking   the use of resources simply to transfer wealth from one group to another without increasing production or total wealth

residual claimants   entrepreneurs who acquire profit or the revenue remaining after all other resources have been paid

resources, factors of production, inputs   goods used to produce other goods, i.e., land, labor, capital, entrepre- neurial ability

roundabout production   the process of saving and accu- mulating capital in order to increase production in the future

rule of reason   to be illegal an action must be unreasonable in a competitive sense and the anticompetitive effects must be demonstrated

saving   not consuming all current production

scarcity   the shortage that exists when less of something is available than is wanted at a zero price

scientific method   a manner of analyzing issues that involves five steps: recognition of the problem, making assumptions, model building, hypothesis formation, and hypothesis testing

sequential game   a situation in which one firm moves first and then the other firm is able to choose a strategy based on the first firm's choices

short run   a period of time just short enough that the quan- tities of all resources cannot be varied

short-run average total cost (SRATC)   the lowest-cost combination of resources with which each level of output is produced when the quantity of at least one resource is fixed

shortage   a quantity supplied that is smaller than the quan- tity demanded at a given price

shutdown price   the minimum point of the average- variable-cost curve

slope   the steepness of a curve, measured as the ratio of the rise to the run.

social costs   the private and external costs of a transaction

social regulation   the prescribing of health, safety, perfor- mance, and environmental standards that apply across sev- eral industries

sole proprietorship   a business owned by one person who receives all the profits and is responsible for all the debts incurred by the business

standardized or nondifferentiated products   products that consumers perceive to be identical

statistical discrimination   discrimination that results when an indicator of group performance is incorrectly applied to an individual member of the group

strategic behavior   behavior that occurs when what is best for B depends on what A chooses and what A chooses depends on what B is most likely to do

strategic deterrence   undertaking an action to prevent cer- tain behavior by rivals

substitute goods   goods that can be used in place of each other (as the price of one rises, the demand for the other rises)

substitution effect   the tendency of people to purchase less expensive goods that serve the same purpose as a good whose price has risen

sunk costs   costs that occurred in the past

superstar effect   the situation where people with small dif- ferences in abilities or productivity receive vastly different levels of compensation

supply   the amount of a good or service that producers are willing and able to offer for sale at each possible price dur- ing a period of time, ceteris paribus

supply curve   a graph of a supply schedule that measures price on the vertical axis and quantity supplied on the hor- izontal axis

supply schedule   a list or table of prices and corresponding quantities supplied of a particular good or service

surplus   a quantity supplied that is larger than the quantity demanded at a given price

surplus (in a balance of payments account)   the amount by which credits exceed debits

tax incidence   who pays the tax?

total costs (TC)   the sum of total variable and total fixed costs

total fixed costs (TFC)   costs that must be paid whether a firm produces or not

total physical product (TPP)   the maximum output that can be produced when successive units of a variable resource are added to fixed amounts of other resources

total revenue (TR) $TR = P \times Q$

total utility   a measure of the total satisfaction derived from consuming a quantity of some good or service

total variable costs (TVC)   costs that rise or fall as pro- duction rises or falls

trade off   to give up one good or activity in order to obtain some good or activity

trade surplus (deficit) exists when imports are less than (exceed) exports

transaction costs the costs involved in making an exchange

transfer earnings the portion of total earnings required to keep a resource in its current use

transfer payment income transferred from one citizen, who is earning income, to another citizen, who may not be

union shop a workplace in which all employees must join a union within a specific period of time after they are hired

utility a measure of the satisfaction received from possessing or consuming goods and services

venture capital funds provided by a firm or individual that specializes in lending to new, unproven firms

voting cycle the situation where a collective decision process does not reach a decision

workfare a plan that requires welfare recipients to accept public service jobs or participate in job training

X-inefficiency the tendency of a firm not faced with competition to become inefficient

zero economic profit (normal profit) total revenue equals the sum of direct and opportunity costs

Credits *(continued from p. ii)*

p. 120 © Jeffrey Markowitz/Sygma; p. 126 © Richemond/The Image Works; p. 137 © Bob Daemmrich; p. 156 © Rob Crandall/Stock Boston; p. 171 © Ulrike Welsch/Photo Researchers; p. 172 © Pablo Bartholomew/Gamma Liaison; p. 187 © David R. Frazier Photolibrary; p. 197 © David R. Frazier; p. 201 © Schiller/The Image Works; p. 227 © Bob Daemmrich/Stock Boston; p. 232 © Robert Rathe/Tony Stone Images; p. 251 © Edrington/The Image Works; p. 267 © David R. Frazier Photolibrary; p. 277 © R. Maiman/Sygma; p. 280 © David R. Frazier Photolibrary; p. 305 © Martha Bates/Stock Boston; p. 307 © Robert Daemmrich/Tony Stone Images; p. 314 © Charles Kennard/Stock Boston; p. 333 © David R. Frazier; p. 336 © Arthur Tilley/Tony Stone Images; p. 338 © Frank Cezus/Tony Stone Images; p. 353 © David Joel/Tony Stone Images; p. 355 © Cameramann International; p. 377 © David R. Frazier; p. 382 © Andy Levin/Photo Researchers; p. 401 © Bob Daemmrich; p. 407 © Compoint/Sygma; p. 425 © Wesley Bocxe/Photo Researchers; p. 436 © Bob Daemmrich; p. 455 © Bob Daemmrich; p. 464 © Mark Gibson; p. 483 © Jim Harrison/Stock Boston; p. 499 © Mulvehill/The Image Works; p. 511 Jerry Howard/Positive Images; p. 518 © M. Vertinetti/Photo Researchers; p. 530 © M. Grecco/Stock Boston; p. 539 © Jonathan Nourok/Tony Stone Images; p. 548 © Nicolas Reynard/Gamma-Liaison; p. 555 © John Elk III/Stock Boston; p. 563 © Robert Daemmrich/Tony Stone Images; p. 571 © David R. Frazier; p. 576 © Ferdinando Scianna/Magnum Photos; p. 587 © Charles Gupton/Tony Stone Images; p. 591 © John Sims/Tony Stone Images; p. 607 © Fred R. Palmer/Stock Boston; p. 619 © David R. Frazier Photolibrary; p. 627 © David H. Wells/The Image Works; p. 649 © Swersey/Gamma-Liaison; p. 654 © Swersey/Gamma-Liaison; p. 657 © Katie Arkell/Gamma-Liaison.

Index

DISCARDED
from
New Hanover County Public Library

NEW HANOVER COUNTY PUBLIC LIB.

3 4200 00407822 6

DISCARDED
from
New Hanover County Public Library

7V76

NEW HANOVER COUNTY PUBLIC LIBRARY
201 Chestnut Street
Wilmington, N.C. 28401

GAYLORD
S

ML